Systems Analysis and Design:

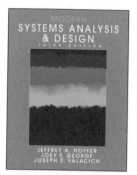

Hoffer/George/Valacich, *Modern Systems Analysis and Design 3/e*

Marakas, *Systems Analysis and Design: An Active Approach*

Valacich/George/Hoffer, *Essentials of Systems Analysis & Design 2/e*

Kendall & Kendall, *Systems Analysis and Design 5/e*

Telecommunications, Networking and Business Data Communications:

Stamper & Case, *Business Data Communications 6/e*

Panko, *Business Data Networks and Telecommunications 4/e*

Security:

Panko, *Corporate Computer and Network Security*

Other Titles:

Awad & Ghaziri, *Knowledge Management*

Marakas, *Decision Support Systems in the 21st Century 2/e*

Marakas, *Modern Data Warehousing, Mining, and Visualization: Core Concepts*

Turban & Aronson, *Decision Support Systems and Intelligent Systems 6/e*

Request desk copies for evaluation through your local Prentice Hall representative or by email at CIS_Service@prenhall.com

KNOWLEDGE MANAGEMENT

KNOWLEDGE MANAGEMENT

Elias M. Awad

Virginia Bankers Association Professor of Bank Management
University of Virginia

Hassan M. Ghaziri

Associate Professor
School of Business
American University of Beirut

PEARSON

Prentice
Hall

Upper Saddle River, New Jersey 07458

Library of Congress Cataloging-in-Publication Data

Awad, Elias M.
    Knowledge management / Elias M. Awad, Hassan Ghaziri—1st ed.
      p. cm.
    Includes bibliographical references and index.
    ISBN 0-13-034820-1
    1. Knowledge management.   2. Information resources management.   I. Ghaziri, Hassan.
  II. Title.
  HD30.2.A98 2003
  658.4′038—dc21
                                                 2002035518

AVP/Executive Editor: David Alexander
Project Manager (Editorial): Kyle Hannon
Editorial Assistant: Maat Van Uitert
VP/Publisher: Natalie Anderson
Media Project Manager: Joan Waxman
Marketing Manager: Sharon K. Turkovich
Marketing Assistant: Scott Patterson
Managing Editor (Production): John Roberts
Production Editor: Maureen Wilson
Production Assistant: Joe DeProspero
Permissions Coordinator: Suzanne Grappi
Associate Director, Manufacturing: Vincent Scelta
Production Manager: Arnold Vila
Manufacturing Buyer: Michelle Klein
Cover Design: Bruce Kenselaar
Cover Illustration/Photo: Gettyimages/PhotoDisc
Composition and Full-Service Project Management: BookMasters, Inc.
Project Manager: Sharon Anderson, BookMasters, Inc.
Printer/Binder: Von Hoffman Owensville

Credits and acknowledgments borrowed from other sources and reproduced, with permission, in this textbook appear on appropriate page within text.

Pearson Education LTD.
Pearson Education Australia PTY, Limited
Pearson Education Singapore, Pte. Ltd.
Pearson Education North Asia Ltd.
Pearson Education, Canada, Ltd.
Pearson Educación de Mexico, S.A. de C.V.
Pearson Education–Japan
Pearson Education Malaysia, Pte. Ltd.

10 9 8 7 6 5 4 3 2 1
ISBN 0-13-034820-1

"The great end of life is not knowledge but action."
—Thomas Henry Huxley

This text is dedicated to the memory of
Firefighter Dana Hannon and his 342 FDNY brothers
who died in the line of duty,
World Trade Center,
September 11, 2001.
—Elias Awad

To my wife Blandine,
who showed me that seeking the truth entails
sharpening the taste of beauty, and
who constantly reminds me that technology
without humanity leads to chaos.
—Hassan Ghaziri

Contents

PART V: ETHICAL, LEGAL, AND MANAGERIAL ISSUES   385

CHAPTER 14:   Who Owns Knowledge? Ethical and Legal Issues   385

Preface

We live in a world that changes by the minute. Change often moves organizations and advances people's intellect. For change to be effective, organizations as well as people must change. However, even the most intelligent individuals can become handicapped in ineffective organizations. People, being creatures of habit, are so busy working the job that they fail to see change around them. They get carried away with behavior that did well in the past, not realizing that it no longer produces effective results in a fast-changing business.

The key to change and growth is awareness, sharing ideas, and coming up with new and innovative ways of staying ahead of the competition. It involves learning, innovating, and adopting behavior designed to improve quality and performance. As McLuhan said, "Everybody experiences far more than he understands. Yet, it is experience, rather than understanding, that influences behavior."

So, smart people need smart organizations. The name of the game is integration and cooperation for competitive advantage. For companies to make use of human experience and intelligence, they must provide a sharing environment, empower people with tools, and create a climate for learning and testing new ways of doing business. As Philip Kotler, professor of marketing, Northwestern University, wrote, "Every company should work hard to obsolete its own line . . . before its competitors do."

Why This Book?

Knowledge management is growing rapidly. More and more companies have built knowledge repositories, supporting such knowledge varieties as customer knowledge, product development knowledge, customer service knowledge, human resource management knowledge, and the like. Even new job titles have appeared—from knowledge developer, to knowledge facilitator, to corporate knowledge officer. Other signs of the growing knowledge management emphasis are in the many newspapers, magazines, journals, conferences, and seminars that appear daily worldwide. Even vendors on the Internet and in established locations tout specialized knowledge management applications of all kinds and aimed at all levels of the organization. By all accounts, knowledge management is becoming a necessary feature of today's business culture.

In our opinion, people change the world; books pave the way. This text is about knowledge, how to capture it, how to transfer it, how to share it, and how to manage it. In this volume, we introduce the many facets of knowledge management—from concepts, to people, to tools, to procedures. In terms of tools, we cover the use of the computer for capturing and sharing tacit knowledge and the network that transfers tacit and explicit knowledge. Consider the following questions regarding one aspect of knowledge and computers:

- Do you know a more effective way to preserve the knowledge of an expert who might be retiring soon than by preserving it through a computer?
- How could today's corporations afford brain drain and loss of knowledge and expertise without a way to capture it so that less-experienced employees could use it to advantage?
- If knowledge is today's best corporate asset, would it not make sense to find a way to preserve, nurture, share, and protect such capital?

The actual carrier of the knowledge, whether it is e-mail, groupware, or peer-to-peer meetings, will involve people with an attitude of sharing common knowledge in the interest of the project or the organization. Technology is only a tool employed to expedite processes.

Another reason for writing this book is dissatisfaction with existing books for the academic sector. There are many good books on the market where each book gives a specialized picture of knowledge rather than a comprehensive view of what knowledge is and how it is embedded in today's organization. For example, one book focuses on common knowledge based on studying a number of established enterprises. Another book brings up the concept of learning in action as a guide to putting the learning organization to work. Another known book discusses how organizations manage what they know. Other books are either extremely behavioral focused or lean heavily toward knowledge automation. This text is neither. It is process oriented. It strikes a balance between the behavioral aspects of knowledge and knowledge management and refers to technology as a medium for knowledge transfer, especially in the e-world.

▪▪▪▪ How the Text Is Organized

This text is about knowledge management—what it is and how to use it for competitive advantage. Figure 1 is a graphic layout of how the text is organized. Part I presents the basics of *knowledge management* and focuses on the concept of *knowledge* and *knowledge management system life cycle.* Chapter 1 introduces the meaning of knowledge, how knowledge came about, the myths, and a summary of the knowledge management life cycle. Chapter 2 addresses cognition and knowledge management, types of knowledge, expert knowledge, and human thinking and learning. Chapter 3 elaborates on the challenges in building knowledge management systems and the knowledge management system life cycle.

Part II addresses the important area of *knowledge creation* and *knowledge capture.* The focus is on the various knowledge tools to capture tacit knowledge as a step to storing it for knowledge sharing. Chapter 4 brings up Nonaka's model of knowledge creation and transformation and knowledge architecture centered on people and technical cores. Chapter 5 lays out in detail the tacit knowledge capture process using the interview as a tool. It also covers how to evaluate and develop a relationship with the expert. Chapter 6 discusses other tacit knowledge capture tools such as brainstorming, protocol analysis, Delphi method, and concept mapping.

Part III examines *how tacit knowledge is codified* and how the resulting knowledge base is implemented. In Chapter 7, we deal with knowledge codification tools such as knowledge maps, decision tables, decision trees, and production rules. Chapter 8 elabo-

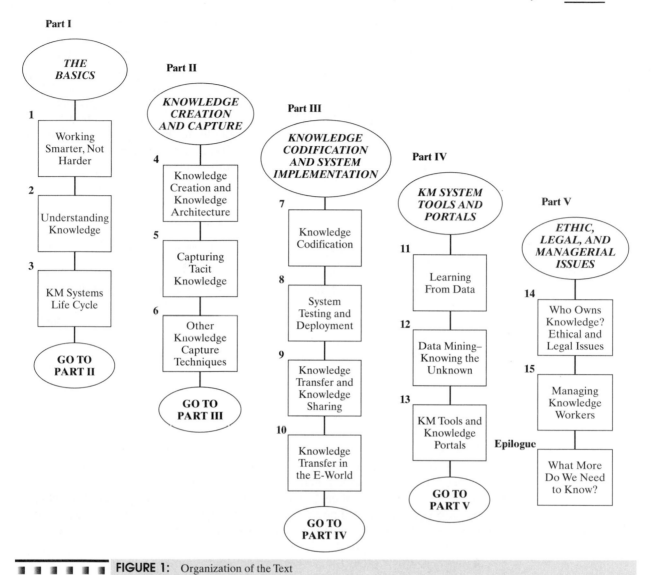

FIGURE 1: Organization of the Text

rates on various approaches to logical and user-acceptance testing, how to manage the testing phase, and issues related to deployment. Chapter 9 expounds on knowledge transfer and knowledge sharing. Specifically, we focus on the prerequisites for knowledge transfer, knowledge transfer methods, and the role of the Internet in knowledge transfer. Finally, Chapter 10 focuses on the e-world in terms of knowledge transfer within a company's intranet, extranet, groupware, and groupware applications. E-business is discussed in terms of knowledge transfer between businesses, supply-chain management, and customer relationship management.

Part IV addresses the more *technical aspects of knowledge management*. The focus is on data mining and knowledge management tools and portals. In Chapter 11, the focus is on learning from data through neural nets, association rules, and classification trees. Chapter 12 deals with data-mining concepts, tasks, processes, and practice. Chapter 13 addresses portals, knowledge portal technologies, and key managerial issues.

Part V brings up the *ethical, legal, and managerial issues* in knowledge management. The question is who owns knowledge—the knowledge worker or the firm? In Chapter 14, we discuss the liability of the knowledge developer, the expert, and the user. We also highlight the meaning of copyrights, trademarks, and trade names. Major threats to ethics in knowledge sharing are also covered. Chapter 15 concludes the text with a focus on the knowledge worker and how to manage knowledge work. Specifically, we elaborate on the skills set of the knowledge worker and how technology can be a critical tool for advancing knowledge work. The Epilogue is a futuristic view of knowledge management and the likely direction it will take to help the learning organization succeed in an increasingly competitive global environment.

▪ ▪ ▪ ▪ Key Features

This text incorporates several key features for easy learning:

- *Learning by example* is evident throughout the text. Concepts, principles, or procedures that are either technical or new are followed by examples or illustrations for easy learning.
- *Boxed vignettes* throughout each chapter are brought in from the field through journals or Web sites.
- *Illustrations* are incorporated where necessary for clearer understanding of the material. Each graph, figure, or table has been carefully sketched to ensure that the key concept being represented stands out clearly. When actual adaptation is used, references are provided so the student can locate the knowledge source.
- *Implications for knowledge management* relates chapter material to knowledge management or management decision making.
- *Knowledge exercises* available at the end of each chapter offer a variety of both straightforward and more thought-provoking applications. The solutions are available in the instructor's manual on the Web site: www.prenhall.com/awad.
- *A summary* at the end of each chapter brings into focus the essence of the chapter. Good summaries can be a useful guide for chapter coverage. Depending on learning preference, reading the summary before reading the chapter can be an effective learning approach.
- *Terms to Know* are selected key terms from each chapter. A glossary of these terms is available on the Web site: www.prenhall.com/awad.

▪ ▪ ▪ ▪ Supplements

COMPANION WEBSITE (www.prenhall.com/awad)

The text's Companion Website includes the Instructor's Manual, Test Item File, and Microsoft PowerPoint slides.

Access to the instructor's section of the site, where the Instructor's Manual and Test Item File are housed, requires a valid user ID and password to enter. You simply need to register yourself as the instructor of the course by going to the Web site and completing the initial instructor registration process. Upon completion of the process, your registration request will be forwarded to your sales representative for validation.

If you have any problem with your authorization, please contact your Prentice Hall sales representative.

INSTRUCTOR'S MANUAL

A specially prepared manual is available for the instructor. The manual provides the following support material:

- A *syllabus* based on a quarter or a semester plan as a guide to teaching the course
- *Lecture assistance,* including the objectives of each chapter, teaching notes, and chapter summary
- *Solutions to knowledge exercises* at the end of each chapter

TEST ITEM FILE

The Test Item File contains multiple choice, true-false, and essay questions. The questions are rated by the level of difficulty and answers are referenced by page number.

POWERPOINT PRESENTATIONS

The slides illuminate and build upon key concepts in the text. They are available for both students and instructors for download from www.prenhall.com/awad.

Acknowledgments

In a nutshell, every effort has been made to make *Knowledge Management* truly understandable, high on lucidity, and practicable. In preparing the manuscript, we kept in mind people, not computers, as the final decision makers. Although the underlying technology in automating knowledge work ensures the availability of tacit knowledge in knowledge bases and other repositories, humans have the final say in the way organizations and society must perform.

Before the manuscript found its way to the publisher, various versions were tested in the classroom over a 2-year period in the United States and abroad. There were successive revisions and updates resulting from student feedback and feedback from professional reviewers and attendees to our many seminars on the subject. We would specifically like to thank the following people:

Mark Addleson—George Mason University
Jim Albers—Pacific Lutheran University
Dorine Andrews—Georgetown University
Frada Burstein—Monash University
David Fearon—Central Connecticut State University
Mike Godfrey—California State University, Long Beach
Barbara Grabowski—Benedictine University
Paul Gray—Claremont Graduate University
William Hafner—Nova Southeastern University
Paul Johnson—University of Miami
Ravi Rao Patnayakuni—Temple University

Shan Ling Pin—National University of Singapore
Steven Ruth—George Mason University
Doug Tuggle—American University
Joanne Twining—University of Denver

Because no knowledge management book is ever complete, future revisions are inevitable. After having gone through this material, you are invited to share your experience, ideas, or thoughts. Feel free to e-mail the authors at ema3z@virginia.edu or ghaziri@aub.edu.lb, respectively.

Elias M. Awad
University of Virginia
Charlottesville, Virginia
Voice: 434-924-3423

Hassan M. Ghaziri
School of Business
American University of Beirut
Beirut, Lebanon
Voice: 961 1 352700

About the Authors

Dr. Elias M. Awad is the Virginia Bankers Association Professor of Bank Management at the University of Virginia. He has over 40 years IT experience in the academic, publishing, and consulting areas. He is one of the world's leading IT instructors and seminar presenters in the banking industry. Dr. Awad is the CEO of International Technology Group, LTD., an IT consulting group with offices in Chicago, New York, Beirut, Damascus, and Bratislava. His book publication record goes back to the early 1960s with best sellers across the IT discipline in systems analysis and design, database management, knowledge management, human resources management, and building knowledge automation systems. His publications have been translated into German, Spanish, Portuguese, Chinese, Arabic, Russian, and Braille. Dr. Awad's publications have earned international recognition for lucidity, logical flow, and presentation of material based on experience in the field. He has delivered professional seminars internationally to major corporations and government agencies in 26 countries, including Korea, Russia, Cambodia, Canada, Mexico, Kazikhstan, Moldova, Uzbekistan, Saudi Arabia, Lebanon, Jordan, and Egypt.

Dr. Hassan M. Ghaziri is an associate professor in operation and information management systems at the School of Business, American University of Beirut. Dr. Ghaziri has 12 years of experience in IT teaching, consulting, and research. He performed his activities for the academic and business communities in American, European, and Middle Eastern cultures. Dr. Ghaziri is the founder of Research and Computer Aided Management–SAL, an IT company providing enterprise integrated systems and focusing on helping companies bridge the gap between business practices and knowledge technologies. His research and development interests include knowledge discovery and building enterprise knowledge systems. He has authored and co-authored over 20 scientific publications in premier journals.

CHAPTER 1

Working Smarter, Not Harder

Contents

Knowing ignorance is strength
Ignoring knowledge is sickness
—LAO TSU

In a Nutshell

Welcome to the twenty-first century and the knowledge society. The business landscape is changing rapidly. The competitive environment is no longer linear or predictable. Survival and success depend entirely on the organization's ability to adjust to the dynamics of the business environment. Changes in information technology (IT) have generated gaps in access and control of information and knowledge. Even when these gaps are bridged, several fundamental challenges remain. How do we apply knowledge for value-added and competitive advantage? How do we convert information into knowledge? How do we use technology to convert challenges into opportunities? Knowledge management is the solution for realigning the firm's technical capabilities to create the knowledge that drives the firm forward.

There is obvious room for change in the way we work and communicate and in relationships and processes among people within and across organizations. To be empowered to face these challenges means not only accessing technology, but also developing the ability to manage knowledge. In the final analysis, the key questions an organization must consider are "Does your company know what you know?" "Do you know what you know?" "How do you make best use of the knowledge you have?" It also means thinking "out-of-the-box," where "the box" is what represents all the tried-and-true procedures that have worked in the past. There is less room for "packaged solutions" to solve most of a firm's problems. Knowledge management means thinking outside the boundaries of current practices, products, services, and organizations. The new and unpredictable business environment puts a premium on innovation and creativity much more so than it has in the past. This explains our chapter title—working smarter, not harder. It is "obsoleting what you know before others obsolete it and profit by creating the challenges and opportunities others haven't even thought about" (Malhotra 2000).

We have progressed from the data processing age of the 1960s to the information age of the 1980s to the knowledge age of the 1990s. The latest transformation represents the most fundamental change since the introduction of the digital computer 4 decades ago. Knowledge and intellectual capital (viewed here as accrued knowledge) represent our corporate and national wealth. Knowledge workers are found in every organization, and they are the backbone of every successful business. Knowledge workers use technology to reason through problems and reach successful solutions. Computer-aided software gives them an edge over workers using conventional methods. In this chapter, we discuss knowledge management, the general concepts and myths surrounding knowledge management, the relationship between knowledge management and management information systems, and how an innovative organization looks at knowledge.

In the past decade, there has been much discussion about the importance of knowledge and knowledge management. Roy Vagelos, the chief executive officer of Merck & Co., told *Fortune* magazine that devoting time and resources to the proper management of knowledge is slowly, but surely, gaining support in many organizations. For a company to manage knowledge, it must first inventory its people, systems, and decisions. Professional knowledge workers within the company must be identified, and their functions must be defined. Knowledge technologies must be incorporated to reengineer the entire business process. Major decisions should be reviewed, and a knowledge system for making each decision should be developed. The company's information system should also be examined to determine how to benefit from emerging knowledge technologies. This self-assessment makes a company more cognizant of its strengths and weaknesses. It should also lead to changes that are more in tune with the competitive nature of the business environment.

▪ ▪ ▪ ▪ What Is Knowledge Management?

Knowledge management (KM) is a newly emerging, interdisciplinary business model that has knowledge within the framework of an organization as its focus. It is rooted in many disciplines, including business, economics, psychology, and information management. It is the ultimate competitive advantage for today's firm. Knowledge management involves people, technology, and processes in overlapping parts (see Figure 1.1).

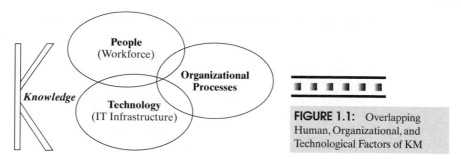

FIGURE 1.1:   Overlapping Human, Organizational, and Technological Factors of KM

As can be deduced from the select definitions in Table 1.1, researchers as well as practitioners have yet to agree on a definition. However, each definition of KM contains several integral parts:

- Using accessible knowledge from outside sources
- Embedding and storing knowledge in business processes, products, and services
- Representing knowledge in databases and documents
- Promoting knowledge growth through the organization's culture and incentives
- Transferring and sharing knowledge throughout the organization
- Assessing the value of knowledge assets and impact on a regular basis

In some ways, KM is about survival in a new business world—a world of competition that increases in complexity and uncertainly each day (see Box 1.1). It is a world that challenges the traditional ways of doing things. The focus is not only on finding the right answers, but also on asking the right questions. What worked yesterday may or may not work tomorrow. The focus is on "doing the right thing" rather than "doing things right" so that core competencies do not become core rigidities in the future (Malhotra 2000).

KM is the process of capturing and making use of a firm's collective expertise anywhere in the business—on paper, in documents, in databases (called *explicit knowledge*), or in people's heads (called *tacit knowledge*). Figure 1.2 implies that up to 95 percent of information is preserved as tacit knowledge. It is the fuel or raw material for innovation—the only competitive advantage that can sustain a company in an unpredictable business environment. It is not intended to favor expert systems of the early 1990s, when computers were programmed to emulate human experts' thought processes. The goal is to present a balanced view of how computer technology captures, distributes, and shares knowledge in the organization by linking human experts and documented knowledge in an integrated KM system.

The goal is for an organization to view all its processes as knowledge processes. This includes knowledge creation, dissemination, upgrade, and application toward organizational survival. Today's knowledge organization has a renewed responsibility to hire knowledgeable employees and specialists to manage knowledge as an intangible asset in the same way that one calls on an investor to manage a financial portfolio. A firm seeks to add value by identifying, applying, and integrating knowledge in unprecedented ways, much like an investor adds value by unique combinations of stocks and bonds. The process is part science, part art, and part luck.

THE KNOWLEDGE ORGANIZATION

A conceptual structure of the knowledge organization is shown in Figure 1.3. The middle layer addresses the KM life cycle—knowledge creation, knowledge collection or capture, knowledge organization, knowledge refinement, and knowledge dissemination.

TABLE 1.1   Alternative Definitions of Knowledge Management

- Knowledge management is the process of gathering a firm's collective expertise wherever it resides—in databases, on paper, or in people's heads—and distributing it to where it can help produce the biggest payoff (Hibbard 1997).
- KM is a newly emerging, interdisciplinary business model dealing with all aspects of knowledge within the context of the firm, including knowledge creation, codification, sharing, and how these activities promote learning and innovation (encompassing technology tools and organizational routines in overlapping parts) (Berkeley 2001).
- KM caters to the critical issues of organizational adaptation, survival, and competence in the face of increasingly discontinuous environmental change. Essentially, it embodies organizational processes that seek synergistic combinations of data and information processing capacity of information technology, and the creative and innovative capacity of human beings (Malhotra 1999).
- Knowledge management is the art of creating value from an organization's intangible assets (Sveiby 2000).
- Knowledge management is the classification, dissemination, and categorization of information and people throughout an organization (Taft 2000).
- Knowledge management is the discipline of capturing knowledge-based competencies and then storing and diffusing that knowledge into business. It is also the systematic and organized attempt to use knowledge within an organization to improve performance (KPMG 2000).
- KM is really about recognizing that regardless of what business you are in, you are competing based on the knowledge of your employees (Johnson 2001).
- KM is a conscious strategy of getting the right knowledge to the right people at the right time; it is also helping people share and put information into action in ways that strive to improve organizational performance (O'Dell et al. 2000).
- Knowledge management is a framework, a management mind-set, that includes building on past experiences (libraries, data banks, smart people) and creating new vehicles for exchanging knowledge (knowledge-enabled intranet sites, communities of practice, networks) (O'Dell et al. 2000).
- KM is accumulating knowledge assets and using them effectively to gain a competitive advantage (Brooking 1996).
- KM is a framework within which the organization views all its processes as knowledge processing, where all business processes involve creation, dissemination, renewal, and application of knowledge toward organizational sustenance and survival (Malhotra 2000).
- Knowledge management includes a combination of software products and business practices that help organizations capture, analyze, and distill information (Craig 2000).
- KM is not about technology; it is about mapping processes and exploiting the knowledge database. It is applying technology to people's minds (Deveau 2000).
- Knowledge management is the sharing of information throughout a company or even between business partners. It creates an environment in which the company leverages all its knowledge assets (Trepper 2000).
- KM can automate the classification of documents while using machine logic that comes as close as possible to human logic (Hersey 2000).
- Knowledge management is a discipline of identifying, capturing, retrieving, sharing, and evaluating an enterprise's information assets (Bair 2001).

▪ ▪ ▪ ▪ ▪ ▪

AN EXAMPLE OF KNOWLEDGE MANAGEMENT.

The predawn silence at the U.S. embassy in Indonesia is shattered by automatic weapons fire, and a small force of U.S. Marines barely prevents the attackers from entering the compound. Within the next few hours, the embassy sends information about the attack to the Combat Development Command in Quantico, Virginia. There, a team analyzes the data and sees that it matches a pattern of activity of a fundamentalist rebel group operating in the region.

Another team in Quantico taps into a Community of Practice knowledge database to review new tactical maneuvers being developed in a modeling game room. Experts from across the U.S. Marine Corps join an online discussion, aided by the latest intelligence information and satellite photographs merged into an electronic work space. Within a few hours, a new urban tactic is developed, tested in the modeling game room, and sent to the Marine command in Indonesia.

The commander coordinates plans with the USS *Winston Churchill*, a guided-missile destroyer some 500 kilometers to the east. Later that day, he calls for fire and, 90 seconds later, the ship launches a dual salvo of Tomahawk missiles at a key rebel communications center 10 kilometers from the embassy.

"It's just a story," says Alex Bennet, the U.S. Navy's deputy CIO for enterprise integration, but such stories are an important ingredient in what observers describe as the largest knowledge management effort in the world. The military's knowledge management programs are so comprehensive, in fact, that the private sector can learn much from them, from more effective ways to apply information technology to new ways of teaching.

Army Knowledge Online will become mission-critical, literally, says program manager Maj. Charles Wells. "Yesterday, we had a very straightforward threat: We knew who the enemy was, and we had a lot of detailed plans to stop an attack," says Wells. "Today, we are faced with a variety of challenges—regional instabilities, economic dangers, and the proliferation of weapons of mass destruction. How are we going to accomplish all these missions with a much smaller force? The senior Army leadership sees knowledge management as the key."

As advice to other knowledge managers, Lt. Cmdr. Judith Godwin, Pacific Fleet knowledge manager, says, "Don't build something and expect people to come. They won't." Instead, she says, "Find communities that are trying to get a task done. Enable them with a specific tool so they can see the value it can bring to what they are doing right now. Then it will grow from there."

SOURCE: Excerpted from Anthes, Gary H. "Charting a Knowledge Management Course," *Computerworld*, August 21, 2000, p. 38ff.

The final step is the maintenance phase, which ensures that the knowledge disseminated is accurate, reliable, and based on company standards set in advance. The outer layer is the immediate environment of the organization—technology, culture, supplier and customer intelligence, competition, and leadership. Such an environment has a lot to do with how well an organization goes about developing and implementing its KM life cycle—also called the KM process.

The ideal knowledge organization is one where people exchange knowledge across the functional areas of the business by using technology and established processes. As depicted in Figure 1.4, people exchange ideas and knowledge for policy formulation and strategy. Knowledge is also internalized and adopted within the culture

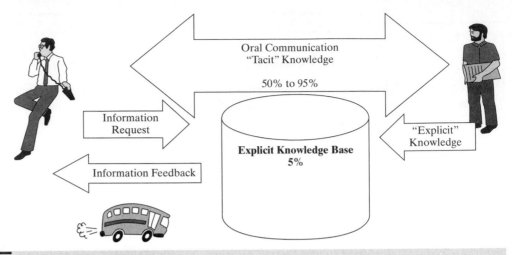

▪ ▪ ▪ ▪ ▪ ▪ ▪ **FIGURE 1.2:**   Uncaptured Tacit Knowledge

SOURCE: Bair, Jim "Knowledge Management Technology: Beyond Document Management."
www.strategy-partners.com/spweb/pages.nsf/all+pages/White%20Page%20%20%20Knowledge%20
Management%20Technology:%20Beyond%20Document%20Management?opendocument September 19,
2001, pp. 1–6. Date accessed August 2002.

of the organization. All knowledge workers (people) are in an environment where they
can freely exchange and produce knowledge assets by using various technologies. This
process influences the company as a whole in a positive way.

A knowledge organization derives knowledge from several sources:

- Customer knowledge—their needs, who to contact, customer buying power, etc.
- Product knowledge—the products in the market place, who is buying them, what
  prices they are selling at, and how much money is spent on such products
- Financial knowledge—capital resources, where to acquire capital and at what
  cost, and the integrating in financial practices
- Personnel practices knowledge—the expertise available, the quality service they
  provide, and how to go about finding experts, especially in customer service

▪ ▪ ▪ ▪ ▪ ▪ ▪ **FIGURE 1.3:**   The Knowledge Organization

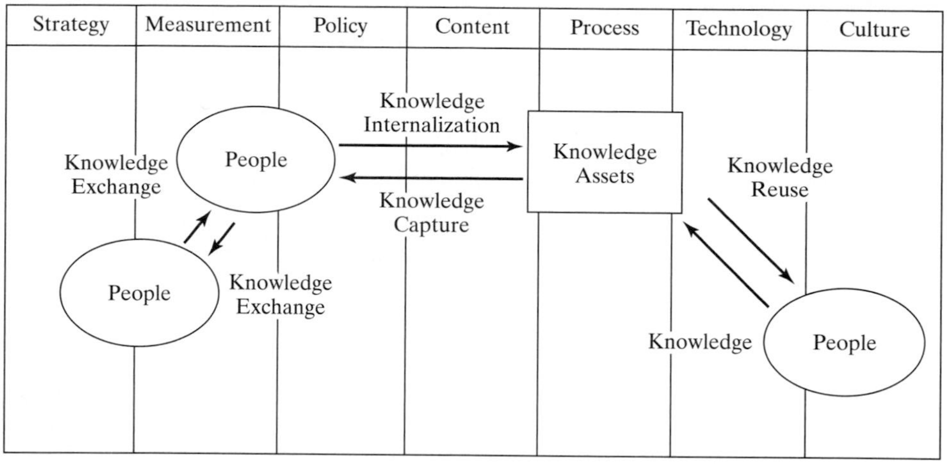

Strategy	Measurement	Policy	Content	Process	Technology	Culture

Knowledge Exchange

People

Knowledge Internalization

Knowledge Assets

Knowledge Reuse

Knowledge Capture

People

Knowledge Exchange

Knowledge

People

▪ ▪ ▪ ▪ ▪ ▪ ▪ **FIGURE 1.4:** Ideal Knowledge Management

SOURCE: Gravallese, Julie. "Knowledge Management," *The MITRE Advanced Technology Newsletter,* April 2000, vol. 4, no. 1. www.mitre.org/pubs/edge/april_00/4, Date accessed August 2002.

The idea of "managing" knowledge is abstract. Knowledge is not something we typically think of as being managed, but rather something that is individually controlled, personal, and autonomous. To be able to manage knowledge, one must first be able to elicit an individual's knowledge from that individual. The human aspect of both knowledge and managing are integral. There is also the issue of measuring knowledge: If you cannot measure it, you cannot manage it.

One unique indicator of KM in action is seeing people think actively, not passively—thinking ahead, not behind. It is an environment where customer service is improved through better problem-solving, where new products are available to the market more quickly, and where the organizational processes that deliver the new products continue to improve through innovation and creativity of the people behind the product and the production process. This is where technology, networking, and data communication infrastructure play an important role. Technology has made knowledge sharing and innovation more feasible (see Figure 1.5).

What KM Is Not About

- *Knowledge management is not reengineering.* Reengineering implies one-shot, drastic "electrical shock" change in organizational processes to improve efficiency. It is a mechanical shift from one stage of operation to a more efficient stage, and it usually involves radical changes of business processes and the people involved. In contrast, KM implies continuous change and addresses future threats and unique opportunities. There is continuous learning, unlearning, and relearning to ensure smooth change from top to bottom. The focus is on change that will generate gradual but solid gains in the competitive environment. Knowledge management is engrained in the day-to-day operations of the business and directed by people who are directly connected with the changing world of their company's business.
- *Knowledge management is not a discipline.* It is another way of improving quality, profitability, and growth.
- *Knowledge management is not a philosophic calling.* KM goes to the core of an organization's intangible asset (knowledge), revisits the knowledge, and taps into it.

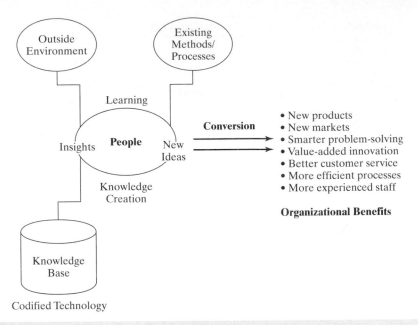

FIGURE 1.5:   Knowledge Management and Innovation

- *Knowledge management is not intellectual capital, per se.* Intellectual capital (IC) represents the value of a company's trademarks, patents, or brand names. Intellectual capital is a company's collective brainpower, or a composite of experience, knowledge, information, and intellectual property—all the property of the organization. Although treated in the literature the same as knowledge, knowledge, per se, is the consequence of actions and interactions of people with information and knowledge exchange based on experience over time (see Box 1.2).
- *Knowledge management is not based on information.* Information can become knowledge after people use it in ways that create value. Knowledge has been viewed as information in action. As we shall explain in Chapter 2, information is context-sensitive; knowledge is consensus-oriented.
- *Knowledge management is not about data.* Data (facts without context) or information (interpretation or patterns of data) is not knowledge. As we shall find in Chapter 2, data by itself is not actionable knowledge (O'Dell et al. 1998, 17).
- *Knowledge value chain is not information value chain.* In information value chains, the key component is a technological system guiding the company's business processes, viewing humans as passive processors. In contrast, knowledge value chains view humans as the key components assessing and reassessing information stored in a technological system. Best practices into organizational business processes are carried out after active human inquiry, and such processes are continuously updated in line with the changing external environment.
- *Knowledge management is not limited to gathering information from the company's domain experts or retiring employees and creating databases accessible by intranets.* KM is a collective concept of the organization's entire core knowledge.
- *Knowledge management is not digital networks.* KM is about improving business processes with people and technology in mind. Effective technology is the enabler of KM, and people must be in the equation from the start to use technology effectively.

▮▮▮▮▮▮ **BOX 1.2** ▮▮▮▮▮▮

INTELLECTUAL CAPITAL

Tracking a company's physical assets is straight-forward enough, as long as you're counting computers, adding salaries, and estimating heating bills. But managing intellectual capital is a different ball game, and one in which few companies consistently hit home runs.

Intellectual capital involves a company's employee expertise, unique organizational systems, and intellectual property. For example, if a company's book value is $10 per share and its stock is selling for $40 per share, the difference is often attributed to intellectual capital. "When you subtract book value from market value, the remaining is all the intellectual and knowledge and market capital. It includes all the patents they might have and all other intangibles," says Vish Krishna, associate professor of management at the McCombs School of Business at the University of Texas at Austin.

Once a company identifies its intellectual capital, the next step is to maintain it. One of the techniques that Dollar Bank uses to manage intellectual capital is to keep employees involved in decision making and planning, says Abraham

Nader, senior vice president and chief operating officer at the Pittsburgh-based bank.

Ron Griffin, CIO at The Home Depot, Inc., says that Atlanta-based home improvement retailer has tried-and-true structures in place for measuring, maintaining, and growing intellectual capital. The company uses a nine-box grid system to measure each employee's performance and potential, and it offers developmental courses to bring employees up to speed on certain issues. The categories measured include leadership ability, how an employee fits into the Home Depot culture, financial acumen, and project management capabilities

For its part, Home Depot posts a bulletin on its intranet with quick references on topics such as how to repair a leaky toilet or build a deck. That way, knowledge is available for employees to remain up to speed and to pass such information along to customers. "It's not just about selling product in our business; it's a lot of the knowledge, and we train on that extensively," Griffin says.

SOURCE: Excerpted from Taylor, Christie. "Intellectual Capital," *Computerworld*, March 12, 2001, p. 51.

▮▮▮▮▮▮

- *Knowledge management is not about "knowledge capture," per se.* Knowledge cannot be captured in its entirety. Problems involving collaboration, cooperation, and organizational culture must be addressed before one can be sure of reliable knowledge capture.

Regardless of the business, a company competes based on the knowledge of its employees. A company also has a management mind-set that relies on past experience (such as smart people, documents, or databases) and creates a new way for exchanging knowledge by using intranets, the Internet, local area networks, and the like. Consider the case of a British supermarket chain that used a customer data-mining application to assess buying behavior. After running correlation analyses among several variables, it quickly discovered a clear association between the purchases of diapers and beer by male customers on Friday afternoons. Armed with this knowledge, the store began to stack diapers and beer together.

It should be clear by now that people are the determinants of KM success. The best software is insufficient if you do not have people willing and ready to cooperate and collaborate. Sharing knowledge based on mutual trust is the critical component in the entire KM process. To illustrate, Lotus describes its Raven as resembling the "collaborative capabilities of Notes" but going further by "defining the relationships between people and content." Raven is a key element of Lotus' overall knowledge management strategy, which includes services, methodologies, and solutions from Lotus and IBM, all captured under the unifying theme of "people, places, and things." The company can create an employee profile detailing the employee's specialty and his or her projects, and then store the profile in a database that can be edited and accessed by users and coworkers via e-mail, instant messaging, and conferencing setups. The requirement with Raven is for employees to update their respective profiles (databases) consistently and regularly to maintain the "knowledge portal." If knowledge is not reinvested in this manner, it cannot be reliably created at a later time. Software update alone is not the answer.

Raven provides a single portal that will allow end users and communities to find and discover useful information and applications on a given subject, make the user aware of other knowledgeable people in the company, and organize all related tasks, teams, and projects. With its unique architecture, it is capable of generating a content map, creating expertise profiles, creating and hosting communities, clustering documents, mining skills, locating experts, and searching and browsing in a user-friendly manner. Such a KM tool can satisfy many of the user's needs that might not be fulfilled currently in the firm. One can plan to use such a product for the KM implementation. However, to fit a firm's needs perfectly, an information technology consultant should be contacted for proper fit.

■■■■ Why Knowledge Management?

A new word for the consumer in today's market, "prosumer," refers to the consumer who is no longer in the passive market where goods are offered at the exact face value. Prosumers are more educated consumers, and they demand more. They provide feedback to manufacturers regarding the design of products and services from a consumer perspective (Bexar 2000). This has initiated new and radical changes in the business world. Even with recent technology developments such as networking, e-mail, and the Web, business has yet to fully respond to the societal, cultural, and technical challenges. However, a positive response to knowledge sharing and knowledge management among growth-oriented firms is beginning to appear.

KM has already demonstrated a number of benefits and has offered justification for further implementation. The Internet facilitated its development and growth via fast and timely sharing of knowledge. By sharing knowledge, an organization creates exponential benefits from the knowledge as people learn from it. This makes business processes faster and more effective and empowers employees in a unique way. For example, Microsoft's Hotmail service advanced the wide use of e-mail that allowed users to exchange information through any Web browser. Today's Web-based interface is the norm for most Internet service providers.

Based on a number of published studies, KM has had a positive impact on business processes. The goal is to capture the tacit knowledge required by a business process and encourage knowledge workers to share and communicate knowledge with peers. With such knowledge, it is easier to determine which processes are more effective or less effective than others. The main constraint in KM, however, is initially capturing it. However, if an organization can succeed in capturing and dispersing knowledge, the benefits are endless. A company can leverage and more fully utilize intellectual assets. It can also position itself in responding quickly to customers, creating new markets, rapidly developing new products, and dominating emergent technologies.

Another benefit of KM is the intangible return on knowledge sharing rather than knowledge hoarding. Too often, employees in one part of a business start from "scratch" on a project because the knowledge needed is somewhere else but not known to them. To illustrate one documented case, a department of AT&T spent close to $80,000 for information that was available in a technical information document from its associate company, Bell Research Corporation, for $13 (Skyrme 1999, 2).

As a result of KM, systems have been developed to gather, organize, refine, and distribute knowledge throughout the business. In his study of Smart Business, Botkin (1999) suggests six top attributes of knowledge products and services:

- *Learn.* The more you use them, the smarter they get and the smarter you get, too.
- *Improve with use.* These products and services are enhanced rather than depleted when used, and they grow up instead of being used up.
- *Anticipate.* Knowing what you want, they recommend what you might want next.
- *Interactive.* There is two-way communication between you and them.
- *Remember.* They record and recall past actions to develop a profile.
- *Customize.* They offer unique configuration to your individual specifications in real time at no additional cost.

During the 1960s and 1970s, technology was focused on automating high-volume static processes such as claims processing, mortgage loan updating, airline reservation systems, and the like. The emergence of e-commerce in the late 1980s and 1990s showed how information technology could implement a new way of doing business effectively. Ever-increasing processing power, high bandwidth data transmission, and networking made it possible to reenvision how business gets done. It has also changed the business environment and introduced new competitive imperatives. Among them are:

- *Reacting instantly to new business opportunities, which led to decentralized decision making (and competency) at the front lines, where the action is.* With that came the desire to build mutual trust between knowledge workers and management and to cooperate in handling time-sensitive tasks.
- *Building better sensitivity to "brain drain."* It has been said that "expertise gravitates toward the highest bidder" (Applehans et al. 1999, 17). More and more companies realize the importance of managing and preserving expertise turnover. For the human resources department, the key question is "How does the firm replace expertise when it retires, resigns, or simply leaves?"
- *Ensuring successful partnering and core competencies with suppliers, vendors, customers, and other constituents.* Today's technology has enabled companies to reengineer the ways to do business. Getting partners up to your speed requires more than fast technology. Knowledge workers and others within the company should ensure that cooperation and coordination of work are practiced for the good of the firm.

With the expected depletion of highly knowledgeable workers due to the retirement of baby boomers, KM will be important in the upcoming years. It is essential that organizations capture and preserve the knowledge of senior colleagues so that younger employees can make immediate use of it and improve upon it to make the business run even more smoothly and more efficiently. Merrill Lynch has worked to incorporate KM to shorten the learning curve of its 18,000 brokers worldwide. The newly developed knowledge-based system facilitates sharing of knowledge and quickly enables less-trained brokers to achieve performance levels ordinarily associated with much more experienced professionals. The system captures and disperses knowledge about transactions, trading rules, yields, securities features, availability, tax considerations, and new offerings. Sharing of this knowledge allows brokers to serve millions of clients worldwide with sophisticated investment advice and detailed, up-to-date information and data. It acts as an instant training vehicle.

Andersen Consulting (now Accenture) provides another example of a well-developed knowledge-sharing system, called *ANet*. This electronic system connects employees and encourages the sharing of knowledge. ANet allows an employee to use the total knowledge of Accenture (formerly Arthur Andersen) to solve a customer problem anywhere in the world through electronic bulletin boards and to follow up with visual and data contacts. In theory, ANet expands the capabilities and knowledge available to any customer to that of the entire organization. It further enhances employee problem-solving capacity by providing access to compiled subject, customer-reference, and resource files available either directly through the system or from CD-ROMs available to all offices. Based on experience, Accenture reported that technological changes alone could not make ANet successfully used by employees. Major changes within the organization, such as changes in incentives and culture, were needed to create participation. A summary of KM justification is shown in Table 1.2.

Companies that fail to embed a viable KM operation probably suffer from several oversights or pitfalls:

- *Failing to modify the compensation system to reward people working as a team.* The traditional method of compensating people based on the old-fashioned "information-hoarding" practice does not work in a knowledge-sharing environment. Merit increases and bonuses should be based on team contribution and team performance rather than quantity or volume.
- *Building a huge database that is supposed to cater to the entire company.* Generalized systems do not usually work well, because information and knowledge are not stratified to address specialized areas of expertise. Ideally, the

---

TABLE 1.2 KM Justification

- Creates exponential benefits from the knowledge as people learn from it
- Has a positive impact on business processes
- Enables the organization to position itself for responding quickly to customers, creating new markets, developing new products, and dominating emergent technologies
- Builds mutual trust between knowledge workers and management and facilitates cooperation in handling time-sensitive tasks
- Builds better sensitivity to "brain drain"
- Ensures successful partnering and core competencies with suppliers, vendors, customers, and other constituents
- Shortens the learning curve, facilitates sharing of knowledge, and quickly enables less-trained brokers to achieve higher performance levels
- Enhances employee problem-solving capacity by providing access to compiled subject, customer-reference, and resource files available either directly through the system or from CD-ROMs available to all offices.

human resources department should first determine who works best with whom based on commonality of job type or job experience and then discover the knowledge that can be shared for each employee to be more successful.

- *Viewing KM as a technology or a human resources area.* This oversight relates to the earlier one—where human resources and information technology efforts are poorly coordinated—and defeats the purpose behind embedding KM into the fabric of the organization. The two departments should work jointly at introducing KM as part of the organizational processes.

- *Placing too much emphasis on technology.* Although intranets, knowledge-based tools, data warehouses, and other computer-based software are part of the way today's organization must adopt, technology is only the enabler of knowledge management. The knowledge it makes available must be organized and disseminated to human decision makers to be of any use.

- *Introducing KM into the organization via a simple project to minimize possible losses.* This is the wrong way to start KM. A company should start with a strategy and a champion, with a focus on a worthwhile, high profile project that can set the tone for the rest of the organization. It is a high risk approach, but one that is most likely to pay dividends in the long run.

- *Pursuing KM without being ready.* Spurred by the paradigm shift in our economy, many corporations pursue KM without evaluating whether they are organizationally ready (Stewart et al. 2000, 45). In other words, corporations that have been operating under classical management principles cannot be successful in adopting KM without major changes in culture, management attitudes, and communication skills.

- *Having poor leadership.* Like any high priority project, KM is best implemented with determined champions and top management commitment. For example, General Electric (GE) recognizes an organizational culture open to ideas from all levels of the company. By encouraging best-practice sharing, the company can grasp the knowledge within the employees and innovate the organization's processes. Jack Welch, former CEO, has established a knowledge management university and frequently teaches the classes himself. Only 10 percent of the 96 companies surveyed by the Conference Board sponsored by PricewaterhouseCoopers identified the CEO as a component of a KM initiative. By integrating the CEO of the company into the KM system, KM acquires a level of importance and respect that would otherwise be lacking. GE has incorporated all levels of the business and is well designed to share knowledge. The company is successfully able to use employee input and knowledge to produce a strategic advantage (Jones 1999, 3–18).

The Drivers

With these justifications to consider, several key KM drivers are worth noting. Each driver makes a compelling case for KM.

Technology Drivers.   The proliferation of technology, data communications, networking, and wireless transmission has revolutionized the way employees store, communicate, and exchange data at high speed. The World Wide Web has changed KM from a fad to an e-business reality. With a personal computer costing less than $600, anyone can access people and information at any time and from anywhere. Today, the same technological infrastructure makes it possible to store, communicate, and exchange knowledge. This makes technology a core capability leveler, leaving knowledge as a competitive differentiator. It means that although technology can move information or knowledge from Chicago to Bombay at lightening speed, it is people who turn knowledge into timely and creative decisions. Tomorrow's successful companies are ones that use information technology to leverage their employees' knowledge in ways that make knowledge immediately available and useful. It also implies quality maximization and cost minimization over the long term.

Process Drivers.   One of the most critical sets of KM drivers is designed to improve work processes. Implied in this area is the elimination of duplicate mistakes by learning from the past and by transferring the best experiential knowledge from one location or project in the firm to another. Starting from scratch with each project makes no sense in terms of efficiency, productivity, and value-added contribution to the company's bottom line. The value of knowledge sharing is shown in Box 1.3.

Another area where KM can improve process is the way companies react to market changes. "Just in time" is one approach to minimizing investment in inventory and more expeditiously meeting the demands of the consumer. Responsiveness that exceeds the competition becomes the key contributor to differentiation. It requires knowledge of control processes. KM means allowing companies to apply unique knowledge that makes them more responsive to market changes by the hour.

Personnel-Specific Drivers.   This area of KM drivers focuses on the need to create cross-functional teams of knowledge workers to serve anywhere in the organization and minimize personnel turnover as a threat to collective knowledge. More and more of what was once viewed as independent firms are now closely coupled. Products and services are jointly handled from diverse disciplinary areas (such as packaging, manufacturing, engineering, and technical skills), where creative cooperation is essential for innovation. Brainstorming, competitive response, and proactive positioning—all require collaboration and coordination of various tasks within and among corporations.

Another personnel-specific driver is minimizing knowledge walkouts. Highly marketable employees with unique knowledge can spell disaster for their employer. Competence drain that goes to the competition is probably the worst that can happen to a company struggling through the new knowledge economy.

Knowledge-Related Drivers.   Several KM drivers relate to the very concept of knowledge sharing and knowledge transfer within the firm. They include revisiting overlooked employee knowledge, making critical knowledge available at the time it is needed, and finding a mechanism to expedite available knowledge for immediate use. Companies often know what they know but have difficulty locating it. Take the case of a customer who wanted to return a product that was initially purchased from the same outfit in a different city to a local chain store. A code had to be entered into the computer to debit the initial store by the price of the product and then credit the local store by the same amount. There was only one employee in the local store who knew the code. She happened to be on vacation. The customer service employee could not find critical existing knowledge in time. So, she had to contact the other store for instructions on how to handle the returned item. Counting wait time and learning the procedure took close to 1 hour, while the customer was waiting.

Financial Drivers.   As an asset, knowledge defies economic theory, where assets are subject to diminishing returns over the long run. Knowledge assets increase in value as more and more people use them. With this in mind, knowledge follows the law of increasing returns—the more knowledge is used, the more value it provides. KM provides a worthwhile opportunity to integrate knowledge in a way that enriches the quality of decision making throughout the organization.

In the final analysis, the goal of KM is to produce a positive return on investment in people, processes, and technology. It means measurable efficiencies in production,

▪ ▪ ▪ ▪ ▪ ▪ **BOX 1.3** ▪ ▪ ▪ ▪ ▪ ▪

AN EXAMPLE OF THE VALUE OF KNOWLEDGE SHARING

LEARNING FROM MISTAKES

Mistakes happen. Best Buy Co., the Minneapolis-based retailer of consumer electronics, personal computers, and home appliances, does speaker installation and similar tasks. For Best Buy, preventing mistakes is a focus for knowledge management. KM is about creating a corporate culture that learns from experience, so if mistakes do happen, they will never be repeated.

To see how quickly the bottom-line benefits of knowledge sharing prove themselves at Best Buy, let's look at the results of one of its original three KM pilots, in the auto service and installation bays. "We have over 400 stores, two car bays per store, 1,400 service technicians, and 400 different audio products," says Allen Meyer, KM program director. "How many different ways can you put a radio in a car? One: the right way. The emphasis on knowledge management and knowledge sharing is to be able to model best practices behavior to avoid cost and improve customer satisfaction."

If, for example, a technician was to set off the Porsche Boxster's airbag, Best Buy would lose revenue and customer confidence. You might say that the retailer that does this the fewest number of times wins. As a matter of fact, no one at Best Buy has made this particular mistake even once. "One of our technicians found the similarity of wires for the airbag and the speakers and disseminated that information," Meyer says. "The hazard was promoted to a top tip and sent to every mobile installer across our enterprise that day." Of course, that glitch is only one of many possible mistakes. Other installations, for example, require drilling close to a car's gas tank.

Today, before an installer ever touches a car, he or she goes to the computer to print out any tips for the specific vehicle and product. If anyone learns something new, a tip is input to be validated by the gatekeeper and disseminated through the system. In these ways, knowledge sharing becomes a process embedded in standard operating procedures. "With a new model where this is always going to be a problem, it may be inevitable that [a mistake] happens once," Meyer admits. "The real tragedy is if it happens even a second time because the information didn't get out. If we avoid that scenario, how much money can we save?"

SOURCE: Excerpted from Barth, Steve. "Learning from Mistakes," *Knowledge Management*, April 2001, pp. 41–47.

▪ ▪ ▪ ▪ ▪ ▪

sales, and services on a daily basis; improving the quality of decision making at the front lines; bringing your business partners up to speed; improving employee morale to ensure low turnover and effective decision making; and improving customer-employee relations through better trust in knowledge workers' expertise.

▪ ▪ ▪ ▪ How It Came About

Traditionally, there has been a predefined "recipe for success," where companies have been run by company mottos and age-old business practices that were accepted as methods for success. Doing the same stuff harder and harder has demonstrated to many leading firms that they are losing touch with the quickly changing business environment and losing market share. The successes of yesterday no longer translate into successes of tomorrow. In today's business world, the heartbeat of the firm depends on the constant revamping of systems to remain competitive. There is tremendous emphasis on quick response instead of planning. Business can no longer rely on preset rules with which to operate, because the business environment is constantly evolving at an alarming speed. To be successful, business firms must redefine and question their current knowledge stored in corporate databases, while creating new practices to fit the business environment. As a reaction to the questionable benefits from downsizing, business process reengineering, and other cost-cutting measures in the 1980s and 1990s, knowledge management surfaced as the best next step to addressing the competition in a hard-to-predict environment.

The information revolution has placed emphasis on sharing huge amounts of information that is now accessible on the Internet. In a time of "e-everything," information is accessible from business-to-business, business-to-consumer, and consumer-to-consumer (Malhotra 2000). Corporate America has begun to use this information availability to their advantage. External relationships such as supply chain management have been successfully used to improve productivity and flexibility based on sharing between suppliers and customers. Companies have taken this idea of information sharing through KM to work within the firm. Aided by technology, employees now can share knowledge internally, in an effort to make the corporation a more productive enterprise.

KM is slowly gaining acceptance across industries. Several factors triggered interest in KM:

- *The pace of change has accelerated dramatically during the past decade.* Companies are looking at innovative ways of taking on the competition. Innovation is the one core competency needed by all organizations (Drucker 1969).
- *Globalization and geographic dispersion changed the organization's scope.* More and more organizations are trying to lean on years of experience to manage their global commitment in a timely and profitable fashion.
- *Downsizing and reengineering resulted in staff attrition and knowledge drain.* This prompted organizations to assess their knowledge core and make more effective use of it. Reengineering assumed a one-time fix to a situation. This created a vicious cycle, where solutions became new problems. It failed to recognize rapid changes in today's market.
- *Networking and data communications made it easier and faster to share knowledge.* Knowledge sharing is becoming the best way to distribute expertise across and around the firm via technology. Technology alone is insufficient.
- *The increasing dominance of knowledge as a basis for improving efficiency and effectiveness triggered many companies to find the means for utilizing the knowledge they have gained from previous experience.*

With these factors, it is easy to see how knowledge management works for the survival of the firm. Knowledge is the key. It is the core competence of any business. It is a function that can and should be embedded into every business process—new products and services, new channels of distribution, new marketing strategies, and new industry definitions. Technology is the backbone, and human components are necessary to utilize it.

In a 2000 survey of 243 domestic and international organizations by a leading consulting firm, the goal was to assess the current status of KM in business. Over two-thirds of the respondents claimed they had a KM strategy in place. Among the highlights of the report are the following:

- KM provides real benefits.
- Companies with KM are better than those without it.

- Organizations are failing to tackle KM's challenges. Failure to integrate KM into everyday work, lack of time to learn and share knowledge, lack of training, little personal benefit, and failure to use knowledge effectively continue to be a problem.
- Organizations are struggling with understanding the cultural implications of KM. They are finding that it complicates their job description.
- Companies still see KM as purely a technological solution. The shift in focus is occurring now, but human importance has yet to be realized.
- There is much to be accomplished in adopting and integrating KM, but the future looks bright (KPMG 2000).

Human resources is commonly identified as having a leading role in knowledge management. When PricewaterhouseCoopers sponsored a survey of 90 companies, they found that 32 percent of employees believed that human resources were involved in knowledge management, with a 25 percent response for information technology. Although information technology and technology in general are a large part of knowledge management, people continue to be the driving force behind knowledge management (Newman 1999).

Key Challenges

The biggest challenge that KM vendors face is explaining what KM is and how it can benefit a corporate environment. To get their foot in the door, vendors must integrate KM into the corporate culture—a shift in both organizational and individual philosophy. The culture comes from the top of the organization. Good or bad, it defines the major aspects of employee behavior on a daily basis. If the culture is not one that encourages cooperation and trust among employees, employees will not cooperate. Many experts suggest that the first objective is to make knowledge sharing profitable for the employee and the firm as well. When one tries to change another person's conditioned behavior, it is best to tie a form of compensation to changes in behavior, performance, or cooperation or to offer some kind of reward as a motivator. Cultural difference and their impact on knowledge sharing are shown in Box 1.4.

After the organizational culture is modified, the next challenge is to evaluate the firm's core knowledge, by employee, by department, and by division. One source compares assessing returns from a KM initiative to "calculating a payback from providing employees with telephones, paper and pens, etc." (Glasser 1999, 17). In evaluating these initiatives, one must look at the human as well as the technological investment.

A third challenge is learning how knowledge can be captured, processed, and acted on. KM must allow an organization not only to "stockpile" and access information, but to get at the history of how decisions were reached as well. Turning knowledge into action requires gleaning the information that has meaning and relevance for a particular organization. Because many executives resist the idea of managing knowledge like other assets, a company has to incorporate KM into the cultural fabric—a shift that requires changes in both organizational and personal philosophy.

A fourth challenge in KM is addressing the still neglected area of collaboration. Sound collaboration capabilities mean helping company employees share documents and needed information for all kinds of projects. Beyond efficiency and productivity, the real benefit of collaboration is *innovation*. It is a natural outcome of people working together for a common cause in a group or an organizational setting. Promoting innovation is the essence of KM. Technology can make this possible via online meetings, discussion databases, and other techniques made available through the IT department. To illustrate, imagine you missed your flight on the way to your home office to

▪▪▪▪▪▪ BOX 1.4 ▪▪▪▪▪▪

CULTURAL DIFFERENCES AND THEIR IMPACT ON KNOWLEDGE SHARING

WEAVING TWO INTO ONE

Making a merger work is not easy. When faced with a different corporate culture, it is not uncommon for the acquiring entity to try to impose its own systems, values, and strategies on the acquired. This approach can produce a defection of talent and a decline in stock price. One example is the unification of Daimler-Benz AG and Chrysler Corp. Touted beforehand as a "merger of equals," in reality it was an acquisition. Daimler-Benz, the dominant partner, has gradually been imposing its will. Observers say that the cultural conflicts between these companies have been particularly damaging when it comes to sharing knowledge. "German engineers are leery of having their 'superior' technology incorporated into 'lowbred' American cars," says Kay Hammer, an entrepreneur and president of Evolutionary Technologies International, Inc. "Similarly, German marketers are having trouble figuring out what the U.S. consumer wants. If they are too arrogant to listen to their American counterparts, there's going to be even more trouble ahead."

Cultural issues and other intangibles can make or break a merger. The decision about buying or selling a company should include analysis of the cultures in the form of a knowledge audit.

Knowledge management techniques and principles are vital to a smooth transition. KM naturally was at the forefront when Sopheon PLC, a London-based developer of KM tools, merged with the Minneapolis-based KM consultancy Teltech Resource Network Corp. In this case, management had to harmonize several core differences that could have undermined the deal. Both sides had to learn the finer points of transatlantic culture differences. "Europeans like to get to know you a little first and then do business, whereas in America it is often the other way round," says Paul Corney, a business and strategic advisor to Sopheon in England, who acted as a facilitator for the merger.

These examples suggest that a smooth merger transition depends on speed of execution and effective communication to resolve cultural barriers. "If the cultures are not meshed quickly, knowledge will exit before it can be harvested," says Barry Calogero, executive vice president at Robbins Gioia, Inc., a management consultancy in Alexandria, Virginia. Following management efforts to assure employees of the wisdom and express the strategic advantages of the mergers, assessing and sharing knowledge management help to cement the deal.

SOURCE: Excerpted from Robb, Drew. "Weaving Two into One," *Knowledge Management*, April 2001, pp. 33–38.

▪▪▪▪▪▪

participate in an important meeting regarding the launching of a new product. Instead of missing the debates and participation in strategic discussions, a KM system with collaborative features can allow you to log on from your hotel room and jump into an online debate about the product in question. You could participate in the meeting as it is taking place. You could even vote on the final decision as if you were there in person.

A fifth challenge is to continue researching KM to improve and expand its current capabilities. The research should discover ways of gathering, storing, processing, and distributing knowledge customized to the unique structure and operation of the firm. Meantime, it should be recognized that the wicked environment of discontinuous change is not temporary. The KM process means cooperation and commitment to change. Organizations must act on what they learn and continually adapt to the dynamic environment to reap the benefits of KM initiatives. Once initiated, there is no

looking back at the classical ways of doing business. A summary of the key challenges is shown in Table 1.3.

A final challenge is how to deal with tacit knowledge. As we shall discuss in Chapter 2, organizational learning helps us deal with tacit knowledge. Unfortunately, most of the time is spent dealing with explicit knowledge. Tacit knowledge is difficult to express and, therefore, difficult to codify, transfer, or share.

Like any other initiative, with challenges come KM tools or methods that take various forms. The most common tools include the Internet and intranets, data warehousing, document repositories, best-practice repositories, database mining tools, work-flow tools, work-flow applications, and online application-processing tools (Taft 2000, 14). These tools connect people to people and people to information on a global basis. Briefly, two key technologies are of special importance:

- *Installing an* intranet *is the first KM tool that allows company employees to access a wealth of information from anywhere at anytime to conduct business.* Active knowledge management assures accuracy, currency, reliability, and integrity of stored knowledge round the clock.
- *Developing a* videoconferencing system *makes it practicable for remote knowledge workers to initiate a face-to-face discussion over a telecommunication network.* Such a setup is ideal for sales staff in the field or workers encountering problems on an offshore oil rig. Later in the text, we discuss the kind of technology required to make this interface possible.

An important question that is often asked is "How would one know that KM initiatives are taking place?" Several indicators are worth watching in a business:

- Employees throughout the organization sharing the best practices—through databases as well as through personal interactions
- A knowledge center that promotes knowledge skills and facilitates knowledge flow for all employees to use in knowledge sharing
- A fine-tuned intranet and groupware facilities to expedite information and knowledge flow at all times, regardless of time, distance, or location.
- Working knowledge teams from all departments or divisions, whose focus is identifying, developing, and promoting ways to apply KM throughout the organization

Related to KM initiatives are KM user issues worth considering. With the user in mind, we need to question the processes required for KM success, organizationally and technologically, and how a KM system is measured to transform individual and team know-how into what the firm should "know." One solution is to develop taxonomies of

---

TABLE 1.3   Key Challenges in KM

Key Challenges in KM

- Explaining what KM is and how it can benefit a corporate environment
- Evaluating the firm's core knowledge by department and by division
- Learning how knowledge can be captured, processed, and acted upon
- Addressing the neglected area of collaboration
- Continuing research into KM to improve and expand its current capabilities
- Learning to deal with tacit knowledge

organizational knowledge for easy knowledge transfer and distribution. Success can be assured with a proven implementation plan based on experience.

Historical Overview

Knowledge has been the staple source of competitive advantage for many companies for hundreds of years. For example, the idea of passing knowledge to an apprentice from a master was used extensively during medieval times. Passing the "family recipe" that makes a certain product unique from one generation to another also attests to the notion of knowledge transfer and knowledge sharing. Although such transfer was extremely slow, it opened the door to modern methods of knowledge management that can exploit faster media of knowledge exchange, such as the Internet.

The recorded history of knowledge dates back to Plato and Aristotle, but its modern-day understanding is credited to scholars like Daniel Bell (1973), Michael Polanyi (1958, 1974), Alvin Toffler (1980), and the Japanese guru, Ikujiro Nonaka (1995). Other writers like Sveiby (1997) and Stewart (2000) promoted the concept knowledge as the core asset of an organization. As we shall find in Chapter 2, Polyani and Nonaka identify two kinds of knowledge: *Tacit* knowledge is highly experiential and is found in the heads of employees, customers, and vendors; *explicit* knowledge can be found in books, documents, data banks, corporate policy manuals, and the like. The learning process involves the intersection of both kinds of knowledge and the resulting knowledge transformation process.

In the 1960s, Drucker coined the terms "knowledge work" and "knowledge worker" when he was discussing the role of knowledge in organizations. He was the first to suggest that the U.S. economy has shifted from an economy of production to a knowledge economy, where the basic resource is knowledge, not capital. This means a shift to market-driven as opposed to product-driven orientation (Drucker 1969).

In the early 1970s, researchers at MIT and Stanford were analyzing ways in which companies produced, used, and diffused knowledge. This was the first essential step in the evolution of knowledge management, as we know it today. The idea of knowledge being a corporate asset had not yet caught on, and it was not until the 1980s that companies truly began to value knowledge. They also began to find ways to manage knowledge through such technologies as artificial intelligence and expert systems. Expert systems had their heyday in the 1980s and early 1990s, when developers focused on trying to develop "thinking machines" to emulate human experts rather than using machines to improve human thinking—the essence of KM.

During the 1990s, the onset of the Internet, the information superhighway, allowed KM to take off. The Internet facilitated access to publications about the concept of KM and how to implement it. With the help of the Internet, KM became a feasible concept for many companies. It provided more opportunities for knowledge sharing and knowledge transfer than there had been in the past. In terms of methodology, KM was briefly presented in total quality management (TQM) and teamwork. Business process reengineering (BPR), downsizing, and outsourcing were also attempts to improve the performance of the firm, although they had limited success. They resolved the productivity factor, but drained knowledge from the organization.

These attempts were more like round one, where companies managed their knowledge assets in the same way they managed physical assets. Physical goods were stored in the warehouse, but for the intellectual equivalent, it was in the knowledge repository. When databases and "warehouses" were full (too many physical assets), they began thinking about supply chain management (SCM), trying to match the supply of goods with demand and reduce inventories to what was actually ordered for production. It was more like rewarding the efficiency-driven prediction of the future based on past trends—doing things right. In contrast, in round two of KM, companies began to realize that to fit the supply of knowledge to the demand for it in products and services, they needed to toy with how knowledge workers did their jobs. To be effective, KM has to be "baked into" the job and be part of the fabric of the work to bring in knowledge when needed and export it anywhere in the organization when it is acquired (Davenport 1999, 2). This is where we began to see a shift from "doing things right" to "doing the right thing"—working smarter, not harder.

Given the progress made in automating procedures in the 1970s and communications and networking (mostly through e-mail) in the 1980s, the focus of technology in the 1990s was on cognitive computing to augment the knowledge work of humans. Of these, the Internet and intranets have had the most profound impact on spreading the know-how. From a knowledge perspective, the Internet and accompanying technologies have demonstrated several characteristics in knowledge management:

- *The Internet is an incredible information source.* Internet access is available worldwide. It means a company's knowledge workers can access information and share knowledge anywhere, anyplace, anytime, without delay
- *With the World Wide Web, every user can share and update information at will.* This is especially attractive with the decreasing cost of communications.
- *The Internet uses a universal communication standard protocol.* This protocol, TCP/IP, makes information access and exchange accessible from anywhere there is a computer and an Internet service provider.
- *The Internet provides quicker interaction and communication with fellow knowledge workers.* This interaction can be one-on-one or as a group.

■ ■ ■ ■ KM Myths

In contrast to what KM is, we have tried to clarify what KM is not. KM is not a separate area or function in a business, represented by a KM department or a KM process. KM is interwoven into all of an organization's processes. Although effective utilization of technology is essential, KM is not constrained by collecting knowledge from domain experts and building networked databases or databases supported by the company's intranet. Finally, KM is not defined in terms of the specific knowledge needs of every employee, the relevant knowledge needed, or the knowledge to be shared.

There are several myths as well:

Myth 1: Knowledge management is a fad. As mentioned earlier, there are many pessimists in industry who doubt the "good fit" potential of KM. Being at a crossroads, vendors push older software products under the KM label. BPR and artificial intelligence had their positive turn, although they suffered from raised expectations. Unlike earlier trends, however, true KM becomes embedded in the way people work in business. So, knowing what you know or what you need to know cannot be a fad.

Myth 2: Knowledge management and data warehousing are essentially the same. The term *data warehousing* implies a repository of data, not knowledge. Knowledge, per se, is how you take information and transform it into action. Data warehousing is critical for KM. It is where data, critical documents, e-mail, and other forms of information are available for eliciting knowledge at the time when it is needed. For example, Sears, Roebuck & Co. has a customer data warehouse with demographic information on over 100 million households to help the sales force improve marketing and sales quality. For example, a repairperson working on a customer's refrigerator notices through the KM system that such a customer is a likely prospect for a new freezer. Data mining serves a similar purpose, in that patterns within a mass of data allow management to better understand trends and directions in a product or consumer preference—a necessary dimension of KM.

Myth 3: Knowledge management is a new concept. As a concept, KM has been practiced by successful firms as far back as the early 1980s. Companies like Ford and General Motors Corporation have been exchanging design information and collaborating on design projects worldwide using technology all along. Today's version of KM goes under customer profiling, where a supermarket clerk scans a store-generated customer card to determine patterns of purchases and consumer preferences by date, by product, and by location. The idea is the same as it has been for the past 2 decades, except that in today's KM, technology has taken on a special role in the way knowledge is shared and disseminated.

Myth 4: Knowledge management is mere technology. This is a serious misconception. KM is really about people, relationships, and a new way of working together as an entity in an organizational setting. It is a unique way of thinking about work and about working. Imagine a knowledge community of employees with common interests sharing information on best practices that help everyone do a more efficient job. KM will work only if there is trust and confidence among coworkers. Over 80 percent of all technology-centered KM efforts have been known to fail because of a lack of attention to people (Whiting 1999, 44).

Myth 5: Technology can store and distribute human intelligence. Data may be stored in a centralized database for employee access, but that does not ensure that employees will use the information. In a turbulent competitive environment, one cannot assume that companies can predict the right information for the right employee. So, it is hardly the case that technology distributes human intelligence. It is impossible to build a KM system that predicts who the right person is and at what time he or she needs specific information for decision making. Tacit knowledge exists within a person's brain; information or "knowledge" stored within the database can be viewed as a valuable exchange between people to make sense of a situation but should not be interpreted as human intelligence. In other words, knowledge repositories stored in computers do not allow for renewal of existing knowledge and creation of new knowledge. KM should be considered as a system to be used with concentration on the human aspect aided by technology for decision making.

Myth 6: Knowledge management is another form of reengineering. Reengineering is efficiency-driven—a one-time attempt at introducing radical change in organizational processes to improve efficiency. The emphasis is on cost reduction and making better use of existing operations. Jump-starting such a business, however, often results in failure. KM is an ongoing renewal of organizational processes to learn in advance about the company's future opportunities and contingencies. The concentration is on value-added activities that demand innovation and creativity. This is ingrained in the day-to-day processes of the business. Technology plays a critical role in the way information becomes available at electronic speed.

Myth 7: Company employees have difficulty sharing knowledge. The answer is yes and no, depending on a number of factors: attitude of the knower, who the requester is, company culture, sensitivity of the knowledge requested, availability of attractive motivators, and trust level among company personnel. Under the traditional business model, employees with unique knowledge accumulated over years of experience tended to protect "turf" by not sharing such knowledge. In a KM environment, where knowledge sharing means great potential for everyone including the organization, knowledge workers need to be sold on how knowledge sharing will bring them mutual benefits. The term *sharing* means "willingly giving away a part" and "holding in common." It is a "give to get" attitude, and because "knowing" is personal, asking someone to share is to ask him or her to give something of themselves. Mature or secure people in a stable work environment tend to share knowledge more than others whose experience is to the contrary. Also, knowledge sharing can improve bonds between people, provided the act of sharing is reciprocal.

Myth 8: Knowledge management works only within an organization. On the surface, this may be true, but some of the most valuable knowledge comes from the outside— suppliers, brokers, government agencies, and customers. The problem with extending KM initiatives to outside sources is incompatible technology, security issues, and complexity of the design.

Myth 9: Technology is a better alternative than face-to-face. We have seen over the years that when it comes to real-life experience and use of human knowledge, technology does not hold all the answers. The emerging mind-set within today's forward-looking, creative organizations is that KM must entail cultural and organizational change as well as technology-based innovations. Data warehousing and data mining are all contributors to extracting and sharing knowledge, but the best knowledge resides in human minds. This makes a face-to-face approach to knowledge acquisition and knowledge sharing a better alternative.

Myth 10: It is a "no brainer" to share what you know. In general, secure and mature people are less reluctant to share what they know with others. Unfortunately, in traditional business, people with years of experience tended to hoard knowledge rather than share it, because it gave them leverage, control, and assurance of a job. Furthermore, "knowing" is personal. To ask people to share knowledge is tantamount to expecting them to give something of themselves. Sharing knowledge often depends on who the requester is, how sensitive is the knowledge requested, the attitude of the "knower," and the motivational forces at play. To share knowledge, the business has to undergo special employee training, instill trust within the business, and give employees and management a chance to cement relationships based on trust. A summary of the KM myths is shown in Table 1.4.

TABLE 1.4   Myths About Knowledge Management

The Myths of Knowledge Management

1. Knowledge management is a fad.
2. Knowledge management and data warehousing are essentially the same.
3. Knowledge management is a new concept.
4. Knowledge management is mere technology.
5. Technology distributes human intelligence.
6. Knowledge management is another form of reengineering.
7. Company employees have difficulty sharing knowledge.
8. Knowledge management works only within an organization.
9. Technology is a better alternative than face-to-face.
10. It is "no brainer" to share what you know.

▪ ▪ ▪ ▪ KM Life Cycle

KM goes through a series of steps, making up an ongoing life cycle. The four-step process, summarized in Table 1.5, includes gathering, organizing, refining, and disseminating. These and alternative approaches to the KM life cycle are explained in detail in Chapter 3.

The capturing phase deals with knowledge capture and includes e-mail, audio files, digital files, and the like. In this phase, it is important to go to all the sources available and never judge the usefulness of the captured knowledge until after it is subjected to exhaustive testing. In this phase, KM systems are an ideal approach to eliciting and representing knowledge into a form that can be available to many users—a key KM process. This process is discussed in detail in later chapters.

After the capturing phase, captured data or information should be organized in a way that can be retrieved and used to generate useful knowledge. One can use indexing, clustering, cataloging, filtering, codifying, and other methods to do the organizing. Speed, user-friendliness, efficiency of access, and accuracy are important elements to consider throughout the organizing phase.

After organizing the information, it should be refined. Data mining can be applied in this phase. Data mining takes explicit knowledge found in databases and transforms it into tacit knowledge. Data-mining software is used to find patterns in data, predict behavior, and warn against future problems based on the data supplied in data warehouses. For example, the sales records for a particular brand of tennis racket might, if sufficiently analyzed and related to other market data, reveal a seasonal correlation with the purchase by the same parties of golf equipment.

TABLE 1.5 Four-Process View of Knowledge Management

Four-Process View of KM

• **Capturing**	—Data entry
	—Scanning
	—Voice input
	—Interviewing
	—Brainstorming
• **Organizing**	—Cataloging
	—Indexing
	—Filtering
	—Linking
	—Codifying
• **Refining**	—Contexualizing
	—Collaborating
	—Compacting
	—Projecting
	—Mining
• **Transfer**	—Flow
	—Sharing
	—Alert
	—Push

▪ ▪ ▪ ▪ ▪ ▪

After the refining phase, knowledge should be disseminated or transferred. This includes making knowledge available to employees via tutorials or guidelines for effective use. Predictive models can be designed to alert users to consequences of certain projects or human resource activities. The key point is not to let stored or available knowledge sit idle in a repository like a database. It should be available to authorized users to contribute to the corporate competitive advantage.

Figure 1.6 shows the relationship between the KM life cycle and four key areas in the organization. Taken together, one can understand a viable set of relationships between KM and management decision making, organizational culture, organizational personnel, and information technology. As we shall see in Chapter 3, each area could have an impact on the way KM is installed and maintained in the organization.

Role of Trust in the KM Life Cycle

Knowledge-based organizations are learning human systems. One of the requirements that encourage the flow of knowledge is establishing an environment where employees feel free to share insights, experiences, and know-how. This boils down to the issue of *trust*. Trust supports the KM process by giving employees clear impressions that reciprocity, free exchange, and proposing innovations will be recognized and fairly compensated. In contrast, lack of trust encourages employees at all levels to hoard knowledge and build suspicion in people and organizational processes.

Trust means integrity, consistent communication, and proven willingness of the organization to integrate employees into the decision-making process. For trust to be effective, an organization must make an overt effort to embed trust in the culture of the business. This means tackling the environment of trust from several angles: human resources, management initiatives, top management support, and demonstrating to knowledge employees that they belong. It becomes the cement that glues an organization together in its effort to address an unpredictable competitive environment. The bottom line is that one cannot have an open, candid dialogue with someone he or she does not trust. If one trusts his or her peers, then there should be no concerns about where they stand.

With trust in mind, the key question is how does a company develop trust? First, trust should be built at all levels of the organization. A summary view is to break down

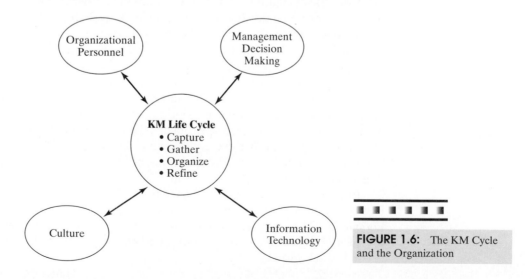

FIGURE 1.6: The KM Cycle and the Organization

the barriers created by traditional organizational structures. Rather than managing by controlling and closely supervising employees, the alternative is to empower them and open lines of communication between managers and workers. During the annual performance evaluation session, each employee should be given a chance to explain what he or she did to build a sense of community in their department, division, or the company as a whole. Some of the suggestions offered include:

- Decentralizing or flattening the organization structure to allow decision making by teamwork
- Reducing control-based management and encouraging management by results so that employees and teams can get their rightful credit for contribution to the company's profitability
- Revisiting the company's mission statement and ethics policy to demonstrate the company's new views about organizational values and opening lines of communications through periodic employee satisfaction surveys, brainstorming sessions, and the like
- Assessing and improving employee responsibilities and accountability on a company-wide basis; eliminating unnecessary directives or barriers
- Recognizing employees through bonus programs, knowledge employee of the month, on the employee bulletin board, or in the newspaper
- Installing an employee training program, especially geared for improving employee commitment to knowledge sharing

It can be concluded, then, that trust is critical to a successful KM program. Despite its value, it continues to be a most difficult intangible to create and maintain, especially in large corporations like Ford, General Motors, IBM, and others. The potential is in its lasting effect once it is properly embedded into the organization and maintained within the corporate policies that make sense for KM.

▪ ▪ ▪ ▪ Implications for Knowledge Management

Any discussion on knowledge management is bound to produce both optimists and doubters. However, we know now that the source of organizational wealth is something specifically human—knowledge. Applying knowledge to what we already do contributes to productivity. In contrast, applying knowledge to what is new is innovation. Knowledge is the key to both goals. This will be the focus of Chapter 2.

The rapid advancement of knowledge exchange tools (such as the Internet, intranets, and groupware) is setting the stage for knowledge management. The great potential of this emerging concept lies in how well we share the "know-how" to augment the decision-making quality and capacity of the organization. For those whose product is knowledge, knowledge workers are distinguished from information handlers by their ability to solve unique problems with renewed effectiveness and add value in an unpredictable competitive environment. The emphasis is on augmenting the abilities of the human user—working smarter, not harder. They use their knowledge rather than data or information.

In most corporations, the management of knowledge is still uncharted territory. Few executives understand how to make the most effective use of their company's knowledge. They may know about tangible assets like the physical plant or existing inventory, but they have trouble putting a price tag on the value of the talent or expertise in the sales force.

To promote a knowledge management environment, companies must consider cultural, social, and organizational changes as well as technological support. They must also add systems and applications in their IT infrastructure in the interest of integration and knowledge sharing. For this reason, more and more companies are beginning to recognize the importance of knowledge management systems. This area is covered later in the text.

One area that a company must address is how to manage its intellectual capital—the sum of knowledge of the human resources of the organization. As we shall find in Chapter 2, the knowledge found in policy manuals, case histories, training materials, and employees' heads is the most valuable asset of the company in terms of replacement costs. To develop and maintain this knowledge is extremely costly. Unless a company reviews its core knowledge and takes steps to manage it, it is subject to potential disaster resulting from resignations, turnover, loss of its competitive edge, and the like.

Finally, in the grand scheme of things, the trend toward knowledge sharing is good for coworkers, for the company, and for society as a whole. The key converter from hoarding knowledge to sharing knowledge is trust. To gain a competitive advantage in an unpredictable environment, we must learn to master the art of knowledge sharing and knowledge management. Efforts can be realized only if there is follow-through. Corporate culture must change first. Knowledge is not a technology, but an activity enabled by information technology and produced by people. Companies must commit to changing their corporate structure by assigning knowledge workers, whose responsibilities include motivating and organizing the corporate, to adapt to a new way of business that transcends the entire landscape.

SUMMARY ▪ ▪ ▪ ▪

- Today's knowledge age brings with it an increasingly complex business environment worldwide. Companies need to address knowledge sharing, knowledge collaboration, and knowledge dissemination to be able to compete in an unpredictable marketplace.
- KM is the process of gathering and making use of a firm's collective expertise anywhere in the business. A firm seeks to add value by creatively identifying, applying, and integrating knowledge in unprecedented ways.
- KM is not about reengineering, discipline, or one based on information only. It is not a fad or a way of appeasing employees around an employee-oriented concept. It is about change, and tomorrow's business is the name of the game. People are the determinants of KM success.
- There is plenty of justification for KM. Knowledge sharing means faster processing, no duplication of effort, and reacting more responsively to new business opportunities. It also means ensuring successful partnering and core competencies with suppliers, vendors, customers, and other constituents.
- Companies that fail to install a KM environment could be guilty of using the old reward system, having a database that lacks focus, having poor coordination of the IT or human resources effort, choosing the wrong project, and having poor leadership.
- There are several drivers that provide a compelling case for adopting KM: technology, process, personnel-specific, knowledge-related, and financial drivers. In the final analysis, the goal of KM is to produce a positive return on investment in people, processes, and technology.

- Several factors triggered interest in KM: need for innovation, globalization, easier navigation with telecommunications, and the increasing dominance of knowledge as a way of improving efficiency and effectiveness of the firm.
- KM dates back to Plato and Aristotle, although its modern-day understanding began in the 1960s. During the 1990s, the onset of the Internet, the information superhighway, allowed KM to take off. Quicker interaction and communications with fellow knowledge workers, whether one-on-one or as a group, made it all possible.
- Several KM myths have been cited in an effort to clarify what KM is not. Once the concept becomes widely accepted and the KM process becomes standardized, most of these myths should disappear.
- The KM cycle essentially begins with knowledge gathering, followed by knowledge organization, knowledge refinement, and knowledge transfer. The role of trust is critical throughout the entire life cycle. In Chapter 3, the KM life cycle, including knowledge maintenance and update, will be discussed in detail.

TERMS TO KNOW ▪ ▪ ▪ ▪

Downsizing: Reducing the physical, personnel, and functional processes of an organization in an effort to improve its efficiency through reduced costs and improved performance.

Financial driver: A driver or a motivator that views knowledge assets as something increasing in value as more and more people make use of it.

Intellectual capital: The value of a company's trademarks, patents, brand names, and the like; a company's collective brainpower or a composite of experience, knowledge, information, and intellectual property.

Internet: A system of interconnected data communication or computer networks on a global basis.

Knowledge management: The process of gathering and making use of a firm's collective expertise wherever it resides—on paper, in databases, or in people's heads.

Knowledge-related driver: A driver or a motivator that relates to the concept of knowledge sharing and knowledge transfer within the firm.

Knowledge-sharing: A process of transferring human knowledge about a process or a procedure to others in the organization; ability and willingness of people to exchange specialized experience with others for the common good of the organization.

Personnel-specific driver: A driver or a motivator that focuses on the need to create cross-functional teams of knowledge workers to serve anywhere in the organization and minimize personnel turnover as a threat to collective knowledge.

Process driver: A driver or a motivator designed to improve work processes through KM.

Reengineering: One-shot drastic "electrical shock" change in organizational processes to improve efficiency; a mechanical shift from one stage of operation to a more efficient stage.

Supply chain management: The integration of all activities associated with the flow and transformation of goods from the raw materials to the customer as well as the related information flows.

Technology driver: A driver or a motivator designed to use technology for storing and transferring knowledge throughout the organization.

Trust: A feeling of confidence in another person; having confidence or faith in another person or in a relationship.

Videoconferencing: A computer-based system designed to simulate face-to-face meetings with two-way full-motion video along with two-way audio. Participants can view one another during long-distance conferences or meetings.

TEST YOUR UNDERSTANDING ▪ ▪ ▪ ▪

1. Select one definition of KM in Figure 1.2 and explain the reason(s) for your choice.
2. KM involves people, technology, and processes in overlapping parts. Explain the KM concept.
3. One unique indicator of KM in action is seeing people think ahead, not behind. Do you agree with this statement? Explain why you agree or disagree.

4. In what way is KM *not* about:
   a. reengineering
   b. a discipline
   c. data
   d. knowledge capture
5. Distinguish between:
   a. KM and intellectual capital
   b. a champion and a manager
   c. the Internet and an intranet
   d. trust and knowledge sharing
6. What factors justify the adoption of KM into an organization?
7. What oversights or pitfalls impede the introduction of KM into an organization?
8. Briefly explain the factors that triggered interest in KM.
9. The chapter explains several challenges in KM. Select three challenges and elaborate on each.
10. How would one know that KM initiatives are taking place?
11. Summarize in your own words the history leading to today's KM.
12. How does the Internet contribute to the use of KM in organizations?
13. Explain five KM myths and the reasons for viewing them as myths.
14. List and briefly explain the key steps in the KM life cycle.
15. How does a company develop trust? Be specific.

KNOWLEDGE EXERCISES ▪ ▪ ▪ ▪

1. Suppose you were asked to do a 15-minute presentation before the managers of a small retailer about the pros and cons of knowledge management. What would you say? Outline the content of your talk.
2. How easy do you think it is to understand knowledge management? Why?
3. Search the Internet and current journals for surveys that show how well companies are adopting (or struggling with) KM. Report your findings in class.
4. How should a company assess its knowledge core? Detail a procedure that can be sold to top management.
5. What do you think distinguishes today's knowledge age from that of the information age of the 1980s and 1990s?
6. Search the literature, including the Internet, and prepare a three-page report on some of the problems in developing and implementing a knowledge management system.
7. In your own words, describe the implications that a knowledge management system has on an industry of your choice.
8. Working with a classmate, conduct an interview or a telephone survey regarding a local business's
   a. familiarity with KM
   b. level of literacy in KM
9. A business manager, a programmer, and a psychologist all want to become KM designers. Which do you feel will have the least difficulty? Why?
10. A car dealer who has just learned about knowledge management thinks it could be ideal for separating "tire-kickers" from serious buyers. Would this be a typical KM application? Why?
11. Visit a small business (such as a hardware store or a bakery) and stay long enough to get a feel for the information exchanged, customer questions, and the way the business is run. Write a short report about the core knowledge of the business. Are there knowledge workers there or just clerks?

12. Find cases or current information on trends in KM by searching the Internet. Locate a company that is reported to have succeeded (or failed) in going the KM route. Write a three-page report summarizing your findings.
13. Visit a local bank (not a branch) and identify knowledge workers. What is unique about knowledge workers? How do you distinguish them from regular employees?

REFERENCES ▪ ▪ ▪ ▪

Applehans, Wayne, Globe, Alden, and Laugero, Graig. *Managing Knowledge*. Boston, MA: Addison-Wesley, 1999.

Bair, Jim. "Knowledge Management Technology: Beyond Document Management," www.strategy-partners.com/spweb/pages.nsf/all+pages/White%20Paper%20%20Knowledge%20Management%20Technology:%Beyone%20Document%20Management?open document, Date accessed August 2002.

Barth, Steve. "Learning from Mistakes," *Knowledge Management*, April 2001, pp. 41–47.

Bell, Daniel. *The Coming of Post Industrial Society*. London: Oxford University Press, 1995.

Bexar County. "Information Technology Industry Trend," www.co.bexar.tx.us/bcis/Documentation/DOC_It_Industry_Trends/doc_it_industry_trends.htm, Date accessed August 2002.

Botkin, James. *Smart Business: How Knowledge Communities Can Revolutionize Your Company*. New York: Free Press, 1999.

Brooking, A. *Intellectual Capital*. London: Thompson Press, 1996.

Craig, Robert. "Knowledge Management Comes of Age." *ENT*, vol. 5, April 2000, pp. 36–37.

Davenport, Tom. "Knowledge Management, Round Two," *CIO Magazine*, November 1, 1999, pp. 1–4.

Deveau, Denise. "Knowledge Is Business Power," *Computing Canada*, vol. 26, no. 8, April 14, 2000, p. 14.

Drucker, P. F. *The Age of Discontinuity*. New York: Harper Publishing, 1969.

Glasser, Perry. "The Knowledge Factor," *CIO Magazine*, January 1999, pp. 12–18.

Gravallese, Julie. "Knowledge Management," *The MITRE Advanced Technology Newsletter*, vol. 4, no. 1, April 2000, pp. 1–3. www.mitre.org/pubs/edge/april_00, Date accessed August 2002.

Hersey, Ian. "Need: Net-Speed Knowledge Tools," *Electronic Engineering Times*, September 4, 2000, p. 90.

Hibbard, Justin. "Knowing What We Know," *InformationWeek*, October 20, 1997, p. 46.

Johnson, Cindy. Director of Collaboration and Knowledge Sharing at Texas Instruments. Interview February 2, 2002.

KPMG Consulting. *Knowledge Report 2000*, November 1999.

Malhotra, Yogesh. "Knowledge Management for the New World of Business," www.brint.com/km/whatis.htm, Date accessed August 2002.

Newman, B. "Managing Knowledge: The HR Role," *HR Executive Review*, vol. 6, no. 4, 1999, pp. 3–18.

Nonaka, Ikujiro. *The Knowledge-Creating Company*. London: Oxford University Press, 1995.

O'Dell, Carla S., Essaides, Nilly, Ostro Nilly (contributor), C. Grayson (preface). *If Only We Knew What We Know: The Transfer of Internal Knowledge and Best Practice*. New York: Free Press, 1998.

Polanyi, Michael. *Knowing and Being*. Chicago: The University of Chicago Press, 1974.

Polanyi, Michael. *Personal Knowledge: Toward a Post-Critical Philosophy*. Chicago: The University of Chicago Press, 1958.

Robb, Drew. "Weaving Two into One," *Knowledge Management*, April 2001, pp. 33–38.

Skyrme, David J. "Knowledge Networking," *The Intelligent Enterprise*, November 1999, pp. 9–15.

Skyrme, David. "Knowledge Management: Making It Work," www.skyrme.com/pubs/lawlib99.htm, Date accessed August 2002.

Stewart, Kathy, et al. "Confronting the Assumptions Underlying the Management of Knowledge: An Agenda for Understanding and Investigating Knowledge Management," *The Data Base for Advances in Information Systems*, Fall 2000, pp. 41–45.

Stewart, Thomas A. *Intellectual Capital: The New Wealth of Organizations*. New York: Doubleday Press, 1997.

Sveiby, Karl-Erik. "Intellectual Capital and Knowledge Management," www.sveiby.com/articles/Intellectual Capital.html, Date accessed August 2002.

Sveiby, Karl-Erik. *The New Organizational Wealth: Managing and Measuring Knowledge-Based Assets*. New York: Berrett-Kohler, 1997.

Taft, Darryl. "Stopping Knowledge Overflow— Knowledge Management Tools Still in Developmental Phase," *Computer Reseller News*, February 2000, p. 14.

Taylor, Christie. "Intellectual Capital," *Computerworld*, March 12, 2001, p. 51.

Toffler, Alvin. *The Third Wave*. New York: Bantam Books, 1980.

Trepper, Charles. "Keep Your Knowledge In-House," *InformationWeek*, September 4, 2000, p. 55.

Whiting, Rick. "Myths and Realities," *InformationWeek*, November 22, 1999, p. 42ff.

Understanding Knowledge

Contents

I think, therefore I am.
— RENE DESCARTES

▪ ▪ ▪ ▪ In a Nutshell

The most critical word in the KM area is *knowledge.* Unfortunately, there is a continuing myth that knowledge resides only in books, reports, or documents. This cannot be true, any more than viewing musical notes on a page constitutes music. What we have here are representations of information and music, respectively. What do we mean when we talk about knowledge? Two key issues are distinguishing between knowledge and information and determining how they are interrelated. Knowledge is neither data nor information, although it is related to both. The terms are not interchangeable, and knowing what is needed often determines organizational success or failure.

This chapter examines the concept of knowledge as the heart of an organization's productivity and growth and discusses the classifications of knowledge. Intelligent behavior implies the ability to understand and use language and to store and access relevant experience at will. Humans acquire expertise—that is, they learn via experience. Expertise incorporates the ability to reason and to make deductions; it also includes the concept of common sense. This makes human intelligence and the knowledge that humans amass over time the primary organizational asset. An organization's technology or telecommunications network is only a vehicle for knowledge transfer and knowledge exchange; it cannot replace human knowledge.

An essential criterion of knowledge and learning is memory. Learning by discovery is less understood than learning by experience or by example. Several approaches to learning are covered later in the chapter. A knowledge base is a critical component of knowledge management. Knowledge developers need to understand the theory and meaning of knowledge early in the knowledge capture phase and become familiar with the unique kinds of knowledge available in the corporation under study. It should be pointed out that an expert's knowledge is not limited to information or complex procedures. Knowledge embraces a wider sphere than information. Likewise, a knowledge base is not the same as a database. A database has a predetermined structure; a knowledge base is a set of facts and inference rules for determining new information and "smarter" knowledge for decision making.

Knowledge as know-how may be either shallow or deep knowledge. It may also be procedural, declarative, semantic, or episodic knowledge. More recently, knowledge has been classified as explicit or tacit knowledge. All these classifications are covered in the chapter.

Another goal of this chapter is to show that human knowledge and logical processes can be captured and represented in a valid way to solve certain kinds of problems. (The words *valid* and *validity* as used in the text do not have the same meaning as *truth.* A conclusion, for example, follows logically from facts and rules using inference procedures; it can be a false, or not correct, conclusion, even though it may still be a valid one.)

■ ■ ■ ■ Definitions

Before discussing knowledge and its many ramifications, *knowledge* needs to be defined in relation to *intelligence, experience,* and *common sense.*

KNOWLEDGE

We define *knowledge* as "understanding gained through experience or study." It is "know-how" or a familiarity with how to do something that enables a person to perform a specialized task. It may also be an accumulation of facts, procedural rules, or heuristics. These elements are defined as follows:

- A **fact** is a statement of some element of truth about a subject matter or a domain. For example, milk is white and the sun rises in the east and sets in the west are facts.
- A **procedural rule** is a rule that describes a sequence of relations relative to the main. For example, always check the traffic when entering a freeway; if the gas gauge indicates less than a quarter of a tank of gas, look for a gasoline station.
- A **heuristic** is a rule of thumb based on years of experience. For example, if a person drives no more than 5 miles above the speed limit, then that person is not likely to be stopped for speeding.

A beneficial aspect of knowledge is that it can compensate for some search time. A human expert who knows a set of solutions can get a job done without much searching for information. Conversely, a human novice in a video game searches a vast number of alternative moves at each juncture because he lacks experiential knowledge. Unfortunately, without the aid of knowledge that allows the novice to immediately eliminate inappropriate approaches, this method encompasses too many approaches to evaluate.

Another aspect of knowledge is specificity; it cannot be transferred from one problem domain to another. Therefore, one must have the surgeon's know-how to repair a heart valve, the auto transmission specialist's know-how to replace a reverse gear, and the painter's know-how to create an accomplished portrait. These kinds of extensive knowledge are referred to as *tacit knowledge* and often take many years to acquire.

Finally, values, beliefs, and integrity are related to knowledge. This has a lot to do with what the knower perceives, accepts, and concludes from the environment. People generally organize and synthesize their knowledge by their values. Nonaka and Takeuchi suggest that "knowledge, unlike information, is about beliefs and commitment" (Nonaka and Takeuchi 1995). More recently, we began to attach integrity to the whole process of knowledge capture, knowledge sharing, and knowledge maintenance. Integrity means reliability, trustworthiness, privacy, and confidentiality. Integrity cuts across the discipline, regardless of company size or resources.

INTELLIGENCE

Intelligence refers to the capacity to acquire and apply knowledge. It is the ability to build or improve upon knowledge, to transform as much of one's knowledge as possible into knowledge that can be used to make good decisions. An intelligent person is one who has the ability to think and reason. This distinction separates the novice from the master in a game like chess. Knowledge conversion is directly responsible for much of the expert's efficiency in applying knowledge and for the difficulty of making it explicit.

Consider this example: Recent research into the true meaning of intelligence illustrates very well the difficulty of defining the term. The organization doing this research decided to get to the bottom of the question once and for all and, given its importance, assigned its most senior scientist to it. The esteemed scholar spent several months conducting this research. At the end of that period, the scientist gathered a number of colleagues together, held up in front of them the artificially intelligent artifact chosen as the subject of the research, and said, "Ladies and gentlemen, this is a thermos bottle. It keeps hot stuff hot, and it keeps cold stuff cold. My question is, how does it know?"

Ability to understand and use language is another attribute of intelligence. Language understanding is not easy to acquire, especially for the existing technology. For example, consider the statement, *The city of Fairmount is under 6 feet of water.* Does this mean that the city is completely underwater, with the tallest building below the water level? Another example is the statement, *The sun broke through the clouds.* How literally should one interpret this statement? Of course, both the meaning of the words and the context of the statements determine how a reader should understand the messages. Prior knowledge and common sense also enter the picture.

Memory, or the ability to store and retrieve relevant experience at will, is part of intelligence. How the brain stores and retrieves information or knowledge is still unclear. Later, the text includes a discussion of knowledge organization and how it is exploited in the KM building life cycle.

Learning is knowledge or skill that is acquired by instruction or study. It is the inevitable consequence of intelligent problem-solving. Intelligent people learn quickly and make effective use of what they learn. Inasmuch as problem-solving and knowledge organization have been successfully demonstrated in the business enterprise, the same success has yet to be shown in technology or computer programs. People learn from experience; to date, computers have not.

EXPERIENCE

Experience relates to what we have done and what has historically happened in a specific area of work. In Latin, the word *experience* means "to put to the test." People with deep knowledge in a given subject have been tested by experience. Experience also leads to expertise. Think of Sherlock Holmes investigating a murder. The goal is to find the murderer. Holmes's reasoning and deductions rely on all evidence collected; he works backward from the goal until the suspect is caught. Expertise is also intuition and the ability to access one's knowledge rapidly to achieve an efficient and successful outcome.

Experience is closely related to knowledge. Knowledge develops over time through successful experience, and experience leads to expertise. An **expert** is someone who knows what he or she does not know and is the first one to tell you so. Firms hire experts to benefit from their experience and proven knowledge in solving complex problems. People use experience to change facts into knowledge, which separates novices from experts. Exceptions do occur, however. Bach, for example, was expert musician at 5 years of age. In general, without experience, one would hardly be considered an expert. Experience in using knowledge allows people to refine their reasoning processes in a knowledge management environment.

COMMON SENSE

Common sense refers to the unreflective opinions of ordinary humans, which comes naturally to a child as young as 3 or 4 years old. For example, most youngsters know that if they touch a hot stove, they will get burned. In contrast, a computer could be told all kinds of things about hot stoves and the effect of heat on the human skin, and it still would not perceive what would happen if it "touched" a hot stove: Machines lack common sense. Common sense is not easily learned or acquired

TABLE 2.1   Basic Knowledge-Related Definitions

Artificial	Emulating or imitating something natural or real
Common sense	Innate ability to sense, judge, or perceive situations; grows stronger over time
Fact	A statement that relates a certain element of truth about a subject matter or a domain
Heuristic	A rule of thumb based on years of experience
Intelligence	The capacity to acquire and apply knowledge; ability to understand and use language; ability to store and retrieve relevant experience at will; learning from experience
Knowledge	Understanding gained through experience; familiarity with the way to do something to perform a task; an accumulation of facts, procedural rules, or heuristics
Procedural rule	A rule that describes a sequence of relations relative to the domain

Lack of common sense makes technology "brittle"; that is, computers rarely go beyond the scope of their data warehouse or knowledge base. Many important projects assumed by humans in business today require common sense, which is only partially understood by today's computer. Table 2.1 summarizes these concepts.

■ ■ ■ ■ Cognition and Knowledge Management

Cognitive psychology provides an essential background for understanding knowledge and expertise. The goal of cognitive psychology is to identify the cognitive structures and processes that relate to skilled performance within an area of operation. Cognitive science in general is the interdisciplinary study of human intelligence. Its two main components are experimental psychology, which studies the cognitive processes that constitute human intelligence, and artificial intelligence, which studies the cognition of computer-based intelligent systems. Our focus in this text is on the first component—how cognition contributes to the performance of intelligent workers.

With these relationships in mind, one can see cognitive psychology's contribution to KM. Understanding the limitations and biases provided by cognitive psychology helps in understanding expertise. Human limitations—such as memory capacity and the physical limits imposed by human sensory and motor systems—must be considered when attempting to understand how the human expert carries out a task.

The process of eliciting and representing expert knowledge typically involves a knowledge developer and one or more human experts. To capture human knowledge, the developer interviews the expert(s) and asks for information regarding a specific area of expertise that the expert is adept at solving. The expert may be asked to "think aloud," to verbalize his or her thought processes, while solving the problem. People cannot always give complete, accurate reports of their mental processes. Experts may have greater difficulty in conveying some kinds of knowledge, such as procedural knowledge (explained later in the chapter). Psychologists have long been aware of problems related to verbal reports, and through research, they have developed methods for circumventing them.

Cognitive psychology research contributes to a better understanding of what constitutes knowledge, how knowledge is elicited, and how it should be represented in a corporate knowledge base for others to tap. Because knowledge developers should take knowledge elicitation (also called *knowledge capture*) seriously, they should have a strong educational and practical background in cognitive psychology and cognitive processes. Knowledge capture techniques are covered in Chapter 4.

▪▪▪▪ Data, Information, and Knowledge

The main benefit of discussing knowledge this early in the text will become obvious later, when the analysis turns to knowledge workers and how knowledge developers capture and codify knowledge from human experts. Knowledgeable experts tend to be adept at explaining how they arrive at decisions or solutions because they have years of experience. They have become experts by adding and refining knowledge, not just by capturing and storing information. Likewise, knowledge developers, whose job is to acquire and represent experts' knowledge, need to understand the many ramifications of knowledge early in order to decide whether a particular expert has the requisite knowledge for building or updating a reliable knowledge base.

DATA

Data are unorganized and unprocessed facts. They are static; they just sit there. For example, *John is 6 feet tall.* This is data; it does not necessarily lead one anywhere. However, the meaning one brings to the evaluation of this data could be important. Such an evaluation may indicate that John's height would make him an asset to the basketball team. This becomes information.

Data is a set of discrete facts about events—structured records of transactions. When a customer goes to the store and buys merchandise, the number of socks and the price he or she paid are all data. The data tells nothing about the motivation behind the purchase, the quality of the socks, or the reputation of the store. Quantitatively, stores evaluate patterns of purchases, number of customers purchasing specific items, and other items those customers purchased. Evaluations such as these can be used to derive information about customer behavior, the price-sensitivity of certain merchandise, and the like. This means that data is a prerequisite to information.

All organizations need data, and some companies depend more heavily on data than others. For example, insurance companies, banks, the internal revenue service, and the social security administration are heavy number crunchers. Millions of transactions are processed daily. The problem with too much data is that it offers no judgment and no basis for action. This means that an organization must decide on the nature and volume of data needed to create information.

INFORMATION

The word *information* is derived from the word *inform*, which means "to give shape to"; information means shaping the data to arrive at a meaning in the eyes of the perceiver. **Information** is an aggregation of data that makes decision making easier. It is also facts and figures based on reformatted or processed data. For example, a profit and loss statement provides information. It is an assembling of facts into a form that shows an organization's state of health over a specific time period. Here is another example of information:

> *Five farmers of northern Beirut, who had switched crops from watermelon to sugarcane with the high hope of a quick profit, could not bear the anguish of crop failures for two consecutive seasons. They committed suicide after having to sell the farm to pay the bank loan.*

Unlike data, information is understanding relations. It has meaning, purpose, and relevance. It has a shape, because it is organized for a purpose. The data may have been reorganized, statistically analyzed, or have had errors removed—all performed to add meaning to a message, a report, or a document. The medium is not the message, although it could affect the message. An analogy: Having a telephone does not ensure worthwhile conversation, although certain telephones make the message clear and more easily understood. Today, having more information technology is not a guarantee for improving the state of information.

Information is accessible to employees and managers through the company's local area networks, intranet, e-mail, Internet, satellite infrastructure, snail mail, or hand delivery. Unlike data that emphasizes quantity and efficiency of processing, the focus of information is qualitative: Does the report tell me something I don't know? Is there new meaning in the semiannual report? The implication is that data becomes information when meaning or value is added to improve the quality of decision making.

KNOWLEDGE

Knowledge has always been an essential component of all human progress. Our ancestors must have employed an enormous amount of knowledge to form an axe-like object. From know-how to use seeds for planting to the invention of machinery, to travel to the moon—all required an accumulation of special knowledge to achieve the task. When it comes to basics, people use their intelligence and creativity to come up with the value-added products and services that take on the competition. Knowledge capital is essentially a reflection of how well an organization leverages the knowledge of its workforce, the needs of its customers, and the knowledge of the suppliers to ensure value-added outcome. Knowledge capital is the way an organization derives wealth from its information resources on a regular basis.

Knowledge is the most cherished remedy for complexity and uncertainty. It is a higher level of abstraction that resides in people's minds. It is broader, richer, and much harder to capture than data or information. People seek knowledge, because it helps them succeed in their work. Tiwana views knowledge as actionable (relevant) information available in the right format, at the right time, and at the right place for decision making (Tiwana 2000).

Knowledge has different meanings, depending on the discipline where it is used. In this text, *knowledge* is "human understanding of a specialized field of interest that has been acquired through study and experience." It is based on learning, thinking, and familiarity with the problem area in a department, a division, or in the company as a whole. The focus is on *sustainable competitive advantage.* Knowledge is not information, and information is not data. Davenport and Prusak (2000) define knowledge as "a fluid mix of framed experience, values, contextual information, and expert insight that provides a framework for evaluating and incorporating new experiences and information." See Figure 2.1 for alternative definitions of knowledge, data, and information. Other characteristics of knowledge are summarized in Box 2.1.

Knowledge is derived from information in the same way information is derived from data. It may be viewed as an *understanding* of information based on its perceived importance or relevance to a problem area. It can also be thought of as a person's range of information. Embracing a wider sphere than information, knowledge includes perception, skills, training, common sense, and experience. It is the sum total of our perceptive processes that helps us to draw meaningful conclusions. For example, an investor requires knowledge to evaluate two companies' profit and loss statements in order to determine which one is the healthier company.

Data	*Information*	*Knowledge*
Statements about reality (Acharya 2001)	Organized, systematized data (Acharya 2001)	Human interaction with reality (Acharya 2001)
Unsorted bits of fact (Dixon 2000)	Data that has been sorted, analyzed, and displayed (Dixon 2000)	Meaningful links people make in their minds between information and its application in action in a specific setting (Dixon 2000)
A representation of a fact, number, word, image, picture, or sound	Data that has been assigned a meaning (Liebowitz and Wilcox 1999)	The whole set of insights, experiences, and procedures that are considered correct and true and that, therefore, guide the thoughts, behavior, and communication of people (Liebowitz and Wilcox 1999)
Measurements (Applehans et al. 1999)	Data that is meaningful or useful to someone (Dickerson 1998)	
A discrete, objective fact about events (Davenport and Prusak 2000)	Potential for action; resides in the user (Malhotra 1998)	An ideational (i.e., conceptual rather than physical) construct generated via the agency of the human mind (Housel and Bell 1999)
	A statement of fact about measurements (Applehans et al. 1999)	Ability to turn information and data into effective action (Applehans et al. 1999)
	Descriptive knowledge (characterizing the state of some past, present, future, or hypothetical solution) (Holsapple and Whinston 1996)	An organizational resource consisting of the sum of what is known (Holseapple 1996)
	Data that makes a difference (Davenport and Prusak 2000)	A fluid mix of framed experience, values, contextual information, and expert insight that provides a framework for evaluating and incorporating new experiences and information (Davenport and Prusak 2000)
		Systematizing and structuring information for a specific purpose (Johannessen et al. 1994)
		Information whose validity has been established through tests of proof (Libeskind 1996)

▪ ▪ ▪ ▪ ▪ ▪ ▪   **FIGURE 2.1:**   Alternative Definitions of Data, Information, and Knowledge

In addition to evaluation, information becomes knowledge with questions like "What implications does this information have for my final decision?" "How does this information relate to other information I received yesterday?" "What value can I derive from this information that adds value to the finished product?" Regardless of the process that organizes knowledge in the individual, it promotes the sought-after expertise for value-added decision making in the business. See Table 2.2 for a summary definition of each of the three terms.

As can be seen, information is all around, but only a fraction of it is useful in problem-solving. Knowledge has to be built and requires regular interaction with others in the know in the organization. It is social, time critical, interactive, evolving, and created for a

▪ ▪ ▪ ▪ ▪ ▪   BOX 2.1   ▪ ▪ ▪ ▪ ▪ ▪

SELECT CHARACTERISTICS OF KNOWLEDGE

- Knowledge involves a *human* interaction with reality (or with information about reality, or information about other knowledge or information), where the human is the subject and acts as the active, creative element, and modifies the latter by way of reconstructing it. Knowledge involves attribution of *meaning and significance* by the knower as a person. In fact, every reconstruction is a reinterpretation as well.

- When I know something, it is relative to me. There can be no knowledge without me. It is always in relation to my existence and my knowing it. With my death dies my world, and with it my knowledge. In knowing something, I individualize, subjectify, and appropriate it and make it my own. What I know, in the process, becomes *my own.*

- Knowledge is essentially social in nature. We need *universal categories* for generation, expression, representation, storage, retrieval, and reappropriation of knowledge. The categories are universal in the sense that (a) they are capable of holding the same meanings for all humans belonging to the same community and (b) the categories can be socialized in terms of being shared, reconstructed, and applied by other humans belonging to the concerned universe of discourse.

- In knowing something, I *believe* it to be *true.* Without this belief, it could just be some information, without that stamp of individualized identity marked on it. This belief is a part of a system of beliefs, values, and rationality, and hence constitutes a *responsibility* and potential *commitment.*

- Knowing takes place in relation to *existing knowledge*—it is placing things in context, in relation to existing constructions of reality, content, and concepts.

- Knowledge involves a *judgment,* a subsumption of the particular under the universal. It involves a certain amount of synthesis and integration of discreet information under a category, a construction, or an attribution of a causality or justifiability, relative to the knower's frame of reference.

- Knowledge has a moment of *categorical imperative* and can induce a cognitive dissonance between belief and practice, between the past and the present, between the present and the future, between what is and what ought to be, and so on, and therefore, can form a springboard for potential action. In other words, *knowledge by definition is driven into practice.*

- Knowledge is always a part of a *dynamic* system. Knowledge has the tendency to go for more of itself, to bypass itself, and to constantly develop itself. It is only limited by mental and environmental constraints.

- Knowledge is *gregarious* by nature and has a tendency to socialize itself. Socialization is the means by which individual knowledge gets reinforced, challenged, modified, improved, and validated.

- Knowledge processes are always a part of an *open* system. It is like a game where the goalpost keeps shifting itself. *The meanings, the dictionaries, and even the rules of the language are always in flux*—as volatile as the turns in modern life. Knowledge creation, by definition, is a process of innovation.

SOURCE: Excerpted from Acharya, Jagabandhu. "What Is Knowledge?" kmx.totalkm.com/whatisk.html, April 27, 2001, pp. 2–5, Date accessed August 2002.

▪ ▪ ▪ ▪ ▪ ▪ ▪

purpose but drawing on experience from other times and domains. Cooperation and productivity are expected as people work to achieve, not to control. Teamwork is a prerequisite for people to talk, compare, and exchange thoughts, leading to a culture that makes it clear that "What is my job?" is less important than "What is the purpose of what I am doing?"

Knowledge, not information, can lead to a competitive advantage in business. Information is thus closer to the decision-making process than is data. For example,

TABLE 2.2   Progression from Data to Information to Knowledge

Data	Unprocessed or raw facts; a static set of transactional elements, such as 211102345.
Information	Processed data; an aggregation of data that have meaning. For example, a financial analysis report that begins with account number 211-10-2345.
Knowledge	A person's range of information, embracing a wider sphere than information. It includes perception, skills, training, common sense, and experience. For example, a financial analyst might say, "All indicators tell me that I'd better pull out of XYZ stock before year end."

▪ ▪ ▪ ▪ ▪ ▪

inventory tracking involves storing, retrieving, and reporting information in a structured format. Decision-making tools that structure information are called **decision support systems (DSS)** (spreadsheets, financial planning, resource allocation, and production scheduling) in which the decision approach is advisory and the problems addressed are semistructured. These systems are used in situations in which the end user makes decisions.

DSS performs the kind of information processing necessary to speed the decision-making process and thereby saves the user from sifting through the information unassisted. The user might query a sales-forecasting software (or DSS) package, "What if I lowered the price of product X by 8 percent?" The software would evaluate the impact of the price cut and might respond, "Your sales should increase by 32 percent." The user would then decide what to do with this information.

Figure 2.2 approaches data, information, and knowledge in support of the definitions in Table 2.2. Data is the raw material for the so-called "number crunching" or data processing. The emphasis is on quantitative capture of facts—the backbone of accounting and payroll applications. For example, an alphabetic list of company employees, the hours worked, and the hourly rates are all data. When we organize data in a format that adds meaning, it becomes information. In this respect, information is more qualitative than quantitative (or algorithmic) than data. Using the same example, when the employee list shows employee earnings by department and titles, it becomes useful information. Information has been defined as data "in formation" (Dixon 2000). It is data that is classified, sorted, displayed, communicated verbally or graphically, or in the form of tables.

In contrast to information, knowledge is viewed as a body of information, processes, and experience that centers on a particular subject. It is actionable information. Knowledge is links that people make between information and how it is applied in action in a specific domain. For example, the employee list (by department and title) may be evaluated by an experienced personnel director for inequity in pay. Inequity in pay is a specific domain of concern to every organization.

Wisdom is the highest level of abstraction, with vision, foresight, and the ability to see beyond the horizon. It is the summation of one's career experience in a specialized area of work. The power of vision is illustrated in Box 2.2.

One can see that knowledge-rich organizations have a reason for adopting knowledge management into their infrastructure. Knowledge management moves a firm to a new level of quality, creativity, and sustainable competitive advantage. Unlike technology, which disappears as a medium of competitive advantage (everyone has it), knowledge advantage is sustainable because over the long haul it generates continuing advantages. To ensure continuity, a corporation with a knowledge management environment must maintain and enhance its knowledge base and knowledge activities on a regular basis.

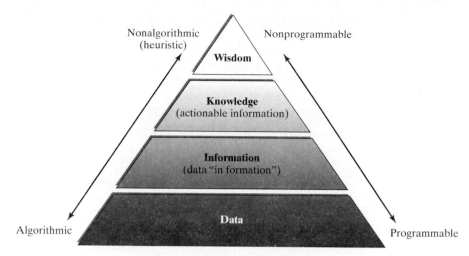

Data, Information, and Knowledge

▪ ▪ ▪ ▪ ▪ ▪ ▪ **FIGURE 2.2:**   Data, Information, and Knowledge

▪ ▪ ▪ ▪ ▪ ▪   BOX 2.2   ▪ ▪ ▪ ▪ ▪ ▪

THE YOUNG MAN AND THE STARFISH—AN EXAMPLE OF VISION

A wise man was taking a sunrise walk along the beach. In the distance, he caught sight of a young man who seemed to be dancing along the waves. As he got closer, he saw that the young man was picking up starfish from the sand and tossing them gently back into the ocean.

"What are you doing?" the wise man asked.

"The sun is coming up, and the tide is going out; if I don't throw them in, they'll die."

"But young man, there are miles and miles of beach with starfish all along it—you can't possibly make a difference."

The young man bent down, picked up another starfish, and threw it lovingly back into the ocean, past the breaking waves. "It made a difference for that one," he replied.

That young man's actions represent something special in each of us. We are all gifted with the ability to make a difference. Each of us can shape our own future. Each of us has the power to help our organizations reach their goals.

Vision without action is merely a dream.
Action without vision just passes the time.
Vision with action can change the world.

—*Joel Arthur Barker*

SOURCE: Anonymous.

▪▪▪▪ Types of Knowledge

Knowledge is classified into a variety of types. When considering knowledge management, the knowledge developer should be familiar with each type and know how to tap into it during knowledge capture.

SHALLOW AND DEEP KNOWLEDGE

One way to classify knowledge is to determine whether it is shallow or deep. **Shallow, or readily recalled** *surface,* **knowledge** indicates minimal understanding of the problem area. For example, approval of loan applications for secured loans of less than $1,000 depending on assets and salary would be based essentially on a few basic rules that hardly require human consultation. In contrast, a loan approval scheme that employs 14 variables (including customer's credit rating, net worth, pattern of paying on time, and college education) would be more complex and more risky. **Deep knowledge** acquired through years of experience would be required to decide on such a loan.

KNOWLEDGE AS KNOW-HOW

Knowledge based on reading and training is much different from knowledge based on practical experience that spans many years. Knowledge based on know-how, or accumulated lessons of practical experience, is what is needed for building expert systems. The problem with practical experience is that it is rarely documented. Capturing such experience requires special tools. Knowledge capture procedures and tools are covered in Chapter 4.

Know-how distinguishes an expert from a novice. If you were told you needed an operation to save your eyesight, you probably would not want an intern to do it. Instead, you would want an expert eye surgeon's seasoned experience based on hundreds of similar operations.

Experts represent their know-how in terms of heuristics, rules of thumb based on their experience—empirical knowledge. In building a knowledge base, heuristics generally operate in the form of if/then statements: "*If* such and such conditions exist, *then* such and such actions result." Lenat has defined *heuristics* as "compiled hindsight" (Lenat 1982). Know-how is not book knowledge; it is practical experience. It can be expressed as rules of thumb or heuristics if one were to build a knowledge base for knowledge sharing within the organization.

REASONING AND HEURISTICS

Humans reason in a variety of ways:

1. Reasoning by analogy: relating one concept to another. For example, a battery is analogous to a reservoir. Both are used to store and provide energy for power.
2. Formal reasoning: using deductive or inductive methods. Deductive reasoning (also called *exact reasoning* because it deals with exact facts and exact conclusions) takes known principles and applies them to instances to infer some sort of a conclusion. For example:

   IF Fred is taller than Nancy **AND** Nancy is taller than Sarah,
   THEN Fred is taller than Sarah.

   Another example:
   IF mothers are women **AND** Sarah is a mother,
   THEN Sarah is a woman.

Deduction makes use of major and minor premises. Almost any argument can be formed using this type of reasoning process. Here are two examples:

a. *Major premise:* Each titanium coil leaving the mill must be 100 percent quality tested.

Minor premise: One part of the coil has not passed the test.

Conclusion: The entire coil should be rejected.

b. *Major premise:* In Turkey, all citizens get a pension from age 60 on.

Minor premise: Kamal Elberlik, age 60, is a citizen of Turkey.

Conclusion: Elberlik is receiving a pension.

As is evident from the examples, the idea behind deductive reasoning is to generate new knowledge from previously specified knowledge. If the original rule is true, then the deduction will be valid. If a knowledge base, for example, uses only deductive inference and the information assimilated is true, then one can depend on all the inferred conclusions to be valid. Unfortunately, much of common-sense reasoning (explained later) is nondeductive by nature.

In terms of inductive reasoning, it works the other way around. Inductive reasoning is reasoning from a set of facts or individual cases to a general conclusion—from specific examples to general rules. **Inductive reasoning** is the basis of scientific discovery. Consider the following examples:

a. *Premise:* Chronic unemployment causes social problems.

Premise: Illiteracy causes social problems.

Premise: Recession causes social problems.

Premise: Drug trafficking causes social problems.

Conclusion: Chronic unemployment, illiteracy, recession, and drug trafficking cause social problems.

b. *Premise:* He is an avid fisherman.

Premise: He is an avid hunter.

Premise: He is an avid mountain climber.

Conclusion: He likes outdoor sports

c. *Premise:* Admission depends on status.

Premise: Admission depends on race.

Premise: Admission depends on appearance.

Premise: Admission depends on financial wealth.

Conclusion: Admission is subjective.

In each example, the inference is an induction: It goes from a finite number of instances to a conclusion about every member of a class.

3. Case-based reasoning (CBR). Suppose a person was diagnosed with a condition that required major surgery. How would that person choose a surgeon? People tend to prefer an older surgeon with years of practical experience over someone fresh out of residency. The younger surgeon might be well versed in book knowledge, but experience is a better predictor of success among surgeons. Their experience is judged based on the number of cases they handled and the success of each case.

The idea of reasoning from relevant past cases is attractive because it is so similar to the process human experts often use to solve problems successfully. The process of choosing a surgeon indicates the perceived importance of case experience in expert problem-solving. Manipulating past problem-solving examples is critical in problem areas such as law, medical diagnosis, prediction, design, and process control. Because experts tend to forget over time, capturing these cases in a knowledge base means reaping future benefits from past successes (and failures) of experts' work.

For years, knowledge developers have claimed that human experts reason about a problem by recalling similar cases encountered in the past. In fact, they reason by analogy: The expert tries to figure out how one case is similar (or dissimilar) to other cases solved in the past. A **case** is knowledge at an operational level. It is an episodic description of a problem and its associated solution. Box 2.3 illustrates an instance of human CBR, in which the reasoner (the father, who is also an attorney) uses previous cases similar to the current case as precedent to get the judge to dismiss the case.

COMMON SENSE AS KNOWLEDGE

Common sense is another type of knowledge that all human beings possess in varying forms and in varying amounts. It is a collection of personal experiences and facts acquired over time and the type of knowledge that humans tend to take for granted. For example, if someone asked you to look up Shakespeare's phone number, you would know that such a task is impossible. Common sense tells you that Shakespeare is dead and that the telephone was not invented until years after his death.

A human expert uses extensive common sense knowledge. Such reasoning is so common to the expert that it is basically ignored. Unfortunately, a computer does not possess common sense. Although computers can calculate *pi* to a thousand decimal places in seconds, they "know" nothing about some of the simplest things that people learn early in life, such as oranges are to eat, but baseballs are not, and that legs are permanently attached to the body.

FROM PROCEDURAL TO EPISODIC KNOWLEDGE

A fourth way to classify knowledge is according to whether it is procedural, declarative, semantic, or episodic (see Figure 2.3).

Procedural knowledge is an understanding of how to do a task or carry out a procedure. It is knowledge contained in the application of a procedure. Procedural knowledge usually involves psychomotor skills, such as holding onto the handrail while riding an escalator.

Some procedural knowledge is not psychomotor, however. For example, when a person learns a language and speaks it fluently, it becomes a natural part of the person. In the case of an expert, when the same knowledge is used over and over again in a procedure, it comes to be used automatically. Knowledge developers must select appropriate techniques for tapping this type of knowledge. Procedural knowledge is covered more fully in Chapter 4.

Declarative knowledge is information that experts can easily discuss. Unlike procedural knowledge, it is "awareness knowledge," or routine knowledge of which the expert is conscious. It is shallow knowledge that is readily recalled, because it is simple, uncomplicated information. This type often resides in **short-term memory**, the part of the brain that retains information for brief periods of time. It kicks in when you are at an airport and decide to call a friend in the area, for example. You look up the friend's phone number in the phone book and memorize it well enough to dial it. Chances are by the time you have boarded the flight, you will have forgotten the number. You remembered it only long enough to dial it.

Shallow, declarative knowledge is also used in diagnosing the electrical system of a car. The rule of thumb is that dim headlights probably indicate a faulty battery. The simple rule that if the headlights are dim, then the battery is faulty is obvious. It does not explain how the electrical system works; it just states a causal relationship between the headlights and the battery. As we shall find in Chapter 4, knowledge developers

------ ▪ ▪ ▪ ▪ ▪ ▪ BOX 2.3 ▪ ▪ ▪ ▪ ▪ ▪ ------

REASONING WITH THE JUDGE

An attorney's 17-year-old son was issued a speeding ticket for driving 72 miles per hour in a 65-mph zone. The young man vehemently denied going that fast, but the radar report unmistakably indicated a speeding violation. Father and son were scheduled to appear in juvenile court later that month.

The week before the scheduled court date, the father went to court. He talked to parents waiting outside the courtroom. He sat in on several cases to size up the judge and plot strategy for defending his son's case. Every parent he talked to—case after case—indicated that the judge almost never let the juvenile off the hook. Penalties ranged from a $60 fine to suspension of the driver's license. The judge dismissed only one case out of 40 that day. The father decided to use it as the basis for his son's defense.

On the scheduled court date, father and son appeared before the judge:

Judge: Young man, how do you plead, guilty or not guilty?

Son: No contest, your honor.

Judge: It sounds like you've been coached. Officer, go ahead with your report. (The officer goes through the ritual of showing the radar report.)

Judge: Young man, tell this court your side of the case.

Son: Your honor, it is impossible to go exactly 65 miles per hour while driving. I kept looking at the speedometer. I know I was not driving at 72 miles per hour the way this cop drummed it up.

Judge: (looks at the father) Sir, are you the father?

Father: I am, your honor.

Judge: Do you have anything to say before I give my decision?

Father: Your honor, we have no quarrel with the radar as an electronic system. It is known for measuring speed but not the driver's attitude or experience. I would like to submit as evidence this young man's academic record (all As) and extraordinary accomplishments (Eagle Scout, president of his class, no prior speeding tickets). A number of cases have been brought before this court to mitigate the severity of the charge. For example, in the case of *Jane Maloney v. Commonwealth of Massachusetts* and *Bill Croll v. Commonwealth of Massachusetts.*

Judge: (quickly scans the record as he remembered both cases cited). Bailiff! Hand the driver's license to this boy's father. (To the father) Sir, you are to keep your son's license for 10 days before he's allowed to drive. Next time, bring your checkbook with you. Case dismissed.

------ ▪ ▪ ▪ ▪ ▪ ▪ ------

find this type of knowledge useful in the early phase of knowledge capture, because it promotes familiarity with the type of expertise of the human expert. The best way to acquire declarative knowledge is with a structured interview.

Semantic knowledge is a deeper kind of knowledge. It is highly organized, "chunked" knowledge that resides in long-term memory. Such knowledge may have been there for years and may have been used so often that the information seems like second nature. Semantic knowledge includes major concepts, vocabulary, facts, and relationships. Returning to the headlight and battery example, semantic knowledge about the system would consist of understandings about the battery, battery cables, lights, the ignition system, and so forth, and their interrelationships. On the basis of this knowledge, one can build rules about causal relationships among those things. In the case of the headlights, one might know that dim headlights can be caused by a loose battery cable, a bad alternator, or a drain on the electrical system. At this point, a real expert (in this case, a certified mechanic) enters the picture (see Figure 2.4).

Shallow Knowledge

Deep Knowledge

Procedural Knowledge

Knowledge of how to do a task that is essentially motor in nature; the same knowledge is used over and over again.

Declarative Knowledge

Surface-type information that is available in short-term memory and easily verbalized; useful in early stages of knowledge capture but less so in later stages.

Semantic Knowledge

Hierarchically organized knowledge of concepts, facts, and relationships among facts.

Episodic Knowledge

Knowledge that is organized by temporal spatial means, not by concepts of relations; experiential information that is chunked by episodes. This knowledge is highly compiled and autobiographical and is not easy to extract or capture.

▪▪▪▪▪▪▪ **FIGURE 2.3:** From Procedural to Episodic Knowledge

▪▪▪▪▪▪▪ **FIGURE 2.4:** A Comparison of Declarative and Semantic Knowledge

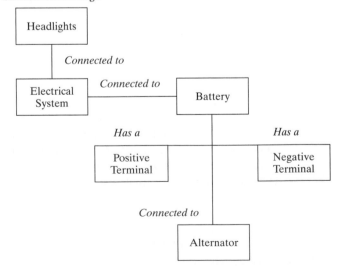

Episodic knowledge is knowledge based on experiential information, or episodes. Each episode is chunked in long-term memory. In general, the longer a human expert takes to explain or verbalize his or her knowledge, the more semantic or episodic it is. In contrast, an expert can recall procedural or declarative knowledge in a relatively short time, because it is readily available in short-term memory.

An interesting aspect about episodic knowledge is that its use is automated. For example, have you ever driven from point A to point B and yet not remembered many details of how you got there? This is a common experience. Driving information is so chunked that most people have trouble remembering and explaining it. In the process of conveying the expert's knowledge, the expert explains by examples, or **scenarios**. Special tools and techniques are required for capturing such knowledge.

EXPLICIT AND TACIT KNOWLEDGE

Another approach to categories of knowledge is whether the knowledge is tacit or explicit (Nonaka and Takeuchi 1995). **Tacit** knowledge is knowledge embedded in the human mind through experience and jobs. Coined by Hungarian medical scientist Michael Polanyi (1891–1976), it includes intuitions, values, and beliefs that stem from years of experience. It is the knowledge used to create explicit knowledge and is best communicated personally through dialogue and scenarios, with use of metaphors. Therefore, knowledge is not private, but social. Socially relayed knowledge becomes part of the real-life experience of the knower.

In contrast, **explicit** knowledge is knowledge codified and digitized in books, documents, reports, white papers, spreadsheets, memos, training courses, and the like. Explicit knowledge can be retrieved and transmitted more easily than tacit knowledge. Because it is knowledge learned directly from experience, tacit knowledge (also referred to as *whispers in the ears*) is difficult to share across space and time. The person with tacit knowledge has no conscious experience of what it is that is causing his or her activity. Chapter 4 elaborates on methods and tools for tapping tacit knowledge.

Tacit and explicit knowledge have been expressed in terms of knowing-how and knowing-that, respectively. They have also been viewed as embodied knowledge and theoretical knowledge, respectively (Sveiby 1997). Knowing-how, or embodied knowledge, is characteristic of the expert who makes judgment or decisions without explicitly going through a set of rules. By contrast, knowing-that, or theoretical knowledge, is when a person learning a skill articulates available knowledge using explicit instruction, rules, principles, or procedures.

On the surface, explicit or documented knowledge is easier to identify, because it is a physical entity that can be measured and distributed. It can be stored as a written procedure or as a process in a computer. With that in mind, it is reusable for decision-making purposes. By contrast, tacit knowledge is personal and hard to formalize and communicate. It is primarily heuristics (rules of thumb), mind-sets, and unconscious values. The downside is that it is occasionally wrong and hard to change. Because the human mind is the storage medium, tacit knowledge is vulnerable to loss. When it is shared, vulnerability is reduced, and it is easier to reuse (Foster 2002).

Understanding what knowledge is makes it easier to understand that knowledge hoarding is basic to human nature. As long as job security is based on the special knowledge that we have, it continues to be a challenge to support knowledge sharing. So, when it comes to building a KM system, the company that assumes "if we build, they will rush" has a surprise coming. A strong incentive and proper change in the culture of the business are part of the planning that must take place before going KM.

▪▪▪▪ Expert Knowledge

Most people realize that knowledge cannot be directly observed. What can be observed is the expertise that relies on knowledge to produce solutions. A person with expert knowledge can solve a complex problem more quickly and more effectively than someone else can. When the expert's advanced skills and years of experience are enhanced by attention to detail, quality results. Not surprisingly, most experts are perfectionists. They want the solution to be exactly what is called for by the problem.

Expert knowledge is not just a head full of facts or a repository of information for the intellect. It is information woven into the mind of the expert for solving complex problems quickly and accurately. Take the case of chess experts. They not merely recognize thousands of chessboard moves, but they consider them in ways relevant to playing the game. These are all finely tuned to the requirements of the game. The patterns experts learn to recognize are also unique, and the possibilities they consider all tend to be good ones. It is obvious that a good problem-solving strategy depends on how much you know.

CHUNKING KNOWLEDGE

Knowledge is stored in an expert's long-range memory as chunks. Knowledge **compilation**, or **chunking**, enables experts to optimize their memory capacity and process information quickly. *Chunks* are groups of ideas or details that are stored and recalled together as a unit. For example, an auto mechanic who had been rebuilding Porsche transmissions for 18 years was able to remember 140 different steps flawlessly. Although the sequences and combinations were difficult for him to describe, he consistently completed each job according to specifications.

Chunking promotes expert performance. The more chunking a person does, the more efficient is his or her recall. The drawback is that chunking makes it difficult for experts to be aware of their own knowledge so that they can describe it to others. For this reason, *decompiling* chunked knowledge and putting it into words is not an easy task.

KNOWLEDGE AS AN ATTRIBUTE OF EXPERTISE

Experts appear to differ from novices by the greater knowledge of their specialties. Our society has always recognized exceptional persons, whose performance is vastly superior to that of the average individual. Speculation about how people acquire extraordinary abilities has been a subject of discussion for many years. Based on current literature, it seems that in virtually all areas of specialization, insight and knowledge accumulate quickly, and the criteria for expert performance undergo continuous change.

To become an expert in a specialized area, one is expected to master the requisite knowledge, surpass the achievements of already recognized eminent people, and make unique contributions to the specialized field. This means that if individuals are innately talented, they cannot easily or quickly achieve an exceptional level of performance without preparation time and years of successful practice. In their classic study of expertise in chess, Simon and Chase (1973) learned that no one had attained the level of international chess master (grandmaster) with less than 10 years of intense preparation with the game. Bobby Fischer and Salo Flohr were only a year shy of the 10-year preparation time (Hayes 1981).

The unique performance of a knowledgeable expert (versus a novice) is clearly noticeable in decision-making quality. This implies that knowledgeable experts are more selective in the information they acquire, are better able to acquire information in a less-structured situation, and agree more than novices regarding the information they consider important for decision making or problem-solving (Shanteau 1988).

Aside from quantifying soft information, knowledgeable experts tend to categorize problems on the basis of solution procedures (as opposed to surface procedures), embedded over time in the expert's long-range memory and readily available on recall. Because of this strategy, experts tend to use knowledge-based decision strategies, starting with known quantities to deduce unknowns. Should a first-cut solution path fail, the expert can trace back a few steps and then proceed again—a valuable process in deciding on the appropriate action(s).

In contrast, nonexperts use means-end decision strategies to approach the same problem situation. They focus on goals instead of essential features of the task, making the job laborious and unreliable (Sweller, et al., 1983). The net effect is that experts seem to demonstrate better-developed procedural knowledge for problem-solving. If procedural knowledge is appropriate for the problem, experts proceed to encode and finalize a decision more quickly and effectively than nonexperts. As a result, experts reason differently and solve problems more quickly than nonexperts. Experienced cab drivers, for example, will recognize a shorter route while traveling to their destinations and tend to take that route even though the rider misinterprets such a maneuver (Awad 1999).

Taken at face value, experts are the beneficiaries of the information or knowledge that comes inevitably from experience rather than innate talent bestowed upon the select few who eventually become experts in their specialty. Experts work harder, rely less fully on routines, and seem to be engaged in extending their knowledge rather than merely exploiting it. With knowledge as an attribute of expertise, the focus is not only on what it includes but also on how it is acquired and how it works. Within the hidden knowledge of experts are declarative, procedural (skill), and episodic (heuristic) knowledge (Awad 1999). Procedural knowledge manifests itself in performance; episodic knowledge is the invisible knowledge lying in long-range memory. It represents years of proven experience in a domain.

In a nutshell, certain individuals consistently perform at higher levels than others and are labeled experts. They possess attributes that account for their outstanding performance. Whether these attributes are innate talent or whether they are acquired through knowledge, practice, and experience, there is reason to believe that experts succeed primarily because of their proven knowledge and how well they apply and upgrade it on a daily basis. The conceptual model in Figure 2.5 essentially suggests that academic knowledge contributes to conceptual knowledge, which is a prerequisite for practical (in the field) knowledge. Practical knowledge is a contributor to experience that over time leads to expertise. Expertise means minimum or no errors in decision making or problem-solving.

The main conclusion regarding corporate experts is for the company to find ways to retain them by various means, such as recognition, bonuses, and giving an opportunity for mentorship, knowledge sharing, creativity, independence, ability utilization, and the like (see Box 2.4). The key phrase is *knowledge sharing*. Mechanisms must be installed to encourage the sharing of expertise throughout the organization, and there must be strong support from upper management. Without such effort, brain drain could be devastating for a forward-looking organization operating in an uncertain environment.

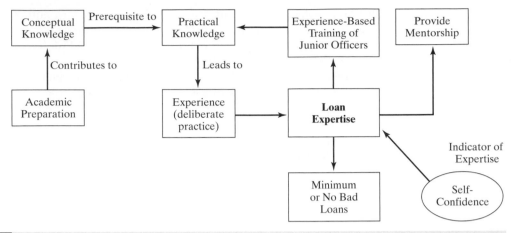

▪▪▪▪▪▪ **FIGURE 2.5:** A Conceptual Model of Expertise

▪▪▪▪▪▪   **BOX 2.4**   ▪▪▪▪▪▪

THE IMPORTANCE OF EXPERTS

TAKING CARE OF EXPERTS

After the initial pride of being recognized as an expert wears off, being on call to an entire company may not seem very attractive to busy professionals. "Many experts' greatest concern about Yellow Pages and other locator software is that they will be swamped with basic questions," says Richard McDermott, a knowledge management consultant in Boulder, Colorado. "So, they often hide out."

An effective knowledge-sharing system should give experts safe, efficient, and pleasant ways to help their coworkers. Knowledge leaders must show these experts how their participation will help their own colleagues, so they don't see it "as some sort of headquarters deal," says Reid Smith, vice president of knowledge management for Schlumberger Ltd. in Sugar Land, Texas. "Explain why you're doing this and what you're trying to achieve."

Recognizing that experts may want to control their availability, some software applications con-

ceal the expert's identity, leaving it up to the expert to participate or communicate directly with an individual once a query is made.

It makes sense for companies to reinforce appreciation of the value of experts' contributions. Peer recognition is a good way to do this, according to Smith. "We implemented a recognition program where engineers vote for the best of the best practices," he says. More tangible incentives can help, too. Some companies, including Schlumberger, offer prizes for sharing and create point systems for collaborative efforts.

Experts also find that they like sharing what they know. "Occasionally, a worker's job changes so much that providing expertise becomes as significant a part of the job as the tasks in the original job description," says Susan Hanley, director of content and collaboration management at Plural, Inc., in Bethesda, Maryland. Some even change careers so they can do it more.

SOURCE: Excerpted from Cuthbertson, Bruce. "Prospective for Experts," *Knowledge Management*, June 2001, p. 30.

▪▪▪▪▪▪

▪ ▪ ▪ ▪ Human Thinking and Learning

Because knowledge is the focus of knowledge management, knowledge developers need to understand how humans think and learn. Scientists have long tried to understand the human brain as part of their process of building computers that may someday duplicate the human expert's thought process in problem-solving. Imagine a child using blocks to build a tower. As soon as the tower is completed, the child takes a whack at the tower, destroying it. Next, the child builds a higher tower and then destroys it as well, and so on. Eventually, the child becomes hungry, and the pattern of BUILD and DESTROY begins to degenerate. The child gives the tower one final swipe, destroying it on the way to the kitchen. These spontaneous activities have proved to be difficult for computers, mainly because no one knows why people do them and, therefore, knows how to instruct the computer to do them.

According to Marvin Minsky (1991), the human mind is a "society of minds" that is hierarchically structured and interconnected so that the BUILD, DESTROY, and HUNGER agents of the child are minds that represent the self, promote intelligence, and provide the basis for acquiring knowledge. The study of artificial intelligence has introduced more structure into human thinking about thinking. So many activities of the computer resemble human cognitive processes that human and machine "thinking" are converging in many applications, despite the differences between the brain's architecture and the computer's. For example, both mind and machine accept data and information, manipulate symbols, store items in memory, and retrieve items on command.

Obviously, humans do not receive and process information in the same way that machines do. For instance, humans receive information via sensing—seeing, smelling, tasting, touching, and hearing. This system of receiving external stimuli promotes a kind of thinking and learning that is unique to humans. On a macro level, computers and humans receive inputs from a variety of sources. Computers receive information from keyboards, speech, touch screens, and other external sensors. On a micro level, both the central processing unit of a computer and the human brain receive all information as electrical impulses. The difference is that computers must be programmed to do specific tasks. Performing one job does not transcend onto other jobs as it does with human.

HUMAN LEARNING

Memory is an essential component of learning, because it accommodates learning. One interesting aspect of healthy human memory is that it never seems to run out of space. Also, as humans acquire more and more knowledge, they generally experience little interference with the recall ability or the quality of the information in memory. In other words, as people learn new facts, they integrate them in some way with what they think is relevant and organize the resulting mix to produce valuable decisions, solutions, or advice. Such learning ability is the basis of accumulating knowledge, experience, and expertise.

For humans, learning occurs in one of three ways: learning by experience, learning by example, and learning by discovery. The next section explores these types in an effort to see how they contribute to human knowledge.

LEARNING BY EXPERIENCE

The ability to learn by experience is a mark of intelligence. When an expert is selected whose knowledge someone wants to acquire, the expert is expected to have years of experience reworking problems and looking into different angles for solving difficult

TABLE 2.3 Three Types of Human Learning

Learning by experience	Trial and error or reworking problems is used to acquire experience in problem-solving. An expert uses experience to explain how a problem is solved.
Learning by example	Specially constructed examples or scenarios are used to develop the concept(s) the student is expected to learn. In knowledge capture, the human expert uses a scenario to explain how a problem is solved.
Learning by discovery	This is an undirected approach, where humans explore a problem area with no advance knowledge of what their object is.

problems. One way of testing potential experts is to observe their recall ability. Experts, who know a lot about a particular problem, have been found to remember facts in that problem area much more easily and more quickly than nonexperts, who presumably have fewer facts to recall. This type of information would be important for the knowledge developer to keep in mind when understanding a human expert's range of knowledge.

LEARNING BY EXAMPLE

Like learning by experience, learning by example is a good contributor to accumulating knowledge over time. In learning by example, specially constructed examples are used instead of a broad range of experience. Much classroom instruction is composed of teaching by example—providing examples, cases, or scenarios that develop the concepts students are expected to learn. Because this method allows students to learn without requiring them to accumulate experience, it is more efficient than learning by experience.

LEARNING BY DISCOVERY

Learning by discovery is less understood than learning by example or by experience. It is an undirected approach in which humans explore a problem area without advance knowledge of the objective. No one understands why humans are so good at this. It is difficult to teach, and it will be years before we can benefit from this approach commercially. Table 2.3 summarizes the three types of learning.

▪ ▪ ▪ ▪ Implications for Knowledge Management

Knowledge awareness benefits entire organizations. With today's emphases on sustainable competitive advantage, added value, and improved productivity, a firm's management needs to create, innovate, monitor, and protect its knowledge inventory. More specifically, a KM environment means a focus on generating new knowledge; transferring existing knowledge; embedding knowledge in products, services, and processes; developing an environment for facilitating knowledge growth; and accessing valuable knowledge from inside and outside the firm. When this happens, it is beyond survival. In fact, it is beyond intranets and databases—the technology that supports KM.

Some sources claim that 20 percent of an organization's knowledgeable personnel can operate 80 percent of the organization's day-to-day business. The human resources manager can play an important role in identifying the knowledge core of the organization, recommending ways to preserve this critical core, and building a robust, long-range plan to ensure top-quality operation. Without such preparation, corporate talent could potentially erode through a brain drain that spells disaster for any business. At the same time, professionals with expertise are naturally drawn to organizations that recognize and reward expertise, especially when that expertise directly contributes to the firm's productivity. Such matches explain the stability and growth of many successful "learning" companies.

Based on the discussion in the chapter, several ideas should be considered for how a company should perform in order to create and maintain sustainable competitive advantage. First, there should be more emphasis on tapping, sharing, and preserving tacit knowledge and the total knowledge base of the company. A company's knowledge base includes explicit and tacit knowledge and exists internally in the business as well as within the firm's external connections. Second, companies should focus on innovation and the processes that convert innovation to new products and services. Knowledge sharing and an emphasis on the total knowledge base promote innovation.

Finally, it is important to consider a renewed focus on organizational learning systems and systemic thinking throughout the organization. This is a realistic expectation, because knowledge is closely related to learning, which is the outcome of regular and continuous interactive learning. Systems thinking means understanding how the various parts of the company work. This includes learning behavioral patterns in the system and the culture or system environment in which employees and administrators operate. In other words, systemic thinking is expected to support innovation and continuous improvement processes, social competence, and interactions, as well as the total knowledge base.

What good is knowledge if it cannot be shared? If knowledge is power, sharing it will multiply power across the business. Unfortunately, sharing knowledge is an unnatural thing. One person's knowledge is an added value to that person's career path. Knowledge management is designed to solve the problem of unrecycled knowledge. Systems have been developed to gather, organize, refine, and distribute knowledge throughout the business. Virtually all such systems should have six key attributes: learning capability, improving with use, knowing what you want, two-way communication between the system and you, recalling past actions to develop a profile, and unique configuration to your individual specifications in real time.

In the final analysis, communication and connection make knowledge sharing an ongoing activity. Technology can only do so much to create a formal system. Success with KM exists when the culture is ready to communicate and connect. The end result is "community," built around knowledge and based on vision.

SUMMARY ▪ ▪ ▪ ▪

- Intelligent behavior has several attributes:
  - The ability to understand and use language
  - The ability to store and retrieve relevant experience at will
  - Learning by example, from experience, or by discovery
- Several key terms are worth noting:
  - *Knowledge*—understanding gained through experience
  - *Intelligence*—the capacity to apply knowledge

- *Heuristics*—rules of thumb based on years of experience
- *Common sense*—innate ability to sense, judge, or perceive situations that grows stronger over time
- *Experience*—changing facts into knowledge to refine a reasoning process

- A distinguishing feature of human learning is that as people learn new facts, they integrate them in some way and use the resulting mix to generate value-added decisions, solutions, or advice.
- Humans learn by experience, by example, and by discovery. Learning by discovery is less understood than learning by example and by experience. Learning continues to be a major concern in knowledge management.
- Knowledge developers, whose job is to capture experts' knowledge, need to be well prepared and to have a clear understanding of the distinctions among knowledge, information, and data. They must focus on knowledge as it relates to the problem area.
- The relative importance of data, information, and knowledge is a function of the importance of the problem, the decision approach, the nature of the problem, and the number of persons affected. Whereas data plays a relatively trivial role in problem-solving, knowledge occupies a major role. The decision approach is advisory and relates to a difficult problem affecting many people in the organization.
- Expert knowledge is clustered, or "chunked," in long-range memory. Chunking promotes expert performance, but can also make it difficult for experts to be aware of their own knowledge in a way that allows them to describe it to others.
- Humans have common-sense knowledge, a collection of personal experiences and facts acquired over time. The fact that common-sense reasoning is so strong in experts makes it difficult for knowledge developers to capture their deep knowledge.
- Knowledge can be classified by procedural, declarative, semantic, or episodic means.

  - *Procedural* knowledge is knowledge that is used over and over again.
  - *Declarative* knowledge is knowledge that the expert is aware or conscious of. It is shallow knowledge.
  - *Semantic* knowledge is chunked knowledge that resides in the expert's long-range memory.
  - *Episodic* knowledge is knowledge based on experiential information. Each episode is chunked in long-range memory.

- Common sense is inferences made from knowledge about the world. Reasoning is the process of applying knowledge to arrive at solutions. It works through the interaction of rules and data.
- Deductive reasoning deals with exact facts and conclusions. The idea behind deductive reasoning is to generate new knowledge from previously specified knowledge. In contrast, inductive reasoning is reasoning from a set of facts to general principles. Induction usually produces results without explanation.
- Knowledge has also been classified as tacit and explicit knowledge. Tacit knowledge, or "know-how," is stored in people's minds and is not so easy to capture or share. By contrast, explicit knowledge is codified and digitized in the form of records, reports, or documents and is reusable for decision making.
- Case-based reasoning is reasoning by analogy. Human experts reason about a problem by recalling similar cases encountered in the past.

TERMS TO KNOW ▪ ▪ ▪ ▪

Case: Knowledge at an operational level; episodic description of a problem and its associated solution.

Case-based reasoning: A methodology that records and documents previous cases and then searches the relevant case(s) to determine their usefulness in solving a current problem; problem-solving a case by analogy with old ones.

Chunking: Grouping ideas or details that are stored and recalled together as a unit.

Common sense: Possessing common knowledge about the world and making obvious inferences from this knowledge.

Compilation: The way a human translates instructions into meaning language or response.

Decision support systems (DSS): Computer-based information systems that combine models and data for solving complex problems with extensive user involvement.

Declarative knowledge: Surface information that experts verbalize easily.

Deductive reasoning: Also called *exact reasoning;* takes known principles (exact facts) and applies them to instances to infer an exact conclusion.

Deep knowledge: Knowledge based on the fundamental structure, function, and behavior of objects.

Episodic knowledge: Knowledge based on experiential information chunked as an entity and retrieved from long-term memory on recall.

Experience: The factor that changes unrelated facts into expert knowledge.

Expert: A person whose knowledge and skills are based on years of specialized experience.

Expertise: The skill and knowledge possessed by some humans that result in performance that is far above the norm.

Explicit knowledge: Knowledge codified in documents, books, or other repositories.

Fact: A statement of a certain element of truth about a subject matter or a problem area.

Heuristic: A rule of thumb based on years of experience.

Inductive reasoning: Reasoning from a given set of facts or specific examples to general principles or rules.

Inferencing: Deriving a conclusion based on statements that only imply that conclusion.

Intelligence: The capacity to acquire and apply knowledge through the ability to think and reason.

Knowledge: Understanding, awareness, or familiarity acquired through education or experience.

Learning: Knowledge or skill acquired by instruction or study.

Learning by discovery: Acquiring new ideas by exploring a problem area with no advance knowledge of what is being sought.

Learning by example: Acquiring new ideas based on specially constructed examples or scenarios.

Learning by experience: Acquiring new ideas based on hundreds of previously stored concepts.

Logic: The scientific study of the process of reasoning and the set of rules and procedures used in the reasoning process.

Memory: The ability to store and retrieve relevant experience at will.

Premise: Provides the evidence from which the conclusion must necessarily follow; evaluates the truth or falsehood with some degree of certainty.

Procedural rule: A rule that describes a sequence of relations relative to the problem area.

Reasoning: The process of applying knowledge to arrive at solutions based on the interactions between rules and data.

Scenario: The formal description of how a problem situation operates.

Semantic knowledge: Highly organized, "chunked" knowledge that resides in the expert's long-term memory and represents concepts, facts, and relationships among facts.

Shallow knowledge: Readily recalled knowledge that resides in short-term memory.

Short-term memory: The part of the human brain that retains information for a short period of time.

Tacit knowledge: Knowledge used to create explicit knowledge; the mind-set of individuals that includes intuitions, values, and beliefs that stem from experience.

TEST YOUR UNDERSTANDING ▪ ▪ ▪ ▪

1. If intelligence is the capacity to acquire and apply knowledge, what is knowledge?
2. Briefly explain the key attributes of intelligent behavior.
3. Distinguish between:
   a. fact and rule
   b. knowledge and common sense
   c. experience and heuristics
   d. learning by example and learning by discovery

4. Define episodic knowledge and semantic knowledge. Give an example of each.
5. Illustrate by example the possible relationship between:
    a. knowledge and information
    b. knowledge and data.
6. Why is knowledge compiled? Discuss its relationship to long-range memory.
7. Review the types of knowledge discussed in the chapter. Use an illustration of your own to show how each type differs from the other types.
8. What is the difference between tacit knowledge and explicit knowledge? Give an example of each.
9. If shallow knowledge is declarative knowledge, what is deep knowledge? Be as specific as you can.
10. Illustrate the differences between deductive and inductive reasoning. Under what conditions is one preferred over the other?

KNOWLEDGE EXERCISES ▪▪▪▪

1. "People do not think in the same way as machines, because people are biological." Do you agree?
2. What type of knowledge is used in each of the following activities:
    a. tying a shoelace
    b. debugging a computer program
    c. baking a pie
    d. replacing a car's flat tire
    e. negotiating peace with a hostile country
    f. driving in congested traffic
    Explain each classification.
3. List five heuristics that you employ in everyday life. By what kind of learning have you arrived at these rules of thumb?
4. Determine the type of reasoning in each of the following cases:
    a. Liz did not deposit money in her checking account.
       Liz is a customer of the bank.
       Liz's check bounced (insufficient funds).
       Conclusion: Checks drawn against a negative account balance will bounce.
    b. Drivers who exceed the speed limit get speeding tickets.
       Donna is a licensed driver.
       Donna drove her car 20 miles over speed limit.
       Conclusion: Donna will get a speeding ticket.
       (What is wrong with this reasoning?)
    c. A customer whose account balance drops below $100 during the month is subject to a $5 charge.
       Bob is a bank customer.
       Bob has a checking account.
       Bob's checking account balance dropped to $98.
       Conclusion: Bob's account will be charged $5.

REFERENCES ▪▪▪▪

Applehans, Wayne, Globe, Alden, and Laugero, Graig. *Managing Knowledge.* Boston, MA: Addison-Wesley, 1999.

Acharya, Jagabandhu. "What Is Knowledge?" kmx.totalkm.com/whatisk.html, April 27, 2001, pp. 2–5, Date accessed August 2002.

Awad, Elias M. *Selected Attributes of the Domain Expert.* Unpublished manuscript 1999, pp. 1–13.

Chiem, Phat. "Trust Matters," *Knowledge Management*, May 2001, pp. 50–52.

Cuthbertson, Bruce. "Prospective for Experts," *Knowledge Management*, June 2001, p. 30.

Davenport, Thomas H., and Prusak, Laurence. *Working Knowledge*. Boston, MA: Harvard Business School Press, 2000, pp. 1–24.

Dixon, Nancy M. *Common Knowledge*. Boston, MA: Harvard Business School Press, 2000, pp. 12–13, 17–32.

Foster, Allan. "Grasping the Tacit Knowledge Nettle." *Knowledge Management*, April 1998, p. 32.

Garvin, David A. *Learning in Action*. Boston, MA: Harvard Business School Press, 1999, pp. 47–90.

Hayes, J. R. *The Complete Problem Solver*. Philadelphia, PA: Franklin Institute Press, 1981.

Holsapple, C. W., and Whinston, A. B. *Decision Support Systems*. Minneapolis, MN: West Publishing Co., 1996, pp. 11–124.

Horibe, Frances. *Managing Knowledge Workers*. New York: John Wiley & Sons, Inc., 1999, pp. 1–18.

Housel, Thomas, and Bell, Arthur. *Measuring and Managing Knowledge*. New York: McGraw-Hill, Inc., 2001.

Johannessen, J. A., Olaisen, Johan, and Olsen, B. *Mismanagement of Tacit Knowledge*, www.program. forskningsradet.no/skikt/johannessen.php3, Date accessed August 2002.

Koulopoulos, T. M., and Frappaolo, Carl. *Smart Things to Know About Knowledge Management*. Milford, CT: Capstone Publishing, 2000, pp. 37–66.

Lenat, Douglas B. *Knowledge-Based Systems in Artificial Intelligence*. New York: McGraw-Hill Book Co., 1982.

Liebeskind, J. P. "Knowledge, Strategy, and the Theory of the Firm," *Strategic Management Journal*, Winter 1996, pp. 93–107.

Malhotra, Yogesh. "Knowledge Management for the New World of Business." *Journal for Quality & Participation*, July/August 1998, pp. 58–60, www.brint.com/km/ whatis.htm, Date accessed August 2002.

Minsky, Marvin. "Conscious Machines." In *Machinery of Consciousness Proceedings*, National Research Council of Canada, 75th Anniversary Symposium on Science in Society, June 1991.

Nonaka, Ikujiro, and Takeuchi, Hiro. *The Knowledge-Creating Company: How Japanese Companies Create the Dynamics of Innovation,* New York: Oxford University Press, 1995.

Pfeffer, Jeffrey, and Sutton, Robert. *The Knowing-Doing Gap*. Boston, MA: Harvard Business School Press, 2000, pp. 5, 12, 181.

Roberts-Witt, Sarah. "Knowledge Everywhere," *Knowledge Management*, June 2001, pp. 36–41.

Shanteau, James, "Psychological Characteristics and Strategies of Expert Decision Makers." *Acta Psychologica*, vol. 68, 1988, pp. 203–15.

Simon, H. A., and Chase, W. G. "Skill in Chess," *American Scientist*, vol. 61, 1973, pp. 394–403.

Sveiby, Karl-Erik. "Tacit Knowledge." December 31, 1997. www.svciby.com/articles/polanyi.html, Date accessed August 2002.

Sweller, John, Mawyer, R. F., and Ward, M. R. "Development of Expertise in Mathematical Problem Solving," *Journal of Experimental Psychology: General*, December 1983, pp. 639–61.

Tiwana, Amrit. *The Knowledge Management Toolkit*. Upper Saddle River, NJ: Prentice Hall, 2000, pp. 55–98.

Witt, Roberts. "Knowledge Management: Know What You Know," *PC Magazine*, July 1, 2000, p. 165.

Knowledge Management Systems Life Cycle

Contents

In a Nutshell
Challenges in Building KM Systems
Conventional Versus KM System Life Cycle
Knowledge Management System Life Cycle (KMSLC)
    System Justification
    Role of Rapid Prototyping
    Selecting An Expert
    Role of the Knowledge Developer
    Role of Quality Assurance
    User Training
Implications for Knowledge Management
Summary
Terms to Know
Test Your Understanding
Knowledge Exercises
References

There is nothing more difficult to plan, more doubtful of success, nor more dangerous to manage than the creation of a new system. For the initiator has the enmity of all who would profit by the preservation of the old system and merely lukewarm defenders in those who would gain by the new one.
—MACHIAVELLI, 1513

▪▪▪▪ In a Nutshell

The building of knowledge management can be viewed as a life cycle that begins with a master plan and justification and ends with a system structured to meet KM requirements for the entire company. A knowledge team representing the thinking of the firm and a knowledge developer with expertise in knowledge capture, knowledge design, and knowledge implementation ensure a successful system. Lack of planning, structure, and order can invite disaster.

The most critical phase of the KM systems life cycle is identifying the immediate, intermediate, and long-term needs for the prospective system. This means reviewing the knowledge core of existing employees; conducting a cost/benefit analysis to determine the justification for and potential benefits of the candidate system; and determining the tools and the procedures to ensure completeness, accuracy, integrity, and operational success of the installation.

The knowledge management systems life cycle (KMSLC) centers around three questions:

1. What is the *problem* that warrants a solution by the KM system? How important is the problem? What clues indicate that the system should be built? What will the user and the company as a whole gain from the system?
2. What *development strategy* should be considered? Who is going to build the system?
3. What *process* will be used to build the system?

These questions are interrelated, and they lead to other questions when the knowledge developer gets involved in the system development process. In deciding on a KM system, it is important to consider top management support early in the planning phase. Employee support and participation through the knowledge capture phase also make it easier to navigate through the development process. This chapter focuses on the strategic planning and the justification for KM system development and the process of building it.

The concept of "life cycle" is not new. It can be applied to virtually every endeavor, personal and business. Here are some examples:

College:	Admission, education, graduation
Term paper:	Introduction, body, conclusion, references
Air flight:	Boarding, takeoff, cruising, landing, disembarking
Faculty:	Assistant professor, associate professor, professor
Information system development:	Problem definition, analysis, design, implementation

These life cycles have some characteristics in common:

- Discipline, order, or segmentation into manageable activities or phases
- Good documentation for possible changes or modifications of the system in the future
- Coordination of the project to ensure the cycle is completed on time
- Regular management review at each phase of the cycle

Structure and order are to KMSLC what chapters and paragraphs are to a book. Can you imagine trying to read this book if the paragraphs occurred in random order? You would be exposed to the same material, but it would lack order and, therefore, meaning. In the same way, a well-defined life cycle is essential for successful development and maintenance of knowledge management in a business environment.

▪▪▪▪ Challenges in Building KM Systems

On the surface, KM seems exciting, but several challenges lay ahead that hinder KM system development. Among the key challenges are the following:

- *Culture.* Changing organizational culture is not an overnight exercise. The number one challenge is getting people to share their knowledge rather than hoarding it (see Box 3.1). To do so means changing people's attitudes and behaviors. The company that develops the right combination of incentives for employees to collaborate and share their knowledge will go a long way toward ensuring a successful KM system. There is no question that knowledge is power, and no one wants to give it up. Traditionally, employees hoard knowledge because they understandably worry that they will lose advantage in the organization. KM has to make knowledge sharing attractive enough to be lasting, not just for the company but for the employees as well.

- *Knowledge evaluation.* The company that tackles the evaluation issue will have both a head start on the employee incentive problem and an edge on refining KM processes for maximum profit. Assessing the worth of information is a crucial step if a company wants to refine its methods or create a reward system for employees who have generated the "best" knowledge (see Box 3.2).

▪ ▪ ▪ ▪ ▪ ▪ ▪   **BOX 3.1**   ▪ ▪ ▪ ▪ ▪ ▪ ▪

THE SHARING OF KNOWLEDGE

Both inside and outside a company's gates, great things often begin at those fortunate moments when people with knowledge and vision pool their dreams. A perfect example: WorldCom, Inc., the company that merged with MCI to form MCI WorldCom, Inc., now the fourth-largest telecommunications company in the world, had its origins at a coffee shop in Hattiesburg, Mississippi, when four executives who knew the business got together exactly 1 month after AT&T's long-distance monopoly was broken by antitrust laws. Is it luck or knowledge?

Of course, businesspeople can meet by design at regular times and places, but the spontaneous appearance of a group that can develop a shared vision has historically been the product of a chance meeting on the stairs, on the elevator, by the coffee machine, or at the water cooler. Knowledge management proponents today believe that those chance interactions that mix and reformulate knowledge can and should be systematically encouraged. It can happen in one office, but time and geography are no longer constraints to collaborative work. The creation of a profitable idea—like MCI WorldCom—always takes hard work but is never just dumb luck. Larry Prusak, executive director of IBM's Institute for Knowledge Management in Waltham, Massachusetts, says, "All of life and business is a game of odds. Just as HR policies increase the odds of employee retention, and good customer service increases the odds toward repeat business, knowledge management is about increasing the odds toward knowledge being transferred, utilized, and contributing to innovation."

SOURCE: Excerpted from Glasser, Perry. "The Knowledge Factor," *CIO Magazine*, December 15, 1998–January 1, 1999, pp. 1–9.

▪ ▪ ▪ ▪ ▪ ▪

▪ ▪ ▪ ▪ ▪ ▪   **BOX 3.2**   ▪ ▪ ▪ ▪ ▪ ▪

ESTIMATING THE WORTH OF KNOWLEDGE

Figuring a return for knowledge management initiatives is like trying to calculate payback from providing employees with telephones, paper, and pens. According to international and U.S. chief knowledge officer Michael J. Turillo, Jr., of KPMG Peat Marwick LLP, the consultancy invested $40 million in a knowledge management initiative called *Kworld* during a 5-month period in 1998. The investment included capital outlays for hardware, software, and the development cost of executive and management time consumed by planning and testing the system for the New York City–based

firm. Though satisfied with Kworld's early operation, a nagging concern for Turillo remains finding a proper way to evaluate the information in KPMG's knowledge repository, the Global Knowledge Exchange. Assessing the worth of information is a crucial step if a company wants to refine its methods or create a reward system for the employees who have generated the "best" knowledge. A simple hit count on information use reveals little about its worth. Instead, the interest is in quality, who is using the information, and whether they are decision makers.

SOURCE: Excerpted from Glasser, Perry. "Knowledge Factors," *CIO Magazine*, December 15, 1998–January 1, 1999, p. 3.

▪ ▪ ▪ ▪ ▪ ▪

Unfortunately, estimating the worth of knowledge is complicated. Reliable metrics have yet to be made available.

- *Knowledge processing.* Many companies do not realize the importance of the human element in KM. Effective KM systems must allow organizations not only to store and access information but to document how decisions were reached as well. Specifically, techniques should be identified that will capture, store, process, and distribute the kind of knowledge that cannot be readily tabulated in rows or columns (see Box 3.3).

▪ ▪ ▪ ▪ ▪ ▪   **BOX 3.3**   ▪ ▪ ▪ ▪ ▪ ▪

THE PROCESSING OF KNOWLEDGE

The merger of Peat Marwick International and Klynveld Main Goerdeler in 1987 produced a babel of cultures in the American, British, Dutch, and German partnership known today as KPMG Peat Marwick LLP. "KPMG was not so much a global company as it was a collection of geographically identified franchises," says international and U.S. chief knowledge officer Michael J. Turillo, Jr.

Kworld—KPMG's knowledge intranet that started in 1997—is the company's strategic bet to make all its pieces work together. The knowledge

base design respects the legacy of KPMG's consulting practice, which remains organized around product, industry, and geography. KPMG users once had to physically locate the work of a specialist senior partner and potentially read through dozens of documents. With Kworld, expert information is available on the desktop. Extracting in-house knowledge about ERP installations for the petroleum industry in Germany, for example, is now only a few mouse clicks away.

(continued)

- *Knowledge implementation.* When it comes to KM, an organization must commit to change, learning, and innovating if it is to realize leadership in the marketplace. Technology has already made it possible to implement knowledge collaboration, regardless of time and place. One of the important tasks in KM is extracting meaning from information that will have an impact on special problems or missions. Lessons learned in the way of feedback are stored for others facing the same problem in the future. That is why prisoners of war are debriefed after their release. Their experience is stored in a repository for future behavioral adjustment that could improve the survival and life style of future prisoners of war.

▪▪▪▪ Conventional Versus KM System Life Cycle

Those who have developed conventional information systems in the past and are now involved in building KM systems need to see the relationship between the conventional systems approach and KM system development. This perspective extends to the role of the systems analyst versus that of the knowledge developer. This section examines these important distinctions.

Key Differences

Some striking differences distinguish conventional systems development from KM system development:

1. The systems analyst deals with data and information obtained from the user. The user is highly dependent on the analyst for the solution (a conventional information system). The knowledge developer deals with knowledge captured from people with known knowledge in the firm. The developer is highly dependent on them for the solution.
2. The main interface for the systems analyst is with the novice user, who knows the problem but not the solution. In contrast, the main interface for the knowledge developer is the knowledgeable person who knows the problem and the solution. There is no comparable expert in a conventional information system process.
3. Conventional system development is primarily sequential; that is, particular steps are carried out in a particular order. Design cannot be initiated without analysis, testing cannot be done without a design, and so on. In contrast, KMSLC is incremental and interactive. A KM system is not built in a few large steps; rather, it evolves toward a final form. Rapid prototyping as a knowledge capture tool plays a major role in KM system evolution. The flowcharts in Figure 3.1 illustrate these differences.
4. In the development of conventional information systems, testing occurs toward the end of the cycle after the system has been built. In KMSLC, the knowledge

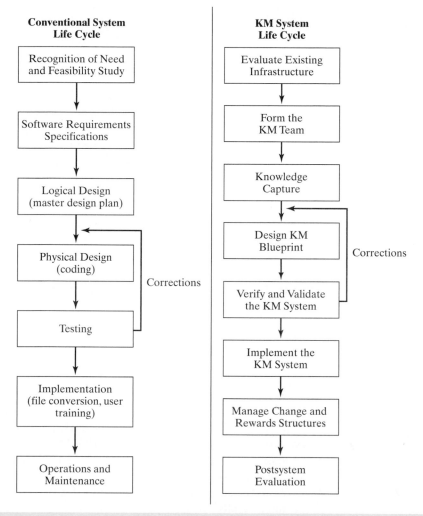

FIGURE 3.1: Comparison of the Development Life Cycles of a Conventional Information System Life Cycle and a KM System Life Cycle

developer tests (verifies and validates) the evolving system from the beginning of the cycle.

5. The discipline of system development and system maintenance is much more extensive for conventional information systems than it is for KMSLC. KM system maintenance is delegated to knowledge editors, whose job is to ensure a reliable system and to upgrade the system to standards.

6. The conventional system life cycle is process-driven and *documentation-oriented,* with emphasis on the flow of the data and the resulting system. It fosters the "specify then build" approach. The KMSLC is *result-oriented.* The emphasis is on a "start slow and grow" incremental process.

7. Conventional system development does not support tools like rapid prototyping because it follows a set sequence of steps. KMSLC utilizes rapid prototyping (to be explain later in the text), incorporating changes on the spot, which augments and refines the KM system until it is ready for use. Thus, the prototype *evolves*

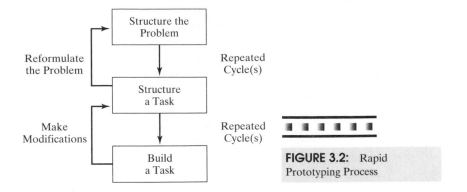

FIGURE 3.2: Rapid Prototyping Process

into the final KM system. As shown in Figure 3.2, in knowledge capture, tasks are structured, and the knowledge sought is reformulated until the knowledge worker or the resident expert judges that it is right. This process promotes verification of the KM system. Verification answers the question, *Is the system built right?* The final test is validation, which ensures that authorized users are satisfied with what the KM system offers.

Key Similarities

Although obvious differences exist between the conventional information system development life cycle and KMSLC, so, too, do certain similarities:

1. Both cycles begin with a problem and end with a solution. The problem solution is pitched to benefit the company user and the organization as a whole.
2. After setting up the strategic plan, the early phase of the conventional system life cycle begins with information gathering to ensure a clear understanding of the problem and the user's requirements. In KMSLC, the early phase requires knowledge capture, which later becomes the foundation of the knowledge base. Both information and knowledge must be represented in order for a system to produce results.
3. Verification and validation of a KM system resemble conventional system testing. Verification ensures that the KM system is clear of errors. This is similar to alpha testing or debugging a conventional system program(s). In contrast, KM system validation and conventional system beta (user acceptance) testing ensure that the system meets the user's requirements prior to deployment.
4. Both the knowledge developer and the systems analyst need to choose the appropriate tools for designing their respective systems. Choice of tools and methodologies will be covered in Chapter 4.

Users Versus Knowledge Workers

Users and knowledge workers have similarities and differences. For example, in terms of cooperation, the user must work with the systems analyst by providing the information or documents needed for building a successful information system. In contrast, the knowledge worker or the expert "owns" the knowledge being shared or given away. Most experts are cooperative, although no knowledge developer should take them for granted. The main difference is that the expert does not have the same vested interest in the system that the user has; in most cases, the expert will not be the final user. Table 3.1 summarizes differences between the user and the expert.

TABLE 3.1   Comparison of Users and Experts

Attributes	*User*	*Expert*
Dependence on the system	High	Low to nil
Cooperation	Usually cooperative	Cooperation not required
Tolerance for ambiguity	Low	High
Knowledge of problem	High	Average/low
Contribution to system	Information	Knowledge/expertise
System user	Yes	No
Availability for system builder	Readily available	Not readily available

▪ ▪ ▪ ▪ Knowledge Management System Life Cycle (KMSLC)

Due to a lack of standardization in the field, several approaches have been proposed for a KMSLC. Some approaches borrow from the conventional system development life cycle; others prescribe steps unique to knowledge management. Table 3.2 lists representative

TABLE 3.2   Alternative Approaches to Knowledge Management Development

Step	*Tiwana (2000)*	*Dixon (2000)*	*Garvin (2000)*	*Liebowitz and Wilcox (1997)*	*Davenport and Prusak (2000)*
1.	Analyze existing infrastructure	Team performs a task	Acquiring knowledge	Build knowledge	Acquisition
2.	Align knowledge management and business strategy	Team explores the relationship between action and outcome	Interpreting knowledge	Organize and hold	Dedicated resources
3.	Design the knowledge infrastructure	Common knowledge gained	Applying knowledge	Distribute and pool	Fusion
4.	Audit existing knowledge assets and systems	Knowledge transfer system selected		Apply knowledge to work object	Adaptation
5.	Design the KM team	Knowledge translated into a form usable by others			Knowledge networking
6.	Create the KM blueprint	Receiving team adapts knowledge for its own use			
7.	Develop the KM system				
8.	Deploy, using the results-driven incremental methodology				
9.	Manage change, culture, and reward structures				
10.	Evaluate performance, measure ROI, and incrementally refine the KMS				

Stage	*Key Question(s)*	*Outcome*
Evaluate existing infrastructure	What is the problem? Is the system justifiable? Is the system feasible?	Statement of objectives Performance criteria Strategic plan
Form the KM team	Who should be on the team? How will the team function?	Standardized procedure for system development
Knowledge capture	What and whose knowledge should be captured? How would knowledge capture proceed?	Acquisition of knowledge core
Design KM blueprint (master plan)	How will knowledge be represented?	Design of KM system Hardware/software implementation details Test plan Security, audit, and operating procedures
Test the KM system	How reliable is the system?	Peer reviews, walkthroughs
Implement the KM system	What is the actual operation? How easy is it to use?	User-friendly system Training program
Manage change and reward structure	Does the system provide the intended solutions?	Satisfied users
Post-system evaluation	Should the system be modified?	Reliable and up-to-date system

▪▪▪▪▪▪ **FIGURE 3.3:** KM System Development Life Cycle

approaches. A cursory examination reveals many similarities and overlaps. We propose a hybrid life cycle that makes best use of the existing ones (see Figure 3.3). A representative knowledge management system is summarized in Box 3.4.

Note that although conventional system development and KM system development differ in some important ways, the two approaches are fundamentally similar. The conventional approach may still be used in developing KM systems, but it is being replaced by iterative design, prototyping, early testing, and other variations.

▪▪▪▪▪▪ BOX 3.4 ▪▪▪▪▪▪

THE LIFE CYCLE OF A KNOWLEDGE MANAGEMENT SYSTEM

BUILDING A KNOWLEDGE MANAGEMENT SYSTEM FROM THE GROUND UP

With the Wall Street scandals of 2002 (Arthur Andersen, Enron, WorldCom), a large commercial bank ordered the development of a knowledge management auditing system to advise the bank on compliance with the federal bank examiners who audit the bank on a quarterly basis. The office of the Comptroller of the Currency (OCC),

(continued)

(continued)

a bureau of the U.S. Treasury, is the regulator of the national banking system. To oversee this system of 4,500 banks, the OCC administers 125 offices across the country, staffed by 2,500 bank examiners. These examiners range from 25-year veterans to novice assistants.

To create a bank knowledge management auditor or BANKOR, the bank's president formed a knowledge management team consisting of the bank's auditor, a representative from each major department, and a member of the board of directors to launch the project. The senior vice president of the loan department chaired the team. BANKOR's knowledge was captured through extensive interviews with six federal examiners over a 15-month period. Fortunately, one knowledge developer was an examiner, and the other was an IT expert in knowledge management system design.

Interviewing the Examiners Given the serious nature of bank auditing and solvency, six seasoned examiners were chosen for the job. With each examiner coming from different states where the bank does business, this strategy helped BANKOR address everyone's concerns and made it easier to gain universal acceptance. Once selected, the knowledge developers scheduled a weeklong session with each examiner. They held the first interview not really knowing what to expect. They had selected several case studies for the examiners to analyze. The first mistake was that the cases were too obvious. After the first interview, it was apparent that it did not take an experienced examiner to analyze the cases and reach conclusions. So, in preparation for the succeeding interviews the developers selected more complex cases that would require the examiners to wrestle with their own decision-making process and apply true expertise.

Following the first interview, it took 3 months to assemble and collate the captured notes. The developers reduced the notes for an individual examiner's cases to a general conclusion about

how that examiner worked. Finally, the developers combined the six methods into one set that described the examiners' consensus.

Taping the sessions was tremendous help. It saved having to write everything down and allowed the developers to concentrate on what was said, and they were better able to probe their thought process for inconsistencies and missing pieces. The transcripts also allowed them to see their responses verbatim.

Three more sessions were held. The fourth and last session used four cases and involved visits to all six examiners. This round was the sign-off for testing the model. During this visit, the examiners analyzed the cases and compared their results with that of the system. After some minor modification, the examiners approved BANKOR as a "fair representation" of their own analyses. At this point, the developers were ready to present the system for final user acceptance testing.

After knowledge capture, the developers designed a blueprint that specified how BANKOR would be codified. They adopted CORVID—a knowledge automation package developed by EXSYS Corporation. In addition, they decided on the implementation and testing details. Testing plays a critical role in the codification of knowledge, using rules. The package is capable of interfacing with databases as well as documented knowledge in various repositories. It also is capable of importing and exporting text information for printout or documentation update.

The bank president turned out to be the best champion of the project. He let it be known that the system must be a winner. He attended several meetings of the KM team and brainstormed issues dealing with auditing procedures and integrity. He also made sure that all details were properly documented for maintenance and future upgrade. The team also became the end user when it was time to test the system. It was totally committed to seeing the system succeed at each phase of the life cycle. The experience turned out to be an effective knowledge-sharing experience.

Evaluate Existing Infrastructure

The basis for a KM system is satisfying a need for improving the productivity and potential of employees and the company as a whole. To do so, we need to gain familiarity with various components making up the KM strategy and supporting technology. Identifying and evaluating the current knowledge environment makes it easier to point out the critical missing gaps and justify the formation of a new KM environment. The psychology behind evaluating the current knowledge infrastructure is giving the perception that the current way of doing things is not conveniently abandoned in preference for a brand new system.

As a part of this phase, we focus on system justification, scoping the evaluation, and determining feasibility. Each step is explained here:

SYSTEM JUSTIFICATION

The goal of this step is for the knowledge developer to justify whether it is worth undergoing the kinds of changes and investment that ensure top management support. KM system justification involves answers to specific questions:

1. *Is current knowledge going to be lost through retirement, transfer, or departure to other firms?* Existing knowledge infrastructure becomes a problem when knowledge workers who have been handling highly complex problems for years suddenly decide to leave or are due to retire, resign, or simply go with the competition. Because replacing company experts whose knowledge has been individually hoarded is not easy to do, a KM system that provides shared expertise could be added assurance for company survival and future growth. In the case of BANKOR (see Box 3.4), the auditing process of existing bank auditors needed verification and possible update to a system that assured federal bank examiner compliance. The need was timely and a necessary step to ensure integrity of operation.

2. *Is the proposed KM system needed in several locations?* If a company has only one expert to handle a particular problem at a given time, similar problems in other locations have to wait for the expert's attention or someone in that location might have to address the problem from scratch. (This is why it took more than 18 months to put out the fires in Quwait's 650 oil wells after the Gulf War.) In such a case, a KM system can be used to distribute application expertise uniformly throughout a company's facilities.

3. *Are experts available and willing to help in building a KM system?* Without reliable knowledge or knowledge workers, there can be no knowledge-based system. For certain complex problems, a knowledge developer may have to work with several knowledge workers, although dealing with several knowledge workers presents all kinds of knowledge capture or validation challenges. With the BANKOR project, multiple examiners were needed to ensure consistency of decision making, especially with the bank doing business in several states.

4. *Does the problem in question require years of experience and cognitive reasoning to solve?* One indicator that a problem might be a candidate for a KM system is its nonprocedural or nontrivial nature. If the knowledge can be learned in a few weeks and the pattern of solution is routine, then the problem is probably not sufficiently heuristic to qualify for a KM system application. With BANKOR, years of practical experience were required for bank auditing.

5. *When undergoing knowledge capture, can the expert articulate how the problem will be solved?* The ability to explain a procedure or illustrate how a problem is to be solved is not a skill everyone possesses. Often, the more of an expert a person

is, the more difficulty that person has explaining a complex procedure or a solution. One of the main obstacles is explaining heuristics. In order to do this, experts must dig into their deep knowledge and verbalize stored heuristics. For the process to work, the knowledge developer must also have good communication and interpersonal skills to elicit the expert's responses.

6. *How critical is the knowledge to be captured?* Criticality of an application has to do with how vital it is to the company's survival or productivity. A project that is considered a reaction to a recent catastrophic failure in an area of the firm's operation deserves close evaluation. The BANKOR project was a reaction to the corporate scandals resulting from devious auditing corruption.

7. *Are the tasks nonalgorithmic?* That is, are heuristics used to solve the problem? The problem domain should be considered a judgment maker rather than a calculation processor. Conventional software performs calculations on data to produce information; a KM system takes information and transforms it into knowledge and practical advice. See Figure 3.4 for a comparative view of the two systems.

8. *Is there a champion in the house?* For a KM system to succeed, it must be supported from within the organization. The organization must have a champion who believes that a KM system can be beneficial for the company and is willing to support its development aggressively. The champion is often in a good position to coordinate the development of the system. Such a person usually has credibility with the employees, understands their concerns, speaks their language, and knows the key people in the organization. With BANKOR, the president was popular with bank officers and employees, even though he had been president for less than 2 years. His enthusiasm and honesty got the team to work overtime many days at a time.

The Scope Factor

When deciding how large the KM system should be, it is important to "scope" the project first. The term *scoping* means "limiting the breadth and depth of the project within the financial, human resource, and operational constraints." The project should

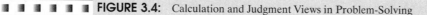

▮ ▮ ▮ ▮ ▮ ▮ ▮ **FIGURE 3.4:** Calculation and Judgment Views in Problem-Solving

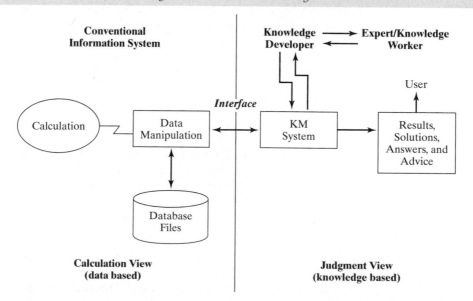

be small enough for the knowledge developer's capabilities, especially if it is the organization's first attempt at developing a KM system. It must also be completed quickly enough for the users to foresee its benefits. A complex, drawn-out project whose development takes months and years is likely to falter on the way to completion or cause the user to lose patience and interest, which makes training and successful use difficult.

As part of the scoping factor, several areas must be included:

- Readiness of the company's current technology. This includes intranet, local area networks, extranet (a company's extended network connecting suppliers, customers, and salespersons), decision support tools, and other information technology tools.
- Identification of gaps and areas needing improvement in current technology to see how well such technology will match the technical requirements of the proposed KM system.
- General review and understanding of the benefits and limitations of KM tools and components that become part of the feasibility study.

The Feasibility Question

The first phase to consider is feasibility. A feasibility study addresses the following questions:

- Is the project *doable?* Can it be completed within a reasonable time?
- Is it *affordable?* Do the system's potential benefits justify the cost of development?
- Is it *appropriate?* Just what can the firm expect to get out of it?
- Is it *practicable?* How frequently would the system be consulted and at what cost?

In BANKOR's experience, the project was clearly doable, affordable, appropriate, and practicable, because the bank wanted to be the leader in demonstrating integrity and reliability to customers, stockholders, and federal examiners. Actually, the project had to be carried out, given the sensitivity of accurate auditing in the banking sector.

Including an assessment of costs against tangible and intangible benefits, these questions evaluate the project in detail. The result of the study is a proposal that summarizes what is known and what is going to be done. Once approved by top management, it paves the way for KM system design. Although a feasibility study is not considered a formal part of KM system development, identifying the proposed system's many ramifications (economic, technological, and behavioral) is necessary front-end work. This way, there should be no surprises. Attempting such a project makes no sense unless the heart and soul of the company are committed to the effort, especially if it is the organization's first KM system.

Economic feasibility, better known as *cost/benefit analysis,* determines to what extent a new system is cost-effective. *Technical* feasibility is determined by evaluating the hardware and supportive software within the framework of the company's IT infrastructure. *Behavioral* feasibility includes training management and employees in the use of the KM system. All these factors must be viewed collectively for a successful installation.

The traditional approach to conducting a feasibility study could be useful in building a KM system. It involves several tasks:

- *Form a KM team.* Forming a KM team means formalizing a commitment to the KM development process. Team members are selected from various areas in the organization; selection is based on criteria designed to bring the best representatives for the duration of the project. This is exactly what was done to form the

KM team for BANKOR. There was fair representation of both talent and departments on a full-time basis.

- *Prepare a master plan.* A master plan lays out the steps to be taken throughout the life cycle of the project. It could be a physical representation like a flowchart that specifies the activities to be carried out and the relationships among the activities.
- *Evaluate cost/performance of the proposed KM system.* In this phase, the key question is "What are we getting in return for the cost of building this new KM system?" The terms used are *breakeven analysis* and *payback analysis.* Breakeven is the point at which the costs of the current and the proposed systems are equal. Beyond that is net savings or net benefits. Payback is deciding how long it will take a system to produce enough savings to pay for developmental costs.

  Essentially, performance criteria are evaluated against tangible and intangible costs to determine the most cost-effective system. Obviously, the more tangible the costs, the easier it will be to measure the benefits. It is often the case that the benefits are more intangible than tangible, which makes it difficult to sell to top management (see Box 3.5).

- *Quantify system criteria and costs.* There are various metrics to do so. One procedure for quantifying system criteria is as follows:

  - Determine a weight factor for each criterion based on its perceived impact on the system.
  - Assign a relative rating to each criterion. For example, on a scale of 1 to 5, 1 is rated "poor" and 5 is rated "excellent."
  - Multiply the weight factor by the relative rating and sum the score for each alternative system. Table 3.3 shows an example of a weighted candidate evaluation system compared to the existing or an alternative one. Assuming the weight and rating factors are accurate, the system with the higher score is judged to be the better system. Additional supportive information would be helpful in reinforcing the choice.

In summary, several factors must be considered in identifying an appropriate KM system. Many such projects fail because of poor front-end evaluation. Also, without a champion or someone within the firm who can support and promote the project at all times, the project is likely to fall by the wayside.

Importance of User Support

In conventional information systems, systems analysts often build the system and then worry about selling it to the user through demonstrations and training. Such "selling" should begin early in the development process. The same is true with KM systems. The user should be sold on it early in the KMSLC. At this stage of the development life cycle, a knowledge developer needs to address a number of questions:

- Does the intended user know the new KM system is being developed? How is it perceived?
- How involved should the ultimate user be in the building process?
- What user training will be required when the KM system is up and running?
- What operational support must be provided?

These questions prompt idea generation. They help determine whether the proposed KM system is doable and justifiable; they also allow a move to the next step, knowledge capture. Without an honest "sell" to the user, all kinds of problems can arise when it is time to implement the system. Upper management should also give its blessing to the project early by allocating sufficient resources for its development.

■ ■ ■ ■ ■ ■ BOX 3.5 ■ ■ ■ ■ ■ ■

VALUATION OF KNOWLEDGE CAPITAL

CALCULATING KNOWLEDGE CAPITAL

The valuation of knowledge capital makes it possible to assess the worth of the people who possess the accumulated knowledge about an organization. They are the individuals who leave the workplace every night (and may never return), storing in their heads the know-how acquired while receiving full pay. Their brains are repositories of knowledge accumulated over untold hours of listening and talking while not delivering any goods or services to paying customers.

The employees' minds, and the files they manage, carry a share of the company's knowledge capital. This makes every employee a custodian of the most important assets a firm owns, even though these assets never show up on any financial reports.

In contrast, the custodianship of financial assets has become a well-defined discipline that depends on procedures and regulations on how to account for and report these resources. Over a period of many years, an elaborate framework involving accounts, auditors, reporting standards, and government oversight has been developed to do that. The financial assets of corporations represent only a small share of total corporate assets. By far, the most important assets are now in the form of corporate knowledge, but the custodianship, accounting, and reporting standards for these resources do not exist.

Financial executives have shown a remarkable reluctance to put numbers on something many consider to be intangible. However, with the rising importance of knowledge assets, the time has come to place the management of knowledge on the agenda of executive managers, financial analysts, and shareholders. To that end, one must start by developing an independently verifiable quantification of the worth of knowledge assets.

The allocation of the respective contributions of knowledge capital and financial capital to profits can be made if one recognizes that financial capital is now a commodity—readily available at a price that reflects the interest rate that a firm pays for its borrowings. However, what makes a company prosper is not financial capital—which anyone can obtain for a price—but the effectiveness with which knowledge capital is put to use. Therefore, the annual returns realized on knowledge capital can be isolated after paying a "rental" for the financial capital and then subtracting that amount from the profits.

What remains is "economic profit," or the economic value-added, because it accounts for those missing elements that represent everything not shown on a conventional balance sheet. By filtering out the contributions of financial capital from the reported profits, we are left with a residual that is entirely attributable to what knowledge capital has actually delivered. In other words, knowledge value-added is the annual yield a firm realizes from its knowledge capital assets.

SOURCE: Excerpted from Strassmann, Paul A. "Calculating Knowledge Capital," files.strassmann.com/pubs/km/1999-10.php, October 1999. Date accessed August 2002.

■ ■ ■ ■ ■ ■

In summary, the first step in the KMSLC is to decide what is wanted, identify the goals of the proposed system, assess feasibility, plan how to begin, locate a champion, inform users and their managers of the project, and gain their support within the scope of the project. Above all, every KM system must begin with ready knowledge, knowledgeable experts ready to work with a knowledge developer in building the infrastructure.

TABLE 3.3   Weighted Evaluation Matrix

Evaluation Criteria	Weight	System A		System B	
		Rating	*Score*	*Rating*	*Score*
Performance					
Knowledge quality	4	5	20	4	16
System reliability	2	4	08	4	08
Knowledge currency	3	4	12	3	09
Costs					
Payback	2	3	06	4	08
System development	4	4	16	3	12
System operation	3	4	12	3	09
User training	5	5	25	3	15
			99		78

Role of Strategic Planning

As with any other application, there are concerns to ponder before launching a new system. Issues such as planning your new KM system, selling it to the employees and top management, providing good service and maintaining security—all take on a new meaning when applied to KM development and support. As a consequence of evaluating the existing infrastructure, the company should devise a strategic plan with vision aimed at advancing the short-term and long-term objectives of the business with the KM system in mind.

What is being emphasized is the ultimate goal of a KM system—connecting users with knowledge content. That is why it is so important to review knowledge needs throughout the company and to inventory knowledge content assets that you wish to capture. It is risky to plunge ahead before strategizing. Consider the following areas:

- *Vision*—What is your business trying to achieve? How will it be done? How will the KM system fulfill the goals? How will you measure success?
- *Resources*—How much can your business afford to build the right KM system? Is there talent aboard that can take the responsibility and assure that vision becomes reality?
- *Culture*—Is your business politically amenable for coordinating efforts to support this new approach to knowledge sharing? Who will ultimately control the KM system's content and user feedback?

Once business strategy is made final, the next step is to demonstrate a viable link between KM and strategy. The idea is to elevate KM to the higher level of strategy and ensure that the final system is in compliance with strategy. Related to this step is the importance of analyzing knowledge gaps (things that need corrections or additions) and relating them to strategic gaps. There is also the need to determine the right questions to ask and to package knowledge as part of the proposed KM system. The upshot is to use knowledge to create value for the product, the service, or the organizational process.

Figure 3.5 illustrates the relationship between and the need to match business strategy with that of KM strategy early in the KM system life cycle. Threats and feedback

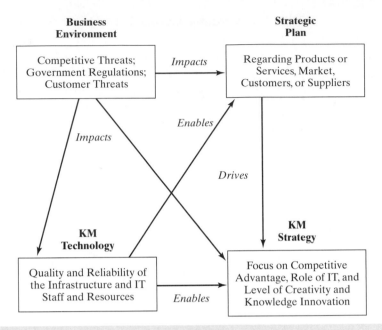

**Business
Environment**

Competitive Threats;
Government Regulations;
Customer Threats

Impacts

**Strategic
Plan**

Regarding Products or
Services, Market,
Customers, or Suppliers

Impacts

Enables

Drives

**KM
Technology**

Quality and Reliability of
the Infrastructure and IT
Staff and Resources

Enables

**KM
Strategy**

Focus on Competitive
Advantage, Role of IT, and
Level of Creativity and
Knowledge Innovation

▪▪▪▪▪▪▪ **FIGURE 3.5:**   Matching Business Strategy with KM Strategy

from the environment (such as government regulations, customers, and competitive threats) impact business strategy on a day-to-day basis. Likewise, the business environment impacts both KM strategy and KM technology, which enable KM strategy. The strategic plan, in turn, drives KM strategy, which means that KM strategy must be within the framework of the company's strategic plan for it to work and be supported by top management.

Form the KM Team

After evaluation of the company's existing infrastructure is complete, a KM team should be formed; this team stays with the building process until the final installation. Forming a KM team means:

- Identifying the key units, departments, branches, or divisions as the key stakeholders in the prospective KM system. Each stakeholder unit has certain knowledge requirements and one or more experts who could represent the unit on the KM team. In forming the BANKOR KM team, a representative from every department involved in the federal examiners' quarterly bank audit was included in the KM team. Each member brought unique knowledge and cited specific audit strategies that were tested through knowledge capture; the outside examiners acted as experts.
- Balancing the team size and competency organizationally, strategically, and technologically. In other words, the KM team should have a balanced complement of experts in each of these areas to collaborate on the multidimensional nature of the KM system building process.

Teamwork can be pleasurable and smooth running or it can be fraught with problems. Team success depends on a number of factors:

- *Caliber of team members in terms of personality, communication skills, and experience.* Engaging personalities with good communication skills usually do better at problem-solving and conflict resolution than laid-back personalities. Also, team members with experience in a specific domain garner attention and respect within the team.

- *Team size.* There should be representation with qualifications. In a large multinational firm, where there are hundreds of departments or divisions, a representative from each area would make teamwork unwieldy and counterproductive. Based on the author's consulting experience, team size from 4 to 20 is manageable. Beyond that, a team is divided into subcommittees with more distinctive assignments. When that happens, things tend to drag, and coordination among subcommittees becomes a challenge.

- *Complexity of the project.* The complexity of a KM system depends on the size of the organization, the nature of the products, the level of sophistication of existing technology, and the expertise of team members. Working against a tight deadline can also make the project more difficult to handle. In the case of BANKOR, the KM system was extremely complex, especially with the tax and regulatory requirements of the states in which the bank conducted business.

- *Leadership and team motivation.* Effective leadership can generate motivation, cooperation, and coordination within the team to ensure a successful outcome. Team motivation means a volunteering spirit and willingness to devote time for the KM system building process. This is influenced by the size of the team, the perceived level of expertise of each team member as compared to other team members, and how freely team members are encouraged to participate.

- *Promising more than can be realistically delivered.* There is nothing worse for a team than to build high hopes for top management when the odds are stacked against such achievement. Underestimating factors such as development costs and outcomes beclouds credence of the team to deliver with integrity.

Knowledge Capture

In the third step in the KMSLC, knowledge capture takes on several directions and meanings. Briefly, explicit knowledge is captured in repositories from documentation, files, and other media. In contrast, tacit knowledge is captured from company experts and from knowledge stored in databases for all authorized employees. Data mining also enters the picture in terms of using intelligent agents that analyze the data warehouse and come up with new findings that could lead to new products or services.

The focus of Chapter 5 is on capturing tacit knowledge by using various tools and methodologies. Knowledge capture involves eliciting, analyzing, and interpreting the knowledge that a human expert uses to solve a particular problem. It corresponds to systems analysis in conventional system development. In both cases, interviews with knowledgeable people are used to capture information and knowledge. Sometimes, interviewing the ultimate user of the knowledge management system is just as important as interviewing the expert whose knowledge you are trying to capture.

In KM system development, the knowledge developer acquires heuristic knowledge from the expert(s) in order to build the knowledge base. In Chapter 4, we discuss problems and procedures in the knowledge capture process. For example, the user has more to gain from the knowledge base than the expert who is helping to build it. The expert hands over years of knowledge for a system that someone else will use. The benefits are not the same, which explains some experts' lack of cooperation and motivation throughout the system development life cycle.

Knowledge capture and transfer are often carried out through teams, not just through individuals. As shown in Figure 3.6, common knowledge is created by asking a

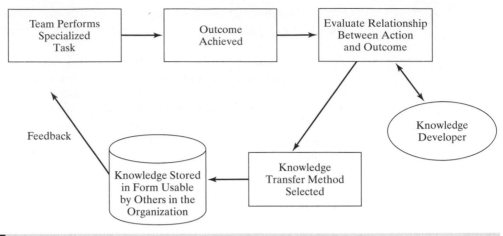

▪ ▪ ▪ ▪ ▪ ▪ ▪ ▪ **FIGURE 3.6:** Knowledge Capture and Transfer Through Teams

team to perform a task. After the outcome is achieved, the knowledge developer explores with the team the relationship between team action and outcome. If the team agrees that common knowledge has been gained, it becomes available in a knowledge base by translating it into a form usable by others in the organization. It can be in the form of a document, a case with rules and parameters, or a scenario.

Knowledge capture plays a unique role in various phases of the KMSLC. As shown in Table 3.4, knowledge capture includes determining feasibility, choosing the expert, tapping the expert's knowledge, and retapping knowledge to plug gaps in the system and to verify and validate the knowledge base after the system is in operation. So, in KMSLC, knowledge capture is an evolving step, not a one-time, front-end step as it is in conventional information system development.

TABLE 3.4 Knowledge Capture Activities in the KMSLC

KMSLC Step	*Knowledge Capture Activity*
1. Determine feasibility	• Seek out a champion • Locate a cooperative expert
2. Capture knowledge	• Apply appropriate tools to capture expert's knowledge
3. Design KM blueprint	• Design KM architecture
4. Verify and validate the KM system	• Correct for knowledge integrity and work closely with expert through rapid prototyping
5. Implement the KM system	• Work with the user to ensure system acceptance and proper training
6. Manage change and reward structure	• Reinforce change and reward compliance through human resources
7. Evaluate postsystem	• Recapture new knowledge and update the knowledge base

▪ ▪ ▪ ▪ ▪ ▪

ROLE OF RAPID PROTOTYPING

Most knowledge developers use an *iterative* approach in knowledge capture, which means a series of repeated actions. For example, the knowledge developer starts with a small-scale system, a *prototype,* based on the limited knowledge captured from the expert during the first few sessions. What turns the approach into rapid prototyping is the following:

- The knowledge developer shows the expert a skeletal procedure based on rudimentary knowledge acquired from the expert during the past two sessions.
- The expert reacts by saying, "This is all right, but there's more to it. Let me tell you what you need to incorporate into this prototype . . ." This is precisely how the knowledge developers in the BANKOR system conducted their interviews.
- While the expert watches, the knowledge developer enters the additional knowledge into a computer-based system that represents the prototype.
- The knowledge developer reruns the modified prototype and continues entering additional knowledge or making modifications as suggested by the expert until the expert says, "This is about right. I think you've got it this time."

This spontaneous, iterative building of a knowledge base is referred to as **rapid prototyping**. The process continues through several sessions and weeks of work until the knowledge base moves out of the prototype stage and becomes a full-fledged knowledge base that is ready for use. Rapid prototyping is essential for large systems, because the cost of a poorly structured system that is unusable can be prohibitive. Other benefits of rapid prototyping include the following:

- It documents for the expert and others that progress is being made on the project.
- Mistakes can be quickly corrected.
- The system is tested each time new knowledge or modifications are incorporated.
- It yields a tangible product at an early stage.
- The system "grows" in step with increasing understanding of what the user will learn and how the expert will provide it.
- It promotes accelerated knowledge capture.
- It demonstrates the capabilities of the resulting knowledge base.

The "smash and grab" approach—in which the knowledge developer "grabs" the attention of the expert for a few hours over a few sessions and ends up with a "workable" knowledge base—is not recommended. Remember that knowledge bases are based on human heuristics (rules of thumb) and human knowledge, not on quantitative or syntactic data. Rapid prototyping fosters maturation and "value-added" activities. It requires patience, concentration, and knowing how to make changes on the fly without errors.

SELECTING AN EXPERT

In expressing their differing views about the nature of expertise, some argue that the entire breadth of human expertise must be studied before attempting to capture the knowledge necessary to build a knowledge base. Others support a narrower focus that limits the role of the expert to knowledge capture activities. In either case, the goal is a knowledge base that represents expertise, rather than the expert.

In working with the expert, the knowledge developer will occasionally run into vague expressions of thought or reasoning processes that must either be clarified by the expert or factored into the system. For example, "fuzzy" expressions can be assigned certainty factors to reflect the extent of "fuzziness" of the expression. Certainty factors require careful analysis to assure proper representation in the knowledge base. In fact, much of the knowledge that the expert provides is based on heuristics, which tend to be qualitative, rather than quantitative.

Finally, a competent and cooperative expert is essential to the success of knowledge capture. The expert must be able to communicate information understandably and in sufficient detail. The questions that face every knowledge base project are as follows:

- How can one know that the so-called expert is in fact an expert? In the example of BANKOR, the examiners were certified and each had more than 10 years' experience.
- Will the expert stay with the project to the end?
- What backup is available in case the expert loses interest, decides to leave, or simply is no longer available?
- How is the knowledge developer to know what is and what is not within the expert's area of expertise?

Sometimes, either because of the nature of the problem or its importance to the organization, more than one expert should be involved in addressing the problem domain. Dealing with several experts is not an easy task. The knowledge developer may have to use different tools in different ways to access the experts' knowledge and promote agreement among them before the captured knowledge becomes part of the knowledge base. Dealing with single and multiple experts is discussed in Chapter 5.

ROLE OF THE KNOWLEDGE DEVELOPER

The knowledge developer is an important player in the KMSLC. As explained in detail in Chapter 4, he or she is the *architect* of the system. This one person identifies the problem domain, captures the knowledge, writes and tests the heuristics that represent the knowledge, and coordinates the entire project from beginning to end.

Such a pivotal job requires certain qualifications. The most important attributes are excellent communication skills, an understanding of knowledge capture tools, familiarity with technology, tolerance for ambiguity, ability to work well with other professionals including experts, being a conceptual thinker, and having a personality that motivates people to work together as a team. The knowledge developer's job requires interaction with a number of individuals throughout the KMSLC. The most frequent interactions, shown in Figure 3.7, are with the organization's knower(s), the knowledge worker, and most likely, the champion. Each person can make or break the project. In the case of BANKOR, the knowledge developers had a great rapport with the president, whose time and effort championed the application through implementation.

Design the KM Blueprint

This phase is the beginning of designing the IT infrastructure and the knowledge management architecture. The knowledge management team relies on such a blueprint to proceed with the actual design and deployment of the KM system. A KM blueprint, referred to as the *KM system design,* addresses several important issues. Once created, the next step is to actually put together the KM system.

1. Aim for system interoperability and scalability with existing company IT infrastructure.
2. Finalize the scope of the proposed KM system with realized net benefits in mind.
3. Decide on the required system components, such as user interface options, knowledge directories, and mining tools.

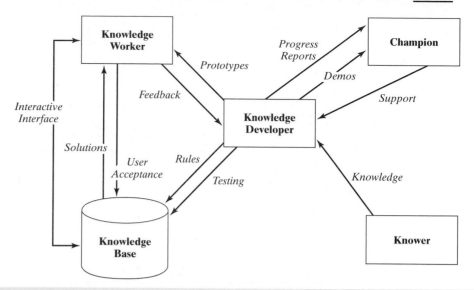

▪ ▪ ▪ ▪ ▪ ▪ ▪ **FIGURE 3.7:**   The Central Role of the Knowledge Developer

4. Develop the key layers of the KM architecture to meet your company's requirements. As shown in Figure 3.8, the key layers are as follows:

a. The *user interface* is what the user sees and works with in terms of accessing and working with the knowledge base and other repositories. Without an effective user interface, even the best KM system is bound to fail. A browser is used to link the user to the Internet.

b. The *authentication/security layer* screens incoming requests for security purposes. For example, firewalls are installed by the company's IT department to ensure that certain files do not leave company premises or certain incoming information does not contaminate existing repositories. Passwords and other authorization protocols are used to ensure integrity of the knowledge base and reliability of the overall systems at all times.

c. *Collaborative agents and filtering* are designed to provide a near-personalized presentation of knowledge or information to meet the user's requirements. **Intelligent agents** (specialized software) are employed to do "intelligent" searches in a database, knowledge base, or other repositories to expedite user requests and display the right information.

d. The *application layer* is used to communicate with the actual application in use. This is where the user begins to do something useful with the networks—browsing a Web site, sending e-mail, or transferring a file between file servers and client computers. It answers the question "What information do I send to my partner?" It is simply two useful programs talking to each other. It also defines request and response formats. For example, an e-mail client browser program talks to the e-mail server program, saying something like "Deliver this message to ema3z@virginia.edu." Remember that each type of program (e-mail, file transfer, and so forth) has its own protocol. The application layer protocol assumes that the next layer down (transport layer) will take care of passing the message along to the destination.

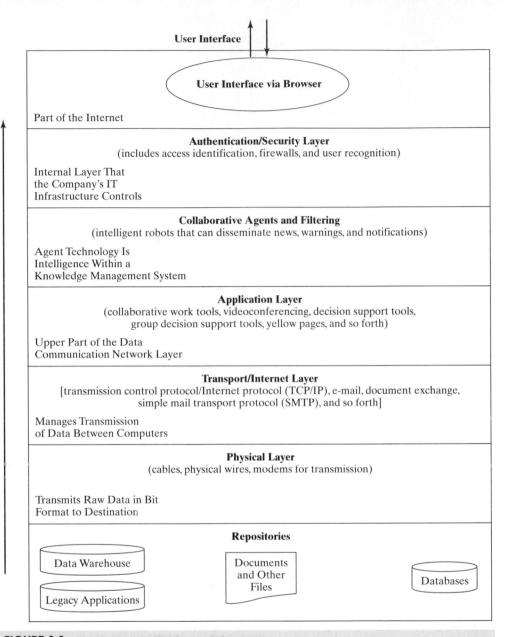

▪ ▪ ▪ ▪ ▪ ▪ ▪ **FIGURE 3.8:** Key Layers of a KM System Infrastructure

SOURCE: Adapted from Tiwana, Amrit. *The Knowledge Management Toolkit.* Upper Saddle River, NJ: Prentice Hall, 2000, p. 309.

Remember that there are standards that specify how two application programs should communicate at the application layer. For example, in Web service, there is a program called "browser" that resides on the client PC and a Web server application program on the Web server. The standard on the application layer is the hypertext transport protocol, or HTTP. Its function is to govern requests and responses between the browser and the Web server application program. It is usually the beginning of a Web address in the form of http://. E-mail uses other applications that use different application layer standards such as SMTP (simple mail transfer protocol) and POP (point of presence) application layer standards to send and receive e-mail, respectively.

e. The *transport Internet layer* is the most critical part of the KM network system. The function of the transport layer is to manage the transmission or the flow control of data between two computers or across a network. It also allows two computers to communicate, even if the computers were made by different vendors. The standard for the transport layer is **transmission control protocol (TCP)**, which specifies how two host computers will work together.

In contrast, the Internet layer routes messages across multiple nodes of networks for delivery. It also handles network congestion to minimize performance problems. A typical message is "Send this packet to computer number 190.172.63.08 via computer number 123.32.12.14, which is on a network one hop away." The standard for routing messages is **Internet protocol (IP)**. TCP and IP work together, and that is the reason that in the literature you always see them as TCP/IP.

f. The *physical layer* is the lowest layer in the journey of a message from source to destination. It converts bits into signals for outgoing messages and signals into bits for incoming messages. It answers the question "How do I use the medium (cable, physical wiring) for transmission?" The physical layer also uses modems (telephone network standards) to transmit the message as raw data to the destination. Modems are used only to link a user host to the first router (a box with intelligent software that routes messages to other routers).

g. *Repositories* are hard disks or storage devices that hold explicit and tacit knowledge and the rules associated with them. Other repositories include legacy (old or traditional applications like accounts receivable) databases, Web databases, e-mail databases, and UNIX databases.

Test the KM System

The testing phase involves two steps: a verification procedure and a validation procedure. A **verification** procedure ensures that the *system is right*—that the programs do what they are designed to do. The internal makeup of the system is checked to see that the right knowledge is available when needed in the format needed and that any rules will fire when they are supposed to fire. In this way, the technical performance of the system is evaluated.

The second procedure is called **validation**. This test ensures that the system is the *right system*—that it meets the user's expectations, that it is user friendly, and that it will be usable and scalable on demand. Validation provides assurance that the solutions or advice derived from the knowledge management system comes close enough to that of the human expert. In other words, the validation process checks reliability of the knowledge management system. In the case of BANKOR, the system was initially tested weekly to see how well the bank met the federal regulatory audit procedures. Several changes had to be made because of oversight on embedding old auditing requirements into the current system. Also, a money laundering module had to be rewritten to reflect the changes made after the federal government began to track Bin Laden's assets in the United States and abroad.

Validation of KM systems is not foolproof. System validation is a long-term item: Human experts must monitor system performance continually. Eventually, systems will be able to renew their certification and vouch for their own reliability.

Implement the KM System

Once the appropriate knowledge has been captured, encoded in the knowledge base, verified, and validated, the next task of the knowledge developer is to implement or deploy the proposed system on a computer or a server. **Implementation** means converting a new KM system into actual operation. **Conversion** is a major step in implementation. The other steps are postimplementation review and KM system maintenance. Another way of looking at implementation is that it is the transformation of a precise representation of knowledge into a machine-executable equivalent—a specific program or software package.

ROLE OF QUALITY ASSURANCE

Quality assurance is the development of controls to ensure a quality KM system. This feature is actually emphasized in every stage of the system development process. The goal is to have as error-free and reliable a system as possible. Knowledge developers under time and budget constraints could compromise quality, especially during knowledge capture. The chief knowledge officer (CKO) has the responsibility to ensure that every step in knowledge management is error-free.

There are several kinds of errors to look for in knowledge base design:

- *Reasoning errors.* Errors can occur in inductive or deductive reasoning. An example of an inductive reasoning error is *This firm has never had a layoff. Therefore, it will never have a layoff in the future.* The likelihood of error is higher if this conclusion is accepted. Likewise, a deductive reasoning error is *If you are pregnant, then you will be overweight.* The deduction that pregnancy causes weight gain does not apply in *all* cases. Even if it did, one must still consider the question of how much weight is "overweight." Such issues are illustrative of fuzzy logic, covered in detail in expert systems courses.
- *Ambiguity.* A statement is ambiguous when it has more than one meaning or can be interpreted in more than one way. For example, "Sell the bad stock" is an ambiguous directive. Which stock is bad? What is meant by "bad"? How bad is "bad"? The subjective nature of decision making in such a case raises questions of validity, reliability, and integrity of the decision and, therefore, the knowledge base.
- *Incompleteness.* A statement that represents some but not all pieces of knowledge is incomplete knowledge. For example, does "Adjust the air conditioner" mean to turn it on or off, or to make it cooler or warmer?
- *False representation.* A statement that incorrectly represents pieces of knowledge is **false representation**. Take the example, "The small key will open the door." Which small key? An incorrect representation presents the possibility of two kinds of errors: false positive and false negative error. With **false positive** error, a rule is accepted when it should be rejected. In the "small key" example, if the small key will not open the door when it should, then accepting the key gives a false positive. In contrast, when a rule is rejected when it should be accepted, it is descriptive of **false negative**.

USER TRAINING

A major part of the implementation phase is training company employees on the new KM system. The level and duration of training depend on the user's knowledge level and the system's attributes. Users range from novices to experts. A *novice* is generally a casual user with limited knowledge of IT. An *expert* is someone with prior IT experience and who keeps abreast of the technology. Users are also classified as tutor, pupil, or customer.

The **tutor user** acquires a working knowledge of an existing knowledge base in order to keep the system current. This end user is responsible for system maintenance. The knowledge developer normally trains the tutor user on procedures for incorporating new knowledge into the knowledge base.

The responsibilities and interest of pupil users and customer users fall within the actual use of the KM system. The knowledge developer's role is to familiarize the end users with the ways in which the system will be best used. The **pupil user** is an unskilled worker trying to gain some understanding of the captured knowledge. The purpose of training pupil users is to gain their acceptance of the KM system. The **customer user** is one with interest in knowing how to use the KM system on a regular basis.

Neither the pupil user nor the customer user needs in-depth training during the early stages of KM system development. Training in the early phases uses development funds inefficiently. During the time between prototyping and a working system, the pupil users and customer users may forget most details.

User training is also influenced by the requirements of the KM system. System requirements range from simple and user friendly to advanced and less user friendly. A user friendly KM system is almost self-instructional with menu-driven features and easy-to-use manuals. The duration of training is usually measured in hours to days. Advanced KM systems require knowledge of queries in high-level programming or artificial intelligence (AI) languages and take days to weeks to learn, even for the experienced user.

Training must be geared to the specific user based on capabilities, experience, and system complexity. The most effective training is supported by a well-written user manual, easy-to-use explanatory facility, and job aids. User manuals can be invaluable training documents, especially if the user is geographically isolated. A well-written user manual is highly illustrated and contains an index for reference. Graphics, photographs, and templates provide quick reference and are invaluable teaching aids. Comparable information should also be available in the software via a help key on the keyboard.

Manage Change and Reward Structure

Regardless of what is being converted or how well deployment is carried out, knowledge sharing does not come easy to many people. *Implementation means change, and people in general resist change.* Implementation of a KM system is the initiation of a new order. People become anxious when they do not know what the system will offer and how it will affect their current jobs and decision-making quality. The result is stress and further resistance to change. The resistors include the following:

- *Experts.* Some domain experts have anxiety about the potential impact of sharing knowledge of their jobs in the organization. Experts on the way to retirement worry less, but they may still lack motivation unless they are properly compensated for their efforts.
- *Regular employees (users).* Participants in general resent lack of recognition (sometimes compensation), especially when they have put time in building the KM system.
- *Troublemakers.* Those left out of building the KM system or chronic complainers tend to obstruct the installation, cause delays, and may even prompt cancellation of the installation.
- *Narrow-minded "superstars."* Technical people in the organization's IT department sometimes resist any change that they did not initiate or approve in advance. Others veto a project not in their area of interest. Without management support, such resistance can spell doom for a new installation.

Resistance is displayed in three personal reactions:

- Projection: hostility toward peers.
- Avoidance: withdrawal from the scene, such as calling in sick.
- Aggression: killing the system, because of uncertainty of its operation or use.

A psychological element that explains resistance to change is the value that users place on knowledge and decision making. In most organizations, knowledge means power. While knowledge developers build KM systems that promote knowledge sharing through knowledge bases, domain experts who stand to lose monopoly on knowledge may resist a new system installation. Most resistance relates to the perceived impact of the system on one's job or status in the organization. Of course, a few people resist change of any kind.

Resistance also has much to do with the individual personality, the organizational structure, and the group relations within the area where the KM system will be installed. User education, training, and participation in the building process can help reduce resistance to change.

Because a major user concern in KM system implementation is how to work the system, users frequently ask such questions as What functions are available? How do I access each function? How do I know if the system has answered my questions correctly? How current is the knowledge base? Another user concern is how the KM system reaches conclusions or lines up with the real-world problem as seen by the user. The knowledge developer must demonstrate the system and provide detailed training.

Postsystem Evaluation

After the KM system has been deployed and the operation is "up and running," the effect of the new system on the organization should be carefully evaluated. System impact must be assessed in terms of its effects on the people, procedures, and performance of the business. More specifically, the main areas of concern are quality of decision making, attitude of end users, and costs of knowledge processing and update.

Several key questions are asked in the postimplementation stage:

- How has the KM system changed the accuracy and timeliness of decision making?
- Has the new system caused organizational changes? How constructive have the changes been?
- How has the new KM system affected the attitude of the end users? In what way? Was it worth it?
- How has the new KM system changed the cost of operating the business? How significant was it?
- In what way has the new system affected relationships between end users in the organization?
- Do the solutions derived from the new system justify the cost of investment?

The objective is to evaluate the KM system against standards and determine how well it meets the goals set in advance. This process is actually related to validation. The user initiates the review, which prompts a procedure for maintenance or enhancement. *Enhancement* means upgrading the system to meet a new set of requirements; *maintenance* means making corrections to meet the initial system requirements.

▪ ▪ ▪ ▪ Implications for Knowledge Management

Assuming the technology is available and ready to use, several managerial factors should be considered:

- An organization considering a KM system as part of its information systems environment must make a commitment to user education and training prior to building the system. Knowledge sharing is not that straightforward in many organizations.
- Top management should be approached with facts about the costs and benefits of the proposed KM system. Being sold on the project means assurance of financial and technical support.
- If a KM system is anywhere on the organization's horizon, human resources or the IT department should begin training knowledge developers and others who have the potential to do knowledge engineering.
- Domain experts must be recognized and rewarded in ways that make them feel it is worth their time to cooperate. Assigning an expert to the project without such rewards can jeopardize the whole process.
- Finally, for an organization to anticipate its future technology needs, it is extremely important to do long-range strategic planning. Such planning can help the firm to attain its desired outcomes. Introducing leading-edge technology such as KM systems can help the organization to achieve competitive advantage.

One of the critical issues raised during implementation is knowledge system maintenance. Maintenance of KM systems continues to be a nebulous area. Some of the questions to be addressed by management include the following:

- Who will be in charge of maintenance?
- What skills should the maintenance specialist have? What is the best way to train him or her?
- What incentives should be provided to ensure quality maintenance?
- What kinds of support and funding are needed?
- What relationship should be established between the maintenance of a KM system and the IT staff of the organization?

The *enhancement* function is closely related to maintenance. Because experts constantly upgrade their knowledge, it makes sense to do the same with the KM system to keep it current. One question is "How quickly does the problem change?" The answer then determines how one would justify the enhancement, given the nature of the solution(s).

Another managerial issue to consider is how one would know whether the implementation would be a success. In addition to technical considerations, one must be aware of the people factor. People rallying behind technology can increase the success of implementation. Additionally, a KM system cannot succeed if the issues of cost and how that cost is going to be absorbed have not been resolved. Any of these issues can inhibit successful implementation.

Other managerial issues affect the direction and outcome of KM system projects. For example, the depth of the knowledge required to solve the problem is often an unknown commodity due to the nature of the expertise and the limitations of the knowledge developer. Forcing clarification too early in the building phase can result in a less-than-satisfactory system. Therefore, managing expectations and scoping the system are crucial early tasks.

Finally, the role of the expert in system implementation is also important. Management should properly compensate the domain expert for his or her effort in developing a KM system. The CKO may also play a proactive role in the implementation phase by simply sharing interest in the KM system. A lack of this kind of enthusiasm and overt support puts a damper on the whole idea of knowledge sharing and knowledge management.

SUMMARY ▪▪▪▪

- Building a KM system can be viewed as a life cycle. The life cycle begins when a knowledge management system is determined to be doable, affordable, and practicable, with value added for company profitability and growth. Knowledge developers interview users and work with experts to develop a system. Discipline, good documentation, coordination, and regular management review characterize the development of KM system life cycle.
- Conventional and KM systems' development life cycles differ.
    - A systems analyst deals with data and information obtained from the user; the knowledge developer deals with tacit knowledge acquired from human experts.
    - The main interface for the systems analyst is the user, who knows the problem but not the solution. The main interface with the knowledge developer is the human expert, who knows the problem and the solution.
    - Conventional system development is primarily sequential; KMSLC is incremental and interactive.
    - Testing is done at the end of conventional information system development; verification and validation are performed throughout the KM development life cycle.
- Conventional and KM systems' development life cycles are also similar.
    - Both begin with a problem and end with a solution.
    - Both begin with information gathering to ensure a clear understanding of the users' requirements or the problem at hand.
    - Both involve testing the system and ensuring that the system is satisfactory.
    - Particular development tools are used to build each system.
- The first step in building a KM system is identifying the problem domain, followed by a feasibility study for evaluating the problem in detail. This includes weighing the total costs against the potential tangible and intangible benefits. Early scoping is important. The project should be of a manageable size, and the organization should be able to foresee its benefits.
- Knowledge capture involves elicitation, analysis, and interpretation of the knowledge that a human expert uses to solve a particular problem.
- Most KM systems begin as small-scale prototypes based on the limited knowledge acquired during the first few sessions with the human expert. The system grows gradually as the knowledge developer gains new insights from the expert and adds them to the prototype.
- Once the KM blueprint is made final, verification and validation ensure that the system is right and that we have the right system, respectively.
- System implementation is the process of organizing the knowledge and integrating it with the testing strategy of verification and validation. A system must be modified or updated as new knowledge is captured.

- Most barriers to the development of a KM system are nontechnical. Lack of support from top management, knowledge developers' limited interpersonal skills, experts' poor communications skills, and users' resistance are all barriers that must be addressed.
- The ultimate goal of every KM system is successful implementation and deployment. Implementation means change, and people in general resist change. The resistors include experts, nonexperts, troublemakers, and narrow-minded technical "superstars." Resistance is displayed in the form of projection, avoidance, and aggression and has much to do with the individual personality, the organizational structure in which the user works, and the group relations in the area where the system will be installed. User education, training, and participation can help reduce or control resistance to change.

TERMS TO KNOW ▪ ▪ ▪ ▪

Aggression: Resistance to KM systems through employee sabotage of the system.

Avoidance: Resistance to KM systems through employee withdrawal from the job or scene.

Champion: Individual within the organization who believes the project will benefit the company and is willing to take risks in supporting its development; has credibility with management, experts, and users; and has access to key persons in the business.

Customer user: A user interested in knowing how to use the system for problem solving on a regular basis.

Deployment: Physical transfer of the technology to the organization's operating unit.

Enhancement: Upgrading the system to meet a new set of requirements.

Implementation: The process of organizing the knowledge and integrating it with the processing strategy for final deployment.

KM system life cycle (KMSLC): The steps through which a knowledge management system project goes before it becomes operational.

Maintenance: Making necessary corrections so that the KM system continues to meet the initial system requirements.

Projection: Resistance to expert systems through employee display of hostility toward peers.

Pupil user: An unskilled employee trying to learn or gain some understanding of the captured knowledge.

Rapid prototyping: Spontaneous, on-the-spot, iterative approach to building KM systems; an iterative process by which the knowledge developer shows the domain expert what the KM system looks like based on the knowledge captured to date.

Systems analyst: A specialist who gathers information from the user or the user's staff in order to define a problem and determine alternative solutions and their consequences within conventional information system development processes.

Tutor user: A user with a working knowledge of the KM system or knowledge base and the responsibility for system maintenance.

Validation: A system test to ensure the right system from a technical view; a system that meets the expert's expectations.

Verification: A system test to ensure the proper functioning of the system; addresses the intrinsic properties of the KM system.

TEST YOUR UNDERSTANDING ▪ ▪ ▪ ▪

1. Why is it helpful to view the building of a KM system as a life cycle?
2. In what ways do conventional and KM systems' development life cycles differ? How are they similar?
3. Distinguish between:
   a. verification and validation
   b. knowledge developer and systems analyst
   c. pupil user and tutor user
   d. projection and avoidance
4. Successful KM system implementation depends on several factors. Briefly explain each factor.
5. How important are organizational factors in system implementation?

6. Why is the place of training important? Why is duration of training important?
7. What do you think determines the success of user training?
8. How do users differ from experts?
9. Of the steps making up the KMSLC, which one do you consider the most critical? Why? Which would be the most time-consuming?"
10. What is rapid prototyping? How is it useful in building KM systems?
11. Elaborate on the main steps of a feasibility study. When should a feasibility study be conducted? Why?
12. What does it mean to "scope" a project? Give an example.
13. What is your understanding of a human expert? How would you select one?
14. Write an essay in which you describe the role of the knowledge developer and his or her relationship with the key persons in the knowledge capture process.
15. Briefly highlight the functions and attributes of the chief knowledge officer (CKO).

KNOWLEDGE EXERCISES ▪▪▪▪

1. Crozet Country Club's use of a knowledge management system can be justified on several fronts. The system captures the human resources manager's knowledge of how she makes her hiring decisions. If she leaves the club, the system will help to ensure that her expertise and know-how are not lost.

    The "Hiring KM System" saves the club time and money by making accurate decisions more rapidly than the normal way of deciding on an applicant. Because the club receives a large number of applications to fill a relatively small number of positions, efficient applicant evaluation is of critical importance. However, handling and sorting the plethora of applications was formerly time-consuming and haphazard. This system reduces the time taken to fill vacant positions. More importantly, it helps to ensure that employees have the necessary qualifications.

    The hiring KM system promotes a higher level of consistency and quality in hiring decisions. Prior to implementing the system, the manager did not have a "wage matrix" to use in determining appropriate wages for employees, and the process was quite random. This led to some conflict within the organization. Furthermore, the manager hired some applicants without focusing enough on their ability, and they turned out to be poor employees. In essence, the KM system helps guarantee that all of the necessary variables are fully considered in each decision.
    a. Is this sufficient justification for the KM system? Why or why not?
    b. Is the system likely to replace the human resources manager, who was instrumental in sharing her knowledge, which is captured in the knowledge base?
2. The goal of this project is to develop a consumer-lending knowledge base to guide the junior bank officer through the decision of whether an auto loan should be approved. In the loan department, there are experienced senior loan officers who are willing to share their knowledge with others.

    You have been assigned the job of building a KM system for the bank. Explain in detail the life cycle of this project.
3. A KM system for a large retailer was designed to help human resources develop a qualified candidate pool from the many applications they receive on a daily basis. The knowledge on hiring available in the KM knowledge base suggests the wage each accepted applicant should receive, based on his or her skills and relevant experience.

    The three positions addressed are (a) floor salesperson, (b) customer service representative, and (c) gift wrap employee. The system encodes the knowledge of the expert in each area and the knowledge of the person who makes the hiring decisions into rules that are used to perform the task. The store's human resources manager played a key role throughout knowledge capture; her experience is stored in a specialized knowledge base. During her absence, a junior human resources person can query the knowledge base for information based on the expert's (human resources manager) opinion in various combinations of circumstances and constraints. This made certain decisions easy to make, which made the hiring process faster and improved the overall efficiency of the human resources department.

   a. Is anything missing from the development life cycle? What made you think so?

   b. Do you think more than one person developed the KM system? Explain.

4. A high-tech firm designed a KM system for the student housing office of a major university in March 2001 and made the system available through the university's intranet; three campuses were involved. After the system passed verification and validation, the knowledge developer held a wrap-up meeting with representative end users from each branch. She spent 2 hours going through the operations manual and running examples through the newly installed system to demonstrate ease of use and ease of access.

   The attendees were quite impressed with the many features—a color screen, easy-to-follow menu, and display of the reasons to justify all kinds of answers. The system also links legacy databases such as tuition adjustment and meal plans, depending on the housing arrangements.

   One month after the 2-hour training session, the knowledge engineer sent a questionnaire to all attendees, who, by then, were end users of the KM system. Some of the questions were as follows:

   • Did the operations manual help you understand the system?
   • Did the knowledge developer give you a working understanding of the system?
   • Did you understand the questions asked by the system?
   • Does the system meet your expectations? If not, please offer any suggestions you might have.
   • Did the system provide adequate and correct answers?
   • Do you think that the system is usable in your environment with immediate change? Be specific.

   a. Based on the information provided, evaluate the training approach followed by the knowledge developer.

   b. Could you deduce a training plan in this case? Explain.

   c. Critique the questionnaire used to follow up on the installation.

REFERENCES   ▪ ▪ ▪ ▪

Angus, Jeff. "Harnessing Corporate Knowledge," *Informationweek*, August 7, 2000, pp. 1–3, www. informationweek.com/798/prknowledge.htm, Date accessed August 2002.

Date, Shruti. "Agencies Create CKO Posts to Get in the Know," *Government Computer News*, November 8, 1999, pp. 1–2.

Davenport, Thomas H., and Prusak, Laurence. *Working Knowledge*. Boston, MA: Harvard Business School Press, 2000, pp. 1–24.

Delio, Michelle. "Stepping Up, Moving On, Getting Smarter," *Knowledge Management*, June 2001, pp. 51–54.

Dixon, Nancy M. *Common Knowledge*. Boston, MA: Harvard Business School Press, 2000.

Flash, Cynthia. "Who Is the CKO?" *Knowledge Management*, May 2001, pp. 37–41.

Foster, Allan. "Grasping the Tacit Knowledge Nettle," *Knowledge Management*, no. 1, April 1998, p. 32.

Frank, Diane. "Feds Ponder CKO Role," *Federal Computer Week*, June 28, 1999, pp. 16–18.

Freeman, Miller. "Applying Knowledge to Profitability," *Intelligent Enterprise*, March 1, 2000, p. 15.

Garvin, James. *A Guide to Project Management Body of Knowledge*. Newton Square, PA: Project Management Institute 2000.

Glasser, Perry. "The Knowledge Factor," *CIO Magazine*, December 15, 1998–January 1, 1999, pp. 1–9.

Housel, Thomas, and Bell, Arthur. *Measuring and Managing Knowledge*. New York: McGraw-Hill, Inc., 2001.

Liebowitz, Jay, and Wilcox, Lyle C. *Knowledge Management*. Ft. Lauderdale, FL: CRC Press, 1997.

Paquette, Pat. "CKO: Trendiest Job in Business," www.hightechcareers.com/doc498e/trendiest498e.html, Date accessed August 2002.

Skyrme, David. "Do You Need a CKO?" www.skyrme.com/insights/27cko.htm, Date accessed August 2002.

Strassmann, Paul A. "Calculating Knowledge Capital," files.strassmann.com/pubs/km/1999-10.php, October 1999, Date accessed August 2002.

Tiwana, Amrit. *The Knowledge Management Toolkit*. Upper Saddle River, NJ: Prentice Hall, 2000.

Trepper, Charles. "Keep Your Knowledge In-House," *Informationweek*, September 4, 2000, pp. 1–3. www.informationweek.com/802/prknowledge.htm. Date accessed November 22, 2002.

Knowledge Creation and Knowledge Architecture

Contents

In a Nutshell
Knowledge Creation
Nonaka's Model of Knowledge Creation and Transformation
Knowledge Architecture
    The People Core
    Identifying Knowledge Centers
    The Technical Core
    Build In-House, Buy, or Outsource?
Implications for Knowledge Management
Summary
Terms to Know
Test Your Understanding
Knowledge Exercises
References

*Where success is concerned, people are not
measured in inches, or pounds, or college degrees,
or family background; they are measured by the
size of their thinking.*
—J. M. CUPELLO

▪▪▪▪ In a Nutshell

In the previous chapters, we discussed the concept of knowledge management, what knowledge is, and the development process that deploys a KM system for a business organization. In this chapter, the key questions are: Where does knowledge reside? How would one create knowledge? What does it take to design a KM system? The literature differs on how to address these questions, because much depends on the type of knowledge, the culture of the organization, and how one strategically makes use of knowledge management. For example, Churchman interpreted the viewpoint of philosophers Leibniz, Locke, and Kant by emphasizing that knowledge resides in the user and not in the collection of information. "To conceive of knowledge as a collection of information seems to rob the concept of all of its life. Knowledge resides in the user and not in the collection. It is how the user reacts to a collection of information that matters" (Churchman 1971). He emphasizes the human nature of knowledge creation in an environment characterized by discontinuous change. Malhotra also discusses the nature of knowledge creation (Malhotra 2001).

The focus on tacit knowledge being the primary type of knowledge to tap is reinforced by Boland, who pointed out that by considering the meaning of knowledge as "unproblematic, predefined, and prepackaged, they ignore the human dimension of organizational knowledge creation" (Boland 1987). In 1995, Gill reinforced the view a different way. He stated that "prepackaged interpretation of knowledge works against the generation of multiple and contradictory viewpoints that are necessary for meeting the challenge posed by wicked environments: This may even hamper the firm's learning and adaptive capabilities."

In this chapter, we also discuss knowledge architecture as a framework of the *people core*. We explore the types of people making up the organization, the knowledge they own, and where they use it. Under the *knowledge sharing core,* the focus is on deciding where knowledge resides and where it is used, and identify those responsible for knowledge sharing. Finally, the *technology core* illustrates how to leverage the Internet and the technical layers for building a technology base for knowledge sharing. With all these issues, the CKO plays a critical role in the KM process.

▪▪▪▪ Knowledge Creation

Most of us live in a world where today's knowledge will not solve tomorrow's problems. This means updating our knowledge on a regular basis. You probably have heard the old joke about the teacher who used the same experience with a course 20 times rather than having 20 years of teaching experience. The two are not the same. Knowledge update is creating new knowledge based on ongoing experiences in a particular problem area and then using the new knowledge in combination with the initial knowledge to come up with updated knowledge for knowledge sharing. Unfortunately, most organizations have a very competitive culture, where no one wants to share. With a change in culture, values, and improved mutual trust, sharing creates a learning culture that feeds itself in terms of improving knowledge sharing—giving away, holding in common, and improving bonds within the firm. In contrast, our view is to look at explicit and tacit knowledge as the two primary knowledge types and learn how to capture them for organizational inquiries and growth in an unpredictable environment. Either type can be created and should be captured. Capturing explicit knowledge is covered later in the text under data warehousing and data mining. In the next chapter, we focus on capturing tacit knowledge, and Chapter 6 elaborates on the main tools used in knowledge capture. We approach knowledge and "knowing" as deeply personal. Keep in mind that KM is not a technology. It is an activity enabled by technology and produced by people. It is also how people share the type of knowledge that will add special value to the growth and competitive nature of the business. The use of technology is a critical aid for processing and deploying knowledge whenever it is needed.

An alternative way of creating knowledge is through teamwork. Figure 4.1 shows how a team translates experience into knowledge. Essentially, a team commits to performing a job over a specific time period, such as weeks or months. A *job* is more than a task. It is a series of specific tasks carried out in a specific order, format, or sequence. In the end, a job is completed, and the results are either successful or disappointing. The team looks back and compares the experience it had when starting the job to the outcome. This comparison is what translates experience into knowledge. When it performs the same job in the future, the team takes corrective steps, modifying actions based on the new knowledge they have acquired.

With either knowledge creation alternative, the outcome is the same. Individuals or teams begin a commitment to a job with specific knowledge. After the job is completed, a comparison of the "before and after" occurs. In most cases, the outcome is extended knowledge that should improve the quality and effectiveness of performing the same job the next time around. In some quarters, this is called *maturation* or *seasoned experience.* Over time, experience leads to expertise, where one person or one team becomes known for handling a complex problem very well. This knowledge can be transferred to others in a reusable format. The receiving individual or team adapts the knowledge for use in a special context.

▪ ▪ ▪ ▪ ▪ ▪ ▪ **FIGURE 4.1:**   Knowledge Creation and Knowledge Transfer via Teams

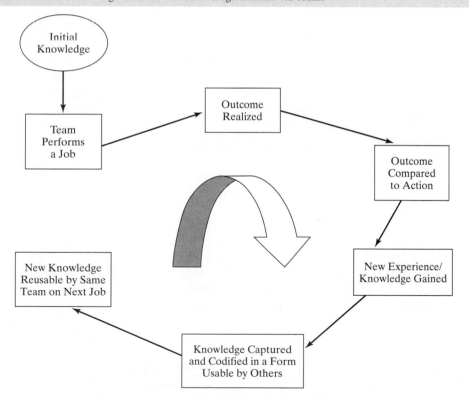

Team formation and teamwork begin with experienced individuals working jointly on a project. In consulting assignments, for example, an experienced individual manages a team of experienced and semiexperienced members (see Box 4.1). The manager assigns tasks and decides how much knowledge sharing will occur. In a way, tacit knowledge begins with the individual, not the team. Real knowledge continues to be held by people (Berry 2000). In a team environment, shared exchange results in collaborative decision making and problem-solving. So, when it comes to knowledge capture,

---

▪▪▪▪▪▪ **BOX 4.1** ▪▪▪▪▪▪

ROLE AND FORMATION OF KM TEAMS

DRAFT YOUR DREAM TEAM

By definition, it takes at least two people to share something. When that something is knowledge applied to the goals of a large enterprise, the sharing multiplies, and the number of people involved must increase. Therefore, most organizations make establishing a project team an early priority in their knowledge management initiatives.

Choosing and recruiting the right people for the team is a vital task that will have enduring consequences. Accomplishing corporate business objectives requires a mix of skills, experience, and stakeholder interests, so the team members usually will come from multiple disciplines. Team developers also must consider issues of trust across departments and business units as well as between individuals.

Successful KM initiatives, experts say, focus first on people business processes and company culture. Only later should the emphasis shift to the technology and tools that facilitate knowledge sharing. Members may need expertise in management, administration, human resources, and business processes as well as in the supporting technologies.

"A knowledge management project must leverage the strengths of each of these professional perspectives to be successful," says Ray Merrill, a consultant at Ariel Performance Centered Systems, Inc., in Fort Lauderdale, Florida. When helping clients to implement knowledge management projects, consultants at Chicago-based Andersen Consulting suggest staffing teams with individuals from the business process in question and from the human resources and information technology departments. According to Christina Schultz, manager of global knowledge services at Andersen Consulting, a team needs members from all three sectors. "You don't find all these skills in one person, so you have to ensure that all are represented," she says.

CASTING ROLES

A team member's primary duty within the group is as important as his or her qualifications. From his KM project experience, Merrill has derived six key roles, which he calls "hats," that one team member or another must play. They are as follows:

Business leads: Specialize in understanding the measurable result to be obtained

Organizational leads: Specialize in communication plans, motivational incentives, and other organizational needs

Super users: Can influence the user community and provide practical feedback

Interface design leads: Specialize in computer/human interaction and integrating content into work processes

Training leads: Specialize in cognitive needs, learning strategies, and repurposing legacy content

Technical architects: Specialize in technology installation and administration

---

SOURCE: Excerpted from Robb, Drew. "Draft Your Dream Team," *Knowledge Management*, August 2001, pp. 44–50.

▪▪▪▪▪▪

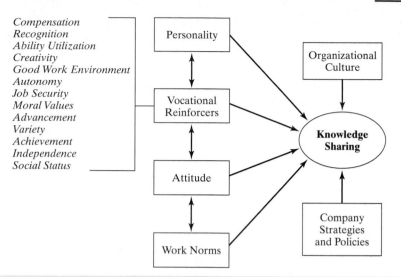

Compensation
Recognition
Ability Utilization
Creativity
Good Work Environment
Autonomy
Job Security
Moral Values
Advancement
Variety
Achievement
Independence
Social Status

■ ■ ■ ■ ■ ■ ■ **FIGURE 4.2:**   Impediments to Knowledge Sharing

the approach is to tap the individual's tacit knowledge, which could be a single expert or multiple experts, as the situation warrants.

With knowledge transfer and knowledge sharing, there are impediments to consider. Whether it is the individual expert or the "expert" team, knowledge sharing is not that straightforward. As shown in Figure 4.2, there are factors that encourage or retard knowledge transfer—from personality and attitude to vocational reinforcers. Whether knowledge sharing causes change in the organizational culture or the other way around continues to be a hotly debated area. In either case, a review of the motivational factors that encourage people to share is important if the KM process has a chance of succeeding.

As shown in the conceptual model in Figure 4.2, personality is one factor in knowledge sharing. For example, people who are extroverts, display self-confidence, and feel secure tend to share experiences more readily than those who are introspective, self-centered, or security conscious. Attitude and work norms are additional considerations. People with a positive attitude, who trust others, and who work in an environment conducive to knowledge sharing tend to be better at sharing than those working in a "cutthroat" environment.

Finally, vocational reinforcers are key to knowledge sharing. Based on the authors' vocational psychology research, people whose vocational needs are met by job reinforcers are more likely to favor knowledge sharing than those who are deprived of one or more reinforcers. One may conclude that the totality of attitude, personality, work norms, and vocational reinforcers determines how likely people are to view knowledge sharing and knowledge transfer in a positive light.

■ ■ ■ ■ Nonaka's Model of Knowledge Creation and Transformation

Another way of looking at knowledge creation and knowledge transformation is to use Nonaka's model. Nonaka (1995) coined the terms *tacit knowledge* and *explicit knowledge* as the two main types of human knowledge. Tacit knowledge is considered the most valuable knowledge. The key to knowledge creation lies in the way it is mobilized and converted through technology. Conversion of knowledge between tacit and explicit knowledge is shown in Figure 4.3.

Tacit to tacit communication, referred to as *socialization,* takes place between people in meetings or in team discussions. Such knowledge sharing, transfer, or collaboration often produces no explicit knowledge. Experience among people in face-to-face business situations is mostly shared, and technology plays a minimal role. However, there is an increasing trend for online groupware tools be used in work groups or teams. In such a synthetic atmosphere, especially in geographically dispersed settings, team members can conduct meetings, listen to presentations, or simply carry out discussions. Lotus Notes is one example of a software product that allows people to share documents and discuss them via video and text-based chat.

Tacit to explicit communication, or *externalization,* is essentially articulation among people through dialogue. Brainstorming, where a team carries out discussions around a specific problem is one example. Comments and suggestions are entered into a PC and displayed on a screen, but no one knows who made the comment. Brainstorming is covered in detail in Chapter 6.

Online discussions can capture tacit knowledge and apply it to an immediate problem (Marwick 2001). The database becomes a repository of useful knowledge. On the surface, the exchange gives the impression that it is purely explicit knowledge. However, the participant first has to decide on the nature of the problem before he or she can give the best solution—both prompting the use of tacit knowledge before such knowledge becomes explicit. After the knowledge has been made explicit and has been stored in a repository, persons facing a similar problem can consult the database at their convenience.

Explicit to explicit communication (also referred to as *communication*) is one transformation phase that is best supported by technology. Explicit knowledge can be easily captured and transmitted to a worldwide audience. For example, sending an attached memo or document via e-mail expedites knowledge sharing in an efficient and effective way. In this respect, technology helps by motivating people to capture and share what they have or what they know.

Explicit to tacit communication (also referred to as *internalization*) is taking explicit knowledge such as a report and deducing new ideas or taking constructive action. Creating technology to help users derive tacit knowledge from explicit knowledge is an important goal of knowledge management. By searching and finding associations, technology makes information more useful by making it easier to derive new tacit knowledge from it. For example, supermarkets profiling customers when they use

Tacit to Tacit *(socialization)* Team Meetings and Discussions	**Tacit to Explicit** *(externalization)* Dialog Within Team Answer Questions
Explicit to Tacit *(internalization)* Learn from a Report	**Explicit to Explicit** *(communication)* E-Mail a Report

▪ ▪ ▪ ▪ ▪ ▪

FIGURE 4.3: Conversion of Knowledge Between Tacit and Explicit Forms

SOURCE: Marwick, A. D. "Knowledge Management Technology," *IBM Systems Journal,* vol. 40, no. 4, 2001, p. 815.

a store-issued card to get discounts is an example of explicit to tacit knowledge. Through data mining, the store can derive a number of new ideas regarding the kind of product that is popular or the preference of customers by age, location, or price. Such tacit knowledge is critical for competitive advantage.

In conclusion, one can see that Nonaka's model divides knowledge creation processes into four categories. It focuses on tacit knowledge and the use of technology in generating or transmitting such knowledge to others. Using electronic meetings or chat rooms for collaboration, knowledge sharing, and transfer are well known in today's knowledge organizations. Despite the advancement of technology, one limitation remains: the ability of technology to support the use of tacit knowledge in face-to-face meetings and direct interactions (Marwick 2001). Human knowledge continues to be a valuable resource, and technology is expected to trickle slowly into a human domain where knowledge creation and knowledge transfer can be expedited for human decision making regardless of time or location.

▪▪▪▪ Knowledge Architecture

Knowledge architecture is a prerequisite to knowledge sharing. We view the infrastructure as a combination of people, content, and technology. As shown in Figure 4.4, these components are interdependent and inseparable. People with knowledge provide content, relying on technology to transfer and share knowledge. This combination provides the efficiency and performance to managing the knowledge core of the corporation.

THE PEOPLE CORE

Knowledge management is about people and the way they creatively perform in an environment conducive to knowledge sharing. By *people,* we mean knowledge workers, managers, customers, and suppliers. The first step in knowledge architecture is to evaluate the current information and documents people use, the applications they need, the people they contact for solutions, the associates they collaborate with, the e-mail they send and receive, and the database they access. All these sources make up an employee profile, which is later used as the basis for designing a knowledge management system that best serve people's long-term needs via technology.

The goal of *profiling* the people part of an organization is to get a handle on existing knowledge exchanges that the organization uses and ways to capture them. As a procedure, it involves not only asking the right questions but also providing answers that become part of the KM system infrastructure. Discovering whom to profile, in what sequence, and for what duration and using the right knowledge capture tool are discussed in Chapter 5.

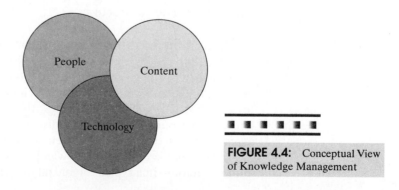

▪ ▪ ▪ ▪ ▪ ▪

FIGURE 4.4:   Conceptual View of Knowledge Management

Profiling can be approached in several ways. The worst way is to send a survey or questionnaire by e-mail. When it comes to knowledge capture, the most important prerequisite is selecting the employees and planning the questions. Planning whom to elicit knowledge from means deciding whether to talk with senior employees only, younger or newer employees, or some mix based on criteria that make sense. The next prerequisite is type of question to ask. Each question should be phrased and intended to elicit information accurately and completely.

Finally, the whole idea behind assessing the people core is to do a good job in assigning job content to the right person and to ensure that the flow of information that once was obstructed by departments now flows to the right people at the right time. For example, customer service need no longer have an exclusive on troubleshooting information, any more than the legal department should have an exclusive on settling customer litigation. To expedite knowledge sharing, a knowledge network should be mapped in such a way as to assign people authority and responsibilities for specific kinds of knowledge content. It means:

1. Identifying knowledge centers (for example, sales, products, or marketing).
2. Activating knowledge content satellites—lower level knowledge centers that hierarchically fall under higher level centers (for example, customer support or product documentation in repositories).
3. Properly staffing experts over each knowledge center. The outcome is a corporation-wide knowledge structure that blends the best of existing organization structure and the best of technology—e-mail, intranets, extranets, and networking—to ensure a smooth, 24-hour knowledge sharing environment.

IDENTIFYING KNOWLEDGE CENTERS

Once you have determined the knowledge that people need, the next step is to identify where knowledge resides and how to capture it. By *knowledge center,* we mean areas in the organization where knowledge is available for knowledge capture. For example, in Figure 4.5, a retail organization might have at least four knowledge centers: sales, customer service, human resources, and marketing. These centers become the skeletal framework for knowledge capture. They also serve to identify individual experts or expert teams in each center who could be candidates for the knowledge capture process.

Activating Knowledge Content Satellites

As mentioned earlier, this step simply breaks down each knowledge center into lower, more manageable levels, satellites, or areas. The focus is on searching for knowledge content, not evaluating departments or divisions in the way we evaluate the traditional organizational structure.

Assigning Experts to Each Knowledge Area

Once the new framework is made final, each knowledge satellite should be assigned a manager to ensure integrity of information content, access, and update (see Figure 4.5). In the assignment process, it is important to identify management-type people for each satellite knowledge center; these people will provide contact sources for knowledge capture. This enforces discipline and quality of information, because managers have vested ownership in their respective departments.

Ownership is critical to knowledge capture, knowledge transfer, and knowledge implementation. In a typical organization, departments tend to be territorial. So-called

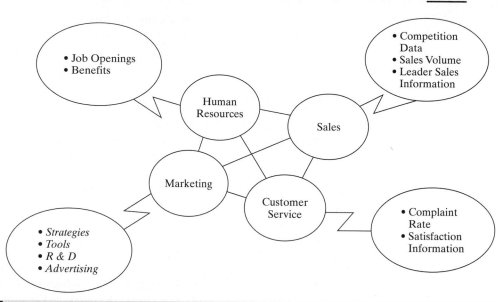

▮ ▮ ▮ ▮ ▮ ▮ ▮ **FIGURE 4.5:**   Identifying Knowledge Content Centers

turf battles occur regularly over budget size or control of sensitive processes. This includes the kind of knowledge a department owns. These reasons justify assigning department ownership to knowledge content and knowledge process. In Figure 4.6, a well-defined knowledge content ensures discipline and order to a company's knowledge base. You can work your way from the major departments down to lower levels in each department. For example, "Operations" shows the main knowledge areas (teller schedules, deposits and withdrawals, and electronic balancing). Likewise, "Loans" owns a variety of loans and loan processing (commercial, unsecured, personal, and auto). For troubleshooting, "Customer Service" has an exclusive on issuing traveler's checks, settling customer complaints, ordering checkbooks, and opening new accounts. From the department level, we can map out each knowledge content in greater detail. Such a step is carried out in knowledge capture.

Adjacent or interdependent departments are expected to be cooperative and ready candidates for knowledge sharing. For example, the bank tellers that accept

▮ ▮ ▮ ▮ ▮ ▮ ▮ **FIGURE 4.6:**   Knowledge Content by Department in a Bank

Knowledge	What	Why	Troubleshooting
Department Owner	Operations	Loans	Customer Service
Knowledge Content	Teller Schedule Electronic Balancing Deposits/Withdrawals ↓ Details	Commercial Loans Unsecured Loans Personal Loans Auto Loans ↓ Details	Traveler's Checks Handling Complaints Order Checkbooks Open New Accounts ↓ Details

mortgage payments are accommodating the loan department that issued the loan in the first place. We need to first identify the commonality of knowledge and then sell the "goodness of fit" between departments for assuring smooth knowledge sharing and knowledge transfer.

THE TECHNICAL CORE

The goal of the technical core is to enhance communication and ensure effective knowledge sharing. Communications is a special area, where technology provides unlimited opportunities for managing tacit knowledge. Communications networks create links within and across databases. Like the telephone, they open up a rich medium for informal communication among employees and managers alike. E-mail, for example, has already demonstrated the rich exchange within and across organizations worldwide.

The phrase *technical core* is used here to refer to the totality of hardware and software and to the specialized human resources required to enable knowledge. Speed, accuracy, reliability, integrity, and security are all expected attributes of successful technology under the technical core. Remember that technology enables knowledge delivery, and it is people who enable knowledge. Because the organization is a knowledge network, the goal of knowledge economy is to push employees toward greater efficiency and productivity by making better use of the knowledge they have.

Once in place, a knowledge core becomes a network of technologies designed to work on top of the company's existing network. The approach to designing the technology core is leveraging and more leveraging of the organization's existing technology. In designing a knowledge management system, it is prudent to tie in what already exists and blend it with what is recommended.

When it comes to leveraging, keep the following in mind:

- Focus on real knowledge of people rather than artificial intelligence that was once unique to expert systems but which has now become a flop.
- Concentrate on a knowledge management system that facilitates finding the sources of know-how, not just the know-how. A user should be able to readily locate people and their respective expertise and use available knowledge as he or she sees fit.
- A successful knowledge management system should be tagged to collaboration. It would be superfluous to think of knowledge sharing, knowledge transfer, or continued creativity without collaborative success.
- People are no longer expected to adapt to the requirements of the machine, but the other way round. Today's human intelligence should make use of the way the machine (computers, networks, and the like) supports intelligent thinking, innovations, and creativity.
- Concentrate on realism, not perfection. A knowledge management system should begin with what you have and try to improve it. Disposing of current infrastructure and replacing it with a new one invites a host of problems that could backfire on the organization for a long time.
- Allow the user to decide on whether the proposed knowledge management system makes sense and how well information is organized and ready for day-to-day access.

The best way to visualize the technical architecture as the building block of KM is in terms of a layer system, starting with the user interface (least technical) and going all the way to the repositories that form the most technical layer of the technical core. They represent technologies of the company's intranet and its interface with the World Wide Web, including the protocols, standards, browsers, and servers. Knowledge exchange and communications within the company and across organizations are made possible via satellite communication, telecommunication networks, and wireless networks. Satellite companies are setting up new broadband networks to reach people where telephone service is not available. Telecommunication companies are developing new technologies for higher-bandwidth communication across existing networks. Wireless networks are also being converted for Internet use. Providers for each technological area play a major role in the expansion of the Internet.

The 7-tier technical layer, forming the overall building blocks of the knowledge management architecture, is shown in Figure 4.7. Each layer is briefly covered in the following sections.

The User Interface Layer

The first layer is the interface between the user and the KM system, usually represented by a Web browser. It is the top layer in the KM system architecture and the only layer with which the user interacts. To the user, beyond this layer is simply a black box. The goal is to move information into and out of the KM system. It simplifies technology for the user by the way graphics, tables, and text are displayed on the screen. It represents knowledge when displayed in a timely, actionable, and nontechnical user friendly universal view. *Universal* means uniform, consistent, and customized navigation. It means no barriers to information and tacit knowledge transmitted from repositories or remote sources.

Practically speaking, technology best supports explicit knowledge, although it should also represent tacit knowledge, as we saw in the 1990s. The user interface layer must provide a way for tacit and explicit knowledge flow. Knowledge transfer between people and technology requires capturing tacit knowledge from experts, storing it in a knowledge base as an intermediate step, and making it available to people as tacit knowledge for solving complex problems (see Figure 4.8).

For years, it has been known in the artificial intelligence (AI) community that human knowledge cannot be fully codified. That is all the more reason why tacit knowledge should be made available by face-to-face, e-mail, or other media. Direct communications allow for context, tone of voice, and nonverbal interpretation. This goes beyond the storage and electronic communication that databases and networks are best known for providing. Capturing tacit knowledge is covered in Chapter 5.

In terms of user interface design, several features should be considered:

- *Consistency.* Menus, icons, and buttons should have the same meaning or representation throughout the KM system, including those used in future upgrades. All information should be consistent in layout and format across all areas of the system.
- *Relevancy.* Any information displayed should be relevant to the user's expectations. It means users should be able to customize information in the way they want. It also means personalization of the Web site.
- *Visual clarity.* Ideally, all information should be presented in one screen, with space-saving features such as pull-down menus available as default. Proper use of color, margins, and text density can add quality and clarity of the displayed information. In today's digital age, people do not like to read text-heavy screens. In designing Web pages, for example, there is an 8-second rule that measures user tolerance to reading a screen full of information or to waiting for one.

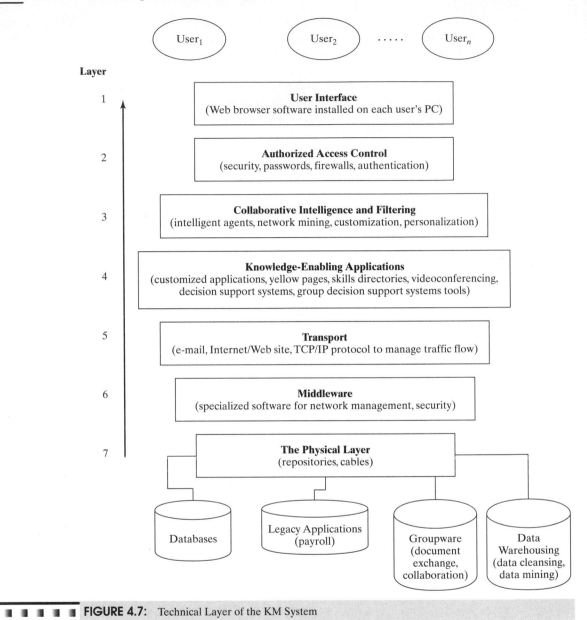

FIGURE 4.7: Technical Layer of the KM System

SOURCE: Adapted from Tiwana, Amrit. *The Knowledge Management Toolkit.* Upper Saddle River, NJ: Prentice Hall, 2000, p. 309.

- *Navigation.* The term *navigation* means how easily a user moves through Web pages, files, or records in a computer-based system. When dealing with different packages or tools within the KM system, the user's view should be a single mode of operation or one where the system tells the user which packages he or she has in operation.
- *Usability.* This feature addresses navigation in terms of how easy it is to use icons and buttons and the speed of access to files or databases.

With this in mind, it is critical that talented user interface designers be hired to build this layer, whether the layer is browser-based or client/server–based. The com-

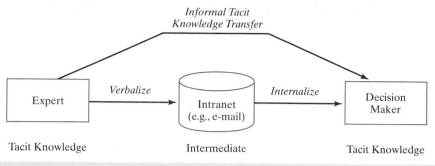

▪ ▪ ▪ ▪ ▪ ▪ ▪ **FIGURE 4.8:** Knowledge Transfer

pany's IT department can be instrumental in the final version of the design, including choice of colors, banners, icons, graphics, and so forth. Usability testing by company users is the final test of the acceptability of the user interface.

Authorized Access Layer

The authorized access layer maintains security and ensures authorized access to the knowledge captured and stored in repositories through the company's intranet, the Internet, and extranet. In essence, the company's traditional client and communication structure is replaced by repositories and knowledge bases that can be accessed from anywhere and at any time.

Figure 4.9 shows the technical access layer, with focus on the use of the Internet, intranet, and extranet as part of the technical infrastructure of the KM system. A company's **intranet** is the internal network of communication systems modified around the Internet. It is a way of thinking about how people in a business work and transfer knowledge. Technically, it is a network connecting a set of clients by using standard Internet protocols. Internet technologies are superior to the conventional means for developing internal communication systems. The Web browser, for example, is readily available and a familiar access tool for immediate use. Documents are easily handled

▪ ▪ ▪ ▪ ▪ ▪ ▪ **FIGURE 4.9:** Technical Access Layer

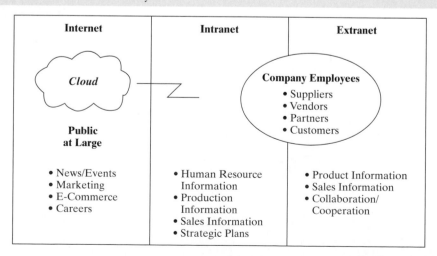

and multiple media can be supported as well. Managers can share documents on inter-departmental and intradepartmental levels. With various operating systems, network protocols, and application suites, trying to ensure homogeneity in managing documents can be quite a challenge. Intranets can handle all these problems with ease.

In contrast, an **extranet** is an intranet with extensions that allow clearly identified customers or top suppliers to reach and access company-related technical educational information. For example, in one electrical corporation the extranet is accessible to 950 electricians and small electrical outlet shops via the company's special Web page. An electrician enters a specially assigned password to access information about new products and special deals that are available to high-volume buyers. Based on 7 months of practice, the company's Net-based practice paid dividends. The company cut down on phone calls and fax orders, and gave sales reps in the field online support when needed. It even improved shipment schedules and deliveries, regardless of distance.

It should be noted that in today's Internet economy, a company's success depends less on the resources within its walls and more on its relationships with suppliers, ven-dors, and customers. Effective management of the company's product traffic is mar-shalling the resources of its employees in line with those of other companies. In this respect, relationships become assets, just as the company's buildings, information, and knowledge (Tapscott 2001).

Intranets and extranets have a lot in common. As shown in Figure 4.10, intranets are more localized within a firm and move data more quickly than the more distributed extranets. The use of Internet (primarily Web) protocols is more common to connect business users and branches. On the intranet, Web administrators prescribe access and policy for a defined group of users. To collaborate via extranet, the applications have to perform consistently on all represented platforms. The same is true for trading partners and suppliers, who may be totally unknown to one another.

▪ ▪ ▪ ▪ ▪ ▪ ▪ **FIGURE 4.10:** General Extranet Layout

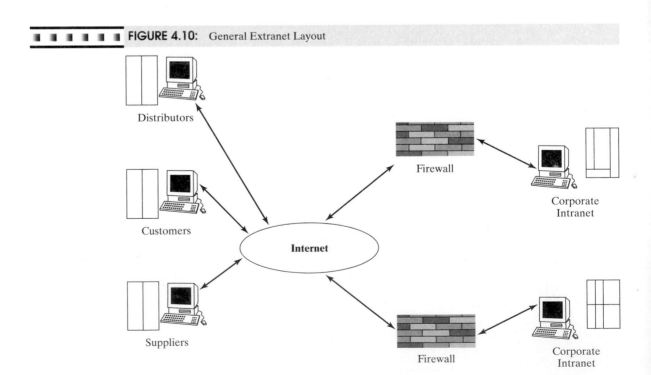

The access layer has taken on a special role in the technical core due to the vulnerability of intranets and heavy traffic on the Internet. The focus of today's access layer is on security, use of protocols like passwords, authentication to ensure users are authorized, and software tools like firewalls to block certain information from leaving the company's repositories or incoming information from contaminating company files. Firewalls are hardware and software tools that define, control, and limit access to networks and computers. They detect intruders, block them from entry, keep track of what they do and where they originate, notify the system administrator of mischievous acts, and produce a report. Specifically, a firewall protects against the following:

- E-mail services that are known to be problems
- Unauthorized interactive log-ins from the outside world
- Undesirable material such as pornographic images, movies, or literature
- Unauthorized sensitive information leaving the company

In contrast, a firewall cannot prevent:

- Attacks that do not go through the firewall (such as taking data out of the company by tape or diskette)
- Weak security policies
- Viruses on floppy disks
- Traitors or disgruntled employees

There are two main issues related to the access layer: access privileges and backups. In organizing access privileges, a network administrator has to authenticate each company user and define the types of files he or she may access. In terms of backups, a knowledge base requires a duplicate in case of fire, security violations, virus attack, or hardware breakdown. A company whose lifeline depends on such repositories must strategize a backup scheme and implement it accordingly.

Biometrics is an evolving technology that is slowly becoming part of the access layer. *Biometrics* is the automatic identification of a person based on physiological or behavioral characteristics. This science along with voice and fingerprint recognition should add reliable muscle to the access layer.

Collaborative Intelligence and Filtering Layer

Layer three is the collaborative intelligence and filtering layer within a KM system. It provides customized or personalized views based on stored knowledge. It is designed to reduce search time for information by combining the knowledge sought with the user's profile. Authorized users registered in the KM system's directory can expect information tailored to their view in format, content, and detail. This is all available through a search mechanism such as the browser or the client/server network of the organization.

Intelligent agents are probably the best contribution that AI has made to the Web. An *intelligent agent* is an active object that can perceive, reason (learn from past mistakes), and act in a situation to assist in problem-solving. Most agents are more mobile than static. They search across servers to find the information requested by the client (user).

Intelligent agents are clusters of precanned bits of intelligence that relate specific needs or attributes to other agents on a network. They are not real agents; they do not knowingly cooperate or share in problem solutions. They must be programmed to do those things, and they "learn" only a few things. They are planned for many kinds of services, from spreadsheets to personal information managers. One can realistically expect intelligent agents of the future to represent users in searching databases. They could conceivably arrange meetings, pay bills, and even wander through virtual shopping malls, suggesting gifts, greeting cards, and so on.

Figure 4.11 illustrates the key differences between traditional client/server infrastructure and that of mobil agent/computing. In client/server, there is direct but more frequent interaction between the client and the network server. This means heavy network load and possible congestion. In mobil agent/computing, the agent picks up the slack; the interaction is between the agent and the server, leaving the overall load vastly reduced.

Think of the mobil agent's role as that of an agent for a professional athlete. Any requests or contract negotiations are handled by the agent, which reduces the direct volume of correspondence for the athlete. In agent/computing, mobility is important. A mobile agent roams around the Internet across multiple servers looking for the right information or synthesis. There are other benefits as well:

- *Fault-tolerance.* When a server or a node in the network fails, an agent is warned in advance; the agent can take special action to complete an activity or relocate on another server to continue operation.
- *Reduced overall network load.* As mentioned earlier, agents reduce the number of interactions between clients and servers. In doing so, they reduce the load and delay on the network, releasing the savings to carrying bandwidth-intensive files such as videoconferencing or sound in the same network.
- *Heterogeneous operation.* With networks handling different hardware and software within the same network, mobil agents operate seamlessly in the same heterogeneous environment; this saves time and effort.

■ ■ ■ ■ ■ ■ ■ ■ **FIGURE 4.11:**   Contrast Between Client/Server and Mobil Agent/Computing

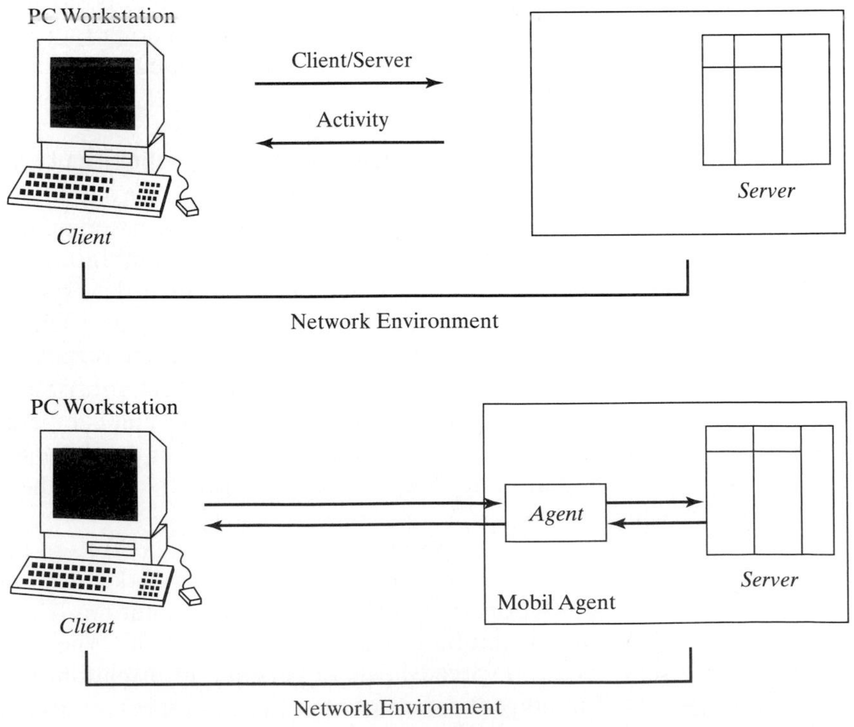

The key components of the collaborative intelligence layer are (1) the registration directory that develops tailored information based on user profile, (2) membership in specialized services such as news service, sales promotion, schedules, and customer support, and (3) the search facility such as a search engine to assist in finding information. Users can search for words, subjects, or single queries for information, regardless of where it is stored. The security feature is that users see only the results for which they have access.

In terms of the prerequisites for an effective collaborative layer, several criteria are considered:

- *Security.* This is a critical feature, especially as an organization becomes increasingly distributed worldwide.
- *Portability.* A collaborative platform must operate in a portable environment across platforms. For example, HTTP and the Web allow different systems to communicate with each other, regardless of architecture, location, or language. The Web browser is the most universal tool that users employ to access repositories.
- *Integration* with existing systems, including legacy applications. The Web is a good example, where a collaborative knowledge-sharing platform integrates with existing systems and mainframe databases.
- *Scalability, flexibility, and ease of use.* These three criteria go together in emphasizing the importance of a knowledge-enabling, upgradable, flexible, and easy-to-use (and to learn) collaborative platform. It boils down to the platform's ability to filter out irrelevant content and display what the user needs to see.

For years, companies have been trying to use computers to capture and manipulate knowledge for productivity and performance. The collaborative and filtering layer relies on a combination of technologies such as expert systems, case-based reasoning (CBR), neural networks, and intelligent agents.

Expert systems are a branch of artificial intelligence or AI. Its main purpose is to assist a person's thinking process, not merely to provide information for a person to consider. When a company faces a critical decision—such as whether to acquire another company, market a new product, or grant a hefty loan to a new customer—it turns to an expert for advice. These experts have years of experience in a particular area and generally know the probability of success for a particular decision. A difficult problem requires a seasoned professional, who is invariably an expensive commodity.

Expert systems are decision-making and problem-solving tools. They consist of computer software programs that emulate or clone the reasoning of a human expert in a problem domain. As shown in Figure 4.12, the knowledge base is the repository of the rules, facts, and knowledge acquired from the human expert. The knowledge is typically represented in the form of IF . . . THEN rules, facts, and assumptions about the problem the system is designed to solve. The developmental environment simply allows a human knowledge engineer to acquire the knowledge from the human expert. Such knowledge is entered into a knowledge base that represents the operational environment.

The user environment consists of a user friendly interface; a **justifier** that explains to the user how and why an answer is given; an **inference engine** that is the problem-solving mechanism for reasoning and **inferencing**; and a **scheduler** that has the unique job of coordinating and controlling rule processing. All these components work together to simulate a near-real environment of a client-expert relationship.

Properly used, expert systems can help a person become wiser, not just better informed. AI encompasses many aspects of human behavior (such as speech, language, and movement); expert systems focus on the task of problem solving. Expert systems utilize the research discipline of AI to create a commercial reality that produces benefits

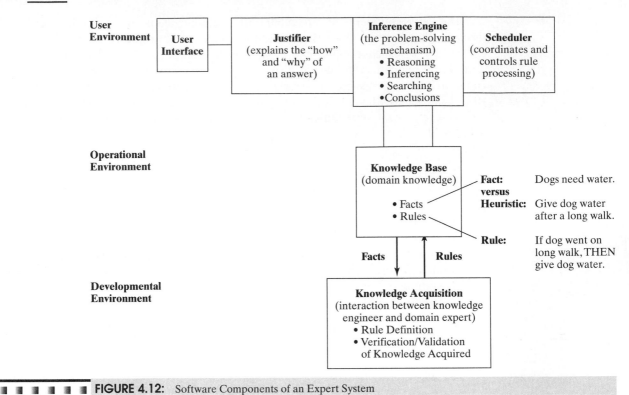

▪ ▪ ▪ ▪ ▪ ▪ **FIGURE 4.12:** Software Components of an Expert System

each day. An expert system is a branch or a commercial spin-off of AI. It contains practical knowledge obtained from a human expert. Its information is explicit and comprehensible, and the system is able to explain its reasoning on demand. In this respect, it is viewed as a problem-solving tool.

Expert systems have not lived up to expectations and have not revolutionized the business environment. The main reason is that human knowledge is too complex to understand, capture, or manipulate. Their applications are also rather restricted. They work best with two simultaneous conditions: express a problem variable in hard terms (such as numbers or speed) and rules cannot overlap.

Case-Based Reasoning.   In this particular area of reasoning, old solutions are adapted to meet new situations by using old cases to explain those new situations. For example, attorneys use case precedents to justify or explain their arguments in new court cases. Doctors often treat patients based on symptoms they have treated in previous patients. Experience with old cases allows an attorney to decide on how to handle the case easily and quickly (see Figure 4.13).

A *case* is a contextual piece of knowledge representing an experience. It is knowledge at an operational level. Case-based reasoning (CBR) is useful to experts with experience in their particular domains, because it helps them reuse the reasoning they have done in the past. CBR also reminds the expert to avoid repeating past mistakes.

Neural networks, or neural nets, are information systems modeled after the human brain's network of neurons—the basic processing elements of the brain. Each neuron has a small amount of local memory and is connected to other neurons to receive input and produce output. Communications among neurons are carried out only through the input-output pathways. A neuron evaluates the inputs, determines their weights, sums

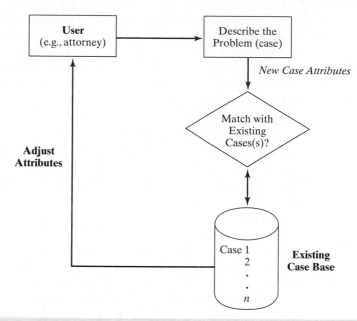

▪ ▪ ▪ ▪ ▪ ▪ ▪ **FIGURE 4.13:** Case-Based Reasoning

the weighted inputs, and compares the total to a threshold. If the sum is greater than the threshold, the neuron fires. Otherwise, it generates no signal. This means it modifies its activity in response to new input until it produces the right results.

Knowledge-Enabling Application Layer

The fourth layer is the knowledge-enabling application layer. It is also referred to as the *value-added layer,* which creates a competitive edge for the learning organization. Most of such applications provide the users better ways to do their jobs. They include knowledge bases, discussion databases, sales force automation tools, yellow pages, decision support, and imaging tools. The ultimate goal is to show how knowledge sharing could improve the lot of employees and the organization as a whole.

The Transport Layer

The transport layer is probably the most technical layer to implement KM architecture. It ensures that the company will become a network of relationships, where e-mail and electronic transfer of knowledge throughout the organization will be as routine as answering the telephone. The key change is a move away from classical transmission processing to knowledge transfer and the sharing of expertise.

Included in the transport layer are local area networks (LANs), wide area networks (WANs), intranets, extranets, and the Internet. The things to consider are multimedia, URLs (Web addresses), graphics, connectivity speeds and bandwidths, search tools, and managing network traffic on a continual basis.

The Middleware Layer

When designing a KM system, concern must be given to how such a system will interface with legacy systems and other programs or applications that reside on different platforms or operate under older operating systems. The term *legacy system* refers to applications that once ran on mainframes or operated under traditional programming languages, such as COBOL. The designer needs to address databases and applications with which the KM system must interface. The middleware layer contains a cluster of programs to do that job—to provide connections between legacy applications and existing and new systems. Essentially, it makes it possible to connect between old and new data formats.

The Repositories Layer

The bottom layer in the KM architecture represents the physical layer where repositories are installed. These include intelligent data warehouses, legacy applications, operational databases, and special applications for securing traffic management and integrity assurance of the knowledge architecture. Each repository has a structure appropriate for the type of knowledge stored.

Once the repositories are established, they are linked to form an integrated repository. For example, knowledge about sales might be in one repository, while sales best practices are stored in another repository. An integrated repository brings together all the knowledge available from the repositories and creates a profile of the next sales strategy for the following quarter or for the remainder of the year. A conceptual model of an enterprise-wide integrated knowledge management system is shown in Figure 4.14.

The main advantage of an integrated knowledge repository is that the user does not care in which repository the knowledge resides. On the other hand, as users add content to various repositories with no clear validation procedure, information overload could cause all kinds of validity and reliability problems. Content in repositories should be proactively managed, not only for adding content, but also for getting rid of old content and eliminating redundancies.

Managing an integrated repository means knowing where content comes from and what information to tap. In a banking installation, for example, the key content centers include the following:

- Operations department (bookkeeping, accounting, payroll, teller work)
- Loan department (commercial, automobile, personal, construction, student, and collateral loans)
- Human resources department (career planning, performance data, skills data, pension)
- Trust department (pension management, investment, stock trading)
- Safe deposit department (box rental, billing, opening/closing new accounts)

As to what information to tap, the same financial institution might consider the following:

- What do outside sources say about our competition?
  - Financial and government agencies: financial data, government reports, and industry data
  - Customer and business community: newspapers, articles, and chambers of commerce
  - Business organizations: vendors, suppliers, users, and industry journals
- What information is generated by the competition?
  - Number of new branches in the area
  - Quarterly annual reports
  - Advertising volume and frequency

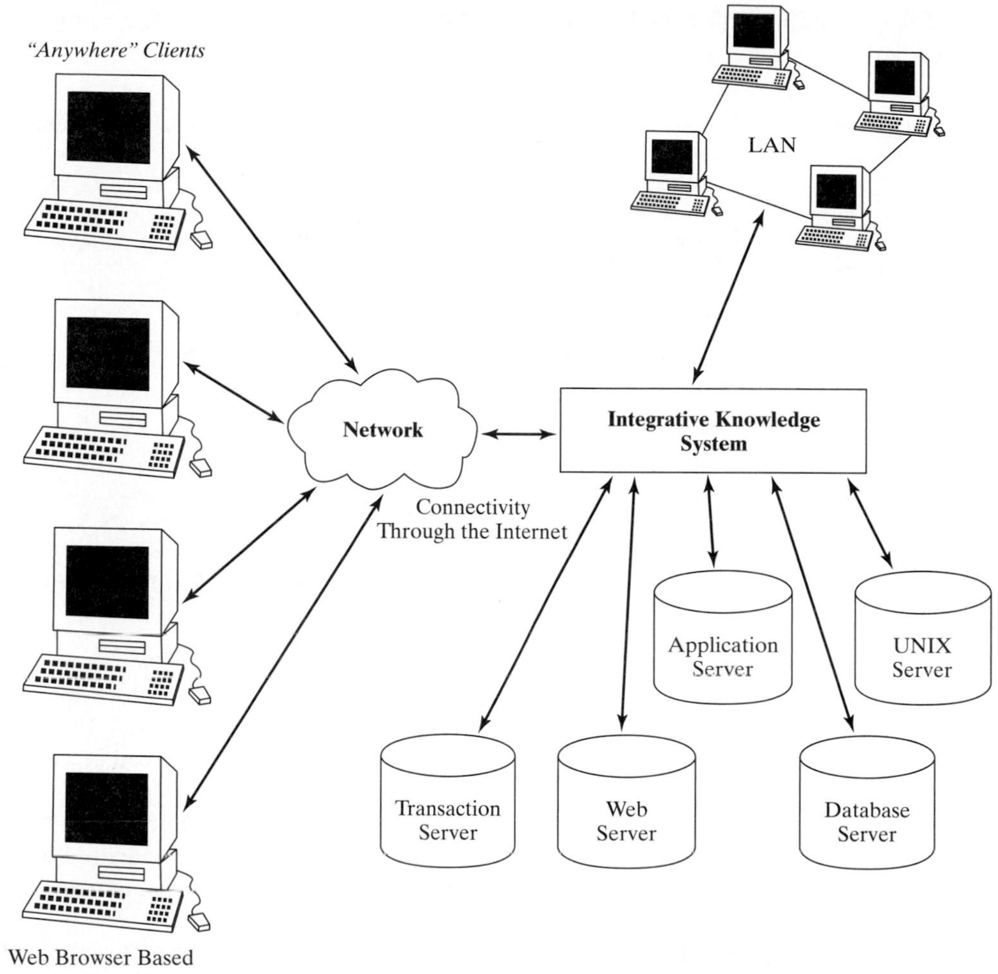

"*Anywhere*" Clients

LAN

Network

Integrative Knowledge
System

Connectivity
Through the Internet

Application
Server

UNIX
Server

Transaction
Server

Web
Server

Database
Server

Web Browser Based

▪ ▪ ▪ ▪ ▪ ▪ ▪ **FIGURE 4.14:**   Enterprise-Wide Integrated Knowledge Management System

BUILD IN-HOUSE, BUY, OR OUTSOURCE?

The question of whether to build a knowledge management system in-house from scratch or adopt an off-the-shelf system involves several options. As summarized in Table 4.1, building a knowledge management system in-house from scratch requires ready professionals in system design, where the development cost is high and the risk of the system not running on the first try is also high. The main benefit is customization, which many firms find well worth the cost. On the other extreme, installing an off-the-shelf system means quick installation and low cost, although customization is usually not quite right in most cases. In between are situations where the end user delves into system design. In most cases, this is not a recommended approach to system development.

The trend in today's software is toward ready-to-use, generalized software packages. Outsourcing is also a trend that allows companies to concentrate on their strengths while technological design and other specialized areas are released to outsiders. Based on the authors' experience, purchasing a software package represents

TABLE 4.1   Key Elements in Build Versus Buy Decision

Option	*Cost*	*Time Factor*	*Customization*	*Comments*
In-house development	Usually high	Much longer than off-the-shelf installation	High, depending on quality of staff	Consultants can be hired to improve quality, but the cost will be higher. Leak of unique system features by consultants is a possibility.
Development by end users	Usually low	Depends on skills set, system priority, and so forth	High to the user specifications	This is not recommended for for first-time users.
Outsourcing	Medium to high	Shorter than in-house	High	The competition might already have the same knowledge system.
Off-the-shelf solution	Low to medium	Nil	Usually up to 80 percent usable	Installation time is short, and installation is not that difficult.

▪ ▪ ▪ ▪ ▪ ▪

roughly 10 percent to 20 percent of the cost of developing the same in-house. A reliable KM software package offers several advantages:

- *Short implementation time.* Installation of a software package is completed in a matter of days rather than the months necessary for "homegrown" packages. It also contains fewer errors and is of higher overall quality than most in-house software.
- *Reduced need for resources.* In-house software can be costly, and completion dates are hard to predict. Incomplete software projects are not uncommon because of turnover among programming staff.
- *Lower development cost.* A package can take years to build, great expense to complete, and even more time to maintain. Users do not have the expertise to cost-justify developing such packages.
- *Greater flexibility.* Users are not saddled with a software package, as they would be with in-house programs. If the package fails the test, there is no obligation to acquire.

Software packages, on the other hand, are not without drawbacks:

- *Shorter track record.* Many of the software houses have been in the knowledge management business less than 5 years. It is difficult to predict how long they will continue.
- *Application incompatibility.* For a sophisticated user, extensive modification of a package can be costly. If the user modifies the software, the vendor may no longer be responsible for any errors that occur.
- *Lack of competition.* Selecting a package is often not straightforward. In some cases, a software package is one-of-a-kind. In other cases, it is the only available software for the problem.

Whether the choice is build, buy, or outsource, it is important to set criteria for the selection. In knowledge management system development, the following components are generally agreed to be crucial:

- *Reliability* has to do with how long software will operate without a failure. It also relates to how accurate and dependable the results are. Software does not fail. It does not even wear out. Invariably, reliability problems are the result of errors overlooked during the development process. In contrast, hardware fails because of wear and tear associated with continued use or inadequate maintenance.

- *Market pressure* to produce software has had an adverse impact on the reliability of software in general. To make things worse, first-time users do not know much about software testing. A demonstration by a sales representative is often all it takes to purchase the package. For this reason alone, inquiring about vendor support is crucial.
- *Modularity* refers to the ease of modifying the software across product lines. Software with high modularity operates in computers across product lines. It should be noted that most of today's software packages are seldom modified by the user. In contrast to modularity, *expandability* has to do with how well the software can be modified to meet a user's changing requirements. Some of the expandability questions related to knowledge management systems are:
  - How easily can knowledge be changed or relocated?
  - Will the knowledge management system be unusable if a part of it fails?
  - What are the recovery features of the knowledge management software?

  Related to expandability are capacity and flexibility. *Capacity* refers to the software's capability for file size, volume of transactions, and additional reports. *Flexibility* is the ease of modifying or extending a software package to address changing requirements.
- *Usability* ensures user friendly software. For example, the popularity of dBase II in the early 1980s was attributed to the fact that a novice user could create and maintain a database file in less than 4 training hours. In this respect, it was highly usable.
- *Portability* is a measure of how well the software will run on different computers. A software package rated high on portability would also be high on usability.
- *Serviceability* emphasizes the importance of vendor services and support. An effective package must be well documented for maintenance and future enhancements. This includes a description of the system logic, input/output file descriptions and layouts, and a readable user manual. Vendor support means technical support, software maintenance, and updates. On-site training and conversion support are part of most commercial software installations.
- *Performance* is one of the most critical criteria of software selection. It is a measure of the software's capacity to meet user requirements and perform under peak loads. The programming language of the software may be a performance factor. For example, a knowledge management package written in C++ or Java usually outperforms substantially a similar package written in BASIC. However, it is cheaper and easier to modify a package written in BASIC.

Buying or even outsourcing a knowledge management system brings up the important question of *ownership*. Most license agreements lease (not sell) the software for an indefinite time period. To protect proprietary rights, the vendor does not provide the source code. However, the availability of the source code becomes crucial when dealing with a software house that could fold without notice. The questions to consider on ownership are as follows:

- What is the user paying for?
- What restrictions are there to copying the software for company branches or other departments within the firm?
- Who modifies the software? What are the charges? How are modifications made if the vendor goes out of business?

Related to the issue of buy versus outsource is evaluating the vendor's services in terms of conversion, backup, maintenance, and upgrade. Vendor-assisted *conversion* provides programming support, file conversion, and user training. *Backup* ensures alternative sites for processing applications in an emergency. *Maintenance* ensures against unexpected system failure. In contrast, *upgrade* revises the system in order to make it more current.

■ ■ ■ ■ Implications for Knowledge Management

A successful knowledge management system cannot exist without a clearly defined architecture. The cost of correcting the "wrongs" at a later stage can be prohibitive. In the early stages of planning such infrastructure, it is important to keep the following in mind:

- *Decide whether to build, outsource, or buy the software.* There is really no best answer. In any case, the company has the right to modify the KM system as the situation warrants. Buying the system rather than leasing also means cash savings from depreciation and lower cash outlay if the system is kept 5 years or longer. The main negative, however, is that maintenance, insurance, and upkeep are borne by the user.
- *Understand what you are building in terms of the components of the KM architecture.* This means evaluating the quality, reliability, performance, and manageability of the user interface, integrative repositories, the collaborative platform, and knowledge directories. The user interface, for example, provides a unique opportunity to see how well the users buy into the system. The IT department or an outside consultant can do the evaluation and inform management of the status quo.
- *Focus on optimization for scalability, performance, and flexibility of the KM architecture.* Prior to committing the KM system to actual operation, rigorous testing of the technology is critical. The system should be tested not only to see how well it works, but also under what conditions it begins to fail. This is called *force-fail testing*—a step that requires experience and patience.
- *Ensure interoperability.* This means that the existing technology and its affiliate components, intranet, extranet, databases, legacy systems, and PCs should all work together in an interactive and integrative environment. The alternative could be fragmented applications, where one application is totally oblivious to the technical and knowledge-based activities of the others.

Another area of importance is managing a KM project. Choosing and recruiting the right specialists for the KM project team is a vital task. Team members come from multiple disciplines representing various areas of the firm. The focus should be first on people, followed by business processes and organizational culture. The technology that ensures knowledge sharing comes next (see Box 4.2).

■ ■ ■ ■ ■ ■   BOX 4.2   ■ ■ ■ ■ ■ ■

DEVELOPING A KM TEAM

WHO IS IN CHARGE?

When many business units are involved in an endeavor, project leadership can become a point of contention. A team leader must be able to balance the various, sometimes competing, demands on the group while keeping it focused on meeting the organization's knowledge needs. The leader must understand the business requirements and problems the company must address and be able to articulate a broad vision that spans the unique needs of the lines of business—and the business processes and technical infrastructure that can meet those needs.

(*continued*)

(continued)

A very large organization should hand the reins of team leadership to a chief knowledge officer (CKO). You need someone with the influence and skills to take the enterprise in the right direction. In any case, team leaders must command respect and trust within the company. This is especially true if team members come from different business units.

Team members who do not view a KM project as a new path to career success will be more willing to give it their all if they see the project as a finite effort with a definite end, after which they can return to their normal duties, observers say. For this reason, it may be a good idea to set a life span for the team at the outset of the project. The duration can vary from a few months for projects that seek to plant the seeds for a more ambitious endeavor to several years for complex projects that involve reengineering business processes.

SOURCE: Excerpted from Robb, Drew. *Knowledge Management*, August 2001, pp. 44–50.

▪ ▪ ▪ ▪ ▪ ▪

SUMMARY ▪ ▪ ▪ ▪

- One way of creating knowledge is based on experience; the other way is through teamwork. Either way, the outcome is the same, because the focus is knowledge sharing. Team formation and teamwork begin with experienced individuals working jointly on a project.
- Knowledge sharing is influenced by personality, attitude, vocational reinforcers, and work norms. The concept also considers organizational culture, company strategies, and company policies. It is not so straightforward, because people are more used to knowledge hoarding than knowledge sharing.
- Knowledge architecture is a combination of people, content, and knowledge sharing. They are interdependent and inseparable. People with knowledge provide content, relying on technology to transfer and share knowledge.
- Part of the people core is profiling. The goal of profiling is to get a handle on existing knowledge exchanges that the organization relies on and ways to capture them. The idea is to assign job content to the right person and to ensure that the flow of information that once was obstructed by departments now flows to the right people at the time needed.
- Once profiling is completed, the next step is to identify where knowledge resides and how to capture it. These centers become the skeletal framework for knowledge capture. At the same time, experts are assigned to each knowledge area to assure continuity and effective management of the knowledge sharing process.
- The goal of the technical core is to enhance communication and ensure effective knowledge sharing. By technical core, we mean the totality of hardware and software, and the specialized human resources required to enable knowledge capture. Once in place, a knowledge core becomes a network of technologies designed to work on top of the company's existing network.
- The best way to visualize the technical architecture as the building block of KM is in terms of a layer system, starting with the user interface and going all the way to the repositories that form the most technical layer of the technical core. In terms

of the user interface layer, consistency, relevancy, visual clarity, navigation, and usability are important design considerations.

- The technical access layer involves the use of the Internet, intranet, and extranet as part of the technical infrastructure of the KM system. Each area has unique contributions to make. Because of the vulnerability of the intranet and extranet, firewalls and other security devices are installed.

- The collaborative intelligence and filtering layer reduces search time for information by combining the knowledge sought with the user's profile. Intelligent agents are used to assist in problem-solving by retrieving the right information. For an effective collaborative layer, security, portability, integration, scalability, flexibility, and ease of use are important design criteria.

- The collaborative layer relies on expert systems, CBR, and neural nets to do its job. Expert systems are a branch of AI, which assist a person's thinking process based on years of captured human experience. CBR is based on real-life cases that allow the decision maker a chance to compare his or her decisions to the ones decided by older cases. Neural nets are information systems modeled after the human brain's network of neurons. They can be trained to improve on the quality and accuracy of decisions.

- The remaining layers are knowledge-enabling application, transport, and middleware layers. Each layer gives the user better ways to do the job. The transport layer is the most technical layer to implement in KM architecture.

- The bottom layer is the one representing the repositories, including intelligent data warehouses, legacy applications, operational databases, and special applications for securing traffic management and integrity assurance of the knowledge architecture.

- Building a KM system in-house provides the benefits of customization and personalization, although at a high cost. The alternative is to outsource or buy an off-the-shelf package. KM software packages usually mean short implementation time, lower development cost, and greater flexibility. The main drawbacks include shorter track record, application incompatibility, and lack of competition

- Finally, the role of the CKO is crucial in developing KM architecture. The key functions of such an officer are maximizing the returns on investment in knowledge, sharing the best practices, promoting and improving company innovations, and minimizing brain drain or knowledge loss at all levels of the organization. Interpersonal and technical skills are also crucial.

TERMS TO KNOW ▪▪▪▪

Artificial intelligence: The science of making machines do things that would require intelligence if done by humans; the capacity to acquire and apply an understanding gained through experience or study in order to imitate or emulate "natural intelligence."

Authentication: Making sure that a cardholder is, in fact, the person authorized to use the card.

Browser: A program designed to search for and bring in Internet resources.

CBR (case-based reasoning): A methodology that records and documents previous cases and then searches the relevant cases to determine their usefulness in solving a current problem; computer systems that solve new problems by analogy with old ones.

Collaborative intelligence: A knowledge management technical layer that provides customized views based on stored knowledge.

Data warehouse: A repository where relational data are specially organized to provide "cleaned" data in a format understandable to the user.

Expert system: A sophisticated computer program that applies human knowledge in a specific area of expertise to create solutions to difficult problems.

Extranet: Network that connects separate companies with a shared database.

Fault-tolerance: In hardware, having a specially designed operating system that keeps the Web site or any application running, even when the central processing unit goes down.

Firewall: A network node consisting of hardware and software to protect or filter certain information entering the company's databases or keep select information from leaving the company.

Inference engine: The "brain" of an expert system; a cluster of computer programs that coordinates through a scheduler the reasoning and inferencing based on the rules of the knowledge base to produce the solution or advice.

Inferencing: Deriving a conclusion based on statements that only imply that conclusion.

Intelligent agent: A cluster of precanned bits of intelligence that relate specific needs or attributes to other agents on a network.

Internet: An infrastructure that links thousands of networks to one another; the information highway that makes the information stored on thousands of computers worldwide available to millions of people everywhere.

Interoperability: Ability to move back and forth between different systems.

Intranet: A network using TCP/IP to share information within an organization.

Justifier: Explains the action (line of reasoning) of the expert system to the user.

Knowledge center: An area in the organization where knowledge is available.

Knowledge creation: Generating experience via teamwork, repositories, or other interfaces.

Legacy application: An application that once ran on mainframes or operated on traditional programming languages such as Cobol.

Middleware: A software layer in the technology core that makes connections between old and new data formats.

Modularity: Refers to the ease of modifying the software across product lines.

Navigation: In Web design, it refers to how easily a user moves through Web pages, files, or records in a computer-based system.

Neural net: An information system modeled after the human brain's network of electrically interconnected processing elements called neurons; a self-programming system that creates a model based on its inputs and outputs.

People core: The human part of a knowledge management environment and the way people creatively perform in that environment.

Performance: A measure of the software's capacity to meet user requirements and perform under peak loads.

POP: Point of presence; a physical location on the premises of a local exchange carrier at which messages are transferred or linked to other carriers for routing to their intended destinations.

Portability: Ability of software to be used on different hardware and operating systems.

Profiling: In knowledge management systems, it is generating a graphic or textual representation of people in terms of criteria such as skills or personality traits.

Reliability: Has to do with how long software will operate without a failure.

Repository: A subsystem such as a database used for data, information, or knowledge storage.

Scalability: Ability of a computer system, a database infrastructure, or a network to be upgraded to new standards.

Serviceability: A criterion that emphasizes the importance of vendor services and support.

SMTP: simple mail transfer protocol; a TCP/IP protocol used on the Internet to deliver messages between electronic mail hosts and to specify message structure.

TCP/IP: Transmission control protocol/Internet protocol; standards architecture used on the Internet and in many other networks.

Technical core: The aspect of the knowledge management system that represents the technology and technical features that make the system operational.

Transport layer: The layer that standardizes exchanges between the operating systems of the computers in the system.

Usability: The degree to which a system is deemed useful by the end user; a criterion that ensures user friendly software.

User interface: A layer that standardizes exchanges between the ultimate user and the system.

Web: Also called World Wide Web; a service on the Internet in which users working with browsers can retrieve Web pages from any Web server around the world. Each page is in hypertext format and contains links to other Web pages.

TEST YOUR UNDERSTANDING

1. What is knowledge creation?
2. A job is more than a task. Do you agree? Give an example.
3. How is knowledge created and transferred via teams?
4. Explain the main impediments to knowledge sharing.

5. Distinguish between:
   a. transport layer and application layer
   b. usability and portability
   c. profiling and repository
   d. collaborative intelligence and intelligent agent
6. Why do we profile people in knowledge management design? Be specific.
7. What is the main difference between an intranet and an extranet? Where does the Internet fit in?
8. Explain in your own words the functions of middleware. How does middleware differ from the user interface?
9. What does it mean to leverage technology?
10. Why is it a critical requirement that a successful knowledge management system be tagged to collaboration?
11. People are no longer expected to adapt to the requirements of machines, but machines are expected to adapt to people. Explain.
12. When it comes to leveraging, what should one keep in mind?
13. Explain the basis for the user interface layer and the services it offers.
14. What design considerations are unique to the user interface?
15. What is involved in authorized access to a knowledge system?
16. Explain the main steps in knowledge transfer.
17. How does an intelligent agent differ from filtering? Be specific.
18. Explain briefly the key components of the collaborative intelligence layer.
19. What distinguishes a Web browser from a client/server network?
20. Cite some prerequisite criteria for an effective collaborative layer.
21. Distinguish between:
    a. scalability and portability
    b. flexibility and ease of use
    c. fault-tolerance and integrity
    d. expert systems and CBR
22. What are the main drawbacks of expert systems? Are there any unique benefits?
23. How do databases differ from legacy systems?
24. Identify a business organization and cite its key content centers.

KNOWLEDGE EXERCISES ▪▪▪▪

1. Arrange a visit to a medium- or large-size firm in your area. In an interview with a company representative, address the following:
   a. Identify the satellite knowledge centers.
   b. Identify managers for each knowledge center within departments or divisions.
   c. Identify the company's KM strategies and specific projects that support overall corporate goals.
   d. Write up strategic plans to higher levels of management and get their buy-in.
2. Access to knowledge is based on profiles derived from the knowledge base. What technology would you recommend to provide access? Who will manage such access?
3. Visit the Internet and review the latest applications based on expert systems, CBR, and neural nets. Write a short report showing how these applications relate to knowledge management.
4. Visit the Internet and look up two articles that explain the role of the CKO. Report your findings to class.

REFERENCES

Berry, John. *Real Knowledge Is Held by People*. New York: CMP Media, Inc., 2000.

Boland, R. J. "The In-Formation of Information Systems," in R. J. Boland and R. Hirschhe (eds.), *Critical Issues in Information Systems Research*. Chichester: Wiley, 1987.

Churchman, C. W. *The Design of Inquiring Systems*. New York: Basic Books, 1971.

Davenport, T. H., and Prusak, Laurence. *Working Knowledge*. Boston, MA: Harvard Business School Press, 1998.

Flash, Cynthia. "Who Is the CKO?" *Knowledge Management*, May 2001, pp. 37–41.

Gill, T. G. "High-Tech Hidebound: Case Studies of Information Technologies That Inhibit Organizational Learning," *Accounting, Management and Information Technologies*, vol. 5, no. 1, 1995, pp. 41–60.

Malhotra, Yogesh. "Knowledge Management in Inquiring Organizations," 2001, www.brint.com/km, Date accessed August 2002.

Marwick, A. D. "Knowledge Management Technology," *IBM Systems Journal*, vol. 40, no. 4, 2001, pp. 814–830.

Nonaka, I., and Takeuchi, H. *The Knowledge Creating Company*. Oxford, UK: Oxford University Press, 1995.

Robb, Drew. "Draft Your Dream Team," *Knowledge Management*, August 2001, pp. 44–50.

Shruti, Date. "Agencies Create CKO Posts to Get in the Know," *Government Computer News*, November 8, 1999, pp. 1–2.

Tapscott, Don. *Growing Up Digital: The Rise of the Net Generation*. Boston, MA: Harvard Business School Press, 2001.

Tiwana, Amrit. *The Knowledge Management Toolkit*. Upper Saddle River, NJ: Prentice Hall, 2000, p. 309.

CHAPTER 5

Capturing Tacit Knowledge

Contents

I suppose it was something you said
That caused me to tighten and pull away
And when you asked, "What is it?"
I, of course, said, "Nothing."
Whenever I say, "Nothing,"
You may be very certain there is something.
The something is a cold, hard lump of "Nothing."
—Lois Wyse

▪ ▪ ▪ ▪ In a Nutshell

Knowledge management systems derive their power from the knowledge they use. When knowledge developers begin the building process, they are confronted with the first step—capturing tacit knowledge (see Figure 5.1). As mentioned in earlier chapters, tacit knowledge resides in the minds of people—the experts in the department, division, or the firm. A knowledge developer converts human know-how into machine-ready "say-how" by using an iterative process of articulation, a series of refinement cycles, or rapid prototyping, in which the computer's performance is compared to that of the human expert.

Capturing tacit knowledge and converting it into rules that the computer can use is a costly business. It requires an extensive time commitment from the domain expert and the special skills of the knowledge developer. At times, the expert might lose interest in the project and even feel like quitting. Perhaps the knowledge developer and the expert just never seem to hit it off because of their interpersonal chemistry, or the knowledge developer may use the wrong tool or approach.

Working with experts in capturing their tacit knowledge is not a straightforward routine. For example, the methods or tools chosen for knowledge capture depend on the temperament, personality, and attitude of the expert and whether the knowledge automation system is being built around a single expert or multiple experts. Another important factor is whether one or more knowledge developers will be involved in the building process.

Before beginning the knowledge capture process, a knowledge developer needs to have an understanding of the expert's level of expertise. The knowledge developer can look at several indicators of expertise as well as specific qualifications to determine whether someone is an expert. One of the most important indicators is the expert's communication skills.

Using either a single or multiple experts each has advantages and limitations. For smaller knowledge management systems, a single expert should suffice. In problem situations with dispersed knowledge, which require synthesis of experience, multiple experts are preferred. In either case, working with experts (and accommodating the

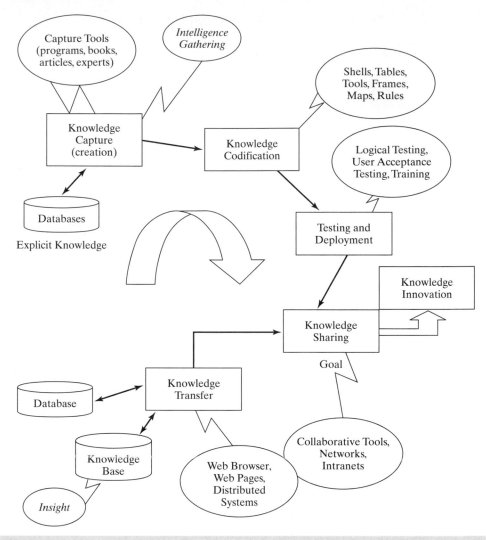

■ ■ ■ ■ ■ ■ ■ **FIGURE 5.1:** Knowledge Codification in the KM System Life Cycle

experts' individual styles of expression) requires special skills. The location at which knowledge capture sessions are held adds another dimension that the knowledge developer must consider.

■ ■ ■ ■ What Is Knowledge Capture?

A review of the literature reveals as many definitions of knowledge capture as there are authors. Some of the definitions are interesting:

- An "applied brain drain"
- A "manual craft that depends on the skill and effectiveness of the knowledge developer"
- The "transfer of problem-solving expertise from some knowledge source to a repository or a program"

- The "process by which knowledge management system developers discover the knowledge that company experts use to perform the task of interest"
- An investigative experimental process involving interviews and protocol analysis in order to build a KM system

In this book, we define knowledge capture as a *process by which the expert's thoughts and experiences are captured.* It is a sort of "mind automation." In a broader view, knowledge capture may also include capturing knowledge from other sources such as books, technical manuscripts, and drawings. In fact, these processes lead to the case-based reasoning used in the building of many KM systems.

Knowledge capture is a demanding mental process in which a knowledge developer collaborates with the expert to convert expertise into a coded program. Three important steps are involved:

1. Using an appropriate tool to elicit information from the expert
2. Interpreting the information and inferring the expert's underlying knowledge and reasoning process
3. Using the interpretation to build the rules that represent the expert's thought processes or solutions

The capture of knowledge can be accomplished in many ways; no single way is best. The process typically entails several refinement cycles. The KM system's task is not simply to display the knowledge but also to codify it at different levels of reasoning or explanation. Box 5.1 illustrates the challenge in knowledge capture.

Knowledge is usually captured when the knowledge developer interviews the expert, who answers the following questions: What do you do as a first step? What information do you consider next? What constraints do you look for? These types of

---

▪ ▪ ▪ ▪ ▪ ▪ ▪   **BOX 5.1**   ▪ ▪ ▪ ▪ ▪ ▪ ▪

THE CHALLENGE IN KNOWLEDGE CAPTURE

Sometimes even the best knowledge development techniques and the most talented knowledge developers cannot get the job done, which happened to two Texas Instruments (TI) knowledge developers who were signed on to capture the knowledge of Thomas Kelly. Kelly, a civil developer with Southern California Edison, is a genuine expert. He can almost feel the presence of danger at the Vermilion hydroelectric dam. This task was a complex one that relied on many rules of thumb. How did Kelly know that a small stream of water on one side of the dam meant a blocked drain at its base? Kelly was unhappy, because the two knowledge developers working with him on knowledge capture were not picking up on what he was saying fast enough.

Too ambitious a scope and poor communication between the knowledge developer and expert crippled the progress of this most interesting system. Today, Project Kelly has finally wound down. A good prototype, but not a deployable one, was built. Southern California estimates that another $200,000 will have to be pumped into Vermilion dam to make it a generic dam knowledge management system. Now it just keeps Tom Kelly company during his lonely vigils.

SOURCE: Awad, E. M. *Building Expert Systems.* Minneapolis, MN: West Publishing, 1996, p. 144.

▪ ▪ ▪ ▪ ▪ ▪

questions lead the expert through scenarios, or case situations. Then, the knowledge developer returns to specific points and questions the expert further until all angles of the problem are explored. Here is a partial session with a loan officer who is trying to capture her experience on how she decides to approve or deny a loan:

STEVE (knowledge developer):	What is your main job as a loan officer?
SANDRA (loan officer):	I review loan applications and recommend which ones qualify for a loan.
STEVE:	How long have you been on this job?
SANDRA:	Eighteen years with this bank and 7 years with another bank before coming here.
STEVE:	The idea of lending and how loans are approved or denied is intriguing. Suppose you receive a loan application. Then what? I mean, what do you do next?
SANDRA:	Well, let me see. This is going to take time to explain. The gist of the process I follow is to mentally plug the information that the applicant provides against criteria I use that help me decide whether to approve or deny the loan.
STEVE:	What criteria do you use?
SANDRA:	The main criteria are the applicant's employment status and how long he or she has been on the job, marital status, annual salary and other sources of income, credit history, monthly expenses, and the like. There is really no set procedure, and nothing is set in concrete. It all depends.
STEVE:	What do you mean?
SANDRA:	Well, I sort of size up the overall application against criteria, strategies, potential, the interest of our bank in the loan, the state of the competition, and so on. I tell you, I don't mind elaborating further, but maybe we should allocate another session or two for the details. What do you think?
STEVE:	(sensing unease by Sandra) I agree. How about next Tuesday, the same time, the same place?
SANDRA:	Fine, unless you hear from me today or tomorrow, let's go ahead and meet then.
STEVE:	Thanks. See you Tuesday. Meantime, if you have any set rules that I can work with regarding the criteria or the decision process, I'd appreciate your sending them to me by e-mail at your convenience.
SANDRA:	I'll see what I can do.

To capture the knowledge used in building complex KM systems, knowledge developers use flowcharts, flow diagrams, decision trees, decision tables, and other graphic representations. Using the loan capture scenario, a partial decision tree is shown in Figure 5.2. You can appreciate the logical flow of a decision tree and how easy it is to codify tacit knowledge based on graphical flow.

Knowing how experts know what they know is the bottom line in knowledge capture. Expert knowledge is cognitively complex and tacitly pragmatic. It is not always easy to capture through a traditional interview process. In many cases in

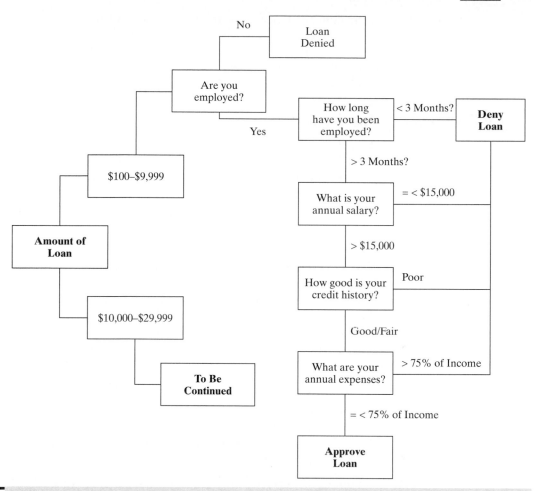

■ ■ ■ ■ ■ ■ ■ FIGURE 5.2:   Partial Decision Tree for a Loan Advisor

which knowledge capture was unsuccessful, the knowledge developer did not quite understand the pragmatic nature of the expertise. Just as the knowledge developer may not fully understand the expert, the expert may be equally unclear about the knowledge developer. Experts sometimes perceive knowledge developers as domain novices, who require patience and who must go through an apprenticeship process that takes them from novice to near-expert status during the building of the knowledge management system. This perception is even more reason for the knowledge developer to devote serious efforts toward preparation and a familiarity in the domain.

The following suggestions can be used to improve the knowledge capture process:

1. Knowledge developers should focus on how experts approach a problem. They must look beyond the facts or the heuristics.
2. Knowing that true expertise takes the form of chunked knowledge, knowledge developers should reevaluate how well they understand the problem domain and how accurately they are modeling it. Can they see patterns and relationships leading to a solution? That is, can the knowledge developer grasp the complexity

of the domain? Conceptual tools (discussed in Chapter 6) provide the developer with a concise, easy way to capture heuristics.

3. The quality of human emulation is best captured through episodic knowledge or knowledge based on previous experience. Therefore, a knowledge developer should elicit the expert's knowledge through concrete case situations or scenarios.

■ ■ ■ ■ Evaluating the Expert

Tacit knowledge capture requires free access to a cooperative and articulate expert. In most cases, the knowledge developer does not have the luxury of deciding on the expert. However, he or she must be able to identify real expertise and how well a particular expert's know-how suits the project (see Box 5.2).

Without a good match of expert and project, the knowledge developer could spend hours questioning someone whose knowledge might be unusable in the proposed system. There are several indicators of expertise:

- Peers regard the expert's decisions as good decisions. The expert commands *genuine respect.*
- Whenever a specific problem arises, people in the company *consult the expert.*
- The expert admits not knowing the answer to a problem. Honesty indicates *self-confidence* and a *realistic view of limitations.*
- The expert avoids information that is irrelevant to the domain and instead sticks to the facts and works with a *focus.*
- The expert demonstrates a *knack for explaining things* and can customize the presentation of information to the level of the individual listener.
- An expert's expertise is apparent to an informed listener. An expert exhibits a certain depth of detail and an *exceptional quality in explanations.*
- The expert is *not arrogant* about personal credentials, years of experience, or strong ties with people in power.

In addition, experts usually exhibit specific qualifications:

1. *Knows when to follow hunches and when to make exceptions.* This quality is a result of experience. Trial and error teaches an expert when to make exceptions

---

■ ■ ■ ■ ■ ■   BOX 5.2   ■ ■ ■ ■ ■ ■

CHARACTERISTICS OF AN AEROBIC FITNESS KM SYSTEM

The domain expert is the fitness program director. She is a certified aerobic and fitness instructor. She has her masters in sports fitness and has been working in this field for more than 10 years in health clubs and at university health centers. She also certifies the aerobic instructors in the city. She is quite energetic and excited about working with me as the "expert" in developing the aerobic fitness knowledge management system. Heather is committed to her career and enjoys helping others achieve fitness whenever she can.

SOURCE: Wakat, Heather. Interview by Mary Hill, knowledge developer of the aerobic fitness knowledge management system. University of Virginia, Spring 2000.

■ ■ ■ ■ ■ ■

and build the episodic memory. Unlike semantic memory, which is the knowledge of facts, episodic memory is the knowledge of cases based on experience. Case-based reasoning is effective in building complex KM systems.

2. *Sees the big picture.* Experts can sift through information and readily determine which factors are important and which are superfluous. In a study of radiologists reading X-rays, novices searched for particular features in the X-ray, looking for each feature's underlying causes. As the radiologists gained more experience, they began to realize that certain features were dependent on other features in the X-ray and learned that the context offered them cues. This process illustrates the complexity of true expertise.

3. *Possesses good communication skills.* A knowledge developer cannot create a reliable expert system if the expert cannot communicate his or her knowledge. Verbal skills facilitate smooth tacit knowledge capture.

4. *Tolerates stress.* Building KM systems can test an expert's patience, particularly when the knowledge developer asks the wrong question, the interview simply stagnates, or the domain is too difficult for the knowledge developer to understand.

5. *Thinks creatively.* An expert should demonstrate a certain inventiveness when solving a problem or explaining the reasoning behind a solution. Creative approaches can clarify the expert's thought processes and ability to convey knowledge to the knowledge developer.

6. *Exhibits self-confidence.* Experts believe in their ability to deliver. A self-confident expert can accept criticism and react without feeling threatened when an answer is not known. Self-confidence also boosts an expert's capacity to handle stress.

7. *Maintains credibility.* Experts who demonstrate competency in the way they field questions gain a reputation for believability based on the experience others have had with them.

8. *Operates within a schema-driven orientation.* The expert does serious schema-driven or structured, thinking in an effort to come up with realistic, workable solutions. (Two examples are provided in Box 5.3.)

9. *Uses chunked knowledge. Chunks* are groups of items stored and recalled as a unit. Several studies have shown that an individual's ability to recall information increases proportionately with the amount of chunking. For example, a study of

---

▪ ▪ ▪ ▪ ▪ ▪ **BOX 5.3** ▪ ▪ ▪ ▪ ▪ ▪

EXAMPLES OF SCHEMA-DRIVEN ORIENTATION

1. A graduate student was interviewing with a Big Six accounting firm for a position in information systems. One of the partners asked, "How many takeoffs and landings occur during a given day at O'Hare Airport?" The recruit snapped, "Fifteen per hour, on the basis of 4 minutes per flight." When later asked how the question should have been answered, the partner replied, "Well, there is no specific answer. The number of flights depends on the number of usable runways, the time of the day, weather conditions, ratio of international to national flights, and the like. For example, international flight takeoffs are heavier in early to late evening than during the day. Landings are heavier during mid- to late afternoons."

2. Two chess players were asked to recall moves of a game in progress. One player recalled the moves by attack and defense strategies; the other player recalled the moves by local position. The first player was the expert and showed evidence of higher-order processing than did the second player.

▪ ▪ ▪ ▪ ▪ ▪

master-level and novice chess players involved in copying board positions of games in progress showed that experts turned back to look at the board fewer times than did novice chess players. The experts took in larger chunks of the game than did the novices. Another study found that baseball experts tended to recall entire sequences of plays much more easily and accurately than did individuals with only surface knowledge of the game. A possible problem with chunking, however, is the difficulty many experts have in describing their knowledge — segmenting chunked knowledge and verbalizing it.

10. *Generates motivation and enthusiasm.* Enthusiastic experts who enjoy what they do generally perform well. Indifference and boredom contribute to poor motivation and endanger the project.

11. *Shares expertise willingly.* A "tight" expert will produce a less-than-complete tacit knowledge. The most effective experts have a volunteering nature and do not fear being eased out of their job.

12. *Emulates a good teacher's habits.* Most people remember one particular teacher because of the way that person delivered information. The best teachers are also good learners, and good learners make sure knowledge is transferred effectively. An effective expert "teaches" how to solve a problem realistically and achieve good results.

Obviously, no person can possibly possess all these attributes. Perhaps the most important ones are acknowledged expertise, the ability to commit a large amount of time, and a gift for communicating knowledge. In return, experts have to be pampered.

LEVELS OF EXPERTISE

The critical role of communication skills cannot be overemphasized. Various studies have shown that different levels of expertise influence communication quality. One can arbitrarily classify experts into three levels: the highly expert person, the moderately expert person, and the new expert.

Highly expert persons generally give concise explanations. They assume the listener has enough knowledge about the problem; therefore, they focus on the key steps, often skipping vital details. Highly expert persons also tend to rate their own expertise highly.

Moderately expert problem solvers may be more tentative in their explanations, but they tend to provide detailed explanations. They are quicker to give answers than the highly expert person and more often adapt their description to the level of the knowledge developer.

New experts are more likely to offer answers that are brief and fragmented, which suggests shallow knowledge of the domain. (See Box 5.4 for a description of characteristics and capabilities of an expert's knowledge.)

Based on the generalizations about the levels of expertise, one can conclude that the more expert the person is, the longer that person will take to communicate an answer. A highly expert person stores years of experience in long-term memory, which may take longer to recall and transform into a verbal response. The challenge for the knowledge developer then is to help the expert "unpack" or "dechunk" the knowledge accurately and quickly. Rechecking and cross-validating the expert's opinions are important steps to follow in the tacit knowledge capture process.

CAPTURING SINGLE VERSUS MULTIPLE EXPERTS' TACIT KNOWLEDGE

To ensure the reliability and quality of the KM system, a prime consideration is whether to tap one expert or a panel of experts. Based on the authors' experiences, this decision is based on several factors: the complexity of the problem, the criticality of the

▪ ▪ ▪ ▪ ▪ ▪   BOX 5.4   ▪ ▪ ▪ ▪ ▪ ▪

CHARACTERISTICS AND CAPABILITIES OF EXPERT KNOWLEDGE

Experts are distinguished by the quality and quantity of knowledge they possess; they know more, and what they know makes them more efficient and effective.

Expert knowledge, whether applied by human or machine, works in situations that do not admit optimal or provably correct solutions. Expert knowledge is used by problem solvers to find an acceptable solution that meets or exceeds requirements with a reasonable expenditure of resources.

Specifically, expert knowledge helps problem solvers improve their efficiency by marshalling relevant facts, avoiding common errors, making critical distinctions between problem types, pruning useless paths of investigation, ordering search, eliminating redundancy, reducing ambiguities, eliminating noise in data, exploiting knowledge from complementary disciplines, and analyzing problems from different perspectives or levels of abstraction.

SOURCE: Hayes-Roth, F., and Jacobstein, N. "The State of Knowledge-Based Systems," *Communications of the ACM*, March 1994, p. 28.

▪ ▪ ▪ ▪ ▪ ▪

project to the organization, the types of experts available, and the funds allocated for building the KM system. Each alternative has advantages and limitations.

ADVANTAGES AND DRAWBACKS OF USING A SINGLE EXPERT

There are several advantages to working with a single expert:

1. *A single expert is ideal when building a simple KM system—one with few rules.* A one-on-one interactive relationship between a single knowledge developer and a single expert promotes close ties quickly and speeds the knowledge capture process.
2. *A problem in a restricted domain calls for a single expert.* For example, David Smith, General Electric's locomotive expert, knew the problems of diesel engines and how to best repair them. His expertise made him the best choice for solving a particularly difficult problem in a restricted domain.
3. *A single expert facilitates the logistics aspect of coordinating arrangements for knowledge capture.* Once an expert agrees to do the work, one can more easily arrange meeting times and schedules than if multiple experts are involved. Prototyping also moves quickly, because only one expert needs to review the work and vouch for its readiness.
4. *With a single expert, problem-related or personal conflicts are easier to resolve.* Communications are usually easier, and the approach to knowledge capture is more consistent when only one expert is involved.
5. *Single experts tend to share more confidentiality with project-related information than do multiple experts.* Part of human nature is sharing information: As more people are party to a session, more opportunities arise for that information to leak. Of course, much depends on both the nature of the project and the standards and integrity of the experts.

As attractive as the single expert approach is, several drawbacks are worth keeping in mind:

1. *Sometimes the expert's knowledge is not easy to capture.* If the expert has difficulty explaining or communicating procedures, the project can die quickly, especially if no backup expertise is available.

2. *Single experts provide a single line of reasoning, which makes it difficult to evoke in-depth discussion of the domain.* If someone sees a doctor and learns that he or she has a serious disease, that person would certainly appreciate a second opinion. Multiple experts are more likely to provide a built-in system of checks and balances (see Box 5.5).

3. *Single experts are more likely to change scheduled meetings than experts who are part of a team.* Unfortunately, people who make the best experts are often the least accessible. Other projects may limit an expert's commitment to a new one. As a result, a reasonable deadline for completing the project may be uncertain.

4. *Expert knowledge is sometimes dispersed.* Relying on a single expert, especially in a complex system, can either create blind spots or result in a system that will have no users. Consider, for example, the area of medicine, in which personnel are trained separately for radiology, gynecology, and internal medicine. Most medical KM systems need to draw upon community knowledge bases and integrate expertise from different areas to be successful. No single expert can realistically address more than one area.

PROS AND CONS OF USING MULTIPLE EXPERTS

Capturing the tacit knowledge of a team of experts has its own advantages and drawbacks. The advantages include the following:

1. Complex problem domains benefit from the expertise of more than one expert, especially if knowledge is dispersed and a number of "partial" experts are available. A pool of experts is most often needed to capture sufficient reliable knowledge to build complex KM systems. For example, building a KM system to predict the next direction of a given stock on the New York Stock Exchange requires the talent of a pool of highly seasoned traders. No single trader could supply a reliable answer to all aspects of this problem.

2. Working with multiple experts stimulates interaction that often produces synthesis of experience. Bringing in a number of experts is bound to enrich the quality of knowledge captured.

3. Listening to a variety of views allows the knowledge developer to consider alternative ways of representing the knowledge. Two heads are usually better than one, provided they agree to work together toward the goals of the project.

4. Formal meetings are frequently a better environment for generating thoughtful contributions.

Possible drawbacks of multiple experts are as follows:

1. *Coordinating meeting schedules for three or more experts can be a challenge.* Because an expert is usually in demand, each expert on a team will probably have to compromise in order for group meetings to be arranged. This area is the one in which interpersonal abilities of the knowledge developer can make or break the project.

2. *Disagreements frequently occur among experts.* The greater the number of experts on a panel who must agree on a procedure or a solution, the higher the probability of disagreement. If the diversity of opinions does not resolve into a

▪▪▪▪▪▪   BOX 5.5   ▪▪▪▪▪▪

THE ADMISSIONS KM SYSTEM

One person was selected as the domain expert for an admissions KM system. The expert is a practicing admissions director of a major university. She was chosen because she is the sole decision maker in the admissions selection process. Plus, the process is unique, making other experts' knowledge invalid for this specific problem domain. The expert also showed enthusiasm for the project and willingness to commit her time and expertise.

Throughout the knowledge capture process, the director was extremely cooperative. She had excellent communication skills and conveyed information in a clear and descriptive manner. Throughout the project, she remained interested

and enthusiastic. This allowed the knowledge developer to conduct efficient and meaningful interview sessions.

The expert was very patient with the continuing questioning. As a by-product of this work, she has become interested in KM systems as a mechanism for training new personnel in the admissions process. Despite her cooperation, however, some problems came up particular to the use of a single expert. One difficulty was bias. The knowledge base will only reflect inputs from her. Without a secondary source of expertise, the expert is both the supplier of knowledge and final authority who validates the KM system.

▪▪▪▪▪▪

consensus, the success of the project could be in jeopardy. Disparity among the experts can also cause the least-senior expert to stifle, edit, or compromise an opinion. The knowledge developer must be sensitive to this issue (see Box 5.6).

3. *The greater the number of people involved, the harder it may be to retain confidentiality.* As mentioned earlier, both the individuals involved and the nature of the problem domain determine the level of confidentiality needed.

▪▪▪▪▪▪   BOX 5.6   ▪▪▪▪▪▪

MULTIPLE EXPERT AGGREGATIONS

In tacit knowledge capture, it is often desirable to aggregate the judgment of multiple experts into a single KM system. In some cases, this takes the form of averaging the judgment of those experts. In these situations, it is desirable to determine if the experts have different views of the world before their individual judgments are aggregated. In validation, multiple experts often are employed to compare the performance of expert systems and other human actors. Often those judgments

are then averaged to establish performance quality of the KM system. An important part of the comparison process should be determining if the experts have a similar view of the world. If they do not, their evaluations of performance may differ, resulting in a meaningless average performance measure. Alternatively, if all the validating experts do have similar views, then the validation process may result in a paradigm myopia.

SOURCE: Awad, E. M. *Building Expert Systems.* Minneapolis, MN: West Publishing, 1996, p. 168.

▪▪▪▪▪▪

TABLE 5.1 Advantages and Drawbacks of Using Single and Multiple Experts	
Single Expert	*Multiple Experts*
Advantages	*Advantages*
1. Ideal for building a simple domain KM system	1. Works best for complex problem domains
2. Works well for problems in a restricted domain	2. Stimulates interaction and synthesis of experience
3. Simplifies logistical issues	3. Presents a variety of views allowing for alternative representations of tacit knowledge
4. Increases the probability of resolving conflicts	4. Generates more thoughtful contributions
5. Decreases risks to confidentiality	
Disadvantages	*Disadvantages*
1. Not easy to capture an expert's tacit knowledge	1. Creates scheduling difficulties
2. Provides only a single line of reasoning	2. Increases the probability of disagreement
3. Increases the chance of schedule changes	3. Raises confidentiality issues
4. Does not accommodate dispersed knowledge	4. Requires more than one knowledge developer
	5. Leads to a "process loss" in determining a solution

4. *Working with multiple experts often requires more than one knowledge developer.* With two interviewers, one can maintain the topic agenda and the recording while the other asks questions and gives feedback to promote discussion or clarify points. Because committing two knowledge developers to a single job can be costly and time-consuming, this practice is usually reserved for complex, priority projects.

5. *The overlapping mental processes of multiple experts can lead to a "process loss."* When two or more experts get together, the nature of the discussion tends to overlap, and the problem-solving process can be colored by other experts' opinions. Sometimes, determining which expert is the closest to the solution is difficult.

A summary of the pros and cons of single and multiple experts is shown in Table 5.1.

■ ■ ■ ■ Developing a Relationship with Experts

CREATING THE RIGHT IMPRESSION

Working with experts can be a complicated business. Perception plays an important role in the early phase of the building process. For example, how does the knowledge developer know whether an expert—whose knowledge is sought, but is not paid for—will cooperate fully and reliably? From the expert's view, the knowledge developer is building a KM system in an area about which she or he knows little. The expert often has a poor perception of what the knowledge developer can do. To reverse this perception, the knowledge developer must learn quickly and use psychology, common sense, marketing, and technical skills to gain the expert's attention and respect.

Related to this point is underestimating the expert's experience. A seasoned expert will explain things simply and clearly. This simplicity can be deceptive, however, and create a false impression that the problem is easy to solve when in reality the expert has barely scratched the surface. To quote Ed Koch, former mayor of New York City, "For every complex problem, there is a solution which is simple, economical, and wrong." For every simple thing the expert says, the details behind it are likely to be more complex. A knowledge developer must keep exploring until the details are understood.

UNDERSTANDING THE EXPERT'S STYLE

Experts express their views in a variety of ways that require special understanding. Knowledge developers should acclimate themselves to the expert's style during the first session. Experts generally use one of four styles of expression:

1. The *procedure type* of expert is verbal, logical, and procedure-oriented. This expert shows a methodical approach to the solution, with emphasis on structure, sometimes at the sacrifice of content. The knowledge developer does not have to encourage the expert to talk but should focus the expert's explanations on the problem at hand, staying within the guidelines of the problem domain. Otherwise, most of the knowledge developer's energy will go toward making sense out of the expert's details.

2. The *storyteller type* of expert focuses on the content of the domain at the expense of the solution. This expressive expert probably came up through the ranks and received little attention or recognition. Such a person is usually willing to repeat a story or a description, but will often go off on a tangent, wander from one aspect of the domain to the next, or bounce between topics without noticing. The knowledge developer must use structured interviews with this type of expert.

3. The *godfather type* of expert, by nature of position and personality, has a compulsion to take over. If allowed, this expert will wrest control from the knowledge developer. No single prescription works every time for this situation, which will often worsen if the knowledge developer attempts to right the balance of power in the wrong way. In fact, the worst scenario occurs when a godfather expert is paired with a manipulative knowledge developer.

4. The *salesperson type* of expert spends most of the knowledge developer's time "dancing" around the topic, explaining why the expert's solution is the best. The knowledge developer can become distracted by this expert's habit of answering a question with another question. The knowledge developer's role is to redirect the conversation and encourage straight answers.

PREPARING FOR THE SESSION

It should be obvious that before making the first appointment, the knowledge developer should know something about both the expert (such as personality, temperament, job experience, and familiarity with the problem) and the problem.

The initial sessions can be the most challenging and the most critical. Not knowing what to expect, the expert may become protective when the knowledge developer begins to "peel" information from the expert's memory. The expert may resent any aggressive prodding. The burden of building trust falls on the knowledge developer, because the responsibility of building the KM system also lies with the knowledge developer, not the expert.

The knowledge developer should become familiar with the project terminology and review existing material, such as a paper written by the expert or a book that details the nature and makeup of the domain. This type of research is also a way to learn the expert's language. Can you imagine building a real estate KM system without knowing terms like *prime rate, variable interest rate,* or *balloon mortgage?* An early grasp of the basics inspires confidence on the part of the expert and allows the knowledge developer and expert to be more productive.

An important beginning step in the first session is personal introductions. The expert is eager to know what type of person the knowledge developer is and what the goals are for the project. The sooner rapport is established, the easier things will move. Honesty is important. The expert and the knowledge developer need to understand each other's experience related to the problem at hand. Humility avoids a situation in which constant questions may appear arrogant.

DECIDING WHERE TO HOLD THE SESSIONS

Location is a matter of preference, but protocol calls for the expert to decide on the meeting site. Because a series of sessions take place over an extended time period, most experts opt for the convenience of meeting on their own turf. The knowledge developer may also find benefit in recording the expert's knowledge in the environment where he or she works. An expert may feel more comfortable in having any necessary tools or information within arm's reach. Moreover, the knowledge developer's willingness to travel to meet with the expert should generate goodwill for the project. An important guideline is to make sure the meeting place is quiet and free of interruptions, such as phones ringing or "urgent" messages.

APPROACHING MULTIPLE EXPERTS

One of the challenges in tacit knowledge capture among multiple experts is deciding the appropriate approach. Three approaches are most often used.

The Individual Approach

The knowledge developer holds sessions with one expert at a time, making it easier for the expert to offer information freely while assuring privacy. The individual approach is also useful in clarifying knowledge or defusing interpersonal problems that crop up when several experts are gathered in one room.

The Approach Using Primary and Secondary Experts

The knowledge developer may decide to hold a session with the senior expert early in the knowledge capture program for clarification of the plan. For a detailed probing of the domain's mechanics, he or she may tap other experts' knowledge. In this approach, the primary expert verifies solutions in the event of diverse responses or conflicting opinions of secondary experts.

Another way of working with primary and secondary experts is to gather information from the secondary experts first and then consult the primary expert to check the reliability of the tapped knowledge. This bottom-up approach is useful when the primary expert is in demand and cannot devote full-time to the project. The primary expert's energies can be saved for the crucial steps as needed.

The Small Groups Approach

Experts are gathered in one place to discuss the problem domain and provide a pool of information. Their responses are monitored at the same time, and the functionality of each expert is tested against the expertise of others in the group. The knowledge developer can decide which expert is more cooperative or more believable. This approach requires experience in assessing tapped knowledge, as well as perception and cognition skills.

One of the issues that the knowledge developer must deal with is power and its effect on the expert's opinions. For instance, how does a "junior" expert openly contradict the senior expert? Protocol may well require the junior expert to let comments go uncontested, which defeats the purpose of having experts share their knowledge.

It should be noted that group performance is closely related to group size. As the size of a group increases arithmetically, one can expect a geometric increase in the total number of relationships. Using the formula $n(2^n/2 + n - 1)$, for a group size of $n = 3$, the total number of relationships is equal to 18. When group size is increased to $n = 4$, the total number of relationships increases to 44. For this reason, the number of experts must be limited to the knowledge developer's capacity to handle the additional interaction and feedback. An increase in group size may also bring out group conflict rather than ready consensus.

▪ ▪ ▪ ▪ Fuzzy Reasoning and the Quality of Knowledge Capture

People reason with words, not numbers, which can lead to a problem commonly encountered in interviewing: Experts are not always easy to understand. Because the problem domain is likely to be technical or complex, decision making often involves rules with many shades of meaning that may be fuzzy to the nonexpert. For example, one can easily understand the following simple rule:

> *In the United States, if you are under 60 years of age, you are not entitled to social security benefits.*

A retirement benefit rule might be more complex, although still understandable. For example:

> *If you are at least 60 years old and have been a state employee for at least 25 years or at least 62 years of age and have worked full-time for more than 5 contiguous years, then you are entitled to collect social security benefits provided you are not handicapped or you are not receiving a salaried income greater than $10,000 or collecting unemployment compensation from a state agency.*

People use IF . . . THEN statements in conversations, but problems that require expertise are not always straightforward, and the solutions cannot be stated in simple IF . . . THEN rules. The words used to express solutions may also have many meanings. For example, consider the word *warm* and the criteria used to characterize weather as warm. The meaning of *warm* depends on the time of year, temperature, and location. What is warm to a person from the mid-Atlantic coast can be judged as hot by someone from the North or even called chilly by someone from the Deep South. Furthermore, a day that is warm in winter can be colder than a day labeled as cold in the summer. Because no definite rules distinguish what is cold and what is hot, this range of temperature can be described as fuzzy.

Take another example. When an expert comments, "The procedure I just explained works most of the time," what does he or she mean by "most"? Is it any number of times over 50 percent? Is it about 75 percent or perhaps more?

Here is a third example. Suppose a heart surgeon said,

> *I don't expect heart trouble in a 20-year-old patient. The occurrence is so rare I would say it is nil. It isn't worth subjecting a person that young to a rigorous heart stress test. Patients that young, I most likely won't do the tests; older patients I'd probably consider it.*

Try pressing the surgeon to explain this statement and see how far you get. Because the English language does not always distinguish clearly between words or the meaning of certain words, the interpretation of words often depends on their context. This fuzziness increases the difficulty of translating what the expert has said into rules that make sense.

ANALOGIES AND UNCERTAINTIES IN INFORMATION

When experts explain events, they use analogies—comparing a problem to a similar one encountered in a different setting months or years ago—to make a judgment. For example, a professor, after listening to a student in a new course, might say,

> *This student reminds me of a student I had in the same course last year. She did great work. Most probably this one will do just as well.*

This pattern matching is another fuzzy comparison that must be clarified before the information acquired can be usable. A knowledge developer who runs into this line of reasoning must learn more about the expert's examples and pay attention to how the expert forms analogies, or pattern matching.

In addition to analogy problems, a knowledge developer may also encounter uncertainties in information. An expert's knowledge or expertise is the ability to take uncertain information and use a plausible line of reasoning to clarify the fuzzy details. One aspect of uncertainty is belief. Belief describes the level of credibility. People generally use all kinds of words to express belief; these words are usually paired with qualifiers such as *very, highly,* or *extremely.* For example, words such as *possible, likely,* and *definite* show relationships between words that express belief. To handle uncertainty expressed in words, the knowledge developer must draw out such relationships during tacit knowledge capture.

UNDERSTANDING EXPERIENCE

Knowledge developers can benefit immensely from an educational grounding in cognitive psychology. The human expert usually follows the same basic reasoning principles as a computing system. To solve a problem, the expert acquires information from the outside world and stores it in the brain. When a question is asked, the expert operates on certain stored information through inductive, deductive, or other problem-solving methods. The resulting answer is the culmination of processing stored information.

When knowledge developers ask an expert how he or she arrived at an answer, they are asking the expert to relive an experience. The right question will evoke the memory of experiences that previously produced good solutions. How quickly the expert responds to a question depends on the clarity of the content, whether the content was recently used, and how well the expert understood the question.

Visual imagery is often represented by phrases the expert uses in a descriptive answer. For example, "something tells me," "sounds O.K. to me," "I heard that," "hmm, let me see—one more time," and "the manual illustrated" are phrases that show the expert is mentally reacting to an image. When the expert uses this type of phrase, the knowledge developer should ask, "When you say something tells you, what do you mean or what do you see?" or "Why did you say it sounds O.K. to you?"

At times, the expert's emotions are involved in the problem-solving process. For example, phrases like "I have a feeling," "my gut feeling is," and "my sixth sense tells me" serve as the conscious representation of sensory memories that have gone dormant for lack of use. The knowledge developer can clarify the content behind these phrases by asking, "How would you describe this feeling?" or "What makes you feel this way?"

People who have difficulty with visual imagery usually have trouble answering questions. When the knowledge developer does not understand an explanation, he or she should ask the expert to go through it again and pay closer attention to the content of the answer as well as any clues to visual imagery. A knowledge developer may need to step back to better understand how the expert thinks through a problem. As a knowledge capture tool, interviewing allows repeated questioning for knowledge capture and verification. Interviewing principles are explained later in the chapter.

THE LANGUAGE PROBLEM

The main concern during knowledge capture is to be able to understand and interpret the expert's verbal description of information, heuristics, and so on. Repeated questioning often clarifies and promotes complete answers. But how well experts represent internal processes varies with their command of the language and the knowledge developer's interviewing skills. For example, take a look at the preceding sentence and review the structure of the sentence: "How well" (how well who? What?), "experts represent" (do they present? Summarize?), "internal processes" (what internal processes? What does it mean?). The sentence was written to convey an idea in words whose meanings the writer hopes the reader understands.

Language may be unclear in a number of ways:

- *Comparative words such as* taller *or* better *sometimes are left hanging.* For example, the expert might say, "This last solution works better for what you're looking for." The question is, better than what? The comparison requires clarification. The knowledge developer might ask, "Better than what?" or "Can you elaborate on that comparison?" or "I don't understand what you mean by *better.*"
- *Certain words or components may be left out of an explanation.* Experts sometimes think that certain things are so obvious that they do not need to spoon-feed every detail. A knowledge developer who is not as familiar with the domain as the expert assumes may be lost without these details. The knowledge developer must ask the expert to clarify and to elaborate. If the expert comments, "To me, that is the key point," the knowledge developer might reply "*That* refers to . . . ?" or "What makes it a key point?" or "How do you know it is the key?"
- *Absolute words and phrases may be used loosely.* For example, be wary when you hear "always," "never," "cannot," or "no way." The expert might say, "This approach will never give you the right combination," "There is no way I can explain this procedure in 1 hour," "Your suggestion will never work," or "This procedure cannot be applied." The knowledge developer might probe by asking, "How does this approach make that combination impossible?" "Can you imagine a situation where it might not clear things up?" "Then, can you briefly explain the procedure?" or "What do you mean this procedure cannot be applied?" These questions will gently push the expert to reconsider.
- *Some words seem to have a built-in ambiguity.* For example, "The titanium shield of the missile performs a protective function during reentry." The question here is "What is a protective function?" or "protective in reference to what?" The knowledge developer should either rephrase the question or ask for further clarification.

The main goal of pointing out these ambiguities is to warn the knowledge developer to be alert to meanings as well as to verbal and nonverbal cues. The success of the subsequent steps in building a KM system is dependent on accurate knowledge capture.

■■■■ The Interview As a Tool

The interview is a tool that is used commonly in the early stages of tacit knowledge capture. It is the oldest and most often used (and abused) tool for capturing or verifying tacit knowledge. Because the knowledge captured through an interview is so important to KM system development, validity is a critical issue. Validity of a given question means that it is logically correct and is understood the same way by different people. It also provides consistency in the way questions are asked. The knowledge developer needs to make special efforts to eliminate interviewer bias that would reduce validity. Often the validity of information is more reliable if it is freely given. For this reason, the voluntary nature of the interview is important; it should be a relationship freely and willingly entered into by the expert. If the interview and participation in the knowledge capture process are requirements, the expert might be giving information with no assurance of accuracy or reliability, which is the measure of truthfulness or credibility.

In an interview, the knowledge developer has an opportunity to verify information and observe the expert's thought process in action. A major benefit of interviewing is behavioral analysis. The expert is asked to act out a case or a scenario in the domain. While the expert goes through the motions, the knowledge developer records the observations and assesses body language, facial movements, and other communication cues. A knowledge developer who is ill trained can create or fail to eliminate problems with the resulting knowledge base.

The interview as a tacit knowledge capture tool has four primary advantages:

1. Its flexibility makes it a superior tool for *exploring areas* about which not much is known concerning what questions to ask or how to formulate questions.
2. It offers a better opportunity than any other tool for *evaluating the validity* of information acquired. The knowledge developer cannot only hear what is said but also how it is said.
3. It is an effective technique for *eliciting information* about complex subjects and for probing an individual's sentiments underlying expressed opinions.
4. Many *people enjoy being interviewed,* regardless of the subject. They usually cooperate when all they have to do is talk.

The major drawback to interviewing, however, is the cost involved in extensive preparation time. Interviews also take a lot of time to conduct. Whenever a more economical way of capturing the same knowledge is available, the interview is generally not used.

Even though interviewing experts is an art learned at school, most knowledge developers develop expertise through experience. Knowledge developers need to pay attention to the primary requirements for a successful interview: the development of a sound, structured strategy and the creation of a friendly, nonthreatening atmosphere that puts the expert at ease. An experienced interviewer elicits credible answers that the expert can offer with no fear of criticism.

TYPES OF INTERVIEWS

Interviews vary widely in form and structure. From a knowledge capture perspective, interviews range from the highly unstructured (neither the questions nor their responses are specified in advance) to the highly structured (the questions and responses are definitive). Of course, a great deal of variation is possible within this range.

The unstructured interview is used when the knowledge developer wants to explore an issue. It allows experts to answer spontaneous questions openly (see Figure 5.3). Unstructured techniques are not easy to conduct, and this kind of interview is difficult to plan. An expert may interpret the lack of structure as permission to avoid preparing for an interview.

The structured interview is used when the knowledge developer wants specific information. It is goal-oriented. In multiple expert knowledge capture, the questions should be presented with the same wording and in the same order to each expert. For example, the question to one expert, "Would you like to see a prototype of what you gave me during the last session?" will not elicit the same response as asking, "How do you feel about showing the material you gave me during the last session in the format of a prototype?" Standardized questions can improve the validity of the responses by ensuring that all experts are responding to the same question.

A structured question is expressed as a set of alternatives. Several variations of structured questions can be used:

1. **Multiple-choice questions** offer specific choices, faster tabulation, and less bias due to the way the answers are ordered. Because most people have a tendency to favor the first choice item, alternating the order of the choices may reduce bias; however, additional time is needed to pick the choice item question (see Figure 5.4).
2. **Dichotomous (yes/no) questions** are a special type of multiple-choice question. They offer two answers (see Figure 5.5). The sequence of questions and content is also important.
3. **Ranking scale questions** ask the expert to arrange items in a list in order of their importance or preference. In Figure 5.6, the question asks the expert to rank five statements on the basis of how descriptive the statement is of the expert's current job.

Finally, with the semistructured technique, the knowledge developer asks predefined questions but allows the expert some freedom in expressing the answers. Here is a dialogue from the Diabetic Foot KM System:

Knowledge developer: What would be your first question to the patient?
Diabetic specialist: Where is the pain?

▪ ▪ ▪ ▪ ▪ ▪ ▪ **FIGURE 5.3:**   Examples of Unstructured (Open-Ended) Questions

From a Publisher KM System:
- Suppose you have the manuscript ready for production. What does the author do between then and the final binding of the book?

From a Diabetic Foot KM System:
- How can you tell if a diabetic patient has charcot?

From a Loan Approval KM System:
- How do you deal with excessive bad loans after a grace period?

From Auto Loan KM System:

- If the customer made a final offer within $100 from your minimum to sell a $10,000 car, what do you do next?
  - ____ Talk the matter over with the sales manager
  - ____ Split the difference with the customer
  - ____ Walk away from the deal
  - ____ Throw in amenities

From Diabetic Foot Knowledge Automation System:

- If a diabetic patient complains about foot problems, who should he or she see first?
  - ____ Podiatrist
  - ____ General practitioner
  - ____ Orthopedic surgeon
  - ____ Physical therapist

From Loan Evaluator KM System:

- Which type of loan brings the highest revenue to your bank?
  - ____ Auto loan
  - ____ Personal loan
  - ____ Mortgage loan
  - ____ Collateral loan

■ ■ ■ ■ ■ ■ ■ **FIGURE 5.4:** Examples of Multiple-Choice Questions

From Publisher KM System:

- Does your book contract prohibit you from publishing on the same subject with another publisher?
  - ____ Yes ____ No

From Real Estate KM System:

- Does the seller or the buyer pay your commission?
  - ____ Seller ____Buyer

From Diabetic Foot KM System:

- Do patients with neuropathy come for regular checkups?
  - ____ Yes ____ No

■ ■ ■ ■ ■ ■ ■ **FIGURE 5.5:** Examples of Dichotomous Questions

■ ■ ■ ■ ■ ■ ■ **FIGURE 5.6:** An Example of a Ranking Scale Question

Please rank the five statements in each group on the basis of how well they describe your job as a loan officer. Give a ranking of "1" to the statement that best describes your job; give a ranking of "2" to the statement that provides the next best description. Continue to rank all five statements, using a "5" for the statement that describes your job least well.

In my job, I

____ Decide on auto loans over $10,000

____ Review each application before authorizing credit checks

____ Interview loan applicants as they come in

____ Cosign all checks sent to local auto dealers

____ Work with local auto dealers to attract more loans

| *Knowledge developer:* | What possible answers do you expect? |
| *Diabetic specialist:* | Ankle, big toe, from kneecap to ankle, or "I'm not sure." |

| *Knowledge developer:* | Suppose the answer is "big toe." What do you do next? |
| *Diabetic specialist:* | I'd look for coloration, swelling, and possible curving of the toe. |

| *Knowledge developer:* | What would be your next question? |

The process continues until the knowledge developer has no more questions to ask. The advantage over the unstructured technique is that the information is well structured and the information solicited is reasonably clear. A disadvantage is that this information may not be complete in other possible ways.

▪ ▪ ▪ ▪ Guide to a Successful Interview

Interviewing should be approached as logically as programming. In tacit knowledge capture using the interview, several steps are considered:

1. Setting the stage and establishing rapport
2. Phrasing questions
3. Listening closely and avoiding arguments
4. Evaluating session outcomes

SETTING THE STAGE AND ESTABLISHING RAPPORT

This first step is an ice-breaking, relaxed, informal exchange. The knowledge developer opens the session by focusing on the purpose of the meeting, the role of the expert, and the agenda for review. During stage setting, the knowledge developer closely observes how the expert cooperates. Both the content and tone of the expert's responses are evaluated. How well the interview goes depends on the knowledge developer's ability to adapt to the expert's style. An expert may be the *friendly* type, who makes everyone involved feel the process will be easy teamwork; the *timid* type, who needs to be coaxed to talk; or the *resident expert* type, who bombards the knowledge developer with opinions disguised as facts.

In one respect, tacit knowledge capture is time-consuming and an intrusion into the expert's privacy. Even when the procedure has management support and the expert is on the company's payroll, the process is still lengthy and taxing. The expert may anticipate some harm from the KM system being developed. It is important to establish rapport with the expert at the beginning and maintain that rapport throughout the knowledge capture process. Although setting the stage has no hard and fast rules to follow, the knowledge developer needs to keep in mind certain guiding factors:

1. *Honesty: Do not deliberately mislead the expert about the purpose of the project.* A careful, well-thought-out briefing should provide honest details regarding the purpose of the project. The briefing should be consistent when dealing with more than one expert.
2. *Confidentiality: Assure the expert that no information offered will be shared with unauthorized personnel.* The sole purpose of the session is to build a KM system in line with the expert's thinking rather than to disclose specific information to other experts or to upper management.
3. *Modesty: Avoid showing off knowledge or revealing information from other experts.* Such action can color the objectivity of the approach and discourage the expert from freely giving information.

4. *Efficiency: Respect the time schedule or commitments of the expert.* The session should not be an extended social event. The expert may not complain, but other people who need the expert might.

5. *Professionalism: Proper dress and demeanor are important.* For example, a conservative gray suit is appropriate attire when you are interviewing a banking expert. A casual outfit may be passable when you are interviewing on the assembly line. If the session takes place in the expert's environment, the knowledge developer should be a courteous guest.

6. *Respect: Be courteous and a good listener.* More than any other advice, respect for the expert is a must. Interrupting the expert can alter the thought process or break the expert's train of thought.

PHRASING THE QUESTIONS

Except in unstructured interviews, each question should be asked in the same order as it appears on the interview schedule. Altering the sequence could affect the comparability of the sessions with the experts. In structuring questions for the expert, the knowledge developer needs to consider the level and sequencing of the questions. A question may be primary or secondary. A primary question is usually a lead question that paves the way for more detailed questions. For example, in the Diabetic Foot KM System, a primary question is "What is the first thing you do when a diabetic patient comes to you with a swollen ankle?" It leads to a series of questions concerning whether to advise the diabetic person to seek self-help, medical treatment, or surgery.

A secondary question usually probes for more details. For example, "So, you find a blister just under the ankle. What does it mean in terms of procedures or treatment of the swelling?" This is a secondary question, because the question asks for more information about the primary question—a swollen ankle. Using secondary questions helps the knowledge developer probe deeper for clarity of details.

Question sequencing determines whether the interview begins with general open-ended questions followed by secondary questions and closed questions, or vice versa. Either approach has benefits and drawbacks. The open-to-closed question sequence helps establish rapport and enables the knowledge developer to assess the quality of the response before asking more focused questions. This assessment often results in discarding unnecessary questions due to redundancy or overlap [see Figure 5.7(a)].

When using the closed-to-open sequence, the knowledge developer begins with a set of well-focused questions, lending a more formal tone to the session. It also allows the knowledge developer to use open-ended questions to end the interview. This approach requires substantial advance preparation [see Figure 5.7(b)].

QUESTION CONSTRUCTION

Regardless of question type, a question must be valid enough to elicit a reliable response. The knowledge developer must focus on question content, wording, and format. Here is a summary checklist:

1. Question content
   a. Is the question necessary? Is it a part of other questions?
   b. Does the question adequately cover the intended area?
   c. Does the expert(s) have proper information to answer the question?
   d. Is the question biased in a given direction?
   e. Is the question likely to generate emotional feelings that might color responses?

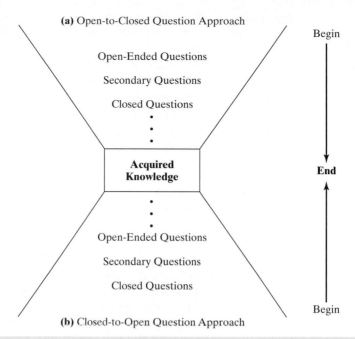

(a) Open-to-Closed Question Approach

Open-Ended Questions

Secondary Questions

Closed Questions

Acquired
Knowledge

Open-Ended Questions

Secondary Questions

Closed Questions

(b) Closed-to-Open Question Approach

Begin

End

Begin

▪ ▪ ▪ ▪ ▪ ▪ ▪ **FIGURE 5.7:**   Sequencing of Open-Ended and Closed Questions

2. Question wording

    a. Is the question worded to suit the expert's background and expertise?
    b. Can the question be misinterpreted? What else could it mean?
    c. Is the frame of reference uniform for all experts?
    d. Is the wording biased toward a specific answer?
    e. How clear and direct is the question?

3. Question format

    a. Can the question be framed in the form of multiple choices (answered by a word or two or by a number) or with a follow-up free answer?
    b. Is the response form easy to use and adequate for the job?
    c. Is the answer to the question likely to be influenced by the preceding question? That is, is it subject to a *contamination effect*?

THINGS TO AVOID

One of the dangers of interviewing is generalizing conclusions on the basis of a few sessions. Transcribing notes into rules often results in verification problems that arise later during the testing of the KM system. Experts are often annoyed when they keep repeating the same rules or procedure or keep repeating the same information. The alternative to note taking is taping the session. The main drawback of this technique is the time it takes to play back the tape. Videotaping is not recommended, because few experts are comfortable in front of a camera. In either case, a knowledge developer should practice with the equipment prior to the session to become familiar with it and to make sure everything is working properly.

An important guideline for a knowledge developer is not to aggressively debate or interrupt the expert's discussions or convert the interview into an interrogation.

Inconsistency should be pointed out in an unobtrusive way. A knowledge developer should also avoid asking questions that put the domain expert on the defensive. For example, a knowledge developer who realizes the expert is being inconsistent should say, "How would this solution relate to an earlier one about the same problem?" rather than "Based on the earlier solution I have here in my notes, this solution doesn't make sense."

Using technical terms such as *data mining systems* or *KM infrastructure* often results in an unfavorable response; it can also put the developer in a defensive position in having to explain the technology or system. Explanations such as "This is more like a system project," "It's a system that captures knowledge offered by people with experience like yourself," or "It's a special system application that uses the expert's knowledge to give the user something to work with to arrive at the same solution" are better alternatives.

A knowledge developer's command of the session is critical to a successful interview. A loss of control is a sign of overaccommodation, an overbearing expert, or poor preparation for the session. Distributing an agenda in advance, keeping the discussion on the topic, summarizing the expert's comments when appropriate, and limiting the interview to a reasonable time period should help control the session.

Being in control also means that a knowledge developer should avoid getting frustrated over ambiguous answers when they are least expected. For example, a cool head is needed when an expert answers, "Because that's the way it works—I don't know why, but it works all the time." Explaining how some things work is often more difficult than one might imagine. The knowledge developer should avoid excessive interpretation of the expert's answers.

The converse, of course, is pretending to understand something. The knowledge developer needs to recapitulate what he or she understands, thereby reinforcing the expert. However, starting from scratch is frustrating for everyone. The expert can help only by knowing exactly where the knowledge developer got lost. One helpful practice for keeping everyone on track is to draw pictures to illustrate a point or a procedure, especially if the expert is a developer or a database designer.

In addition to honesty about understanding the expert's information, the knowledge developer should avoid promising something that cannot or should not be delivered. For example, during the first session, a knowledge developer should not say, "A couple of sessions and we should be beyond the halfway mark" if the project is obviously going to take several more sessions. As an alternative response, "I don't know how many sessions we need, but chances are it will be several sessions before we can wrap things up," is much better. Figure 5.8 summarizes the things to avoid in a knowledge capture interview.

RELIABILITY OF INFORMATION FROM EXPERTS

The knowledge captured from the expert is presumed to correspond accurately to the actual way solutions are produced in the domain. However, several uncontrolled sources of error may reduce the information's reliability:

1. *The expert's perceptual slant.* Perceptual abilities vary; the reports of a single event given by several experts often have little resemblance to one another.
2. *The expert's failure to remember just what happened.* As time passes, the exact details of an event generally become more difficult to describe.
3. *An expert's fear of the unknown.* Experts often distort descriptions of events for fear that the KM system will replace him or her. These distortions defeat the purpose of knowledge capture that is based on mutual trust.
4. *Communication problems.* Some experts have difficulty communicating their knowledge. In a related vein, the knowledge developer is sometimes unable to

1. Never aggressively debate or interrupt the expert's interpretations or opinions.
2. Avoid asking questions that put the expert on the defensive.
3. Stay away from using technical or special terms just to show off.
4. Try to be specific, rather than general.
5. Avoid losing control of the session.
6. Avoid getting frustrated over ambiguous answers.
7. Avoid bringing up items or details that are not on the agenda.
8. Avoid pretending to understand something.
9. Avoid promising something that cannot or should not be delivered.

▪ ▪ ▪ ▪ ▪ ▪ ▪ **FIGURE 5.8:**   Things to Avoid in a Knowledge Capture Interview

elicit the information that the expert is qualified to provide. Verbalization conveys the information that is available in working memory, also called *spoken protocol.*

5. *Role bias.* The risk of role bias increases when the expert is aware of his or her importance as the critical element in building the KM system. The expert might wonder, "What type of person should I be as I answer this question?" and then select a role to fit the expectations of the knowledge developer. Research has shown that experts with limited formal schooling tend to exhibit "put on" behavior and are more likely to distort the knowledge elicited than highly educated experts.

Various validation and cross-validation methods should be applied before captured knowledge can be represented. For example, one way to cross-validate an expert's opinions is to ask another expert and check for similarities between the two opinions. Another way to validate an opinion is to ask the question again at the next session to see if the expert gives the same answer.

ERRORS MADE BY THE KNOWLEDGE DEVELOPER

In addition to possible bias originating with experts, knowledge developers can also contribute to the reliability problem. Validity problems often stem from what is called the *interviewer effect:* Something about the knowledge developer colors the response of the domain expert. Some of the effects include the following:

- The **age effect**: In the eyes of a much older domain expert, a 20-something knowledge developer is not viewed as experienced enough to take on the building of a knowledge management system. The wrong perception of age can color responses of the domain expert.
- The **race effect**: Unfortunately, people can be biased because of race. In a professional environment, biases should not exist, but they do. The best option for earning an expert's respect is for a knowledge developer to demonstrate competency, integrity, and determination to do quality work. If race continues to be a serious barrier, perhaps an alternative expert or an alternative knowledge developer is the best course of action.
- The **gender effect**: The gender of the knowledge developer can alter the way the interview is conducted. Research in the social sciences has shown that male interviewers obtain fewer responses than female interviewers, regardless of race, and white females obtain the highest number of responses from men. The exception is young women who interview young men; they get fewer responses than older women.

The knowledge developer must watch for biased responses from the expert early in the capture process and find ways to correct the tendency.

PROBLEMS ENCOUNTERED DURING THE INTERVIEW

Other difficulties are not uncommon during the interview. They range from biased responses and the way the questions are phrased to personality clashes between the expert and the knowledge developer.

Response Bias

A response bias occurs when experts answer questions on the basis of their interpretation of the question and in response to certain constraints: lack of time, lack of motivation, perceived hostility, an attempt to please the knowledge developer, and so on. A combination of wording and tone of voice can also promote response bias. For example:

KNOWLEDGE DEVELOPER:	Isn't it true that when a diabetic comes in with a blister, you pretty much decide that she will be making more than one visit?
DOMAIN EXPERT:	Well, as a general rule, I'd say yes.
KNOWLEDGE DEVELOPER:	Don't you think that following your verification procedure results in disapproval of loans for minority applications?
DOMAIN EXPERT:	I'd probably say yes, but we have good reasons for this.

The questioner coaxed an unintended "yes" answer by prefacing the question with "Isn't it true" or "Don't you think."

Another response bias stems from the order of the questions asked, which is called the *contamination effect.* For example, a question that is asked following another question is answered one way; if it were asked later or earlier in the questioning sequence, the answer could be totally different.

One test to reveal bias is the circular triad. For example, when the expert for the Diabetic Foot KM System says, "I consider vascular disease more serious than neuropathy," and then says, "I consider neuropathy more serious than charcot," and then states, "I consider charcot more serious than vascular disease," it is called a *circular triad*. This type of contamination is usually the result of long interview sessions, loss of motivation or interest, fatigue, or faking, which provides even more reason for pretesting the questions.

Inconsistency

The problem of inconsistency is most likely to occur when the knowledge developer interviews two domain experts and is inconsistent when asking the questions. For the sake of validity, the questions and their order should be standardized. Validity is related to reliability; they are two faces of the same coin. Validity is addressed when one asks, "Does the question mean the same thing to all of the experts being interviewed?" If it means different things to different people, then the question is not valid. No invalid questions obtain accurate responses. Reliability, on the other hand, occurs when the question elicits the same response at different times. The reliability of an expert's answer can be revealed by answering the question, "How much credence can we place in this answer?" If the question is not valid, one can assume that the answer is not reliable. Knowledge developers often rephrase questions and ask a variety of questions about the same process to ensure the reliability of the information captured.

Communication Difficulties

Not everyone has a knack for explaining things. The knowledge developer may need to resort to analogies or other tools to stimulate the expert's thought process. For example, the knowledge developer may say, "If I understand you correctly, you would require the application to be a homeowner and have an average income of $50,000 to qualify for a $30,000 car loan?" or simply ask the expert "I am not sure I follow what you just explained. Can you go through it one more time?"

Communication problems can also stem from the knowledge developer, who may not have been listening or did not understand. However, when a knowledge developer admits to these lapses, most experts do not mind repeating or simplifying the points just explained. Next time, the knowledge developer had better get it right, because pretending to understand is a destructive habit. Asking the expert to repeat the same thing three times could cause tempers to flare and threaten the end of the whole process.

Hostile Attitude

Nothing is more problematic to an interview process than hostility. Various factors cause hostility: bad chemistry between the expert and the knowledge developer, an expert's "forced" participation, or time wasted on repeated deadends. Unfortunately, no quick fixes work for reducing hostility.

Standardized Questions

On the surface, the task of standardizing questions does not appear difficult. However, even if the wording is the same, the way the question is asked, the tone of voice, and the facial expression can elicit a different response.

Length of Questions and the Duration of the Interview

No written rules provide the ideal number of questions or minutes in an interview. Much depends on the preference of the expert, the expectations of the knowledge developer, and the nature of the constraints surrounding the whole project. Ideally, each interview should last no more than 1 hour. Any longer, and the participants' attention spans begin to break down, and the quality of the thought process degenerates.

ENDING THE INTERVIEW

Ending an interview requires sensitivity to the domain expert's preferences, use of proper verbal and nonverbal cues, and efforts to maintain ties with the expert even after the interview is finished. When the knowledge developer has elicited all the knowledge needed, common tendency is to cut the session abruptly. This action can easily be misinterpreted. The better practice is to carefully plan the end of the session.

One common procedure calls for the knowledge developer to halt the questioning a few minutes before the scheduled ending and to summarize the key points of the session. This practice allows the expert to comment and schedule a future session. If the procedure is carried out naturally, the expert will feel good about time well spent, and the next session is more likely to flow just as smoothly.

Several verbal and nonverbal cues can be used to close an interview. Table 5.2 summarizes some of the verbal closing cues that have been found to be successful in ending a knowledge capture session. Nonverbal closing cues that may be used with verbal cues to end a session are listed in Figure 5.9.

TABLE 5.2 Verbal Closing Cues for Ending an Interview

Verbal Cue	Meaning
1. This is my summary of the session. Do you have any questions?	I'm ready to end the session unless you have questions.
2. I think I've asked all the questions I had in mind. I appreciate your time and input.	I'm ready to call it a day.
3. My time allowance is up. I know you have another meeting soon.	Time's up.
4. I learned a great deal from this session. I appreciate your support.	I don't need any more information. The session is over.
5. This covers pretty much what I had in mind. Did I miss anything?	I am ready to end the session.
6. This turned out to be an informative meeting. How about scheduling another meeting sometime next week?	Session is over. I'd like to schedule another one.

▪ ▪ ▪ ▪ ▪ ▪

ISSUES TO ASSESS

During the interview, several issues may arise. To be prepared for the most important issues, a knowledge developer should consider the following questions:

- *How would one elicit knowledge from experts who cannot say what they mean or mean what they say?* Sometimes, the expert is knowledgeable but has difficulty explaining things. Whether this difficulty stems from lack of knowledge usually becomes apparent during the first meeting. Unless it is a one-time blunder on the part of the expert, an alternative expert should be considered immediately.

- *What does one say or do when the expert says, "Look, I work with shades of gray reasoning. I simply look at the problem and decide. Don't ask me why or how."* Unless a knowledge developer is well prepared to handle unexpected situations, this type of answer could very well end the interview. The expert probably knows the solution so well that the details are an unconscious part of it. The knowledge developer must work around this unconsciousness and look for ways to get at the details indirectly.

- *How does one set up the problem domain when one has only a general idea of what it should be?* One rule of thumb is to ask the expert to illustrate or explain—through scenarios—the general procedure of the domain. The knowledge devel-

▪ ▪ ▪ ▪ ▪ ▪ ▪ **FIGURE 5.9:** Nonverbal Cues for Ending an Interview

1. Look at watch and uncross legs.
2. Put cap on pen and uncross legs.
3. Put cap on pen and close folder.
4. If taping session, stop taping and rewind tape.
5. Stop taking notes, uncross legs, put cap on pen, and look at watch (strongest nonverbal cues).
6. Place writing materials in briefcase and close briefcase.
7. Close folder and uncross legs.
8. Use any combination of these cues.

oper should then feed back his or her understanding of what the expert said and work from there.

* *What does one do if the relationship with the domain expert turns out to be difficult?* Perhaps the expert is not only uncooperative, but he or she also seems to be trying to sabotage the project. The expert may react defensively to the knowledge developer's queries. The expert may have been told by management to participate in the project. Unless the expert can be coaxed into a more positive frame of mind, the resulting sessions could be strained at best. It should be noted that personality differences that surface quickly could work against the capture process. Personality clashes can be triggered by a number of things: a series of jumbled questions with no end in sight, "grilling" the expert as if on the witness stand, or reminding the expert too frequently of prior successes in building expert systems. If the situation reaches a deadlock, the best solution is to replace the knowledge developer or scrub the project.

* *What happens if the expert dislikes the knowledge developer?* This issue also addresses personality clashes. For example, on one project a young knowledge developer with a Ph.D. was assigned a senior loan officer to capture the decision-making process regarding jumbo loans (loans over $275,000). From the beginning, the expert was reluctant to cooperate beyond cursory information. Well into the fourth session, the knowledge developer learned that the expert had not been able to complete his doctorate and had difficulty working with younger consultants.

Ways of gaining the respect of an expert vary from person to person. Sometimes, young knowledge developers do not do well with experts 20 years their senior. In other cases, the expert may feel his or her time is being wasted when talking to a novice. For these situations, an accommodating personality, finesse, and advance planning are critical in reaching the expert. A relationship that does not jell in the first session could make the entire capture process an uphill battle.

▪ ▪ ▪ ▪ Rapid Prototyping in Interviews

One approach to building KM systems is rapid prototyping, or the build-as-you-go approach, in which knowledge is added with each knowledge capture session. This incremental or iterative approach allows the expert to verify the rules as they are built during the session (see Box 5.7). Some people have likened rapid prototyping to the miracle of birth: An 8-pound baby is the prototype of a 180-pound person, who has essentially all the same features, but with a more complete and mature configuration. Each stage of KM system development has its own problems, requires its own modifications, provides its own excitement, and results in its own contributions.

BENEFITS AND DRAWBACKS

Rapid prototyping can open up communication through its demonstration of the KM system. Because of its instant feedback and modification, it also reduces risk of failure. Another benefit is allowing the knowledge developer to learn every time a change is made in the prototype. Its iterative nature encourages discovery of better ways to build the KM system.

Rapid prototyping depends on the teamwork spirit of the knowledge developer, the expert, and the end user. It is highly interactive, and its continuous feedback leads to improvements and refinements all the way to completion, which creates a KM system that corresponds as closely as possible to its stated requirements. An obvious

▪▪▪▪▪▪ **BOX 5.7** ▪▪▪▪▪▪

ROLE OF RAPID PROTOTYPING

In some beliefs, everything began in Genesis. God created the world in 6 days and rested on the seventh. Everything else occurred through evolution. Genesis is an excellent model for rapid evolutionary development, because we want to create a deliverable, functioning prototype in as little time as possible and begin the endless additions, changes, and deletions required to keep the system in balance and evolving to meet the needs of the business.

Rapid evolutionary development relies on speed, simplicity, and a shared vision to create a desired product. Prototypers create a working system that does work and provides the essential, initial elements of the system. Then a series of step-wise improvements—evolution—turns the system into the customer's desired paradise.

Can you imagine what would have happened if God had tried to specify the requirements for this earthship and then built it from scratch will all the bells and whistles? It could have taken 150 million years just to get started. Instead, God chose to *rapid-prototype* the initial version in 6 days and grow it from there.

Unlike the traditional development life cycle, speed is required more than direction in rapid prototyping. Once you are rolling, you can change course at will. If you are not moving, you have no feedback to guide your first steps.

SOURCE: Excerpted from Arthur, L. J. *Improving Software Quality: An Insider's Guide to TQM.* New York: John Wiley & Sons, Inc., 1992.

▪▪▪▪▪▪

problem, however, is lack of clear guidelines for rapid prototyping use. Another drawback is that the prototype itself can create user expectations that, in turn, become obstacles to further development efforts. As a result, users refuse to buy into it, and the transition to an operational KM system never materializes.

▪▪▪▪ Implications for Knowledge Management

For success in building KM systems, several things must fall into place. First, complex applications require time and talent of the knowledge developer. By the time knowledge capture begins, all the preliminaries should be established, including the budget approval, the expert's availability, and the company's commitment.

Many KM systems are built by using teams. A team includes a champion, system users, an expert, one or more knowledge developers, and a scribe. The champion is a respected executive who believes in the project and sells the idea to those who control the purse strings. Executive support is usually assured if the project promises a fair return on investment and the availability of expertise in several locations. A prototype of the KM system can be built to sell the change early in the life cycle of the product, which also makes it easier to train the user and gain their acceptance.

A key managerial issue centers around who owns the knowledge of the expert. Some organizations form contracts with their experts, under which the knowledge gained on the job belongs to the firm and cannot be sold to or shared with the competition within a specified time period after the expert leaves the firm or retires. In the absence of an agreement, the organization cannot claim knowledge ownership, except in the case of investment in special training that actually promoted the expertise.

Interviewing itself carries several managerial implications. First, managing knowledge capture means managing the expert's time, which is precious. The knowledge developer should make the most efficient use of the expert's time in the fewest number of sessions. Management must also provide the right atmosphere and support if the interviewing process is to succeed, which is actually the responsibility of the champion. Finally, to what extent can the expert provide time for the capture phase? Experts who are on the company payroll often draw high salaries. Advance planning by the knowledge developer is necessary to make the most efficient use of the expert's time.

In terms of rapid prototyping, management should be educated about the potential of the product well before it is ready to be installed. Demonstrating the prototype at some point can be a good "selling" technique. Without such occasional feedback, funds and support may dwindle, often resulting in half-baked or incomplete systems.

SUMMARY ▪ ▪ ▪ ▪

- The goal of tacit knowledge capture is to extract problem-solving knowledge from the human expert in order to build a KM system. The scope of the domain should be well defined, the domain should contain common-sense knowledge, and the resulting KM system must be a manageable size.

- Experts have definite qualifications. They include perceptual ability to discern the relevant from the irrelevant, communication skills, creativity, self-confidence, and credibility. Motivation, enthusiasm, and willingness to share the expertise are also important. The right expert does not guarantee a successful expert system, however.

- Three levels of experts are emphasized: the highly expert person, the moderately expert problem solver, and the new expert. Each level carries its own contributions and constraints. The best situation occurs when the knowledge developer is able to work with the most qualified expert available.

- Using a single expert or multiple experts both have pros and cons. Single experts are ideal for simple and relatively quick KM systems; they entail fewer conflicts to resolve and make logistical arrangements easier. The main risk is that the credibility of the expert system depends entirely on the thought processes of one expert. In contrast, multiple experts are typically used in problem domains with diffused knowledge. They provide a synthesis of experience that is critical for the reliability of the system's solutions. However, scheduling difficulties, process loss, and the need to involve more than one knowledge developer can make the use of multiple experts problematic.

- A common problem encountered in interviewing is an expert who cannot easily convey the knowledge even though he or she may be quite competent at the specialty. To the nonexpert, an expert's pattern matching or analogy can resemble fuzzy reasoning.

- Ambiguities of language during interviewing or when interpreting the expert's descriptions or explanations is a common problem a knowledge developer must be aware of and work to avoid.

- A structured interview has several variations: multiple-choice, dichotomous, and ranking-scale questions. Each variation has its own format and goals.

- Interviewing should be approached logically, using stage setting, proper phrasing of questions, good listening, and evaluating the session outcome. Question sequencing as well as probing the expert for details are also important.

- Reliability of an expert's information can be affected by question construction, which requires a careful review of question content, wording, and format. Reliability is also affected by uncontrolled sources of errors: the expert's perceptual slant, failure to remember just what happened, fear of the unknown, communication problems, and role bias. Errors can also originate with the knowledge developer; these can include age, race, and gender effects.
- Several problems may be encountered in interviews: response bias, inconsistency, communication difficulties, hostile attitude, and standardized questions.
- Several issues that may arise during the interview must be assessed. For example, how would one get knowledge from experts who do not say what they mean or mean what they say? How can one set up a problem domain while knowing little about it? What does one do when the relationship with the expert turns out to be difficult?

TERMS TO KNOW ▪▪▪▪

Age effect: Bias against a person due to age.

Analogies: Comparing a problem to a similar one encountered previously.

Closed question: A question that asks for specific responses.

Dichotomous question: A question answerable by one of two answers, usually yes or no.

Gender effect: Bias against a person based on gender.

Interview: A face-to-face interpersonal situation in which a person called the *interviewer* asks another person questions designed to elicit certain responses about a problem domain.

Multiple-choice question: A question that offers the expert specific answer choices.

Novice: An individual with skills and solutions that work some of the time but not all of the time.

Open-ended question: A question that asks for general rather than specific responses.

Primary question: A question that elicits the most important information in one area during the interview; leads to further questions to obtain pertinent details.

Race effect: Bias against a person due to race.

Ranking scale question: A question that asks the respondent to arrange items in a list according to preference or importance.

Reliability: Dependability; truthfulness of the response or answer to a given question; credibility; how well the KM system delivers solutions with consistency, accuracy, or integrity; detecting or removing anomaly.

Response bias: Bias resulting from the subjective responses of the expert to any given question.

Role bias: An altered attitude resulting from the expert's awareness of his or her importance in the building of a KM system.

Scribe: A person who takes notes during interviews and maintains all the documentation related to the project.

Secondary question: A question used to probe for further details or for follow-up on an area under discussion.

Uncertainty: Lack of adequate information to make a decision.

Unstructured interview: An approach in which the questions and the alternative responses are open-ended.

Validity: The logical correctness of a question, which is worded in order to elicit the information sought.

TEST YOUR UNDERSTANDING ▪▪▪▪

1. In your own words, define tacit knowledge capture. What makes it unique?
2. Are there any particular steps involved in knowledge capture? Explain briefly.
3. "The problem solution should be based on symbolic knowledge rather than numerical computation." Do you agree? Explain.
4. How would one identify expertise?
5. Working with experts requires certain skills and experience. What suggestions or advice would you give to an inexperienced knowledge developer concerning:
   a. working with or approaching an expert
   b. preparing for the first session
6. Working with multiple experts has definite benefits and limitations. Cite an example in which the use of multiple experts is a must. Explain your choice.

7. Use an example of your own to illustrate the conditions under which you would be willing to build a KM system based on a single expert. Justify your choice.
8. Why should the knowledge developer understand the differences among the levels of experts? Isn't an expert an expert regardless of level?
9. Explain the relationships between an expert's:
   a. motivation and willingness to share knowledge
   b. credibility and perceptual ability
   c. creativity and well-developed perceptual ability
10. How does pattern matching adversely affect the quality of an interview?
11. In what ways is visual imagery helpful in recalling chunks of experience?
12. Distinguish between:
   a. validity and reliability
   b. multiple-choice and dichotomous questions
   c. question format and question content
   d. question wording and question content
13. Briefly explain each of the uncontrolled sources of error that the knowledge developer needs to consider. Which source do you consider most serious? Why?
14. What is the interviewer effect? How likely is the occurrence of this problem?
15. Review briefly some of the problems encountered during an interview. Which problem do you consider most serious? Why?
16. The chapter suggests a guide to a successful interview. Does it allow enough flexibility? That is, what determines how strictly one should follow the guide?
17. Experience teaches that how questions are phrased can determine the nature of the answers. In knowledge capture, explain how the following are related:
   a. question phrasing and question sequence
   b. primary and secondary questions
   c. open-ended and closed questions
18. In what way is rapid prototyping related to interviewing? Be specific.

KNOWLEDGE EXERCISES ▪ ▪ ▪ ▪

1. What suggestions can you make for improving knowledge capture?
2. Which of the prerequisites for knowledge capture described in the chapter do you think is the most crucial? Why?
3. Do you think knowledge capture can be fully or easily automated? Why or why not?
4. "An expert exhibits a certain depth of detail and exceptional quality in explanations." How important is the "exceptional quality" of an expert's explanations in knowledge capture? Explain.
5. When the expert tells you what he or she does not know, does that indicate expertise?
6. Why are good communications skills so important in knowledge capture? Is this quality a prerequisite for experts only? For knowledge developers? Why?
7. If you were asked to select an expert, how would you proceed? What characteristics would you look for? What other factors would you consider?
8. "Knowledge developers can benefit immensely from an educational grounding in cognitive psychology." Do you agree? Why or why not?
9. If you were building a KM system using a single expert who had been coaxed for weeks to participate, what things would you avoid in interviewing such an expert?

10. Select two other people to form a group of three. One person will be A, the second person will be B, and the third person will be C. Have A ask a question of B. B will then ask a question of C. C will ask a question of A. Questions may cover areas pertaining to the course material or a KM system project you would like to work on. Review the following questions:
    a. How well have you learned about one another?
    b. What were you doing when the other two people were talking to each other?
    c. What experience did you have when you asked one question at a time? Be specific.
    d. In general, how did you spend most of your time?

11. Interviewing is sometimes similar to conversation. Get into a conversation with another person for 15 minutes. Choose a topic in advance. How many times did the topic change? What triggered the change in the topic?

12. Watch an interview on TV between a news reporter and an expert in the field (such as a police or government official). Record how the interview was started. What types of questions were asked? Do you agree with the question sequence and construction? Explain.

13. Determine whether the following questions are leading questions or neutral questions:
    a. You like to operate on patients, don't you?
    b. When was the last time you had less than satisfactory surgery?
    c. How does an auto loan differ from a commercial loan?
    d. Would you classify yourself as an orthopedic surgeon or a specialist in hip replacement?
    e. How do you feel about applicants lying on their application form?

14. Write the name of one person you admire and one person you dislike or distrust. The person could be someone you know, a celebrity, or a national figure. Make a list of traits each person possesses. Which of these traits are critical aspects of credibility? How would the distrusted person proceed to change his or her image in your eyes?

15. Publisher KM System:
    The goal of the first session with the expert was to develop a master list of the variables that the expert considered important in deciding on whether a manuscript should be published. These variables were condensed into 20 possibilities and then ranked in order of importance. The ranking was presented to the expert for verification. The variables were reduced to the five most important:
    a. marketability of the work
    b. reviewers' opinions of the manuscript
    c. author's prior publishing record
    d. author's requirements before signing a contract with the publisher
    e. cost of manufacturing the book
    In preparation for the first interview, the knowledge developer reviewed published articles about book publishing, what manuscripts get published, the criteria used in making favorable decisions, and the book production process. This background provided a number of prefatory questions that were included in the first session.

    Assignment:
    For this project, set up a list of questions to ask the expert (book editor) during the first interview. Explain the reason(s) for choosing these questions. What variables or parameters have you been able to conclude from the session?

16. Multiple experts were used to capture knowledge for the Residential Real Estate KM System. The reasons are:

   a. One objective of this KM system is to integrate the expertise in real estate tax and finance, which requires two separate experts.

   b. The procedure of making a buy-or-lease decision is a complex and intense process for a single expert to provide all necessary information to come up with a decision. The nature of the problem also suggests that to make a decision, one has to consider both tax and financial issues. Thus, multiple experts are necessary to divide the scope into manageable pieces.

   c. Multiple experts give the ability to compare and contrast the knowledge captured. The real estate finance expert has deep knowledge in the real estate tax field as well. He was particularly helpful in confirming the tax information captured from the tax expert. Confirming the validity of the proposed recommendation and solution is critical considering the continuously changing tax law. One expert might not be aware of the change, while the other is.

   Questions:

   a. In your opinion, is the use of a multiple expert approach justified for this project? Explain.

   b. Can the use of two knowledge developers to tackle the problem be justified? What are the conditions for a multiple knowledge developer approach to building this system? Explain.

REFERENCES ▪ ▪ ▪ ▪

Arthur, L. J. *Improving Software Quality: An Insider's Guide to TQM*. New York: John Wiley & Sons, Inc., 1992.

Awad, Elias M. *Building Expert Systems*. Minneapolis, MN: West Publishing Co., 1996, pp. 134, 168.

Davenport, T. H., and Prusak, Laurence. *Working Knowledge*. Boston, MA: Harvard Business School Press, 2000, pp. 137–140.

Eisenhart, Mary. "Gathering Knowledge While It's Ripe," *Knowledge Management*, April 2001, pp. 49–54.

Gill, Philip J. "The Ancient Art of Storytelling Emerges As a Tool for Knowledge Management," *Knowledge Management*, May 2001, pp. 24–30.

Hayes-Roth, F., and Jacobstein, N. "The State of Knowledge-Based Systems," *Communications of the ACM*, March 1994, p. 28.

Hill, Mary with Dr. Heather Wakat, University of Virginia, Spring 2000 (personal interview).

Johannessen, Jon-Arild, Olaisen, Johan, and Olsen, Bjorn. "Mismanagement of Tacit Knowledge," www.program. forsknningsradet.no/skikt/johannessen.php3, Date accessed April 2002.

Pfeffer, Jeffrey, and Sutton, Robert I. *The Knowing-Doing Gap*. Boston, MA: Harvard Business School Press, 2000, pp. 1–28.

Sherman, Lee. "Managing the Modern Document," *Knowledge Management*, September 2001, pp. 48–52.

Stewart, Kathy A., Storey, Veda C., and Robey, Daniel. "Plugging the Knowledge Drain: Strategies and Technologies for Acquiring Knowledge in Lean Organizations," *Journal of Information Technology Management*, vol. 10, no. 3–4, 1999, pp. 59–67.

Other Knowledge Capture Techniques

Contents

"I don't think like you do."
—DANIEL KORKILL

▪▪▪▪ In a Nutshell

Like any other professional, the knowledge developer must be well versed in the use of specialized knowledge capture tools. Each tool has a unique purpose, depending on whether the capture process revolves around a single expert or multiple experts. Among the tools are computer-based tools designed to promote accuracy and integrity of the knowledge capture process.

A knowledge developer might want to observe the problem-solving process in a situation in which an on-site observation would be a proper tool. When dealing with two or more experts, brainstorming followed by consensus decision making is preferred. Whatever tool is chosen, the knowledge developer must follow a preestablished procedure for conducting the session.

A unique knowledge acquisition technique for single experts is protocol analysis or the think-aloud method. In essence, it involves listening to the spoken protocol of the expert. During the session, the expert speaks aloud whatever thoughts come to mind while answering a question or solving a problem. In contrast, a repertory grid uses a grid or a scale to represent the expert's way of looking at a particular problem. The number of gradations on a scale can be increased to reflect a more accurate rating.

Other techniques for multiple experts include the nominal group and Delphi methods. Each method has unique features and a procedure to make its use operational. The nominal group method is an interface between consensus and brainstorming; the Delphi method is a polling of experts' opinions via questionnaires.

An attractive computer-based method for multiple experts is the blackboard. Also called *groupware,* this global memory structure promotes privacy and equality among participating experts. It attempts to get the experts to agree on a solution, and it is ideal for complex problem-solving involving several experts.

▪▪▪▪ Overview

A knowledge developer must recognize that many complex problems cannot be solved by single experts. For example, the prototype for the Diabetic Foot KM System described in the preceding chapter will involve two other specialists in the field to agree on medical and surgical treatment before the KM system can be medically certified. To be sure that knowledge is reliable, multiple experts are often required.

When dealing with multiple experts, the knowledge developer must be familiar with the tools and techniques that are unique to the task. Chapter 5 focused on ways to ensure a successful interview with a domain expert. The use of this tool requires a customized approach to both the expert and the process. This chapter examines other tools used in knowledge capture: on-site observation, protocol analysis, and consensus methodologies, including brainstorming, consensus decision making, the repertory grid, nominal group technique, and the Delphi method for multiple experts. A more recent knowledge capture tool, blackboarding, will be discussed at the end of the chapter.

Acquiring knowledge from multiple experts requires experience and special-purpose techniques. Without this combination, serious problems often arise, such as experts walking out, faking solutions to end the session, and so on.

▪▪▪▪ **On-Site Observation**

This specialized knowledge capture technique has been borrowed from the social sciences, where the knowledge developer observes the daily work of a domain expert. **On-site observation**, or *action protocol,* is a process of observing, interpreting, and recording an expert's problem-solving behavior while it takes place. It requires concentration on the overall steps that the domain expert takes as well as the more subtle details of the process. In addition to observing and recording the expert's behavior, the knowledge developer asks the expert questions about the problem-solving process.

On-site observation carries with it a certain protocol. The knowledge developer does more listening than talking; avoids giving advice and does not pass judgment on what is observed, even if it is incorrect; and does not argue with the expert while the expert is performing the task.

On-site observation was used by one knowledge developer to build a teller KM system for a commercial bank, a project that took 2 months to complete. She sat in a booth adjacent to a senior teller with 7 years of experience. The purpose of the project was to build a KM system to determine when a check exceeded the set limits ($500, in this case) and what to do about the problem without requiring an officer's signature. This particular teller's success rate (the check did not bounce) for the decision was 95 percent; the average bank officer's success rate for the same decision was 70 percent.

In this example, on-site observation gave the knowledge engineer a visual or a live exposure to the kind of information that can also be gathered through the interview. In the teller KM project, the knowledge developer conducted brief informal interviews with the teller when no customers were waiting. The answers during those interviews verified the information picked up through participant observation.

Observation of behavior enables the knowledge developer to seek knowledge within the working world of the expert. In comparison to the interview, observation places the knowledge developer closer to the actual steps and procedures used by the expert to solve the problem. One problem with this capture technique is that some experts do not like to be observed. They prefer to talk about their thought process rather than show them in practice. Sometimes, experts fear that observation will give away years of experience in one quick look.

The reaction of others in the observation setting can also be a distracting problem. During the early stages of the teller KM system project, other tellers' curious and occasionally hostile feelings were conspicuous. One teller with 18 years' experience was quite irritated at the bank for allowing such a "ridiculous automation of the human mind." She guarded her own actions closely after commenting during a lunch break that the teller "expert" was being used as a guinea pig and wondering, "How can they tell us to follow procedure, and here they are trying to automate the procedure?" However, in the case of the teller KM system project, the teller expert thrived on attention. She was not at all distracted by the presence of the knowledge developer or the reservations of coworkers. Participant observation went on for 2 weeks without any problems.

Another problem with on-site observation is the accuracy or completeness of the captured knowledge. Although the general assumption may be that the recording of an event and the event itself occur simultaneously, in reality a time gap separates what is observed and its recording. The event is first transcribed into a mental image before that image is translated into the knowledge developer's own words. It becomes a retrospective process, which inevitably invites errors.

To form a mental picture of the event, the knowledge developer attempts to integrate his or her perception of the situation with the expert's perception. That mental picture is then recorded. What happens is a continuous **shuttle process**; the knowledge developer mentally moves back and forth from the initial impression of the event to the later evaluation of the event. What is finally recorded is the evaluation made during this retrospective period. Because a time lapse can make details of a situation less clear, the information is not always valid.

▪ ▪ ▪ ▪ Brainstorming

Unlike on-site observation, which focuses on the work of a single expert, **brainstorming**—an unstructured approach to generating ideas about a problem—invites two or more experts into a session in which discussions are carried out and a variety of opinions are tossed around. The primary goal of this process is to think up creative solutions to problems. In brainstorming, all possible solutions are considered equally. The emphasis is on the frequency of responses during the session. Anything related to the topic can be brought up, and everything is valued. Questions can be raised for clarification, but no evaluation is made at the moment.

In brainstorming, the first look is on idea generation, followed by idea evaluation. Similarities begin to emerge across opinions, which are then grouped logically and evaluated by asking several questions:

- If one followed up on this idea, what benefits would ensue? (All ideas are itemized or prioritized.)
- What problem(s) would a selected idea solve?
- What new problem(s) would arise?

In the evaluation phase, the knowledge developer explains each idea and treats any comments or criticisms accordingly.

The general procedure for conducting a brainstorming session is as follows:

1. *Introduce the brainstorming session.* Explain what it is and what it is not designed to accomplish, the role of each participant, the "rules of the game," and the expected outcomes. Starting with the wrong objective or the wrong step can doom the entire process.
2. *Give the experts a problem to consider.* The problem approved by the organization is in the experts' domain of expertise. The knowledge developer must give them time to think it through and then be a good listener and show enthusiasm but also set reasonable time limits.
3. *Prompt the experts to generate ideas.* The experts can do this either by calling out their ideas or by establishing some order in which each expert will have a turn to speak. The knowledge developer must keep pace with the expert.
4. *Watch for signs of convergence.* Ideas often trigger counteropinions or reinforcements that should eventually coax the experts to converge onto the final four, the final two, and the final solution. When experts begin to pass or the rate and quality of ideas presented declines, the process moves on to convergence.

If experts cannot agree on the final solution from two or three alternatives, the knowledge developer may call for a vote or a **consensus** in order to reach agreement on the best final solution; this does not guarantee success. The intensity of the discussion just prior to such a vote, the temperament of the experts, and how willing they are to resolve conflicts all influence whether a consensus can be reached.

ELECTRONIC BRAINSTORMING

A relatively new development in brainstorming is a computer-aided approach to dealing with multiple experts. Desks in a U-shaped layout hold PCs networked through a software tool that serves as a catalyst in the meeting, promotes instant exchange of ideas between experts, and sorts and condenses those ideas into an organized format. Such a tool also allows experts to elaborate and vote on ideas (see Figure 6.1).

For example, an electronic brainstorming process begins with a **presession plan** that identifies objectives and structures the agenda, which is presented to the experts for approval. During the live session, each expert chooses a PC and engages in a predefined approach to resolving a focused issue and then generates ideas or plans. The experts gain leverage from anonymity, focus on content (not personalities), and engage in parallel and simultaneous communication. This format allows two or more experts to provide opinions through their PCs without having to wait their turn. The software displays the comments or suggestions on a huge screen without identifying the source.

This method protects the shy expert and prevents tagging comments to individuals. The overall benefits include improved communication, effective discussion of sensitive issues, shorter meetings, and closure of meeting with concise recommendations for action. The sequence of steps is summarized in Figure 6.2. The expert's ideas are priori-

■ ■ ■ ■ ■ ■ FIGURE 6.1: Electronic Brainstorming Environment

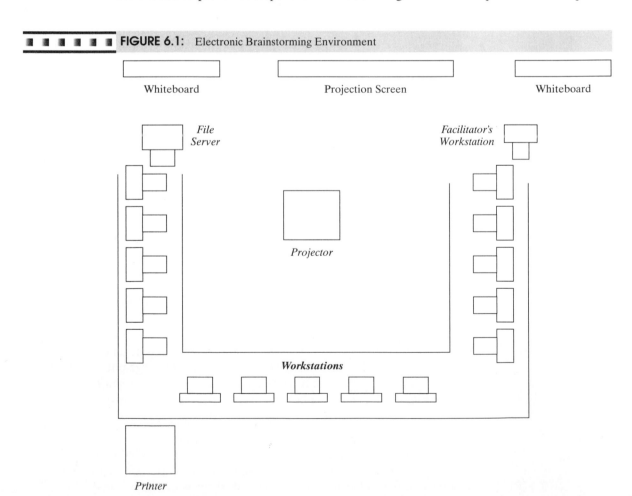

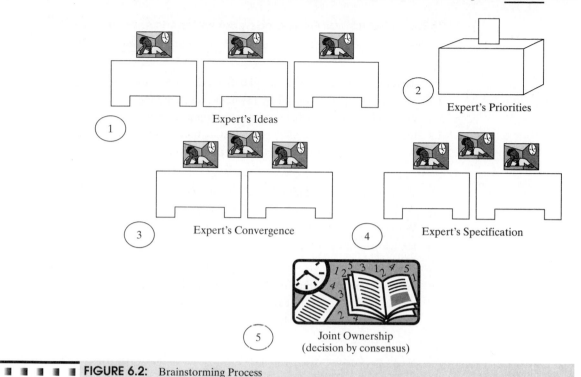

■ ■ ■ ■ ■ ■ ■ **FIGURE 6.2:** Brainstorming Process

tized. This eventually leads to convergence and setting final specifications. The result is joint ownership of the solution.

To illustrate the process used in electronic brainstorming, a group of graduate professors met one day to discuss the field research topics for MIS graduate students. The 1-day session using IBM's Electronic Brainstormer began with a focused topic: Generate a portfolio of field research projects for graduate MIS students. The facilitator (the role taken by the knowledge developer) asked each professor to list as many topics as desired through the PC. Each professor was assigned an ID that was not visible on the screen when the questions were entered or displayed.

Table 6.1 shows the resulting input of the seven participants.

After the questions had been listed on the screen, they were discussed, and redundancies were removed. Afterwards, the key topics remained, as shown in Figure 6.3. The questions listed were reviewed and arranged in order of priority. Then a vote was taken. The resulting matrix shown in Table 6.2 provides the voting results.

■ ■ ■ ■ Protocol Analysis

Suppose you want to understand the diagnostic process of a medical expert; the knowledge he or she uses; and the cognitive actions they take. How would you go about it? One obvious approach is to ask the expert questions about diagnosis. Chances are the expert will not find it easy to answer questions. One of the authors found out that his orthopedic surgeon is more used to doing the job than explaining it. The surgeon tried to explain diagnosing a diabetic foot in terms of the formal procedure he learned in medical school, which is not quite the diagnosis he follows with each patient. The alternative is to observe an examination of a real patient and then listen to the spoken protocol.

TABLE 6.1 Questions Generated by Seven Experts Anonymously

Problem Domain: Generate a portfolio of field research for graduate MIS students.

Participant 1:

1.1 Develop an interactive graphical data model query selection

1.2 Analyze group decision support systems; e.g., team focus

1.3 Develop a manufacturing database to support Comm 326

1.4 Develop an executive information system that uses real-time data feeds

1.5 Analyze Dave Smith's office (Can he possibly be productive in his environment?)

Participant 2:

2.1 Work with physical plant on cost estimating system

2.2 Assist athletic department in establishing an injury database

2.3 Work with local IBM office to sell more PCs

2.4 Develop database of nine in-class speakers from industry

Participant 3:

3.1 Work with medical imaging specialists on patient database

3.2 Explore use of COBOL to access distributed database

3.3 Establish a database of MIS internships

Participant 4:

4.1 Analyze communication media (e.g., electronic and/or voice mail), perhaps using the Commerce School as a case study

4.2 Study the allocation of computer resources in the University of the Comm School

4.3 Determine the effect of various levels of DSS on player performance of a management simulation game

4.4 Reconcile use of university and Comm School e-mail

4.5 Evaluate the impact of GDSS on Comm student group productivity

Participant 5:

5.1 Study graphics applications in GDSS (Can we integrate graphics input?)

5.2 Analyze issues of migration to graphic user interfaces for end users

5.3 Automate commerce student registration

Participant 6:

6.1 Analyze new CASE tools

6.2 Examine use of simulation tools for dataflow modeling

6.3 Evaluate use of GDSS tools in an academic environment

Participant 7:

7.1 Explore implementation issues of electronic mail

7.2 Simulate knowledge acquisition session with multiple experts

7.3 Implement a neural network to evaluate mortgage applications

Analyze group decision support systems (1.2)

Develop executive information systems (1.4)

Do projects that add to technical capabilities of our school

Simulate rapid prototyping through brainstorming with experts

Implement e-mail for graduate MIS students (4.4)

Simulate knowledge capture session for multiple experts (7.2)

Build interactive knowledge-based system to train med students (3.1)

Develop electronic rosters and grad submissions (7.1)

Evaluate current case tool (6.1)

▪ ▪ ▪ ▪ ▪ ▪ ▪ ▪ **FIGURE 6.3:**   Final Set of Questions Agreed Upon by the Experts

In working with multiple experts, the problem-solving process is bound to vary. Two experts might give the same answer, but they might use two different problem-solving strategies. A think-aloud protocol provides a clear insight as to how each expert arrived at the solution through the individual expert's verbalizations. The think-aloud method avoids interpretation by the experts.

Box 6.1 illustrates how two solvers interpreted an arithmetic word problem. The two solvers arrived at the same answer, but each used a different solving strategy. The cognitive processes of experts are difficult to obtain by other means. The **protocol**

TABLE 6.2   Voting and Rank Key Topics

Key Topics	*Number of Votes in Each Position*									
	1	*2*	*3*	*4*	*5*	*6*	*7*	*8*	*9*	*Mean*
Anal	4	1	—	2	—	—	—	—	—	2.00
Exec	1	2	1	1	—	—	1	1	—	3.86
Do p	2	—	—	2	—	1	1	—	1	4.57
Doin	—	—	1	—	5	1	—	—	—	4.86
Impl	—	1	2	—	—	2	—	1	1	5.29
Know	—	2	—	—	—	3	1	1	—	5.29
Buil	—	1	—	1	1	—	2	2	—	5.86
Deve	—	—	2	—	—	—	2	2	1	6.43
Shou	—	—	1	1	1	—	—	—	4	6.86

Rank

Sum

Analysis of group decision   56

Executive information system   43

Do projects that add to   38

Doing rapid prototyping   36

Implement e-mail for   33

Knowledge acquisition session   33

Build interactive knowledge   29

Develop electronic roster   22

▪ ▪ ▪ ▪ ▪ ▪

▪▪▪▪▪▪ BOX 6.1 ▪▪▪▪▪▪

COGNITIVE APPROACH TO PROBLEM SOLVING

A father, a mother, and their daughter have a combined age of 70 years. The father is three times as old as the daughter. The mother is the same age as the father. How old is the daughter?

SOLVER 1

1. This sounds complicated—I'll give it a shot.
2. Assume F for father, M for mother, and D for daughter.
3. F + M + D = 70
4. F is 3 times D.
5. M = F
6. So far, I have three equations and three unknowns.
7. D + 3 times D (or F) + 3 times D (or M) = 70
8. 7 D = 70
9. D = 10
10. Ages of father and mother total 70 - 10 or 60.
11. Because both are the same age, father is 30 years old and mother is 30 years old.

SOLVER 2

1. Father, mother, and daughter are 70 years old, total.
2. How can this be?

3. If father is 25 years old and mother is 25, then the daughter is 20 years old.
4. This doesn't make sense, because 25-year-old parents cannot have a 20-year-old daughter.
5. Also, the father is not 3 times the age of the daughter.
6. Father and mother must be older.
7. If father and mother are 27 years old, then the daughter must be 16.
8. The daughter is not 3 times the age of the father.
9. A 27-year-old father cannot logically have a 16-year-old daughter.
10. This is not the right combination. I'll have to change ages.
11. What if the father is 30 years and the mother is 30 years? This will make the daughter 10 years old.
12. This adds up to 70 all right.
13. At 30, the father is exactly 3 times the age of the daughter, who is 10 years old.
14. The mother is also the same age as the father, which is 30.
15. The whole thing makes sense. A 30-year-old father can have a 10-year-old daughter.

▪▪▪▪▪▪

analysis or think-aloud method shows clearly how the solvers approached the problem one step at a time. It is a useful technique for knowledge capture.

WHAT IS A SCENARIO?

In protocol analysis, protocols (also known as *cases* or *scenarios*) are collected by asking experts to solve a problem and verbalize what goes through their heads, stating directly what they think. In other words, the expert keeps talking, speaking out loud whatever thoughts come to mind, while they answer a question or solve a problem. Unlike their role in other techniques, knowledge developers do not interrupt or ask questions in the interim. The solving process is carried out in an automatic fashion while the expert talks. Structuring the information elicited occurs later when the knowledge developer analyzes the protocol.

The term *scenario* is used to refer to a detailed and sometimes complex sequence of events. Mission scenarios, for example, are a detailed specification of a flight plan, a series of aircraft maneuvers and pilot tasks. These can be used to train pilots or to consider the performance requirements of an aircraft.

A scenario refers to a situation or, more precisely (because it has a temporal component), an episode. A scenario involves individuals, objects, and courses of events. One important characteristic of scenarios is that they describe particular states of affairs and events. They can be used to describe possible worlds in which certain yet to be considered actualities could occur. This is the case with mission scenarios, where a pilot is being trained for certain anticipated events. It is also true of design scenarios, in which a designer imagines what it would be like to interact with a system using a particular kind of device.

The purpose of a scenario is to provide an explicit concrete vision of how some human activity could be supported by technology. Scenarios are one good reference point for making design decisions. By showing the actual circumstances under which people work, scenarios provide guidelines on how a technology should perform. The very act of making things explicit and clear also helps in making design choices.

For a scenario to be good, it must realistically depict some actual human activity. It must "bring to life" for its users the activity that is to be supported. Scenario developers need interviewing and writing skills as well as technical imagination and understanding. These skills could be distributed between two people; for example, one researcher might be an especially good interviewer, while the other has strong writing skills and technical depth.

PROTOCOL PROCEDURE OF THE DIABETIC FOOT KM SYSTEM

This KM system stores knowledge that directs a diabetic foot patient to seek either self-help, medical help, or surgical help.

Case Description

1.	Sex	**female**
2.	Age	**45–48**
3.	Complaint	**blister does not heal; pain in left foot when standing or walking**
4.	How much does patient weigh?	**230 pounds**
5.	How long has patient had the blister?	**2 weeks**
6.	Has patient had blisters before?	**no**
7.	Does the blister get worse when walking?	**yes**
8.	Where is pain located?	**left foot below ankle**
9.	How strong is the pain?	**quite strong**
10.	How long has patient had pain?	**over a week**
11.	Did patient use any medication for pain?	**no**
12.	Does pain change with movement?	**no**
13.	What does patient think is wrong?	**poor shoe fit**

Protocol

1. This is a woman in her mid- to late 40s.
2. Being quite overweight and a diabetic, blisters are common occurrences.
3. Pain is symptomatic of the blister.
4. Patient is experiencing this blister for the first time. She's probably more worried than in pain.

5. Being diabetic, blisters take a long time to heal. It is not likely to get worse.

.

.

.

40. I don't see skin broken or pus accumulating, which is a good sign.
41. I'm going to recommend NSD and soaking the foot in warm water before going to bed and after getting up in the morning.
42. Her husband is going to have to help.
43. I'm going to recommend that patient wear wide-toed shoes.

.

.

.

64. So, for the moment, I am going to tell the patient to see me in 2 weeks.
65. Right now, I wouldn't recommend any medical treatment. Surgery is the last thing on my mind.
66. I'll relay this diagnosis and decision to patient.

In summary, think-aloud or protocol analysis is a knowledge capture method that consists of asking experts to think aloud while going through a problem solution and analyzing the resulting verbal protocols. It is an effective source of information on cognitive processes and for building knowledge management systems. In fact, think-aloud makes the expert (in this example, the surgeon) cognizant of the process being described, which is a contribution to the validity of the practice or procedure used in the diagnosis. It also provides a wealth of information toward knowledge representation.

■■■■ Consensus Decision Making

The term *consensus* refers to a clear agreement regarding the best solution to a problem. As a tool, **consensus decision making** follows brainstorming. It is effective only when each expert in the team has had adequate opportunity to air their views. To arrive at a consensus, the knowledge engineer conducting the exercise tries to rally the experts toward one or two alternatives while fostering the experts' feelings of the ownership of the alternative(s) so that they want to support it.

In consensus decision making, a knowledge developer follows a procedure designed to ensure fairness and standardization in the way experts arrive at a consensus:

1. The knowledge developer explains the solutions generated earlier, possibly through brainstorming. After a problem is presented to the panel of experts, they are asked to vote on the alternative solutions they generated. Voting takes place in rounds, with each round devoted to reducing the number of alternative solutions.
2. In round 1, the knowledge developer explains that each expert has three votes to cast: one vote per option for a maximum of three options among the total number of options. The options with fewer than the agreed-upon number of votes are deleted.
3. In round 2, the knowledge developer questions the experts to see if any of the remaining options can be deleted or merged. Then, the experts are given two votes each to vote on the remaining options. That is, each expert votes on two of the total number of options that remain after round 1.
4. As with round 1, those options that receive fewer than the required number of votes are deleted. This process of voting by rounds continues until only two options

are left. During the last round, each expert is allowed to cast only one vote for the final option. The option that carries the majority vote is selected as the solution.

The consensus method is quite effective and works well most of the time, but it is not without problems. First, it is a bit tedious and can take hours; at any time during the round, an expert may call for a discussion of the remaining options before further voting. Second, some experts complain that each option unfairly carries the same weight; some options are more serious than others and should be adopted or rejected by every expert on the panel. Third, experts have been known to walk out on the whole capture process because of the rigidity of the consensus method. Although this tool promotes a democratic process of decision making, some experts allow personalities and personal agendas to interfere.

▪▪▪▪ The Repertory Grid

The **repertory grid** is another tool used in knowledge capture. The domain expert is viewed as a scientist who classifies and categorizes a problem domain using his or her own model. The grid is used to capture and evaluate the expert's model or the way the expert works through the solution. Two experts in the same problem domain will produce different sets of results that are personal and subjective. Experts see problems based on reasoning that has stood the test of time and are able to use this deep knowledge in the problem-solving process. For example:

NOVICE LOAN CUSTOMER: The bank tried to charge more interest than they promised. Now I am in a bind.

EXPERT LOAN CUSTOMER: The issue is whether their last interest quote was an estimate or a binding rate for the loan

A novice may have a general sense of the effects of certain actions, but the expert foresees cause and effect in a specific way. The goal of knowledge capture is to identify the underlying principles the experts use so that they can be captured and later used by the user.

The repertory grid is a representation of the experts' way of looking at a particular problem. A grid is a scale or a bipolar construct on which elements are placed within gradations. The knowledge developer elicits the constructs and then asks the domain expert to provide a set of examples, called *elements*. Each element is rated according to the constructs that have been provided. The following are examples of bipolar constructs:

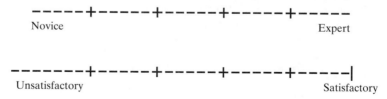

Gradations break down the scale for more accurate ratings. In the following unsatisfactory-satisfactory construct, a 1–5 point scale is used.

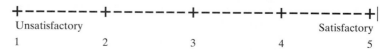

Once a particular scale has been adopted, it should stay the same throughout the grid, although the terms that describe the rating vary from construct to construct. The rating is useful in comparing individual rankings. For example, if John is rated "1," Ann is rated "3," and Bob is rated "4," it does not mean that Bob is four times as satisfactory as John. It only means that Bob is more satisfactory than either John or Ann. It is a comparative subjective rating of elements along a scale.

One of the benefits of the repertory grid is that it may prompt the expert to think more seriously about the problem and how to solve it. The main drawback is that it tends to be a difficult tool to manage effectively when large grids are accompanied by complex details. Large grids defeat the tool's goals of clarity, simplicity, and manageability. For this reason, knowledge developers normally use the grid in the early stages of knowledge capture.

The practical use of the repertory grid can be demonstrated by the following interview, in which the human resources director compares bank tellers in order to decide on potential promotions or transfers. The expert is the human resources director. The comparative rating of the tellers is shown in Figure 6.4.

KD: As I understand it, we're here to discuss the selection process and selection criteria for the bank's tellers.

EXPERT: Yes, I'm interested in reviewing all of the tellers to get a better understanding of our selection procedure.

KD: Which tellers do you consider prime candidates for the purpose of the selection procedure?

EXPERT: I have in mind Dixie, John, Barry, Curt, Lester, and Joanne.

KD: If you take the first three tellers (Dixie, John, and Barry), which two are about the same but differ from the third?

EXPERT: I'd say Dixie and John are similar, but Barry is quite different.

KD: If experience is the similarity factor, what word would describe their dissimilarity?

EXPERT: Inexperience

KD: Suppose we place "experience" and "inexperience" on a scale of 1 to 3, where 1 represents "inexperienced" and 3 represents "experienced." How would you rate the tellers?

EXPERT:

Dixie	3	
John		3
Barry	1	
Curt		1
Lester	1	
Joanne		1

▪ ▪ ▪ ▪ ▪ ▪ ▪ **FIGURE 6.4:** A Repertory Grid Rating Job Performance of Bank Tellers

Construct		T1	T2	T3	T4	T5	T6	Construct	
1	Inexperience	3	3	1	1	1	1	Experienced	1
2	Academically Ill-Qualified	2	1	2	1	1	3	Academically Qualified	2
3	Poor Appearance	3	2	1	2	1	3	Good Appearance	3
4	Late	2	3	2	3	1	1	Punctual	4
5	Introverted	2	3	3	2	1	1	Extroverted	5
T1	Dixie								
T2	John								
T3	Barry								
T4	Curt								
T5	Lester								
T6	Joanne								

KD: Let us now take the last three tellers, Curt, Lester, and Joanne. How would you compare them?

EXPERT: These tellers, I'd want to compare in terms of academic qualifications. I'd say Joanne is better qualified than Curt or Lester. Using the 1 to 3 scale you suggested earlier, I'd rate the six tellers as follows:

Dixie		2
John		1
Barry	2	
Curt		1
Lester	1	
Joanne		3

KD: Next, let's take Joanne, Dixie, and Barry. How would you rate them?

EXPERT: I guess I'd want to rate them based on appearance—how well they look in the eyes of the customers. Based on customer feedback, I'd rate Joanne and Dixie the same. Barry is not in the same league. I'd rate them as follows:

Dixie		3
John		2
Barry	1	
Curt		2
Lester	1	
Joanne		3

KD: Let's take one more group—John, Curt, and Lester.

EXPERT: These tellers remind me of attendance. John and Curt are hardly ever late to work. Lester is often late. So, using the 1 to 3 scale (1 is tardy; 3 is prompt), I'd rate them as follows:

Dixie		2
John		3
Barry	2	
Curt		3
Lester	1	
Joanne		1

KD: Do you have other ratings you want to include?

EXPERT: Just one dealing with John, Barry, and Lester. John and Barry are extroverts; Lester isn't. I'd use the 1 to 3 scale (1 = introvert; 3 = extrovert) and rate them as follows:

Dixie		2
John		3
Barry	3	
Curt		2
Lester	1	
Joanne		1

▪▪▪▪ ## Nominal Group Technique (NGT)

In some problem domains, more than one expert might be available as a source of knowledge for building the KM system. However, for situations in which several experts have overlapping expertise, each expert's opinion must be interpreted in line with the problem domain. In fact, a single expert is used precisely to avoid potential contradictions between experts and possible misinterpretations on the part of the knowledge developer. The nominal group technique and Delphi method have been shown to mitigate some of the process losses associated with multiple experts.

An alternative to the consensus technique, the **nominal group technique (NGT)** provides an interface between consensus and brainstorming. In this technique, the panel of experts becomes a "nominal" group whose meetings are structured in order to effectively pool individual judgment.

NGT is an ideawriting or idea generation technique. **Ideawriting** is a structured group approach used to develop ideas and explore their meaning for clarity and specificity; the result is a written report.

The NGT procedure begins as follows:

1. The knowledge developer explains the technique and provides to each expert information about the problem or alternative solutions.
2. Instead of discussing the problem, the knowledge developer asks each expert to list on paper the pros and cons of the problem or alternative solutions. This is silent generation of ideas in writing.
3. The knowledge developer compiles a list of all pros and cons without making comments regarding their merit. Any overlapping ideas are either reworded or deleted.
4. Each expert is given a copy of the compiled pros and cons and asked to rank them on the basis of their priorities.
5. The knowledge developer then leads a discussion of the pros and cons and their respective ranks. The discussion focuses on the priorities placed on each item and the reasoning behind them, which leads to a listing of possible solutions.
6. The knowledge engineer compiles the alternative solutions. This is followed by a group discussion that should lead to agreement of the "best" solution.

Unfortunately, NGT can be time-consuming and tedious. It has been known to promote impatience among the experts who must listen to all kinds of discussions with other experts, some of whom will lobby aggressively for their own ideas. One way to expedite this procedure is to have the experts vote as a group on the set of possible problems to work on, and later on which solution(s) to use

On the other hand, as experts share expertise, things can really jell in adopting the best solution. NGT is ideal in situations of uncertainty regarding the nature of the problem domain. It is also effective in multiple expert knowledge capture, especially when minimizing the differences in status among experts is important.

NGT is similar to brainstorming, except that it is based on the understanding that certain group goals can be best achieved by writing rather than by discussion. Each expert has an equal chance to express ideas in parallel with other experts in the group. Because discussion is accommodated in sequential order, NGT can be a more efficient and productive approach than brainstorming.

▪▪▪▪ The Delphi Method

Another tool used in multiple expert knowledge capture is the **Delphi method.** Essentially, it is a survey of experts. Experts are polled concerning a given problem domain. A series of questionnaires are used to pool the experts' responses in order to solve a difficult problem. Each expert's contributions are shared with the rest of the experts by using the results from each questionnaire to construct the next questionnaire.

The Delphi method gets its name from the ancient Greek oracle at Delphi, who was said to be able to look into the future. It works this way:

1. A panel of experts is asked to prepare an anonymous opinion about a focused problem domain. Each person is usually given a short written explanation of the problem. For example, one problem could be to estimate when air cargo revenues of XYZ airline would equal its passenger revenues.
2. For the second round, each expert is given a summary of the results of the first round and is asked to make a second (still anonymous) estimate on the same issue based on the additional information and reasons provided in the summary of the preceding anonymous opinions. Knowing how the other experts responded, an expert may stick to or change his or her initial answer.
3. Step 2 is repeated two or more times, and then a final summary is prepared. By this point, all extreme estimates will have been deleted, and those that remain will converge on a narrow range of answers.

The Delphi method has three important features:

1. *Anonymous response.* Because opinions are obtained anonymously, the danger that the response of one expert will bias another is removed. For example, a top executive will have no influence on a subordinate who may be part of the group.
2. *Controlled feedback.* Through a controlled set of rounds, the Delphi method allows each expert to rethink any previous answers in light of the anonymous feedback received from other experts.
3. *Statistical group response.* The final opinion of the experts is an aggregate of each expert's response in the final round.

The Delphi method has two main limitations. First, experts often lack the necessary knowledge on which to base their final judgment. The problem could be one of communication. Second, poorly designed questionnaires have been known to be less than effective in developing an understanding of the complexity of the problem domain. The knowledge developer must exercise care in assessing in advance the likely consequences of using the Delphi method.

▪▪▪▪ Concept Mapping

A unique tool to represent knowledge in graphs is **concept mapping**. It is a network of concepts that consists of nodes and links. A node represents a concept, and a link represents the relationship between concepts (see Figure 6.5). Similar to a semantic network, concept mapping can be done for several reasons: to design a complex structure (such as large Web sites); to generate ideas (for example, brainstorming); to communicate complex ideas (such as finding petroleum); or to diagnose misunderstanding. Initially developed by J. D. Novak at Cornell University in the 1960s, concept mapping is designed to transform new concepts and propositions into existing cognitive structures related to knowledge capture.

As can be seen, concept mapping is a structured conceptualization, where a topic of interest involving input from one or more experts produces a clear pictorial view of their ideas, their concepts, and how they are interrelated. It is an effective way for a group to function without losing their individuality. In contrast to concept mapping is **mind mapping,** which consists of a key word or concept. The knowledge developer draws around the central word several main ideas that relate to that word. From each "child" word, several main related ideas are further drawn. A mind map has only one main concept; a concept map may have several.

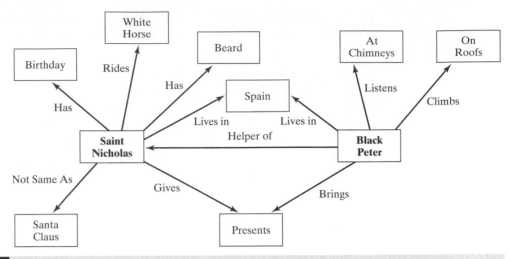

▪▪▪▪▪▪▪ **FIGURE 6.5:** Conceptual Map—An Example

SOURCE: Adapted from Lanzing, Jan. "Concept Mapping." Article posted on users.edte.utwente.nl/lanzing/cm_home.htm, Date accessed October 18, 2002.

PROCEDURE

Using a concept map as a tool involves a 6-step procedure. As shown in Figure 6.6, these steps are as follows:

- *Preparation,* which centers around identifying the participants and developing a focus for the knowledge capture project. For example, in the Diabetic Foot KM System, the orthopedic surgeons decided to focus on defining gangrene before discussing it. A schedule for the mapping is also agreed upon.
- *Idea generation.* In this step, the participants generate a series of statements that address the focus and expected outcomes as a result of the participation. This is where brainstorming and nominal group tools may be useful.

▪▪▪▪▪▪▪ **FIGURE 6.6:** Steps in Concept Mapping

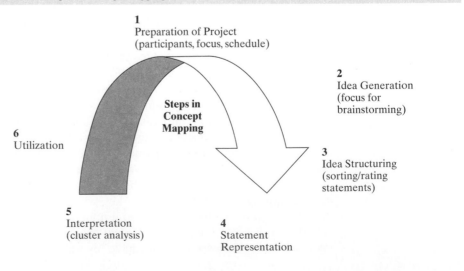

- *Statement structuring.* Once the statements are assembled, they are sorted into piles of similar ones, with one statement on each standard-size card. Then, each pile is given a unique descriptive label, and each participant rates each statement on an agreed-upon scale, such as 1 to 5 (1 = unimportant and 5 = extremely important).
- *Representation.* This step represents idea analysis. It is where the sort and ratings are represented in map form. One form of analysis, called *cluster analysis,* takes the output of the point scaling and partitions the map into clusters. The statements that are specific outcomes are viewed as outcome clusters.
- *Interpretation.* In this step, the knowledge developer or facilitator works with the participants to arrive at their own labels and how each map is interpreted.
- *Utilization.* This is where the maps are actually made operational, and the results are displayed.

CONCEPT MAPPING AND SEMANTIC NETS

One graphic tool used to encode relationships to capture knowledge is the semantic net. Similar to concept mapping, a **semantic net** is a collection of nodes linked together to form a net. Through a net, a knowledge developer can graphically represent descriptive or declarative knowledge. Each idea of interest is represented by a node linked by lines called **arcs** that show relationships between nodes. It is merely a network of concepts and relationships.

Figure 6.7 presents a partial semantic net representing an airline's personnel KM system; it shows a specialist in pilot testing. The knowledge of the expert (Jim Harding) is expressed in basic elements rather than complex statements. The personnel knowledge base includes elements such as Olesek's (flight instructor) license, a list of the

■ ■ ■ ■ ■ ■ ■ **FIGURE 6.7:**   Semantic Net of a Personnel Knowledge Base

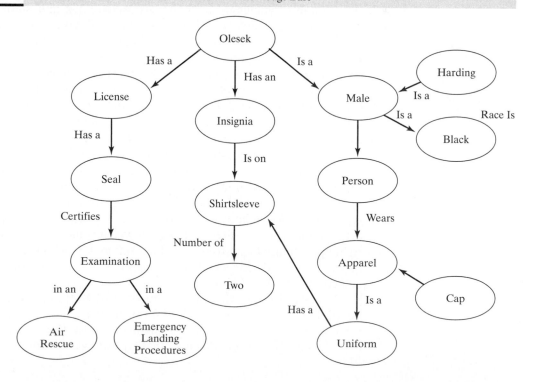

characteristics of each element, and a way to link things together. For example, the knowledge base would indicate that the insignia on Olesek's shirtsleeve signifies a flight instructor.

▪▪▪▪ Blackboarding

Imagine bringing a group of experts together in a room with a large blackboard. The experts work together to solve a problem, using the blackboard as their work space. Initial data are written on the blackboard for all to see. Each expert has an equal chance to contribute to the solution via the blackboard. The process of blackboarding (also called *groupware*) continues until the problem has been solved.

One important assumption of a blackboard system is that all participants are experts, but they have acquired their own expertise in situations different from those of the other experts in the group. Because each expert's experience is unique, no one need feel either inferior or superior in offering a possible solution. The essence of this technique is the independence of expertise in an atmosphere that discourages compliance or intimidation.

There are several characteristics of blackboarding:

1. *Diverse approaches to problem-solving.* The fact that the experts have different ways of thinking does not prevent them from solving the problem. Each expert (called a *knowledge source,* or *KS*) in this technique is similar to a black box whose internal thinking process is hidden from other KSs in the meeting. It does not really matter how each KS thinks through a solution. Each KS can make contributions within the framework of the blackboard.
2. *Common language for interaction.* The KSs participating in this technique should share a common language (including use of diagrams and charts) so that they can interact, interpret, and contribute to the final solution. Private jargon or abbreviated phrases should be discouraged, because they limit the involvement of other KSs in the solution process.
3. *Flexible representation of information.* An expert's suggestion of an alternative or a partial solution in graphics versus text is allowable by the software as long as it can be understood by all experts concerned. No prior restrictions on the information limit its content or how it should be represented on the blackboard.
4. *Efficient storage and location of information.* Virtually all of the information contributed by the KSs is stored somewhere in the blackboard. To ensure quick access to an updated version of the blackboard, the blackboard is organized into regions, each representing a specific type of information. Once the type of information required is determined, the KS can go directly to the suitable blackboard region and scan the information stored in it. Remember that experts do not interact with one another directly. Each KS watches the blackboard, looking for the right opportunity to contribute to the solution. KSs who see a new change on the blackboard can decide whether they agree with it, and if not, they can go ahead and contribute their opinion.

   KSs are also motivated by events other than those displayed on the blackboard. For example, a KS might inform the blackboard about an event of personal interest, which is entered on the blackboard. The blackboard then directly considers the KS owner whenever that type of event occurs.

5. *Organized participation.* One benefit to blackboard technology is that two or more experts cannot respond to an event simultaneously. Only one expert at a time is allowed, which promotes control and gives each KS a chance to mull over the changes before they decide to contribute. The knowledge developer can be used to restore order by considering each KS's request to approach the blackboard with the proposed change.

6. *Iterative approach to problem-solving.* The solution to the problem domain is approached step by step, like building blocks from bottom up or from basic to advanced. In this situation, no single KS has a full answer to the problem. Each KS refines and adds something of value to someone else's contribution, and the whole group moves toward the solution incrementally. A summary of the characteristics of blackboarding is provided in Figure 6.8.

A typical blackboard system consists of three parts: knowledge sources (KSs), the blackboard, and a control mechanism. The inference engine and the knowledge base are part of the blackboard system. A **knowledge source** is the expert—a unique module that has the knowledge to solve the problem.

The **blackboard** is a global memory structure, a database, or a repository that stores all partial problem solutions and other data that are in various stages of completion. It serves as a communication medium and triggers a KS into action or controls the necessary information for the blackboarding process.

Blackboard processing is based on the concept of independent cooperating experts. Each KS is an independent expert who observes the status of the blackboard and tries to contribute a higher level partial solution based on the knowledge it has and how well such knowledge applies to the current blackboard state. In this respect, the blackboard is useful for structuring complex problem-solving jobs that require multiple experts.

The **control mechanism** coordinates the flow and pattern of the problem solution. It monitors the changes on the blackboard and decides on the next action(s) to take. The problem-solving behavior of the whole process is encoded in the control module (see Figure 6.9).

The blackboard approach is useful in situations involving multiple expertise, diverse knowledge representations, or uncertain knowledge. It can be particularly valuable when working with complex applications or prototyping an application. Unfortunately, blackboard systems have too short a history to provide a good rationale for advocating their use. This is compounded by a lack of commercial software specifically designed for building blackboard applications and a shortage of developers experienced in this area.

▪ ▪ ▪ ▪ ▪ ▪ ▪ **FIGURE 6.8:** Key Characteristics of Blackboard Systems

Diverse approaches to problem-solving
Common language for interaction
Flexible representation of information
Efficient storage and location of information
Organized participation
Iterative nature of problem-solving

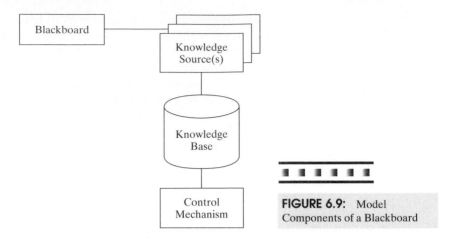

FIGURE 6.9: Model Components of a Blackboard

▪▪▪▪ Implications for Knowledge Management

The knowledge developer has a number of challenges in choosing knowledge capture tools. First, the technique that best taps the knowledge of the domain expert must be determined. Certain techniques are ideal for single experts, and others are more suitable for multiple experts. Second, advance planning and preparation for knowledge capture can best be carried out through using the most efficient tools, thereby making the best use of the expert's time and resources.

The managerial aspects of tool selection have to do with the organization's commitment to providing proper training and support for the knowledge developer. The knowledge developer should be an effective manager of time. Selecting the right knowledge capture techniques means saving time and ensuring reliable representation of the knowledge. The knowledge developer must also be able to communicate with experts, regardless of their background or expertise. Communication breakdown could spell disaster for any project, large or small.

Finally, the knowledge developer's success depends on cultivating good relations with management in general. In other words, a knowledge developer must be aware of the organization's politics, its grapevine, and what steps are necessary to get systems accepted. The support of a champion could make the entire knowledge process easier.

Management support also includes continued commitment to fund the project. Lack of proper financial support can lead to a low-quality product, an incomplete system, or dissatisfied users. In the final analysis, management must see the KM system project as an investment from beginning to end and gauge its support according to the gain it hopes to realize.

SUMMARY ▪▪▪▪

- On-site observation is a process of observing, interpreting, and recording based on observation of the expert's problem-solving behavior while it takes place. The technique carries with it a certain protocol. It requires more listening than talking and enables the knowledge developer to seek knowledge within the working world of the expert. The main problem is that some experts do not like to be observed. Some question as to the accuracy of the captured knowledge may also arise. The shuttle process allows room for possible errors.

- Brainstorming invites two or more experts into an idea generation session in which discussions are carried out and a variety of opinions are tossed around. The procedure includes introducing the brainstorming session, presenting a problem for the experts to consider, prompting the experts to generate ideas, and watching for signs of convergence. This technique dictates that the expert cannot be cut short, yet some experts talk too long for comfort. Electronic brainstorming tends to improve the efficiency with which brainstorming is conducted and evaluated.

- Protocol analysis or think-aloud is a knowledge capture method that allows cases and scenarios to be collected by asking experts to solve a problem while verbalizing what goes through their heads—stating directly what they think. The expert speaks out loud whatever thoughts come to mind while answering a question or solving a problem.

- Consensus decision making is used to arrive at a clear agreement regarding the best solution to a problem. As a tool, it follows brainstorming. Experts converge toward one or two alternatives for a final consensus. This technique is quite effective and works well most of the time, but it is a bit tedious and can take hours to conclude. One of the drawbacks is that options unfairly carry the same weight. Some participants are uncomfortable with its rigidity.

- The repertory grid is used to capture and evaluate the way the expert works through a solution to a problem domain. The grid is a scale with elements described by the gradations. Gradations break down the scale to allow for more accurate rating. Once adopted, the scale should stay the same throughout the grid, although the terms that describe the rating vary from construct to construct. One of the benefits of the grid is that it may prompt the expert who sees it on paper to think more seriously about the problem and how to solve it. On the other hand, the grid can be difficult to manage.

- An alternative to the consensus technique is the nominal group technique or NGT. It is an ideawriting or idea generation technique used as an interface between consensus and brainstorming. A panel of experts becomes a nominal group. The idea is to structure small group meetings so that individual judgments can be effectively pooled. NGT is time-consuming and tedious. One way to expedite this procedure is to have the experts vote as a group on the set of possible problems to work on, and later on which solution(s) to use. The tool is ideal in situations of uncertainty regarding the nature of the problem domain.

- The Delphi method is a series of surveys that poll experts concerning a given problem domain. Questionnaires pool the experts' responses in order to solve a difficult problem. The procedure begins by asking a panel of experts to prepare individual anonymous opinions about a focused problem domain. For the second round, each expert receives a summary of the results of the first round and is asked to make a second estimate on the same issue based on the additional information provided in the summary. This second step is repeated two or more times, and then a final summary is prepared. The main feature of this tool is anonymous response, controlled feedback, and statistical group response. A poorly designed questionnaire can be a serious constraint.

- Blackboarding offers a diversity of approaches to problem-solving and a common language for interaction. It also has the characteristics of flexible representation of information, efficient storage and location of information, organized participation, and an iterative approach to problem-solving. The blackboard approach is useful in situations involving multiple expertise, diverse knowledge representations, or uncertain knowledge.

TERMS TO KNOW ▪▪▪▪

Active participant observation: Switching back and forth between asking questions and observing the domain expert.

Blackboard: A shared database in which various knowledge sources work together to solve a problem.

Blackboarding: Experts work together in a common work area to come up with a solution.

Brainstorming: An unstructured approach to generating ideas by which two or more experts generate ideas about a problem domain.

Consensus: Finding a clear agreement on the best solution to a problem.

Consensus decision making: A knowledge developer conducts the exercise after brainstorming to rally the experts toward one or two alternatives and to convey the impression that all of them are part owners of the alternative(s).

Control mechanism: Coordinates the flow and pattern of the problem solution in a blackboard model.

Delphi method: A series of surveys that poll experts concerning a given problem domain.

Electronic brainstorming: A computer-aided approach to dealing with multiple experts through a network of PCs, which promotes live exchange of ideas between experts; the ideas can be sorted and condensed into an organized format.

Grid: A scale or a bipolar construct on which elements are placed within gradations.

Ideawriting: A structured group approach used to develop ideas, explore their meaning for clarity and specificity, and produce a written report.

Knowledge source: A unique module that has the knowledge to solve the problem.

Nominal group technique (NGT): Small group meetings in which individual judgment can often be effectively pooled; interface between consensus and brainstorming.

On-site observation: Observing, interpreting, and recording an expert's problem-solving behavior as it occurs in the expert's domain.

Passive participant observation: Act of only observing the domain expert, in which the knowledge engineer refrains from asking questions as the situation arises during the observation.

Protocol analysis: Systematic collection and analysis of protocols; synonymous with think-aloud protocol.

Repertory grid: Knowledge capture tool by which the problem domain is classified and categorized around the domain expert's own model; a representation of the expert's way of looking at a particular problem.

Shuttle process: The back and forth aspect of the knowledge developer's recollection of an event as it was mentally registered at the time of the retrospection.

Think-aloud: Knowledge capture method in which the expert speaks out loud whatever thoughts come to mind while answering a question or solving a problem; synonymous with protocol analysis.

TEST YOUR UNDERSTANDING ▪▪▪▪

1. Explain in your own words the distinctive features of on-site observation. What kinds of problems does it pose?
2. Distinguish between:
   a. brainstorming and consensus decision making
   b. protocol analysis and Delphi method
   c. repertory grid and nominal group technique
   d. blackboarding and electronic brainstorming
3. How is brainstorming conducted? Provide an example.
4. If no interruptions are allowed or no questions asked while the expert is answering a question or solving a problem, how does the facilitator control a protocol analysis session?
5. In what way does consensus decision making follow brainstorming? Be specific.
6. Give an example of your own to illustrate the procedure followed in consensus decision making.
7. "The grid is used to acquire and evaluate the expert's model—the way the expert works through the solution." Do you agree? What is unique about the grid? What are some of its drawbacks?
8. In what way is the nominal group technique an alternative to the consensus technique?
9. Illustrate by an example of your own the procedure followed in NGT.

10. If you were asked to apply the Delphi method involving four experts, what procedure would you follow? What limitations would you expect in this knowledge capture technique?
11. Blackboarding offers certain characteristics. Explain each briefly. What makes up the basic model?

KNOWLEDGE EXERCISES ▪ ▪ ▪ ▪

1. Divide into small groups of five to seven people. Select a group discussion leader and a person to record responses. Use the brainstorming guidelines to conduct a 5-minute brainstorming session on the following topic. Your goal is to identify creative solutions to the problem:

    Employees in large companies often complain that personal worth perception is low. They feel that the company does not overtly reward them for their contributions or set procedures that allow them to be most productive and creative.

2. Based on the situation presented in problem 1, complete the following tasks:
    a. *Brainstorm* how the company can reward efforts and increase the perception of personal worth other than issuing pay increases.
    b. Use *nominal group technique* to find the best solution to the employee personal worth perception problem. Consider the solutions from the brainstorming activity and select the "best" solution from that set.
    c. Use *consensus decision making* with the goal of selecting a solution to the employee personal worth perception problem to which all members of the group can commit.

3. Publisher KM System:

    Knowledge capture uses a variety of tools. In the Publisher KM System (discussed in Chapter 5), several knowledge capture tools were used.

    Knowledge was captured from a series of four interviews with the expert. The first two interviews encompassed fairly broad questions about the expert's decision-making process. The last two interviews elicited more detailed information about the expert's decision process by discussing the outcome of specific sample case scenario decisions, to which confidence levels were assigned.

    In one interview, an attempt was made at rapid prototyping, but the format of the table used was difficult for the expert to understand. It was not used as productively as expected.

    An induction table (similar to a decision table) was developed, which included possible combinations of the five variables and their outcomes—accept, defer, or reject a book manuscript (see Table 6.3). Evaluate the approach taken in the knowledge capture process to determine the rationale and reliability of the tools used.

4. A total of six knowledge capture sessions were conducted with the expert at the expert's location, except for the few occasions when the session required use of the system.

    In the first session, the knowledge developer became familiar with the domain expert, elaborating on the admissions materials previously provided. This overview made it possible to establish a basis of knowledge, which evolved into the concept dictionary. In the second session, the interview was used to extract basic parameters and then had the expert organize these parameters according to her view of the domain. This organization was transformed into a visual concept diagram of the domain. The concept diagram was referred to and refined throughout the entire acquisition process. This diagram provided a clear direction for the acquisition process. It also became the foundation for the knowledge representation structure (see Figure 6.10).

TABLE 6.3 Induction Table

Rule #	Market	Author's Reputation	Reviewers' Comments	Author's Requirements	Publisher's Decision	Confidence Level
0	High	Excellent			Offer contract	0.90
1	High	Average	Very good	Average or below average	Offer contract	0.80
2	High	Average	Very good	Above average	Offer contract	0.85
3	High	Average	Mixed	Average or below average	Offer contract	
4	High	Average	Mixed	Above average	Get sample chapters	
5	High	Average	Below average	Average or below average	Get sample chapters	
6	High	Average	Below average	Above average	Reject manuscript	
7	High	Poor	Very good	Above average	Offer contract	0.75
8	High	Poor	Very good	Average	Offer contract	0.85
9	High	Poor	Very good	Below average	Offer contract	
10	Moderate	Poor	Mixed	Above average	Reject manuscript	
11	Moderate	Poor	Mixed	Average or below average	Get sample chapters	
12	Moderate	Poor	Below average	Above average	Reject manuscript	
13	Moderate	Poor	Below average	Average	Reject manuscript	
14	Moderate	Poor	Below average	Below average	Reject manuscript	
15	Moderate	Average	Very good	Above average	Offer contract	0.65
16	Moderate	Average	Very good	Average	Offer contract	0.75
17	Moderate	Average	Very good	Below average	Offer contract	0.90
18	Moderate	Average	Mixed	Above average	Get sample chapters	
19	Moderate	Average	Mixed	Average	Offer contract	0.70
20	Moderate	Average	Mixed	Below average	Offer contract	0.75
21	Moderate	Average	Below average	Above average	Reject manuscript	
22	Moderate	Average	Below average	Average	Reject manuscript	
23	Moderate	Average	Below average	Below average	Reject manuscript	
24	Moderate	Poor	Very good	Above average	Offer contract	0.70
25	Moderate	Poor	Very good	Average	Offer contract	0.80
26	Moderate	Poor	Very good	Below average	Offer contract	
27	Moderate	Excellent	Very good		Offer contract	0.90
28	Moderate	Excellent	Mixed	Average or below average	Offer contract	0.90
29	Moderate	Excellent	Mixed	Above average	Get sample chapters	
30	Moderate	Excellent	Below average		Get sample chapters	
31	Low	Excellent	Very good	Above average	Offer contract	0.60
32	Low	Excellent	Very good	Average	Offer contract	0.70
33	Low	Excellent	Very good	Below average	Offer contract	0.70
34	Low	Excellent	Mixed	Average or below average	Get sample chapters	
35	Low	Excellent	Mixed	Above average	Reject manuscript	
36	Low	Excellent	Below average		Reject manuscript	
37	Low	Average	Very good	Below average	Offer contract	0.70
38	Low	Average	Very good	Average	Offer contract	0.60
39	Low	Average	Very good	Above average	Reject manuscript	
40	Low	Average	Mixed	Average or below average	Get sample chapters	

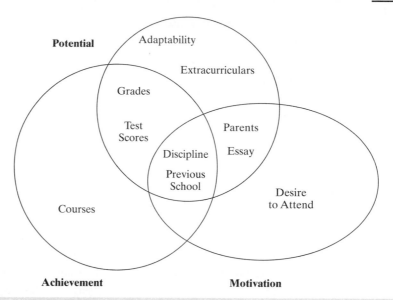

FIGURE 6.10: Concept Diagram for Undergraduate Admission

Other tools employed were process tracing and case scenarios. I used process tracing by asking the domain expert to provide an example of a typical admissions decision. From following her decision-making process, I began to understand how the parameters interacted with one another. This helped me assign parameters to groupings based on the domain concept diagram. This also alerted me to the minimum and maximum values that could be assigned to each parameter. In addition, I was able to derive the minimum requirements for consideration in which the applicant would be immediately rejected. A list of parameters is shown in Table 6.4.

In order to capture the expert's heuristics, I devised a matrix of parameters and their potential values. This allowed me to vary parameters in relation to each other. This proved to be a formidable task. Ten multivalued parameters, each with three or more permissible ranges, produced more scenarios than could easily be generated via manual means. The difficulty of this task also had implications for completeness of the rule base; therefore, scenarios could easily be overlooked. To assist me in generating scenarios, I discovered Logic Gem, a logic processor software that made life easier for the rest of the capture process.

Questions

a. Based on the nature of the problem domain, evaluate the tools used in this project.
b. How important is listing parameters early in the knowledge capture phase? Explain.
c. Convert the concept diagram to a concept diagram for Publisher Advisor. *Hint:* Focus should be on the author's past record, standing in the university, motivation as reflected in the number of books he or she has published, and so forth.

REFERENCES ▪▪▪▪

Aiken, Milam, Krosp, Jay, Shirani, Ashraf, and Martin, Jeanette. "Electronic Brainstorming in Small and Large Groups," *Information and Management*, September 1994, pp. 141–149.

Aouad, G. F., et al. "Knowledge Elicitations Using Protocol Analysis in a Workshop Environment," *Constructions Management and Economics*, May 1994, pp. 271–278.

TABLE 6.4 ADMIT Parameters

Name	Type	Values
ENGLISH	Number	0–3
SCIENCE	String	Biology, Chemistry, Physics
LANGUAGE	Boolean	Yes/No
US HIST.	Boolean	Yes/No
WORLD	Boolean	Yes/No
MATH	String	Algebra I, Algebra II, Geometry
GRADES	String	A-A, A-B, B-C, C-C, C-D, D-F
PSAT	Number	0–160
SAT	Number	0–1600
AP_ESSAY	String	Excellent, Good, Fine, Poor
TM_ESSAY	String	Excellent, Good, Fine, Poor
MOTIVATION	String	Over Achiever, On Target, Under
CHALLENGE	Boolean	Achiever
DESIRE	String	Yes/No
P_SUPPORT	String	Enthusiastic, Positive, Unsure, Negative
EXTRA_C	Boolean	Excellent, Average, Weak
SCHOOL	String	Yes/No
DISCIPLINE	String	Above, Equal, Below
DEMEANOR	String	Acceptable, Unacceptable
MINORITY	Boolean	Excellent, Average, Difficult
LEGACY	Boolean	Yes/No
FACKID	Boolean	Yes/No
STAYED	Boolean	Yes/No
BOARD	Boolean	Yes/No
SIBENROLL	Boolean	Yes/No
NEW	Boolean	Yes/No
		Yes/No

CHANGES (from Session #4)
1. Remove RELIGION
2. Remove FORMER
3. Add NEW
4. Remove ERB, SSAT
5. Remove ACCSIB (same as SIBENROLL)
6. Remove individual language, add LANGUAGE

▪ ▪ ▪ ▪ ▪ ▪

Awad, E. M. *Building Expert Systems*. Minneapolis, MN: West Publishing Company, 1996, pp. 214–238.

Dixon, Nancy M. *Common Knowledge: How Companies Thrive by Sharing What They Know*. Boston, MA: Harvard Business School Press, 2000, pp. 127–141.

El-Sherif, Helmy H., and Tang, Victor W. "TeamFocus—Electronic Brainstorming," *Training and Management Development Methods*, vol. 8, no. 3, 1994.

Garvin, David A. *Learning in Action: A Guide to Putting the Learning Organization to Work*. Boston, MA: Harvard Business School Press, 1999, pp. 155–165.

Horibe, Frances. *Managing Knowledge Workers*. New York: John Wiley & Sons, Inc., 1999, pp. 57–90.

Kambouri, Maria, Koppen, Mathieu, and Vilano, Michael. "Knowledge Assessment: Tapping Human Expertise by the QUERY Routine," *International Journal of Human-Computer Studies*, January 1994, pp. 119–151.

Lanzing, Jan. "Concept Mapping," users.edte.utwente.nl/lanzing/cm_home.htm, Date accessed October 18, 2002.

Ono, Ryota, and Wedemeyer, Dan L. "Assessing the Validity of the Delphi Technique," *Futures*, April 1994, pp. 289–304.

Tiwana, Amrit. *The Knowledge Management Toolkit*. Upper Saddle River, NJ: Prentice Hall, 2000, pp. 147–193.

Ward, Lewis. "Collaborative KM Tools: Putting Customer Care Online," *Knowledge Management*, April 2001, pp. CS1–CS6.

CHAPTER

7

Knowledge Codification

Contents

> *All you have to do is write one true sentence.*
> *Write the truest sentence that you know.*
> —ERNEST HEMINGWAY, *A MOVEABLE FEAST*

▪▪▪▪ In a Nutshell

In the previous chapter, we talked about knowledge capture and the tools that make this initial KM system building process possible. The next step is to find a way to codify and organize knowledge into a form for others to use when needed. Getting the right knowledge to the right people at the right time is the whole idea behind knowledge codification (see Figure 7.1).

Codification comes in many forms, depending on the type of knowledge and its specificity. A common way of displaying knowledge processes is via knowledge maps. Others refer to the process as storyboarding knowledge. Essentially, the goal is to link KM projects to identifiable corporate objectives that add value to the company's bottom line. The overall emphasis is on intellectual capital, company users, and the consumer. The knowledge map diagrams the relationships among people, processes, and knowledge on a project basis, department-specific or company-wide. This chapter details the reasoning and mechanics of knowledge mapping, tacit and explicit knowledge codification, and the tools of codification as a step for knowledge transfer. Knowledge and skills requirements of the knowledge developer are also covered.

In addition to codification justification and process, the chapter highlights the knowledge developer's skill set—the characteristics and criteria for codifying tacit knowledge—because it originates with people and is interpreted by the people who explain it. The key point is that it is one thing to know what to codify and how to codify, but it is another thing to know how to deal with people's attitudes and motivation during the knowledge capture phase to ensure reliable knowledge for codification. Without the interpersonal skills, the question of reliability of the knowledge capture would be severely questioned.

▪▪▪▪ What Is Knowledge Codification?

As an emerging trend, knowledge management systems are slowly succeeding in standardizing terminology and meanings for the common user. As a matter of procedure, after knowledge is captured, it is organized and codified in a manner amenable for transfer and effective use. Knowledge codification is organizing and representing knowledge before it is accessed by authorized personnel. The organizing part is usually in the form of a decision tree, a decision table, or a frame, as we shall see later in the chapter. Codification must be in a form and a structure that will build the knowledge base. It must make it accessible, explicit, and easy to access.

From a knowledge management view, codification is converting tacit knowledge to explicit knowledge in a usable form for organizational members. From an information system view, it is converting undocumented to documented information. Regardless of the view, codification is making corporate-specific knowledge (tacit and explicit) visi-

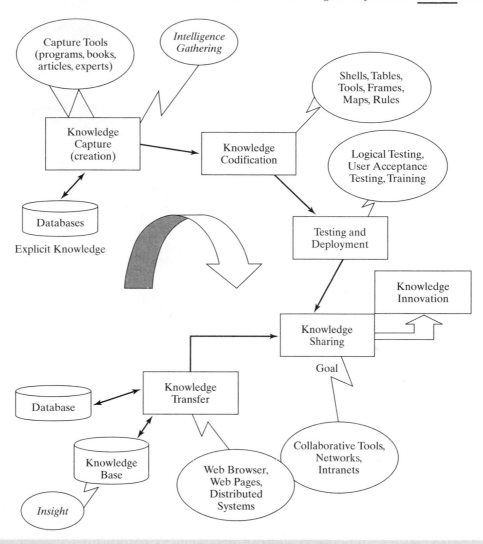

▪ ▪ ▪ ▪ ▪ ▪ ▪ **FIGURE 7.1:** Knowledge Codification in the KM System Life Cycle

ble, accessible, and usable for value-added decision making, no matter what form it may take. This means that:

- Tacit knowledge such as human expertise is identified and leveraged through a form that delivers the highest return to the business. It may be through knowledge-sharing events, organized directories, yellow pages, or other means that will connect the ones who need the expertise to the source of expertise.
- Explicit knowledge should be organized, categorized, indexed, and accessed via the company's intranet or some other means to make it visible, accessible, and usable. As conceptualized in Figure 7.2, we cultivate new organizational communities and keep them aligned around the company's intranet. This includes the social, interpersonal, financial, managerial, legal, and marketing systems. Such a "constellation" encompasses all knowledge roles performed within the firm. The connectors are facilitators that make the linkages among the "islands" viable and bind the constellation together.

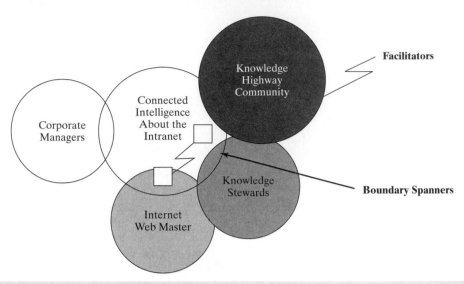

▪ ▪ ▪ ▪ ▪ ▪ ▪ ▪ **FIGURE 7.2:** Select Communities in the Intranet Knowledge of the Enterprise

Think of a legal knowledge base, where precedents are codified and made explicit to authorized users—lawyers, judges, and lay people. Such knowledge can be made available on diskette and CD-ROMs or it can be downloaded from the Internet for a charge. Precedents may be available as a model, a knowledge map, a simulation, or a set of rules. Each approach has unique features and limitations. Technology expedites action, but no format encompasses the tacit knowledge of attorneys and judges. Codified knowledge simply makes available articulated legal knowledge.

▪ ▪ ▪ ▪ Why Codify?

Like a chameleon, organizations constantly adapt to changing situations—changes in market, changes in customer tastes and preferences, turnover among company specialists and experts, and new developments in technology. In codifying knowledge, the resulting knowledge base serves in several important training and decision-making areas. Among the important ones are the following.

DIAGNOSIS

A diagnostic KM system is given identifiable information through the user's observation or experience. Built into the system's knowledge base is a list of all identifiable symptoms of specific causal factors. For a medical diagnostic system, for example, the goal is to identify the patient's illness. It starts by assuming that the patient has a particular illness. It proceeds by reviewing the rules and their actions and asks the patient for additional information about unique symptoms in order to create a description of the illness. If it cannot prove an illness exists on the basis of the symptoms, the system takes up another possible illness as the assumed illness and proceeds in the same fashion. All previous responses by the patient are retained in working memory so that repetitive questioning of the patient is avoided.

INSTRUCTION/TRAINING

The basic concept of this type of codified knowledge base is to promote training of junior or entry-level personnel based on captured knowledge of senior employees. Most training KM systems have explanatory capabilities; they display the reasoning behind their solutions. Some systems allow students to pose hypothetical "what if" scenarios, enabling them to learn by exploration.

INTERPRETATION

Interpretive codified knowledge systems compare aspects of an operation to preset standards. Typically, they use sensor data to infer the status of an ongoing process or to describe a given situation. Much of the reasoning is coupled with *confidence factors*. For example, one knowledge rule in an auto knowledge advisor reads, "If water temperature is over 50 percent of max and oil pressure is less than 9, then there is .78 certainty that engine is low on oil." In such a case, the system flashes a warning message, "CHECK ENGINE OIL."

PLANNING/SCHEDULING

A planning KM system maps out an entire course of action before any steps are taken. The system creates detailed lists of sequential tasks necessary to achieve two or more specific goals. An example is a system used by the U.S Air Force in the Afghanistan war. It makes 5-day projections of the missions to be launched and materiel to be used in reducing the enemy's military capability over a designated geographical area. Once a plan is completed, the system refines each step to arrive at the optimal schedule. The system rejects any out-of-line approach that is not within the prescribed constraints.

PREDICTION

Predictive KM systems infer the likely outcome of a given situation and flash a proper warning or suggestions for corrective action. The system evaluates a set of facts or conditions and compares it by analogy to precedent states stored in memory. The knowledge base contains several patterns on which predictions are based. These systems are used in hurricane prediction, for example. They are capable of estimating damage to real estate, and they can predict the nature of the hurricane by evaluating wind force and ocean and atmospheric conditions.

In summary, justification for codifying knowledge is to address the areas where codified knowledge results in efficient, productive, and value-added knowledge bases and knowledge applications. It means improving an organization's competitive advantage by reducing its dependence on human experts, who are expensive, hard to come by, inconsistent, and mortal. Codified knowledge and the resulting knowledge base mean allow organizational users to perform at a level closer to that of a human specialist in the domain. In the least, knowledge bases can be used as training grounds for junior employees to go through the thought process of the seasoned specialists and learn from it.

THINGS TO REMEMBER

As a process, knowledge codification is neither easy nor straightforward. There are things for the knowledge developer to remember before beginning to codify. As shown in Figure 7.3, they include the following:

- Recorded knowledge is difficult to access, either because it is fragmented or poorly organized.
- Diffusion of new knowledge is too slow.
- Knowledge is not shared, but hoarded. This has political implications, especially when knowledge cuts across departments.
- People are oblivious to who has what knowledge.

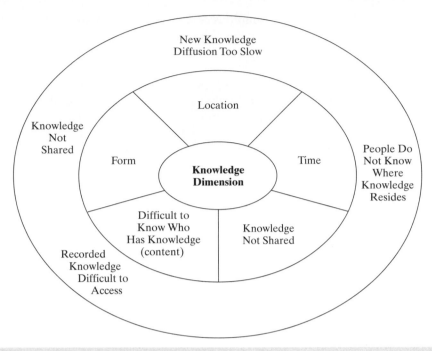

▪ ▪ ▪ ▪ ▪ ▪ ▪ **FIGURE 7.3:** Knowledge Dimensions and Bottlenecks

- Knowledge is often
  - not present in the proper form (form)
  - not available when needed (time)
  - not present where the knowledge process is carried out (location)
  - not complete (content)

With these constraints, a knowledge developer should plan carefully, as we shall see later in the chapter.

▪▪▪▪ ## Modes of Knowledge Conversion

Before we delve further into knowledge codification, it is important to distinguish between knowledge capture and knowledge creation and how they are treated in the knowledge codification phase. In knowledge creation, the basic assumption is that individuals create knowledge and that organizational knowledge creation is the amplification of the knowledge created by organizational members. In contrast, knowledge capture is viewed as part of knowledge creation. In knowledge capture, usefulness is often more important than originality and must be followed by codification and adaptation to the organization's needs.

The literature also looks at tacit and explicit knowledge as the two major types of knowledge and combines them into four modes of knowledge conversion. As shown in Table 7.1, they are as follows:

TABLE 7.1 Modes of Knowledge Conversion			
From	*To*	*Tacit*	*Explicit*
Tacit		Socialization	Externalization
Explicit		Internalization	Combination

Source: Adapted from Marwick, A. D. "Knowledge Management Technology," *IBM Systems Journal,* vol. 40, no. 4, 2001, p. 815.

- *From tacit to tacit knowledge* produces socialization, where experience is what a knowledge developer looks for in knowledge capture. Observation and practice are two important knowledge capture tools.
- *From tacit to explicit knowledge* is externalizing, explaining, or clarifying tacit knowledge via analogies, models, or metaphors. Explicit knowledge can then be stored in knowledge bases or repositories for day-to-day use.
- *From explicit to tacit knowledge* is internalizing or fitting explicit knowledge into tacit knowledge. An example is learning to ride a bicycle by practicing again and again.
- *From explicit to explicit knowledge* is more or less combining, reorganizing, categorizing, or sorting different bodies of explicit knowledge to lead to new knowledge. An example of this would be sorting an employee master file to see how many employees are older than 65 years of age, fall between the ages of 50 and 64, and so forth.

Knowledge capture is part of knowledge creation, which requires group work, recognition of the value of tacit knowledge, and support for socialization and internalization. Knowledge creation also requires experience, which over time leads to expertise. Human experts become candidates for tapping their tacit knowledge via knowledge capture.

▪ ▪ ▪ ▪ How to Codify Knowledge

The key question in this chapter is how to retain knowledge and its distinctive properties. Before any codification, an organization must focus on the following:

- What organizational goals will codified knowledge serve? For example, if the intent is to improve quality sales, then the sales knowledge base should be codified to improve sales quality. Because codifying puts knowledge in a usable form, a corporation should have a specific strategic reason for its use. Firsthand knowledge alone is not enough. Different goals for a knowledge management project require different perspectives. At this point, we need to assess an organization's knowledge and needs in order to develop a strategy for fulfilling its unmet needs.
- What knowledge exists in the organization that addresses these goals? It means starting with a survey of various aspects of knowledge—presence, availability, transfer, use, and so forth. At this stage, we need to understand the knowledge and work practices of an organization and then use these insights to help transform the organization into what it intends to be. Such knowledge must be

identified and put into some usable form before sharing it outside the organization. The goal is to look for relevance of knowledge, not completeness. Knowledge codification requires specific aims rather than merely making knowledge available.

- How useful is existing knowledge for codification? As we shall see later, one way to make existing knowledge useful is via knowledge maps—diagramming the logic trail to a major decision.
- How would one codify knowledge? That is, what medium or tool would be the most appropriate for codification? Mapping corporate knowledge is an essential part of the codification process. To do the job, the knowledge developer must identify the type of knowledge—rich versus schematic, tacit versus explicit, rule-based or frame-based, and so forth. What can be done with the knowledge depends on the level of importance, its type, and how labor-intensive it will be for proper evaluation.

CODIFYING TACIT KNOWLEDGE

We should know by now that tacit knowledge is complex. It is the type of knowledge that was developed and internalized in the mind of the human expert over a long time period. Because of that, it is not easy to codify it in its entirety in a knowledge base or a repository. The distinctive style of the expert can barely be described or externalized in a set of rules as part of the codified knowledge. In brief, it requires special knowledge capture skills to codify tacit knowledge effectively.

One conclusion is that certain knowledge is more of an art than a science, and art is difficult to codify into rules and formulations. To process and fully codify an expert's years of intuitive experience would be too laborious and futile. That is why when the knowledge base project is completed, the best that the knowledge developer can say about it is "It's good enough"; it is neither complete nor final. Maturation with human knowledge over time continues to be the missing area in codified tacit knowledge. If you do not believe this, try to explain to a child how to ride a bicycle.

For these reasons, we codify tacit knowledge by relying heavily on a willing expert with the knowledge and a knowledge developer to capture such knowledge. Dealing with experts is not easy, but once chosen, a knowledge developer needs to assess the expert's style of expression. The expert may be the procedure type who thrives on explaining by procedure, the storyteller type, the parental type, or the salesperson type who sells his or her way of solving a problem. The knowledge developer must adopt knowledge capture and codification methods accordingly.

It should be noted that many organizations lack the transparency of company-wide knowledge. Critical knowledge is often available, but no one seems to know where to find it. Because of that, knowledge identification and knowledge capture improve knowledge transparency, which is a prerequisite for knowledge sharing. To identify knowledge, one needs to create a codified form of it. In this respect, codification means representing knowledge in a useful and meaningful way so that it can be transferred and shared by any authorized user of an organization.

■■■■ Codification Tools and Procedures

Several different ways of encoding facts and relationships to codify knowledge exist. Some schemes are graphical, others are tabular, and others are descriptive statements of facts. Knowledge can be categorized, described, modeled, mapped, or embedded in rules and recipes. The codification schemes included in this section are knowledge maps, decision tables, decision trees, rules, case-based reasoning, and intelligent software agents. The knowledge developer's skill set is also covered.

Before getting into codification tools and procedures, it is important to note that knowledge managers must decide on the business goals that the codified knowledge will serve and identify existing knowledge appropriate to the goals. They must also evaluate codified knowledge for usefulness and appropriateness for codification and the medium for codification and distribution.

KNOWLEDGE MAPS

In tacit knowledge capture, it has been said, "You can't verbalize unless you visualize." One way to codify knowledge is to visualize it via knowledge maps. Knowledge maps arose from a belief that people act on things that they understand and accept. They simply do not like to be told what to think. This means self-determined change is sustainable. Instead of telling employees what to do to succeed, knowledge maps are tools to transform employees into knowledge partners for effective decision making.

A knowledge map is a visual representation, not a repository of knowledge. Typically, it is a straightforward directory that points to people, documents, and repositories. It does not contain them, however. The main purpose of knowledge maps is to direct people where to go when they need certain expertise. Such maps usually recognize explicit and tacit knowledge captured in documents, repositories, and in experts' heads. Knowledge maps can represent explicit or tacit, formal or informal, documented or undocumented, and internal or external knowledge. In terms of tacit knowledge, codification effort is generally limited to locating the person with the knowledge, pointing the seeker to it, and making the expert available for interaction.

Without a "knowledge highway" map to access knowledge locations, finding knowledge would be difficult. In addition to the guiding function, knowledge maps may also identify strengths to exploit and missing knowledge gaps to fill. For example, codifying a corporate strategic plan for a new product may make it clear that the sales force has been using a successful procedure that was never part of the plan. Not capturing and storing but using knowledge is the aim of knowledge maps. They should be integrated into knowledge management tools such as intranets and groupware to support operational processes.

How Knowledge Maps Work

As a process, there are five key elements that work together to ensure a knowledge map experience:

- The map depicts visually the business issue or problem at hand. It is designed to be fun, easy to follow, engaging, and clearly reflecting the material to be covered.
- The pace of the group's collaborative discussions should be guided by a set of questions that hopefully create shared knowledge. The process allows each employee to find out how the process or the problem applies to him or to her and what the employee should be doing differently.
- Facts are presented to the group to focus on the realities of the problem. They often come up with the same conclusions that senior leaders do.

- The nature of the collaborative discussion among peers should be an open and trusting environment, facilitated by a coach. Otherwise, knowledge maps will not work.
- Finally, postsession follow-up activities are reviewed, and conclusions are drawn.

The Building Cycle

Building a knowledge map is easy. Once you know where knowledge resides for a problem, you simply point to it and add instructions on how to get there. Keep in mind that quality knowledge must first be available. Then it must be accurate and easy to use and navigate. A company's intranet is a common medium for publishing knowledge maps. Often, the human resources package interface with the company's intranet provides knowledge capability. In one partial knowledge map, this author was using Microsoft Word, but the tab somehow would skip 10 spaces instead of the normal five. After clicking on a special help key, a screen asked him to enter the problem. When he entered "tab problem," the response was "call Brad at 4-3775." Brad happened to be the Word specialist in the department. He was also the faculty-IT liaison.

A more complex student health compensation map is illustrated in Figure 7.4. The benefits of this map are as follows:

- *Sensible reduction of time to prepare paperwork and approval to be reimbursed for medical expenses.*
- *Reduction of division among departments.* The knowledge map cuts across several departments—department where the employee works, the human resources department, payroll, company-approved physicians, the hospital, and the health insurance carrier.
- *Helps the employee acknowledge various knowledge sources.*

▪ ▪ ▪ ▪ ▪ ▪ ▪ **FIGURE 7.4:**   Question Knowledge Map for Organizing the Content

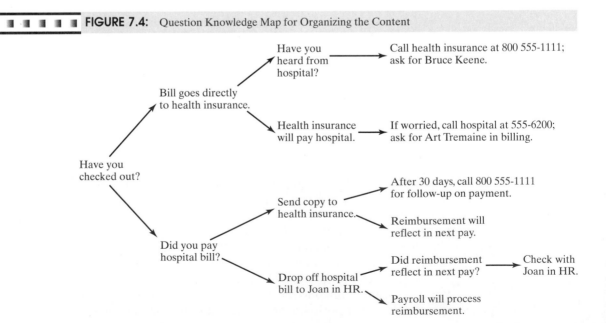

Employees that experience a knowledge map learning process are asked to challenge their attitudes, seek understanding, and collaborate with others to acquire new knowledge about products, customers, and internal performance. They can then come up with new conclusions and internalize specific action steps in dealing with business issues. They will also discover what it will take to create success for the employer and for their career paths.

There are different approaches to codifying knowledge into systems. The more bounded and rule-based the knowledge, the easier it is embed it into a computer-based system. This includes knowledge-based systems, expert systems, case-based systems, and software agents. Each system is explained later in the chapter. It should be noted that a knowledge system should not be viewed as automating expert tasks but rather *informing* about such tasks. A knowledge system is not necessarily an expert system either, although we can codify tacit knowledge in an expert system format, using rules or heuristics.

Select Building Guidelines

A knowledge map is often put together in bits and pieces—some facts are documented and others are informal. In a large organization, asking the question more than once can cause waste. FAQs (frequently asked questions) are appropriate when tagged to a computer-based environment, but FAQs also tend to get longer and more tedious. Being primarily text-oriented, certain questions are not easy or quick to look up. In contrast, knowledge maps are generally graphic, more specific, and easier to follow than FAQs. The focus of a knowledge map is on procedure rather than on fragmented questions and answers.

To illustrate, revisit Figure 7.4, which shows a procedure employees must follow to get reimbursed for hospital care. A knowledge map maker initially follows a trail of fragmented recommendations, beginning with the human resources department as the primary knowledge source. Then, he or she talks to another person in charge of health insurance claims and then follows up with the people in compensation and payroll, respectively. The widening cascade of referrals eventually links the fragmented knowledge in some sequence that makes sense to employees who expect to be reimbursed after a hospital stay.

Another popular knowledge map in the human resources area is a skills planner, where the goal is to match employees to jobs. Once the knowledge map maker has an idea what knowledge is required of employees, they can be selected for educational training and other offerings. Building the map requires four steps:

1. *Develop a structure of the knowledge requirements.* For example, the requirement might be 1 year of experience in teller operations for basic knowledge and 5 years of experience in teller operations plus 2 years of Excel for a junior officer's position.
2. *Define the knowledge required of specific jobs.* For example, knowledge required may be 3 years of cost accounting in retailing and a minimum of 1 year of supervisory experience for entry-level management.
3. *Rate employee performance by knowledge competency.*
4. *Link the knowledge map to a training program for career development and job advancement.*

With this in mind, a knowledge map may be set up as a 4-tier knowledge structure to evaluate employee competency and identify within the structure tacit and explicit knowledge for each competency. As shown in Figure 7.5, basic knowledge is expected

	Knowledge Structure	Knowledge Category
Global	Company-wide knowledge competency	Applies to all company employees. For example, knowledge of company policies and business practices.
	Department or division level competency	Applies to all employees within a function or a department. For example, every employee in the IT department should be well versed in computer technology.
	Working knowledge competency	High-level skills unique to a specific job type. For example, a loan officer to decide whether to approve a loan.
Local	Basic level knowledge competency	Foundation knowledge. For example, ability to send and receive e-mail as part of a job.

▪ ▪ ▪ ▪ ▪ ▪ ▪ **FIGURE 7.5:** Knowledge Structure and Categories for Knowledge Mapping

as entry-level knowledge competency. For example, each employee is expected to know how to send and receive e-mail. The next higher level is working-level knowledge competency, when high-level skills are unique for a specific job type. For example, a loan officer of a bank should be able to decide whether to approve a loan.

After basic and job-specific knowledge competency comes the division or department level knowledge type, where certain knowledge applies to all employees in that department or division. For example, all IT employees should be familiar with computer technology. Finally, the highest knowledge type competency is company-wide knowledge, where all company employees should be familiar with company policies and practices.

The resulting knowledge map is loaded in a computer-based environment, where a manager building a new team may query the computer database. The manager may ask the database to "SELECT all candidates with advanced skills above 90 percent of the knowledge competency for job = senior analyst and location = Richmond, Virginia." The system goes to a knowledge repository via the company's intranet and lists on a screen (in a matter of seconds) those who meet the criteria.

Another popular area where a knowledge map can be used is plotting company strategy against the company's current knowledge to determine the knowledge required to successfully implement strategy. In Figure 7.6, a company begins by identifying the strategy that it must implement for a new product or a new approach to compete. Next, it specifies the knowledge required to execute the strategy. These two items establish the strategy-knowledge link before searching within the company to scan for the strategic and knowledge gaps to plug. Comparing what the company knows to the required knowledge measures the knowledge gap. In contrast, comparing the "must do" strategy to what the company "can do" determines the strategy gap. In other words, a knowledge map describes a company's strategy against the current company knowledge base and displays the missing knowledge that will ensure successful execution of the strategy.

Overall, one can conclude that the criteria of a good knowledge map are clarity of purpose, ease of use, and accuracy of content. Although technology is involved in its application and availability, technology alone cannot guarantee that the knowledge map will be accepted or used effectively in an organization. Most maps have a political catch. They cannot be interpreted as favoring one view over others. They cannot be perceived as giving away power or influence, either. In the final result, a knowledge map should represent equity and fairness in the way it is designed. It is not the terri-

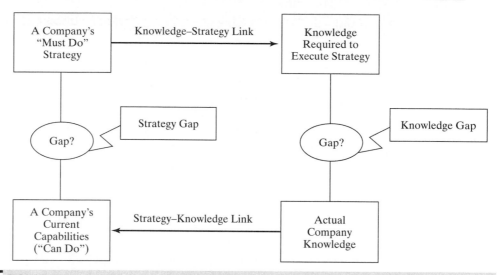

■ ■ ■ ■ ■ ■ ■ **FIGURE 7.6:**   Use of a Knowledge Map in Executing Strategies

SOURCE: Adapted from Tiwana, Amrit. *The Knowledge Management Toolkit.* Upper Saddle River, NJ: Prentice Hall, 2000, p. 153.

tory, but it can influence the territory in the way it defines it and represents it. FAQs on knowledge maps are presented in www.appliedlearninglabs.com/kmaps/faqs.html.

DECISION TABLES

Another scheme used for knowledge codification is the decision table. A **decision table** is more like a spreadsheet; it is divided into two parts: (1) a list of conditions and their respective values and (2) a list of conclusions. The various conditions are matched against the conclusions. A simple example that determines the discount policy of a book publisher is shown in Table 7.2.

Note that the answers are represented by a "Y" to signify "yes," an "N" to signify "no," or a blank to show that the condition involved has not been tested. In the action entry quadrant, an "X" or check mark indicates the response to the answer(s) entered in the condition entry quadrant. Each column also represents a decision or a rule. For example, rule 1 states:

IF customer is bookstore and order_size > 6 copies
THEN allow 25% discount

The decision table example provides six decisions and, therefore, six knowledge rules.

DECISION TREES

Another knowledge codification scheme is the **decision tree**. A decision tree is a hierarchically arranged semantic network and is closely related to a decision table. It is composed of nodes representing goals and links that represent decisions or outcomes. A decision tree is read from left to right, with the root being on the left. All nodes except the root node are instances of the primary goal. To illustrate, the decision table in Table 7.2 is shown as a decision tree in Figure 7.7. The primary goal is to determine a discount policy. The equivalent rule is IF customer is a bookstore and order size is greater than 6 copies, THEN discount is 25 percent. Several other rules can be extracted from the same tree.

TABLE 7.2   Decision Table of Publishing Company Discount Policy

	Condition Stub	1	2	3	4	5	6
		Condition Entry					
IF (condition)	Customer is bookstore	Y	Y	N	N	N	N
	Order size > 6 copies	Y	N	N	N	N	N
	Customer is librarian/individual			Y	Y	Y	Y
	Order size 50 copies or more				Y	N	N
	Order size 20–49 copies					Y	N
	Order size 6–19 copies						Y
THEN (action)	Allow 25% discount	X					
	Allow 15% discount				X		
	Allow 10% discount					X	
	Allow 5% discount						X
	Allow no discount		X				X
	Action Stub			**Action Entry**			

FIGURE 7.7:   Decision Tree Representing Publishing Company Discounts Policy

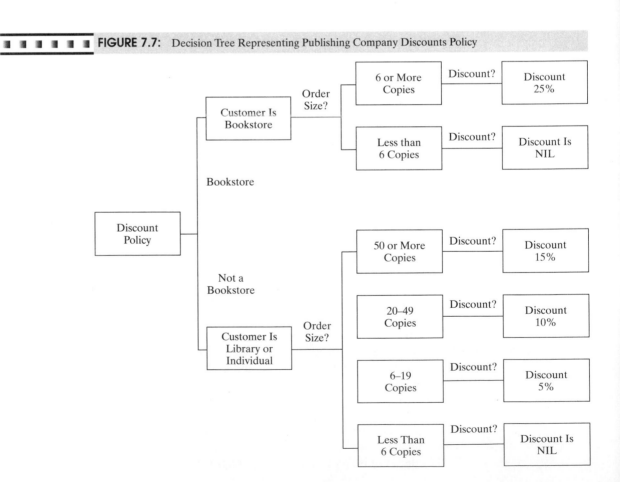

Decision tables and decision trees are commonly used as a first step before actual codification. Decision tables are especially useful in verifying rules, a task for which special software is available. A major advantage of a decision tree is its ability to verify logic graphically in problems involving complex situations that result in a limited number of actions. A major drawback of decision trees is the lack of information in the tree format that might indicate what other combinations of conditions could be included. This is where the decision table is useful.

FRAMES

A **frame** is a structure or a codification scheme for organizing knowledge through previous experience. It handles a combination of declarative and operational knowledge, which makes it easier to understand the problem domain. A frame represents knowledge about an entity in the real world, such as an employee, a person, or person type.

Frames were developed by Marvin Minsky of MIT, and they are based on the idea that people use analogical reasoning to build new systems by taking a previous collection of structures from memory. A frame can contain information about various aspects of the situations that people describe.

A frame is like a cookbook recipe: Its "slots" contain both the ingredients for the recipe and the procedural details ("cook over medium heat," "toast until brown,") to make the data operational or to fill the slots, within or between frames. The idea is to catalog the requirements for membership of certain elements of a knowledge scheme. In other words, it is a data structure with a name, a type, and a set of attributes, called *slots*.

Frames have two key elements:

- A **slot** is a specific object being described or an attribute of an entity. For example, in a personnel knowledge base, some of the slots are "instructor," "unique feature of employee verification," and "training certification."
- A **facet** is the value of an object or a slot. As shown in Figure 7.8, the facet (value) of slot type "instructor" is "Olesek"; "verification" is "training license"; and so forth.

Figure 7.9 shows a frame describing automobiles. The frame consists of six slots (attributes): manufacturer, city of origin, year, color, miles per gallon, and owner. One or more facets are associated with each slot. They include *range* (set of possible values), *default* (value to assume if none were specified), *if-needed* (how to determine actual value), and *if-changed* (what to do if the slot's value changes). If-needed and if-changed are called *demons* or procedures that allow procedural knowledge to be combined with the declarative knowledge part of the frame. They specify the actions that should take place if certain conditions occur during processing. If-needed means "the demon lays waiting until needed," and at that point it is "triggered."

▪ ▪ ▪ ▪ ▪ ▪ ▪ **FIGURE 7.8:** A Frame Representing Olesek's Training License

Object: License	
Slot	**Facet**
Instructor	Olesek
Verification	Training license
Unique feature of verification	State seal
Teaching certification	In air rescue

Object: Automobile

Slot	
Manufacturer	Range: Default
City of origin	Range: Default
Year	Range: (1960–2001) (value cannot be modified)
Color	Range: (white, black, burgundy, blue) If-needed: (examine title or view–automobile)
Miles per gallon	Range: (10–35)
Owner	Range: (person's name)

▪ ▪ ▪ ▪ ▪ ▪ ▪ **FIGURE 7.9:** A Frame Representing the Object of Automobile

When all the slots are filled with values, the frame is considered **instantiated**, which means an instance of the frame is created. The value of the slot could be a string, an integer, or a pointer to another frame instance.

The problem-solving technique used by a frame-based system is called **matching**, in which the values associated with a given entity are matched with the slot values of frames. With a sufficient match, the frame-based system assumes that an instance has occurred.

Frames represent knowledge about a particular idea in one place. They provide a framework or structure, in which new information can be interpreted. They are especially helpful in dealing with hierarchical knowledge, because their organization of knowledge makes inferences easy to describe.

Frames can also be linked—one frame may inherit properties of a higher-level frame. In the example shown in Figure 7.10, a "performance review" is a type of "session" with an "informal" nature. The director, attendance, and frequency are attributes special to the performance review. Relying on the concept of "inheritance," the *child frames* of "session" and "manager" are a specialized type derived from the more general *parent frame*. Because of this relationship, one can assume that the child frames inherit attributes of the parent frame. The "child" may also have properties of its own not shared by the parent. The inheritance mechanism means only information specific to a given frame will be specified. Knowledge-based systems using frames determine the particular process for operating inheritance relationships.

PRODUCTION RULES

A popular form of tacit knowledge codification is based on **production rules**, commonly known as **rules**. Rules represent the major elements of a modular knowledge codification scheme, especially when using specialized computer-based software packages. Rules are conditional statements that are easy to understand and write; they specify an action to be taken if a certain condition is true. They also express relationships between parameters or variables. In expert systems vocabulary, production rules are also called *premise-action, cause-effect, hypothesis-action, condition-action, test-result, IF . . . THEN,* or *IF . . . THEN . . . ELSE.* In the latter form, IF is the rule's antecedent, THEN is some consequent, and ELSE is some other consequent.

Child Frame

Session	
Type	
Nature:	Informal
Time:	10:10 A.M.
Place:	Office

Parent Frame

Performance Review	
Type Is a	**Session**
Nature:	Informal
Director Is a	**Manager**
Attendance:	?
Frequency:	?

Child Frame

Manager	
Type Is a	**Conference**
Seniority:	Member of Evaluation Review Committee

▪ ▪ ▪ ▪ ▪ ▪ ▪ **FIGURE 7.10:**   Set of Interlinked Frames

The basic idea of using rules is to codify tacit knowledge in the form of premise-action pairs as follows:

Syntax: IF (premise) THEN (action)
Example: IF income is "average" and pay_history is "good"
           THEN recommendation is "approve loan"

Knowledge-based rules differ from the traditional if-then programming statements. In knowledge-based systems, rules are relatively independent of one another and are based on heuristics or experiential reasoning rather than algorithms. Rules can carry some level of uncertainty. A *certainty factor* is represented as *CNF* or *CF* and is synonymous with a confidence level, which is a subjective quantification of an expert's judgment. In the preceding example, the rule means: "IF the applicant's income is average and pay history, which implies a previous loan, is good, THEN the recommendation is approval of the loan at the 80 percent level of confidence." Eighty percent is the default. Figure 7.11 specifies the structure of a rule, which consists of a premise and an action. The premise has three expressions or clauses, each of which has an attribute, an object, and a value. The action has one expression or a clause with an attribute, an object, or a value.

A Premise

The IF . . . THEN structure of the rule language is represented by *premise* and *action* clauses or statements. The **premise** is a Boolean (yes/no, true/false) expression that must be evaluated as *true* for the rule to be applied. It is composed of one or more statements separated by AND or OR connectors. A specialized software package

| Premise: | IF | \multicolumn{3}{l}{Cloud site is black and wind force > 35 mph and wave height > 18 feet} |
| Action: | THEN | \multicolumn{3}{l}{There is .6 evidence that classification of storm is hurricane.} |

		Attribute	**Object**	**Value**
Premise	IF	Site	Cloud	Black
		Force	Wind	> 35 mph
		Height	Wave	> 18 feet
Action:	THEN	Classification	Storm	Hurricane

▪ ▪ ▪ ▪ ▪ ▪ ▪ **FIGURE 7.11:** Structure and Elements of a Rule

processes a rule by testing its premise for truth or falsity. The test must be satisfied before any action of a rule can be executed. Examples of a rule premise are as follows:

If GPA is "high" THEN . . .
IF car_motor is "bad" or car_body is "fair" THEN . . .
IF income > \$50,000 and assets > \$300,000 or payment_history is "good"
THEN . . .

In multiple premises, processing proceeds from left to right. AND has a higher precedence than OR. Parentheses may be used to change or specify precedence. The default order of precedence is X and /(divided by), + and −, left association. For example $2 + 3 \times 5 - 6/8 \times 7$ is evaluated as $\{[2 + (3 \times 5)] - (6/8 \times 7)\}$.

An Action

The action part of a rule is the second component, separated from the premise by the keyword THEN. The **action** clause consists of a statement or a series of statements separated by ANDs or commas (,) and is executed if the premise is true. It could be either a list of commands to be carried out if the premise evaluates to *true* or it could be a Boolean expression that evaluates to *true* whenever the premise is true. If any part of the premise were false, then the action would not be true or would be true at a specific level of uncertainty. Examples of rule action include the following:

IF owns auto = "false" THEN potential_insurance = "high"
IF income > \$100,000 THEN federal_tax_rate > .35
IF loan holder = "late payer" THEN add "penalty = .5" to premium

For multiple action clauses, statements must be linked with AND or commas. For example:

IF GPA = "HIGH" and SAT > 1400
THEN admission = true and financial_aid = \$6,000

In this example, two values are assigned to admission with financial aid. Two actions are also fired. In most business-oriented knowledge-based systems, rules are used almost exclusively. They are a natural expression of "what to do" knowledge or "how to do" knowledge. They are easy to understand and to represent the expert's know-how. Their main drawback is the way they are expressed at a fine level of detail. Such fine-grained representation makes the know-how involved difficult to understand. Also, the amount of knowledge that can be expressed in a single rule is limited. This limitation depends largely on the shell. For example, EXSYS Corvid (a knowledge-based software package) allows as many as 126 conditions in the IF and the THEN parts of a rule.

Loan Advisor—An Illustration

To follow up on the partial loan advisor represented in a decision tree in Figure 5-2, the partial tree can easily be converted into a set of rules using EXSYS Corvid, as follows:

```
1employment = yes
        2               emp_length = 4_to_9, 10_to_18, over_19
        3                 [salary] >=15000
        4                   credit_history = Good, Fair
                                 employment = yes
                      AND   emp_length = 4_to_9, 10_to_18, over_19
                      AND   [salary] >=15000
                      AND   credit_history = Good, Fair
        5                       [expenses} <(.75*([salary]/12))
        6                          → [approve] = 1
7[approve] !=1
8 ----> [deny] = 1
9 ----> RESULTS
```

Rule-based systems made their debut when expert systems were popular in the 1990s. Expert systems represent human knowledge by a formalized rule-based programming setup. They play a limited role in knowledge codification. From a practical point, the more unambiguous and rule-based tacit knowledge is, the more easily it can be embedded in an expert system environment.

Role of Planning

For some time, writing rules was viewed as being synonymous with expert systems development. Later, complex projects required greater coordination and organization. A lack of planning was reflected in poor quality solutions, incomplete answers, or inefficient systems. Planning is an important part of the knowledge management development process. It ensures proper transition from knowledge capture to knowledge codification, verification, validation, and implementation. For example, in knowledge codification, knowledge developers sort out the rules, decide on their sequence and content, determine which rules belong in which modules, and so on. A knowledge developer is also responsible for planning the development and execution phases and how the user will interface with the resulting KM system—activities that are difficult to carry out without a plan.

In knowledge-based systems, planning involves the following aspects:

- Breaking the entire KM system into modules or manageable components
- Looking at partial solutions
- Linking partial solutions through rules and procedures to arrive at final solutions that make sense
- Deciding on the programming language
- Selecting the right software package
- Arranging for the verification and validation of the system
- Developing user interface and consultation facilities before installing the KM system
- Promoting clarity and flexibility

- Reducing unnecessary risks
- Making rules easier to review and understand

Unfortunately, plans can go awry, which means that the knowledge developer must monitor the results, compare plans with system results, assess the discrepancies, and make the necessary changes to ensure system integrity. Without this type of monitoring, the value of planning is lost.

Role of Inferencing in Knowledge-Based Codification

In an expert system environment, once the knowledge base is built, the system begins to make inferences. **Inferencing** means deriving a conclusion based on statements that only imply that conclusion. The program that manages the inferencing strategies for controlling the application of knowledge is the **inference engine**. It is the reasoning component that decides when certain inference rules should be accessed or fired (executed). **Reasoning** is the process of applying knowledge to arrive at solutions. To reason is to think clearly and logically, to draw reasonable inferences or conclusions from known or assumed facts. It works through the interaction of rules and data.

To illustrate inferencing, read the following sentence:

Brothers and sisters have I none,
But that man's father is my father's son.

Drawing the conclusion, "That man is my son," may be viewed as an inference from the riddle, based on our knowledge of relationships between brothers and sisters, parents and children, and so on.

Take an example related to reasoning:

The victims were stabbed to death in a dance hall in the mall. The suspect was on a nonstop flight to Chicago when the murder occurred.

You would probably conclude that the suspect was innocent. This typical day-to-day reasoning illustrates two important phenomena:

1. Reasoning depends not just on the premise but also on general knowledge. In the example, the suspect could not be in two places at the same time. There are no dance halls on board flights to Chicago (or to anywhere else).
2. People generally draw informative conclusions. Although several valid conclusions may follow from any set of premises, most of them are probably trivial.

No one can say precisely what mental processes lead to the conclusion that the suspect is innocent, because humans can only observe the results of another's conscious thoughts. In any case, people take for granted that deduction depends on a mental logic containing rules of inference based on experience.

Although rule-based systems look straightforward, their application is somewhat restricted. They work when one knows the variables in the problem and can express them in hard terms (numbers, dollars). The rules to apply must cover all the variables, and they cannot overlap. Before the rule-based system is operational, the rules must be validated to ensure reliability. Table 7.3 summarizes the relative fit of rule-based systems in a KM environment.

CASE-BASED REASONING

One type of reasoning that is a promising candidate for knowledge management is case-based reasoning or reasoning by analogy. A **case** is knowledge at an operational level. It is an episodic description of a problem and its associated solution. **Case-based**

TABLE 7.3 Relevant Fit of Rule-Based System in a KM Environment	
Attributes	**Limitations in a KM Environment**
Flexibility	Rule-based systems are OK for small systems, but inflexible in bases with complicated problems requiring new variables.
Scalability	With maturity over time, rule-based systems require change in rules, which means working with the expert again.
Speed of development	Rule-based systems can be developed quickly, provided you have a willing expert. Unfortunately, knowledge capture is very time-consuming.
Dependence on domain expert	Knowledge capture comes in stages, often requiring several drafts before the system is ready for final testing.
Response time	As rule-based systems increase in complexity, response time usually takes a hit. This means upgrading the hardware and software, which can be costly.

▪ ▪ ▪ ▪ ▪ ▪ ▪

reasoning or **CBR** is reasoning from relevant past cases in a manner similar to humans' use of past experiences to arrive at conclusions. An expert, for example, relies on previous cases for solving a current problem through a process of recalling the closest cases in memory, making inferences based on comparisons of the cases, and asking questions when inferences cannot be made. From an algorithmic view, CBR is a technique that records and documents cases and then searches the appropriate cases to determine their usefulness in solving new cases presented to the expert (see Figure 7.12).

Day-to-day examples of CBR are numerous:

- A doctor sees a patient with unusual symptoms. The doctor remembers previous patients with similar symptoms and prescribes the old diagnosis as a solution.
- An auto mechanic facing an unusual electrical problem is likely to recall other similar cases involving the same year or make and consider whether the old solution corrects the current problem.
- When updating a corporate pension fund, an estate-planning attorney relies on previous pension fund experience to expedite the completion of the current one.

Referring to old cases is especially advantageous when dealing with recurring situations. Because no old case is exactly the same as the new one, old solutions must often

▪ ▪ ▪ ▪ ▪ ▪ ▪ **FIGURE 7.12:** General CBR Process

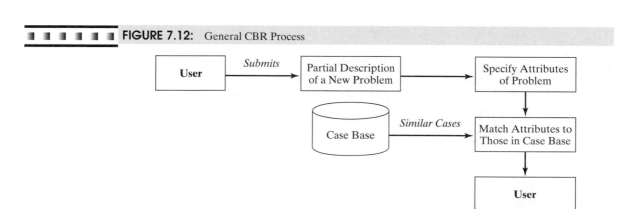

be adapted to fit a new case. In every case, some reasoning and some learning are involved. The success rate of problem solving improves with recurring CBR.

One obvious advantage of CBR over rule-based systems is its time savings. Knowledge developers can spin their wheels in manually capturing knowledge from human experts for building the KM system. In CBR, less time is needed to retrieve representative cases for performing knowledge development. CBR allows the reasoner to come up with solutions to problems quickly, without having to start from scratch. CBR is most advantageous when rules are difficult to formulate and when cases are readily available, particularly when the domain expert is uncertain, not available, inconsistent, or uncooperative.

Another advantage is its maintenance requirements. In rule-based systems, the cost of maintaining and enhancing the system stem from the difficulty in structuring rules into a workable system. In CBR, maintenance entails simply adding more cases that offer features similar to the case in question.

CBR has a downside, as well. Using CBR means rigorous initial planning that takes into account all possible variables. Also, because cases age, it is almost mandatory that recent cases be incorporated into the case base on a regular basis. Although a case provides accurate and consistent documentation, it lacks the dynamics or the best decision based on maturation that a human expert can provide.

The goal of CBR is to bring up the most similar historical case that matches the current case—not an easy task. For example, in the analogy "a flashlight battery is like a reservoir," the size, color, shape, or make of the battery is not the relevant aspect. The relevant aspect is the fact that both the battery and a reservoir store and provide energy as power. In this situation, only relationships dealing with these two attributes would be useful in this analogy.

Another problem is the difficulty in mechanizing a person's insight and ability to see an analogy between a previously encountered case and a current case. No general representation procedure prescribes how to reason by analogy. As a consequence, reasoning by analogy tends to introduce errors, biases, and inconsistencies into the formulation of rule-based systems. To improve the usefulness and reliability of rule-based systems, a better understanding of human reasoning is needed.

A third problem is maintenance of appropriate indexes. Adding new cases and reclassifying the case library most often expand knowledge. A case library broad enough for most CBR applications requires considerable database storage with an efficient retrieval system. CBR can be fully automated, depending on how much creativity is required to derive solutions and how much complexity is involved. Regardless of the level of automation, the biggest factor in making CBR work is its case library. Table 7.4 uses the attributes in Table 7.3 to summarize the limitations of CBR in a KM environment.

KNOWLEDGE-BASED AGENTS

In software language, an intelligent agent is a program located in a computer-based system that is capable of performing autonomous action in a timely fashion. It is not intended to replace human intelligence, but to support it. In addition to acting in response to their environment, intelligent agents are capable of exhibiting goal-directed behavior by taking initiative. They can also be programmed to interact with other agents (or humans) by some agent communication language.

In terms of knowledge-based systems, an agent can be programmed to learn from the user behavior and deduce future behavior in order to assist the user. Because they can take some control, agents need to have access to decision knowledge. Such knowl-

TABLE 7.4   Attributes of CBR in a KM Environment

Attribute	*Limitations in a KM Environment*
Flexibility	As the number of attributes increases, CBR begins to show degradation and inaccuracy, especially when there is interaction among multiple attributes.
Scalability	Attributes are not easily scalable. All future attributes must be carefully defined for accuracy.
Dependence on domain expert	An expert must be employed to ensure attribute matching and retrieval.
Response time	Adding more cases could result in degradation in the system's response time.
Solution accuracy	As more cases are added to the case base, accuracy improves.

edge can be about the user as a personal assistant or the domain, as is the case in expert systems.

Information agents are unique in the way they search on behalf of their users or other agents. The search involves evaluating, retrieving, or integrating information from multiple information sources (for example, knowledge bases). They learn user preferences and provide appropriate information based on these preferences. They can automatically execute special tasks such as filtering unwanted e-mail messages. In essence, they learn by "looking over the shoulder" of the user while he or she is working. They can provide suggestions when the user reaches a useful level of success in their predictions.

■ ■ ■ ■ The Knowledge Developer's Skill Set

To perform knowledge codification, a knowledge developer is expected to have various technical, procedural, and interpersonal skills. Some skills are taught; others are innate. Table 7.5 summarizes the knowledge and skills requirements of the knowledge developer. The literature is still sketchy on this subject. The list is culled from a review of the research and a brief survey of practicing knowledge developers in two select organizations. Other surveys being conducted will help standardize the job requirements of this important job.

KNOWLEDGE REQUIREMENTS
Computer Technology

The knowledge developer should be well-versed in hardware and software, how operating systems work, and issues regarding legal matters, security, testing, documentation, and maintenance. A general background in science and computer architecture is helpful.

Domain-Specific Knowledge

The knowledge developer must be familiar with the nature of the problem, the business of the user organization, and the factors surrounding the problem domain, such as the organization's political climate, level of management support, and the users' computer literacy. For example, if the problem domain is mortgage loan analysis, the knowledge developer should have a basic understanding of lending practices and

TABLE 7.5 Knowledge and Skill Requirements of the Knowledge Developer	
Knowledge Required	*Skills Required*
• Computer technology and operating systems	• Interpersonal communication
• Domain-specific knowledge	• Ability to articulate the project's rationale
• Knowledge repositories and data mining	• Rapid prototyping
• Cognitive psychology	

■ ■ ■ ■ ■ ■

procedures before approaching the loan specialists. A knowledge developer who builds knowledge bases for oil exploration would probably be the wrong choice for this assignment.

Knowledge Repositories and Data Mining

Among the technical prerequisites for a knowledge developer are familiarity with knowledge repositories and what the market offers in terms of off-the-shelf packages for knowledge management, data warehousing, and data mining.

Cognitive Psychology

The knowledge developer should have a basic familiarity with the principles of cognition, the understanding of knowledge in general and of how human experts think or reason. Cognitive skills are important in capturing and codifying complex, ill-defined, and judgmental knowledge and understanding the domain expert's thought processes such as decision making under conditions of uncertainty. Background in this field improves communications, interviewing, and listening skills.

SKILLS REQUIREMENTS

Interpersonal Communication

The most pervasive factor in a knowledge developer's success is the ability to communicate. If he or she cannot understand and relate the expert's intent or meaning accurately, the reliability of the resulting knowledge base will be questionable.

Persons with poor interpersonal skills cannot be effective knowledge developers; their deficiency cannot help but detract from their relationships with experts, users, management, and others. This also applies to domain experts. They must enunciate concepts and procedures in simple, clear terms so that the knowledge can be codified accurately. Interpersonal skills enable one to work with people to achieve common goals or to help others work together as a team. Interpersonal behavior is closely related to personality and dictates a person's management style.

Ability to Articulate the Project's Rationale

Part of the knowledge developer's job is to discuss project feasibility, justify investment in the project, and sell the proposed change to management. Persuasive articulation of the rationale is developed with experience. Actually, this ability is important in working with management at all levels.

Rapid Prototyping Skills

The knowledge developer will occasionally sit down with the user or the specialist with the tacit knowledge to get feedback on how the knowledge base is shaping up. Rapid prototyping is an iterative process in which the knowledge developer shows what the knowledge base looks like on the basis of the knowledge codified to date. The knowledge developer can make changes to the system on the spot in the presence of the audience. Rapid prototyping requires experience and quick thinking, and it promotes respect and trust between the knowledge developer and the expert or the user, respectively.

Personality Attributes

When it comes to personality attributes, knowledge developers should exhibit the attributes described here.

- *Intelligence.* An intelligent knowledge developer develops KM systems efficiently. He or she is constantly learning from experience and from exposure to the various specialists and users. Intelligence enables him or her to keep abreast of advances in technology and to learn and think quickly and well, especially when various procedures must be integrated.
- *Creativity.* A creative mind enables a person to generate ideas and react quickly to new methods for solving problems. Creative knowledge developers are more adept at selecting appropriate reasoning strategies and ways of capturing knowledge.
- *Tolerance for ambiguity.* The willingness to probe further and further into an unclear issue or procedure until it is clear and usable demands a degree of patience that some people do not possess. This process takes time, and the expert or knower may require much encouragement.
- *Realism.* Experienced knowledge developers understand that not every expert they deal with will be cooperative or motivated and that some projects will be more onerous than others. These knowledge developers tend to be more tolerant.
- *Cognitive ability.* The ability to reason by analysis, association, and inference characterizes knowledge developers. They are able to "see through things," to perceive the reality of a situation.
- *Persistence.* Knowledge developers have the determination to try new things and maintain their commitment to a project. Self-confidence is a component of this persistence. When dealing with ill-structured problems, the knowledge developer must remain positive, saying, "I can do it if I keep at it." The poem in Box 7.1 addresses the importance of a positive state of mind.
- *Logical thinking.* The ability to learn new technology and continue to improve the codification process is essential to a knowledge developer. When codifying knowledge, he or she must be willing to argue reasonably in order to resolve inconsistencies. Otherwise, the resulting system will be illogical and unreasonable.
- *Good sense of humor and optimism.* Light-hearted, cheerful people are easier to work with and make attractive collaborators.

Job Roles

The knowledge developer plays a variety of roles, depending on the nature of the knowledge project, the type of knowledge, and the organization's climate. Some of the key roles are those of change agent, investigator, diplomat, architect, builder, tester, accountant, and salesperson. He or she may also be a project planner, contractor, motivator, quality inspector, and adept at conflict resolution. These roles relate to personality attributes as well as knowledge and skills requirements.

▪ ▪ ▪ ▪ ▪ ▪ ▪   BOX 7.1   ▪ ▪ ▪ ▪ ▪ ▪ ▪

ALL IN THE STATE OF THE MIND

If you think you are beaten, you are;
    If you think you dare not, you don't;
If you would like to win and don't think you can,
    It's almost a cinch you won't.
If you think you'll lose, you're lost;
    For out in the world you'll find
Success begins with a fellow's will.
    It's all in the state of the mind.
Full many a race is lost
    Ere even a step is run,
And many a coward fails
    Ere even his work is begun.

Think big and your deeds will grow;
    Think small and you'll fall behind;
Think that you can and you will.
    It's all in the state of the mind.
If you think you are outclassed, you are;
    You've got to think high to rise.
You've got to be sure of yourself before
    You can ever win a prize.
Life's battles don't always go
    To the stronger or faster man;
But sooner or later, the man who wins
    Is the fellow who thinks he can.

SOURCE: Awad, E. M. *Expert Systems.* Minneapolis, MN: West Publishing Co., 1996, p. 129.

▪▪▪▪ Implications for Knowledge Management

In traditional terms, management means planning, organizing, directing, and coordinating the efforts of people, procedures, and technology in an organizational setting. The work of knowledge codification involves more than codification schemes or tools. It means planning the codification phase, planning the use of specific tools within the framework of a programming environment, and making the most efficient use of the knowledge developer's and the expert's time and talent.

In addition to the front-end phase of management, the knowledge developer should sense the user's expectations and determine how the user can be part of the codification phase of the knowledge management system development life cycle, especially during knowledge codification. Partnership or cooperation can be accomplished through rapid prototyping or inviting the user to join in the day-to-day routines of codification. In addition, the knowledge developer needs to foster the relationship with the champion, whose role continues to be vital to the future acceptance and success of the knowledge-based system.

Finally, in preparation for the detailed writing of the coding, rules, and procedures, the knowledge developer would be well advised to begin promoting the goodness of fit and exciting features of the knowledge management system to the key person in the area where the system will be installed. In fact, the selling effort is best begun early in the process, especially when the knowledge-based system is likely to take months rather than weeks to build. The ultimate goal is user acceptance and willing commitment to long-term use of the system.

From the human resources and career path view, encouraging signs suggest a career for the knowledge developer. Building knowledge management systems can provide higher pay and the opportunities for doing more creative work. Professionals in the IT field who want to move to a career in knowledge development should determine the level of support for building knowledge management systems in their employing organization. They may be able to stay with their current employer as a knowledge developer.

Given the increasing demand for knowledge developers, an organization can now consider long-range training programs, by which the talent for knowledge development may be tapped from its existing pool of IT and other professional areas in the business. Another alternative is for the organization to support academic IT programs that offer courses in knowledge management or knowledge engineering.

Knowledge development allows a firm to preserve its intellectual capital for problem-solving and competitive advantage. A learning company understands and capitalizes on its human resources. To incorporate knowledge management without knowledge development as the core competency would be like building automobiles without qualified assemblers.

The knowledge developer is a person who is committed to this evolving technology and who pursues a goal of building quality systems. Without quality assurance, reliability, and integrity, the whole process remains questionable. For knowledge development to become an established area of system building, organizations must provide rewards sufficient to minimize voluntary resignations. Knowledge developers are expensive to train and hard to replace. Motivating technical people requires regular performance, monitoring, and feedback for reinforcement. Providing opportunities for advancement, creativity, utilization of abilities, recognition, higher compensation, and the like promotes employee loyalty to the firm and its objectives. This level of concern for people counts in the final results.

SUMMARY   ▪ ▪ ▪ ▪

- Knowledge codification is organizing and coordinating knowledge before the user can access it. It must be in a form and a structure meaningful for access at any time, from anywhere, by any authorized person.
- Codification is a prerequisite to knowledge transfer. The resulting knowledge base serves several useful areas such as diagnosis, scheduling, planning, instruction, and training. However, there are bottlenecks such as difficulty in accessing knowledge and slow diffusion of new knowledge. Bottlenecks can also be created when knowledge is not in the proper form, not available in a timely manner, incomplete, or not present at the right location.
- The four modes of knowledge conversion tag the four possible relationships between tacit and explicit knowledge and the resulting outcomes of socialization, externalization, internalization, and combination.
- Before codification begins, an organization must address several questions: What organizational goals will codified knowledge serve? What knowledge exists in the organization that addresses these goals? How useful is existing knowledge for codification? How would one codify knowledge?
- Codifying tacit knowledge is complex and is more of an art than a science. Several different ways of encoding facts and relationships to codify knowledge exist. They include knowledge maps, decision tables, decision trees, frames, production rules, and software agents. Each has a unique approach to knowledge codification.
- A knowledge map is like a knowledge highway to access knowledge location. It identifies strengths to exploit and missing knowledge gaps to fill. Building the map requires three steps: Developing a structure of the knowledge requirements,

defining the knowledge required of specific jobs, and rating employee performance against knowledge requirements.

- A decision table scheme is divided into two parts: (1) a list of conditions and their respective values and (2) a list of conclusions. In contrast, a decision tree is a hierarchically arranged semantic network that is closely related to a decision table. It is composed of nodes representing goals and links that represent decisions or outcomes.

- A frame is a structure for organizing knowledge. It handles a combination of declarative and operational knowledge and makes the current problem domain easier to understand. It represents knowledge about an entity in the real world and catalogs the membership requirements of certain elements of a knowledge scheme. The two key elements of a frame are a slot, which is a specific object being described or an attribute about an entity that holds a value or facets, and a facet, the value of an object or slot. When all slots are filled with facets, an instance of a frame is created.

- Rules represent the major elements of a modular knowledge codification scheme. They are conditional statements that specify an action to be taken, if a certain condition is true. They express relationships between parameters and represent the human expert's tacit knowledge in the form of premise-action pairs.

- Knowledge developers are more than talented programmers or knowledge capture people. They are professionals with skills in tapping human expert knowledge and using tools to codify that knowledge. They perform several key functions. They identify knowledge-based applications, develop project proposals, capture knowledge, oversee testing and implementation, perform user training, and maintain knowledge systems.

- Knowledge development requires certain knowledge and skills. Knowledge requirements include computer technology knowledge of the domain, programming knowledge using special tools, and cognitive psychology. Skills requirements include communication and interpersonal skills.

- The personality attributes of the knowledge developer typically include intelligence, creativity, patience, realism, persistence, and a good sense of humor.

TERMS TO KNOW ▪ ▪ ▪ ▪

Action: Consists of a list of commands to be carried out if the premise evaluates to *true,* or a Boolean expression that evaluates to *true* whenever the premise does; conclusions to be drawn with some appropriate degree of certainty or instructions to be carried out.

Agent: Also called *intelligent agent;* a bit of intelligence that represents specific attributes to other agents in a knowledge base or on a network.

Case: Knowledge at an operational level; episodic description of a problem and its associated solution.

Case-based reasoning: A methodology that records and documents previous cases and then searches the relevant case(s) to determine their usefulness in solving a current problem; computer systems that solve new problems by analogy with old ones.

Certainty factor: A measurement of belief or a subjective quantification of an expert's judgment and intentions.

Decision table: A list of conditions with their respective values matched against a list of conclusions.

Decision tree: A hierarchically arranged semantic network that is closely related to a decision table; composed of nodes representing goals and links that represents decisions or outcomes.

Facet: The value of an object or a slot.

Frame: A structure or a codification scheme for organizing knowledge through previous experience.

Inference engine: The "brain" of a knowledge-based system; a cluster of computer programs that coordinate reasoning and inferencing based on the rules of the knowledge base to produce the solution or advice.

Inferencing: Deriving a conclusion based on statements that only imply that conclusion.

Inheritance: An instance of a particular class is assumed to have all the properties of more general classes of which it is a member.

Instantiate: Create a frame by filling its slots.

Knowledge codification: Organizing and coordinating knowledge in a form and a structure meaningful to the user.

Knowledge developer: A specialist responsible for planning the development and execution phases of a knowledge management system.

Knowledge map: A directory that points to people, documents, and repositories.

Logic: The study of reasoning; the scientific study of the process of reasoning and the set of rules and procedures used in the reasoning process.

Matching: The values associated with a given entity paired with the slot values of the frames to signify that an instance has occurred.

Premise: A Boolean expression that must be evaluated as *true* for the rule to be applied.

Production rule: Knowledge codification method in which knowledge is formalized into rules.

Rapid prototyping: Spontaneous, on-the-spot, iterative approach to building knowledge-based systems; an iterative process by which the knowledge developer shows the domain expert or the user what the system looks like based on the knowledge captured to date.

Reasoning: The process of applying knowledge to arrive at solutions based on the interactions between rules and data.

Rule: A conditional statement that specifies an action to be taken if a certain condition is true; a formal way of specifying a recommendation directive, or strategy, expressed as IF (premise).

Rule of inference: A deductive structure that determines what can be inferred if certain relations are taken to be true; facts known to be true and used to derive other facts that must also be true.

Slot: A specific object being described or an attribute of an entity.

TEST YOUR UNDERSTANDING ▪ ▪ ▪ ▪

1. What assumptions can be made about knowledge codification?
2. Distinguish between:
   a. rule premise and action
   b. slot and facet
   c. decision table and decision tree
3. Two key elements make up a frame. Use an example of your own to illustrate these elements.
4. How can frames be linked?
5. Summarize the pros and cons of decision tables versus decision trees. Under what conditions would you use one tool over the other?
6. In your own words, write a short essay explaining the importance of knowledge codification.
7. In your own words, explain knowledge codification. How does it differ from knowledge creation?
8. Present justification for knowledge codification. How important a step does it play in building knowledge management systems?
9. How important is planning in knowledge codification? Be specific.
10. In what way(s) do the four modes of knowledge conversion result in socialization and externalization?
11. What is a knowledge map? How does it differ from a decision tree?
12. Discuss the role of inferencing in knowledge-based codification.
13. Why do we call software agents "agents"? Where do they fit when it comes to knowledge codification?

KNOWLEDGE EXERCISES ▪ ▪ ▪ ▪

1. Using the Internet, research case-based reasoning. Write a 2-page essay describing the CBR process.
2. Review the employment ads in two consecutive Sunday editions of a major newspaper. What pattern in knowledge management jobs may be significant?

What types of jobs relate to knowledge management? What types of organizations are looking for knowledge developers or specialists in the field?

3. The knowledge developer's work is to model the expertise, not the expert. Do you agree with this sentence? Discuss its meaning.

4. Write a basic set of three rules showing how rules are constructed. Use at least one AND and one OR operator in your rules.

5. If you were trying to explain to a novice the meaning and role of rapid prototyping, what would you say? Give an example to illustrate.

6. Examine the following profiles of knowledge developers and discuss their qualifications:

   a. Erika and Lori have been contracted to build a knowledge-base system for a country club. The system is designed to improve the process of evaluating the applications that the club receives for snack bar worker, lifeguard, and coach. Erika and Lori hold bachelor of science degrees in IT and are well versed in two knowledge software packages. Erika is quite congenial and loves to talk to people. Lori is more introspective and enjoys building knowledge systems without involvement with the user or the company's human experts. In addition, they are both well versed in Pascal and C++. Neither has ever built a knowledge-based system for a club.

   b. Jeanine holds a master of science in management information systems from a university in Florida. She is well versed in expert systems and database design. Her favorite database package is Oracle. She enjoys working with people and seems to thrive under stress. She has developed several small knowledge bases. She tends to be pushy when she needs information. People who worked with her in the past said she is good at what she does but can be intimidating. She gives the impression that she has to be in command at all times, using others to do the "leg work."

   c. Bob is 26 years old and has a master of science degree in computer science from a premier university in New York. He served in the military for 3 years prior to going to graduate school. Someone who worked with Bob on a recent knowledge-based project for the military commented, "Bob has patience for complexity. He is a good listener and is highly intelligent, but he has a tendency to spin off on his own when the project falls behind schedule, leaving the rest of his team behind." He has trouble delegating authority. He knows his technology inside out and feels he can do the work on his own.

   d. Ray earned a doctorate in information technology from a midwestern graduate school in 1974. He has a master's degree in social psychology from the same school. Until the mid-1980s, Ray designed information systems in the banking sector. He started working with software agents and knowledge-based systems in 1997 and found it both challenging and lucrative. Recently, he worked on a medical application with a renowned specialist. The two did not get along well. Ray accused the expert of being uncooperative, and the expert told Ray he was arrogant. The knowledge-based medical project ended in disaster.

7. Someone suggested two types of potential knowledge developers:
   "Send me a well-developed computer programmer or a programmer competent in several languages, and we'll make him or her into a successful knowledge developer."
   and
   "Send me a talented generalist with well-developed interpersonal skills—or somewhat more delicately, 'user friendly person'—and a rigorously analytical mind, and we'll team him or her with a competent knowledge developer."
   In your opinion, which approach would be more successful in knowledge development? Why?

8. Develop a set of general frames to codify the following:
   a. A horse
   b. A student
   c. An airline pilot
   Use these frames and describe the following:
   a. Flashdance, an 18-hand thoroughbred
   b. Brenda, a medium-height, fourth-year liberal arts student
   c. Fred, a 30-year veteran airline captain

REFERENCES ▪ ▪ ▪ ▪

Awad, E. M. *Expert Systems.* Minneapolis, MN: West Publishing Co., 1996, p. 129.

Brown, E. Donald, et al. "Expert Systems," February 1999, agents.gsfc.nasa.gov/ papers/pdf/es.pdf, Date accessed April 2002.

Davenport, Thomas H., and Prusak, Laurence. *Working Knowledge.* Boston, MA: Harvard Business School Press, 2000, pp. 68–87.

Dixon, Nancy M. *Common Knowledge.* Boston, MA: Harvard Business School Press, 2000, pp. 143–160.

Gallupe, R. Brent. "Knowledge Management Systems: Surveying the Landscape," April 2000, business.queensu.ca/docs/fp_00-04.pdf, Date accessed August 2002.

Haley, Paul, and LeFebvre, Peter. "Knowledge Management and Knowledge Automation Systems," Gallagher Financial Systems, Inc., www.dmreview.com/whitepaper/wid274.pdf, Date accessed August 2002.

Lamont, Judith. "Expert Systems and KM Are a Natural Team," *KMWorld*, October 2000, www.kmworld.com/publications/magazine/index.cfm?action=readarticle&Article_ID=944&Publication_ID=42, Date accessed August 2002.

Marwick, A. D. "Knowledge Management Technology," *IBM Systems Journal,* vol. 40, no. 4, 2001, p. 815.

Tiwana, Amrit. *The Knowledge Management Toolkit.* Upper Saddle River, NJ: Prentice Hall, 2000, pp. 146–185.

Applied Learning Labs, www.appliedlearninglabs.com/kmaps/faqs.html, Date accessed August 2002.

CHAPTER 8

System Testing and Deployment

Contents

The quest for quality is a race without a finishing line.
—NORMAN RICKARD
XEROX VICE PRESIDENT OF QUALITY

▪▪▪▪ In a Nutshell

The time comes to put a KM system to the test. What good is a system that has not proven its worth or reliability? Imagine using one in a critical real-time application, such as manned space missions, without proving that it will not make catastrophic errors. At each level of the KM system life cycle, testing and evaluation of the finished product are critical steps before deployment (see Figure 8.1).

System reliability is one of the most important testing issues in knowledge-based systems. **Reliability** refers to how well the system delivers the information or solution with consistency, accuracy, and integrity. It also means detecting and removing anomalies (such as redundancy, ambivalence, and deficiency). As KM systems become larger and more complex, reliability is emerging as a significant issue in developing KM systems.

Two prime considerations behind reliability are quality assurance and maintainability of the system after deployment. The primary goal of the knowledge developer is to ensure that the system says what it means and means what it says. In other words, quality representation of the knowledge requires exhaustive testing. It provides a way of checking that the user's requirements are not misunderstood at the conceptual, capture, or codification phases of the KM system development.

The building process of most KM systems often generates anxiety and concern. In the rush to build and deliver the system, many knowledge developers cut corners when it comes to testing. The reasons range from not knowing how to test to running out of time or funds. Regardless of the reasons, ethical and legal obligations prompt knowledge developers to subject the system to rigorous testing prior to deployment.

Testing KM systems calls for informal, subjective, time-consuming, and often arbitrary creation and execution of test cases. In this chapter, the various aspects of testing are discussed: who should do the testing; what testing criteria should be used; issues in testing of the KM system; and how to promote objectivity and order.

In this chapter, we shall find that the logical part of testing is a process that analyzes the program(s) and their relationship to one another. In contrast, user acceptance testing is a process that assumes that the KM system works fine, but it tests for how well the system meets user requirements. The problems with the two kinds of tests are lack of standardization and reliable specification—deciding what constitutes an error and the sources of test cases. For logical testing, cases must address circular and redundant errors and verify system functionality. User acceptance testing begins with a person or a testing team armed with test criteria using realistic test cases.

No single technique detects all logical or clerical errors in a KM system. Some tools work better than others, depending on the type of KM system. Known user acceptance tools include face validation and test cases provided by the knowledge developer or the user. The key issue in user acceptance testing is planning and managing a test

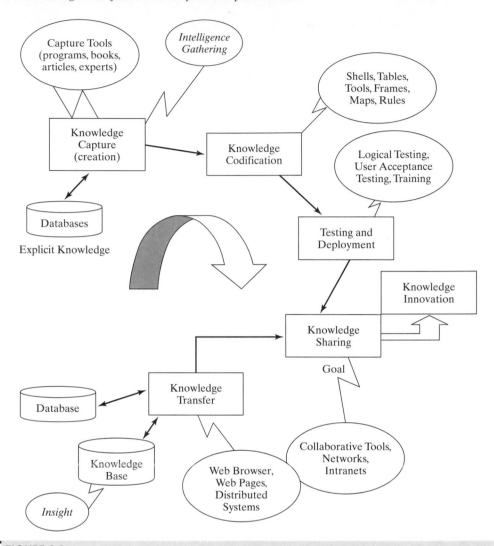

▪ ▪ ▪ ▪ ▪ ▪ ▪ **FIGURE 8.1:** Knowledge Testing and Deployment in the KM System Building Life Cycle

plan that includes decisions on how, when, and where to evaluate the knowledge base and who should do the testing; these are consistent evaluation criteria for various kinds of errors. Once planned, testing becomes a matter of time.

The latter part of the chapter covers implementation issues and procedures. An important aspect is user training. The questions often pondered are "How should the user be trained?" "Where should training be conducted and for how long?" "Who should do the training?" Obviously, how user friendly and how well documented the system is has much to do with training ease and success. User motivation, proper funding, and the role of the champion are additional success factors.

▪▪▪▪ Quality and Quality Assurance

Developing quality KM systems is a goal shared by knowledge developers as well as users. The quality of performance must be demonstrated in a systematic way in order to promote user acceptance of the technology. The KM system must meet or exceed user expectations. Performance capabilities are equated with the quality of the knowledge (tacit and explicit) stored in the knowledge base.

The definition of quality depends on whether the viewpoint is that of the expert, the user, or the knowledge developer. For the expert, quality is a reasoning process that gives reliable and accurate solutions within the framework of the KM system. For the user, quality is the system's ability to be quick, easy to use, easy to understand, and forgiving when the user makes mistakes. For the knowledge developer, quality is how well the knowledge source and the user's expectations are codified into the knowledge base.

▪ ▪ ▪ ▪ Knowledge Testing

The most challenging part of building KM systems is testing. The basic motivation is to control performance, efficiency, and quality of the knowledge base. The goal is compliance with user expectations, human expertise, and system functioning. When a KM system is built via prototyping, each phase of the building process can be properly tested during building instead of waiting until the end, as is usually done in testing information systems. The comments made at each stage could save time, money, and the unnecessary embarrassment of reworking the final version of the system. Prototypes are perhaps the least used form of "rejection insurance" that a knowledge developer or a development team can ever acquire.

KEY DEFINITIONS

The two main types of testing for knowledge bases and knowledge base systems are logical testing and user acceptance testing. **Logical testing** answers the questions, "Are we building the system right?" "Was the system developed using well-established knowledge development principles?" It means checking the system to make sure it gives solutions or results correctly. It looks for anomalies, such as redundant or deficient knowledge, and ensures a bug-free knowledge base.

Logical testing addresses the intrinsic properties of the KM system and its components. *Intrinsic* refers to the syntactic or mechanical aspects of the knowledge base programs. A logical process analyzes codified tacit and explicit knowledge for sequence, structure, and specifications. Because no external factors are considered, the quality of this type of testing can be objectively measured by answering questions such as "What is . . . ?" "How many . . . ?" This is usually done in a static (paper and pencil) mode, even when the system is not yet operational. Its goal is error-free codification.

User acceptance testing follows logical testing and checks the system's behavior in a realistic environment. As a user acceptance phase, these tests ignore the internal mechanics of the system. Meaning and content of the codified tacit knowledge must meet codified criteria of adequacy. The quality measurement of user acceptance testing tends to be subjective. For example, questions based on tacit knowledge such as "What do you think of . . . ?" "How well do you like . . . ? are often asked when conducting user acceptance testing (see Box 8.1).

It is important to note that user acceptance testing is carried out only for technical verification. When the system is modular, each module goes through both steps in building the KM system. See Box 8.2 for an illustration of user acceptance testing.

In today's practice, no standardization, specific tools, or methodologies guide the testing of a knowledge-base system. The process is complex and unique at the same time. Intelligence and knowledge are hard to define, let alone evaluate. Consequently, the whole testing process is subjective and error-prone. Table 8.1 provides a summary of select features of logical acceptance and user acceptance testing criteria.

BOX 8.1

TESTING THE TRAVEL PROFILER

KM SYSTEM TESTING

For user acceptance testing, we assumed the KM system to be a black box—we could see what went in and what came out, but not internal processes. Knowledge developers, experts, and potential users provided the system with inputs and determined if the outputs were correct. For logical (technical) checking, we performed two procedures with hard copy of the program and its knowledge base. First, we read through the lines of code one by one to determine if each was correct. Second, we took examples of what would be a set of correct inputs and manually walked through the knowledge base to see which rules would be applicable; if they would be used correctly, that the function of these rules was correct; and that their left-hand sides were necessary and sufficient to determine the appropriate trueness of the right-hand side of each rule. We also checked to make sure that all of the interfaces between the knowledge base and the user's view were correct.

We look at user acceptance testing as a process of substantiating that a system performs with an acceptable level of accuracy. Logical testing involves whether system performance satisfies the requirements and whether the right system has been built. We validated our system each time we tested it with the knowers. For every inputted problem, we compared the system's output with the knowers' decisions.

During logical testing, we found sets of test cases to run through the system, ran them against a baseline of the software's configuration, and saw how the software reacted. Company experts developed the test cases for us, and we used them not only to determine if the system was running properly, but also to ensure that any modifications we had made had not altered correct operation of the system from prior versions. In other words, we had test cases to ensure that our extensions were correct and that the work of the past developments had not been adversely affected (otherwise known as *regression testing*). Each time new pieces of logic were added (for example, the addition of handling trips to Cuba), new test cases were developed by company experts and run by the knowledge developers and potential users.

We ran another set of tests to ensure that travel agents would understand and be able to use the system and that it would fit their intuitive understanding of the travel problem. From this standpoint, we were testing the system not for its correctness, but for its usability by the company's 27 travel agents in seven locations. In all cases, we were able to get the application to the point where the logic was correct enough for the company experts, efficient enough for the knowledge developers, and usable enough for the travel agents.

SOURCE: Awad, E. M. "*Building Travel Advisor System, Using EXSYS Resolver*," Unpublished manuscript, June 2001.

ISSUES TO CONSIDER

The best KM system test is not so much ensuring how well the system functions, but determining under what conditions it will begin to fail. This is called **force-fail testing**. During planning, the knowledge developer puts together a strategy that uses a minimal set of test cases to discover a maximal set of failures. It is a time-consuming and difficult process to follow. In fact, it is impractical when marginal cost is measured against marginal benefits.

■ ■ ■ ■ ■ ■   **BOX 8.2**   ■ ■ ■ ■ ■ ■

ADEQUACY AS A USER ACCEPTANCE TESTING CRITERION

Adequacy is a measurement of the fraction of actual conditions included in the knowledge base system. For example, the breath gas monitoring system diagnosed 12 waveform patterns of CO_2. Each waveform pattern corresponded to a particular physiological condition. The adequacy of the system was judged according to the total desired number of conditions to diagnose.

In this knowledge base, adequacy was expressed as a simple fraction. The breath gas monitoring system was able to diagnose 12 of 27 important physiological conditions, so the system was $100 \times (12/27) = 44\%$ adequate. As an alternative, subjective weights may be added to particular conditions that are more important to recognize (such as cessation of breathing).

SOURCE: Awad, E. M. "*Validation and Verification of a Breath Gas Monitoring System,*" Unpublished manuscript, August 2001.

■ ■ ■ ■ ■ ■

There are several issues to consider in knowledge-based testing:

- *Subjective nature of tacit knowledge.* Intelligence is difficult to measure. With human experts or a team of specialists, intelligence changes over time due to ongoing upgrades and maturation of abilities and judgment. Solutions for many problems often call for subjective decisions rather than straightforward categorizations of right or wrong. Because tacit knowledge always gives an answer based on the heuristics, it does not "blow up," as do traditional information systems.
- *Lack of reliable specifications.* Ill-defined specifications make knowledge-base testing arbitrary and unreliable. Without testable specifications, a knowledge developer might give in to the tendency to make up specifications for what the system can do instead of figuring out the conditions under which the system will *not* function well. This is an important distinction to keep in mind.
- *Problem of establishing consistency and correctness.* To make sure the performance of the knowledge-base system is correct, the knowledge developer needs to verify both the knowledge base and the reasoning processed by the programs. The

TABLE 8.1   Select Features of User Acceptance and Logical Testing

	Logical (Knowledge Developer Acceptance)	*User Acceptance (User Acceptance)*
Meaning	Building the *system right*	Building the *right system*
Time performed	During knowledge codification or prototyping	During prototyping or when the system is technically operational
Sequence	First	Second
Nature of checking	Syntactic (intrinsic properties of the system)	Semantic (extrinsic properties of the system)
Quality measurement	Primarily objective (technical)	Primarily subjective (judgmental)

■ ■ ■ ■ ■ ■

complex tasks of verifying correctness and consistency are challenging; a knowledge-base system is heavy on tacit knowledge and continues to give answers even though part of the knowledge is incorrect.

- *Negligence in testing.* A vicious cycle begins when no one requires system testing. Part of the problem stems from the difficulty in providing reliable test cases. Another reason is that knowledge-based systems with so many possible states or conditions make exhaustive testing impossible. As a result, user acceptance and logical testing take on "surface" commitment.
- *Lack of time for knowledge developers to test the system.* Many parameters with many potential values cause a combinatorial explosion of rules and test cases, making exhaustive testing difficult. With the simplest tool, tabular checking, rules are grouped into tables similar to IF . . . THEN decision tables. Inside each table, a comprehensive comparison of the rules is made, which checks for inconsistency, redundancy, subsumption, and the like. These types of errors are explained later in the chapter.
- *Complexity of user interfaces.* Some KM systems have complex user interfaces, where inputs are not easy to reproduce, making the potential solution highly inaccurate. The user interface is an important part of the KM system development effort. Through it, the user determines how easy, user friendly, or useful the system is and, therefore, how successful it will be.

One conclusion that knowledge developers should take from these challenges is the need for a seriously designed logical testing strategy. It is a formal statement on how to proceed with the logical testing phase. The test design should meet all the requirements of the client. A force-fail test strategy requires careful choice of test cases that look for missing, ambiguous, or redundant rules with the potential for incorrect answers. These types of rules are discussed later in the chapter.

▪▪▪▪ Approaches to Logical Testing

Two approaches can be used to verify knowledge-base systems:

- Verify knowledge base *formation.*
- Verify knowledge base *functionality.*

Under knowledge base formation, the structure of the knowledge as it relates to circular or redundant errors is verified. Consistency, correctness, and completeness of knowledge base rules are also verified. Logical testing of functionality has to do with confidence and reliability of the knowledge base (see Figure 8.2). Rules and attributes are defined in Table 8.2.

CIRCULAR ERRORS

Carelessness often results in rules that employ circular reasoning. A circular rule tends to be contradictory in meaning or logic. For example, suppose rule 1 states that A is greater than B, and rule 2 states that B is greater than C. If rule 3 states that C is greater than A, then rule 3 is circular and contains an error in logic. The best solution in this case is to remove rule 3.

Here is another example of a circular error:

R5   IF John and Rob are co-owners of company A
        THEN John and Rob own the same company

R6   IF John and Rob own the same company
        THEN John and Rob are co-owners.

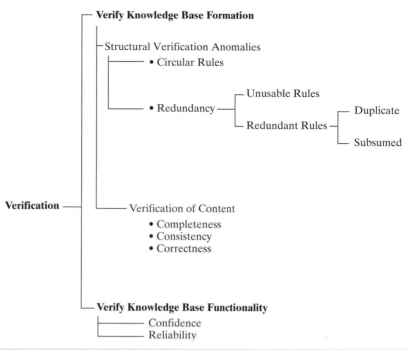

Verify Knowledge Base Formation

Structural Verification Anomalies
- Circular Rules
- Redundancy — Unusable Rules
  - Redundant Rules — Duplicate
    - Subsumed

Verification

Verification of Content
- Completeness
- Consistency
- Correctness

Verify Knowledge Base Functionality
- Confidence
- Reliability

▪ ▪ ▪ ▪ ▪ ▪ ▪   **FIGURE 8.2:**   Approaches to Logical Testing

TABLE 8.2   Attributes in Logical Testing

Circular	A situation where the action(s) of one piece of knowledge may lead back somehow to the condition statement of the same piece of knowledge
Completeness	Answers the question, "Does the system deal with all possible situations with its knowledge base environment reasonably well?"
Confidence	The level of trust or dependence one can put on the system's answers to problems; related to system integrity, with emphasis on system reliability and consistently accurate answers
Correctness	Described as accuracy
Consistency	A check to ensure that the system produces similar answers to all input data at all times with no contradiction
Inconsistency	An anomaly or an error that occurs when an item of knowledge has different value(s) within the knowledge base
Redundancy	Two or more knowledge facts or rules that are written differently but provide the same solution; a duplication of knowledge; absence of redundancy provides greater specificity to the notion of completeness
Reliability	How well the system delivers solutions with consistency, accuracy, and integrity; the probability of failure-free operation of the knowledge base system in a specified environment for a specified time period; synonymous with dependability or trustworthiness
Subsumption error	The conclusion(s) of two pieces of knowledge are the same, except that one piece of knowledge has fewer condition statements

▪ ▪ ▪ ▪ ▪ ▪

If R6 finds a match, its premise part will cause R5 to match and fire. The problem here is that the premise part of R5 matches the action of R6, causing R6 to fire and so on, resulting in useless firing of the two rules.

As a simple example of logical testing, consider a KM system that has several cases involving a house with a living room. We can evaluate cases to determine that there is something incorrect with a case that has a bathtub in the living room. There is probably redundant knowledge in the case if the living room contains two sofas. Likewise, the case of a living room without a sofa probably would be considered incomplete. Finally, we might find it inconsistent if two identical items were labeled the same name. For example, a sofa for one item is labeled a couch for another item.

REDUNDANCY ERRORS

Redundancy errors are ones that offer different approaches to the same problem. There is actually duplication of knowledge. One gets the same results either way—the "dinosaur" effect. For example, study the following rules:

    IF (Salary > 60,000 OR Home > 100,000)
        AND (Loan < 10,000 AND Mortgage < 40,000)
    THEN Max = 100,000

    IF (Salary > 60,000 OR Home > 100,000)
    THEN Assets = 'yes'

    IF (Salary >50,000 AND Dividend > 10,000)
    THEN Assets = 'yes'

    IF (Loan < 10,000 AND Mortgage < 40,000)
        AND Assets = 'yes'
    THEN Max = 100,000

In this example, we find two approaches to the same problem of determining Max. We also do not need to use dividends in the second approach to establish assets. Redundancy can cause difficulties in maintaining the KM system. One version of the rule could be revised; another version could be left as is.

UNUSABLE KNOWLEDGE

An unusable knowledge in the form of a rule is one that only "fires" (executes) if the conditions succeed or fail, one that never fires, or one that has one or more contradictions. They are all in error and, therefore, unusable. An example of an unusable rule that is always false is:

    IF humidity is 5% AND heavy_rain = yes
    THEN conclusion

This rule cannot succeed. If a rule premise (IF) will be false for all valid values, the rule will never succeed. In this example, heavy rain cannot occur in 5 percent humidity. Unusable rules are also called *conflicting rules*.

SUBSUMPTION ERRORS

In **subsumption**, if one rule is true, one knows the second rule is always true. Consider this example:

    R1: IF A AND B, THEN D
    R2: IF A AND B AND C, THEN D

If R1 is true, then R2 is useless, because R2 is subsumed by R1. Both have identical conclusions, but R2 contains an additional (and thus unnecessary) premise clause.

INCONSISTENT KNOWLEDGE

In inconsistency errors, the same inputs yield different results. For example,

IF (Salary > 50,000 OR Home > 100,000)
   AND (Loan < 10,000 AND Mortgage < 40,000)
THEN Max = 100,000

IF (Salary > 50,000 OR Home > 60,000)
   AND (Loan < 3,000 AND Mortgage < 20,000)
THEN Max = 50,000

A user will get different answers, depending on which rule is used. Tests conducted for consistency can also be used to test for completeness. The whole idea is to make sure all the parameters included in the rules are codified correctly and consistently.

▪ ▪ ▪ ▪ Approaches to User Acceptance Testing

As mentioned earlier, user acceptance testing follows logical testing. Its focus is on testing the behavior of the integrated KM system to see if it is satisfactory in the eyes of the user. Even when individual pieces of knowledge are correct, something in their interactions can cause the system to act up.

User acceptance testing includes several steps:

1. *Select a person or a team for testing.* A testing plan should indicate who is to do the testing. Should it be the knowledge developer? The user? Top management? The plan should determine the user acceptance technique(s) appropriate for the system.
2. *Decide on user acceptance test criteria.* The key user acceptance criteria are ease of use, accuracy, adequacy, adaptability, face validity, and performance. See Table 8.3 for definitions of the criteria.
3. *Develop a set of test cases unique to the system.* The test cases should include subtle and obvious cases, boundary conditions, and obviously meaningless combinations of valid and invalid information. The test results are then evaluated against the criteria.
4. *Maintain a log on various versions of the tests and test results.* Documentation can be very important; errors are more easily detected at one test level by simply going back to the previous version. Without this backup, the system would have to be tested from the beginning every time an error occurs—a frustrating and time-consuming job.
5. *Field-test the system.* Once the system has passed the test process, it should be field-tested with user involvement. Field-testing should go smoothly.

TEST TEAM AND PLAN

A successful testing effort requires a commitment to human resources beyond the knowledge developer or the human expert. Commitment begins with management support and a test team with a test plan. The team oversees test activities. The team should:

- Be independent of the design or codification of the system
- Understand computer technology and knowledge base infrastructure
- Be well versed in the organization's business and how the system being tested will fit into the designated area of operation

TABLE 8.3   Select Criteria for User Acceptance Testing

Accuracy	Does the outcome of the system match reality or expectations? Emphasis here is on correctness of the outcome, which is measured by comparing the number of correct answers against known answers.
Adaptability	How well does the system adapt to changing situations? This criterion relates to flexibility and capability to modify facts or rules when new information becomes available. Can the system be customized for particular user needs?
Adequacy	Are the solutions produced by the KM system satisfactory or "good enough" to be acceptable to the user? It is a measurement of the fraction of actual conditions included in the knowledge base.
Appeal	How well does the KM system match the user's intuition and promote useful ideas. Usability is also related to practicability, marketability, and user friendliness.
Availability	Do other KM systems that solve the same problem exist? Availability is related to appeal.
Ease of use	Does the system incorporate human engineering and high quality in its human-machine interaction/interface?
Face validity	How well does the system pass the real-life test on the surface? It is another term for credibility.
Performance	Does the system function as expected? It is related to reliability and quality assurance and the overall quality of the solutions provided by the KM system.
Reliability	See Table 8.2.
Robustness	Is the system able to function near the limits of its coverage?
Technical/ operational test	How well do the system's technical and operational states meet the user's requirements? It indicates the capability of the knowledge base to produce empirically correct answers.

▪ ▪ ▪ ▪ ▪ ▪

Team members normally represent a variety of the users' areas of operation, especially in the final testing phase. The entire procedure should be guided by a plan that defines the roles and responsibilities for everyone involved in the system's life cycle, and it should provide documentation with respect to testing. The plan should:

- Identify the aspects of the KM system that require testing
- Determine when user acceptance testing is appropriate
- Define the test method that will lead to user and company approval
- Provide the guidelines for documenting test results

Having the knowledge developer do the user acceptance testing poses limitations. In user acceptance testing, the problem for most knowledge developers is that they have only limited knowledge in developing test cases that meet user acceptance criteria. The human expert can be consulted to approve the procedure and the acceptability of the solution. In the end, whoever ends up being the tester depends on the availability of expertise, motivation, time, and funds allocated for the testing phase. A test team representing the users' interests and based on a plan would be the best choice.

USER ACCEPTANCE TEST CRITERIA

User acceptance test criteria guide the focus of what to test. As a general rule, all systems are valid against certain criteria and invalid against others. The question is how does one know what criteria to use for evaluating the KM system? This is especially important when certain systems (such as a medical diagnosis knowledge base) require more stringent user acceptance test criteria than other systems (such as one that assists in the selection of roses for Valentine's day). The alternative criteria compare system results against historical cases, against the expert's prediction of the final results, or against some theoretical standard. In any case, user acceptance test techniques contain imperfections and cannot guarantee 100 percent performance.

To illustrate, suppose test cases are chosen from a KM system test plan. Several questions are raised:

- How many test cases should be used to assure that the system is satisfactory to the desired confidence?
- How should the test cases be developed objectively and reliably?
- What objective measures should be determined for the selected criteria?
- Should a performance measure be included—other than that of the human expert—against which test case results should be evaluated?
- What mix of easy versus difficult test cases should be considered in the final test cases? That is, what type of test cases should be used?
- How should the test cases be evaluated? By a panel of experts? By knowledge developers?
- If multiple experts are involved, how should the KM system be validated against differing human opinions?

Addressing criteria measures can assist in test planning. Sound and reliable measures also mean easier deployment and improved user acceptance. Actually, user involvement in testing the user interface generally increases user acceptance of the finished product.

USER ACCEPTANCE TEST TECHNIQUES

No single user acceptance test technique is best for detecting all errors in a KM system. Some techniques work better for certain types of problems and for certain types of knowledge codification (for example, rule-based versus frames or decision trees). Several test techniques are worth reviewing:

- Face validation
- Test cases
- Subsystem validation

Face Validation

In face validation, a knowledge developer, along with users and company experts, evaluates the performance of the KM system at its face value. System solutions are compared with those of the human experts, and a value judgment is made about the reliability of the results.

Face validation can be used to test chunks of knowledge at any phase of the development life cycle. It is mainly a group effort of the knowledge developer, the expert, and the end user. This ad hoc tool is quite useful for testing user-system interfaces, user friendliness, and assist facilities. However, it is not a rigorous user acceptance technique. As such, it offers no measurable assurance of performance or reliability.

Test Cases

A popular test technique is executing a set of prepared test cases on the KM system. The results are examined for agreement with those of an independent expert or a panel of experts that solves the same problem. Only system inputs and outputs are significant (see Box 8.3).

In addition to those provided by the human expert, test cases may be provided by the knowledge developer and the user. Those provided by the developer have been known to be more effective than those provided by others. The domain expert, the

---

▪ ▪ ▪ ▪ ▪ ▪ ▪   BOX 8.3   ▪ ▪ ▪ ▪ ▪ ▪ ▪

TEST CASES FOR THE KNOWLEDGE RECRUITING PROFILER

The test design was created to ensure that all the user's requirements were met. We created a form from which to collect decision data from individual past cases. The form included all seven variables with the corresponding choices, an area to write in Ms. Burgess's (personnel director) past decisions, and an area to write in what the knowledge hiring profiler recommended. Thirty copies of the form were given to the manager to be filled out. A set of cases was selected from her past decisions to represent the good decisions and bad decisions. In order to make this process effective, Ms. Burgess looked through some of her previous applications to see what she had decided.

Good decisions included those applicants with whom Ms. Burgess was satisfied with her decision to either hire or not to hire. Likewise, bad decisions included applicants with whom the manager was dissatisfied with her final decision. Bad decisions resulted from either a Type I error or a Type II error. Results of case testing are as follows:

SAMPLE SIZE = 30	Number Hired	Number Not Hired
Type I error	9	0
Type II error	0	1

Without the use of the hiring profiler, there was a 33.3 percent (10 out of 30) error rate. The utilization of the knowledge base improved the manager's hiring process by ensuring that Ms. Burgess considered all of the required variables before making her decision. This system removed ambiguity and inefficiencies in the decision-making process. In essence, it succeeded in eliminating both Type I and Type II errors recognized in the cases being utilized. We tested this by running each of the 30 cases through the hiring advisor using the following criteria:

- The past cases with applicants identified as good employees who were actually hired were determined to be qualified by the recruiting profiler.

- The past cases with employees who were not hired but were qualified were determined to be qualified by the recruiting profiler.

- The past cases with applicants who were hired and ended up being poor performers were not determined to be qualified by the recruiting profiler.

- The past cases with applicants who were not hired because it was believed they would be poor performers were not determined to be qualified by the recruiting profiler.

The chief limitations of the previous decision-making process included the lack of emphasis on ability and the lack of standardization in the wage placements.

SOURCE: Awad, E. M. "*Test Cases For the Knowledge Recruiting Profiler,*" Unpublished manuscript, January 2002.

▪ ▪ ▪ ▪ ▪ ▪

knowledge developer, and the user are somewhat like three blind men describing an elephant. Each looks at a different aspect of the KM system and tries to make sense out of it. Test cases from all three sources are considered to be the best combination, because they provide a more comprehensive test of the system. They also tend to increase the objectivity of the testing process.

Like other techniques, testing a knowledge base that is based on test cases has its own share of limitations. When the expert who writes the test cases is also the tester, the credibility of the test process can be undermined. Bias—based perhaps on personality conflicts or on ignoring nontechnical aspects such as user interface or ease of use—can filter into them, especially if test case generation is done in an ad hoc manner.

▪ ▪ ▪ ▪ Managing the Testing Phase

The critical issue in KM system testing is planning for completeness of testing that will vouch for system adequacy and lead to user acceptance. Another important issue is managing the test plan. This includes the following tasks:

- *Decide when, what, how, and where to evaluate the knowledge base.* The reliability of answers, explanation, training capability, and the like must be evaluated. Timing and duration of testing in the hands of specialists are crucial to a successful system test and eventual implementation.
- *Decide who should do the logical and user acceptance testing.* All indicators point to having the expert handle the whole process. The next best approach is to have an outside expert or a team do independent tests of the knowledge base.
- *Draft a set of evaluation criteria in advance.* This task involves knowing what to test for. One can get the system to run, but what are you proving or looking for? What are the hard criteria?
- *Decide what should be recorded during the test.* When it comes to testing rule-based tacit knowledge, among the important statistics to record are the following:
  - Rules that always fire and succeed
  - Rules that always fire and fail
  - Rules that never fire
  - Test cases that have failed
- *Review training cases, whether they are provided by the expert, the knowledge developer, or the user.* Appropriateness of the test cases should be emphasized in this task.
- *Test all rules.* This task ensures that every parameter is correct. Testing looks for two types of errors in rules:
  - *Type I error*—A rule that fails to fire when it is supposed to fire. This is tantamount to failing to detect a problem and similar to a false negative in statistics.
  - *Type II error*—A rule that fires when it is not supposed to fire. This is similar to a false positive in statistics.

Finally, generating test cases is so time-consuming and costly that this phase is often viewed as a chore rather than a challenge. It takes a certain know-how and objectivity to generate test cases. Even then, users have been known to accept the system, regardless of how lax the test process has been. With this attitude, testing can go forward with no difficulty.

▪▪▪▪ KM System Deployment

The goal of every KM system development is successful deployment. Even the best system will fail if deployment concerns are not addressed. At issue is how well the knowledge developer coordinates the deployment with the end user. Depending on how knowledge codification was carried out, the end user might have been a regular participant all along, which means deployment stands a good chance of user acceptance and successful deployment.

Deployment is affected by organizational, technical, procedural, behavioral, economic, and political factors, especially where the organization is large and the existing technology is too established to allow change to occur easily. KM system deployment is especially complex. In this next section, we examine deployment issues as they relate to managing KM system projects as well as user training. Knowledge transfer is covered in the next chapter.

The two aspects of deployment are the transfer of the KM system as a technology from the knowledge developer to the organization's operating unit and the transfer of the system's skills from the knowledge developer to the operating person in the organization. This step may also include training an organization's operating unit for system maintenance and upgrade. The issues, prerequisites, and techniques for both of these aspects will also be discussed in this section.

▪▪▪▪ Issues Related to Deployment

Once the system is designed and fully tested, the final step is the physical transfer or deployment of the technology to the organization's operating unit. Whether or not the developer will be the one to deploy, certain issues need to be addressed at the beginning of each KM system development project. These relate to the selection of the knowledge base problem, ease of understanding the KM system, and organizational factors.

SELECTION OF THE KNOWLEDGE BASE PROBLEM

The success of KM system deployment has a great deal to do with the way the problem domain was selected. For example, if the domain was selected with end user involvement and management support, one can expect smooth deployment and cooperation in user training. KM system users can be assured of system success if:

- The user has prior experience with computer applications, which tends to reduce the inherent fear that automated systems will replace people or add stress to their job life.
- The user has been actively involved in defining and identifying the specific functions of the KM system.
- The user is involved in user acceptance testing and the final evaluation of the KM system to assure its accuracy, completeness, and reliability.
- The payoff from the development of the KM system is high and measurable and leaves little room for arguments that it is draining the budget or is unnecessary.
- The KM system can be implemented in the working environment without much interruption of ongoing activities.
- The champion has done a great job selling the user's staff on the potential contributions of the KM system.

By now, the importance of involving the user in the early phases of the development process should be evident. Using rapid prototyping can also offer a way of selling the system and its potential benefits when it is deployed. Front-end commitment requires dedicated users, managers, company experts, and a champion to firm up the planning and provide the support necessary to carry out knowledge codification. Once commitment is secured, deployment is generally easier to accomplish (see Box 8.4).

EASE OF UNDERSTANDING THE KM SYSTEM

The acid test of knowledge codification is when the system is deployed and the user realizes how easy it is to understand. Documentation also plays a key role. When changes must be made, a troubleshooting guide, a step-by-step procedure, or a flow-chart in the form of an easy-to-follow technical or operations manual can guide the user into unlocking the system and correcting glitches.

Reliable documentation, especially during user training, is especially important during deployment. Documentation heavy on illustrations, examples, and graphics reduces training time. Of course, a human trainer who provides face-to-face, inter-active, on-site training is always an asset to the training process.

With this in mind, successful KM system deployment depends on several user-related factors:

- *Level of motivation of the user.* Good documentation cannot compensate for poor attitude and low motivation. Promoting motivation and commitment takes time and must be worked on in advance.
- *Computer literacy and technical background of the user.* A computer-literate user can be easier to work with than someone with no such background. First-time users often require education and training before they are able to support development and use of knowledge-based systems.
- *Communication skills of the trainer.* Selling people on change is sometimes considered more of an art than a science. Communication skills can make the difference between a user's acceptance of or resistance to the new system.
- *Time availability and funding for training.* A training program that is run on a shoe-string is usually a loser. Squeezing training time to the bare minimum often results in trainee impatience, resistance to learning, or nonuse of the system. Training should be part of the deployment phase offered around the convenience of the user.
- *Place of training.* The location of training can make a difference. On-site versus off-site training continues to be an issue, with pluses and minuses for each alternative.

▪ ▪ ▪ ▪ ▪ ▪   **BOX 8.4**   ▪ ▪ ▪ ▪ ▪ ▪

INSTALLATION AND TRAINING ON TRAVEL PROFILER

Participation in the deployment and maintenance of Travel Profiler included two senior managers who had been involved in the knowledge capture phase. This was quite a break for implementation, because they made it difficult for the travel agents to say "no" to using the system. The way it turned out, entry-level agents found the system a great training tool that reinforced what they do on the job. The actual installation and basic training took less than 2 days on a weekend.

SOURCE: Awad, E. M. "*Building Travel Advisor System, Using EXSYS Resolver,*" Unpublished manuscript, June 2001.

▪ ▪ ▪ ▪ ▪ ▪

Off-site training is generally dedicated, uninterrupted learning. Its positive benefits include privacy and focus on the projects. The feasibility of off-site training depends on distance, location, and funding. In contrast, on-site training means no out-of-town transportation or room and board expenses. However, it can be interrupted by telephone calls, secretaries, and uninvited gawkers.

- *Ease and duration of training.* This aspect depends on the caliber of the trainer and the attitude and motivation of the trainees. "Chemistry" often affects how well all parties work with one another. Also, the training period should be reasonable and able to meet measurable goals. A long, drawn-out 3-week training period does not promote the same excitement as a 4-day session.
- *Ease of access and explanatory facilities of the KM system.* KM systems should be easy to access and work with. A feature that provides adequate online explanations satisfies most users and provides convincing evidence of the integrity of the answers provided by the system.
- *Ease of maintenance and system update.* At this stage, good documentation and easy-to-follow procedures in a module-oriented KM system can make the difference between easy maintenance and a nightmare. *Maintenance* ensures that the system stays on course. It means making corrections to meet the initial system requirements. *Enhancement* means upgrading the system to meet a new set of requirements.
- *Payoff to the organization.* A KM system's benefit to the organization is usually measured in cost reduction, improvement in sales or overall performance, and so on. Measured payoff early in the development life cycle promotes successful deployment.
- *Role of the champion.* Solid top management support and a champion pushing for system adoption can make the difference between a successful and a lukewarm installation.

These success factors of KM system deployment are interrelated. Organizational and technical factors also come into play (see Figure 8.3).

KNOWLEDGE TRANSFER

Two approaches can be used to transfer KM system technology in implementation. In the first approach, the KM system is actually transferred from the knowledge developer directly to the working unit (end user) in the organization. The other approach simply means installing the system on the resident hardware. It includes dropping off the user's manual and help facility, a technical manual containing a line-by-line printout of the knowledge codification, and copies of the knowledge base for backup. This step may or may not include user training. Actually, training the user on the KM system is relatively easier than training on a conventional information system because of the unique technical and procedural facilities embedded in the KM system.

In the second approach, which transfers KM system technology skills, the knowledge developer transfers to a group within the organization the knowledge and necessary know-how to maintain and upgrade the system in the future. Such a transfer may include special technical training in the diagnosis and test procedures necessary to make changes in the system. Once completed, the developer is out of the picture, except perhaps in a consultative role.

Transfer of KM systems can be approached in one of two ways: (1) an abrupt, one-time transfer that results in a permanent installation on a specific day or (2) a gradual transfer over a given time period. In the latter case, most often through rapid prototyping, a receiving group becomes part of the developer's team. Once one phase of the

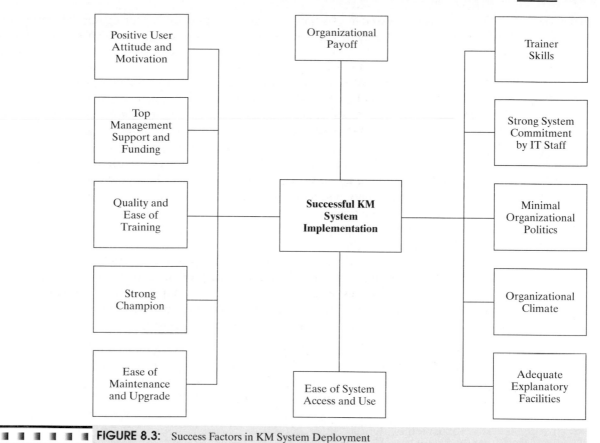

▪ ▪ ▪ ▪ ▪ ▪ ▪ **FIGURE 8.3:** Success Factors in KM System Deployment

system is verified and ready to use, responsibility is transferred to the receiving group, which then examines the makeup of the partial system. The transfer involves the sharing of training, methodologies, experiences, and techniques. Eventually, the rest of the system is transferred, allowing the receiving group to take full responsibility for the system's operation and maintenance.

Implementation can also be approached as a stand-alone KM system installation on a PC or as a fully integrated application that interfaces with other applications or databases. KM systems should be designed on platforms that are compatible with other KM systems in the organization. The compatibility feature makes explanation or justification of the new system easier. It also makes user training easier, because most users presumably look at the new system as "a system just like the others."

INTEGRATION ALTERNATIVES

A KM system can be integrated into the organization's existing operations through the following methods:

- **Technical integration** occurs through the company's local area network environment, the resident mainframe, or existing information system infrastructure. This job is not exactly straightforward. Management must decide on a system's level of priority for access in the network. For example, in one organization's IT department, a LAN–based KM system was given a low priority access, because the course that used the system was taught only during weekends. During regular workdays, employees frequently experienced considerable delays (more than 20 seconds) in response time. They complained that work assignments were always late coming off the printer.

- **Knowledge-sharing integration** is required, for example, in a firm that needs to make a KM system available to each of its 17 branches in an equitable way. This level of availability often requires upgrading the local area network, the mainframe, or lines to ensure equitable service. For example, in the case of the Travel Profiler, after the travel agency installed a LAN, it made plans to have the KM system available to all travel agents at the same time with the same response time.

- **Decision-making flow integration** suggests that the way the KM system assesses a problem situation should match the user's style of thinking. Providing such a match can be crucial to user acceptance and satisfaction.

- **Workflow reengineering** considerations come into play when implementation of a new KM system triggers changes in the workplace or within jobs in the user's domain (such as merging jobs or deleting positions). This type of situation can occur because the actual building of the product leads the KM system and the user, during their interactive sessions, to develop new insight into the problem domain and to a more creative way of dealing with it. One can expect a certain amount of backlash as a result of job reengineering.

The attractiveness of change depends greatly on management's perception of its potential contribution to the productivity of the area in which the new system will reside. The concept of reengineering is evolutionary and usually takes weeks or even months to firm up. In other words, for a KM system to survive, it must be amenable to change. It must also provide built-in flexibility to accommodate the kind of change expected by the user.

THE ISSUE OF MAINTENANCE

An important aspect of KM system development that gets little attention is **maintenance**. The term *maintenance* means "making the necessary corrections that continue to meet the user's expectations." In rule-based KM systems, for example, it means adding, removing, and rewriting certain rules so that the reasoning is more consistent with today's expert's solutions. Although this type of change is carried out during the initial testing phase, one can expect corrections resulting from the user's real-time experience with the system. Whatever mode the knowledge base is codified in, maturation over time tells us that knowledge needs close attention to reflect the best ways to update, transfer, and share knowledge.

System maintenance can be improved in several ways. For example, if the knowledge base is organized into several well-defined modules, one can easily go to a specific module and make the necessary changes. In this respect, a single developer in charge of knowledge codification can promote consistency and uniformity in programming the knowledge base.

For knowledge-based system deployment to succeed, it must facilitate easy and effective maintenance in several ways:

- The system must have a feature to allow changes to be added or deleted as needed, which brings up the importance of the modular approach to KM systems.
- The system must be capable of allowing inconsistent, conflicting, or redundant errors to be easily identified. Removing redundancies ensures improved system performance.

- The system's help facilities must satisfy the user's requirements as closely as possible. User acceptance of the solution is easier with the availability of clear presentation of the solutions.
- The availability of a qualified person or a team can ensure that maintenance is carried out effectively and on schedule. With large organization-wide KM systems, maintenance could be a full-time job.

To assure successful maintenance, responsibility for it needs to be assumed by a qualified person within the organization. Otherwise, the maintenance function should be contracted to a freelance specialist. Part of the maintenance function establishes a change-order procedure with proper documentation that includes the authorized requester, the person who made the change, and the outcome of the change.

ORGANIZATIONAL FACTORS

Of all the deployment issues, a prime consideration is a firm commitment to the project by top management and the user. It means strong, senior-level leadership, because there will be challenges that arise. Management can support system deployment by providing adequate funding, ensuring the availability of technology and personnel, and allowing the champion to function throughout the development process. The second organizational factor is user participation in the building process. Participation improves commitment, enhances system quality, and fosters a sense of ownership of the KM system.

Commitment is not the same as contribution, however. Anyone can make a contribution through system participation without having to make a commitment to system use. Commitment to a project means taking responsibility for its outcome, which is expected to contribute to successful deployment. The anecdote in Box 8.5 illustrates the distinction.

Other organizational factors include organizational politics and organizational climate. This could mean turf war. Different departments (such as purchasing and production) may support the overall goal of the new KM system but have conflicting priorities. *Politics* is jockeying for leverage to influence one's domain and control procedures, technology, or the direction of an area of operation. The prevalence of politics, especially in a negative sense, is often ignored or deemphasized. The knowledge developer must remain neutral within the political arena of the firm.

▪ ▪ ▪ ▪ ▪ ▪   BOX 8.5   ▪ ▪ ▪ ▪ ▪ ▪

THE CHICKEN AND THE PIG VENTURE

A chicken and a pig grew up together on a farm and came to know each other very well. One day, the two met and discussed a joint venture.

The quick-thinking chicken told the pig, "I have a great idea for a breakfast restaurant near a local school. Between the two of us, we have all the ingredients we need — eggs, ham, and sausage. Just think how excited the customers will be to get the freshest ham and eggs in the area."

The slower-thinking pig pondered this ingenious proposal and, after a long pause, said, "My dear friend, your proposal sounds great, although lopsided. All you're offering to do is to make a *contribution* to the venture. You're asking me to make a *commitment.*"

▪ ▪ ▪ ▪ ▪ ▪

The organization's climate dictates whether a KM system's time has come. The key questions that the knowledge developer should ask are "Is today, this week, or this month the right time to implement the product?" "Is the organization ready for this particular environment?" Timing and readiness factors must be assessed in advance. For example, in banking, most computer-based systems are installed during weekends so as not to interfere with the weekday business activities. A KM system, including training, should be completed in an environment devoid of interruptions.

User readiness can also influence deployment success. Foot dragging and delaying the inevitable are not solutions. Users who know that work will accumulate during their training make poor trainees. This suggests that deployment must be planned in advance.

OTHER FACTORS

There are several other implementation factors to consider. The return on investment (ROI) factor is not easy to measure. If it is simply "greater customer loyalty and improvement in employee satisfaction," it is a hard sell with the board of directors. The costs are not hard to quantify, but the benefits are intangible and soft. A company may decide to spend a $1 million on a KM system, but if it does not make its quarterly figures, the quick fix is to shelve expensive projects. When that happens, momentum is lost, consultants leave, and the KM system dies a natural death.

Another factor worth considering is quality information. The number-one requirement for a successful KM system is an infrastructure capable of sharing real-time and accurate information. Content is a critical part of KM system implementation, especially when the knowledge developer is trying to meet deployment deadlines, cut down on costs, or do a quick sell to the user.

ROLE OF THE CHAMPION

When all is said and done, the underlying factor for successful implementation of a KM system is the role of the champion. A champion is someone in an organization who, because of position, power, influence, or control, secures the organization's support of the new system from inception to deployment. Without a champion, a KM system is vulnerable throughout the development process. The champion needs to be at the executive level or a senior steering committee to act as the project's board of directors. Politics, budgetary problems, deficient support, or conflict of interest can stand in the way of deployment.

To illustrate, a KM system designated to help VISA/MasterCard personnel decide on approval of applicants met stiff resistance from the department's manager. The problem caught the attention of the bank's operations vice president, who had a good rapport with the officers of the bank as well as the chairman of the board. The vice president had a long talk with the manager and assured her that the new KM system would "speed things up" rather than replace her final judgment. The vice president concluded the meeting by saying, "Look, let's give this project a try and see how it turns out."

When time came for deployment, the knowledge developer met with the manager and asked to proceed with training her staff on the new system. The manager replied, "That's not necessary. Because I've gone through the process and am familiar with the way it works, just load the package on the server and I'll take it from there."

Concerned about possible delays or improper training, the knowledge developer took up the matter with the bank's vice president, who called a meeting with the senior staff of the VISA/MasterCard division. At the meeting, the vice president explained the importance of the KM system and how it would improve the reliability of issuing credit cards to prospective applicants. He appointed a staff member to undergo the initial training. She, in turn, trained a volunteer as backup.

Training went well. After the system was successfully installed on the local area network's server, the vice president called for an area meeting to announce the official operation of the applicant assistant and to recognize the contributions of the division manager in the development process. A similar announcement was also placed in the bank's employee newsletter on the intranet later that month.

In a situation where resistance could kill a worthwhile project, a champion makes a difference. The KM system cost the bank $80,000. Based on the bank's past records, it paid for itself in 7 months by eliminating high-risk applicants.

▪ ▪ ▪ ▪ User Training and Deployment

A major component of system deployment is user training. The level and duration of training depend on the user's knowledge level and the system's level of complexity. User training is also influenced by the requirements of the KM system. Knowledge-based system requirements range from simple and user friendly to advanced, which requires special vendor training. A user friendly KM system is almost self-instructional, with menu-driven features and easy-to-follow online and hard copy manuals. The duration of training is usually measured in hours to days. Advanced company-wide systems require knowledge-based infrastructure, use of queries, and so forth, which take days to weeks to learn, even for the experienced user. The level of user training depends on the following:

- The user's knowledge of knowledge-based systems
- The complexity of the KM system and how well it accommodates the user
- The trainer's technical experience and communication skills
- The environment where training is carried out

One way or another, training must be customized to the specific user after considering capabilities, experience, and system complexity. In situations in which both the user and the system are new, training procedures are introduced in stages. For example, training first-time users on a stand-alone KM system begins with showing the user how to turn on the system, enter a query, load files, display solutions, update rules, and so on.

The most effective training is supported by a well written help file, easy-to-use explanatory facility, and job aids. A help feature can be an invaluable training document, especially if the user is geographically isolated. It is usually highly illustrated and contains an index for reference. Graphics, photographs, and templates provide quick learning and are invaluable teaching aids.

PREPARING FOR KM SYSTEM TRAINING

Introducing a KM system into the organization affects personnel responsibilities and, in some cases, can alter the structure of an organization. The very concepts underlying a KM system often change the way employees think about tasks. When a system is introduced, the initial goal is to educate the user about the new system. A strategic education plan prepares an organization to adopt it as it becomes ready to deploy. Such a plan takes place before development and cannot be a substitute for training. Hands-on training provides specific skills to operate a system. The combination of a strategic education plan and well-planned training means quicker organizational acceptance, which assures successful deployment.

One way to promote successful KM system deployment is to follow a few simple steps:

- Define how the KM system agrees with the organizational mission.
- Demonstrate how the KM system can help meet organizational goals.
- Allocate adequate resources to a feasible project.
- Advocate positive effects of KM systems, but do not create unrealistic expectations.
- Perform cost/benefit analyses of KM system technology and sell the company on the system's benefits and potential.

To raise awareness, a company might distribute Post-it notepads reading "KM System, (name of the company)" to all employees everywhere.

COMBATING RESISTANCE TO CHANGE

A big mistake many companies make is that they assume that the intrinsic value of a KM system will be welcomed with open arms. This assumption is often shot to pieces. Regardless of what is being converted or how well deployment is carried out, final implementation means change, and people tend to resist change. KM system deployment is the initiation of a new order of things. People understandably become anxious when they do not know what the system will do and how it will impact their job and career path. The result is often stress and increased resistance to change. The resistors are at several organizational levels:

- *Knowledge hoarders* are usually ambivalent about the value and potential of knowledge sharing. Those on the way to retirement worry less, but they may still lack motivation unless they are properly compensated for their efforts.
- *Company employees* in general resent lack of recognition (sometimes compensation), especially when they have been involved in building the KM system from its inception.
- *Troublemakers* are those left out of the system building cycle or chronic complainers who tend to obstruct the installation, cause delays, or force cancellation of the system.
- *Narrow-minded "superstars"* are usually technical people in the organization's IT division. They often resist any change that they did not initiate or approve in advance. Others veto a project not in their area of interest. This is where lack of management support can spell doom for a KM system.

Resistance is displayed in three psychological reactions:

1. *Projection:* Hostility toward peers
2. *Avoidance:* Withdrawal from the scene, such as calling in sick
3. *Aggression:* Killing the system because of uncertainty about its direct benefits

One category that explains resistance to change is the extrinsic or intrinsic value that users place on knowledge and decision making. In most organizations, knowledge means power. Although knowledge developers build systems that promote knowledge sharing through knowledge bases, company experts who stand to lose monopoly on knowledge may resist a new KM system installation. Most resistance relates to the perceived impact of the new system on one's job or status in the organization.

Resistance also has much to do with the individual personality, the organizational structure, and group relations within the area where the KM system will be in use. User education, professional training, and participation in the building process can help reduce resistance to change.

Another resistance category comes from the system itself rather than people. If a KM system offers poor user interface and requires extensive training to master, it could spell disaster for effective deployment. There is no doubt that user friendly, knowledge-based systems are a sure way to overcome resistance to KM system deployment. Ideally, what is needed is a user who has an open mind about change and is "friendly" to technology and the concept of knowledge sharing via technology. Overconcentration on technology and overlooking behavioral issues have resulted in many KM system failures.

Because a major user concern in system deployment is how to work the system, users frequently ask, "What functions are available?" "How do I access each function?" "How do I know if the system has answered my questions correctly?" Another user concern is how the KM system selects the right knowledge—how it reaches conclusions or lines up with the problem at hand. The knowledge developer must demonstrate the system and provide detailed training in a timely manner.

With these ideas in mind, there are various methods to promote KM system deployment:

1. User-attitude survey
2. Communication training
3. Training sessions
4. Role negotiation

In a **user-attitude survey**, opinions are collected from actual users to learn how well they liked the system and how closely it met their requirements. Poor communication skills could be a problem, but the survey is still worth the effort. **Communication training** can prove to be invaluable for enhancing user–knowledge developer relationships and successful system deployment.

For small to medium-sized KM systems, **training sessions** are normally run by the knowledge developer. For larger systems, they are conducted by a knowledge specialist who is expected to be a skilled communicator. In either case, the trainer should address the user's training needs and gear the pace of training accordingly. Some users may learn the system in one day; others take much longer.

Resistance to change becomes obvious when users perceive adverse changes in their jobs. An interesting technique, called **role negotiation**, attempts to clarify what the user expects the altered job to offer. Once understood, users have been known to accept their roles in the change more readily.

In summary, for a new KM system to ensure user support, knowledge developers and users must improve communication channels and jointly discuss the new system's features and how the change can improve their jobs. Users should also participate in all phases of deployment. Sensitivity to user expectations is a step toward "deployment without tears."

▪ ▪ ▪ ▪ Postimplementation Review

After the KM system has been deployed and the operation is up and running, the effect of the new system on the organization should be carefully evaluated. System impact must be assessed in terms of its effect on people, procedures, and performance of the business. More specifically, the main areas of concern are quality of decision making, attitude of end users, and cost of knowledge processing. For example, a post-implementation study of the Travel Profiler showed an increase in the number of overall travelers accommodated by a factor of 2.5. It also showed that travel agent time had improved by 20 percent.

In the postimplementation stage, several questions should be considered:

1. How has the KM system changed the accuracy and timeliness of decision making?
2. Has the new system caused organizational changes? How constructive have the changes been?
3. How has the new system affected the attitude of the end users?
4. Has the new system changed the cost of operating the business? In what way?
5. Has the new system affected the organization's decision-making process? What measurable results can be demonstrated?
6. In what way has the new system affected relationships among end users in the organization?

The objective is to evaluate the KM system against standards and determine how well it meets company requirements. This process is actually related to user acceptance evaluation. The user initiates the review, which prompts a procedure for maintenance or enhancement.

SECURITY CONSIDERATIONS

Safeguarding the KM system against unauthorized access is a necessary system deployment issue. Similar to a conventional information system, at a minimum, the new system should provide password or protocol protection so that only users with the correct code can log onto the system. One aspect of user training is to ensure that passwords and security procedures are consistently observed. Beyond this point, restricted access regarding the update of the knowledge base itself can be secured through the existing LAN or the server in operation.

▪ ▪ ▪ ▪ Implications for Knowledge Management

The main goal of KM system testing is to assure continuous quality and high performance. The term *performance* implies quality. The model shown in Figure 8.4 suggests that the quality of a KM system is affected by the nature of the problem, technical considerations, the people involved, and organizational factors. For example, if the problem is complex and the organizational climate or politics is amenable to the prospective system, then a knowledge developer can expect cooperation from the expert and the user during knowledge codification. This cooperation should contribute to quality testing. The end result should be a high performance, quality-oriented KM system.

One of the main issues raised during deployment is maintenance. Maintenance of KM systems continues to be a nebulous area. Some of the questions to be addressed by management are as follows:

- Who will be in charge of maintenance?
- What skills should the maintenance person have? What is the best way to train him or her?
- What incentives should be provided to ensure quality maintenance?
- What type of support and funding is needed?
- What relationship should be established between the maintenance of a KM system and the IT staff of the organization?

Another managerial issue to consider is how one would know whether deployment will be a success. In addition to technical considerations, one must be aware of the people factor. People rallying behind technology can increase the success of deployment. Additionally, a KM system cannot succeed if the issue of cost of technology and

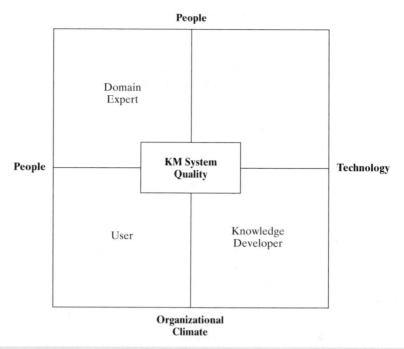

▪ ▪ ▪ ▪ ▪ ▪ ▪ **FIGURE 8.4:**   Internal and External Factors Affecting Knowledge-Based System Quality

how it is going to be absorbed has not been resolved. Any of these issues can inhibit successful deployment.

Other managerial issues affect the direction and outcome of KM system projects. For example, the depth of the knowledge required to solve the problem is often an unknown commodity due to the nature of the expertise and the limitations of the knowledge developer. Forcing clarification too early in the building phase can result in a less-than-satisfactory system. Therefore, managing expectations and scoping the system are crucial early tasks.

Finally, the role of the human expert in system deployment is also important. Management should properly compensate the expert for efforts in developing a KM system. A manager may also play a proactive role in the deployment phase by simply sharing interest or excitement in the system. A lack of this type of enthusiasm and overt support puts a damper on the whole project.

SUMMARY ▪ ▪ ▪ ▪

- KM system reliability is one of the most important issues in knowledge-based systems. Reliability means how well the system delivers information with consistency, accuracy, and integrity. The prime emphasis beyond reliability is quality assurance and maintainability of the system after installation.
- The most important part of building KM systems is testing. Logical testing answers the question, "Are we building the system right?" and its goal is an error-free program or software. User acceptance testing answers the question, "Are we building the right system?" and tests the system's behavior in a realistic environment. Such testing is done only after the system is operational.

- Some important challenges or issues that are considered during testing include the following:

  - The subjective nature of knowledge-based testing
  - Lack of reliable specifications
  - The problem of establishing consistency and correctness
  - The determination of what constitutes an error
  - Sources of test data
  - The danger of negligence in testing
  - Adequacy of automatic logical testing tools
  - The complexity of user interfaces

- A circular error tends to be contradictory in meaning or logic. Redundancy errors offer different approaches to the same problem. An unusable rule always fires and fails, never fires, or has one or more contradictions. In a subsumption error, if a rule is true, one knows the second rule is always true. In inconsistency errors, the same inputs yield different results.

- The steps for user acceptance testing are as follows:

  - Select a person or a team for testing.
  - Decide on user acceptance testing criteria.
  - Determine objective measures for the selected criteria.
  - Develop a set of test cases and scenarios unique to the problem.
  - Maintain a log or various versions of the test and test results.

- Some user acceptance testing tools are face validation, test cases, and subsystem validation.

- Three important deployment issues are worth noting: selection of the problem, knowledge codification and deployment, and organizational factors.

- Technology transfer includes actual transfer of the KM system from the developer to the working unit or the transfer of KM system technology skills. Deployment can be approached as a stand-alone installation on a PC or as a fully integrated application that interfaces with other applications.

- A KM system can be integrated into an organization in a number of ways:

  - Technical integration
  - Knowledge-sharing integration
  - Decision-making flow integration
  - Reengineering considerations

- The level of user training depends on the user's knowledge of the KM system, complexity of the system, the trainer's experience and communication skills, and the environment in which training is carried out. In any case, training should be geared to the specific user and, in some cases, introduced in stages for a lasting impact.

- Regardless of what organizational aspects are being changed, deployment means change, and people in general resist change. The resistors included experts, nonexperts, troublemakers, and narrow-minded technical superstars. Resistance is displayed in the form of projection, avoidance, and aggression and has much to do with the individual personality, the organizational structure in which the user works, and the group relations in the area where the system will be installed. User education, training, and participation can help reduce or control resistance to change.

- Deployment can be promoted in a number of ways: user-attitude survey, communication training, training sessions, and role negotiation. In any case, sensitivity to user expectations is a step toward implementation without tears.

TERMS TO KNOW ▪▪▪▪

Aggression: Resistance to KM systems through employee sabotage of the system.

Avoidance: Resistance to KM systems through employee withdrawal from the job or scene.

Circular rule: A rule that has embedded contradiction in meaning or logic.

Deployment: Physical transfer of the technology to the organization's operating unit.

Enhancement: Upgrading the system to meet a new set of requirements.

Exhaustive testing: A procedure in which all possible combinations of input values are tested.

Face validity: Testing a system at its face value; comparing a human domain expert's value judgment to test results for reliability.

Inconsistency: A rule that has the same input but different results.

Knowledge-sharing integration: Integrating the expert system in such a way that it can be accessed by different branches of the company, allowing them to share information.

Logical testing: A system test to ensure the proper functioning of the system; addresses the intrinsic properties of the KM system; alpha test.

Projection: Resistance to KM systems through employee display of hostility toward peers.

Pupil user: Unskilled worker trying to learn or gain some understanding of the captured knowledge.

Redundancy rule: A rule that offers a different approach to the same problem; duplication or meaning the same.

Reliability: Dependability; truthfulness of the response or answer to a given question; credibility; how well the system delivers solutions with consistency, accuracy, or integrity; detecting or removing anomaly.

Subsumption: In rules, if one knows one rule is true, one also knows the second rule is always true.

Technical integration: Integrating an expert system into an existing operation through the firm's local area network environment, the resident mainframe, workstations, and other information system applications.

Testing: Time-intensive logical and user acceptance testing of KM systems.

Unusable rule: A rule that only fires if the conditions succeed, one that never fires, or one that has one or more contradictions.

User acceptance testing: A system test to ensure the right system from the user's perspective; a system that meets the user's expectations; beta test; user acceptance test.

User-attitude survey: A survey in which opinions are collected from users to learn how well they like the system and how closely the system meets user requirements.

TEST YOUR UNDERSTANDING ▪▪▪▪

1. What is the goal of logical testing? What is the goal of user acceptance testing?
2. In your own words, explain the various phases of KM system testing.
3. Distinguish between:
   a. logical and user acceptance testing
   b. circular and redundant rules
   c. force-fail test and exhaustive test
4. The chapter discusses two approaches to verifying knowledge-based systems. Discuss each of them briefly.
5. How does verification of knowledge base formation differ from knowledge base functionality?
6. Give examples of the following:
   a. circular error
   b. redundant error
   c. subsumed error
   d. unusable rule
7. In terms of securing test cases for user acceptance testing, where should the test cases come from? How would one assure their reliability or relevance?
8. Who should do the user acceptance testing? Should it be the end user or the domain expert? The knowledge developer? Explain.
9. In what way(s) is each of the following validation tools useful:
   a. face validation
   b. test cases

10. If you were coordinating user acceptance and logical testing, what guideline would be useful before the actual test?
11. How can system users be assured of system success?
12. In what way(s) is knowledge codification related to user acceptance testing?
13. "Successful KM system implementation depends on several factors." Briefly explain each factor.
14. Elaborate on the role of maintenance in the life of an expert system.
15. Distinguish between:
    a. maintenance and enhancement
    b. pupil and tutor user
    c. projection and avoidance
16. How would one approach transfer of technology in system implementation? Which approach do you suggest for implementing a small system on a stand-alone PC? Why?
17. There are several alternatives for integrating KM systems into the organization. Briefly explain each alternative. Under what condition(s) would one choose one alternative over the others?
18. Why is place of training important? What about duration of training? Explain.
19. What determines whether user training will be successful? Be specific.
20. How would one promote successful KM system implementation?
21. What is postimplementation review? Why is it important to carry out this step?

KNOWLEDGE EXERCISES ▪▪▪▪

1. Discuss the key issues during logical and user acceptance testing. Is one issue necessarily more critical than all others? Be specific.
2. Discuss the role of security in KM system use. How important is KM system security compared to security measures in conventional information systems?
3. If you were asked to coordinate the implementation phase of a KM system in a department where users are not that interested in the change, what approach or procedure would you follow to combat resistance to change? Cite a specific situation or the conditions under which you would handle the assignment.
4. If a KM system is user friendly and has the necessary help facility, how necessary is a user's manual?
5. How important are organizational factors in system implementation?
6. Discuss the main steps to user acceptance testing. How and why are they important?
7. "A strategic education plan prepares an organization to adopt a KM system." Do you agree? Why or why not?
8. If testing is never that perfect or complete, why test anyway?
9. When a KM system is finally installed and ready to go, is the knowledge developer released from further obligations to the system? Why?
10. Consider the following rules:
    R1   IF $a = 10$
            AND $b = 15$
            THEN $c = 20$
    R2   IF $a = 10$
            THEN $c = 20$
    Of the two rules, which rule is subsumed by the other?
11. Consider the following rules:
    IF   temperature $>$ warm AND
              humidity is high AND
              atmospheric pressure is low
    THEN   there will be thunderstorms

If   temperature > warm AND
            humidity is high
Then   there will be thunderstorms

Which rule is subsumed by the other? Why?

12. Consider the following rules:

    R1   IF $a = 10$
               AND $b = 15$
               THEN $c = 20$

    R2   IF $b = 15$
               AND $a = 10$
               THEN $c = 20$

    Are these two rules redundant? Why? Which rule is made redundant by the other?

13. Consider the following rules:

    R1   If $a = 10$
               AND $b = 15$
               THEN $c = 20$

    R2   IF $a = 10$
               AND $b = 15$
               THEN $c = 35$

    These rules are said to be in conflict. Do you agree? Why or why not?

14. Consider the following rules:

    R1   IF   temperature > warm AND
                     humidity is high
           THEN there will be no thunderstorms

    R2   IF   humidity is high AND
                     temperature > warm
           THEN there will be no thunderstorms

    In what way(s) are these rules redundant? Will they always succeed?

15. Consider the following rules:

    R1   IF   humidity is high AND
                     temperature > warm
           THEN there will be thunderstorms

    R2   IF   temperature > warm AND
                     humidity is high
           THEN there will be sandstorms

    Are these rules redundant? In what way(s)?

16. Identify whether the following rules are redundant, conflicting, circular, or subsumed rules:

    a. R1   IF $a = x$ R2   IF $b = y$
                 AND $b = y$ AND $a = x$
                 THEN $c = z$ THEN $c = z$

    b. R1   IF $a = x$ R2   IF $b = y$
                 AND $b = y$ AND $a = x$
                 THEN $c = z$ THEN $c = w$

    c. R1   IF $a = x$ R2   IF $b = y$
                 AND $b = y$ THEN $c = z$
                 THEN $c = z$

    d. R1   IF $a = x$ R2   IF $b = y$ R3   IF decision = yes
                 THEN $b = y$ AND $c = z$ THEN $a = x$
                                 THEN decision = yes

17. A KM system is being designed to assist a computer retailer's customer service clerks with managing calls related to replacement of Pentium 4 chips in PCs. How should the performance of the KM system be evaluated? Explain.

18. Implementing the Real-Estate Advisor:

In November 2000, a real-estate firm expressed interest in a KM system to train new agents and advise senior ones on the best match between a prospective home owner and the available homes in the area. The firm had 14 offices in eight major cities in the Commonwealth of Virginia. A contract was drawn to do the work with deployment by mid-October.

The resulting knowledge base consisted of 165 rules involving 17 parameters. Testing the package took 2 months before it was ready for deployment. The first step was to meet with two volunteer agents from the main office to demonstrate what the system could do and how easy it was to use. They asked how long it would take. The reply was "3 to 4 hours, total." They suggested a meeting with the knowledge developer the following Sunday to give the system a try.

On Sunday morning, the two real-estate agents came on time and were eager to see what the KM system could do to improve their sales potential. After 2 hours of practice, they began to make suggestions about expanding the system to include variables that had not been raised earlier. For example, they wanted the system to ask if the prospective buyer would object to living in an integrated neighborhood, whether the buyer had transportation to and from work, and so forth.

The result of the 3-hour session was frustration. The agents were courteous, but they did not indicate that they would use the system. Because they worked on commission, there were under no immediate obligation to try it.

A strategy meeting with the president of the firm led to the decision to hold a session with the 11 real-estate agents the following week and discuss the deployment plan. During the 1-hour session, several questions were raised regarding the system's capabilities and how it was built. Luckily, the single most experienced agent used in building the system was a highly respected agent with 18 years of successful experience. The expert was there and offered his opinion of the system.

Suddenly, the president cut into the discussion and said, "Look, we can beat the system over the head and still not agree on a direction. I have an idea for you to consider. Why don't you give this system a try, and after you feel you have a handle on the way it works, see if it can help you match a buyer with the right house. I am willing to increase anyone's commission from 50 percent to 60 percent for every documented match that results in a sale. I am willing to do this for 90 days."

By the end of the session, 6 out of the 11 agents underwent a 1-day training session at company expense. That was in February 2001. By June, 46 successful matches had been made that resulted in 38 documented sales.

The word got around to the branches regarding the usefulness of the Real-Estate Profiler. During the succeeding 5 months, several suggestions were incorporated into the system under a maintenance agreement with the firm. In December 2001, the system became available to the branches under the 60 percent commission plan. Training became easier, as more agents expressed interest in the system.

Questions
1. Evaluate the approach used in deploying the Real-Estate Advisor.
2. Should one expect changes in the system to take place during deployment? What went wrong, if anything? Explain.
3. In what other ways might this system have been deployed?

REFERENCES ▪ ▪ ▪ ▪

Awad, E. M. "*Building Travel Advisor, with EXSYS Resolver*," Unpublished manuscript, June 2001.

Awad, E. M. "*Test Cases For the Knowledge Recruiting Advisor*," Unpublished manuscript, January 2002.

Awad, E. M. "*Validating and Verification of a Breath Gas Monitoring System*," Unpublished manuscript, August 2001.

Ayel, M., and Laurent, J. P. "SACCO-SYCOJET: Two Different Ways of Verifying Knowledge-Based Systems," in M. Ayel and J. P. Laurent (eds.), *Verification and Validation of Knowledge-Based Systems*. New York: John Wiley & Sons, Inc., 1991, pp. 63–76.

Freedman, Roy S. "Knowledge-Based Software Testing," *The Journal of Knowledge Engineering*, Spring 1991, pp. 47–65.

Gupta, Uma G. "Successful Development Strategies: Moving to an Operational Environment," *Information Systems Management*, vol. 9, no. 1, 1992, pp. 21–27.

Horibe, Frances. *Managing Knowledge Workers*. New York: John Wiley & Sons, Inc., 1999, pp. 109–126.

Jafar, Musa, and Bahill, Terry A. "Interactive Verification of Knowledge-Based Systems," *IEEE Expert*, February 1993, pp. 25–32.

Tiwana, Amrit. *The Knowledge Management Toolkit*. Upper Saddle River, NJ: Prentice Hall, 2000, pp. 99–109.

CHAPTER 9

Knowledge Transfer and Knowledge Sharing

Contents

A man has no ears
for that to which experience
has given him no access.
—FRIEDRICH NIETZSCHE

■ ■ ■ ■ In a Nutshell

We have seen that for knowledge to be shared, it must first be captured, codified, and deployed in a format acceptable to the user. The goal is to turn knowledge into action or to transform individualized learning into organizational learning. This is why this material was placed after the KM system life cycle. In most instances, the life cycle is a prerequisite to knowledge transfer and knowledge sharing

Knowledge sharing is more than simply knowing the right thing to do. Knowledge and information are obviously critical to performance. However, we live in a new millennium, where there are a growing number of organizations in the business of capturing and transferring best practices. The goal is to narrow the gap between what they know and what they do.

Part of a changing environment is first to gather intelligence (such as information, added value, and tacit knowledge) that triggers insight (responsiveness) to generate innovation in products, services, and processes. As part of the KM system life cycle, once knowledge is captured, codified, tested, and deployed, the next step is to demonstrate how it is transferred to the right party in the right format and at the time needed. Knowledge transfer is a prerequisite for knowledge sharing for competitive advantage, performance, and profitability. Knowledge sharing is making available what is now known. Knowledge transfer's role in the building life cycle is shown in Figure 9.1. It may come from knowledge bases, databases, or via the Internet. A knowledge-based system that helps a user answer technical questions on the job is an example of knowledge that is being shared with that user.

Of course, there are other ways to transfer and share knowledge. Knowledge may be transferred between persons and computers, computers and computers, teams and individuals, or between individuals. In this chapter, each option is covered in detail to reflect the multifaceted nature of knowledge transfer. We also discuss transfer strategies and methods, inhibitors to knowledge transfer, and how explicit and tacit knowledge are transferred.

■ ■ ■ ■ Knowledge Transfer As a Step in a Process

Knowledge transfer is part of organizational life. It is carried out whether the process is managed or not. It is transmission of knowledge (experience, lessons learned, know-how) and use of transmitted knowledge. It is conveying the knowledge of one source to another source. Merely making knowledge available is not considered to be knowledge transfer. It is transmission plus absorption. The goal is to promote and facilitate knowledge sharing, collaboration, and networking. It is access to scarce resources, new insights, new expertise, cross fertilization of knowledge, and creating an organizational environment of excellence. Collaboration means the ability to connect diverse assets into unique capabilities in pursuit of new opportunities for personal, group, and organizational growth.

Knowledge transfer is done directly by working together, communicating, learning by doing, apprenticing, through face-to-face discussions, or embedding knowledge through procedures, mentoring, or documents exchange. It is not done solely from knowledge bases or repositories. Knowledge can be transferred from repositories to people, from teams to individuals, and between individuals. When an IT employee asks another how to read an HTML page, she is requesting a transfer of knowledge. If a loan officer asks another in the office down the hall if he has ever dealt with a graduate student loan, the second loan officer, if interested, is transferring his knowledge. In any case, even transmission and use of knowledge have no useful value if the acquired knowledge does not result in some new behavior or value-added learning.

It is obvious that knowledge transfer is part of everyday organizational life. Discussing a problem with someone next door is generally by convenience. It is rare

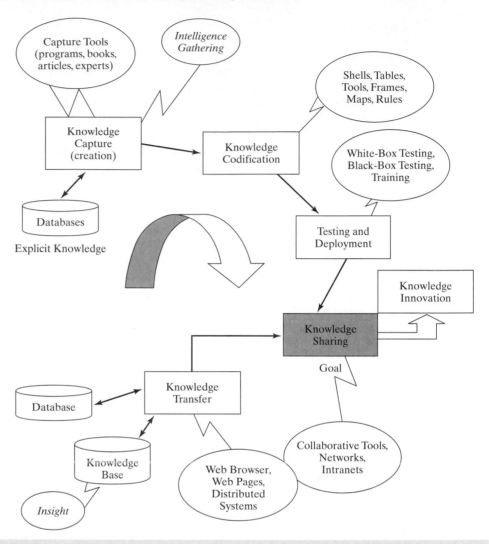

▪▪▪▪▪▪▪ FIGURE 9.1: Knowledge Transfer in the KM System Building Life Cycle

that one looks organization-wide for the best expert or the one with the deepest knowledge. This brings up the concept of *bounded rationality*. Herbert Simon, a renowned behavioral scientist at Carnegie Mellon University, coined the term to recognize human limits to a person's knowledge of all alternatives and their consequences. The hope is to get "good enough" information from someone nearby. The "good enough" view is referred to as *satisficing* rather than optimizing.

To transfer knowledge, we consider three factors:

1. Where knowledge is transferred from—knowledge bases, innovations, lessons learned, programs, books, experts, articles, or data warehouses
2. The media used in knowledge transfer—local area networks, wireless transmission, secure versus unsecured lines, or encrypted or plain text
3. Where knowledge is transferred to—apprentice, user, another computer, a team, any authorized individual, a manager, a customer, or an automated product maker

It should be noted that only a limited amount of human expertise can be captured as explicit knowledge to be part of a knowledge base application. This means that most of human expertise is tacit knowledge, with practical limits as to how much or what types of knowledge can be transferred between people or within a team configuration.

In any case, knowledge transfer facilitates knowledge sharing. The collective knowledge of an organization is gleaned from the learning of its members as well as its stakeholders and customers. Knowledge transfer enhances knowledge flows through collaborative technologies, especially the intranet and the Internet. Hard, high-tech communications technologies and networks serve as the enablers of knowledge transfer and assure constant availability of knowledge on demand. This is best enforced by support from top management (see Box 9.1).

Figure 9.2 shows a partial view of select knowledge transfers and their respective knowledge management applications. Knowledge transfers distribute to points of action—support education and training, act as customer service representatives, and so forth. In contrast, knowledge applications use knowledge to deliver products and services—assist knowledge workers to perform unique functions in a real-time environment, make knowledge available to solve difficult problems, and the like.

▪▪▪▪▪▪   **BOX 9.1**   ▪▪▪▪▪▪

A FRAMEWORK FOR KNOWLEDGE TRANSFER

One of the challenges of managing an ERP (enterprise resource planning) implementation is understanding that not all entities within the organization will instinctively see the value of knowledge capture and management. Farsighted executives, however, are beginning to appreciate this shift to a knowledge-based economy and are investing wisely in building both knowledge content and the technologies that facilitate sharing, management, and access to knowledge.

An ERP system contains a great deal of codified knowledge, both in the software structures provided by the vendor and in process knowledge and business rules developed by the enterprise. However, a corresponding set of auxiliary knowledge is captured only in the form of project documents (formal and informal), training documents, data models, additional business rules and formulas, and in the brains of the project team. You cannot easily access or derive this valuable knowledge from software or the operational system.

To gain the benefits inherent in this auxiliary knowledge, organizations must create and deploy a knowledge system. The starting point for this system is the development of a knowledge transfer framework. Such a framework identifies which information you should retain, who will eventually use that information, and how you will capture that information at each stage of the ERP implementation. In addition, the knowledge transfer framework provides a model of the knowledge environment over the life cycle of a system implementation and illustrates the relationships and dependencies of people, business processes and events, and knowledge domains. With this framework in place, you can anticipate and plan for knowledge requirements of subsequent phases of the ERP project. You can also develop mechanisms for transferring or transforming the knowledge base from one phase to another.

SOURCE: Excerpted from Clark, Linda E. "A Stitch in Time," *Intelligent Enterprise Magazine*, October 20, 2000, p. 2.

▪▪▪▪▪▪

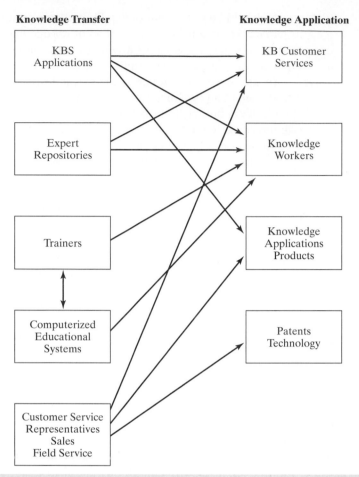

▪ ▪ ▪ ▪ ▪ ▪ ▪ **FIGURE 9.2:** A Partial View of a KM System for Knowledge Transfer and Knowledge Application

Related to this view is the role of knowledge-based system applications in support of knowledge management. Knowledge-based applications impact both the quality of results obtained and the effort required to complete knowledge management tasks. Of course, knowledge-based applications are no match for the human mind, where tacit knowledge resides. Only a limited amount of a person's expertise can be elicited for incorporation into knowledge-based applications. However, there is a growing trend in artificial intelligence that is beginning to add more "smart" to such applications, which are becoming closer and closer to the human way of decision making.

THE KNOWING-DOING GAP

Many organizations know what to do, but for various reasons ignore the information that is available and perform differently—creating the "knowing-doing" gap. Recognizing this problem should help firms make corrections and set up a knowledge transfer environment for all employees to benefit. Even knowledge is not always a solution. To illustrate, in the spring of 2001, one of us gave a 1-day seminar to senior officers of a Miami–based banking group. The topic was "Employees Come First"—a topic that is paramount in a service industry like banking. It has been known for years that employee attitudes and morale affect turnover, customer satisfaction, and profitability.

At the end of the seminar, one senior executive vice president of loans made complimentary remarks about the good ideas she got from the session, but added that none of those ideas would work at the bank. The bank's president, she said, had no appreciation for the rank-and-file staff (tellers, bookkeepers, and customer service clerks) of the bank. Every time he passed by her employees, in the hallways or lunchroom, all he wanted was to make sure employees did not take too much time off. At the end of the year, it was always a big fight to get him to approve salary increases based on performance that was carefully assessed by the human resources department. All he worried about was what his bonus would look like based on the bottom line. Short of replacing the president, there was not much that could be done to implement change.

An hour later, there were two senior officers from another bank still in the seminar room. Although their bank recently implemented performance measures due to a recent acquisition of a smaller bank, they had condensed their notes on paper napkins to take back to the office for follow-up. One officer said, "Although we have activated much of what you covered, the seminar gave us a different way of finalizing the performance measures. To tell you the truth, we did a lousy job in sharing the information with those whose jobs will be affected by the change." The other officer was already on her cell phone, reporting to her boss the changes she wanted to make first thing next Monday.

The first episode illustrates a knowledge-hoarding, manipulative organization under tight top management control. In contrast, the latter episode is an example of a learning organization on the rise. The spirit of cooperation and collaboration was obvious in the way the officers worked together, clarified their notes, contacted the head office, and showed interest in doing something positive for the good of the organization. It is an environment where knowledge transfer and knowledge sharing should be no problem.

PREREQUISITES FOR TRANSFER

The terms *transfer* and *share* are interrelated. *Knowing* is considered deeply personal. In one respect, it asks someone to give something that is his or her own property. *Knowledge transfer* is a mechanistic term, which provides knowledge for someone else. The term *share* is an exchange of knowledge between individuals, between or within teams, or between individuals and knowledge bases, repositories, and so forth. Knowledge sharing recognizes the personal nature of people's knowledge gained from experience. What triggered the writing of this book is the growing trend of more and more organizations that began doing more than mere talking about sharing knowledge. They started to install knowledge bases and processes to transfer knowledge to others to get around the problem of reinventing the wheel. E-mail notices from colleagues such as "Does anyone know where to . . . ?" and "Would anyone know how to . . . ?" are examples of using the technology to promote knowledge sharing.

It should be noted that technology alone is not a sure prerequisite for knowledge transfer or knowledge sharing. The myth that "once you build it, they will use it" does not work that well in most organizations. The image of a huge high-cost repository that contains all the knowledge ever needed offers a feeling of comfort and control. However, neither cooperation nor retrieval occurs with much excitement. When organizations find that not much is happening, they begin to use the incentive system to encourage participation. The consulting firm KPMG coined the "give to get" scheme, where employees cannot take any knowledge without putting something into the knowledge base or into the relationship that provided them the knowledge. In any case, for knowledge transfer to work, it takes a change in culture, in politics, and attitude to make things happen.

As can be seen, transferring knowledge into action is not straightforward. There are interpersonal, political, leadership, and organizational issues to consider. There are also assumptions to be made about the organization and its processes. However, there are recurring episodes and guidelines that help us evaluate the gap between knowledge transfer and knowledge sharing and how to overcome it.

Instill an Atmosphere of Trust in the Organization

Trust is the foundation of knowledge transfer. It is a psychological state, where people feel confident about sharing ideas, experiences, and relationships with others. For decades, people in organizations have learned to hoard knowledge rather than to share it. There is still inherent fear that once knowledge is shared, the knower (person who has the knowledge) becomes vulnerable. In a local retail store, the manager asked the shoe department supervisor of 9 years if she would train a new employee before she would be a candidate to manage another department in a store being built in a new mall on the other end of town. Toward the end of the 5-week on-the-job training, the store manager heard from headquarters that the proposed store would not open due to recent financial difficulties of the chain. The decision was made to retain the newly trained supervisor for less salary. The word got around that neither the manager nor the retail chain could be trusted. It was not the first time this type of episode took place.

Fix the Culture to Accommodate the Change

The trust factor has cultural and political implications. An organizational culture that promotes and rewards cooperation and collaboration is a better candidate for knowledge sharing than a competitive culture that drives employees to performance through the fear of punishment (such as layoffs or dismissal). There is the case of a 2000 graduate from a premier MBA school who accepted a 6-digit salary with a fast growing consulting firm. When the recession hit in 2001, the company laid off 40 percent of its staff without notifying anyone. Early in the year, this graduate sensed things were not on the level. Managers kept information to themselves, and partners were working feverishly to attract new clients. He soon decided to keep to himself his technology-based knowledge required for installing two major projects for *Fortune* 500 clients. That strategy saved him from being axed by the sudden layoffs.

Culture is usually embedded in a company's core values, policies, mission, consistent behavior, treatment of employees, and tradition. A trusting organization tends to attract trustworthy employees who perform well within the cultural values of the business. Those who do not fit voluntarily leave or are soon asked to resign. With that in mind, the "learning organization" notion should be transmitted through the organization's culture. Becker (1998) cites several dimensions of values and beliefs making up an organization's culture:

- Authority
- Collaboration
- Commitment
- Compensation
- Competence
- Conflict resolution
- Consistency
- Cooperation
- Creativity
- Empowerment
- Fairness

- Motivation
- Mistake tolerance
- Participation
- Partnering
- Teams
- Truth, openness
- Self-management
- Risk tolerance
- Innovation
- Change
- Focus

Positive cultural values include the following:

- *Leadership.* For example, a leader is a champion who promotes change and one who is highly regarded by the employees.
- *Understanding company mission.* For example, a company can have a clear mission statement regarding knowledge management and how it plans to embed it in the organization.
- *Culturally internalized management practices.* For example, a company can have enthusiastic management that is optimistic about the changing environment.
- *Culturally internalized operational practices.* For example, a company can make decisions and solve problems by using collaboration and teamwork.
- *Culturally driven forces.* For example, employees must trust one another in a shared learning atmosphere. Trust in others generates honesty and fairness for all participants.

In contrast, the key factors that retard cultural values include the following:

- *Culturally driven forces.* For example, specialists may hoard knowledge or deny that they have sought after knowledge. It is also the attitude of "I don't care" or "It is not my job."
- *Understanding company priorities.* For example, employees and management have a fuzzy understanding of the company's mission, policies, and strategies. Any out-of-the-ordinary ideas or innovations are perceived as unnecessary work.
- *Questionable values.* For example, the company may value money or financial goals as the ultimate goal of the business.
- *Questionable beliefs.* For example, a business may view employees as being replaceable (Wiig 1993).

There is the chicken-or-egg issue of whether to fix the culture and then get the employees to share or vice versa. There is no consensus on one approach or the other. The myth that knowledge sharing happens only in organizations that have a collaborative culture does not pass muster in every case. The authors are of the belief that a learning culture makes it both convenient and efficient to implement knowledge transfer in the interest of knowledge sharing. Knowledge exchange, no doubt, impacts the culture, but going that route could mean a long haul toward fixing the culture on a permanent basis. Either alternative presupposes an ongoing environment of trust in the approach or process.

Push Reasoning Before Process

It never seems to fail that employees undergoing training show greater interest in process ("how to do") than the reasoning ("why") behind process. For example, in database training using Microsoft Access, greater attention is given when trainees learn how to create tables, access data, and enter records than is paid to knowing why a database is designed and why you need a database for decision making. We experience the same situation every time we teach the database management system in school. Students think it is an answer rather than a process.

When people are hired into an organization, supervisors and managers introduce themselves, tell the newcomer who they are, what the company philosophy is, and what they hope the new employee will be expected to achieve. That should be the first thing to provide before employees are shown how to do the job. In our many studies in organization design, we have heard employees say, "I have been with the company 15 years, and I have yet to meet the president or know who the board members are." We often respond, "You should tell management how you feel so that they understand that it is not enough to know what to do, but for whom and why you're doing it." A learning organization begins with employee queries, feedback, and transfer of experience across the board.

A learning organization may also begin with a set of guidelines about how it will operate. In one large Virginia bank, top management have set three core values for tellers in 38 branches that guide their behavior: fairness, cordial treatment, and willingness to share experience with other tellers. The same bank has a set of core assumptions about its employees in general:

- Respected as humans and treated fairly
- Intrinsically creative and capable of thinking and learning, if given a chance
- Can be responsible and be held accountable
- Will make mistakes and can gain experience from trial and error
- Willing to make a contribution, if given a chance

In summary, it is important to remember that when it comes to knowledge transfer, people should be equipped with an attitude and a philosophy and that precedence should not be allowed to substitute for thinking. What creates longevity and combats turnover in a business is making use of the untapped potential within the employees and transferring the training to help each employee work at peak performance. As a result, a firm can learn and communicate with newcomers, regardless of job or distance, and do so in a way consistent with its philosophy and core values. This is what creates success and boosts performance.

Remember That Doing Is Far Better Than Talking

Once a philosophy is understood, the next guideline is to teach and train employees as a way of knowing—not merely talking, conceptualizing, and thinking. Learning from doing things together brings up the concept of knowledge transfer via teams. In most of today's consulting firms, for example, junior staff just out of college are assigned to teams with field knowledge to be mentored by senior team members as a step toward more responsibilities in the future. Likewise, new graduates from medical schools serve residency under certified professionals before they can take on the challenge of independent decision making. This is where they receive experience, knowledge, know-how, and the many ways to handle complex decisions.

Teaching, explaining, and mentoring are ways of transforming and sharing knowledge. So is doing the work and experimenting with different ways to do a job. Once you do it, you will *know*. Being involved in the actual process is the best way to learn it. Consider the case of a new car salesman who served once as an auto mechanic. He could share his knowledge with a prospective customer about the way the car works, how reliable it is, and where you get value for the car under consideration. In a way, this is creativity and a unique way of using knowledge to serve a goal. If the job becomes routine, motivation, morale, and attitude begin to degenerate toward the company, the product, and self. In the case of the auto salesman, he has a way of sizing up the customer, customizes his pitch, and delivers accordingly. His creativity and focus on customized selling earned him the salesman of the year award year after year.

We live in an era of distance learning, where employees can acquire knowledge by learning on their own. There are also jobs that are best learned by first-hand, tangible, physical experience. The traditional way of teaching and learning is for the trainer to stand up, show concepts and procedures through transparencies or slides, and expect people to go back to the job and do something with it. A better way of learning is to form a team with experienced members who show novices why a job is needed and how it is done before they are released to do the job. Unfortunately, knowing by doing is a costly and time-consuming way of transferring knowledge. Going that route, however, will certainly shrink the knowing-doing gap in most jobs.

Actions speak louder than words and are more effective than concepts or theory not tested by experience. Talk without action is no longer workable in a learning organization. To think that because a decision is made through discussion that action will follow is also losing viability.

Know How the Firm Handles Mistakes

Mistakes are bound to be made, and they are a cost for the firm to incur. Tolerating and forgiving mistakes in the interest of learning are important. A story is told about a young IBM executive who caused a $10 million mistake in the way he managed a high-risk project. When brought before Dr. Watson, the founder of IBM, the young man snapped, "I guess I am here because you will want my resignation." Dr. Watson replied, "You have to be kidding. We just blew $10 million to train you."

There is rarely any "doing" without mistakes. In fact, some of the best learning in business is by trial and error, which implies some failure or taking steps backward to move forward. The question is in how the firm reacts. Being human, certain mistakes are forgivable as long as the employees owns up to them. There is the story of a dairy company that set a guideline for its truck drivers to continue on payroll. It is called "the 3-star life cycle" or three red stars and you are fired. If a truck driver is involved in an avoidable accident, a red star is placed next to his name on the employee bulletin board for all employees to see. The accident report is placed in his employee file with a warning to be more careful the next time. In the second avoidable truck accident, another red star is placed on the bulletin board with a warning that the next accident will be the last straw—he will lose his job. When the third accident takes place, he is asked to leave, with the final paycheck to follow in the mail.

Tolerance for mistakes allows room for learning to take place. The truck driver example shows two chances for the driver to learn from the previous mistake. However, there are risks involved in empowering employees to be thinking drivers to stay alert under stressful conditions. The upshot is that companies that succeed in turning knowledge into action usually inspire respect and admiration, rather than fear or intimidation. Managers and executives who bridge authority and power differences induce less fear. General Electric authorized its executives and employees in the mid-1990s to come to work in casual attire in order to reduce the visibility of hierarchical signs. Even the special executive dining room got merged with the cafeteria to eliminate the status gap between managers and employees.

Ensure That Cooperation and Collaboration Are Not Competition or Internal Rivalry

For years, we have known competition to be the great motivator of our economic system. We have even incorporated this theme into the way we manage employees and reward the few based on the most efficient, the most productive, the best contributor, or the most loyal. As a result of the internal rivalry, to compete within the firm, employees became knowledge hoarders rather than knowledge sharers.

Today's growing trend is that the best projects are accomplished via teamwork, cooperation, and collaboration of company specialists committed to produce the best product or service against outside competition. The product is based on common effort and shared goals; the success of each employee depends on joint cooperation and knowledge sharing by everyone in the group. Employees begin to learn from one another and build an attitude or a belief that the best way for them to succeed is if their peers succeed. They also begin to build a culture of cooperation that makes the final product competitive in the marketplace.

Turning away from internal rivalry to cooperation and collaboration is good for any business that can see beyond the horizon. This is especially true when teamwork is based on commonality of goals and the aspiration of its members. When teams are properly formed, team members freely exchange ideas, knowledge, and resources and manage any conflict that stands in the way of doing an excellent job as a team. With the increasingly complex nature of global business in a business organization, it is teamwork and groupware that count. It is fine to hire and retain human talent, but talented people cannot do multifaceted projects alone. They need talented help.

In summary, one can easily foresee the benefits and potential of turning knowledge into action in businesses that have replaced fear and internal rivalry with trust, a sharing attitude, cooperation, and mutual respect for peers and the organization. Market competition continues to be a factor in organizational performance, but with knowledge sharing, the focus is now on fighting the competition rather than one another inside the organization.

Identify What Counts and What Makes Sense

An organization relies on reports and computer-based information to assess what happens over time. All reports represent historical events, transactions, or developments. Unfortunately, nothing is presented that analyzes the reasoning behind the information or why the resulting business turned out the way it did. In addition, there seems to be no prioritization of what should be acted on or what changes should be made that make sense to create a better future for the firm.

In many studies conducted in this area, it was found that organizations spend more time on outcome than on process. Managers look at outcomes, but they do not take time to discuss why it is so good or so bad. For knowledge management to succeed, focus should be on the stock of knowledge—processes and process improvement that might lead to a better outcome.

Take the example of a bank president who asked the board of directors for approval to replace the drive-in machines because tellers had been reporting increasing complaints from customers that the lines were long and the service was slow. The board was about to approve the $160,000 replacement cost when a board member who was a specialist in the field asked if she could take a look at the facility before approval was made. After a 20-minute on-site observation and a brief discussion with the tellers, it turned out that the problem was not in the machines but with the landscaping that narrowed the six lanes to two lanes upon entering the drive-in lot. This forced a lot of the drive-in traffic to wait on the road rather than in the bank's drive-in area. Removing the bushes, widening the entrance to four lanes, and giving out dog biscuits to customer's dogs in the cars brought customer complaints to a halt.

Take a Close Look at the Managers and How They View Knowledge Transfer

Managers and leaders set the tone for how a department, a division, or the entire firm should perform. Within the framework of knowledge management practices, managers are expected to create a culture or an organizational climate that sets work norms and values the transfer of knowledge to produce value-added products and services. It is an effective way to bridge the knowledge-action gap.

In order to make the change possible, managers are put through specialized training to understand the transformation process. Knowing about the knowing-doing gap is superficial without the action that must follow. The mind-set has to change before change can be made in the business. Much depends on management practices that come from the company's philosophy that values innovation, creativity, and an attitude of action. Those who have been with the organization a long time may find it difficult to adopt the change. As a result, they have to be replaced, transferred to stand-alone jobs, or offered an early retirement package.

Assess Employee Job Satisfaction and the Stability of the Workplace

The success of knowledge transfer and knowledge sharing depends to a great extent on how satisfied employees are on the job and the turnover rate in the workplace. For knowledge transfer to be effective, employees have to work in a culture that accommodates transfer, and they must apply and share transferred knowledge in an environment of trust and trustworthiness. Regardless of these factors, employees must be satisfied with the status quo if they are to cooperate and collaborate with others as a team.

Job satisfaction is derived from the degree of match between an employee's vocational needs and the requirements of the job. The major known vocational needs include the following:

- Ability utilization
- Achievement
- Activity
- Advancement
- Authority
- Compensation
- Creativity
- Independence
- Moral values
- Recognition
- Responsibility
- Security
- Status
- Supervision—human relations
- Supervision—technical
- Variety
- Working conditions

As proposed in Figure 9.3, job satisfaction is a function of the degree to which employee vocational needs are met by what the job offers to satisfy the needs. For example, if an employee values recognition highly and the job does not recognize

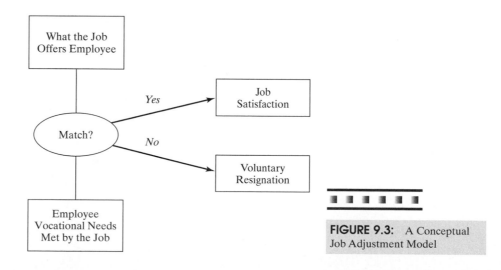

FIGURE 9.3: A Conceptual Job Adjustment Model

employee performance, the mismatch makes an employee wonder if it is worth continuing on the job. The same view applies to all other needs listed earlier. The sum of the squared difference of these needs becomes an index of satisfaction. The lower the satisfaction index, the higher the employee's job satisfaction.

▪▪▪▪ Transfer Methods

Once knowledge is captured and codified or otherwise becomes available, the final step is to transfer it for use by others in the organization. Recipients could be a team, a group, or individuals. Knowledge transfer makes it possible to convert experience into knowledge. As shown in Figure 9.4, a team sets out to perform a specific task. Team action results in an outcome (a finished product, a completed repair, and so forth). This experience is captured and fed back to the team in a form and a language the members understand. The new knowledge serves to reinforce or improve the quality and performance of the team the next time it faces a similar task. It is also transferred to a repository for new recipients whenever it is needed.

It should be obvious that there is no single best transfer method for all tasks. Much depends on factors such as the nature of the problem, the type of knowledge to transfer, and the barriers to transfer. Each factor is briefly explained.

NATURE OF THE PROBLEM

One factor to consider in transfer method selection is the nature of the problem. Some problems are routine problems; others are nonroutine. There are problems that recur once a day; others occur once a month or rarely. There are problems that are complex and critical; others are basic and can wait. Finally, there are problems that have a combination of constraints. A typical example is a customer who brings her year-old automobile to the dealer because of squeaky brakes. On the surface, the problem seems nonroutine, especially when the brakes never squeaked during the first year of operation. However, this kind of problem could occur in cars that are driven in a hot climate

▪▪▪▪▪▪▪ **FIGURE 9.4:**   Converting Experience into Knowledge

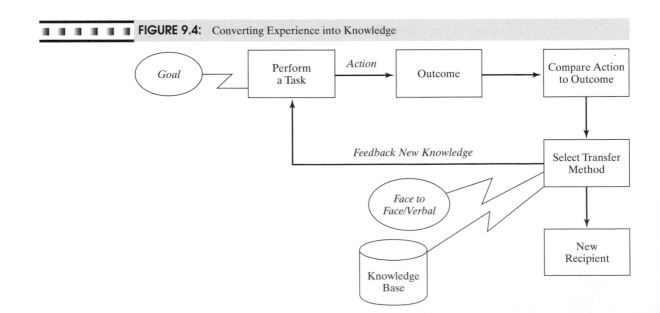

or could occur when braking down a long steep hill in heavy rain. Sand, dust, grease spots, or other matter accumulating on the drums could be routine factors to consider in solving the problem.

The procedure for repairs is considered routine, because all the mechanic has to do is to replace the brake pads, the drums, or both. To do so, he pulls the wheels and the brake assembly; he looks for foreign deposits, inspects the hubs, and checks the brake lines for leaks. However, this often turns out to be the wrong solution. An experienced mechanic may quickly find nothing wrong with the brakes or the deposits anywhere. He knows from similar cases with the same model, though, that after 10,000 to 15,000 miles of driving in the local climate, the hubs get hot and have a tendency to warp or get out of round. Once that happens, it cause unevenness in the braking process; therefore, the squeak. The best action is to replace the front hubs, hopefully with a better quality product.

The nonroutine, infrequent nature of the problem found a solution with the experienced mechanic. If he is working with or collaborating with other less experienced mechanics, the tacit knowledge of the experienced member can be verbally and directly transferred to the rest of the team for future use. If the squeak problem happens to be a chronic complaint and more customers bring in their cars for repairs, the diagnosis and procedure can be automated or stored in a knowledge base to be accessed when needed. Even when the mechanics take notes about the new procedure, they are transferring new knowledge on paper for later reference or use. In any case, we experience knowledge transfer as a step for knowledge sharing.

TRANSFER STRATEGIES

Knowledge management implies formalized knowledge transfer and requires specific strategies to ensure successful transfer. Knowledge is transferred via documents, an intranet, groupware, databases, knowledge bases, and a lot more. By far, the most effective channel for knowledge transfer is face-to-face meetings in the business place (see Box 9.2).

One formalized strategy is codifying and storing tacit knowledge that is neither easy to transfer nor guaranteed to be up to date, compared to the human expert from whom such knowledge is captured. Perhaps the best way to absorb tacit knowledge is to be in the domain where tacit knowledge is practiced. This is done through job rotations, job training and retraining, and devoting specialized focus on on-site learning. It involves on-site decision making, absorbing the mechanics and the heuristics as they occur, and coming up with a new knowledge base that emulates the domain in a unique way. The main limitation of such strategy is time, especially when certain problems cannot wait a year or two before knowledge becomes available for a solution.

The traditional management attitude in most of today's organizations is "stick your nose in the job, minimize the chatter, and get to work." For example, one multinational firm placed a sign by each watercooler that read, "For safety reasons, the company discourages any prolonged meetings or discussions around the watercoolers or anywhere in the hallways, cafeteria, or around the elevators." When asked by one manager the reason for the notice, a senior executive replied, "It means don't kill time when you should be in your office at work." For years, employees have used the watercooler or cafeteria (and rest rooms) as a place to exchange views and resolve problems. The company in question had no conference rooms or a place for group discussions. Management had the attitude that such meetings promote gossip and feed the rumor mill.

In contrast to the traditional view, the knowledge management view is not "stop talking and get to work," but "start talking and get to work." The watercooler get-together could be the enabler of serendipity. Watercooler-type chats are a hit with

▪ ▪ ▪ ▪ ▪ ▪ ▪   BOX 9.2   ▪ ▪ ▪ ▪ ▪ ▪ ▪

WIRING A CORPORATION'S KNOWLEDGE INFRASTRUCTURE

WIRING THE CORPORATE BRAIN

Born of the merger in 1996 of two venerable Basel–based companies, Sandoz and Ciba-Geigy, Novartis is the newest and richest beneficiary of Basel's confluence of scientific learning, industry, and culture. From two tiny makers of specialized dyestuffs 150 years ago, Novartis has become a $24 billion corporation that calls itself a "life sciences company," a conceptual catchall for an entity whose products include such diverse items as pharmaceuticals, genetically engineered seeds, baby food, contact lenses, and animal health products.

However, Novartis's breadth of products and its success in the global economy make for its greatest challenge: How can a company that depends on innovation to survive find ways not just to share but to increase its knowledge? This problem faces any knowledge-intensive, global industry. Novartis addresses it with a three-pronged strategy: using Web-based technology to foster collaboration within its worldwide workforce; creating a system of development grants (think of in-house Fulbrights) for projects that will make different business units work together; and hosting periodic knowledge fairs to spark ideas. Jack Staeheli, who heads this effort, prefers to call it *knowledge networking,* because that sounds less hierarchical than *knowledge management* (the usual term for a strategy to make the whole of a workforce's contribution greater than the sum of its individuals' knowledge). Likewise, Staeheli's title is "officer of the science boards." Senior officer of corporate knowledge management, the role he acknowledges to outsiders and which he in fact performs, would sound too much like he controlled the process, he says. He prefers to see himself as a shepherd rather than a director. The wording is more than symbolic. Novartis's president, Dan Vasella, asserts that knowledge transfer and creation will determine the company's future competitiveness. "Knowledge networking" shows that Novartis understands that making the most of an organization's intellectual assets is more of a cultural than a technological challenge.

SOURCE: Excerpted from Abramson, Gary. "Wiring the Corporate Brain," *Enterprise Magazine*, March 15, 1999, pp. 2–8.

▪ ▪ ▪ ▪ ▪ ▪

teams transferring or sharing focused knowledge during a break away from the office. Spontaneous, brief sessions are door openers for generating ideas and exchanging views; they have the potential for generating new ways of problem-solving. This is one approach to creating exchanges that could produce unique results.

Knowledge transfer should adopt or adjust the organization's culture to facilitate knowledge transfer and knowledge sharing. Management in the Japanese culture sets up talk or conference rooms to encourage dynamic knowledge exchange. Japanese managers spend time together after work. From group dinners to social clubs and sports, they practice knowledge transfer. They function as a mechanism for establishing trust and take time for constructive criticism. They prefer meeting face to face over e-mail and on-the-job experience over learning via a computer-based knowledge base. The whole process, which includes company standards of performance and highly respected protocols, is followed on a regular basis with value-added results.

With this in mind, it would be difficult to fit the Japanese culture with American business. In so many ways, e-mail is an American invention for efficiency and productivity. The notion of "Why call for something you can attach to an e-mail message?" is the American way of promoting performance at the cost of informal or personal knowledge transfer. An employee who spends hours leafing through and responding to e-mail is viewed as being hard at work. An employee found reading a professional magazine as a way of capturing knowledge is frowned upon as being "waste at work." A company that supports knowledge exchange, on the one hand, and discourages reading or talking on company time confuses many employees. Irrespective of culture, "slack time" should be used for knowledge sharing to the advantage of employees and company alike.

INHIBITORS OF KNOWLEDGE TRANSFER

There are several organizational and cultural factors that inhibit reliable knowledge transfer. Some inhibitors are easier to correct than others. The following are the key areas where friction occurs and ways to correct it.

- *Lack of trust.* A major element in the success of any knowledge transfer project is the commonality of language people have with one another. A shared language can only strengthen trust among the participants, whether they are professors, surgeons, attorneys, or night watchmen of a high-rise building. Trust develops after people share proprietary knowledge and feel the reciprocal to be at least intrinsically rewarding. The more people assess one another and have a feel for where they stand, the easier it is to decide how much they can trust one another. In the final analysis, we shall find that cultural, language, status (who gives the knowledge), and location mismatches could be "make or break" of trust for successful knowledge transfer.

- *Lack of time and conference places.* People tend to find knowledge nearby or get the closest source, not the best one. To expedite knowledge transfer, people must show interest, take time, and find meeting places where they can exchange ideas. The "I don't have time because I am snowed under" excuse is rarely a valid excuse. A volunteering spirit of cooperation, collaboration, and coordination is a powerful enabler of knowledge transfer.

- *Status of the knower.* People decide to act on knowledge or information based on who gives it to them. A senior vice president sent by the president to attend a union meeting gives an impression that the company cares. Status refers to the individual's position within a group or an organization, compared with those of fellow employees. One attribute that tends to give a person status, for example, is age. If a company does not want age to be given status, it will have promotions and reward policies that favor youth and work against age.

    Status and status symbols (title, size of office, office views, type of furniture in the office, the floor the office is located on, the kind of company car assigned, and so forth) are important management factors that affect the behavior of individuals and groups. We should look at what status can and cannot do for an organization.

    People who consider status and still are reluctant to put transferred knowledge to good use could have several reasons for feeling that way: not respecting or trusting the knower, not considering the knowledge to be important, pride, lack of interest, lack of time, sheer stubbornness, and reluctance to take unnecessary risks. When this happens, it does little good to push knowledge transfer for the mere show that knowledge is freely shared.

- *Quality and speed of transfer.* When knowledge is transferred from a reliable, high-profile source, it is expected to be of the quality that promotes its use. Unfortunately, that is not always the case. The quality of transfer can be influenced by factors such as mentorship, on-the-job training, job rotation, and career paths that define the way, timing, and duration of job experiences. In contrast, knowledge downloaded from a database or a knowledge base is not a match for the on-site, person-to-person knowledge transfer.

In addition to quality of transfer is the speed of acquiring and making use of knowledge. This is where technology can be a tremendous help, especially if the knowledge transferred affects employees and procedures company-wide. Both quality and the efficiency with which it is transmitted and received would be of concern to management in deciding how well the firm uses knowledge capital.

HOW KNOWLEDGE IS TRANSFERRED

Once the foregoing elements are put into place, knowledge transfer should turn into new action. The question is what types of knowledge can be transferred. The three main types are as follows:

- Collective sequential transfer
- Explicit interteam knowledge transfer
- Tacit knowledge transfer

Each category is explained next. When it comes to design considerations, each type requires a unique design, depending on the recipient, the type of knowledge transferred, and the complexity of the project. The goal is to ensure that the delivery mechanism will meet the requirements of the users of the knowledge.

Collective Sequential Transfer

This is one of the easiest and most straightforward types of knowledge transfer. An ongoing team specialized in one specific task moves to other locations and performs the same tasks. For example, in building new homes in the suburbs, septic systems are installed by a team that does nothing else. Based on the local code, a team of three to five members digs up a designated area with a backhoe; installs pipes, feeders, a trap, and so forth; buries them; and reseeds the area to blend with the rest of the landscape. This know-how requires decisions on the size of the pipes, the direction and slope of the flow, and provisions for venting and future repairs. Once the system is completed, the same team reuses the same knowledge; goes to another new home site; and builds the same septic infrastructure, with variations to meet the local codes. The procedure remains the same. Change occurs only if the county or city alters the regulations or the septic codes.

What is unique about collective sequential transfer is that knowledge is transferred from one site to another by the same team. There is no knowledge transfer from one team to another team, but there is transfer of knowledge from a team member to another member within the team. This is where collaboration is carried out. The focus is on collective knowledge rather than individualized knowledge. With the job carried out in sequence, each member's knowledge and performance affects the next member who has to do the work based on the work completed by the previous member. This means quicker transfer of knowledge with closer adherence to quality of the resulting installation. As shown in Figure 9.5, after each job, a team talks about any new knowledge gained, discusses what should go into the next installation, and adjusts the commitment of each member accordingly.

Each time a team performs a job, each member transfers his or her unique experience into the team so that the resulting transformation can be incorporated into the entire process. It means evaluating and redesigning collectively the new team knowledge every time a job is completed. Once completed, the team is expected to function more effectively on the next job.

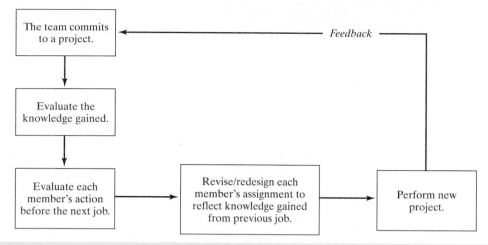

▪ ▪ ▪ ▪ ▪ ▪ ▪ **FIGURE 9.5:**   Collective Sequential Transfer—Transferring Experience to Knowledge

When performing a job, team members are on constant alert regarding the following:

- How did a member's task affect others in the team?
- How did a member's way of performing a task contribute to the performance of others?
- What factors affect a member's performance on the job?
- How does a member's job impact the team's overall performance?

These observations are usually stored in each member's mind until the next time the team meets and exchanges experiences. During the meeting, the sharing of experience and the transformation of experience into new or updated knowledge is what a team should take with it onto the next job. The knowledge transfer process also facilitates the conversion from personal knowing to group knowing. When that occurs, it contributes to the achievement of team goals.

Transfer Protocol.   In every team setting, there is a protocol or a way to specify how a team should function. With a focus on collaborative sequential knowledge transfer, where jobs are interdependent and performed in some sequence, each team member is expected to carry a "suitcase" of knowledge. There is also an assumption that each member has vested interest in sharing rather than hogging knowledge. Any activity carried out by members is done in fulfilling team goals—completing a project collectively, efficiently, and effectively.

The unique features of collaborative sequential knowledge transfer include the following:

- Team meetings are usually brief, but are held regularly as time and the occasion permit. Meeting formats are understood, based on the way the team has conducted previous meetings. There is usually a facilitator or an informal leader who initiates the meeting, monitors the discussions or exchanges, and makes sure things do not drag unnecessarily. Facilitators are routinely rotated among the members. Some of the questions raised center around what happened during the job just completed, whether there were any differences that should be discussed, and why things happened the way they did.
- Meetings are held with all participants being equal. There are no discrimination or hierarchical priorities set as to who speaks first, how influential one's comments

are compared to the rest, and the like. With this in mind, team members are expected to be proactive rather than reactive and assertive rather than laid back, with no attitude such as "Look, this was not my job, so I can't comment" or "My job is to lay pipes, no more no less."

- Whatever takes place in meetings is kept within the team. There is no reporting relationship to the organization's higher-ups. This eliminates the fear that a negative report might prompt layoffs or dismissals. It means that team members begin to understand and trust the circumstances under which they can or cannot share knowledge.

- A unique feature of collaborative sequential knowledge transfer is focus on the project, not the person or the personality. The approach, the setting, and the seating arrangements are not army style (one row behind the other) or classroom style. Team members face one another, and anyone can make a comment anytime within reason. The goal is to fine-tune performance, improve quality, and assure integrity of the work performed by the team (see Box 9.3).

Even with all these advantages, this type of transfer also comes with its own set of problems. A team could be overcommitted or overworked; fatigue or boredom could set in; or the team might be operating under a tight budget. All of these circumstances will make it difficult for the team to meet. Another problem is the level of fluency of

---

■ ■ ■ ■ ■ ■   **BOX 9.3**   ■ ■ ■ ■ ■ ■

GUIDELINES FOR FACE-TO-FACE MEETINGS IN COLLECTIVE SEQUENTIAL TRANSFER

MAKING IT WORK

Setting up effective face-to-face meetings requires a clear game plan. Here are some pointers to consider:

- *Set the agenda.* Clearly communicate the purpose and intention of your meeting. Before the meeting, tell the participants about the meeting time and desired goals.

- *Keep it small.* Sometimes a large meeting is necessary, especially if you need to involve participants from many disparate locations. In most cases, though, smaller is better. KM experts agree that six to eight participants are ideal.

- *Invite the right people.* Filter your attendee list to include only participants whose thinking responses and direct participation are key to your success. Consider having less crucial personnel join remotely in "listening" mode.

- *Facilitate the process.* Find a neutral facilitator who can keep the participants on track through-

out the meeting. Ideally, the facilitator should have no personal stake in the meeting apart from helping the process to flow.

- *Take breaks.* Because attention can easily wander, do not force participants to go much past an hour without time to stretch and relax. Focus on discussing specific, manageable tasks in each session.

- *Socialize.* To help in building trust, try to schedule at least one nonbusiness event. When participants become familiar with each other in an informal setting, they are more likely to share their knowledge productively during work time.

- *Show accomplishments.* Arrange for participants to leave the session with something tangible in hand, even if it is something as simple as a checked-off copy of the completed agenda. It serves to mark progress and emphasize the worth of what they have done.

SOURCE: Excerpted from Dell, Pamela. "Getting the Most out of Getting Together," *Knowledge Management*, August 2001, p. 1.

■ ■ ■ ■ ■ ■

the members. It takes a certain amount of communication skills to exchange experiences and to express opinions about new ones.

Finally, it is not so easy to hold a meeting after a full day's work. Most members are eager to head home, especially when meeting times are not compensatory. The so-called "suitcase" of knowledge carried by each team member will have to wait another day or longer, which tends to age the experience.

Explicit Interteam Transfer

This type of knowledge transfer simply allows a team that has done a job on one site to share the experience with another team working on a similar job on another site. For example, take the case of the septic system. A contractor might have two teams of workers working on a septic system for two houses in two separate subdivisions. As shown in Figure 9.6, team A in subdivision has installed the system more quickly than before, even with a new twist to the installation. While digging a trench for the major pipe that goes to the trap, they had to reroute the pipe around the roots of a 120-year-old maple tree.

▪ ▪ ▪ ▪ ▪ ▪ ▪ **FIGURE 9.6:** Explicit Interteam Knowledge Transfer

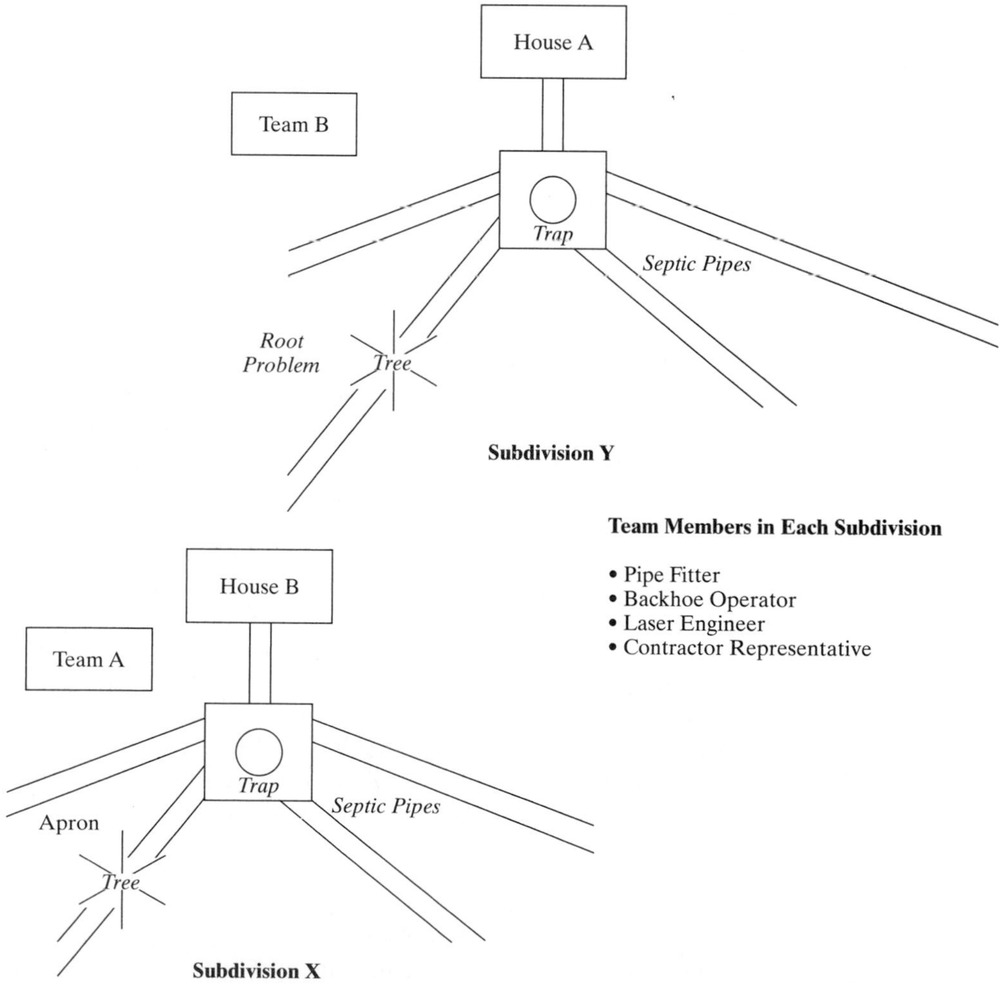

They designed a special apron to protect the tree from any damage should the pipe burst or corrode. This new discovery was shared with another team in subdivision Y, which has a similar problem but was about to cut the tree and dig up the roots to allow the inflexible pipes to lay straight to the trap. The new experience from team A was shared in time to save the tree.

Interteam knowledge transfer is explicit knowledge, because most of the knowledge transferred is routine work and the procedure is precise. Tacit knowledge is transferred in situations where the team might have found a new or a creative way to get around problems. In our example, in Figure 9.6, the tree got in the way in both subdivisions. Team A designed an apron to save the tree without compromising the quality of the work. The apron is something team B never thought of; team B was about to cut the tree. When the two teams met or a representative of team A met with team B, the apron design was shared in time to be of use.

Personal interaction is ideal in projects that are timely and can benefit from quick feedback. It is also useful in situations that reinforce relationships and solidify cooperation and coordination between teams. E-mail or other electronic transmissions of "news and views" cannot be a satisfactory substitute. It can be useful to supplement personal interaction in interteam knowledge transfer.

Despite the benefits, there are human relations and other factors that make it difficult to implement explicit interteam knowledge transfer. One factor is the organizational subculture of the receiving team. In the case of the apron, team B might feel too proud to accept any suggestions or ideas from an outside team, especially if the innovation is simple or if it is something that team members should have thought of on their own. A team may simply be reluctant to share explicit or tacit knowledge, especially in situations where their innovation and productivity will bring bonuses or special awards. Finally, lack of time can be the worst enemy of knowledge transfer or knowledge sharing. For reasons of their own, the team with the new experience might not have the motivation to take extra time after work to spoon-feed another team with the change that it took time and collaboration to invent.

Tacit Knowledge Transfer

This type of knowledge transfer is unique in complex, nonalgorithmic projects, where knowledge is mentally stored. The team receiving tacit knowledge is different by location, by experience, by technology, and by cultural norms. This means that whatever knowledge is being transferred has to be modified in language, tone, and content to be usable by the receiving team.

Take the case of Kuwait's oil wells, which were set on fire by Saddam Hussein's Iraqi troops retreating from Kuwait in 1991. To douse the oil fire, specialized teams from the United States, Russia, the United Kingdom, and Holland attempted to find a solution. Fire control depends on the pressure of the oil, the depth of the well, wind conditions, oil temperature, and the like. The most successful team was that of Red Adair of Texas. Red and his team extinguished 117 of the burning oil well fires in the Ahmadi, Magwa, and Burgan fields—the highest producing fields in Kuwait.

There were logistical problems in the entire fire-fighting operation, which was unlike the hundreds of other oil fires in the United States, in underwater wild wells, or in the 1977 Bravo offshore blowout in the North Sea. The years of experience and the stored tacit knowledge of Adair and his seasoned team allowed them to come up with the combination that was most successful in capping the oil wells; every other foreign team failed to do so. After the work was done, the foreign teams were astounded at Adair's approach and the combination of standard and creative methods he used to

FIGURE 9.7: Tacit Knowledge Transfer

control the fire and the smoke that had virtually covered the skies and sand dunes of Kuwait. American ingenuity, skill, and self-discipline combined to master the seemingly impossible. Adair's tacit knowledge was translated to the Kuwaiti fire-fighting team in a form different from what they had used before the war. Adair formed a new company in 1993 to provide consulting services to fire-fighting teams on a global basis. In every consulting job, he transfers his tacit knowledge to similar teams unrelated to his and in areas and locations foreign to Texas.

Adair's team demonstrated the ability to understand a specific situation and then customize their response to that situation. His team members evaluated the new situation, which triggered memories of past episodes and their respective solutions for the final decision on the approach used to control the unique Kuwaiti fires. What distinguishes this approach from explicit knowledge transfer is the fact that transfer of tacit knowledge goes to another team doing a similar kind of work (extinguishing oil fire), but the knowledge is customized to the location, culture, ability, and constraints of the receiving team (see Figure 9.7).

One of the problems in tacit knowledge transfer is the understandable difficulty in tapping tacit knowledge. Adair's case was no exception. His temperament, tolerance for ambiguity, and patience for explaining details were barriers to his knowledge transfer. The process unique to the Kuwaiti fires was very difficult to capture on paper or to train overnight. Unlike explicit knowledge transfer, tacit knowledge transfer is not practically transferred electronically.

▪ ▪ ▪ ▪ Role of the Internet in Knowledge Transfer

Since 1960, when the first business computer appeared, information technology has changed the way commerce is conducted around the globe. From mainframes to accounting systems, the personal computer revolution, local area networks, electronic data interchange, client/server design, and enterprise resource planning have all had a hand in shaping today's business organization. The past decade has been the Internet decade, however, when companies worldwide have embraced a change without equal. It is a change that promises to have more impact and be more lasting than anything else we have seen to date. Technology is setting the pace for how a company does business, how it exchanges knowledge with suppliers, and how it communicates with customers and others in the new marketplace. Any way you look at it, business will never be the same again.

The primary technology for this transformation is the Internet—a global data, information, and knowledge network that moves closer and closer to the ubiquity of the telephone with each passing day. What makes the Internet so powerful is that it is more about knowledge exchange and communication than it is about technology. It is a medium and a market. It is virtually unstoppable, forcing all kinds of businesses to reexamine their practices and their futures.

There is one feature of the Internet that you will not find on the telephone. The Net allows you to send messages to multiple persons at the same time, much like television or radio broadcasting. The Internet began with message communication, but now it is possible to transmit and receive information containing graphics, voice, photos, and even full-motion videos. The part of the Internet that can accomplish these tasks is called the *World Wide Web,* also known as *WWW* or *the Web.*

The Internet today offers a variety of services including e-mail, access to remote computers, news, and the quick and easy transmission of information between computers worldwide. Many federal agencies now allow anyone to access timely information. These agencies include the Social Security Administration, Veterans Administration, and the U.S. Postal Service.

INTERNET SERVICE PROVIDERS

To link the rapidly growing commercial Internet landscape, the Internet service provider (ISP) industry was born in the mid-1990s. It offers a variety of services, including the following:

1. Linking consumers and businesses to the Internet (for example, America Online, Microsoft Network, and CompuServe)
2. Monitoring and maintaining customers' Web sites
3. Network management and system integration
4. Backbone access services for other ISPs, such as PSI and UUNET
5. Payment systems for online purchases

As public demand for access to the Internet surged, ISPs began to add more lines and better access to accommodate the traffic. Initially, the cost for Internet access often exceeded $1,000 per month, but with new ISP arrivals and competition, prices plummeted. Many of today's ISPs offer unlimited access for as low as $5 per month. Many local governments are funding the use of the Internet because of its political, educational, and commercial benefits. Once on the Internet, there are no additional charges. The place of the ISP in the Internet architecture is shown in Figure 9.8.

You can contact anyone, anywhere, anytime for that monthly fee. The exceptions are Web sites that charge a membership fee or a fee for access to privileged information.

Almost everything one needs on the Internet is free. Among the free services are the following:

- *Hotlists,* which tell the user what is popular and what is not
- *Comics* that focus on entertainment events
- *Software archives* that list the latest free software available
- *Weather services* that provide free weather forecasts anywhere in the world
- *Magazines and broadcasting stations* that constantly update the news
- *Searchers* that help locate items or subjects on the Internet
- *Dictionaries* that include thesaurus and "fact" books on almost all subjects
- *Government services* that publicize what is available from them

The problem for some ISPs is sudden growth without advance planning to accommodate the growth. As a result, response time slows down, which triggers customer complaints. The challenge is to maintain profitability and meet or beat the competition while maintaining customer satisfaction. To do all this well requires professional man-

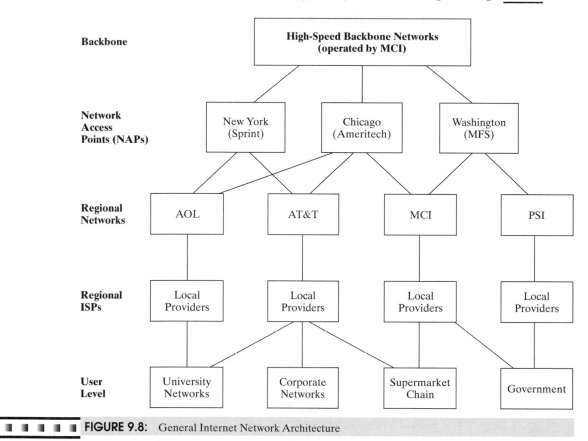

FIGURE 9.8: General Internet Network Architecture

agement, a highly skilled technical staff, and a healthy budget to bring the technology in line with the voracious appetite of today's consumer. The trick is to ensure a balance between creativity and control and between managing growth and a stable technical infrastructure.

STABILITY AND RELIABILITY OF THE WEB

No single agency or company owns the Internet. Each company on the Internet owns its own network. Telephone companies and ISPs own the links between these companies and the Internet. The organization that coordinates Internet functions is the Internet Society. It does not operate any of the thousands of networks that make up the Internet, but works with ISPs by providing information to prospective users. This association's Internet Architecture Board consists of work groups that focus on TCP/IP and other protocols. Various committees also handle technical issues and day-to-day operational aspects of the Internet.

The Web itself, because it resides everywhere and nowhere at the same time, simply cannot cease functioning by itself. Also, because it is based on the Internet, its stability is as good as that of the Internet, which is fairly good so far. The Internet is designed to be indefinitely extendable. Reliability depends primarily on the quality of the service providers' equipment. Inadequate phone lines, bandwidth, or mediocre computers can affect the reliability of the overall service.

UNIQUE BENEFITS OF THE INTERNET

The Internet is the enabler of knowledge transfer and knowledge sharing worldwide. Managers use it to glean intelligence about rivals, monitor sales, and so on. At Cisco Systems, for example, the company's chief executive required executives from various departments to demonstrate how they would use the Web. Cisco and other companies like Dell Computers and Microsoft's Expedia Travel Service use Internet technology in their businesses. Dell, for example, sells more than $6 million worth of computers a day from its Web site, and Expedia's service generates more than $16 million a month from its Web site.

For all the directions the Internet has taken and all the companies it has spawned, this technology was first developed as a tool for scientists to exchange knowledge and keep in touch with one another. This is the way many of us use the Internet today. On the business side, the rise of the Internet as the enabler of e-commerce is changing how companies manage their knowledge and business. Closed enterprise systems are giving way to open system environments, where customers connect to the company's Web site and trading partners connect by the extranet and the Internet.

Among the uses and advantages of the Internet as they relate to knowledge management are the following:

- *Doing business fast.* Knowledge transfer is conducted in minutes rather than hours or days, compared to waiting on the phone or meeting as a team. This speed compresses transfer time and promotes the growth of knowledge sharing.
- *Gathering opinions and trying out new ideas.* The Internet is an ideal place for trying out new ideas at low cost. Interactive surveys provide quick feedback. Opinions can be gathered from just about anywhere. Many online opinion polls provide real-time statistics to the user after a computer package analyzes the user's response in real time.
- *Leveling the playing field.* When a company advertises its products or services on the Internet, it is on equal footing with larger companies. The nice feature about the Internet is that it allows your business to appear alongside big-name companies. Here is a case in point: Caribbean Tour wanted to put its business on the Internet, but it did not have much money to spend. It designed a basic Web site, just to have a presence, and spent only $800 per month to gain experience with online commerce. The Web site broke even after 2 years.

  Even mere presence is a benign way of creating new selling opportunities to a unique type of customer who otherwise would have gone to the competition. The Internet is a great equalizer. A business might be small, but it encourages that business to be very good at what it does.
- *Providing a superior customer service and support resource.* Most Web sites generate customer feedback in the way of comments, suggestions, and complaints. The challenge for the online merchant is to have adequate staff to address this feedback in a timely fashion. A common support resource is an FAQ (frequently asked questions) list. A FAQ eliminates having staff answer the same questions over and over again. If a new question comes up, the answer is added to the list. Using e-mail to handle customer support also frees company personnel from being tied to a telephone.
- *Supporting managerial functions, spreading ideas.* The traditional managerial functions of planning, organizing, directing, and controlling require managers to collect, evaluate, and distribute management information, especially in organizations with branches worldwide. The Internet sends business information through a company's networks and across networks around the globe. E-mail is a convenient tool for managers to reach employees, bosses, customers, and suppliers quickly and at no charge.

The Internet has spawned discussion groups, chat rooms, and online interactive sessions in which technical and managerial staff evaluate products and processes and arrive at value-added decisions that result in lower costs and increased performance.

Better technical support is one of the key benefits of linking to the Internet. IBM, for example, offers customer and technical support and handles software upgrades on the Internet. There are thousands of free software programs available for anyone to download.

Market research firms are a natural for the Web. Credit bureaus, lawyers, private detectives, accountants, baby-sitters, and teachers are all examples of people or agencies that use the Internet for scheduling or advertising their services. The Internet contains thousands of databases containing information about everything from medicine, vehicles, and food preparation to hundreds of research and development (R&D) discussion groups. For thousands of research journals, automated searches through current and back issues are available in minutes rather than the days and weeks it once took to find the information in a brick-and-mortar library. White papers that research centers place on their Web sites provide current information about the latest developments in various fields.

Company research is no different. Companies use the Internet to seek information about customer tastes and preferences, to profile a customer base for a new product, or to test a new concept to see if it is worth developing. All of this can be done in a matter of days.

LIMITATIONS

Like any system with unique benefits, the Internet and the World Wide Web also have unique limitations. The following paragraphs highlight the importance of continuing to work on these limitations in the interest of advancing use of the Internet in general and the Web in particular as a knowledge transfer and exchange medium.

The main limitations of Internet use for knowledge exchange are security and privacy. Key questions that are continually asked by online consumers are "How do I know I am sharing knowledge on a secure line?" "How do I know the Web site assures me privacy for the information I am seeking?" In terms of privacy, according to a study of major Web exchanges by the Federal Trade Commission (FTC), only 20 percent met FTC standards for protecting consumer privacy. However, the study also found a 90 percent compliance rate by Internet companies (for posting their privacy policies).

In addition to fakes and forgeries, there are other threats. Hackers, worms, Trojan horses, viruses, and zombies threaten the security and integrity of any information or knowledge exchange. Viruses are the best-known malicious software. These programs secretly attach themselves to other programs and then infect and reproduce in a manner similar to biological viruses.

Because hackers (those who access others' computer systems illegally) continue to threaten the integrity of files and transactions, hacking schools that teach students how to hack or break into software to protect their own computer systems have begun to appear in various cities. In one typical 4-day seminar, students (usually network administrators) pay $3,500 to learn the tricks of the trade. They are provided with hacking tools that are available over the Internet for free (for example, an information gathering tool, Sam Spade, and a port-scanning tool, SuperScan, that sends queries to Internet servers to check their security status). At the completion of the course, students sign an affidavit that they will use their experience appropriately.

Despite sophisticated FAQs, e-mail, and other technologies, companies still have a problem with simple issues like securing information. In customer service, the heavy demand also puts added pressure on customer service personnel.

▪▪▪▪ ## Implications for Knowledge Management

Knowledge transfer, whether it is face to face, through an electronic knowledge base, or is team-based, involves management support. Any transfer should be carried out with the larger goals of the organization in mind. The link between knowledge and goals should be clearly defined and effectively implemented within the framework of the organization's knowledge management strategic plans.

In addition, a knowledge management system that accommodates knowledge transfer on an ongoing basis should have the facility to monitor its progress, report and promote its benefits to participants, and ensure continuity by the knowledge developer or the chief knowledge officer (CKO). In the final analysis, the process and outcome become a compliance based on choice.

If top management is serious about knowledge management and knowledge transfer, several steps should be taken to ensure a reliable infrastructure that will serve the organization's long-term needs. First, a candidate department or company division with interest in knowledge sharing should be selected to set the tone for the enterprise. As we do in major projects, a committee representing the entity should be formed to begin strategic thinking about how to build a knowledge management environment and launch knowledge sharing. This might involve changes in policy, procedures, training and retraining, and addressing the cultural and work norms to effect a change from knowledge hoarding to knowledge sharing.

Once a steering committee is in place, the next task is to undertake knowledge assessment—evaluating existing knowledge, where it resides, how it is being used, and what part of it needs to be updated, deleted, and so forth. Following this critical step, a procedure should be designed for knowledge transfer, and the types of knowledge and how they should be transferred should be determined. Doing that means looking more closely at existing technology, the company intranet, e-mail technology, and security status. To complete the transfer, receiving individuals or receiving teams must begin to share their knowledge with the right people so that everyone in the division will enrich their experience, improve their productivity, and add value to the strategic goals of the organization. In doing so, the organization as an ongoing venture should begin to realize benefits and grow exponentially in the competitive environment in which it operates.

SUMMARY ▪▪▪▪

- Knowledge transfer is part of everyday organizational life and a step in the KM building life cycle. Knowledge can be transferred from repositories to people, from teams to individuals, and between individuals.
- To transfer knowledge, we consider where knowledge is transferred from, the media used in knowledge transfer, and where the knowledge is transferred. In any case, this transfer facilitates knowledge sharing and enhances knowledge flows through collaborative technologies.
- Knowledge transfer distributes to points of action. It supports education and training, substitutes as customer service representatives, and so forth.
- The knowing-doing gap is a situation where an organization knows what to do, but for various reasons ignores the information available and performs differently. Knowing about this problem should help firms make corrections and set up a knowledge transfer environment for all employees to benefit.
- The terms *transfer* and *share* are interrelated. Knowing is considered deeply personal; it is asking someone to give something that is his or her own property. It is

a mechanistic term, which provides knowledge for someone else. The term *share* is an exchange of knowledge between individuals, between or within teams, or between individuals and knowledge bases, repositories, and the like.

- Translating knowledge into action is not straightforward. To overcome the gap between knowledge transfer and knowledge sharing, the following guidelines are useful:

    - Instill an atmosphere of trust in the organization.
    - Fix the culture to accommodate the change.
    - Push reasoning before process.
    - Remember that doing is far better than talking.
    - Know how the firm handles mistakes.
    - Ensure that cooperation and collaboration are not competition or internal rivalry.
    - Identify what counts and what makes sense.
    - Take a close look at the managers and how they view knowledge transfer.
    - Assess employee job satisfaction and the stability of the workplace.

- There is no single best transfer method for all tasks. Much depends on factors such as the nature of the problem, the type of knowledge to transfer, and the barriers to transfer. The upshot of knowledge transfer is to adopt or adjust the organization's culture to facilitate knowledge transfer and knowledge sharing. Irrespective of culture, "slack time" should be used for knowledge sharing to the advantage of employees and company alike.

- The key inhibitors of knowledge transfer are lack of trust, lack of time and conference places, status of the knower, and quality and speed of transfer. Each inhibitor should be seriously considered before knowledge transfer can be expected to take hold reliably among participants.

- The three main types of knowledge transfer are collective sequential transfer, explicit interteam knowledge transfer, and tacit knowledge transfer. In collective sequential transfer, an ongoing team specialized in one specific task moves to other locations and performs the same task. Once the task has been completed, the same team reuses the same knowledge, goes to another new site, builds the same system, and so forth. Team meetings are generally brief; meetings are held with all participants being equal; whatever takes place in meetings is kept within the team; and the focus is not on the person, but the process.

- Explicit interteam knowledge transfer allows a team that has done a job on one site to share the experience with another team working on a similar job on another site. Interteam knowledge transfer is explicit knowledge, because most of the knowledge transferred is routine work and the procedure is precise; it must follow preset guidelines. Personal interaction is ideal in projects that are timely and can benefit from quick feedback.

- Tacit knowledge transfer is unique in complex, nonalgorithmic projects, where knowledge is mentally stored. The team receiving tacit knowledge is different by location, by experience, by technology, and by cultural norms. This means that whatever knowledge is being transferred has to be modified in language, tone, and content to be usable by the receiving team. One of the problems with this type of knowledge transfer is the difficulty in tapping tacit knowledge. Unlike explicit knowledge transfer, tacit knowledge transfer is not practically transferred electronically.

TERMS TO KNOW ■ ■ ■ ■

Authority: The right to decide or to act.

Belief: A way of thinking; feeling or impression.

Bounded rationality: Tendency to select less than the best objective or alternative; engage in a limited search for alternative solutions; have inadequate information and control of the factors influencing the outcomes of a decision.

Collaboration: Sharing in the decision-making process for solutions considered to be mutually beneficial.

Collective sequential transfer: Transferring knowledge from one team specializing in one task to other locations where the same task is needed.

Culture: Those acquired and learned behaviors that have persisted in human groups through traditions; the shared characteristics and values that distinguish the members of one group of people from those of another.

Empowerment: The leader's sharing of power with subordinates.

Explicit interteam transfer: The transfer of explicit knowledge from a team that has done a job on one site; sharing the experience with another team working on a similar job on another site.

Knowing-doing gap: Ignoring available information and performing a given job differently.

Knowledge transfer: Transmission of knowledge and use of transmitted knowledge.

Learning organization: An organization that uses and shares its knowledge to promote creativity and innovation; learning from the resulting experiences to advance and grow in a competitive environment.

Satisficing: The practice of selecting an acceptable objective or alternative, which might be easier to identify and obtain, less controversial, or otherwise safer than the best object or alternative available.

Tacit knowledge transfer: Transferring knowledge on a complex project stored in a human's mind.

Value: A basic belief about a condition that has considerable import and meaning to persons within a society and is relatively stable over time.

TEST YOUR UNDERSTANDING ■ ■ ■ ■

1. Where does knowledge transfer fit in the KM system building life cycle?
2. In what way(s) is knowledge transfer a step in a process?
3. "Knowledge transfer is not only from knowledge bases or repositories." Do you agree? Why or why not?
4. What is "bounded rationality"? How does it relate to satisficing?
5. Cite and explain briefly the factors that affect knowledge transfer.
6. Distinguish between:
   a. explicit interteam knowledge transfer and tacit knowledge transfer
   b. values and beliefs
   c. authority and empowerment
   d. knowing-doing gap and bounded rationality
7. Explain briefly the key prerequisites for knowledge transfer.
8. List and briefly explain some of the positive cultural values in an organization.
9. How does employee satisfaction affect knowledge transfer?
10. Explain the factors that determine the effectiveness of knowledge transfer.
11. Elaborate on the key inhibitors of knowledge transfer.
12. What are the distinctive features of collective sequential transfer?
13. Give an example of your own tacit knowledge transfer.
14. Summarize the uses and limitations of the Internet as they relate to knowledge management.

KNOWLEDGE EXERCISES ■ ■ ■ ■

1. How would one instill trust in an organization?
2. In your opinion, does one fix the culture and then get the employees to share or vice versa?
3. Discuss the difference(s) between collaboration and commitment. How are they related?
4. In what way(s) is it difficult to fit the Japanese culture onto American business?
5. How important do you think trust is in the process of knowledge transfer?

REFERENCES ▪ ▪ ▪ ▪

Abramson, Gary. "Wiring the Corporate Brain," *Enterprise Magazine*, March 15, 1999, pp. 2–8.

Becker, Rick. "Taking the Misery Out of Experiential Training," *Training*, February 1998, p. 80.

Clark, Linda E. "A Stitch in Time," *Intelligent Enterprise Magazine*, October 20, 2000, p. 2.

Dell, Pamela. "Getting the Most out of Getting Together," *Knowledge Management*, August 2001, p. 1.

Dixon, Nancy M. *Common Knowledge: How Companies Thrive by Sharing What They Know*. Boston, MA: Harvard Business School Press, 2000, pp. 33–142.

Horibe, Frances. *Managing Knowledge Workers*. New York: John Wiley & Sons, Inc., 1999, pp. 21–44.

Koulopoulos, Thomas M., and Frappaolo, Carl. *Smart Things to Know About Knowledge Management*. Oxford, UK: Capstone Publishing, Ltd., 1999, pp. 127–165.

Pfeffer, Jeffrey, and Sutton, Robert I. *The Knowing-Doing Gap*. Boston, MA: Harvard Business School Press, 2000, pp. 89–106.

Wiig, Karl. *Knowledge Management Foundations— Thinking About Thinking—How People and Organizations Create, Represent, and Use Knowledge*. Arlington, TX: Schema Press, 1993.

CHAPTER 10

Knowledge Transfer in the E-World

Contents

The real questions are how
Do we stay connected?
How do we share knowledge?
How do we function any time,
any where, no matter what?
—ROBERT BUCKMAN

In a Nutshell

Knowledge management does not operate in a vacuum any more than it is only about technology. A learning organization is driven by intelligence, and knowledge is voluntarily shared via teams, between individuals, face to face, and electronically. Technology is an inescapable part of most knowledge management success stories. The company's technology—including an intranet, groupware, and extranet—plays a major role in knowledge transfer and knowledge sharing when distance is a problem within the firm and between firms worldwide. External stakeholders such as vendors, customers, and government are considered partners in a company's global integrated knowledge management system, where knowledge sharing is part of a geographically dispersed environment.

One area where knowledge transfer has gained popularity is in e-business and e-commerce. It is an environment where external stakeholders form a networked relationship with a company's knowledge bases or organizational members. In e-business, there are e-merchants, e-vendors, and the knowledge automation tools that make each relationship a value-added reality. Supply chain management is the architecture that makes such relationships possible. In this chapter, we discuss knowledge transfer through technology that facilitates knowledge sharing. These electronic relationships involve the company's intranet and the Internet. Intranets and extranets as part of an integrated knowledge management environment are also discussed.

In terms of knowledge transfer, e-business helps create knowledge markets through intelligent exchange of information, strategies, and processes. Small groups inside big firms can be funded with seed money to develop new ideas. DaimlerChrysler created small teams to look for new trends and products. A Silicon Valley team is doing consumer research on electric cars and advising car designers. Sooner or later, these groups create electronic linkups with outside affiliates.

Today's electronic marketplaces improve knowledge sharing between merchants and customers and promote quick, just-in-time deliveries. Customers and merchants save money; are online 24 hours a day, 7 days a week; experience no traffic jams and no crowds; and do not have to carry heavy shopping bags. However, security continues to be a problem for online knowledge transfer. In a 2000 *Economist* article, 95 percent of Americans expressed reluctance to give out their credit card number via the Internet.

▪▪▪▪ The E-World

By e-world, we refer to the electronic facilities available to a company that accommodate knowledge transfer and knowledge exchange, regardless of place, location, or dialogue. The facilities include the intranet, extranet, groupware, e-commerce, and e-business. These are the commonly used technologies that address knowledge management solutions. Most of them handle the explicit side of knowledge transfer.

INTRANETS

Intranet is a term used when we apply Internet technology to serve the internal needs of an organization. It can be viewed as Internet-like capability at the internal organizational level. The user can simply point and click to access the available information. The drill is easy. Click on an icon, a button, or a link on the screen and go to different pages.

Internet technology is superior to conventional internal communication systems. The Web browser, for example, is a readily available and familiar access tool. Documents are handled easily, and multiple media can be supported as well. Mid- to large-sized organizations are spending thousands of dollars just to keep their documents under control. Managers constantly share documents and knowledge on an inter- and intradepartmental level. With various operating systems, network protocols, and application suites, trying to ensure homogeneity in managing knowledge can be quite a challenge. Intranets handle all transfers and exchanges with ease.

The following scenario is typical of an intranet. Flameless Electric, the second largest manufacturer of electrical parts in Virginia, needed to roll out and sell two major products in 2002. Its strategy used the Internet, intranet, and extranet. The Internet part was easy. The company's Web site displayed the products, which were explained by a company expert for customers to see and order. The company's intranet was accessible only by its 743 knowledge workers. Its priority was to support its 112 sales reps statewide. The intranet supplied them with marketing and technical information about the products and an automated sales application that minimized paperwork, regardless of location or size of order. They were also in touch with product designers and other experts who could explain each product as needed.

The third part was Flameless' extranet. An extranet is an intranet with extensions that allow clearly identified customers or top suppliers to access company-related technical and educational knowledge bases. The company's extranet was accessible to 950 electricians and small electrical parts dealers via a special company Web page. An electrician, for example, could enter an assigned password to access information about new products and special deals that were available to high-volume buyers. There was also a knowledge base, called CRM (customer relationship management), that addressed customer relations. The system stores customer complaints and weaves their solutions into more intelligent answers for future complaints. Answers to customer complaints are based on refined past knowledge of the same.

After 7 months of use, Flameless' Net-based system was paying dividends. It cut down on phone calls and fax orders and gave sales reps in the field immediate online support for the knowledge they needed to transact business. It even improved shipment schedules and deliveries. A summary view of that intranet is a way of thinking about how knowledge workers in a business transfer and share knowledge (see Figure 10.1).

Intranet operation is a communication project designed by a technical staff. It is a network of people, not of wired machines. The focus is the message, not the media. Concentrating on the technology of the intranet is like an author worrying about the presses and typesetting rather than the manuscript.

▪ ▪ ▪ ▪ ▪ ▪ ▪ **FIGURE 10.1:** Corporate Intranet—A Conceptual Model

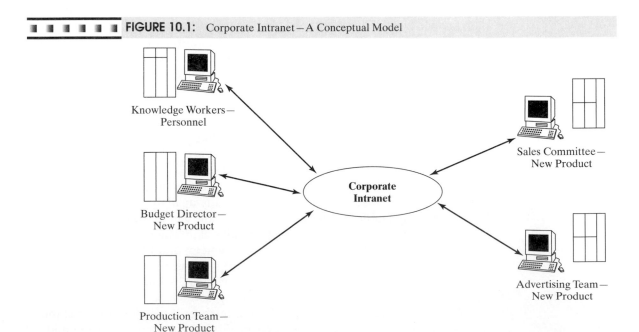

Benefits

An intranet provides many benefits and has distinctive features. It links knowledge workers and smart managers around the clock and automates intraorganizational traffic. Today's face-to-face communication and knowledge transfer systems are labor-intensive, although they are effective once the parties go beyond the exchange of pleasantries. An intranet makes it possible to gain better access to the knowledge and experience of the decision makers who work within it. It is a creative and empowering tool for a company and the foundation for developing an enterprise-wide knowledge-based interactive environment. It is a model for collaborative knowledge transfer and knowledge sharing (see Box 10.1).

An intranet is not for every business. First, from a cost/benefit analysis view, the investment is justified when there are 100 or more employees. One major application is listing employee benefits, company news and views, vacation schedules, job openings, and recognizing special employees. A company needs an intranet when:

- It has a large pool of information to share among hundreds of employees. It is an effective way of cutting the cost of producing conventional multiple hard copies.
- Knowledge transfer must reach its destination in a hurry. Because intranets operate across platforms such as Windows, UNIX, and Mac, they are the easiest way to get people communicating.

Other than human resources, an intranet facilitates knowledge transfer and knowledge sharing in other intelligent applications. They include detailed e-mail for inter-office communication, internal company office circulars, bulletin board service, a daily to-do list and assignments from a central desk to all connected desks, and a channel for

---

▪▪▪▪▪▪ **BOX 10.1** ▪▪▪▪▪▪

THE MARK OF A SUCCESSFUL INTRANET SITE

BEST INTRANET SITE

Bud Mathaisel makes no apologies for the way Ford Motor Co. cajoled thousands of employees to use the Web as the engine for all kinds of business activities. First, the IT department gave workers a kick-start by seeding the intranet with tons of data and easy-to-use templates. Then, senior management applied the real pressure. "Group vice presidents ask—no, direct—their staff to publish all of their knowledge and best practices on the Web," says Mathaisel, Ford's CIO. "The Web is the critical conduit for just about all activities."

That might explain how, 2 years after its launch, the Ford intranet has lured 101,000 employees to use the Web as the central medium of collaboration. The Ford intranet is the repository for all "corporate knowledge." Every vehicle team has a Web site where they post questions and results and resolve business issues. Employees in 800 facilities worldwide report that 90 percent of the critical data they need to do their jobs is available in the Web knowledge base. The intranet has reduced the time it takes to bring new models into production, improved quality, and cut travel costs, Mathaisel says. "In my career, I have seen many promised silver bullets," he says. "None has produced the value that the intranet has."

SOURCE: Joachim, David. "Best Awards Business on the Internet," *InternetWeek*, April 19, 1999, p. 47.

confidential exchange of strategic decisions made by key executives. Intranet facilities also include a chat room, where employees can post ideas for other employees in the hope of coming up with a new product, a better policy, and the like.

EXTRANETS AND KNOWLEDGE EXCHANGE

If a company Web site links two or more trading partners, it is referred to as being business-to-business (B2B) or an extranet. It is a B2B intranet that lets limited, controlled business partners interact with the firm for all kinds of knowledge sharing (see Figure 10.2). Intranets, extranets, and e-commerce have a lot in common. Intranets are more localized within a firm and move information more quickly than the more distributed extranets. Internet (primarily Web) protocols are commonly used to connect business users. On the intranet, Web administrators prescribe access and policy for a defined group of users. On a B2B extranet, system designers at each participating company must collaborate to make sure there is a common interface with the company they are dealing with. One participating business partner might be using Microsoft Explorer; another may be using Netscape Navigator 6.0. To collaborate via extranet, the applications have to perform consistently on all represented platforms. The same is true for e-commerce, where trading partners may be totally unknown to one another.

Extranets are not a passing trend. They are already the backbone of the e-business future. Extranet technology was initially adopted by corporations that had a vision. These corporations realized that knowledge sharing contributes to productivity, profitability, and growth. The obvious benefits are faster time to market, customer loyalty, increased partner interaction, and improved processes. The easiest way to quantify return on investment in extranets is to identify a business unit with the company that might benefit from an extranet. This means identifying a business goal (such as increasing revenue or improving customer base) before deciding on feasibility, justification, and return on the investment.

▪ ▪ ▪ ▪ ▪ ▪ ▪ **FIGURE 10.2:** General Extranet Layout

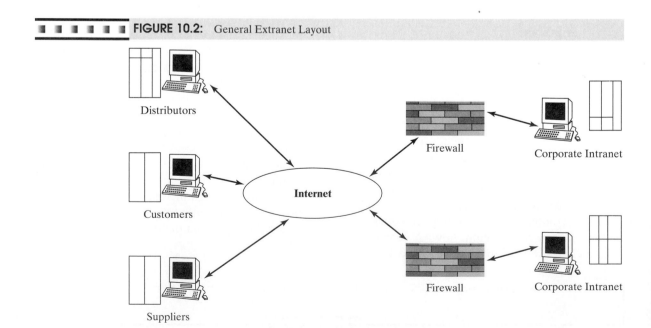

Once a business goal has been established, the next step is for IT departments to discuss feasibility. In a vertical industry like manufacturing, the focus is on improving operations through the existing supply chain; in vertical companies like retail chains, the focus would be on improving revenue. Working with the IT group should bring both technical and business information together for a master design of the extranet. Understanding corporate business processes is the key to a successful deployment of an extranet. By planning the deployment around a well-defined business plan, it is easier to prove how technology will help the bottom line (see Box 10.2).

▪ ▪ ▪ ▪ ▪ ▪   BOX 10.2   ▪ ▪ ▪ ▪ ▪ ▪

EXTRANET AT KODAK

E-COMMERCE TRENDS: KODAK'S EXTRANET PUSH

Eastman Kodak Co. is rapidly expanding its use of extranets to cut costs and boost sales by sharing critical information with major business partners. Kodak has created extranet links to about 25 organizations, including dealers, contractors, joint venture partners, and subsidiaries, and is adding new extranets at the rate of two per week. It is considering linking electronically to key suppliers and retail chains as well, says VP and CIO John Chiazza.

To boost its revenue via e-commerce, Kodak is also developing virtual private networks over which customers such as major retailers can place product orders using a Web browser. About 40 Kodak retail customers accounting for about $1.3 billion in annual revenue already use the networks. "The initial focus is on the consumer business," Chiazza says.

The extranets are being used mainly to exchange information. Kodak continues to rely on electronic data interchange for transactions, but the company is talking to some partners about the potential for conducting transactions over the extranets. "We've been involved in B2B e-commerce for many years as a user of classic EDI, but what has been emerging recently is more intimate interactions through the use of extranets, where we or our customers can reach

into certain internal applications, so that, for example, we can learn how products are moving through their stores and do a better job planning for future orders from them," says Chiazza.

The extranets let authorized users at other companies "tunnel" under Kodak's firewall to access specific servers and even specific applications, Internet, intranet, extranets, and groupware users. Authorized outsiders can get past Kodak firewalls and run applications, as they need to do so. Joint venture partners have access to even more resources, such as intranets, databases, and mailboxes. Some of the networks give Kodak access to its partners' applications.

The extranets enable Kodak and its partners to automatically post product pricing, immediately update product literature, manage inventory, exchange information on jointly developed products, access accounts, and check the status of orders and shipments. To ensure that only authorized users get under the firewall, Kodak uses an extranet management and security system that includes integrated VPN (virtual private network) services, as well as data encryption and authentication for security. Administrators can define privileges based on user identification, the method of authentication and encryption, the information resource being accessed, company affiliation, and day and time.

SOURCE: Awad, E. M. *Electronic Commerce: From Vision to Fulfillment.* Upper Saddle River, NJ: Prentice Hall, 2002, p. 372.

▪ ▪ ▪ ▪ ▪ ▪

Security varies with the type of user, the sensitivity of the knowledge transferred, and the communication lines used. Security questions deal with access control, authentication, and encryption. Access control relates to what users can and cannot access, what can be accessed from what server(s), what accessible data are for display only, and what accessible information can be restricted to certain times of the day. In terms of authentication, decisions must be made regarding the level of authentication for each user, whether passwords and user names are adequate security, and how well other security measures complement the authentication. Is encryption required? If so, how strong should it be? What type of communication line or information should be encrypted?

Extranets are changing how organizations share internal resources and interact with the outside business world. Built with technology and used by people, they can ensure lasting bonds between business partners and corporate members. The entire commitment should be viewed as a knowledge management asset rather than a mere networking expense to expedite business. This is where a champion becomes a critical part of the installation.

A champion who best promotes an extranet is someone who knows the organization's processes, goals, and politics and has technical experience and leadership qualities. This person is an advocate with ability to build company-wide support for the extranet. It is a demanding role, requiring a detail-oriented expert who can sell top management on the viability and potential of the extranet. The key to making his or her case heard is to demonstrate how an extranet can meet the company's revenue goals. Specifically, there should be a convincing argument for how the extranet will generate revenue, how the technology will solve the business problems defined in advance, and how the work will get done through the proposed extranet.

A champion must drive home the key advantages of an extranet:

- An extranet helps the organization ensure accountability in the way it does business and exchanges knowledge with partners.
- An extranet promotes more effective collaboration with business partners, which improves the potential for increased revenues.
- An extranet is a long-term investment in competitive advantage. Sooner or later, having an early start on the competition is bound to pay off.

Think of a manufacturing organization with an e-business environment that allows its business partners, distributors, contractors, and suppliers to access extranet resources through some preestablished interface. Two of the applications could be an e-commerce storefront for suppliers (or an integrated application) and a procurement system. The extranet can be used to manage and tie together all these applications into one integrated system for deriving real value from the company's entire business relationships. The extranet is bound to be the technical community that will eventually generate revenue and ensure competitive advantage.

GROUPWARE

One of the most popular technologies that facilitate intermediation is groupware. By intermediation, we mean connections between people and how knowledge is transferred between knowledge seekers and knowledge providers. Groupware is software that helps people work together, especially for organizations that are geographically distributed and less likely to encounter face-to-face exchange among knowledge workers. Through this specific class of technology, people rely on groupware to communicate ideas, cooperate in problem-solving, coordinate work flow, or negotiate solutions. It seems logical to invest in an intranet that can perform locally within the company and link globally via e-mail and the Internet. Groupware applications on a company's intranet can help the organization do more for less (see Box 10.3).

Groupware is categorized according to (1) whether users of the groupware are working together in the same place (face to face) or in different locations (distance) and (2) whether they are working together at the same time or different times (see Figure 10.3).

Groupware goes beyond cooperation or work by teams. In designing the technology, the prime consideration is learning about group concepts and how group members behave in a group setting. The goal is to identify the tasks, understand how the group communicates, and decide on group structure and member roles. Once understood, the next step is to have a feel for networking technology and how it can assure a productive user's positive experience.

▪ ▪ ▪ ▪ ▪ ▪ ▪   **BOX 10.3**   ▪ ▪ ▪ ▪ ▪ ▪ ▪

GROUPWARE IN ACTION

What attorney Bill Wright was facing was a failure to communicate. First, one of his three partners suddenly up and left, taking 17 employees of the Bellmawr, New Jersey, law firm and lots of clients with him. Then, within days of his departure, the prodigal lawyer sued his former partners. Of course, Wright's firm turned around and filed a countersuit. What with impromptu hallway discussions, emergency meetings, news flashes, urgent requests for background, and the rest of their caseload, the remaining staff at Farr, Burke, Gambacorta & Wright barely had time to breathe. "We had to find a way to help us handle the flood of information," says Wright. "And we had to find it fast." Simple e-mail, he knew, would not suffice. He needed something that would organize and catalog information, not just zap bulletins around the office.

What Wright and his colleagues did was to turn to groupware, a category of software used, as the name suggests, to help people work in groups. Instead of holding one meeting after another, they bought and installed a program called TeamTalk (from Trax Softworks) on their network and started using it to discuss business. When Wright had to produce a draft of a proposed settlement, for example, he no longer had to rummage through notes from previous discussions and interrupt his partners with time-consuming questions. Instead he simply looked in the program's database for a record of earlier memos and messages relating to the topic.

A year after the suits were settled, groupware had become the interactive glue holding Wright's firm together. Their application now has 14 users (partners, lawyers, paralegals, and the office manager) and covers 32 topics, from legal procedures to new cases. If, for example, a bankruptcy judge makes an idiosyncratic procedural ruling about foreclosures, an associate adds that tidbit to the pertinent topic. Some topics are available to everyone; others, like the one that disseminates confidential information about management, are open only to partners. A pregnant attorney created a subject area related to her cases so that others could track her cases while she was on maternity leave and so that she could get up to speed quickly when she returned to work.

SOURCE: Excerpted from Field, Anne. "Group Think," www.inc.com/articles/hr/manage_emp/productivity/1995-6.html, Date accessed November 23, 2002.

▪ ▪ ▪ ▪ ▪ ▪

	Same Place (face to face)	Different Place (distance)
Same Time	Voting, Presentation Support	Chat Room, Teleconferencing
Different Time	Peer-to-Peer, Shared Computers	Work-Flow Process, E-Mail

▪ ▪ ▪ ▪ ▪ ▪ ▪ **FIGURE 10.3:** Groupware Categories

SOURCE: Adapted from Brinck, Tom. "Groupware: Introduction," www.usabilityfirst.com/groupware/intro.txl, 1998, Date accessed August 2002.

Companies want to use groupware for several reasons:

- Groupware works well with groups having common interests or work and where it would not be practical for the same number of people to meet face to face.
- Certain problems are best solved by groups, not individuals.
- Groups can bring multiple opinions and expertise to a work setting.
- Groupware facilitates telecommuting, which can be quite an effective time-saver.
- Joint meetings are often faster and more effective than face-to-face meetings.

Prerequisites for Success

Most groupware systems cannot succeed unless the group of users decides to accept the system. Having a teleconferencing system is useless if only one side has it. The two most critical prerequisites for system success are compatibility of software and perceived benefit to every member of the group. In the early 1980s, IBM and UNISYS introduced workstations, but their systems could not communicate with each other. This meant that anyone who wanted to communicate with others in the organization or elsewhere had to make sure that the other party had the same make. The problem continued until a decade later, when open system standards made it possible for anyone using any make to communicate with any other make, regardless of distance or location.

The second prerequisite for groupware success is the benefit perceived by group members. Each group member must be convinced that the system will generate explicit benefits in the way it transacts ideas across the board. Otherwise, there is the danger of defection. For example, in a chat room, where a common problem is presented for discussion, if a member perceives that his contributions are not fairly represented for others to consider, there is a chance that such a member will minimize or simply refuse to contribute to the problem solution. Of course, the group may apply social pressure to encourage groupware use. Any disparity of individual and group benefit should be hashed out before the final groupware system design.

Communication Structure

In a typical face-to-face session, the protocol is standard. Communication is highly structured. Someone asks a question or explains a situation while the others listen. There is usually a question, then a response, and so on. When a communication structure is known, a groupware system takes advantage of it to speed up communication and improve the performance of the exchange. This communication environment is referred to as a *technologically mediated communication structure*. The expectation is order, discipline, and following a known protocol of question-response.

An alternative communication structure is what we call a *socially mediated communication structure*, where individuals send a request through technology like e-mail, with no control over how soon or whether the recipient will respond. This communication exchange is good for certain problem-solving situations, but not for others. The important point is for the designer to set up a groupware system to fit the specific requirements of the group that will use it. Unless the prerequisites are identified, there is the risk that any groupware technology might backfire.

Session Control

Groupware systems require that sessions be conducted within the framework of protocols designed to ensure privacy, integrity, and successful completion of each session. A **session** is a situation where a group of people agrees to get together to conduct a meeting in person, over the telephone, or in a chat room. Session control is more like a bouncer standing at the door of a private club and checking identification, determining whether the person is wearing the proper attire, and so forth. Session control determines who can enter and exit the session, when they can enter, and how. Once inside, the rest of the group should be aware of the newcomer and his or her role. Some of the rules used in session control include the following:

- Make sure users do not impose a session on others. Like a telemarketer call with no filter such as caller ID or an answering machine, a resident feels vulnerable not knowing who the caller is.
- Conversational group members should be identified before being allowed into a session. This way, other participants have an idea who is included in the session and the role they play.
- The system should control unnecessary interruptions or simultaneous transmissions that might result in confusion or chaos.
- A group member should be allowed to enter and leave at any time. However, participants should know when such a situation occurs.
- Make sure there is a ceiling on how many people can participate and how long the session should last.
- Assign a moderator who controls access to a shared whiteboard or a repository and how long access should last.
- Ensure anonymity, privacy, and accountability at all times. Each user should have control over the information to be shared; other communications should be private or confidential.

When people use technology like groupware to communicate, various types of information are communicated through channels, implicitly and explicitly. Awareness information such as documents and location and tasks of coworkers should all be considered in groupware system design. This suggests that a groupware system designer should be well versed in human interaction and communication skills and in the technology that emulates human exchange. To find such a person is not easy and requires special training and experience in the domain.

GROUPWARE APPLICATIONS

E-Mail and Knowledge Transfer

Besides the traditional telephone, e-mail is the most common groupware application. Unlike the telephone, which involves two persons exchanging information via a dedicated cable, an e-mail system provides much more. It can send and receive messages, forward messages, file messages, and create mailing groups. It can also attach files to a message. Most e-mail systems provide features for sorting and processing messages. A message can easily be routed to any number of destinations.

The intranet and e-mail is a marriage made in "cyberheaven." E-mail is what a company's intranet is best known for; it is "the Net's killer app" (Dell 2000). Almost 90 percent of Net users report e-mail as the most frequently used online contact between knowledge workers. It is a major communication platform in business and government. Scott McNealy, chief executive officer of Sun Microsystems, Inc., once commented: "You can take out every one of the 300 to 400 computer applications that we run our company on and we could continue—but if you took out our e-mail system, Sun would grind to an immediate halt."

Over 200 million in-boxes are active worldwide. Frequent e-mailers already recognize that their in-box is as much a database of appointments and news as it is a place to store messages. With e-commerce volumes on the rise, this knowledge transfer and communication tool is becoming part of e-marketing and sales.

E-mail is also becoming smarter: It can now manage data and documents with ease. It can direct specific messages to defined folders and be a place to check voice, text, and fax messages. This is called *content management* or *unified messaging services*. Managing information with e-mail is more efficient than dealing with the flood of letters, faxes, and bills we handle today. As e-mail becomes the standard for content dissemination of all kinds, it should attract more and more users and become as popular as the cell phone.

Newsgroups and Work-Flow Systems

Similar to e-mail in concept, newsgroups cater to large groups receiving the same message on demand. That is, messages are available to a participant only when he or she requests it. In contrast, a work-flow system is a smart technology for cognition. It is designed to route information (documents, messages, reports) to specific people in the organization and convey the business rules that govern the use of the knowledge. For example, an employee returning from a 2-day conference submits an expense report electronically to her manager, who approves it and forwards it to the accounting department for processing. Another unique feature is the system's capability to analyze a work-flow process and assess the status of documents (where they are, who should have them next, and so on).

Chat Rooms

This groupware system allows many people to participate in a session, where they write messages that appear to all participants on the bottoms of their respective screens. In one chat session, the author was invited to give a talk on e-commerce applications to an Association for Computing Marketing (ACM) chapter 300 miles away via the host university's chat room. The monitor displayed a text message that seven participants were present. It began with a message from the moderator: "Now the meeting will come to order. I am pleased to present our speaker for the evening." A message was displayed every time someone connected to the chat room or exited. As the presentation was entered electronically in text, the presenter was informed of what was going on by participants through the chat room. For example, when a question was entered, it was displayed on one corner of the monitor. At the end, an "applaud, applaud" message was displayed with a thank-you note, which concluded the chat session.

One thing worth noting about the text version of chat is that there is a transcript of the presentation, which makes it easier for participants to react at any time. As a result, in most chat sessions, participants are engrossed in listening, thinking, and responding to the ongoing exchange. It simulates a live session in a human group.

Video Communication

Another groupware application that is gaining in popularity is video communication. This system is essentially a phone system with video hardware. This application is ideal in discussions requiring a video display or when visual information is being discussed. It also projects a view of activities going on at a remote site. Video communication systems allow live video for two-way or multiple locations, depending on the requirements of the group session.

Knowledge Sharing

Knowledge-sharing groupware is unique in small business situations; it allows you to store and share information through a resident knowledge base. The attraction of such a system is that it involves a few steps that are easy to learn and apply; everything resides in the knowledge base and is easily accessible (Field 1996).

Group Calendaring and Scheduling

This application provides unique features related to scheduling, project management, and coordination of schedules among several people involved in a given project. One of the intelligent features is detecting when a schedule is in conflict and finding a meeting time that will accommodate each participant. This includes locating people and synchronizing their availability.

▪ ▪ ▪ ▪ E-Business

E-business brings the universal access of the Internet to the core business process of exchanging information between businesses, between people within a business, and between a business and its many clients. From an *interface* perspective, e-business involves various knowledge exchanges: business-to-business, business-to-consumer, and consumer-to-consumer. Each type is explained later in the chapter.

The focus of e-business is on knowledge transfer and knowledge sharing. It means connecting critical business systems directly to critical constituencies—customers, vendors, and suppliers—via the Internet, extranets, and intranets. The technology-based environment provides electronic information to boost performance and create value by forming new relationships among businesses and customers. E-business is more than a Web site, in that it affects all aspects of business, from strategy and process to trading partners and the ultimate consumer. It combines the resources of traditional knowledge-based systems with the global reach of the Web.

From a knowledge management viewpoint, e-business enables learning organizations to accomplish the following goals:

1. Create new products or services and, consequently, new market knowledge
2. Build customer loyalty through knowledge exchange and knowledge sharing
3. Enrich human capital by more direct and immediate knowledge transfer
4. Make use of existing technologies for research and development and creation of new knowledge for new and more advanced products and services
5. Achieve market leadership and competitive advantage

E-business means exchange of information with anyone, anywhere, anytime. It breaks two traditional rules of knowledge sharing: Companies do not share knowledge with competitors, and suppliers do not share knowledge with buyers, especially knowledge that determines pricing. One of the drivers that promotes e-business is change in organizations. Today's learning organizations empower front-line workers to do the kind of work once performed by junior management. There is also a trend toward partnering owners and managers across departments to develop a chain of relationships and knowledge sharing that adds value to the enterprise. Downsizing of larger organizations, outsourcing of specialized tasks, and encouraging cross-functional business processes all require better communication between the departments that perform these functions. E-business, which makes communication easy, is an ideal method of making these connections (see Figure 10.4).

■ ■ ■ ■ ■ ■ ■ **FIGURE 10.4:** Changes in Organizational Makeup

- Empowerment of Front-Line Workers
- Informating of Key Business Activities
- Outsourcing and Downsizing of Large Organizations
- Partnering Between and Among Knowledge Workers
- Cross-Functional Business Processes

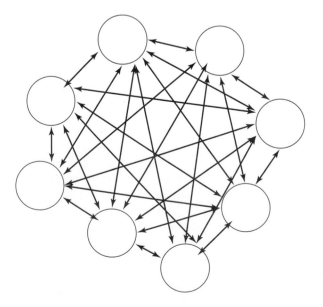

E-business helps create knowledge markets. Small groups inside big firms can be funded with seed money to develop new ideas. For example, a Boston firm formed a team of specialists to do consumer research on electric cars and car comfort.

Electronic marketplaces improve knowledge sharing between merchants and customers and promote quick, just-in-time deliveries. Convenience for the consumer is a major driver for changes in various industries: Customers and merchants save money; are online 24 hours a day, 7 days a week; experience no traffic jams and no crowds; and do not have to carry heavy shopping bags. Control is another major driving factor. For example, instead of banks controlling the relationship with the customer, customers today can have more control over their banking needs via Internet Web sites. Banks like Bank of America, Wells Fargo, and hundreds of others now give customers access to their accounts via the Web.

Even though we can generate a long list of advantages and benefits, there are still problems and drawbacks to consider before using the Web business for knowledge exchange or knowledge transfer. The main problem is system and knowledge integrity. Computer viruses are rampant, and new viruses are discovered every day. Viruses cause unnecessary delays, file backups, storage problems, and the like. The danger of hackers accessing files and corrupting accounts adds more stress to an already complex operation.

Another limitation is corporate vulnerability. The availability of knowledge regarding products, design specifics, and other information about a business through its Web site makes it vulnerable to access by the competition. The idea of extracting business intelligence from the competition's Web pages is called *Web farming,* a term coined by Richard Hackathorn.

THE VALUE CHAIN

In 1985, Michael Porter wrote a book entitled *Competitive Advantage,* in which he introduced the concept of a value chain. A value chain is simply a way of organizing the primary and secondary activities of a business so that each activity provides "value added" or productivity to the total operation of the business. It is a way for businesses to receive raw materials as input, add value to them through various processes, and sell the finished product as output to consumers. Competitive advantage is achieved when an organization links the activities in its value chain more cheaply and more effectively than do its competitors. For example, the purchasing function assists the production activity to ensure that raw materials and other supplies are available on time and meet the requirements of the products to be manufactured. The manufacturing function, in turn, has the responsibility to produce quality products that the sales staff can depend on for "sale without pain." To do the job, the human resource function must hire, retain, and develop the right talent personnel to ensure continuity in manufacturing, sales, and other areas in the business. Bringing in qualified people is value added to stability, continuity, and integrity of operations throughout the firm.

The knowledge-based value chain is a useful way of looking at a corporation's knowledge activities and at how various knowledge exchange adds value to adjacent activities and to the company in general. Everywhere value is added is where knowledge is created, transferred, or shared. By examining the elements of the value chain, corporate executives can also look at ways of incorporating information technology and telecommunications to improve the overall productivity of the firm. Companies that do their homework early and well ensure themselves a competitive advantage in the marketplace (see Figure 10.5).

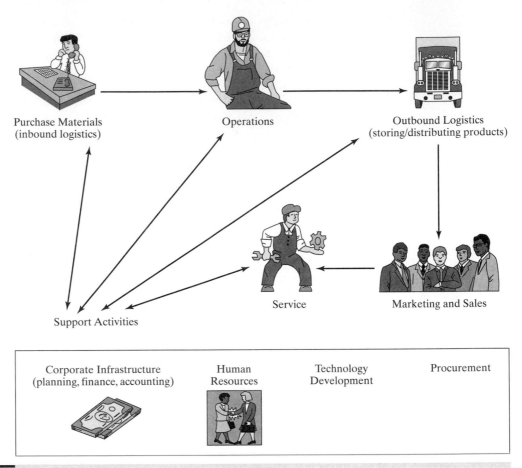

Purchase Materials
(inbound logistics)

Operations

Outbound Logistics
(storing/distributing products)

Service

Marketing and Sales

Support Activities

| Corporate Infrastructure (planning, finance, accounting) | Human Resources | Technology Development | Procurement |

▪ ▪ ▪ ▪ ▪ ▪ ▪ **FIGURE 10.5:** A Knowledge-Based Value Chain

The trend in e-business is to integrate the knowledge management life cycle, from knowledge creation (such as seeking information from the customer, vendor, or employees) to knowledge distribution (such as providing reports, analysis, or forecasting to top management) via three major applications: business-to-consumer (B2C), business-to-business (B2B), and business-within-business. These are also known as the Internet, extranet, and intranet, respectively (see Table 10.1).

Business to Consumer (Internet)

The focus of this e-business application is on the use of a merchant's Web storefront or Web site. Consumers anywhere can browse, learn about products, and order goods or services online anytime. This approach is modeled on the traditional shopping experience found in stores like Safeway, Kroger, and Kmart. For example, a shopping cart is used to hold goods until the customer is ready to check out. Checkout is order and payment processing. B2C is the electronic equivalent of the traditional mail order or telephone-based ordering system. This system involves knowledge exchange between the consumer and the e-merchant through the Web site.

TABLE 10.1   Key Elements of Internet, Extranet, and Intranet E-Commerce

Element	Internet	Extranet	Intranet
E-commerce type	Business-to-consumer (such as mail order via the Web)	Business-to-business (procurement and shipment)	Internal procurement and processing
Access	Unrestricted (anyone can access a URL address)	Restricted to internal company employees, staff, and business partners	Restricted to company customers, employees, and staff
Security	Generally minimal, except for verifying credit cards and financial transaction integrity	Firewalls and restricted access to data and applications for partners	Firewalls to eliminate non-company employees
Payment method	Credit card or electronic cash	Predefined credit agreement between businesses	Within-business charges

▪ ▪ ▪ ▪ ▪ ▪

Business to Business (Internet and Extranet)

Having a Web storefront is not a big deal anymore. Everyone has one. The real power of knowledge management in e-commerce lies not in the direct sale of products to customers but in the integration of relationships among merchants and suppliers for prompt, quality customer service. Business-to-business is industrial marketing: As soon as an online purchase is entered and payment is approved through a credit card clearance procedure, a message is generally displayed that says, "Thank you for your order. The amount of $000 will be charged to your credit card. The product should reach you within 5 to 7 working days." The moment the message is displayed on the customer's monitor, an electronic order is sent to the vendor to fill the order and ship it directly to the customer. Doing this electronically means reduced inventory and quicker service.

SUPPLY CHAIN MANAGEMENT (SCM) AND KNOWLEDGE EXCHANGE

The concept of supply chain management (SCM) means having the right product in the right place, at the right time, at the right price, and in the right condition. This is an integral part of the business-to-business framework. SCM cuts across application infrastructures and business relationships. It transforms the way companies exchange information with suppliers, partners, and even customers. The goal is to improve efficiency and profitability, but it also means creating new opportunities through knowledge sharing for everyone involved.

Supply chain management employs powerful tools that allow companies to exchange and update information (such as inventory levels and sales trends) in an effort to reduce cycle times, to have quicker delivery of orders, to minimize excess inventory, and to improve customer service. This communication is done quickly from one knowledge base or database to another. According to an *InformationWeek* research survey of 300 IT executives using supply chain systems, the majority of the respondents said the most strategic advantages of supply chain systems are better collaboration with business partners, lower operational costs, and reduced cycle times. See Box 10.4 (Stein and Sweat 2000).

In SCM, the name of the game is *collaboration* among business partners, *knowledge sharing* of logistics for timely delivery of goods or products, and *consensus* among

▪▪▪▪▪▪ BOX 10.4 ▪▪▪▪▪▪

SUPPLY CHAIN MANAGEMENT

KILLER SUPPLY CHAINS

For most retailers, one of the trickiest links in the supply chain is moving goods from the supplier to the warehouse and then on to the store. The Home Depot, Inc., has found a simple way around that problem: Remove it. The Atlanta-based building supplies retailer now moves 85 percent of its merchandise—nearly all of its domestic goods—directly from the manufacturer to the storefront. Product no longer languishes in warehouses, saving both suppliers and Home Depot money. "We're treating each of our stores as if it were a distribution center, says CIO Ron Griffin. Because of Home Depot's high volume—its stores average $44 million in sales and 5½ full inventory turns a year—the products frequently ship in full truckloads, making the system even more cost-effective.

Associates walk store aisles, watching for goods that need replenishment. As they enter orders directly into mobile computing devices, called the *Mobile Ordering Platform,* the requests can go almost instantly via EDI connections to more than 80 percent of Home Depot's manufacturers, which can respond immediately. Home Depot offers its partners recognition incentives to get them on board.

Short-term forecasting is handled locally; with up to 65 weeks of data at the store level, store managers are given latitude to adjust for demand based on merchandising programs. Home Depot prepares long-range forecasts of 3 to 5 years on a national level for its suppliers; they contain product-volume data, of course, as well as where growth is expected and where Home Depot plans to build new stores. That helps suppliers decide where to build new plants and distribution centers, and it puts Home Depot in the position of helping to determine facility location instead of simply working around it. "Rather than assume fixed capacity, we help shape it," Griffin says.

Home Depot opens up even more data to its biggest partners. Electric-tool manufacturer Black & Decker is Home Depot's largest supplier, and Home Depot is its largest customer, so it benefits both companies to share information. Home Depot passes point-of-sale data to Black & Decker, which helps the Baltimore company analyze sales and determine future manufacturing volume.

SOURCE: Stein, Tom, and Jeff Sweat. "Killer Supply Chains," *InformationWeek*, January 16, 2000, pp. 1–3.

▪▪▪▪▪▪

knowledge workers and suppliers to make sure orders and inquiries are filled correctly. More and more, companies are extending their focus from internal operations like scheduling and enterprise resource planning to relationships with external customers and suppliers. They are looking for the perfect virtual enterprise that will link their supplier's suppliers to their customer's customers to operate together under one umbrella with seamless connections among knowledge bases, databases, manufacturing, inventory systems, and Web servers (see Box 10.5).

As you can see, B2B exchanges pave the way for a new model of the digital economy. It is a distinct network of suppliers, distributors, Internet service providers, and customers that use the Internet for communications and transaction handling. As communication tools get better and cheaper, transaction costs should drop. With the Internet, many transaction costs are approaching zero. People around the world can now quickly and cheaply access the information they need almost instantly. Companies can also add value to a product or service from any location, at anytime, day or night.

▪ ▪ ▪ ▪ ▪ ▪ ▪ **BOX 10.5** ▪ ▪ ▪ ▪ ▪ ▪ ▪

USES OF SUPPLY-CHAIN MANAGEMENT

- Integrated Web-based systems give companies a better view of their global supply chain, speeding delivery of products from around the world.

- Established companies still rely heavily on electronic data interchange (EDI) to transmit and receive order requests along the supply chain.

- Companies employing Web technologies such as XML can exchange data with less technologically sophisticated overseas partners that lack the resources to handle EDI.

- RosettaNet, a group of companies in the computer and electronic components industry, is implementing standards based on XML to facilitate information exchange over the supply chain.

- Lucent Technologies' Microelectronics Group created a supply system with DHL Airways to deliver silicon chips halfway around the world in 2 days.

SOURCE: Chadbrow, Eric. "Supply Chains Go Global," *InformationWeek*, April 3, 2000, p. 52.

▪ ▪ ▪ ▪ ▪ ▪

To illustrate, General Motors (GM), Ford, and DaimlerChrysler announced in early 2000 that they were moving all their business-to-business activity, involving more than $25 billion and 60,000 suppliers, to the Internet. The new system will replace a mammoth procurement process built on phone calls and fax processing. For GM, the average processing cost of a purchase order is $125. With the Internet, the cost is expected to drop to $1. Bidding will also drive down the cost of some goods. Parts such as tires and headlights are already purchased through online reverse auctions, where the automaker names the price of the part that it needs, leaving it to a supplier to accept the price. This approach should capture millions of dollars in savings.

The serious task is overhauling the way work gets done in a company, which for large corporations can take years and cost millions of dollars. For example, Ford wants to revamp its manufacturing plants to begin building customized cars for consumers; a consumer will have a new car just 2 weeks after the order has been placed. This means major changes for employees, dealers, and suppliers worldwide. Early in 2000, General Motors Corporation launched an SCM project with similar goals. The work is scheduled for completion by 2003 and will cost well over $100 million. It could mean reengineering almost all of GM's business processes and a big investment in new technology, but the payback is expected to be in the hundreds of millions (Violino 1999). The top 10 e-business innovators are shown in Table 10.2.

Customer Relationship Management (CRM)

Related to SCM is customer relationship management or CRM. The goal of this concept is for a company to enhance its relationship management with customers and supply chain partners. CRM is a business strategy used to learn more about customers' needs and behaviors in order to develop stronger relationships with them. It relies on technology to bring various pieces of customer information to knowledge workers. By doing so, companies would be able to create a more holistic view of their customers and, in turn, tailor services to their specific needs.

CRM is about changing a company's business processes to support a new customer focus and applying technologies to automate those new processes. The technology

TABLE 10.2 The Top 10 Electronic Business Innovators

Rank	Company	URL Address	E-Business Profile
1	Office Depot	www.officedepot.com	This office-supply company integrates e-business technology across all channels of its business, increasing customer self-service and order sizes while reducing transaction costs.
2	IBM	www.ibm.com	The world's largest computer company practices what it preaches, employing an e-business infrastructure to link customers, employees, and business partners.
3	Cisco Systems	www.cisco.com	This is one of the first companies to succeed in using the Internet for e-commerce. Eight of 10 orders the networking company receives are via the Web, with online sales topping $1 billion.
4	Army & Air Force Exchange Service	www.aafes.com	World's eighth-largest retailer, 9 percent of catalog sales come via the Web. To reach the unconnected, the exchange for military personnel, family, and veterans employs Web-tied kiosks at retail outlets.
5	E-Trade Group	www.etrade.com	This is the leading online brokerage, touted for its high degree of customization, which lets clients tailor the service to their own needs.
6	Dell Computer	www.dell.com	The granddaddy of customization sites, the PC maker provides an easy-to-use Web site, where customers can configure, purchase, confirm, and track orders for desktops, notebooks, and servers.
7	Lockheed Martin	www.lockheedmartin.com	An Internet pioneer in the days before the Web, this defense contractor's intranet is among the world's largest, with more than 1,100 internal sites linking 185,000 users to 13 enterprise resource planning systems.
8	Avnet	www.avnet.com	The e-business structure of this global electronic-components distributor includes online point-of-use replenishment systems, accounts for 20 percent of customer transactions and more than 90 percent of supplier transactions.
9	Insight Enterprises	www.insight.com	This supplier of computer hardware and software products lets customers—mostly small and midsize businesses—customize online catalogs, which helped boost unassisted Web sales by 222 percent in 1999.
10	Marshall Industries	www.marshall.com	This electronic-components distributor uses an online supply chain management program—combined with data warehousing solutions—which reduces expenses and increases responsiveness.

■ ■ ■ ■ ■ ■

SOURCE: Violino, Bob. "The Leaders of E-Business," *InformationWeek*, December 13, 1999, p. 72.

allows multiple channels of communication with customers and supply chain partners and uses customer information stored in databases and knowledge bases to construct predictive models for customer purchase behaviors. Companies provide a robust network system in order to support a successful CRM implementation. The main benefits include the following:

- Increased customer satisfaction
- Cross-selling products efficiently
- Making call centers more efficient
- Helping sales staff close deals faster
- Simplifying marketing and sales processes
- Discovering new customers

The two critical elements of CRM software are operational and analytical technologies. The operational component uses portals that facilitate communication between customers, employees, and supply chain partners. As shown in Figure 10.6, the portal resides in the presentation layer of the CRM technical architecture. Some of the basic features included in the portal product are as follows:

- Personalization services to develop a user profile based on user cached clickstream information
- Secure services to enforce security rules of the organization for external and internal users
- Publishing services—an interactive mechanism for users to document the location and meaning of business content
- Access services to help users find and access portal content
- Subscription services to deliver business content on a regularly scheduled basis via e-mail, fax, or other media

In contrast, the analytical component uses data-mining technologies to predict customer purchase patterns, which enables the company to apply proactive marketing toward its target customers. Data kept at different parts of the organization, such as sales, customer services, and billing, is organized for efficient retrieval and update.

All factors considered, the architectural imperative for CRM is to do the following:

- Allow the capture of a very large volume of data and transform it into analysis formats to support enterprise-wide analytical requirements
- Deploy knowledge—an intuitive, integrated system; rapidly enables processing of the intelligence gathered from analytical environments
- Calculate metrics by the deployed business rules; identifies pockets of activity by a consumer in real time, enabling truly strategic targeting

Once operational, communications within the organization allow different parts of the organization to share knowledge with one another. For instance, a salesperson might retrieve a historical telephone conversation between one customer and a service representative and then develop a sales pitch based on that particular customer's interests. Another example would be a customer service representative who creates a notice to postpone the invoice for a customer due to an error in the billing cycle. The billing department must then recognize the notice and process the changes made by the customer service representative. Local area network technologies are implemented at most small businesses or at branch offices of larger organizations. Wide area networks

The portal serves as a window to the wealth of information contained within the organization. It is the key to a successful CRM architecture.

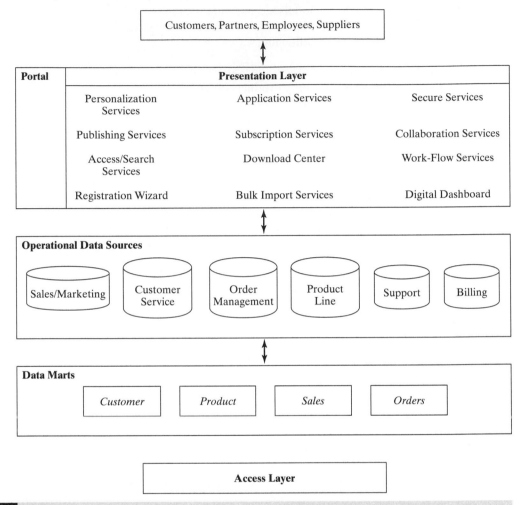

■■■■■■■ **FIGURE 10.6:** Operational and Analytical Components of CRM in Its Technical Configuration

SOURCE: Adapted from Zurell, Nancy. "Operational and Analytical Technologies for Optimizing Your CRM System," *DM Review*, February 2002, p. 82.

(also known as intranets) operate over the Internet and connect departments that are located at remote areas. The overall CRM infrastructure that provides communications within the organization and with outside entities is illustrated in Figure 10.7.

■■■■ Implications for Knowledge Management

The Web has changed the way business and information technology work. E-commerce is transforming the Internet from a "browse-and-surf" environment into a mammoth knowledge exchange. Given the challenges posed by today's e-business and its potential, when it comes to success in this emerging field, it is knowledgeable people and managerial talent that matter. It is people with vision of the future who know how to

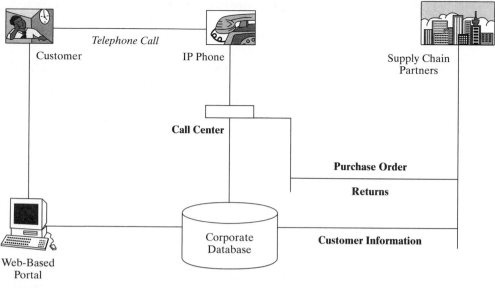

▪ ▪ ▪ ▪ ▪ ▪ ▪ **FIGURE 10.7:** Typical Diagram of CRM Network

handle the speed of change. The person who figures out how to harness the collective genius of the organization will blow the competition away.

Intranets are tools to manage corporate intelligence. They offer unique leverage and a competitive advantage at all levels of the organization. Among the key success factors are strong leadership, a focus on users, and effective management of the intranet project. From a managerial view, change may not be immediate and should be nurtured with care. This author spent 7 weeks designing and implementing a $700,000 intranet site for a foreign central bank with 950 employees. After 3 months of training, coaching, selling, and demonstrating the uses of the new intranet, less than 20 percent of the employees made a habit of using the new system. The rest of the staff continued to deliver memos, documents, reports, and messages the old-fashioned way—in person.

Change is closely related to employee satisfaction, and the effect of the intranet on the way employees do their jobs is important. Those who are forced to use a new system will find a way to get back at the company. For example, gripe sites are available on the Internet that employees use to state their dissatisfaction with the employer. For example, www.vault.com and www.aolsucks.com are gripe sites that accept such complaints. They are normally started by competitors, disgruntled employees, whistle-blowers, or activists. The motive ranges from sheer anger to venting frustration or getting revenge by spreading damaging information. Anyone with an ax to grind can smear the employer for the public to read. IT and company recruiters should review such sites and check what is posted about their company.

Another implication for management is the strategy for recruiting qualified technical personnel. The trend used to be offering significantly higher salaries than the industry average for that job title. However, most organizations today look for applicants with stability, loyalty, and commitment to the work ethic. They offer bonuses based on performance rather than raises, because they do not have to repeat them in later years.

Extranets are career enhancers for many IT professionals. Those who work on a successful extranet project usually end up having the biggest impact on their employer. In one case, an extranet designer deployed an extranet with the goal of driving down costs. The extranet met the goal by automating processes, improving overall efficiencies, and decentralizing functions for faster and better quality decision making. In addition to knowledge of the company's business processes, her skills included client/server technology, data communication and networking, and HTTP. She saw a way of securely linking customers, suppliers, and vendors to the corporate network. When the extranet was implemented, the company recognized the change in revenue, which translated into a hefty raise for the 23-year-old newcomer.

With change being accepted as a way of life, the human resources department has the option of changing the staff or changing the people already on staff. There is a new focus for building productive organizational culture, managing change and results, building intellectual capital, creating future leaders, managing organizational learning, and pushing for growth and innovation. As someone said, "If you are not the lead elephant, you'll never charge."

In terms of success in today's digital economy, the real asset is not money; money is just a commodity. Our real value is knowledge sharing and how knowledge is used to create value for the customer. More than half of doing business is on the soft side—the core personnel of the firm and the customer. Having employees be part of the organization and improving their skill sets adds value and contributes to the success of the firm.

Attracting qualified technical people is a challenge, but finding ways to retain them is a full-time job. In its annual job satisfaction survey, involving 575 respondents, *Computerworld* reported that overall job satisfaction had decreased in 1999. More than two-thirds of the IT workers said they were not working to their potential and more than 25 percent said they planned to look for a job elsewhere. With the economic downturn in 2001, the situation has not improved much. The ability of IT team members to work well together contributes to their retention and productivity. Recognition and flexible hours were found to be extremely important in technology-based work. Stress stemming from heavy workloads was cited as the main drawback.

Finally, the top challenge in managing knowledge through e-commerce is in understanding the customer. Most of the successful companies form a 360-degree customer view by gathering data from every possible source and analyzing it to shed light on the kinds of details that mark the way consumers shop and buy. Obviously, companies that better understand their customers' preferences can sell more. They know which customers are most important, most profitable, and most loyal.

SUMMARY ▪▪▪▪

- The Web is the fastest growing, most user friendly, and most commercially popular technology to date. Internet service providers link commercial traffic to its destination. This involves paying for transactions, managing networks, and linking consumers and businesses to the Internet. As the enabler of e-commerce, the Internet has many uses; it also has many limitations. It can be a tool for gathering opinions, exchanging knowledge, and trying out new ideas. It can also be a vehicle for inexpensive, easy mass distribution of information, products, and services. There are limitations as well: security and privacy issues, hackers, worms, Trojan horses, viruses, and customer relations problems.

- An intranet is a network connecting a set of company clients by using standard Internet protocols, especially TCP/IP and HTTP. Intranets can handle all kinds of communication with ease.
- An extranet or company Web site links two or more trading partners. When contemplating an extranet installation, there are five key factors to consider: identifying the user, listing the technology components, specifying the security requirements, setting up the administration, and understanding the usability.
- There are several benefits to an intranet: It links employees and managers around the clock; companies gain access to their primary resources; and it is the foundation for developing an enterprise-wide information system and a model for internal information management and collaborative computing. In addition, there are cost advantages and ease of access, plus portability and scalability.
- Electronic business connects critical business systems directly to key constituents—customers, vendors, and suppliers—via the Internet, intranets, and extranets. One of the main advantages of electronic commerce is knowledge sharing and the ability to swap information within organizations, between organizations, and between organizations and their suppliers and customers worldwide. The main limitations are concerns about knowledge protection and the integrity of the system that handles the knowledge.
- Groupware is essentially people using technology to communicate various types of information implicitly or explicitly.
- There are several groupware applications worth noting: e-mail, newsgroups and mailing lists, work-flow systems, calendaring and scheduling, video communication, and knowledge sharing.
- A value chain is a way of organizing the activities of a business so that each activity provides added value or productivity to the total operation of the business.
- Supply chain management (SCM) means having the right product, in the right place, at the right time, and in the right condition. The goal is to improve efficiency and profitability.
- CRM allows companies to establish multiple channels of communication with customers and supply chain partners and uses customer information stored in databases and knowledge bases to construct predictive models for customer purchase behaviors.
- The knowledge transfer and knowledge-sharing life cycle includes three major e-commerce applications: business-to-consumer (B2C), business-to-business (B2B), and business-within-business.
- An intranet wires the company for knowledge exchange and links a company's knowledge network electronically. E-mail replaces paper.

Terms to Know ▪ ▪ ▪ ▪

Architecture: The hierarchical physical structure of the Internet.

Browser: A program designed to search for and display Internet resources.

Business-to-business (B2B): The networking of businesses and their respective suppliers to exchange information, execute orders, and obtain supplies.

Business-to-consumer (B2C): The interface where consumers access a merchant's Web site for the purpose of buying merchandise or requesting service.

Electronic business (e-business): Connecting critical business systems and constituencies directly via the Internet, extranets, and intranets.

Electronic commerce (e-commerce): Ability to conduct business via electronic networks such as the Internet and the World Wide Web.

Extranet: Extended intranets that share information with business partners via the Internet.

Groupware: A way to use computer technology to enhance the group work process and decision making through support in the time and place dimensions; technology that facilitates the work of groups.

Internet: An infrastructure that links thousands of networks to one another; the information highway that makes the information stored on thousands of computers worldwide available to millions of people everywhere.

Intranet: A private network based on the same technology as the Internet, but restricted to an organization, its employees, and select customers.

Primary activity: The key functions of a business, including inputs, operations, outputs, marketing and sales, and service.

Supply chain management (SCM): Integrating the networking and communication infrastructure between businesses and their suppliers so that

there is the assurance of having the right product in the right place, at the right time, at the right price, and in the right condition.

Support activity: The activities of a business that support its primary activities.

Value chain: A way of organizing the activities of a business so that each activity provides added value or productivity to the total operation of the business.

Web farming: Systematically refining information resources on the Web for business intelligence capture.

World Wide Web: Also known as *WWW* or the *Web;* the whole constellation of resources that can be accessed by using tools such as HTTP; an organization of files designed around a group of servers on the Internet, programmed to handle requests from browser software that resides on users' PCs.

Test Your Understanding ■ ■ ■ ■

1. What is e-commerce? How does it relate to knowledge management, knowledge transfer, or knowledge sharing?
2. Contrast e-commerce with e-business.
3. Do you think the advantages of e-commerce outweigh the limitations? Explain.
4. What is groupware? How does it differ from e-mail or the telephone?
5. What guidelines are involved in controlling chat room sessions?
6. In what way is security a limitation of e-commerce?
7. Distinguish between:
   a. value chain and supply chain management
   b. intranet and extranet
   c. e-commerce and Internet
8. Cite the key benefits of an intranet. Is it beneficial in every type of knowledge exchange? Why or why not?
9. Briefly describe the uses of the Web.
10. What is the relationship between an intranet and groupware?

Knowledge Exercises ■ ■ ■ ■

1. How does the Web fit with knowledge sharing? Discuss.
2. "Technically, there is no difference between the Internet and an intranet, except that only select people are allowed to connect to the intranet." Evaluate this statement in the light of the way intranets are designed.
3. Do you think having an intranet environment is the best way to communicate within the firm? Assess alternative modes of communication, and report your findings in class.
4. If intranets offer so many benefits, why do you think some companies resist having them? Is it the size of the firm? The nature of the product? The caliber of personnel?
5. How does the Web affect our traditional sales channels, partners, and suppliers?
6. How can a company best prepare to use the Web as a channel for knowledge sharing?
7. Find a company that chooses not to use e-business in its business. What factors or problems does it consider in staying away from e-commerce?

8. Go on the Internet and find a tutorial on the World Wide Web. Review the tutorial and explain why you think it is easy (or difficult) as a learning tool.

9. Is the Internet different from other media for knowledge transfer?

10. Give an example of how e-business can help a firm reach its customers in a very low-cost fashion.

11. Access a chat room of your choice on the Internet, and report your experience.

12. Check the following Web sites to learn more about practices in electronic commerce:
    a. Let customers help themselves: www.got.com and www.edmunds.com
    b. Nurture customer relationships: www.amazon.com
    c. Target markets of one: www.wsi.com
    d. Build a community of interest: www.cnet.com

13. Discuss the value chain by visiting the FedEx Web site at www.fedex.com. How does it relate to knowledge transfer? Knowledge sharing?

14. Internet participation will alter the traditional form of knowledge sharing. Do you agree? Locate information on the Internet that might support or negate this statement.

15. Interview a businessperson or a technical person who is involved with e-business. What has been his or her experience in incorporating the technology into the company's day-to-day media for knowledge transfer? What performance criteria are used to judge the success (or failure) of e-business in the business? Write a short news release for the college or university newspaper to share your knowledge.

16. You are an Internet consultant to a company that wants you to do a 1-hour presentation to top management about the importance and potential of the Internet in the company's electronic knowledge creation and exchange. What information do you need before you prepare the presentation? Write a 3-page report detailing the content of the speech.

17. Visit a large firm on an intranet site. Identify the technology that operates the site.

18. Identify a large retailer in your area and determine whether it is ready to adopt an intranet and an extranet. Interview the head of the IT division and learn about the technology in use. Report your findings to class.

19. Design an intranet (on paper) for a small bank of 65 employees. Explain the details of the infrastructure to a local IT specialist. What did he or she find right and wrong with your design? Write a 4-page report summarizing your experience.

REFERENCES ▪ ▪ ▪ ▪

Anton, Kathleen. "Effective Intranet Publishing: Getting Critical Knowledge to Any Employee, Anywhere," *Intranet Design Magazine*, August 12, 2000, pp. 1–5.

Awad, E. M. *Electronic Commerce: From Vision to Fulfillment*. Upper Saddle River, NJ: Prentice Hall, 2002, p. 372.

Brandel, Mary. "Demise of the Skill Premium," *Computerworld*, July 31, 2000, p. 62.

Brinck, Tom. "Groupware: Introduction," www.usabilityfirst. com/groupware/intro.txl, 1998, Date accessed August 2002.

Brown, Eric, and Candler, James W. "The Elements of Intranet Style," *Intranet Design Magazine*, August 12, 2000, pp. 1–5.

Chadbrow, Eric. "Supply Chains Go Global," *InformationWeek*, April 3, 2000, p. 52.

Deck, Stewart. "The ABCs of CRM," *CIO.com*, February 23, 2001, pp. 1–4.

Deck, Stewart. *What Is CRM?* www.cio.com/research/ crm/edit/crmabc.html, Date accessed December 2002.

Dell, B. J. "The Net's Killer Application," *Knowledge Management*, December 2000, p. 34.

Downes, Larry and Mui, Chunka, *Unleashing the Killer App*. Harvard Business School Press, 1998.

Elbel, Fred. "General Guidelines and Tips (How to Get Rid of Junk Mail, Spam, and Telemarketers)," www.ecofuture.org/jmnews.html, Date accessed May 26, 2001, pp. 1–3.

Ewalt, David M. "Strong Growth Predicted for CRM Services Market," *InformationWeek.com*, April 9, 2002.

Field, Anne. "Group Think," www.inc.com/articles/hr/ manage_emp/productivity/1995-6.html, Date accessed October 15, 2002.

Joachim, David. "Best Awards Business on the Internet," *InternetWeek,* April 19, 1999, p. 47.

Koulopoulos, T. M., and Frappaolo, Carl. *Smart Things to Know About.* Milford, CN: Capstone Publishing, Inc., 1999, pp. 67–98.

Mandell, Janette. "E-Mail Etiquette," *Software Magazine*, July 1998, p. 20.

Porter, Michael. *Competitive Advantage.* Brookline, MA: The Free Press, 1985.

Spence, Rob. "Considering an Extranet? Consider This," *Extranet Strategist*, Spring 2000, p. 1.

Stein, Tom, and Sweat, Jeff. "Killer Supply Chains," *InformationWeek*, January 16, 2000, pp. 1–3.

Tao, Paul I. "Roadmap to a Successful Intranet," *Intranet Design Magazine*, August 12, 2000, pp. 1–13.

Violino, Bob. "The Leaders of E-Business," *InformationWeek*, December 13, 1999, p. 72.

Violino, Bob. "Kodak's Extranet Push," *Extranet Strategist*, Spring 2000, p. 17.

Zurell, Nancy. "Operational and Analytical Technologies for Optimizing Your CRM System," *DM Review*, February 2002, p. 82.

CHAPTER

Learning from Data

Contents

> *"Unlearning must often take place*
> *before learning can begin."*
> —GARY HAMMEL
> *COMPETING FOR THE FUTURE*

■■■■ In a Nutshell

Learning is an iterative process, where the final model results from a combination of prior knowledge and newly discovered information. The improved model gives a business an important competitive advantage. Learning tools are critical for developing a knowledge-management environment. The approach is to identify whether such tools are theory-driven or data-driven. Theory-driven learning tools require the user to specify a model based on prior knowledge and to test that model for validity. Data-driven learning tools automatically create the model based on patterns found in the data. However, the newly discovered model must be tested before it can be considered valid.

Inadequate or incomplete knowledge for decision making often plagues managers at all levels. In this chapter, we demonstrate how certain processes coordinate fragments of knowledge to enable learning organizations to function effectively. It is important to understand how certain mechanisms, procedures, and processes mobilize the knowledge needed to generate quality decision making. We start with the concept of learning, and learning from data, as one aspect of the learning process in an organization.

In this chapter, we cover three major techniques employed in data mining: neural networks, association rules, and classification trees. The data-mining process is covered in Chapter 12.

■■■■ The "Learning" Concept

The collaborative intelligence layer of KM infrastructure relies on several technologies, including artificial intelligence, expert systems, data warehousing, case-based reasoning (CBR), intelligent agents, and neural networks. Case-based Reasoning was covered earlier. Data warehousing is a unifier of databases and will be covered in Chapter 12. In this chapter, we focus on neural networks and their role in knowledge management systems.

Using "learning" technology tools provides a collaborative environment for humans to enhance the processes that are important to them, such as new product development or other tasks that are regularly performed across industries. The goal is to improve the quality of communication and decision making within the firm. Learning tools and procedures provide new knowledge about a product or service, or produce specific knowledge in the way of a solution, a remedy, or an outcome.

When testing learning tools, the competitive market is fertile ground for knowledge validation, which is a prerequisite for knowledge use. The unifying concept of learning is the specific mechanism that helps companies determine the kind of knowledge required for decision making.

In a knowledge automation environment, learning is a process of filtering ideas and transforming them into valid knowledge, having the force to guide decisions. Knowledge validation is a two-step process: model validation and consensual approval. **Model validation** involves testing the logical structure of a conceptual or operational model for internal consistency and testing the results for external consistency with the observable facts of the real world. **Consensual approval** means approval of a special reference group or the user of the results.

Learning from data and data patterns produces knowledge that can be used in business decision making. In general, the goals of the learning process are as follows:

- Discovering new patterns in the data,
- Verifying hypotheses formed from previously accumulated real-world knowledge, and
- Predicting future values, trends, and behavior.

Learning from data requires models that automatically improve with experience. There are two approaches to building learning models: top-down or bottom-up. In the top-down model, one starts with a hypothesis derived from observation, intuition, or prior knowledge. For example, a hypothesis could be, "Tourists visiting Egypt earn an annual income of at least $50,000." The hypothesis is then tested by querying the databases and performing some statistics. If the tests do not support the hypothesis, then the hypothesis must be revised and tested again. The strategy is straightforward: generate ideas, develop models, and evaluate them for validation.

In the bottom-up approach, there is no hypothesis to test. Learning techniques are used to discover new patterns by finding key relationships in the data. An example of pattern discovery is analysis of the shopping basket, whereby purchasing transactions are collected and stored in the database. The goal is to identify products that are purchased together. Extraction of unknown buying patterns can be used to understand the buying habits of customers and perform actions that may increase sales, such as adjusting inventions or modifying floor layouts. For example, in one study, patterns of sales data in a supermarket chain showed that married males between the age of 21 and 27 who went shopping for diapers also bought beer. As a result, the store began to stack beer cases next to the diaper shelf.

▪ ▪ ▪ ▪ Data Visualization

Before building effective models, we must become familiar with the stored data structure, relationships, and meaning. The first step is to gather a variety of numerical summaries and perform some descriptive statistics in order to get averages, standard deviations, and so forth. For example, we might find meaning in learning about the average sale of a leader product or the rate of the sale of one product, such as suits to the sale of another, such as neckties. Exploring the data means searching visually or numerically for groups or trends. This includes the following:

- Distribution of key attributes, for example, the target attribute of a prediction task,
- Identification of outlier points that are significantly outside the expected range of the results,
- Identification of initial hypotheses and predictive measures, and
- Extraction of interesting grouping data subsets for further investigation.

The problem in using visualization stems from the fact that models have many dimensions or variables, but we are restricted to showing these variables on a 2-dimensional computer screen or paper. This means visualization tools must use clever representations to collapse a number of dimensions into just two.

The role of data visualization in understanding phenomena and solving real problems is illustrated in the historical experience of Florence Nightingale and John Snow (see Box 11.1).

▪ ▪ ▪ ▪ Neural Networks As a Learning Model

As an evolving technology, neural networks have been modeled after the human brain's network. The technology attempts to simulate biological information processing via massive networks of processing elements called *neurons*. Neural nets and digital computers are not the same. Neural nets are neither digital nor serial; they are analog and parallel. They learn by example, not by programmed rules or instructions. Digital computers do not evolve as such.

LEARNING TO SAVE LIVES IN THE NINETEENTH CENTURY VIA DATA VISUALIZATION

FLORENCE NIGHTINGALE:

The Crimean War in March 1854 saw the allies (Britain, France, and Turkey) declaring war on the Russians. Many medical facilities were put up, and their conditions were criticized as being beyond appalling. The heroic Italian-born Florence Nightingale was asked to assist in Scutari as a nurse. Initially, the doctors did not ask for the help of nurses, but conditions forced things to change.

In 1858, Florence Nightingale returned to England and wrote a report addressed to the British government describing the unsanitary conditions and offering recommendations for improvement.

The report included a "rose-shaped," polar-area diagram, which compared the number of monthly deaths in two hospitals: one in Crimea, the other in Manchester, England. Each segment, which corresponds to a time period of 1 month, has an area proportional to the number of deaths. In the left-hand corner, the segments after the new sanitary improvements can be seen, and the diagram shows substantial decreases in the number of deaths. More importantly, the visualization of the data showed the medical body that the deaths were mainly due to hygiene problems in the medical facilities, not from wounds or general sickness.

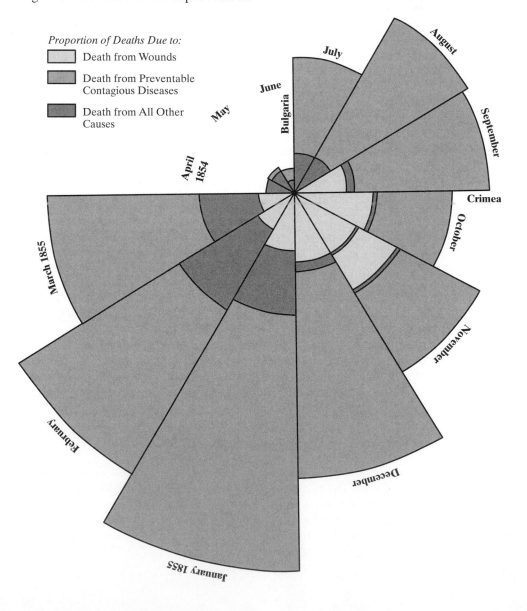

Proportion of Deaths Due to:

- Death from Wounds
- Death from Preventable Contagious Diseases
- Death from All Other Causes

Nightingale's use of visual statistics furthered the progress of the nursing profession as an integral and essential part of every medical facility.

JOHN SNOW:

In 1845, an outbreak of cholera hit the London/Soho area (see figure on facing page). The medical officer commissioned to investigate the disease was Dr. John Snow. He attempted to locate the source of the cholera by drawing the map shown here and pinpointing in black those areas with reported cholera deaths. He was able to locate a large cluster of deaths (over 500 in 11 days) around a water pump on Broad Street. The pumps were immediately disabled, and the number of deaths decreased substantially. Surprisingly, John Snow also noted that workers at a nearby brewery on the same street were relatively unaffected by cholera. This was due to the workers' drinking beer instead of water.

Snow's use of spatial analysis was revolutionary at the time. Today, spatial mapping is used in medical geography to locate, corner, and identify deaths related to all forms of diseases.

SOURCES: Tobler, W. "John Snow's Original 1854 Map on the Location of 578 Deaths from Cholera," www.ncgia.ucsb.edu/pubs/snow/snow.html, Date Accessed November 2002; Evans, D. H. "The Story of Florence Nightingale," www.florence-nightingale.co.uk/biography.htm, 1933, Date accessed December 2002.

One of the areas where neural nets make a definite contribution to decision making is in knowledge automation systems. Neural nets show superior performance over that of human experts for eliciting functional relationships between input and output values. In a comparison of the two technologies, neural nets prove to be better at learning by example rather than by rules, and they continue to learn as the problem environment changes. This capability makes them well suited to deal with unstructured problems and inconsistent information. Neural nets can also handle fuzzy data without losing accuracy. Knowledge automation systems largely depend on complete data before they offer a final solution. In summary, knowledge automation systems offer structure, explanatory capability, and validity, whereas neural nets offer the creative part of problem-solving. They learn from experience in much the same way that a human expert develops decision-making skills.

THE BASICS

The human brain consists of 10 billion or so neurons; each neuron interacts directly with 1,000 to 10,000 other neurons. A neuron fires or does not fire. The rate of firing determines the magnitude of information. When the brain accepts inputs, it generally responds to them. The responses are a combination of learning and what has been genetically programmed over time.

A **neural network (NN)** is an information system modeled after the human brain's network of electronically interconnected basic processing elements called neurons. It is viewed as a self-programming system based on its inputs and outputs. Each neuron has a **transfer function** that computes the output signal from the input signal. A typical neuron building block, or **node**, is shown in Figure 11.1. The neuron evaluates the **inputs**, determines their strengths or **weights**, "sums," the combined inputs, and compares the total to a **threshold** (transfer function) **level**. The threshold could be something as simple as zero or could mirror the input within a given range (0–1). If the sum is greater than the threshold, the neuron fires. That is, it sends **output** from that particular neuron. Otherwise, it generates no signal.

Interconnecting, or combining neurons with other neurons, forms a layer of nodes or a neural network. The interconnection is analogous to the synapse-neuron junction in a biological network.

▪ ▪ ▪ ▪ ▪ ▪ ▪ **FIGURE 11.1:** A Single Node with Weighted Inputs and Summation Function

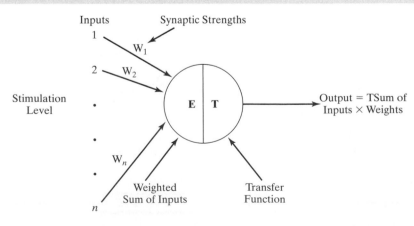

In a real-world problem, inputs represent variables, and the connecting weights are relationships between variables. Once input values are received by a trained network, the output value of each unit is computed by the output function. In Figure 11.2, the neural network model predicts a firm's status; solvent versus bankrupt. Five input variables are fed into the system with two possible outcomes as outputs. The hidden units adjust the weights to the right threshold and are used to support the transformation from input to output.

SUPERVISED AND UNSUPERVISED LEARNING

The most interesting feature of artificial neural networks is their ability to learn. Learning may be supervised or unsupervised. In **supervised learning**, the neural network needs a teacher, with a **training set** of examples of input and output. Each element in a training set is paired with an acceptable response. That is, the actual output of a neural network is compared to the desired output. The network makes successive passes through the examples, and the weights adjust toward the goal state. When the weights represent the passes without error, the network has learned to associate a set of input patterns with a specific output. This is more like learning by reinforcement.

In **unsupervised** (also called *self-supervised*) **learning**, no external factors influence the adjustment of the input's weights. The neural network has no advanced indication of correct or incorrect answers. It adjusts solely through direct confrontation with new experiences. This process is referred to as *self-organization*.

▪ ▪ ▪ ▪ ▪ ▪ ▪ **FIGURE 11.2:**   Neural Network Model Predicting a Firm's Bankruptcy

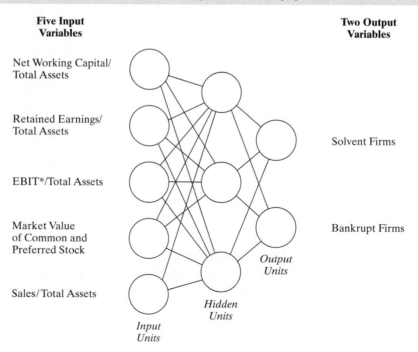

* Earnings Before Interest and Taxes

SOURCE: Awad, E. M. *Building Expert Systems*. Minneapolis, MN: West Publishing, 1996, p. 437.

BUSINESS APPLICATIONS

Neural networks are best applied in situations having a need for pattern recognition, where data are dynamic. Even though this technology has been applied in virtually every industry, the business sector has experienced significant successes with neural networks. Financial institutions, for example, are using neural networks to simulate cash management, asset and personnel risk management, and capital investments. In the capital investment arena, neural networks are used to simulate the reaction of investors to changes in organizational concerns such as capital structure, dividend policy, and reported earnings.

The following applications demonstrate neural networks' contributions to solving business problems in various industries.

Risk Management

A major New York bank uses a neural network to appraise commercial loan applications. The network was trained on thousands of applications, half of which were approved and the other half rejected by the bank's loan officers. From this experience, the neural net learned to pick risks that constitute a bad loan. It identifies loan applicants who are likely to default on their payments.

CitiBank London

CitiBank London needed to develop a successful system to forecast the fluctuations of the foreign exchange market. They needed a very complex nonlinear system suitable for pattern recognition and neural networks.

FX trader is a hybrid system that combines the strong searching ability of genetic algorithms with the detailed pattern recognition abilities of neural nets. Genetic algorithms (GA) were used to identify combinations of technical indicators that were most accurate at forecasting FX exchange rate changes by screening and selecting those that offered the most forecasting power. The values produced by these combinations of indicators were then used as inputs to a neural network. Following this, the system advised on a buy or sell decision. The system was trained for the exchange rates of the U.S. dollar against the Swiss franc and the Japanese yen, using data from the first 6 months of 1990. Then it was tested over an 8- to 11-week period.

The results revealed a return on capital of about 20 percent, an attractive record, given that the best human traders could make 15 percent per year. Moreover, the system correctly forecasted the market direction 57 percent of the time, far surpassing the best human traders. Citibank plans to develop this system for other markets, including U.S. interest rate markets and the Nikkei Index. It also hopes to license the forecasting technology to fund managers and preferred customers.

Fidelity Investment

Fidelity Investment needed both to save time and to maintain high standards in the screening of stocks for its portfolio. A universe of 2000 stocks was scanned to select about 50 stocks for its portfolios. The scan was based on objective criteria and data about the studied companies, such as stock prices, dividends, historical earnings, and balance sheet information. This data was fed to the neural network, which was able to issue a signal indicating which stock was suitable for further consideration.

The neural network system is simple and could easily be transferred to other populations of stocks given the data and the skills indicated. The performance of the mutual fund is quite impressive. The portfolio has five stars, and only 18 funds in the United States have that number of stars. Since December 1988, the stock market has gone up 71 percent, while the Fidelity Funds portfolio has gone up 99.8 percent and has out-performed the market every year since then.

Mortgage Appraisals

One of the most promising applications is a neural network system called AREAS, which reviews mortgage appraisals. The program uses the data in the mortgage loan application with a sophisticated statistical model of real estate valuations for the immediate neighborhood, the city, and the country where the property is located. Then, the system comes up with a valuation for the property and a risk analysis for the loan. For each valuation, the cost has been less than one-half of the manual method, which was also time-consuming and subject to various errors.

Innumerable neural network applications pop up each year. In business, applications identify qualified candidates for specific positions, optimize airline seating, and determine fee schedules. In finance, applications identifying forgeries, interpreting handwritten forms, and assessing credit risks have already justified the necessary investment for these neural networks. In manufacturing, neural network applications control quality and production line processes, select parts for an assembly line, and perform quality inspection of finished products.

A common thread running through these applications is pattern recognition. The neural network looks for a pattern in a set of cases, classifies and evaluates patterns, and reconstructs the correct pattern with a high degree of accuracy. This technology offers businesses a chance to assist decision makers in the kind of work that was once relegated to human perception and judgment.

Perhaps the best a neural network can do is to advise rather than replace humans in problem-solving. The fact that humans can still veto a neural network's decisions attests to the higher-level of learning capacity and intelligence of humans.

RELATIVE FIT WITH KNOWLEDGE MANAGEMENT

There are several characteristics of neural networks that fit in a knowledge management system. The main characteristics are as follows:

- *A neural net exhibits high accuracy and response speed.* After a period of training, a neural net can be quite accurate, although both accuracy and response speed tend to degrade with increased complexity of the problem being solved.
- *High input preprocessed data is often required for building a neural net.* Unfortunately, this is what requires so much data, although the system has high tolerance for "bad" data and usually ends up with accurate solutions.
- *A neural net must start all over with every new application.* It has to be retrained for each specific problem undergoing analysis. A critical condition for using neural nets in KM is the level of knowledge needed to apply the technology. Some technology requires seasoned knowledge from the user, while others assume a novice user with no specific knowledge to contribute at any time. Another factor is the time dimension expected before receiving a satisfactory solution from the KM technology. For example, case-based reasoning requires a high level of user knowledge, but the solution can be arrived at in a short time period. In contrast, expert and rule-based systems require a low level of user knowledge, but it takes much longer to arrive at a solution.

▪▪▪▪ Association Rules

Another knowledge-based tool is the association rule technique, which generates a set of rules to help understand relationships that may exist in data. The main types of associations are as follows:

- *Boolean rule:* If a rule consists of examining the presence or the absence of items, it is a Boolean rule. For example, if a customer buys a PC and a 17-inch monitor, then he will buy a printer. The presence of items (computer and 17-inch monitor) implies the presence of the printer on the customer's buying list.
- *Quantitative rule:* In this rule, instead of considering the presence or absence of items, we consider the quantitative values of items. For example, if a customer earns between $30,000 and $50,000 and owns an apartment worth between $250,000 and $500,000, he will buy a 4-door automobile.
- *Multidimensional rule:* This rule refers to several dimensions. For example, if a customer buys a PC, then he will buy a browser. This rule is a single dimensional rule, because it refers to a single attribute, that of buying. If a customer lives in a big city and earns more than $35,000, then he will buy a cellular phone. This rule involves three attributes: living, earning, and buying. Therefore, it is a multi-dimensional rule.
- *Multilevel association rule:* A transaction can refer to items with various levels of abstraction.

For example,

If a customer earns $50,000, he will buy a laptop.
If a customer earns $50,000, he will buy a computer.

These rules refer to different levels of abstraction. The first one is at the lower level of abstraction, because buying a laptop also means buying a computer, and buying a computer could also mean buying a laptop or PC, see Figure 11.3.

An association rule assumes a larger number of items, such as computers, monitors, and printers, appearing together in a buying list or in a market basket. This concept could be extended to text analysis. In this context, a market basket is the sentence, and the items are the words making up the sentence. Similarly, one can consider the document as the basket and the sentences forming the document as the items.

▪ ▪ ▪ ▪ ▪ ▪ ▪ **FIGURE 11.3:** Items Categorized According to Various Levels of Abstraction

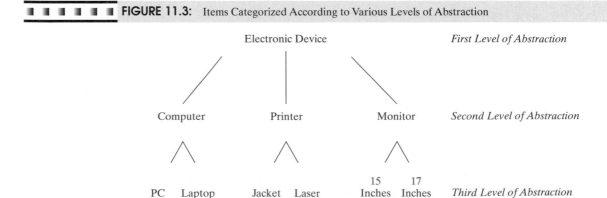

Association rules are statements of the form: When a customer buys a computer, in 70 percent of the cases, he or she will also buy a printer. This happens in 14 percent of all purchases. This statement shows an association rule consisting of four elements:

Rule body: When a customer buys a computer
A confidence level: In 70 percent of the cases
A rule head: He will buy a printer.
A support: It happens in 14 percent of all purchases.

The rule body is the condition of the rule, and the rule head is the result.

Other terminologies exist to define a rule. The left-hand side (antecedent) may be used to replace the rule body. The right-hand side (consequent) may be used to replace the rule head. The confidence level is the ratio of the total number of transactions, with the items of the rule body, to the number of transactions, with the items of the rule body, plus the items in the result.

Consider the previous rule: A confidence level of 70 percent means that when buying a computer occurs in a transaction, there is a 70 percent chance that the item, "printer," occurs at the same time. More formally, let us consider the rule: If A and B, then C. If this rule has a confidence level of 30 percent, it means that when A and B occur in a transaction, there is a chance (likelihood) of 0.3 that C occurs in the same transaction.

The second measure of a rule is called *support*. The first rule states that it has a support of 14 percent. This measures how often items in the rule body occur together as a percentage of the total transactions.

Here is another example:

11,000 transactions
  2,000 transactions contain a PC
    500 transactions contain a laptop
  1,500 transactions contain a printer
  1,000 transactions contain a PC and a printer
    150 transactions contain a laptop and a printer

PCs and printers appear together in 1,000 transactions out of 11,000. The support of the rule, "When a customer buys a PC, he will buy also a printer," is equal to 1,000/11,000 = 0.09. Therefore, 9 percent is the support of this rule. The confidence of this rule is 2,000/1,000 or 50 percent. It is equal to the number of transactions containing PCs and printers divided by the number of transactions containing PCs. To find an association rule linking computer rules to printer rules, we can say:

"A customer buying a computer in 57 percent of the cases will buy a printer. It happens in 1.5 percent of all the purchases."

Here, we have considered a new type of item—namely, computers with a higher level of abstraction than PCs and laptops.

The confidence is calculated as follows:

$$\frac{\text{Number of transactions containing computers (PCs or laptops) and printers}}{\text{Number of transactions containing computers}} =$$

$$\frac{1,000\ +\ 150}{2,000\ +\ 500} = 0.575$$

The support is calculated as follows:

$$\frac{\text{Number of transactions containing a computer and a printer}}{\text{Total number of transactions}} = \frac{1,150}{11,000} = 0.115$$

Sometimes the rules are stated in a different way, for example, when people buy PCs, they also buy a printer half of the time. The confidence level is computed as follows: 1,100/2,000 = 0.5; the support is equal to 1,100/11,000 = 0.09.

MARKET BASKET ANALYSIS: PETCO

Founded in 1965 and incorporated in the state of Delaware, PETCO is a leading specialty retailer of premium pet food and supply items. PETCO stores carry more than 11,000 items, including premium foods, vitamins, toys, and other supplies for dogs, cats, birds, fish, rabbits, reptiles, and other small companion animals. PETCO also provides veterinary services, obedience training, and grooming services.

The Challenge

PETCO needed a way to make it possible for them to obtain company information in a quick and accurate manner. They needed a store analysis to get an in-depth look at the sales and margins section, and the base stores' performance for the last 2-year period. They also wanted to have access to inventory levels at all times, in order to accommodate customers with the appropriate products and services. Identification of store uniqueness was needed to allow for pricing and store assortment for proper product placement and sale. A suitable solution needed to be put into practice in order to properly target their market and track down customers to evaluate their specific buying habits. Promotional, product, and vendor divisions also needed to be analyzed to gain full interpretation of the business.

The Solution

Systech delivered an enterprise business intelligence solution, which aided ad hoc detail merchandising to allow for reporting of data based on specific merchandising units and also aided in overall store analysis across all reporting components. The primary platform and framework built were necessary for the data warehouse to function completely.

Another important component was the development of the market basket analysis. PETCO wanted to be able to totally understand their customers' buying habits and to be able to cross-sell and up-sell to their customers. In order for the implementation of the business intelligence solution to be successful, Systech had to carefully craft seven crucial stages and understand each one to the fullest extent, to give PETCO the solution they needed.

Results

Because of the business intelligence solution, PETCO now has the ability to accomplish store and merchandising analysis. This results in better tracking of products and services. The evaluation of vendor performances can also be obtained with the new solution. This helps to analyze which vendors give better and faster service, allowing for PETCO to have all the necessary products in stock to provide better customer service. Promotional analysis is now effectively generated, which helps PETCO enhance their sales and improve their margins. Systech delivered an enterprise solution, which aided ad hoc detail merchandising. This is the reporting of data based on specific merchandising units. Inventory reports drawn out by the solution are efficiently used to address key issues, such as the fill ratio. This effectively shows the quantity sold in a particular store to quantity received from the distribution center. Some of the key reports, which are done by executives and are available through the data warehouse, are active store comparisons, a store Merchandising Performance Report, (MPR), daily sales (showing the distribution of sales for a particular store based on each sku, subclass, or department by month, week, or day), the daily margin, and department sales comparisons. A market basket analysis was also developed to fully understand customer-buying habits and to allow for cross-sell and up-sell. Targeted marketing helped PETCO properly market their products to specific customers to give them the full customer experience. Systech's implementation of the business intelligence solution will aid PETCO in delivering better analysis across all reporting components (Systech 2002).

▪ ▪ ▪ ▪ Classification Trees

Classification trees are powerful and popular tools for classification and prediction. The attractiveness of the classification trees method is basically due to the fact that, in contrast to NN, classification trees represent tools. Rules can be explained so human beings can understand them or they can be created in a database access language like SQL, so that records falling into a certain category can be retrieved easily.

This point is crucial for situations where interaction is involved. For example, it is equally important for the loan officer and the bank customer to understand the reason behind denying a credit application. For the banker, it is important to find a reasonable argument, even if it is generated by a computer, to justify the decision.

DEFINITION

The concept of "tree" is derived from graph theory. A *tree* is a network of nodes connected by areas, sometimes called *branches,* so that there are no loops in the networks. In general, there is a *root node* that is considered to be the starting node of the tree. The ending nodes of the tree are called the *leaf nodes.* The root and leaf nodes are separated by a certain number of intermediate node organizations in layers, sometimes called *levels.* Figure 11.4 shows a tree with two intermediate levels.

▪ ▪ ▪ ▪ ▪ ▪ ▪ **FIGURE 11.4:**   A Binary Tree with Two Levels

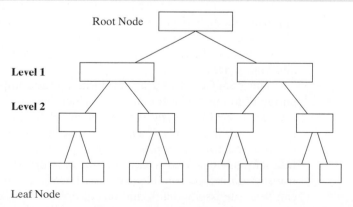

When two nodes branch out from each node, this tree is called a *binary tree*. Adding concepts to the nodes and to the branches transforms the tree from a theoretical network to a decision-learning tool. The decision tree is a tree where nodes represent actions and areas represent events that have a certain probability to occur.

DECISION FOR GRANTING A LOAN

Let us consider the following rule:

> If the savings account > $\$\alpha$ and the assets owned > $\$\beta$, then grant the loan; otherwise, do not grant the loan.

The problem lies in how to reach such a rule, in other words, how to construct such a tree. The bank has to start by collecting data about previous customers, relying on its historical data stored in a customer database. In the historical database, the bank has the needed information about previous customers both who failed to honor their debt and those who were able to honor their debt.

In such a simple case, the two classes of customers are clearly separated. In addition to the rule governing the classification, it is easy to induce what would happen in more complex situations; a systematic technique for tree construction is needed.

TREE CONSTRUCTION

Many elements should be considered when constructing a classification tree. At each level, nodes will split data into groups until they reach the ending node, where the classes are identified. The first question is how to assign attributes to nodes. More specifically, if we consider the root node, one of the attributes has to be assigned to this node. For example, we added the attribute, "savings account," to the root node in the bank loan cases. We could have selected the attribute, "assets owned," for that node. Assigning an attribute to a node that will split the data is the first task to be achieved by classification tree algorithms. The second task is to decide when a classification tree is complete. The third task is to assign classes to the ending nodes. Finally, the fourth task is to convert the classification tree into a set of rules.

▪▪▪▪ Implications for Knowledge Management

Neural networks represent a wide range of applications in knowledge management, knowledge automation systems, and business in general. They enter as stand-alone applications or they can be integrated with knowledge automation systems. Despite obvious successes, they are not a cure-all. They involve several considerations worth discussing: cost/benefit analysis, the nature of neural learning and artificial intelligence, and maintenance.

The benefits of neural networks include improving speed, quality, and "good enough" judgment in the areas in which human judgment might deteriorate due to fatigue, lack of motivation, or problems of recall. The benefits are both tangible and intangible. For example, if a neural network designed to evaluate paint quality and finish of a new car is to replace the human expert inspector, it will likely return tangible financial savings. Likewise, a neural network that "decides" whether a credit card transaction is a reasonable purchase based on the credit card holder's buying habits can save the issuing bank millions of dollars each year by detecting fraud. Of course, intangible benefits include better corporate image when quality and reliability of the product resulting from a neural network contribute to customer satisfaction. Indirectly, it can also contribute to image building in the long run.

The other side is the cost factor. The question is how much is a corporation willing to spend to gear up the technology? Tangible costs involve user training, hardware-software, backup, support, and maintenance. Intangible costs are user resistance and the time it takes to sell change. This is especially if neural networks are trained as artificial learners trying to compete with long-term specialists or experts in the area covered by the neural network. Management must be prepared for these problems and take the appropriate steps to alleviate them.

Another issue relates to the concept of neural networks as adaptive learning systems. Given the iterative process of training a neural network, is artificial learning a "good enough" replacement for humans who learn "on the fly" by using intelligence and common sense? Human decision making and problem-solving are also based on their perceptions, attitudes, and beliefs in addition to methodology, use of tools, and the following of procedures. Human cognitions are modified by experience, which contributes to a maturation that artificial learning lacks.

Perhaps the best function a neural network can serve is to advise, rather than replace, humans in problem-solving. The fact that humans can still veto a neural network's decisions attests to the higher-level of learning capacity and intelligence of humans.

Finally, organizations must address the issue of maintenance. For a neural network to stay up to date in a changing environment, it has to be retrained, which means modifications in the training set, retraining, and ongoing evaluation of the neural network. A firm that relies heavily on applications supported by this technology would need to consider maintenance and enhancement as part of the total commitment to quality assurance.

The level and frequency of maintenance often reflect the adequacy of the initial design of the neural network. Like conventional systems, a poorly thought-out problem definition or scope requires greater and more frequent changes in the system than a well-designed system. This suggests that, for a neural network to succeed, proper attention should be given to the early phases of the development life cycle. This includes problem definition, problem justification, and gathering the right training data for the job. Effective management of the front end of the development life cycle could minimize unnecessary maintenance.

SUMMARY   ▪ ▪ ▪ ▪

- Learning tools are divided into two groups: theory-driven and data-driven. Theory-driven learning, often called *hypothesis testing,* attempts to substantiate or disprove preconceived ideas. Data-driven learning tools automatically create the model based on patterns found in the data.
- There are several types of associations:
  - *Boolean rule.* If the rule considered consists of examining the presence or the absence of items, it is a Boolean rule.
  - *Quantitative rule.* In these rules, instead of considering the presence or absence of items, we consider the quantitative values of items.
  - *Multidimensional rule.* These are rules referring to several dimensions.
  - *Multilevel association rule.* A transaction can refer to items with various levels of abstraction.

- A neural network is a knowledge-based tool of electronically interconnected basic processing elements called *neurons*. Neural networks are ideal for solving cumbersome problems that traditional information systems have difficulty tracking, but they are terrible at problems that computers can do well.
- Neural networks can be contrasted with knowledge automation systems as follows:
  - Knowledge automation systems learn by rules, and neural nets learn by example.
  - Knowledge automation systems are sequential in nature and explain their decisions, where neural nets do not have an explanatory facility.
  - Neural nets continue learning as the problem environment changes, and knowledge automation systems depend on complete data before offering a final solution.
  - A neural network is more effective than knowledge automation systems at developing a knowledge base with experimental data.
- A neural network consists of neurons, connected by axons that receive inputs from other neurons. Communication between neurons is carried out by these input-output pathways. A neuron evaluates the inputs, determines their weights, sums the weighted input, and compares the total to a threshold. If the sum is greater than the threshold, the neuron fires. Otherwise, it generates no signal.
- Learning occurs when the network changes weights and modifies its activity in response to its inputs. Making weight adjustments by backing up from the output is called *back propagation*. Learning may be supervised or unsupervised.
- Classification trees are powerful and popular tools for classification and prediction. The attractiveness of the classification trees method is basically due to the fact that in contrast to NN, classification trees represent tools.
- Many elements should be considered when constructing a classification tree. At each level, nodes will split data into groups until the ending node is reached, where classes are identified.

TERMS TO KNOW ▪▪▪▪

Antecedent: When an association between two variables is defined, the first item (or left-hand side) is called the antecedent.

Associations: An association algorithm creates rules that describe how often events have occurred together. For example, "When prospectors buy picks, they also buy shovels 14 percent of the time." Such relationships are typically expressed with a confidence interval.

Classification tree: A decision tree that places categorical variables into classes.

Confidence: Confidence of rule, "B given A," is a measure of how much more likely it is that B occurs when A has occurred. A 95 percent confidence interval for the mean has a probability of .95 of covering the true value of the mean.

Consequent: When an association between two variables is defined, the second item (or right-hand side) is called the consequent.

Input: Stimulation level in a neural network.

Neural network: A knowledge-based technology modeled after the human brain's network of electrically interconnected processing elements called neurons; a self-programming system that creates a model based on its inputs and outputs.

Supervised learning: A learning strategy that specifies the correct output for a certain input.

Support: The measure of how often the collection of items in an association occurs together as a percentage of all the transactions. For example, "In 2 percent of the purchases at the hardware store, both a pick and a shovel were bought."

Transfer function: A function that transforms the neuron input into an output value.

Unsupervised learning: A learning strategy in which the correct output is not specified.

Weight: An adjustable value associated with a connection between neurons or nodes in a network.

TEST YOUR UNDERSTANDING ▪▪▪▪

1. Define a neural network in your own words. What does the technology attempt to do?
2. "The interesting aspect of a neural net is its known contributions in solving cumbersome problems that traditional computers have found difficult to track." Do you agree? Why or why not?
3. Explain how a neural network functions. Give an example of your own.
4. In your opinion, how severe are the limitations of a neural network?
5. How are neural networks different from knowledge automation systems?
6. Explain in some detail how neural networks learn.
7. How are inputs and outputs used to contribute to a solution?

KNOWLEDGE EXERCISES ▪▪▪▪

1. Search on the Internet or in related literature and write an essay detailing a neural network application in business. What did you learn from this exercise?
2. Suppose you have a small kiosk database of purchased items.
   The available food items in the kiosk are as follows:
   - Coca-Cola
   - Pepsi-Cola
   - Sprite
   - Budweiser beer
   - Guinness beer
   - Estrella chips
   - Pringles chips
   - Taffel chips

   The database contains the following purchase transactions:

Item	*Items Bought*
1	Coca-Cola, Budweiser beer, Pringles chips
2	Coca-Cola, Taffel chips
3	Budweiser beer, Pringles chips
4	Pepsi-Cola, Budweiser beer, Guinness beer, Estrella chips
5	Sprite, Estrella chips
6	Pepsi-Cola, Budweiser beer, Estrella chips

Item	*Items Bought*
7	Sprite
8	Budweiser beer, Guinness beer, Estrella chips
9	Pepsi-Cola, Estrella chips
10	Coca-Cola, Pringles chips

   What kind of rules do you get with a confidence threshold of 0.0 and a support threshold of 0.2?
   Create a hierarchy for the food items in the kiosk, and try to determine if you could get more meaningful information by using multilevel association rules. Is it possible to set different support thresholds on different hierarchy levels?
   Source: Han and Kamber 2000
3. Using a realistic example, discuss in detail how neural networks can be used to solve real-life problems.

4. An insurance company is planning to launch the sale of a newly developed insurance product. As a promotional exercise, the company wishes to identify several potential customers from the local area and send them details of this new product, together with special discount offers. In the past, the company has conducted similar promotional exercises, and the results were not good. The promotion cost was high due to an extremely low response rate. Very few people who responded to the promotions actually purchased the products. This time, the company aims to reduce promotion cost and have an increase in response rate. The company possesses about 2,000 historical records on the previous promotions. The data set stores details of the prospective customers, such as age groups, income bands, occupations, and so forth. The records can be categorized into "response with purchase," "response without purchase," or "no response."

   If the company wants to use a classification technique to identify the people who are likely to purchase the new product, describe the life cycle of such a data-mining project.

5. Review the neural network literature and cite one application of supervised learning and another of self-supervised learning. What do you conclude is the difference between the two forms of learning?

6. Identify whether each of the following applications is a candidate for knowledge automation or a neural network:
   a. Prediction of weather conditions,
   b. Diagnosis of a diabetic condition by a specialist,
   c. Verification of check signature, and
   d. Recognition of characters on an invoice.

7. You have a set of six alphabetic characters: A, S, T, U, T, and E. Like a Scrabble game, your job is to generate as many words as possible from these characters. If you were to do it manually, you would have to think of a word, verify it with the dictionary, and move on to the next word. How would a conventional computer go through the same process? Is this kind of job a candidate for neural network?

8. If the company chooses to use the decision tree induction technique to build a classification model, describe the main activities that need to be performed during the project development.

REFERENCES ▪▪▪▪

Awad, E. M. *Building Expert Systems*. Minneapolis, MN: West Publishing, 1996, p. 437.

Cherkassky, Vladimir, and Mulier, Filip. *Learning from Data: Concepts, Theory and Methods*. New York: John Wiley & Sons, Inc., 1998.

Han, J., and Kamber, M. *Data Mining: Concepts and Techniques*, section 6.3. New York: Morgan Kaufmann Publishers, 2000.

Michalski, Ryszard S., Bratko, Ivan, and Kubat, Miroslav. *Machine Learning and Data Mining: Methods and Applications*. New York: John Wiley & Sons, Inc., 1998.

Mitchell, Tom M. *Machine Learning*. New York: McGraw Hill, Inc., 1997.

Smith, Reid G., and Farquhar, Adam. "The Road Ahead for Knowledge Management: An AI Perspective," *AI Magazine*, vol. 21, no. 4, Winter 2000, pp. 17–40.

Systech, PETCO case study, www.systechusa.com/clients/pop_pet.htm, Date accessed December 2002.

WEB SITES ▪▪▪▪

www.dsi.unifi.it/neural   This site covers recent topics in neural networks and machine learning.

www.inns.org/nn.html   *Neural Networks* is an international journal that serves as a central, interdisciplinary publication. Its editors represent a range of fields including psychology, neurobiology, mathematics, physics, computer science, and engineering.

www.ncaf.co.uk   The Natural Computing Applications Forum runs meetings (with attendees from industry, commerce, and academia) on applications of neural networks.

www.ewh.ieee.org/tc/nnc/index.html   The IEEE Neural Networks Society advances and coordinates work in neural networks. It is exclusively scientific, literary, and educational in character.

www.ime.usp.br/~cesar/revision/neural.htm   This source covers a series of issues related to vision, including computer vision, image processing, computer graphics, neuroscience, artificial intelligence, and many other areas.

www1.ics.uci.edu/~mlearn/MLRepository.html   This is a repository of databases, domain theories, and data generators that are used by the machine learning community for the empirical analysis of machine learning algorithms.

CHAPTER 12

Data Mining—
Knowing the
Unknown

Contents

When knowledge stops evolving,
it turns into opinion or dogma.
—THOMAS DAVENPORT
AND LAURENCE PRUSAK

▪▪▪▪ In a Nutshell

In the previous chapters, we discussed knowledge management and building a KM system from capturing tacit knowledge to codifying, testing, transferring, and sharing it. One important issue discussed in Chapter 4 was how to create knowledge. Our perspective is to look at explicit and tacit knowledge as the two primary types of knowledge. Tacit knowledge is created and captured through teamwork and from one's experience. Explicit knowledge is knowledge codified in books, documents, reports, and the like.

Data mining (DM) is becoming a fundamental component of the global business infrastructure that assists firms in the decision-making process and helps them capture the multifaceted aspects of the new economy. In this chapter, we consider data as a source of undiscovered knowledge. We discuss the process of extracting knowledge from data and information stored in databases, data warehouses, and other repositories. This process is called *data mining*. We also discuss the role of DM in the decision-making process.

The challenge for KM is to find a way to exploit huge amounts of transactional data that might add value and intelligence to decision making and operational business processes. It is estimated that the amount of information in the world doubles every 20 months. Clearly, little can be done to take advantage of this flood of raw data, unless an automated approach is elaborated. This is where DM provides a viable source of knowledge discovery and an efficient way to deliver new added value for business. From this perspective, DM is an essential component of the corporate knowledge architecture.

▪▪▪▪ What Is Data Mining?

Gaining insight to improve business functions remains a major concern of any manager or decision maker. The past 2 decades have seen a wide diffusion of information technologies in all business activities. The intensive use of new electronic devices such as point of sale, remote-sensing devices, ATMs (automated teller machines), and the Internet has contributed to the explosion of available data. It is similar to the gold rush: A new source of wealth was available to all kinds of miners. Suddenly, managers and decision makers became conscious of this wealth of data. It was natural to think about the best way to benefit from it. This is where data mining enters (see Box 12.1).

From a business point of view, DM has gained appeal; as a field, it has yet to reach maturity. The many definitions of data mining show lack of consensus among the

▪▪▪▪▪▪   BOX 12.1   ▪▪▪▪▪▪

SAMPLE USES OF DATA MINING

DATA MINING IN THE FEDERAL AGENCIES

From predicting how many Marines will leave the corps to rooting out fraudulent health-care bills for the Health Care Financing Administration, data mining is becoming a popular technological tool for agency managers trying to make sense and better use of mounds of government data. Data mining is accomplished with commercial off-the-shelf software applications that use sophisticated statistical analysis and advanced modeling to turn volumes of data into usable information. By uncovering subtle trends or patterns in data, the application can enable users to draw conclusions or make predictions. "Data mining is getting the 'aha' out of data," says Adam Crafton, a data-mining manager for IBM's public-sector operations in Bethesda, Maryland.

Commercial retailers first developed data-mining software nearly 30 years ago to track consumer buying habits. By combining those early models with advances in artificial intelligence over the past decade, data-mining firms have moved beyond helping retailers to assisting many businesses. Data mining's uses now range from predicting production breakdowns for large manufacturers to helping financial institutions uncover patterns of money laundering.

Many agencies are already using data mining to make better management decisions and improve services. The Justice Department has used it to find crime patterns so it can focus its money and resources on the most pressing issues. The Veterans Affairs Department has used it to predict demographic changes among its 3.6 million patients so it can prepare more accurate budgets. The Internal Revenue Service uses the technology at its customer service center to track calls in order to pinpoint the most common customer needs. The Federal Aviation Administration uses it to scour plane crash data to find common causes so future failures can be avoided.

MAKING PREDICTIONS

Data mining is more than slicing and dicing data; it is doing predictive work as well. The Marine Corps is using data mining to predict which types of officers and enlisted members will stay in the corps and which will bail out. "We want to use historical data to predict our loss rates in specific areas," says Major Joe Van Steenbergen, a manpower manager for the Marine Corps. By mining a data warehouse containing career and biographical information for every officer and enlisted member in the past decade, the Marine Corps expects to find answers to questions such as "Are married or single Marines more or less likely to leave the service?" "Are members in high-skill career fields like information technology more likely to leave than members with jobs that require less training?"

By answering those questions and many others, the Marine Corps can create a profile of those likely to stay in various positions and use it to make better management decisions when recruiting, assigning, and promoting personnel.

IMPROVING SERVICE

The Centers for Disease Control and Prevention's National Immunization Program in Atlanta is installing data-mining software that allows better tracking of reactions to vaccines. The program has a huge database of adverse reactions to vaccines reported by physicians, clinics and hospitals, patients, and pharmaceutical companies across the nation. Federal researchers and statisticians monitor the data regularly to find problems caused by a single vaccine or vaccine combinations. Data mining has helped the agency recover millions of dollars in fraud cases.

SOURCE: Excerpted from Cahlink, George. "Data Mining Taps the Trends," www.govexec.com/features/1000/1000managetech.htm, September 18, 2000, Date accessed October 16, 2002.

▪▪▪▪▪▪

business community. Even the term *data mining* is subject to controversy. Other than *data mining,* the literature uses knowledge discovery from databases (KDD), information discovery, information harvesting, data archeology, and data pattern processing. The term *KDD* appeared in 1989 to refer to extracting knowledge from databases. It has mostly been used by artificial intelligence and machine learning researchers. In contrast, statisticians, data analysts, and the MIS community have used the term *DM.* There is actually no difference between the two, although DM is not restricted to the mechanism of discovering knowledge (Fayyad et al. 1996).

DEFINITIONS

DM definitions are derived from the interaction of three entities (Figure 12.1):

1. A body of scientific knowledge accumulated through decades of forming well-established disciplines, such as statistics, machine learning, and artificial intelligence
2. A technology evolving from high volume transaction systems, data warehouses, and the Internet
3. A business community forced by an intensive competitive environment to innovate and integrate new ideas, concepts, and tools to improve operations and DM quality

A review of the literature reveals a wide variety of definitions:

- The search for relationships and global patterns that exist in large databases but are hidden among the vast amount of data (Holsheimer and Kersyen 1994)
- A set of techniques used in an automated approach to exhaustively explore and bring to the surface complex relationships in very large data sets (Moxon 1996)
- The process of finding previously unknown and potentially interesting patterns and relations in large databases (Fayyad et al. 1996)

▪▪▪▪ Data Mining and Business Intelligence

Data mining is producing knowledge and discovering new patterns to describe the data. DM is also predicting future values and business behavior. Sending queries to the transactional databases used to be the only way to transform data into information. The major limitation of this approach was the incapability of extracting meaning. "Mining" the data was relegated to the human expert. With the increasing volume of data and the shrinking time for timely decisions, intelligent automated systems such as DM became a necessity to mine the data. Box 12.2 illustrates how data mining and KM can be integrated.

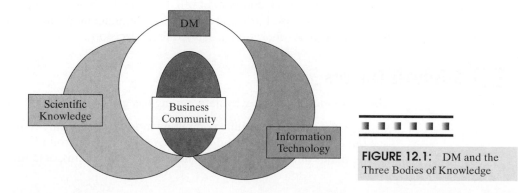

FIGURE 12.1: DM and the Three Bodies of Knowledge

■ ■ ■ ■ ■ ■   BOX 12.2   ■ ■ ■ ■ ■ ■

THE INTEGRATION OF DM AND KM

Knowledge management and data mining developed independently of each other, and their relationship has not yet been fully recognized, much less exploited. Born of the understanding that knowledge is one—if not the most—important asset of an organization, both knowledge management (KM) and data mining (DM) grew and flourished at the convergence of information technologies (machine learning, knowledge-based systems, databases), statistics and data analysis, and the business and management sciences.

KM and DM embody distinct if not opposite perspectives on different knowledge-related issues. One is knowledge capture in the broadest sense of the term. The KM community has traditionally focused on knowledge acquisition from humans, either directly (through manual ontology construction, expert interviews, and authoring tools) or indirectly, as when human know-how is mimicked by a program that observes a human expert in action (such as learning apprentices or programming by demonstration).

In data mining, databases and data warehouses are the ultimate sources from which knowledge is extracted. Machine learning emerged precisely as a way of alleviating difficulties raised by knowledge elicitation from humans. In addition, the exponential growth of process-generated data has spurred the development for more scalable—hence, more thoroughly automated—ways of generating useful knowledge from data.

A second issue is knowledge refinement and revision. The typical KM approach is again manual: The knowledge engineer readjusts domain ontologies, rewrites rules in collaboration with domain experts, and so forth. Although DM research has yielded a promising harvest of automated techniques for knowledge revision and theory refinement, these have been demonstrated on highly circumscribed domain theories and have yet to be validated on medium and large-scale applications. What is needed, then, is an integrative approach that exploits synergies between knowledge management and data mining in order to monitor and manage the full life cycle of knowledge—its capture and discovery, representation, storage, retrieval, revision or refinement, and reuse—in an organization or community of practice.

SOURCE: First Conference on Integrating Data Mining and Knowledge Management, Geneva 2002.

Business intelligence (BI) is a global term for all processes, techniques, and tools that support business decision making based on information technology. The approaches can range from a simple spreadsheet to an advanced decision support system. Data mining is a component of BI. Figure 12.2 shows the positioning of different BI technologies used at different levels of management and for different purposes, including tactical, operational, and strategic decisions.

■ ■ ■ ■ ■ Business Drivers

There are many reasons why data mining has grown substantially in the last few years.

- *Competition.* Successfully competing in today's economy requires an understanding of customer needs and behavior, and a great flexibility to respond to market demands and competitors' challenges. To achieve this, data must be transformed

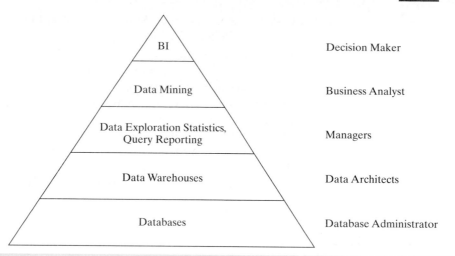

FIGURE 12.2:   Data Mining and Business Intelligence

into knowledge that is leveraged in the business processes. To survive, companies must find quick answers to questions such as "Who is likely to remain a loyal customer, and who is likely to churn?" "What service makes the most profitable customers happy?" "What products should be promoted to which prospects?" Finding the right answers to these questions will differentiate a business from its competitors.

- *Information glut.* Most companies have a glut of information. In fact, many are drowning in information. Today's manager is confronted with increasingly large volumes of data, which has been collected and stored in various databases and constitutes a challenge for decision making. The proliferation of data is a feature of the e-economy. To illustrate, a customer places an order on the phone to buy some items. Such a seemingly simple transaction involves a large number of transactions in various systems at different companies:

  - The merchant knows the items ordered, the shipment method, the credit card used, and so on.
  - The telephone company knows who called, from what location, for how long, and so on.
  - The credit card company knows the amount charged, the approval number, the vendor code, and the available credit.

The information systems of the three companies must exchange information, update records, and store data to perform each transaction properly. Each company has the opportunity to learn from the collected data. The consumer goods company can apply DM to improve its sales process. The telephone company can build churn models to focus on existing customers and select a promotional strategy. The credit card company can leverage its vast warehouse of customer transaction data to identify customers most likely to be interested in a new product.

- *The need to serve the knowledge workers efficiently.* The databases provide the firm with transactional memory. However, memory is of little use without intelligence. Intelligence is the capacity to acquire and apply knowledge. DM incorporates intelligence in its techniques, but DM is worthless if it is not used to make better decisions. Every organization has different types of knowledge workers. These workers include the following:

- Some knowledge analysts are researchers or experts. They demand sophisticated tools for their investigations and research analysis.
- Some knowledge users are executives and decision makers. They need tools that help them review and analyze data. They rely on easy-to-use and powerful systems.
- Other knowledge consumers might be account managers, customer service representatives, or members of the sales force. They require easy to access information.
- DM can provide the right environment to satisfy the requirements of all these people.

▪▪▪▪ Technical Drivers

New developments in analytical methods provide advanced learning capabilities. Answering the question "Why?" means identifying the factors that cause a certain result. The manager can use his know-how and expertise in making decisions and drawing sound conclusions. Analytical methods allow managers to draw hypotheses and test them, predict events and adapt decisions accordingly, find unexpected patterns and exploit them, and discover hidden associations and undertake appropriate actions. Without analytical methods, there is no effective analysis. Without analysis, there is no business intelligence. Without business intelligence, there is no hope to assimilate gigabytes of data and consistently make decisions that keep one's business ahead of the competition. The objective of DM, then, is to optimize the use of available data and reduce the risk of making wrong decisions. Statistics and machine learning are considered to be the analytical foundations upon which DM was developed.

ROLE OF STATISTICS

Statistics embraces concepts, such as hypothesis testing and correlation. The statistician has to start her analysis by assuming a hypothesis about the relationships among the data attributes. With databases organizing data records of hundreds of attributes, the statistics methodology of the hypothesize-and-test paradigm becomes a time-consuming process. DM helps by automating the formulation of new hypotheses.

MACHINE LEARNING

As a subfield of AI, machine learning (ML) has focused on making computers learn things for themselves. Over time, attention has focused on the technological applications of machine learning. Machine learning is the automation of the learning process that is a crucial function in any intelligent system. Its methodology includes learning from examples, reinforcement learning, and supervised or unsupervised learning. Machine learning is a scientific discipline considered to be a subfield of artificial intelligence. In contrast, data mining is a business process concerned with finding understandable knowledge from very large real-world databases.

DATA WAREHOUSES

For years, companies recognized that the volume of data generated by operations such as online transaction processing (OLTP) systems, point of sale (POS) systems, automated teller machine (ATM) systems, and the Internet could be a volatile asset. The challenge is to make data available anytime and anywhere for the decision-making process. For example, Midwest Card Services (MCS) is a rapidly growing financial products services company, with more than 1,000 employees and 200,000 clients. Very quickly, MCS developed the technology infrastructure to meet business needs and provide clients with real-time information. Unfortunately, the company had the technology in place, but lacked the integration of a multitude of stand-alone systems. They had a lot of data available but could not cross-reference among systems. Bringing together data from disparate transactional systems and providing consistent decision-making capabilities across the various functional systems was a real challenge.

As can be seen, data warehousing (DW) is extracting and transforming operational data into informational or analytical data and loading it into a central data warehouse. The major features of DW are as follows:

1. *Subject oriented.* Data warehouses are organized around subjects such as customers' vendor products. In contrast, operational systems are organized around business functions such as loans, accounts, and transactions.
2. *Integration.* Data loaded from different operational systems may be inconsistent. The date in one application may be "yymmdd" and "mmddyy" in another. Integration shows up in consistent naming of variables, in some measurements of variables, and so forth.
3. *Time variant.* Data may be stored but not updated for several years. These are considered historical data and used for prediction, forecasting, and trend analysis purposes.
4. *Nonvolatile.* There are two kinds of operations performed on data warehouses: the initial loading and the access of data. In the operational environment, inserting, deleting, and changing are done regularly. These DW features lead to an environment that is very different from the operational environment. Hence, there is no redundancy between operational data houses and data warehouses.

OLAP

The need for nonstatic reporting systems has led to the development of online analytical processing (OLAP). Data is now used in a proactive way that provides value for the firm. This approach uses computing power and graphical interfaces to manipulate data easily and quickly at the convenience of the user. The focus is showing data along several dimensions. The manager should be able to drill down into the ultimate detail of a transaction and zoom up for a general view.

OLAP has several strengths:

- It is a powerful visualization tool.
- It is an easy-to-use interactive tool.
- It can be used as a first step in understanding the data.

It has also some limitations:

- It does not find patterns automatically.
- It does not have powerful analytical techniques.

These limitations are actually the main strengths of DM. It appears from this analysis that data warehousing, OLAP, DM, and operational systems can be integrated in a single framework to serve the needs of knowledge workers. This model is shown in Figure 12.3.

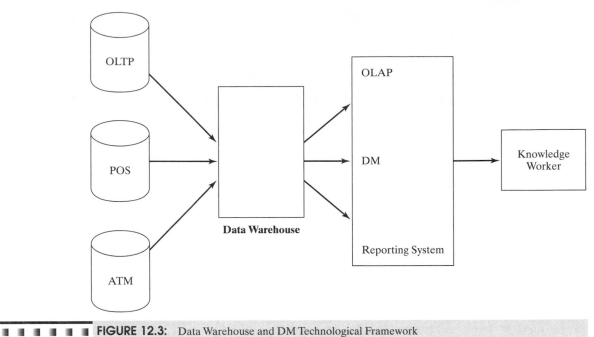

▪ ▪ ▪ ▪ ▪ ▪ ▪ **FIGURE 12.3:**   Data Warehouse and DM Technological Framework

EVOLUTION OF THE DECISION-MAKING ARCHITECTURE

DM is a component of the business intelligence architecture. Business intelligence makes it possible to take action that will ultimately result in measurable benefits. Traditionally, it includes querying and reporting, online analytical processing (OLAP), data visualization, and data analysis. DM complements these tools and provides a global approach that integrates the conventional tools in a whole process that leads to new insights and actionable knowledge for managers and decision makers. It allows users to access information from different sources through client/server or Web-based query systems to visualize models and interact with the results of those queries to gain new business knowledge. Figure 12.4 shows the traditional approach for the decision-making process in contrast with the new approach, which is shown in Figure 12.5.

The integration of decision processing into the overall business process is achieved by building a closed-loop system where the output of decision processing applications is delivered to business users in the form of recommended actions (product pricing changes, for example) for addressing business issues. In the e-business environment, many companies are looking to extend this closed-loop processing to *automatically* adjust business operations based on messages generated by a decision engine.

▪▪▪▪ DM Virtuous Cycle

The goal of DM is to allow a corporation to improve its internal operations and its external relationships with customers, suppliers, and other entities. The virtuous cycle of DM is about harnessing the power of data and transforming it into added value for the entire organization. It incorporates DM into the context of corporate business processes and provides the following capabilities:

- Response to extracted patterns
- Selection of the right action

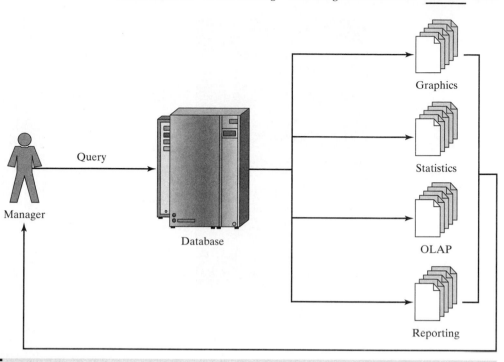

▪ ▪ ▪ ▪ ▪ ▪ ▪ **FIGURE 12.4:** Conventional Approach to Corporate Decision Making

- Learning from past actions
- Turning action into business value

Although the mechanism for extracting patterns from data is important, DM is more than a set of intelligent techniques. What is more important is to apply DM in the right area and deliver the right data to the right people at the right time. The virtuous cycle incorporates DM into other business processes. Its main focus is to extract maximum benefit from data and to gain better understanding of customers, suppliers, and the market. It helps transform an organization from reactive to proactive.

The virtuous cycle is formed by the four steps shown in Figure 12.6.

BUSINESS UNDERSTANDING

The first step in the virtuous DM cycle is identifying the business opportunity, which means defining the problems faced by the firm. The goal is to identify the areas where data can provide values. This stage is the most crucial and the most delicate stage in conducting a DM project. Finding interesting answers for a meaningless business problem is of no use to the company. That is why defining the problem should involve the technical people and the business experts. The DM project manager is expected to possess a combination of skills, including a good command of technical and business cultures. For example, one of the insurance industry's major challenges is fraud, which tends to take different forms—claim fraud, premium fraud, and indemnity fraud. Other important challenges are customer retention or loyalty enhancement programs. Table 12.1 lists business challenges facing different industries and the corresponding DM goals. Identifying these goals is actually the outcome of the business understanding phase.

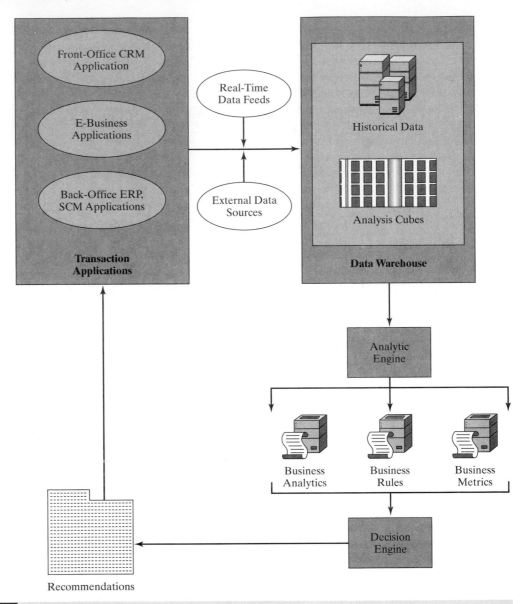

▪ ▪ ▪ ▪ ▪ ▪ ▪ **FIGURE 12.5:** DM in the Context of the New Corporate Business Model

DEVELOP THE DM APPLICATION

Once the business understanding phase is completed, the next step is to develop the application. The goal is to extract knowledge from data and make the mechanism of discovering a new pattern operational. This stage includes four activities:

- Define the adequate data-mining tasks.
- Organize data for analysis.
- Use the right DM technique to build the data model.
- Validate the model.

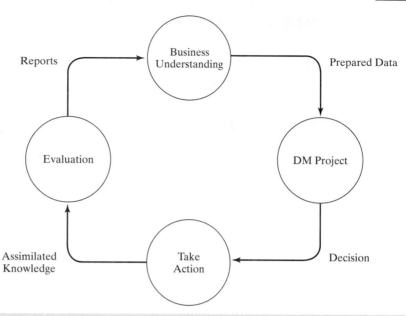

▪ ▪ ▪ ▪ ▪ ▪ ▪ **FIGURE 12.6:** The Virtuous DM Cycle

The development process begins with identification of the outcomes expected from the DM application. The outcomes are called *DM tasks* and consist of the following:

- *Clustering.* Clustering is a tool that divides a database into different groups. The tool finds groups that are very different from each other, but whose members are similar to each other. Unlike classification, we do not know what the clusters will be when we start or by which attributes the data will be clustered. Consequently, someone knowledgeable in the business must interpret the clusters. After the clusters that reasonably segment the database are found, they may be used to classify new data.

- *Classification.* The classification function identifies the characteristics of the group to which each case belongs. This pattern helps us understand the existing data and predict how new instances will behave. For example, we may want to predict whether individuals can be classified as likely to respond to a direct mail solicitation, as vulnerable to switching over to a competing long-distance phone service, or to be a good candidate for a surgical procedure.

- *Affinity grouping.* Affinity grouping is a descriptive approach to exploring data that can help identify relationships among values in a database. The two most common approaches to affinity grouping are association discovery and sequence discovery. **Association discovery** finds rules about items that appear together in an event, such as a purchase transaction. Market-basket analysis is a well-known example of association discovery. **Sequence discovery** is similar to association discovery, in that a sequence is an association related over time.

Once the expected outcomes are identified, the next step is to collect and gather the data needed to start the analysis and match the results to the expected outcomes before releasing the results for decision making.

TABLE 12.1 Business Challenges Faced by Different Industries and the DM Goals

Industry	*Business Challenge*	*DM Goals*
Customer services	The main challenge is understanding that the individual preferences of the customers is the key to satisfying them. What one customer may consider as being "attentive" customer service, another may deem "oppressive." That is why it is extremely crucial to understand these differences and know how to address them in the proper and suitable way.	Customer acquisition profile Customer retention profiling Customer-centric selling Inquiry routing Online shopping Scenario notification Staffing level prediction Targeting market Web mining for prospects
Financial services industry	Retaining customer loyalty is of the utmost importance to this industry, and it is currently the key business challenge.	The financial services industry is a leader in applying DM applications. Very focused statistical and DM applications are prevalent. Risk management for all types of credit and fraud detection are among the DM applications in financial services companies.
Health-care business	Keeping pace with the rate of technological and medical advancement provides a significant challenge. Cost is a constant issue in this everchanging market.	Early DM activities have focused on financially oriented applications. Predictive models have been applied to predict length of stay, total charges, and even mortality.
Telecommunications industry	Keeping pace with the rate of technological change provides a significant challenge to businesses throughout the telecommunications industry. In addition to this, deregulation is changing the business landscape, resulting in competition from a wide range of service providers. Finding and retaining customers is important to telecommunications providers.	In addition to customer profiling, subscription fraud and credit applications are utilized throughout the industry. Concerns about privacy and security are likely to result in DM applications targeted to these areas.

▪ ▪ ▪ ▪ ▪ ▪

▪ ▪ ▪ ▪ Data Management

The most challenging part of a DM project is the data management stage. It is important to know the sources from which data are gathered, the types of data involved in the application, and how to prepare them for the DM techniques. At least 40 percent of a DM project is spent on this stage.

DATA SOURCES

Before data is mined, it must be accessible in an easy format. Here are some examples of data sources:

- *Flat files.* These are the most common source of data. They have a simple structure and are easy to manipulate by the data-mining algorithms. Various types of data can be found in such files.
- *Relational databases.* Relational databases are a set of tables containing rows and columns representing values of entity attributes.
- *Data warehouses.* Data warehouses are repositories of data collected from various data sources.
- *Geographical databases.* Geographical databases combine the relational databases with geographical information from maps.
- *Time series databases.* These databases contain time-related data such as stock market and financial data. Time series databases are continuously fed new data and require real-time analysis.
- *World Wide Web.* The World Wide Web is a dynamic repository with thousands of authors and documents. Mining the Web is a challenging task, which can be helpful in tracing the profile of the Web user or in finding a relevant document to a specific search.

TAXONOMY OF DATA

Various types of data can be collected. Numerical measurements and text documents are simple types; geographic data and hypertext documents are complex types. They can be found in several forms:

- *Business transactions.* Every business transaction, whether it is related to internal business functions like purchasing or external business operations such as relationships with clients, is recorded in large databases. For example, supermarkets, through the bar-coding system, store millions of transactions daily; this helps managers reduce inventory costs.
- *Scientific data.* Scientists collect huge amounts of data from their experiments or observations; this data may include astronomical data and weather data for later analysis and better predictive outcomes.
- *Medical data.* Hospitals keep patients' medical records for years. This type of data is continuously updated based on the health situation of the patient. It is extremely helpful to physicians in diagnosis or prescribing treatments.
- *Personal data.* Government and other institutions collect information about individuals, groups, and communities for security or planning purposes. This has become especially noticeable and critical since the September 11, 2001, attacks.
- *Text and documents.* Most of the communications between companies are based on reports and written documents that are exchanged, communicated, and stored for later use.
- *Web repositories.* For the last decade, the Internet has been a huge vehicle for data stored and organized in repositories.

DATA PREPARATION

The purpose of this step is to change or modify data in order to fit exploration findings. At this point, the following operations are performed on the data:

- Evaluating data quality
- Handling missing data

- Processing outliers
- Normalizing data
- Quantifying data

During the data preparation phase, we begin to understand the importance of some variables and the irrelevance of others. The result is more like a filter, eliminating useless variables and focusing on the significant ones. New variables could be introduced in order to understand more accurately groupings of customers that appeared unexpectedly during the exploration of the initial set of data. This task is called **feature extraction and enhancement**. It consists of selecting the field to use from each record. The chosen fields are called *features*. Various methods are used to ensure the selection of the best set of features. This task is not easy; many tools have been developed for this purpose

MODEL BUILDING

In this phase, various modeling techniques are selected and applied, and their parameters are calibrated to optimal values. Typically, for the same data-mining problem type, there are several techniques, some of which have specific requirements on the form of data. Therefore, stepping back to the data preparation phase is often needed.

Once data is prepared, a model is built to explain patterns in data. The first step is to select the modeling technique. The most popular techniques are as follows:

- Association rules
- Classification trees
- Neural networks

These techniques were covered in Chapter 11.

There are situations where more than one technique is applied. Each technique is applied separately. The results are then compared in terms of performance, business advantage, and gain. Sometimes, there are constraints and requirements that limit the choice of possible techniques. Among the reasons that restrict the use of a certain technique are the assumptions that the technique makes about the data. The assumptions must be compared to the description of the data. If the assumptions do not agree with the data, the designer may have to step back to the data preparation phase and readapt the data. If this cannot be done, the technique then is rejected.

PARAMETER SETTINGS AND TUNING

With any modeling technique, there are several parameters to be adjusted. Most of the time, they are adjusted empirically. The set of initial and intermediate parameters must be recorded for eventual use and comparison. The selection of the parameters must also be explained, and the process of reaching the final values must be documented. The testing and validating samples are used for this task.

MODEL TESTING AND ANALYSIS OF RESULTS

At this point, the prepared data is used, and the model is put to the test using test criteria. If it fails the test, the entire model is rejected or its parameters are adjusted for further testing. After the test phase, the model is validated. Before proceeding to final deployment, the model is thoroughly reviewed to ensure integrity, reliability, and usability.

A key objective is to determine if there are issues that have not been sufficiently considered.

In summary, the tasks of this phase are as follows:

- Reviewing the business objectives and success criteria
- Assessing the success of the DM project to ensure that all business objectives have been incorporated and identifying any factors that have been overlooked
- Understanding the data-mining results
- Interpreting the results
- Comparing the results with common sense and the knowledge base to see if there are any new or worthwhile discoveries

TAKING ACTION AND DEPLOYMENT

At this point, the results obtained from the data-mining application need to be acted upon. Remember that a model is not the reality. It is a representation of the real situation. Like a map, it shows the roads, but it is not the actual road. The model is designed to manipulate data and help in selecting the right action. Unless an action is taken, no transformation is achieved.

Creation of the model is not the end of the project. Knowledge of the data must be organized and presented in a way that the manager can use. Depending on the requirements, the deployment phase can be as simple as generating a report or as complex as implementing a repeatable data-mining process. In many cases, it is the manager, not the data analyst, who will carry out the deployment steps. It means the manager must understand up front what actions will be carried out in order to make use of the created model.

The deployment phase involves several tasks:

- Summarizing the deployable results
- Identifying the users of the discovered knowledge and finding out how to deliver and propagate it
- Defining a performance measure to monitor benefits obtained by the implementation of the DM results (This task is of extreme importance, because it can reduce the risk of misusing the data-mining results. To that end, a monitoring strategy has to be put in place.)

Regarding the procedure or intent, deployment means incorporating the results obtained into the business operation. For example, a cellular telephone company discovered from a data-mining project that profitable customers are the most likely to use their call center. In response, the executive manager decided to improve the services of their call center to keep their customers happy.

POSTDEPLOYMENT PHASE

The purpose of this stage is to provide feedback resulting from the deployment of the newly created model. Measurements are often used to provide feedback. The question is what to measure and how to do it. One important measure is the return on investment (ROI). It measures the financial impact, the response rate, and other impacts resulting from the DM project.

▪ ▪ ▪ ▪ ▪ DM in Practice

DM can be used in two ways: to improve the internal business functions and to address the company's relationship with its customers. Most efforts are being made to understand customer behavior and adjust a company's products and services accordingly. Over 70 percent of marketing departments currently conduct DM projects (see Box 12.3).

▪ ▪ ▪ ▪ ▪ ▪ BOX 12.3 ▪ ▪ ▪ ▪ ▪ ▪

LESSONS LEARNED FROM DM APPLICATION IN SUPERMARKETS

INFORMATION JACKPOT WAS IN THE CARDS

Dick's Supermarkets uses data-mining tools from Datasage, Inc., in Reading, Massachusetts, to gather purchasing-history information from shoppers' scan cards. The company then uses this data to identify product relationships and customer buying patterns.

Kenneth L. Robb, senior vice president of marketing at the Platteville, Wisconsin-based Brodbeck Enterprises, Inc., which operates the eight-store supermarket chain, recently talked to *Computerworld* about the project.

WHAT HAS DATA MINING DONE FOR DICK'S SUPERMARKETS?

It has made us smarter about our customers, smarter marketers—and made us more efficient in our marketing and merchandising investments.

WHAT'S THE BASIS OF A GOOD DATA-MINING PROGRAM?

You have to establish the integrity of your data because that's important to the decisions you'll make. For us, that means getting our customers to use their scan cards with each purchase so that we have good and thorough data about what goes on in our stores.

HOW DO YOU GET THEM TO USE THEIR CARDS AND WHAT KIND OF RESPONSE RATES ARE YOU CURRENTLY GETTING?

We developed several incentive programs for customers using the card. We have given away prizes such as lawn mowers and computers. Currently, 90 percent of our total store [sales are] captured by these cards.

ARE THERE SOME GENERAL THINGS YOU'VE LEARNED ABOUT YOUR SALES?

We discovered that 45 percent of our customers represent close to 90 percent of our volume. Using this information, we can offer the best discounts to the best customers so that we deliver value to those customers who represent the bulk of our business.

WHAT ELSE HAVE YOU LEARNED?

We looked over 1½ years' worth of data and displayed the top product correlations. In our stores, we found a high correlation between yogurt and granola bars and also pie filling and canned milk. We placed a display of granola bars adjacent to the yogurt and measured a 60 percent difference in sales between that type of display and a regular display in the store.

SOURCE: Deck, S. "Data Mining," *Computerworld*, March 29, 1999, www.computerworld.com/hardwaretopics/hardware/desktops/story/0,10801,43509,00.html, Date accessed August 2002.

▪ ▪ ▪ ▪ ▪ ▪

This is explained by the evolution of a company's culture. Being customer-centric rather than service- or product-centric, most companies are driven by the necessity of getting closer to their customers and gaining their loyalty. Customers are extremely volatile; they have access to a huge variety of products and brands through the Internet, regular mail, and other means. These ideas and concepts are illustrated in Box 12.4. It shows how HSBC Bank is using data mining to improve its relationship with the customers in terms of proximity and efficiency.

Building customer loyalty is a challenging task for most companies. DM is among the tools that provide insight about customers and ways to increase sales. A successful

▪▪▪▪▪▪ BOX 12.4 ▪▪▪▪▪▪

DATA MINING IN THE BANKING SECTOR

HSBC Bank USA, a member of the global HSBC Group, serves more than 1.4 million retail banking customers, providing a variety of checking, investment, loan, and other financial products through 380 New York banking locations. HSBC Bank USA, with $35 billion in assets, also serves business and commercial customers.

IDENTIFYING THE BUSINESS PROBLEM

Retail banking is a highly competitive business. A typical branch of a neighborhood bank might have many competitors in close proximity. It creates a continuous competition to attract—and keep—potential customers in the surrounding area. Recent deregulation has also implied an additional competition coming from financial services companies of all kinds. With so many organizations working the same customer base, the value of customer retention is greater than ever. The issue of how to maximize sales and minimize marketing costs has become critical for HSBC Bank USA. This is a typical challenge arising in the retail industry at large.

APPLYING DATA MINING

In the past, HSBC Bank USA often promoted its products to both new and existing customers by using lifestyle segmentation information purchased from market research companies, such as studies that predict income and buying behavior based upon the neighborhood or subdivision.

"That kind of external segmentation scheme has its place and can be valuable when soliciting new customers. However, we realized that we already had much more specific and potentially valuable information on the buying habits and needs of our 1.4 million customers already locked in our database," explained Joe Somma, HSBC Bank USA's manager of customer acquisition and research.

In response to this situation, the bank decided to evolve from a mass-marketing approach in which selected services could be suggested to reflect more closely the real needs of a particular customer. "It was just a matter of mining the data and analyzing the patterns to learn more about who needs what and when. This predictive analysis helps us contact the right people at the right time with the right offer," said Somma.

According to him, the key is using DM to find customers that "look like" those that have demonstrated a particular buying behavior in the past. The previous tools such as OLAP were not able to satisfy his demand. "OLAP is a nice way to get a sense of the characteristics of a data set, but I can't find the strength of the associations and I can't do predictive modeling, and that's the meat of what I need," he said. "OLAP is a good reporting tool, but without a statistical engine, it can only tell me where I've been, not where I need to go."

THE RESULTS

Somma and his colleagues in the bank's individual product departments have created successful marketing strategies based upon the data-mining predictive models. In just 3 years, he reports that sales have risen by up to 50 percent across the bank's numerous product lines, and marketing costs have been reduced by 30 percent. Somma notes that by targeting customers more accurately, he has been able to uncover the most promising prospects for a particular product and to save money by not contacting those customers who do not fit the predictive profile.

THE BENEFITS

"If I'm doing a direct mail campaign, for example, I can mail out fewer pieces in a more targeted manner, get a higher percentage response rate, and bring in about the same amount of money," he said. "Avoiding the traditional 'shotgun' approach, in one recent promotion, we reduced a mail program by more than a third, saving thousands in postage and printing costs, but still brought in 95 percent of the revenues of the previous mailing. So our ROI was enormously improved."

(continued)

(continued)

"If you run just one good model, you can easily pay for the software." In addition, Somma notes there is also a strong customer care "bonus" to his predictive modeling efforts. "No one likes to be inundated with messages about products they don't want or need. Thus, by data mining, we are less likely to annoy our customers with what they might consider junk calls or mail," he said. "And that, I believe, pays off in customer loyalty for the long term."

SOURCE: Adapted from SPSS case studies, www.spss.com/success/pdf/HSB-0200.pdf, Date accessed August 2002.

DM application must bring data and information from various sources and business departments. DM is a required component for various business applications, as shown in Figure 12.7.

The most popular DM applications are as follows:

- Market management applications: Market segmentation, target marketing, churn prediction
- Sales applications: Trends analysis, forecasting, pricing strategies
- Risk management applications: Fraud detection, customer retention, detecting inappropriate medical treatments
- Web applications: Web analytics where DM is applied to the activity logs of Web servers to gain insights about Web surfers' behavior
- Text mining: Mining customers' letters to reveal major complaints, mining maintenance documents to match with a specific failure, mining customers' e-mails to automate responses

▪ ▪ ▪ ▪ ▪ ▪ ▪ **FIGURE 12.7:** DM as a Required Component for Various Applications in Different Departments

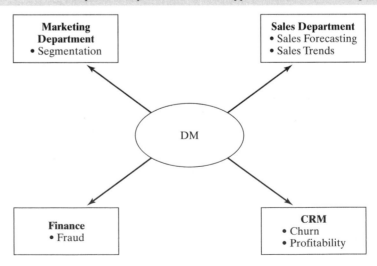

▪ ▪ ▪ ▪ ▪ Role of DM in Customer Relationship Management

Most marketers understand the value of collecting customer data, but they also realize the challenges of leveraging this knowledge to create intelligent, proactive pathways back to the customer. Data mining—technologies and techniques for recognizing and tracking patterns within data—helps businesses sift through layers of seemingly unrelated data for meaningful relationships, where they can anticipate, rather than simply react to, customer needs.

Figure 12.8 shows knowledge integration from disparate sources. Knowledge for marketing decision support can come from customer knowledge, retailers, market research, or market knowledge from third parties. Among the many data-mining applications that enhance an organization's customer services are the following.

CUSTOMER ACQUISITION

This type of application involves finding customers who previously were not aware of the product, who were not candidates for purchasing the product (for example, baby diapers for new parents), or who in the past have bought from competitors. Data mining segments prospective customers and increases the response rate that an acquisition marketing campaign can achieve.

Customer churn is another significant problem in many industries. It is generally far more cost-effective to retain existing customers than to secure new ones. It is desirable to identify customers who are at risk of changing service to a new provider and offer them incentives to retain their existing service.

Customer historical data contains information that can be extremely valuable to retention specialists. Historical data holds usage patterns and other important customer

▪ ▪ ▪ ▪ ▪ ▪ ▪ **FIGURE 12.8:**   Integrated Knowledge Management System for Marketing

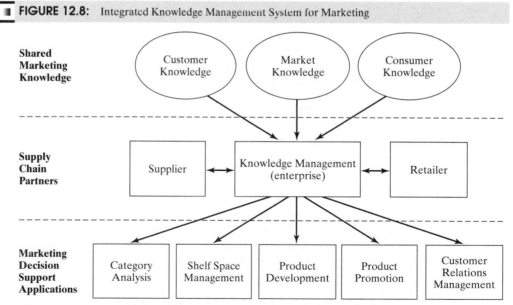

SOURCE: Shaw, M. J., et al., "Knowledge Management and Data Mining for Marketing, *Decision Support Systems*, vol. 31, 2001, pp. 127–137.

characteristics that can be used to identify satisfied and dissatisfied customers. By identifying which customer renewed their service, which did not renew their service, and what incentives were offered to both groups, a predictive model can be built to predict customers who will not renew their service and to make recommendations as to the most effective incentives to offer.

CAMPAIGN OPTIMIZATION

In most marketing organizations, there are many ways to interact with customers and prospects. Besides the offers made, there are multiple communication channels (direct mail, telemarketing, e-mail, the Web) that can be used. The process of marketing campaign optimization takes a set of offers and a set of customers, along with the characteristics and constraints of the campaign, and determines which offers should go to which customers, over which channels, and at what time. The key to satisfying customers, optimizing their experience, and thereby quite possibly their loyalty lies in understanding their individual preferences. Twenty-first century customer relationships are based on mass customization rather than mass production. What one customer may consider "attentive" customer service another may deem "oppressive." Being able to recognize the differences between these two types of customers and making effective use of such information remains a challenge. It is a challenge that data-mining techniques are uniquely well suited to address.

CUSTOMER SCORING

Once a model has been created by a data-mining application, the model can then be used to make predictions for new data. The process of using the model is distinct from the process that created it. Typically, a model is used many times after it is created to score different databases. Identifying customers who are at risk of changing their service and subsequently determining the appropriate actions to take that will encourage customers to retain their service presents a significant challenge to organizations responsible for customer care and customer retention. It is often unclear exactly what characteristics dissatisfied customers exhibit and, therefore, difficult to predict exactly which customers will not renew their service. In addition, even when it is known that a specific customer is dissatisfied, it is difficult to determine what incentives can be offered that will encourage that customer to retain their service.

DIRECT MARKETING

Direct marketing is one of the most popular applications of data mining, because the results can be readily applied to obtain a better campaign response and a higher return on investment. For example, a trained statistician or consultant can develop a response model by using data from a past direct marketing campaign to predict those most likely to respond to the next campaign. By contacting only those most likely to respond, that marketer can substantially increase the percentage of responses and generate higher profits.

Direct marketing campaigns extend beyond the retail merchandising industry to other consumer and business services. The convergence of direct marketing and Internet-based electronic commerce provides a rich resource for future applications of data mining.

INTEGRATING DM, CRM, AND E-BUSINESS

Figure 12.9 shows how DM applications for CRM are integrated with e-sales functions in order to create the customer-centric firm. DM applications are the first line in understanding the customer and an integral key to segmenting the market. An intelli-

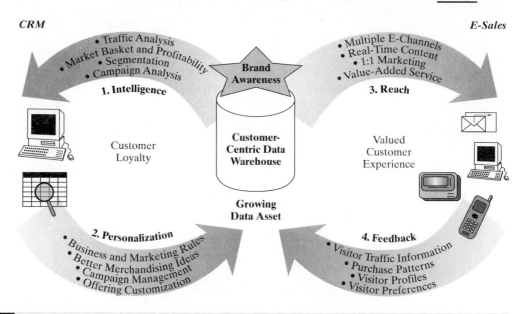

▪▪▪▪▪▪▪ **FIGURE 12.9:**   Customer-Centric Data Warehousing Enables Next Generation E-Commerce

SOURCE: Microstrategy, Inc. "E-Business Elevating Customer Relationships," p. 6, a white paper, August 2002.

gent e-business system enhances CRM by enabling a level of responsiveness and proactive customer care not achievable through other channels. The age of mass customization is now at hand. Through personalization, corporations can build successful 1-to-1 relationships with customers. Customers are now able to receive relevant information derived from complex factors and inputs and enjoy a personalized purchasing experience that meets their needs.

The ability to reach customers is fundamental to a successful e-business, because customers have so many options to buy when and where they wish. Businesses must bring the point of sale to a larger customer base and track buying patterns through a variety of electronic and data channels.

Finally, feedback is an integral process that measures the overall effectiveness of CRM. Assessing performance is required to meet growing challenges from the environment, competitors, and stakeholders.

▪▪▪▪ Implications for Knowledge Management

A DM project is definitely not a straightforward project. While conducting such a project, companies may face many problems, obstacles, and pitfalls that prevent them from gaining returns on investing in a DM project. The main issues and challenges faced by a company are illustrated in Figure 12.10.

What is often forgotten in the scramble to put DM into place is that the technique chosen should reflect what the company wants to find out and the value it puts on acquiring that information. The more powerful techniques have a cost both in project effort and in the difficulty of interpreting results. An organization is wise to take a conservative approach to DM, investigating whether the information required can be extracted by using a less costly approach before launching a project to implement a

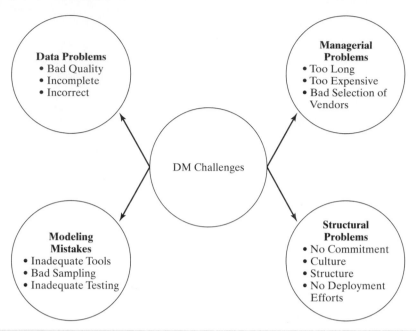

▪ ▪ ▪ ▪ ▪ ▪ ▪ **FIGURE 12.10:** Data-Mining Challenges

neural network when they cannot be sure it will pay off. Conversely, if the potential payoff is sufficient, these techniques may be fully justified or they may indeed be the only ones with the power to provide the required results.

Many DM projects falter because they are championed by the technical department, which understandably wants to try out a new and exciting technique on some interesting data that it holds. The results the project delivers may intrigue the user department to which they are offered. Ultimately, however, because the user has no real business justification for the results and cannot act upon them in a timely manner, there is no impetus to follow up on the project.

Problems that most data-mining project managers stumble across are listed here:

- *Insufficient understanding of business needs.* Many organizations are leaping onto the DM bandwagon; they know who their competitors are. The "me too" approach to the technique is a mistake: Companies should have a business justification for DM, just as they would for any other new technology. The organization will only reap the benefits of DM if there is a real business case to answer because only then will the project be bound tightly into a business process. It should not be an experiment for experiment's sake. In other words, a business needs to resist the technology push of tools, vendors, and technical departments—which often argue for a particular technique regardless of how appropriate it is—and look for user pull.
- *Careless handling of data.* Data that are carelessly handled and conditioned can mislead data miners by deceptively revealing irrelevant patterns and even destroying existing patterns. Data mishandling errors include the following:

  a. *Overquantifying data.* This can lead to the "hiding" of relationships.
  b. *Miscoding data.* This can lead to the creation of pseudopatterns.
  c. *Analyzing without taking precautions against sampling errors.* For example, some data miners use the first *x* number of records as the training data and

blindly assume that the total population of records is randomly distributed and independent.

d. *Loss of precision due to improper rounding of data values.*

e. *Incorrectly handling missing values.* For example, a blank field replaced with a "0" should not be used if a mean average of all the fields is to be taken.

Data visualization and reporting tools should always be used to "see" and statistically analyze data sets to determine if the information is damaged. Additionally, a domain expert, such as a data owner, should check to determine if obvious patterns are still existent in the postconditioned data. This can be done by questioning the postconditioned data set by asking, "Are the relationships *still* there?" "If this was to replace the original data set, can I *still* make sense out of it?" "Is it precise, and does it *still* answer what we already know?"

- *Invalidly validating the data-mining model.* Validating the data-mining model is of utmost importance. This involves testing that a model is properly running as expected by feeding it a large representative data set not used previously in training. Additionally, auditing and using multiple samples from a population can be used to assure the validity of the model.

    Most data miners will face either abundant amounts of testing data or, as often seen, extremely scarce amounts. It is important to never ignore suspicious findings, even if we are hastily trying to meet deadlines. Haste can lead to believing everything the data owners tell us about the data and, even worse, believing everything our own analysis tells us. It is important to question the irrational-sounding voice that asks, "Can this be truly right? I don't think so."

    A good habit is to go through individual records before mining data to get a feel for the information. Many times, a simple examination of the records will raise the awareness of data miners and even bring to their attention to new fields and relationships. Remember: The devil is in the details.

- *Believing in alchemy.* Many data owners believe that data mining is a form of an alchemic process that will magically transform their straw databases into golden knowledge. Data-mining efforts that find nothing are seen as "fool's gold" by data owners. However, they may not necessarily be failures. All data-mining efforts are motivated by the human-induced suspicions that something exists; therefore, the failure may be in the suspicion, not in the data to be mined or the techniques used. Additionally, it could be that the data given to data miners are not suited for the purpose. The technology used might also be inadequate to handle the mass of data available or it may simply have been misapplied. The overall expectations of the project may also play a role in making the gold *seem* to be fake. For example, a company that wants to reduce all customer churn might drop a project that has reduced it only 10 percent, even though this could be a first step.

Challenging and rechallenging the outcomes is the best way to guarantee that real ROI is being achieved. In a rapid prototyping methodology, attacking and analyzing the system as a whole led to finding that the data itself was the problem. In addition, while developing a DM project, managers should consider the following issues:

- Select the right application.
- In-house development or outsourcing: The attraction of in-house DM is to gain skills enhancement, reduce costs, and retain critical information. Outsourcing can reduce the time to develop the project and assure the use of the most advanced technologies.

- Assessing vendor selection: This task is quite difficult because the DM market is still immature and lacks industry standards.
- Team building: Select the right people to participate in the project.

SUMMARY ■ ■ ■ ■

- Data mining is the process of extracting useful patterns and regularities from large bodies of data (that is, bodies of data that are too large to be analyzed by hand).
- Data mining is an umbrella term that covers the tools and techniques used in the analysis of large databases. Data mining is the process that is transforming raw food into blood that nourishes the various functions of the corporation.
- Business intelligence tools are software products that provide the opportunity to take action that will ultimately result in a measurable business benefit. They include a range of tools such as reporting, OLAP, statistical analysis, data visualization, and data mining. Business intelligence tools encompass all tools that could be useful for supporting end users in their analysis and decision-making processes.
- Historically, the term *data mining* appeared in the 1990s, after a long maturation process involving statistics, artificial intelligence, machine learning, and data warehousing. Tracing history to its roots, DM is a double-path discipline originating from the birth of data organization and analytical techniques. On the data organization side, before DM can be applied, data must be properly collected and stored. One such method is data warehousing. Data warehousing collects data from various operational systems, organizes it, transforms it, and makes it available for further DM investigation.
- The primary goals of data mining are prediction (predicting unknown or future values) and description (finding human-interpretable patterns to data). The two goals can be used to carry out primary DM tasks such as classification, regression, clustering, summarization, and dependency modeling.
- The DM process is best illustrated by a seven-step methodology: business understanding, data understanding, data preparation, data modeling, analysis of the results, knowledge assimilation, and deployment evaluation.

TERMS TO KNOW ■ ■ ■ ■

Categorical data: Categorical data is either nonordered (nominal) such as gender or city or ordered (ordinal) such as high, medium, or low temperatures.

Classification: refers to the data-mining problem of attempting to predict the category of data by building a model based on some predictor variables.

Classification tree: A decision tree that places categorical variables into classes.

Cleaning (cleansing): Refers to a step in preparing data for a data-mining activity. Obvious data errors (such as improbable dates) are detected and corrected, and missing data is replaced.

Clustering: Clustering algorithms find groups of items that are similar. For example, clustering could be used by an insurance company to group customers according to income, age, types of policies purchased, and prior claims experience. It divides a data set so that records with similar content are in the same group, and groups are as different as possible from each other.

Cross validation: A method of estimating the accuracy of a classification or regression model. The data set is divided into several parts, with each part in turn used to test a model fitted to the remaining parts.

Data: Values collected through record keeping or by polling, observing, or measuring; typically organized for analysis or decision making. More simply, data are facts, transactions, and figures.

Data accuracy: Refers to the rate of correct values in the data.

Data format: Data items can exist in many formats such as text, integer, and floating-point decimal; refers to the form of the data in the database.

Data mining: An information extraction activity whose goal is to discover hidden facts contained in databases. Using a combination of machine learning, statistical analysis, modeling techniques, and database technology, data mining finds patterns and subtle relationships in data and infers rules that allow the prediction of future results. Typical applications include market segmentation, customer profiling, fraud detection, evaluation of retail promotions, and credit risk analysis.

Data-mining techniques: Procedures and algorithms designed to analyze the data in databases.

Deployment: After the model is trained and validated, it is used to analyze new data and make predictions.

Discrete: A data item that has a finite set of values. Discrete is the opposite of continuous.

External data: Data not collected by the organization, such as data available from a reference book, a government source, or a proprietary database; effect on the dependent variable of the other.

Internal data: Data collected by an organization, such as operating and customer data.

Missing data: Data values can be missing because they were not measured, not answered, were unknown, or were lost.

Model: A model is a road map using data to help understand what is happening or predicting what might happen.

Model accuracy: Refers to the degree of fit between the model and the data. This measures how error-free the model's representations are. Because accuracy does not include cost information, it is possible for a less accurate model to be more cost effective.

OLAP: Online analytical processing tools give the user the capability to perform multidimensional analysis of the data.

Outliers: Outliers are data that fall outside the boundaries that enclose most other data items in the data set.

Pattern: A pattern is a relationship between two variables.

Range: The range of the data is the difference between the maximum value and the minimum value. Alternatively, range can include the minimum and maximum, as in "The value ranges from 2 to 8."

Sampling: Creating a subset of data from the whole. Random sampling attempts to represent the whole by choosing the sample through a random mechanism.

Sensitivity analysis: Varying the parameters of a model to assess the change in its output.

Sequence discovery: The same as an association rule for the market basket analysis except that the time sequence of events is also considered. For example, "Twenty percent of the people who buy a VCR buy a camcorder within 4 months."

Test data: A data set independent of the training data set, used to fine-tune the estimates of the model parameters.

Training: Another term for estimating a model's parameters based on the data set at hand.

Training data: A data set used to estimate or train a model.

Transformation: Reexpression of the data such as aggregating it, normalizing it, changing its unit of measure, or taking the logarithm of each data item.

Validation: The process of testing the models with a data set different from the training data set.

TEST YOUR UNDERSTANDING ▪ ▪ ▪ ▪

1. Why is DM a process and not an end in itself? Explain.
2. Describe the differences and similarities among DM, machine learning, and business intelligence. How are they related?
3. "DM can be thought of as a form of advanced statistical techniques." Do you agree with this statement? Why or why not?
4. "DM is a tool to develop intelligent systems." Define intelligence, explain how systems could have intelligent behavior, and discuss this statement.
5. Describe the differences between OLAP and DM. When would you use each tool?
6. What are the limitations of OLAP? How is DM able to overcome them?
7. What is the role of DM in e-business?
8. Describe, with examples, when you would use predictive DM and when you would use descriptive DM.
9. Explain how DM is used in the health sector and in the telecommunications industry.
10. Explain how companies are using DM to understand their customers' behavior and predict their intentions.
11. Describe the major pitfalls faced by companies when implementing DM solutions.

KNOWLEDGE EXERCISES ▪▪▪▪

1. Discuss what types of industries can best benefit from DM. Which ones cannot? *Hint:* Think of the ones having the most transactions and accessible data.

2. Statistical and DM applications both produce different results for management, even though they might use the same historical data. Discuss the similarities and differences in reporting capabilities.

3. A large online bank needs to mine data coming from many sources, including marketing, accounting, and customer databases. Discuss the best way to collect and prepare multisource data.

4. Minetise.com is an Internet company specializing in online banner ads. The company is developing an application that customizes a banner according to a customer's historic profile. Discuss how DM can be used to develop such an application.

5. Your manager is extremely worried about integration problems that might arise from implementing a DM application on your company's SQL database. Some of the questions bothering him include the following: How will it integrate into the current computing environment? Will it work on our existing SQL database, or do we need anything else? How easily will the system work on our intranet? Discuss the problems and possible solutions to these questions. What other problems might your company face?

6. Finance Trance is a stock brokerage firm. They are thinking of using DM in their customer services department. Suggest some uses and services they can offer. Also, discuss the DM tasks that are to be used.

7. An online bookstore has asked your company to develop a DM application to recommend books to customers. Your manager wants you to analyze how the company works and see what data you can pull from their data warehouses. How would you go about understanding the business and data available before starting the project? What part does this fulfill in the overall project?

8. How could a mobile phone company use DM to lower customer churn? Can it use DM to increase variables such as product development speed, marketing effort, or even customer retention?

9. During the data preparation stage, a supermarket omitted certain data fields that were later shown to have significant adverse effects on the overall DM application. Which stages of the DM process will be affected? At which stage could this problem have been detected? How do you think the problem was detected?

10. Design a survey to glean trends from several companies that are planning to develop DM applications. This survey should help clarify the role of executive managers, the characteristics of the planned project, and the return expected from it.

11. Conduct an in-depth case study with a company that has implemented a DM solution to identify the best practices and common pitfalls.

12. Carrier Corp. is using data mining to profile online customers and offer them cool deals on air conditioners and related products. By using services from WebMiner, Inc., the air-conditioning, heating, and refrigeration equipment maker has turned more Web visitors into buyers, increasing per-visitor revenue from $1.47 to $37.42.

    Carrier, part of $26 billion United Technologies Corp., began selling air conditioners, air purifiers, and other products to consumers via the Web in 1999. However, it sold only about 3,500 units that year, says Paul Berman, global e-business manager at the Farmington, Connecticut, company. Not knowing just who its customers were and what they wanted was a big part of the problem. "We were looking for ways to raise awareness [of Carrier's Web store] and convert Internet traffic to sales," Berman says.

Last year, Carrier gave WebMiner a year's worth of online sales data, plus a database of Web surfers who had signed up for an online sweepstakes the company ran in 1999. WebMiner combined that with third-party demographic data to develop profiles of Carrier's online customers. The typical customer is young (30 to 37), Hispanic, and lives in an apartment in an East Coast urban area.

WebMiner matched the profiles to ZIP codes and developed predictive models. Since May of 2002 Carrier has enticed visitors to its Web site (www.buy.carrier.com/), with discounts. When they type in their ZIP codes, WebMiner establishes a customer profile and pops up a window that offers appropriate products, such as multiroom air conditioners for suburbanites or compact models for apartment dwellers. "It's the first time we've intelligently delivered data-driven promotions," Berman says.

Online sales have exceeded 7,000 units this year, Berman says, compared with 10,000 units for all of last year. Carrier chose the WebMiner service because it was quick to implement and is relatively inexpensive—$10,000 for installation and a $5 fee to WebMiner for each unit sold, compared with 6-figure alternatives.

a. The DM application used by Carrier was one that was predictive in nature. Could a descriptive model also be used? How would you use it, and what outputs would you expect? Would they be of any use to Carrier?

b. What other data-driven promotions could Carrier come up with using other data mining techniques?

c. What manufacturing-driven applications can Carrier implement using data mining? *Hint:* How can it be used to forecast manufacturing defects?

d. What finance-driven applications can Carrier implement using data mining? *Hint:* How can Carrier use DM to distinguish on-time paying customers from doubtful ones?

SOURCE: Whiting 2001.

13. IAURIF, a French regional studies organization, needed to predict what mode of transportation Parisians would use—and why they would use it—from a large data set not originally collected for data mining.

With Clementine's rule-induction algorithms, IAURIF uncovered unexpected insights and proved the group's first assumption, which was based solely on experience, to be untrue. Instead, Clementine's rapid modeling environment revealed the most important travel factors and derived accurate results based on fact.

Results were as follows:

- Accomplished more accurate traffic forecasting
- Improved transportation planning

Analyzing and predicting traffic flows and growth is a complex process. For IAURIF, this process started with an existing database of 400,000 records. These previously collected data, from a detailed Parisian transport survey, were not originally intended for data mining. That meant a more complex task right from the start, because IAURIF had to complete extensive preprocessing before it could begin data mining.

Armed with Clementine's data manipulation capabilities, IAURIF began by grouping the 200 original fields under general headings, such as place of residence and socioeconomic class. Then, analysts selected a representative variable for each group of fields and ensured the groups were independent of their effect on transport mode. This important preprocessing enabled IAURIF to pinpoint 26 fields, a core set of relevant variables that would simplify and significantly help the group's data-mining efforts.

IAURIF analysts then used Clementine's rule-induction algorithms, which predicted a three-way variable — whether someone would walk, drive, or take public transportation for a specific journey. With Clementine's powerful modeling techniques, analysts identified the factors behind each choice. Based on experience, IAURIF had first thought sociological factors, such as income and class, would combine with the journey's purpose to be the most important causal factors.

However, Clementine uncovered a very significant, and surprising, finding. The most important factors proved to be journey distance and trip time — not factors the group had predicted on experience alone. To be sure, IAURIF proved Clementine's high accuracy by testing results with a validation data set. In the end, Clementine and this new modeling process increased IAURIF's ability to plan future transport.

a. Describe the case from the perspective of the 7-step DM process. Which parts were not covered? What recommendations do you have?

b. What difference would using online transaction data, instead of survey data, have on the overall IAURIF project? What suggestions would you give?

c. What other DM projects could you implement for IAURIF? Which DM techniques would you use? Why?

REFERENCES ▪ ▪ ▪ ▪

Adriaans, Pieter, and Zantinge, Dolf. *Data Mining*. Boston, MA: Addison-Wesley, 1996.

Cabena, Peter, et al. *Discovering Data Mining: From Concept to Implementation*. Upper Saddle River, NJ: Prentice Hall, 1998.

Cahlink, George. "Data Mining Taps the Trends," www.govexec.com/features/1000/1000managetech.htm, September 18, 2000, Date accessed October 16, 2002.

Deck, S. "Data Mining," *Computerworld*, March 29, 1999, www.computerworld.com/hardwaretopics/hardware/esktops/story/0,10801,43509,00.html, Data accessed 2002.

Delmater, Rhonda, and Hancock, Monte. *Data Mining Explained*. Boston, MA: Digital Press, 2001.

de Ville, Barry. *Microsoft Data Mining: Integrated Business Intelligence for E-Commerce and Knowledge Management*. Boston, MA: Digital Press, 2001.

Dhar, Vasant, and Stein, Roger. *Seven Methods for Transforming Corporate Data into Business Intelligence*. Upper Saddle River, NJ: Prentice Hall, 1997.

Fayyad, Usama M., et al. *Advances in Knowledge Discovery and Data Mining*. Menlo Park, CA: AAAI Press, 1996.

Groth, Robert. *Data Mining: A Hands-On Approach for Business Professionals*. Upper Saddle River, NJ: Prentice Hall, 1998.

Groth, Robert. *Data Mining: Building Competitive Advantage*. Upper Saddle River, NJ: Prentice Hall, 2000.

Han, Jiawei, and Kamber, Micheline. *Data Mining: Concepts and Techniques*. San Francisco, CA: Morgan Kaufmann, 2001.

Hansen, Morten T., Nohria, Nitin, and Tierney, Thomas. "What's Your Strategy for Managing Knowledge?"

Harvard Business Review, vol. 77, no. 2, 1999, pp. 106–116, harvardbusinessonline.hbsp.harvard.edu/b02/en/common/item_detail.jhtml?id=4347, Date accessed October 19, 2002.

Holsheimer, M., and Kersten, M. L. Architectural Support for Data Mining. KDD Workshop 1994, pp. 217–228.

Hunt, E., Marin, J., and Stone, P. *Experiments in Induction*. New York: Academic Press, 1966.

Inmon, Bill. *Managing the Data Warehouse*. New York: John Wiley & Sons, Inc., 1996.

Kaplan, Abraham. *The Conduct of Inquiry: Methodology for Behavioral Science*. Chicago: Chandler Publishing Company, 1964.

Kaplan, Robert S., and Norton, David P. *The Balanced Scorecard: Translating Strategy into Action*. Boston, MA: Harvard Business School Press, 1996.

Kass, G. V. "Significance Testing in Automatic Interaction Detection," *Applied Statistics*, vol. 24, no. 2, 1976, pp. 178–189.

Kass, G. V. "An Exploratory Technique for Investigating Large Quantities of Categorical Data," *Applied Statistics*, vol. 29, no. 2, 1980, pp. 119–127.

Kluge, Jurgen, Stein, Wolfram, and Licht, Thomas. *Knowledge Unplugged: The McKinsey & Company Global Survey on Knowledge Management*. New York: Palgrave, 2001.

Kuhn, Thomas. *The Structure of Scientific Revolutions*, 3d ed. Chicago: University of Chicago Press, 1996.

Loshin, David. *Enterprise Knowledge Management: The Data Quality Approach*. San Francisco, CA: Morgan Kaufmann, 2001.

Mena, Jesus. *Data Mining Your Website*. Boston, MA: Butterworth-Heinemann, 1999.

Michael, J. A., Linoff, Berry, and Linoff, Gordon. *Data Mining Techniques: For Marketing, Sales, and Customer Support*. New York: John Wiley & Sons, Inc., 1997.

Michael, J. A., Linoff, Berry, and Linoff, Gordon. *Mastering Data Mining: The Art and Science of Customer Relationship Management*. New York: John Wiley & Sons, Inc., 2000.

Michalski, Ryszard S., Bratko, Ivan, and Kubat, Miroslav. *Machine Learning and Data Mining: Methods and Applications*. New York: John Wiley & Sons, Inc., 1998.

Michie, D. "Methodologies from Machine Learning in Data Analysis and Software," *The Computer Journal*, vol. 34, no. 6, 1991, pp. 559–565.

Microstrategy, Inc., "E-Business Elevating Customer Relationships," white paper, p. 6, 2001.

Millaer, William L., and Morris, Langdon. *Fourth Generation R&D: Managing Knowledge, Technology, and Innovation*. New York: John Wiley & Sons, Inc., 1999.

Mizuno, Shigeru. *Management for Quality Improvement: The Seven New QC Tools*. Cambridge, MA: Productivity Press, 1979.

Morgan, J. N., and Sonquist, J. A. "Problems in the Analysis of Survey Data, and a Proposal," *Journal of the American Statistical Association*, vol. 58, June 1963, p. 415.

Moxon, B. "Defining Data Mining," *DBMS Online, Data Warehouse Supplement*, www.dbmsmag.com/9608d53.html, August 1996, Date accessed 2002.

O'Dell, C., Hasanali, F., Hubert, C., Lopez, K., and Raybourn, C. *Stages of Implementation: A Guide for Your Journey to Knowledge Management Best Practices*. Houston, TX: APQC, 2000.

Payne, L. W., and Elliot, S. "Knowledge Sharing at Texas Instruments: Turning Best Practices Inside Out," *Knowledge Management in Practice*, vol. 6, 1997. www.apqc.org/prodserv/km-06.pdf, Date accessed August 2002.

Pyle, Dorian. *Data Preparation for Data Mining*. San Francisco, CA: Morgan Kaufmann, 1999.

Quinlan, R. "Discovering Rules by Induction from Large Collections of Examples," in D. Michie (ed.), *Expert Systems in the Microelectronic Age*. Edinburgh, 1979, pp. 168–201.

Rud, Olivia Parr. *Data Mining Cookbook*. New York: John Wiley & Sons, Inc., 2001.

Shaw, M. J., Subramaniam, C., Wan Tan, G., and Weldge, M. "Knowledge Management and Data Mining for Marketing," *Decision Support Systems*, vol. 31, 2001, pp. 127–137.

Smith, Reid G., and Farquhar, Adam. "The Road Ahead for Knowledge Management: An AI Perspective," *AI Magazine*, vol. 21, no. 4, Winter 2000, pp. 17–40.

Sonquist, J. A., Baker, E., and Morgan, J. *Searching for Structure*. Ann Arbor, MI: Institute for Social Research, 1973.

Spence, Robert. *Information Visualization*. Boston: Addison-Wesley, 2001.

SPSS, HSBC Bank USA, www.spss.com/success/pdf/HSB-0200.pdf, Date accessed August 2002.

Stewart, Tomas A. *Intellectual Capital—The New Wealth of Organizations*. New York: Doubleday-Currency, 1997.

Sturm, Jake. *Data Warehousing with Microsoft SQL Server 7.0 Technical Reference*. Redmont, WA: Microsoft Press, 2000.

Thuraisingham, Bhavani. *Data Mining: Technologies, Techniques, Tools, and Trends*. Ft. Lauderdale, FL: CRC Press, 1999.

Tiwana, Amrit. *The Knowledge Management Toolkit*. Upper Saddle River, NJ: Prentice Hall, 2000.

Westphal, Christopher, and Blaxton, Teresa. *Data Mining Solutions: Methods and Tools for Solving Real-World Problems*. New York: John Wiley & Sons, Inc., 1998.

Whiting, R. "Carrier Fans Sales With Data Mining," *InformationWeek*, August 6, 2001, www.information week.com/story/IWK20010802S0005, Date accessed November 2002.

Witten, Ian H., and Frank, Eibe. *Data Mining: Practical Machine Learning Tools and Techniques with Java Implantations*. San Francisco, CA: Morgan Kaufmann, 2000.

Selected Web Sites ▪ ▪ ▪ ▪

www.dmg.org   The Data Mining Group is a consortium of industry and academics formed to facilitate the creation of useful standards for the data-mining community. The site provides a member area and a software repository, and it also provides news and announcements.

www.kdnuggets.com   KD Nuggets is a leading electronic newsletter on data mining and Web mining. Its monthly release provides up-to-date news items on developments in data mining and knowledge discovery.

www.oasis-open.org   The Organization for the Advancement of Structured Information Standards (OASIS) is a nonprofit international consortium that creates interoperable industry specifications based on public standards such as XML and SGML. OASIS members include organizations and individuals who provide, use, and specialize in implementing the technologies that make these standards work in practice. OASIS provides information on such emerging standards as predictive model markup language (PMML) in the separate XML cover pages site www.oasis-open.org/cover.

www.xml.org   This is an independent resource for news, education, and information about the application of

XML in industrial and commercial settings. Hosted by OASIS and funded by organizations that are committed to product-independent data exchange, this Web site offers valuable tools, such as a catalog to help you make critical decisions about whether and how to employ XML in your business. For business-people and technologists alike, this Web site offers a uniquely independent view of what's happening in the XML industry.

www.microsoft.com/sql   This is the homepage for Microsoft SQL Server. This particular URL provides a list of Microsoft online businesses. You can learn how to get real-time access to the most powerful data in business intelligence, how to manage your business partnerships more effectively, or how to share information within your organization through knowledge management. You may also read how companies plan to use wireless and other mobile technologies.

www.mlnet.org   This site is dedicated to the field of machine learning, knowledge discovery, case-based reasoning, knowledge acquisition, and data mining. This site provides information about research groups and persons within the community. You may browse through the list of software and data sets and locate the events page for the latest calls for papers. This Web site also has a list of job offerings if you are looking for a new opportunity within the field.

www.mdcinfo.com   This site provides information on the Meta Data Coalition, an organization originally set up by Microsoft to provide metadata solutions in data warehousing, business intelligence, and data mining.

www.icpsr.umich.edu/DDI   The Data Documentation Initiative (DDI) is an effort to establish an international criterion and methodology for the content, presentation, transport, and preservation of metadata (data about data) in the social and behavioral sciences. Metadata constitute the information that enables the effective, efficient, and accurate use of those data sets. The site is hosted by the ICPSR (Interuniversity Consortium for Political and Social Research) at the University of Michigan.

www.dhutton.com   David Hutton Associates are consultants in quality management. They are specialists in the Baldrige-style business excellence assessment as a tool to drive organizational change and improvement.

www.salford-systems.com   Salford Systems are developers of CART and MARS data-mining, decision tree, and regression modeling products. The site contains information about these products, white papers, and other technical reports.

Knowledge Management Tools and Knowledge Portals

Contents

In a Nutshell
Portals: The Basics
    What Are Portals?
    Evolution of Portals
    Key Characteristics
    Illustration
The Business Challenge
    Portals and the Business Transformation
    Market Potential
Knowledge Portal Technologies
    Key Functionality
    Collaboration
    Content Management
    Collaboration Versus Categorization: The Case of the World Bank
    Intelligent Agents
Implications for Knowledge Management
    Who Is Building Enterprise Portals?
    Who Sponsors Enterprise Portals?
    Implementation Issues
    Bandwidth
    Portal Product Selection
Summary
Terms to Know
Test Your Understanding

> *What gets measured is what gets done.*
> —ANON

▪▪▪▪ In a Nutshell

This chapter is concerned with the identification of the right tools to set up the infrastructure, services, and applications needed by the enterprise to manage effectively the flow of information and the various activities related to the acquisition, production, and dissemination of knowledge. The goal is to provide an in-depth analysis of the technology trends and issues related to the implementation of knowledge management solutions.

In previous chapters, we focused on knowledge management consisting of three main processes: capture, codification, and integration. A variety of tools are emerging to provide an enterprise with needed capabilities. The capacity to create knowledge begins with collecting and organizing information. The value of information depends on accuracy and timely accessibility. The more accurate and timely information is, the more valuable it becomes for analysis and the creation of insight and new knowledge. To be useful in creating knowledge, information must reach knowledge workers in the most convenient, complete, and accurate way.

Portals are among the latest and most powerful tools to help achieve these goals. A KM solution must employ a tool for capturing knowledge wherever it exits (in documents, in experts' minds, in databases, or as historical data). Another important tool is a user interface that makes knowledge available to a larger community of knowledge workers. By providing an integrated framework for linking people, processes, and knowledge, portals can play a central role in simplifying managerial complexity, increasing operational productivity, and adding value to a company's business operations. Portals employ distribution channels such as the Internet, intranets, and extranets. These distribution channels enable companies to grasp potential advantages that are lying dormant in a company's information and knowledge-based systems. Portals evolved from pure information providers to sophisticated interfaces containing knowledge management features such as content management for knowledge categorization, collaboration tools for knowledge sharing, and personalization capabilities to facilitate the search function. Box 13.1 illustrates the impact of knowledge management portals on performance.

▪▪▪▪ Portals: The Basics

WHAT ARE PORTALS?

Portals are considered to be virtual workplaces that:

- Promote knowledge sharing among different categories of end users such as customers, partners, and employees
- Provide access to structured data stored in data warehouses, database systems, and transactional systems
- Organize unstructured data such as electronic documents, paper documents, lessons learned, stories, and the like

■ ■ ■ ■ ■ ■ BOX 13.1 ■ ■ ■ ■ ■ ■

PERFORMANCE OF KNOWLEDGE MANAGEMENT PORTALS

FRITO-LAY: THE KNOWLEDGE CRUNCH

THE PROBLEM: UNLOCKING KNOWLEDGE

Corporate executives knew that capturing best practices and corporate information would give employees something they could sink their teeth into. However, information was scattered around the company in disparate systems, and there was no easy way for the geographically dispersed sales force to get at it. "We had knowledge trapped in files everywhere," says Mike Marino, vice president of customer development at Frito-Lay, an $8.5 billion division of PepsiCo in Plano, Texas. Marino says that he knew if the 15-member sales team could only access the same information, it would solve its ongoing problems within information sharing and communication.

Additionally, much valuable knowledge was squirreled away on each salesperson's system. There were many idiosyncratic methods of capturing information, "none of which were terribly efficient," Marino says. The sales team also lacked a place for brainstorming and collaboration online. If somebody got a piece of research and wanted to get input from account executives in Baltimore and Los Angeles, the ability to collaborate [online] just was not there.

THE SOLUTION: A KNOWLEDGE MANAGEMENT PORTAL

The answer, Marino's group realized, was to build a knowledge management portal on the corporate intranet. A KM portal is a single point of access to multiple sources of information, and it provides personalized access. Companies are starting to pay attention to portals, because they offer an efficient way to capture information, says Carl Frappaolo, executive vice president and cofounder of the Delphi Group, a consultancy in Boston. A KM portal at Frito-Lay would give the sales department a central location for all sales-related customer and corporate information and cut down on the time it took to find and share research. In addition to different types of information about the team's customers—including sales, analysis, and the latest news—the portal would contain profiles on who's who in the corporation, making finding an internal expert a snap.

THE IMPLEMENTATION: BUILT FROM SCRATCH

Marino's group established three goals for the Frito-Lay portal: to streamline knowledge, exploit customer-specific data, and foster team collaboration. He brought in Navigator Systems, a consultancy based in Dallas, which had worked with Frito-Lay in the past and had some experience building knowledge management portals. Navigator built a prototype in about 3 months using technologies previously approved by Frito-Lay's IS department.

Marino and Navigator essentially had to start from scratch when it came to populating the portal. "Never before at Frito-Lay had they tried to capture expertise systematically in one place," notes Todd Price, a consultant at Navigator. Marino and Price did an audit within the company and then created expertise profiles on the portal so that sales staff in the field would have an easy way to learn who's who at headquarters in Plano. That way, people who have expertise in areas such as promotion planning, activity planning, costing, or new product announcements can be readily tracked down and contacted for information.

The portal went live in January 2000. Since then, three additional sales teams, or *customer communities* as they are called internally, have been given access to the portal with different content—including research abstracts and what Marino calls performance scorecards, which evaluate account performance. "If somebody in sales or market research did a study in a particular area like private-label trends, [the user] would be able to click to that abstract and get a summary of that study." Users access the portal, known as the *Customer Community Portal (CCP)*, through a Netscape Navigator browser and enter their name and password on the Frito-Lay intranet.

(*continued*)

(continued)

THE RESULTS

The CCP has paid off with increased sales. "What we expected to see was that the pilot team would outperform others in terms of sales and profitability," Marino says. While he declined to give figures, he says the test team doubled the growth rate of the customer's business in the salty snack category. It also made the sales team happier. For example, the pilot team members reside in 10 different cities, so the tool has become extremely valuable for communication and helps cut down on travel. A year after implementing the portal, the pilot group has been able to share documents concurrently instead of having to send faxes around the country to different offices. "It's almost a distance learning tool as much as anything else," he says.

The CCP has also helped foster a sense of camaraderie and relationship building. For example, the portal homepage lists the team members' birthdays. People can also share best practices—on anything under the sun. If someone developed an effective sales presentation for a potential customer in Boston, a salesperson in San Francisco could co-opt the information. Salespeople can also find the latest news about their customers, and theirs is an automatic messaging feature that tells team members who is online.

For Ackerman, the portal has also been an invaluable tool for helping him assess employee skill sets, because each salesperson is required to catalog his or her strengths and areas of expertise. "As a team leader, it helps me analyze where people's gaps might be without having to travel to another member's location," he says.

The portal has also helped boost employee retention rates, says Ackerman. Turnover used to be terrible, he says, because salespeople felt pressured to find vital information and communicate with the rest of the team. Marino adds that salespeople felt frustrated and disconnected because there was no way to efficiently collaborate with the rest of their group unless they flew into a central location.

Since the portal has been in place, not one person on the 15-member team has left. Part of that can directly be attributed to the portal, says Ackerman, because it helps build the connection. In company surveys, salespeople previously complained about geographic constraints and how they did not feel connected and part of a team, he says.

The portal has proven so successful that its use has now become a PepsiCo initiative, says Marino. That means it will soon have added functionality so that employees across all three divisions—including Tropicana—can take advantage of product performance information on a jointly shared customer like a supermarket, he says. Marino says the different PepsiCo divisions will have the ability to co-promote and co-merchandise multiple products that are consumed together—such as carbonated beverages and salty snacks—to drive greater sales internally, naturally and for its customer. That's talking more than just peanuts.

SOURCE: Shein, E., " The Knowledge Crunch," *CIO*, May 1, 2001, www.cio.com/archive/050101/crunch.html, Date accessed August 2002.

▪ ▪ ▪ ▪ ▪ ▪

Portals are Web-based applications providing a single point of access to online information. They assure secure and reliable interface to participants in a business process and collaborate with users through the integration of external Web-based applications or internal back-office systems.

Portals are emerging as the most promising tool that could:

- Simplify access to data stored in various application systems
- Facilitate collaboration among employees
- Assist the company in reaching its customers

From a business perspective, portals provide the company's employees with task-relevant information. They can also quickly supply partners and customers with knowledge. The goal of such a portal is the transparent enterprise, reducing the complexity for reaching needed information.

EVOLUTION OF PORTALS

Initially, portals were mere search engines. They employed simple search technology to find information on the Web. The next phase transformed the portals to "navigation sites" to describe the functions available at sites like Quicken, MSN, Lycos, and Yahoo!. Those portals categorize personal interests in groups (such as news, sports, finance, education, science, and others). An example of the logical hierarchy of groups is shown in Figure 13.1. They are referred to as Internet public portals.

Because of the increasing amount of information accessible internally and externally, the need for more personalized information is becoming more critical and urgent. To facilitate access to large accumulations of information, portals evolved to include advanced search capabilities and taxonomies. Because emphasis was on information, they were called *information portals*.

The evolution of the portal concept is shown in Figure 13.2.

Information portals provide the next step in the portal technology evolution. In November 1998, Christopher Shilakes and Julie Tylman of Merrill Lynch's Enterprise Software team introduced the concept of "enterprise portal." The concept was described as "applications that enable companies to unlock internally and externally stored information and provide users a single gateway to personalized information needed to make informed business decisions. They are an amalgamation of software applications that consolidate, manage, analyze, and distribute information across and outside an enterprise, including business intelligence, content management, data warehouse, data mart and data management applications" (Shilakes and Tylman 1998).

Companies are becoming more aware of the opportunities for using and adding value to the information lying dormant in scattered information systems. Companies need to use both "publish" (pull) and "subscribe" (push) media to ensure that the right information is available or distributed to the right people at the right time. The main

▪ ▪ ▪ ▪ ▪ ▪ ▪ ▪ **FIGURE 13.1:**   Yahoo! Home Page

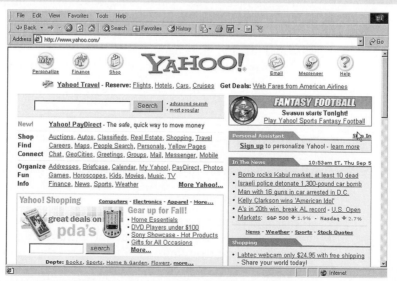

SOURCE: www.yahoo.com, Date accessed September 5, 2002.

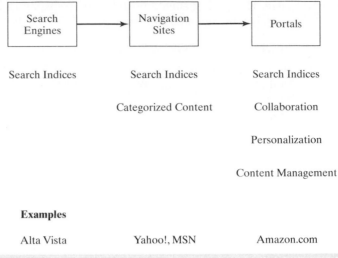

benefits for companies include lowered costs, increased sales, and better deployment of resources. Integration is the key feature of enterprise portals. Portals integrate applications by combining, standardizing, analyzing, and distributing relevant information and knowledge to end users, whether they are customers, employees, or partners.

The effectiveness of information portals can be enhanced by building applications that combine the search, analysis, and dissemination of information. This goal is achieved through knowledge portals.

In the **knowledge portal**, the focus is not on the content of information but on the way knowledge workers will use it. The knowledge portal is a key component in the knowledge management architecture. It is the central piece, allowing producers and users of knowledge to interact. A major trend in knowledge management systems is the move to online knowledge portals.

Knowledge portals provide information on various topics, and they can be customized to meet a user's individual needs. Portals make it easy to access knowledge because of their universal interface—a Web browser. Online portal systems let IT organizations access a variety of back-end systems (such as process management software and methodology databases).

Knowledge portals provide two kinds of interfaces:

- *The knowledge producer interface.* It facilitates the knowledge worker's job of gathering and analyzing information, collaborating with peers or colleagues, and finally generating new knowledge.
- *The knowledge consumer interface.* It facilitates the dissemination of knowledge across the enterprise. A key feature of knowledge portals is a sophisticated personalization facility that takes into account the consumer profile.

KEY CHARACTERISTICS

Knowledge portals provide information about all business activities and also supply metadata for decision making. Enterprise knowledge portals (EKP), therefore, distinguish knowledge from information. They provide a facility for producing knowledge from data and information. They also provide a better basis for making decisions than do enterprise intelligence portals. Those who have knowledge gain competitive advantage

▪ ▪ ▪ ▪ ▪ ▪   **BOX 13.2**   ▪ ▪ ▪ ▪ ▪ ▪

THE NEXT GENERATION OF PORTALS

THE SECOND WAVE OF EIP

The second wave is shifting the primary focus of the enterprise intelligence portal (EIP). Whereas EIP did emphasize broadly based and generalized decision processing and mass dissemination of corporate information, it now targets collaboration and highly targeted and personalized distribution of content, bundled with multiple types of specialized expertise-oriented services. These trends, happening over the past year or so, indicate that the EIP concept is on the verge of an explosion along four key directions:

- *Enterprise business intelligence portals (EBIPs)* provide the central launching point for corporate decision-processing and content-management applications. Their primary focus is to connect users with structured and unstructured content relevant to them.

- *Enterprise collaborative processing portals (ECPPs)* connect users not only with all the information they need, but also with everyone they need. ECPPs consolidate groupware, e-mail, work-flow, and critical desktop applications under the same gateway as decision-processing and content-man-

agement applications. ECPPs are characterized by "virtual project areas" or communities.

- *Enterprise mission management portals (EMMPs)* provide a "digital expertise-oriented workplace"—a highly specialized and personalized Web site where everything a user team needs (such as access to ERP applications, productivity and analysis tools, and relevant internal and external content) to effectively manage mission-critical management activities such as customer relationship management (CRM) is consolidated and made accessible via the Web.

- *Enterprise extended services portals (EESPs)* do everything the first three types do, but focus on providing comprehensive job support from the standpoint of "virtual enterprises" by creating communities and "virtual service spaces" of channel partners, suppliers, distributors, and customers.

The convergence of the first and second EIP waves will occur within 1½ years. This time will be spent on extending architectural frameworks that guide technology from the search-based, first-wave portals to a fully functional architecture capable of enabling expertise- and service-based, second-wave portals.

SOURCE: Excerpted from Davydov, Mark M. *Intelligent Enterprise*, vol. 3, no. 4, March 1, 2000. Accessed from www.intelligent enterprise.com/000301/supplychain.html. August 2002.

▪ ▪ ▪ ▪ ▪ ▪

over those who have mere information. The essential characteristics of enterprise intelligent portals and enterprise knowledge portals are shown in Table 13.1.

ILLUSTRATION

Let us illustrate using the case of the army's knowledge online portal. The objective of this portal is to transform the army into a networked organization that leverages its intellectual capital to better organize, train, equip, and maintain a strategic land combat force. More specifically, the army needs to do the following:

- Allow its enterprise information to be accessed more quickly and easily for less cost
- Use information technology to leverage army-wide innovation in services, processes, and knowledge creation

Figures 13.3, 13.4, and 13.5 show the capabilities of the army knowledge portal, the communities of practice that were created, and their features.

TABLE 13.1 Knowledge Portals Versus Information Portals

Enterprise Information Portals	*Enterprise Knowledge Portals*
• Use both "push" and "pull" technologies to transmit information to users through a standardized Web-based interface • Integrate disparate applications including content management, business intelligence, data warehouse/data mart, data management, and other data external to these applications into a single system that can "share, manage, and maintain information from one central user interface" • Have the ability to access both external and internal sources of data and information, and the ability to support a bidirectional exchange of information with these sources	• Are goal-directed toward knowledge production, knowledge acquisition, knowledge transmission, and knowledge management • Are focused on enterprise business processes such as sales, marketing, and risk management • Provide, produce, and manage information about the validity of the information they supply • Include all EIPs functionalities

SOURCE: Firestone, J. "Enterprise Knowledge Portals," White Paper 8, www.dkms.com, Date accessed August 2002.

■ ■ ■ ■ The Business Challenge

Businesses from all sectors of the economy confront new market realities daily. At the same time, there is inherent pressure to optimize the performance of operational processes in order to reduce costs and enhance quality. Customer-centric systems allow companies to understand the customer, predict customer behavior, and offer the right product at the right time. Companies also need to commercialize their products at the lowest price possible.

FIGURE 13.3: The Army Knowledge Portal

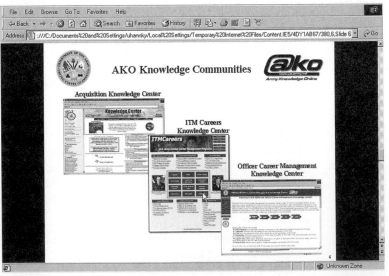

SOURCE: E-Gov Knowledge Management Conference. "Using Army Knowledge Online for Mission Success," April 11, 2000, www.army.mil/ako/webbriefing.ppt, Date accessed August 2002.

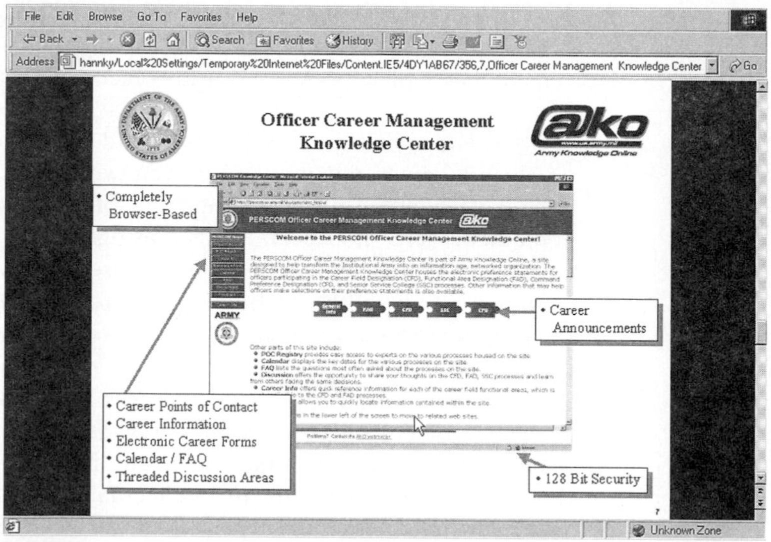

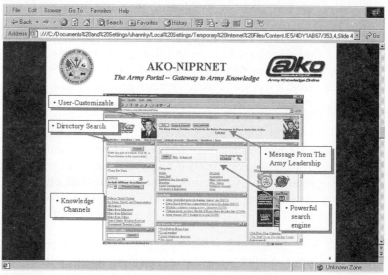

▪ ▪ ▪ ▪ ▪ ▪ ▪ ▪ **FIGURE 13.4:**   The Army Communities of Practice

SOURCE: E-Gov Knowledge Management Conference. "Using Army Knowledge Online for Mission Success," April 11, 2000, www.army.mil/ako/webbriefing.ppt, Date accessed August 2002.

PORTALS AND THE BUSINESS TRANSFORMATION

The problems arise from two fundamental aspects underlying the current computing environment. First, the explosion in the quantity of key business information already captured in electronic documents has left many organizations literally losing their grip on information as they transform into new systems and process upgrades. Second, the speed by which the quantity and kinds of content is growing means that what is

▪ ▪ ▪ ▪ ▪ ▪ ▪ ▪ **FIGURE 13.5:**   Features of Officer Career Knowledge Management Center

SOURCE: E-Gov Knowledge Management Conference. "Using Army Knowledge Online for Mission Success," April 11, 2000, www.army.mil/ako/webbriefing.ppt, Date accessed August 2002.

required to meet these challenges is a rigorous internal discipline to expose and integrate the sources of enterprise knowledge. As a result, organizations are facing tremendous challenges. Consider these pressures faced by just about all organizations:

- *Shorter time to market.* New products and services have to be conceived, developed, and delivered in months, or even weeks.
- *Knowledge worker turnover.* When a pivotal person leaves, the pain is widely and quickly felt. "It's becoming increasingly difficult to acquire and retain employees, and a company's strongest asset is its people," says Chris Moore, chief technology officer at Training Server, Inc. "Organizations that do not tap into their mind share and take advantage of the knowledge within will quickly fall behind."
- *More demanding customers and investors.* For virtually every organization, the squeeze is on customers wanting to pay less while investors want more value from their portfolios. This means that all the resources to which an organization can lay claim, including its intellectual resources, must be managed for the best result.

To sustain competitiveness, organizations carefully craft processes to efficiently manufacture products and care for their customers—all in an effort to effectively exploit valuable resources. However, Ernst & Young estimates that up to 80 percent of a company's intellectual resources—the knowledge residing within it—is not systematically applied to business processes.

Today, more companies realize that they must develop strategies and processes designed to best utilize intellectual resources at both the strategic and operational levels. Ten years ago, companies began using groupware (such as e-mail, discussion forums, and document libraries) for coordinating activities. Now, they are inundated with new tools for communicating, sharing knowledge, and interacting electronically. They are deploying next-generation information, application platforms (such as enterprise portals), and real-time tools (such as instant messaging, Web conferencing, streaming audio/video) while struggling to manage process engineering across partners and suppliers as another aspect of collaboration.

Research from International Data Corp., for example, indicates that 50 percent of companies adopting data warehousing are planning or already implementing knowledge management. According to a survey by Cambridge Information Network (a division of Cambridge Technology Partners) of its 3,500 member CIOs, 85 percent believe that knowledge management generates competitive advantage. Figure 13.6 reports reasons for launching KM projects.

Organizations are looking for solutions to support their new e-business models. As a result, the demand for tools to more effectively negotiate, plan, decide, and collaborate has dramatically increased. However, most organizations are meeting collaboration requirements on a piecemeal basis, fulfilling requests as they emerge from business units or partners without an overall blueprint. The result is a hodgepodge of overlapping and redundant technologies (Meta Group 2000).

The benefits companies are expecting from their EKP initiatives are shown in Figure 13.7.

In the late 1990s, enterprises started to implement intranets to satisfy the enterprise requirements for information access, sharing, and dissemination. However, they are still poorly equipped to take advantage of the rapid development of intranets, enterprise applications, and electronic business.

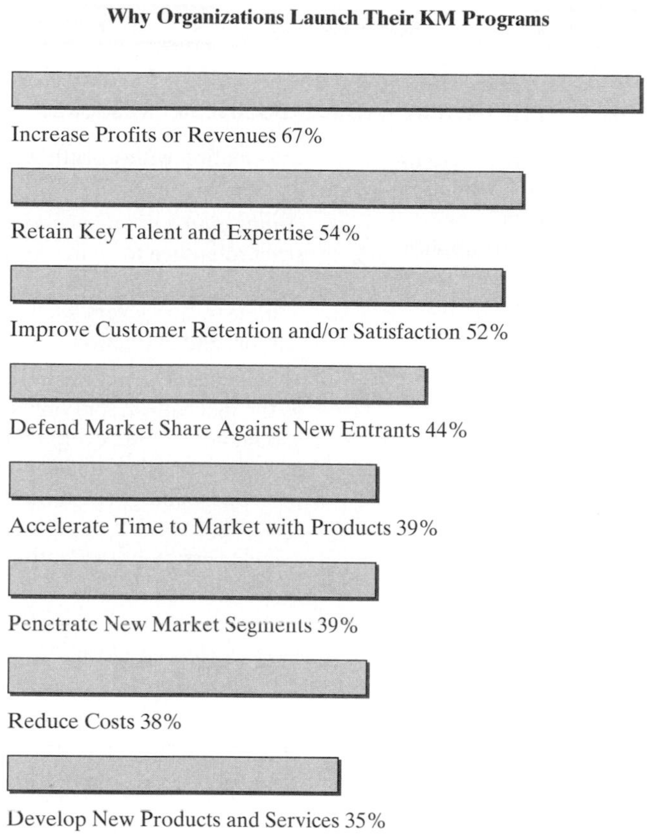

Why Organizations Launch Their KM Programs
Increase Profits or Revenues 67%
Retain Key Talent and Expertise 54%
Improve Customer Retention and/or Satisfaction 52%
Defend Market Share Against New Entrants 44%
Accelerate Time to Market with Products 39%
Penetrate New Market Segments 39%
Reduce Costs 38%
Develop New Products and Services 35%

FIGURE 13.6: Main Reasons for Launching KM Projects

SOURCE: International Data Corporation, *1999 Knowledge Management Survey*, 1999.

MARKET POTENTIAL

Knowledge portals have emerged as a key tool for supporting the knowledge workplace. According to David Folger, a senior program director at WCS, "Portals are big business. More than 85 percent of organizations plan to invest in portals during the next 5 years. The median expenditure is $500,000. We believe that as the world becomes more networked, these estimates are bound to climb. Why? Portals can provide easier,

FIGURE 13.7: The Benefits Knowledge Portals

Benefits of Knowledge Portals
Productivity
Locating Documents
Collaboration
Better Decisions
Quality of Data
Sharing Knowledge
Identifying Experts
E-mail Traffic
Bandwidth Use
Time in Meetings
Phone Calls
Response Times
Redundant Efforts
Operating Costs
Time to Market

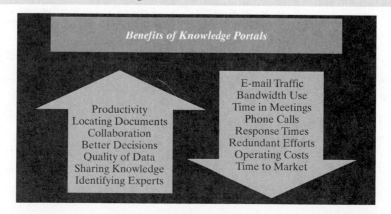

▪ ▪ ▪ ▪ ▪ ▪ **BOX 13.3** ▪ ▪ ▪ ▪ ▪ ▪

THE ROLE OF PORTALS IN FACING BUSINESS PRESSURES

- *Business integration versus information integration or application integration.* Integrating information and applications is the first step to supporting business integration. A portal can support application and information integration, but the weakness at this point can be a lack of providing business context, or meaning, to the information. Business integration is the integration and translation through the metadata layer of information and applications to provide context.

- *Process integration.* In addition to providing context, the portal solution should support process integration. Process integration includes workflow, categorization, and taxonomy services. These services provide the foundation for context.

Information with workflow, categorization, and taxonomy equals context.

- *Application and information integration.* This is a strict reference to source systems from which information is generated. It also includes the data administration layers, such as cleansing, transformation, and extraction.

- *Enterprise metadata repository.* Metadata is vital as the mechanism for context. The repository should not include every piece of information that exists, only the information that will be utilized to provide meaning. The repository then becomes the "single version of understanding," not just the "single version of the truth."

SOURCE: Bolds, Robert. "Enterprise Information Portals: Portals in Puberty," a white paper *KMWorld*, vol. 2, July/August 2001.

▪ ▪ ▪ ▪ ▪ ▪

unified access to business information, and better communications among customers and employees". See Box 13.3 for sample pressures facing portals.

The EIP market is comprised of the following infrastructure components:

- Content management
- Business intelligence
- Data warehouses and data marts
- Data management

An example of a portal in action is explained in Box 13.4.

▪ ▪ ▪ ▪ ▪ ▪ **BOX 13.4** ▪ ▪ ▪ ▪ ▪ ▪

FORD MOTOR COMPANY BUSINESS-TO-EMPLOYEE PORTAL

A BUSINESS-TO-EMPLOYEE PORTAL AT FORD MOTOR COMPANY

Ford Motor Company's Internet portal, using the Plumtree portal, is an example of a business-to-employee (B2E) Internet portal. This case

study example won DCI's Annual Portal Excellence Award for the Internet portal category, announced in January 2001.

(continued)

(*continued*)

Ford used Plumtree to implement an expansive framework for its ambitious business-to-employee e-business strategy. The world's second largest automaker chose Plumtree to create a single, simple, Web destination for 200,000 employees enterprise-wide to find and share the content and services they need to support customers and speed products to market. Ford is deploying the Plumtree corporate portal as part of an initiative to modernize the world's largest intranet, hub.ford.com, which spans 800 Ford facilities and 150 manufacturing plants worldwide. The portal enables Ford to integrate the hundreds of thousands of Web pages that comprise hub.ford.com in one enterprise-wide Web destination. Now, Ford employees anywhere can draw on a common base of best practices, market news, product specifications, performance metrics, and policy and procedures for the information they need to make confident business decisions and act quickly on revenue opportunities. Information is available for customer relationship management, order fulfillment, customer satisfaction, sales and volume tracking, economic assessments, competitive information, and Ford community initiatives.

FEATURES OF FORD'S B2E PORTAL

Personalization. Each hub.ford.com user tailors the portal experience to his or her role. To assemble a complete view of business, Ford employees can select gadgets for embedding e-mail, real-time news feeds, stock reports, sales histories, personnel directories, self-service travel booking, corporate expense reporting, and pay and benefits in personalized portal pages.

Collaboration. The portal enables Ford employees to use a Web-based workplace for drag and drop file sharing, multithreaded discussions, real-time messaging, and polling that Ford is deploying enterprise-wide. For example, paint shop workers from manufacturing departments on different continents can share skills and ideas easily, shortening development cycles and increasing product quality.

Community of practice. To foster collaboration, project mangers at Ford create community pages of content and services shared by entire business units.

BENEFITS TO FORD

Increased ROI on information technology. The Plumtree-powered hub.ford.com organizes scattered intranet sites into a framework that everybody can use, anywhere, and broadens the audience for applications previously limited to specialists, increasing return on Ford's electronic assets. Ford will integrate multiple data sources into the Plumtree corporate portal, including Documentum, whose content management platform is deployed throughout the enterprise.

Increased productivity. A single, personalized destination for corporate content and services helps focus everyone on company strategy, brands, and competitors, increasing the impact of every employee. Hub.ford.com users know what is happening across the enterprise and can stay on top of their customers, products, and markets, driving sales. The portal is also the framework for a broad e-learning initiative to foster employee competency, leadership, and advancement.

Close collaboration. Desktop access to digital workplaces is driving business-to-employee and business-to-business collaboration across Ford's enterprise. Now, Ford engineers can easily communicate with one another and with suppliers and product designers, and executives can conduct secure meetings across time zones and borders.

SOURCE: Finkelstein, C. "Building Enterprise Portals Using XML," The Data Warehouse Institute Conference, 2001.

▪ ▪ ▪ ▪ **Knowledge Portal Technologies**

In this section, we discuss the technologies needed to build portals. We proceed by identifying the functionalities to be included in a portal solution. For each capability, we describe the corresponding technology.

KEY FUNCTIONALITY

The main goal of a portal is to provide a single point of access to all information sources. Therefore, portals must be the ultimate tools for universal integration of all enterprise applications. At the same, because every individual has different information needs and knowledge uses, portals have to deliver a personalized interface. Given the complexity of this challenge, portals must include the following functionalities:

- *Gathering.* Documents created by knowledge workers are stored in a variety of locations (such as files on individual desktops, Web sites on the network, and databases on servers). In order to be accessible, data and documents need to be captured in a common repository.
- *Categorization.* This facility profiles the information in the repository and organizes it in meaningful ways for navigating and searching. Portals should support categorization at all levels, including the employee, partner, and customer levels. It should also support categorizations in various dimensions, including the process, product, and service dimensions.
- *Distribution.* This facility acquires knowledge, either through an active mechanism (search interface) or a passive mechanism (push). This facility supports the distribution of structured and unstructured information in the form of electronic or paper documents.
- *Collaboration.* Collaboration is achieved through messaging, workflow, discussion databases, and so forth. This facility expands the role of portals from a passive information provider to an interface for all types of organizational interactions.
- *Publish.* This facility publishes information to a broader audience, including individuals outside the organization.
- *Personalization.* Personalization is a key component of the portal architecture because it allows individuals to enhance their productivity. It is becoming a necessity for successful portals. This is due to the proliferation of information available through the portal. To take advantage of this facility, knowledge workers must be able to manage and prioritize the delivery of information on task-function or interest bases.
- *Search/navigate.* This component provides tools for identifying and accessing specific information. The knowledge worker can either browse or submit a query.

Figure 13.8 shows the most common features of portals. It shows also their business benefits.

Box 13.5 shows the Microsoft portal architecture.

COLLABORATION

The goal of the collaboration tool is to create a basic, collaborative knowledge management system that supports sharing and reusing information. To support the requirement of capturing undocumented knowledge, the messaging and collaboration module is a perfect tool. If writing e-mail, sending documents, or participating in discussions are easy tasks for knowledge workers, the motivation to act with knowledge manage-

Common Features	Business Benefits
Search	Quick access to hidden information to **facilitate business processes**
Categorization	Ability to organize information assets by business process, group, or job category thus **promoting access to relevant information**
Query, Reporting, and Analysis	**Better decision support** as well as information dissemination and sharing
Integration of Information and Applications	Ability to access through a single interface, all applications and information required for **increased job throughout**
Publish and Subscribe	Maturation of business processes by collaborating with others, sharing information, and **improving business performance**
Personalization	Arranging the interface to meet an individual's needs and desires for **increased job productivity**

▪ ▪ ▪ ▪ ▪ ▪ ▪ **FIGURE 13.8:**   Portal Features and Their Corresponding Benefits

SOURCE: Bolds, Robert. "Enterprise Information Portals: Portals in Puberty," *KMWorld*, July/August 2001, www.kmworld.com/publications/whitepapers/portals/bolds.htm, Date accessed December 2002.

ment in mind is much higher than in infrastructures that do not support this or that make it hard to use collaborative features. In a well-designed collaborative environment, this knowledge flow can be easily captured in e-mail, stored in document and discussion databases, and archived in the knowledge management system for later reuse.

Collaboration in the knowledge management context is the ability for two or more people to work together in a coordinated manner over time and space using electronic devices. One has to distinguish between two types of collaborations: asynchronous and synchronous collaboration.

- Asynchronous collaboration is human-to-human interactions via computer subsystems having no time or space constraints. Queries, responses, or access occur anytime and anyplace.
- Synchronous collaboration is computer-based, human-to-human interaction that occurs immediately (within 5 seconds). It can use audio, video, or data technologies.

Table 13.2 describes the requirements for a successful collaboration component.

Another important distinction to make is that of "push" versus "pull" technologies. Push technology places information in a place where it is difficult to avoid seeing it. E-mail is a classic example of a push technology. Pull technologies require you to take specific actions to retrieve information. The World Wide Web is a good example of a pull technology. An electronic mailing list that uses the push technology of e-mail is extremely powerful as a collaborative tool because it requires little learning or behavior change on the part of the user. In spite of its relative simplicity when compared to sophisticated Web-based collaborative forums, electronic mailing lists are the most popular collaborative tool.

Table 13.3 shows the advantages and disadvantages of the different technologies available to perform asynchronous and synchronous collaboration.

▪ ▪ ▪ ▪ ▪ ▪ **BOX 13.5** ▪ ▪ ▪ ▪ ▪ ▪

LAYERS OF THE PORTAL ARCHITECTURE

MICROSOFT'S KM PLATFORM

The knowledge management platform offers a typical, but extended, 3-layered architecture that allows a company to build a flexible, powerful knowledge management solution that is capable of being scaled. The knowledge desktop layer consists of familiar productivity tools, such as Microsoft Office, and integrates tightly with the knowledge services layer.

- The knowledge services layer provides important knowledge management services such as collaboration, document management, and search and deliver functionality, with modules for tracking, work flow, and data analysis.

- The system layer is a foundation that includes administration, security, and directories for managing the knowledge management platform. All services run on the system layer and benefit from the integrated communication services that connect with external solutions, platforms, and partners.

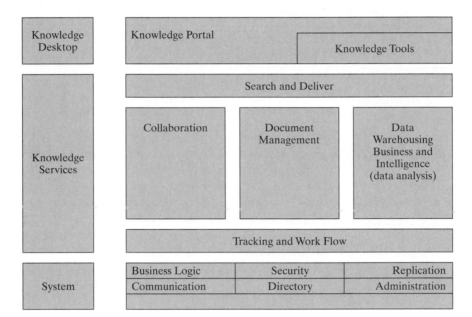

SOURCE: Honeycutt, Jerry. "Knowledge Management Strategies," Redmond, WA: Microsoft, p. 167.

▪ ▪ ▪ ▪ ▪ ▪ ▪

CONTENT MANAGEMENT

Content management requires directory and indexing capabilities to automatically manage the ever-growing warehouse of enterprise data. This component addresses the problem of searching for knowledge in all information sources in the enterprise. This knowledge includes structured and unstructured internal information objects such as office documents, collaborative data, MIS and ERP systems, and experts, as well as information from outside sources. This component handles how knowledge assets get into the knowledge management information base. To handle this new complexity of

TABLE 13.2   Requirements for Successful Collaboration Tools

Requirements for Successful Collaboration

- Comfortable e-mail systems that support collaborative services such as shared calendars, task lists, contact lists, and team-based discussions
- A Web browser for browsing and presenting the documents to the user
- Simple search functionalities such as file services integrated with the operating system or search services integrated with an application (e-mail, discussions)
- Collaboration services with a multipurpose database for capturing the collaborative data
- Web services for providing the access layer to documented knowledge
- Indexing services for full-text search of documents
- Well-organized central storage locations such as file, Web server, and documents databases

▪ ▪ ▪ ▪ ▪ ▪

SOURCE: Honeycutt, Jerry. "Knowledge Management Strategies," Redmond, WA: Microsoft, p. 176.

TABLE 13.3   Advantages and Disadvantages of Synchronous and Asynchronous Collaboration Tools

Synchronous Collaboration	*Asynchronous Collaboration*
Teleconferencing	**Electronic Mailing Lists**
In use extensively by senior management and staff, conference telephone calls represent an effective (if relatively expensive) collaboration technology. *Advantages:* personal, immediate feedback *Disadvantages:* expensive, often does not work well across time zones	Lists have been in use for a number of years and represent an extremely cost-effective collaboration technology. *Advantages:* cheap *Disadvantages:* limited communication medium
Computer Video/Teleconferencing	**Web-Based Discussion Forums**
Computer-based teleconferencing and video-conferencing is a rapidly evolving technology that has tremendous potential for distributed organizations.	There are a number of different online discussion forum applications in use. *Advantages:* same as electronic mailing lists except requires slightly faster Internet connection *Disadvantages:* cultural resistance
Online Chat Forums	**Lotus Notes**
Allow multiple users to communicate simultaneously by typing messages on a computer screen.	Lotus Notes is a comprehensive collaboration tool that includes e-mail and groupware. *Advantages:* comprehensive collaborative solution employing state-of-the-art technologies for communication, document management, and work flow *Disadvantages:* expensive to deploy when compared with other collaboration technologies

▪ ▪ ▪ ▪ ▪ ▪

the knowledge management information base and to help the knowledge workers to stay focused on solving business problems (without disappearing in technology), a sophisticated knowledge management taxonomy needs to be built based on metadata (data that describes other data). Metadata is needed to define types of information. The content management component also needs to publish information in the knowledge base (for example, categories and attributes).

Another important issue handled by content management is the way documents are analyzed, stored, and categorized. Once the documents have been gathered, they must be analyzed so that their content is available for retrieval and use by the system or end users. As documents enter the portal system, they are stored for later retrieval and display. However, it is not useful to simply put the documents away in their raw form. Systems typically analyze the document content and store the results of that analysis so that subsequent use of the documents by the system and users will be more effective and efficient.

As the number of documents under management grows, it becomes increasingly important to gather similar documents into smaller groups and to name the groups. This operation is called *categorizing*. All automatic categorizing methods use features to determine when two documents are similar enough to be put into the same cluster.

Because document collections are not static, portals must provide some form of taxonomy maintenance. As new documents are added, they must be added to the taxonomy at appropriate places, using a classification technology. As the clusters grow, and especially as the conceptual content of the new documents changes over time, it may become necessary to subdivide clusters or to move documents from one cluster to another. A portal administrator, using the taxonomy editor, can monitor and implement these suggestions and can periodically assess the health and appropriateness of the current taxonomy and document assignments within it (Mack, Ravin, and Byrd 2001). In the publishing process, several things should be considered concerning the knowledge management taxonomy. Although tagging documents with metadata is important for the quality of content in this stage of document publishing, it is a burden to submit information if tagging the metadata is a complex or time-consuming process. This is where the XML language comes into play. Box 13.6 provides a brief description of this language.

COLLABORATION VERSUS CATEGORIZATION: THE CASE OF THE WORLD BANK

The World Bank's main activity has been that of lending. It lends some $15 billion to $30 billion a year, receiving profits of about $1 billion a year. Knowledge management has become a strategic thrust. In fact, the World Bank is regarded as a leader in the knowledge management arena. In 1996, the World Bank was drowning in information, and even though it was spending a fortune on classifying all this knowledge, there was very little information flow within the organization (see Figure 13.9) (Sestina 2000).

An electronic document management system (EDMS) represents a substantial undertaking for any organization. The World Bank case provides a good example of the inherent opportunities and difficulties. The bank employs a state-of-the-art, XML–enabled Oracle data engine to drive a document management system linked to Lotus Notes groupware. In spite of the leading-edge nature of this technology, it is impossible to get staff to consistently and correctly file documents. The bank has employed a staff of 100 catalogers internationally to see that information is correctly codified. By ensur-

▪ ▪ ▪ ▪ ▪ ▪ **BOX 13.6** ▪ ▪ ▪ ▪ ▪ ▪ ▪

THE ROLE OF XML

WHAT IS XML?

XML is a subset of the standard generalized markup language (SGML) defined in ISO standard 8879:1986 that is designed to make it easy to interchange structured documents over the Internet. XML files always clearly mark the start and end of each of the logical parts (called *elements*) of an interchanged document. XML restricts the use of SGML constructs to ensure that fall-back options are available when access to certain components of the document is not currently possible over the Internet. It also defines how Internet uniform resource locators (URLs) can be used to identify component parts of XML data streams.

By defining the role of each element of text in a formal model, known as a *document type definition* (DTD), users of XML can check that each component of the document occurs in a valid place within the interchanged data stream. An XML DTD allows computers to check, for example, that users do not accidentally enter a third-level heading without first having entered a second-level heading, something that cannot be checked using the hypertext markup language (HTML) previously used to code documents.

However, unlike SGML, XML does not require the presence of a DTD. If no DTD is available, either because all or part of it is not accessible over the Internet or because the user failed to create it, an XML system can assign a default definition for undeclared components of the markup.

XML allows users to do the following:

- Bring multiple files together to form compound documents
- Identify where illustrations are to be incorporated into text files, and the format used to encode each illustration
- Provide processing control information to supporting programs, such as document validators and browsers
- Add editorial comments to a file

It is important to note, however, that XML is not:

- A predefined set of tags, of the type defined for HTML, that can be used to mark up documents
- A standardized template for producing particular types of documents

XML was not designed to be a standardized way of coding text. In fact, it is impossible to devise a single coding scheme that would suit all languages and all applications. Instead, XML is a formal language that can be used to pass information about the component parts of a document to another computer system. XML is flexible enough to describe any logical text structure, whether it be a form, memo, letter, report, book, encyclopedia, dictionary, or database.

SOURCE: Bryan, Martin. "An Introduction to the Extensible Markup Language (XML)," SGML Centre, 1997, www.personal.u-net.com/~sgml/xmlintro.htm, Date accessed December 2002.

▪ ▪ ▪ ▪ ▪ ▪

ing rigor in classification through the use of controlled vocabulary, resource discovery is much more efficient, both in terms of searching and browsing.

With regard to building knowledge bases (comprehensive knowledge repositories), the overwhelming message from the World Bank is that this is a difficult, extremely labor-intensive process. After 4 years of investment in knowledge management,

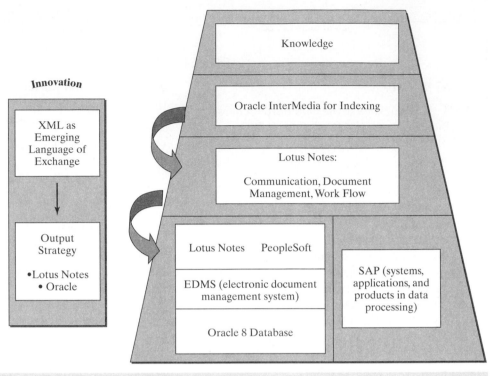

Innovation

■ ■ ■ ■ ■ ■ ■ **FIGURE 13.9:** KM Architecture at the World Bank

SOURCE: Sestina, A., Graham, H. et al. "Technology for Knowledge Management," www.bellanet.org/km/report/KMFinal14.doc?ois=y;template=lists_word.htm, Date accessed August 2002.

the bank reports that they have had much more success with collaboration strategies than with codification.

Although codifying knowledge is a fundamental activity of any knowledge-based organization, the cost of comprehensive codification technologies such as EDMS needs to be evaluated in terms of a return on investment with respect to both technology and people (Denning 1998).

INTELLIGENT AGENTS

Intelligent agents are tools that can be applied in numerous ways in the context of EKPs. As a tool, intelligent agents are still in their infancy. Most applications are experimental and have not yet reached the efficient commercial stage. However, there is no doubt that they will play a crucial role in all aspects of EKPs, especially in intelligent search and filtering the right documents according to some criteria. One application is the use of intelligent agents in ERPs such as CRM portals, specifically in areas of competition.

As the relationships between companies and their customers become more complex, the enterprises need more information and advice on what these relationships mean and how to exploit them. Intelligent agent technology offers some very interesting options for addressing such needs.

Customers set certain priorities while purchasing products and services. Intelligent agents can master individual customers' or customer groups' demand priorities by learning from experience with them, and they can quantitatively and qualitatively analyze those priorities. Agents are software entities that are able to execute a wide range of functional tasks (such as searching, comparing, learning, negotiating, and collaborating) in an autonomous, proactive, social, and adaptive manner. The term *intelligent* in this context means only that we are dealing with entities that are able to adjust their behavior to the environment. In other words, intelligent agents are able to learn from previous situations and replicate the behavior of the customer to predict purchasing patterns. There is a vast range of services customers require that intelligent agents can address. Some of these services may include the following:

- Customized customer assistance with online services: news filtering, messaging, scheduling, making arrangements for gatherings, ordering, and so on
- Customer profiling, including inferring information about customer behavior based on business experiences with the particular customer
- Integrating profiles of customers into a group of marketing activities
- Predicting customer requirements
- Negotiating prices and payment schedules
- Executing financial transactions on the customer's behalf

These examples represent a spectrum of applications from the somewhat modest, low-level news filtering applications to the more advanced and complicated customer relationship management applications that focus on predicting customer requirements. The main point is that an intelligent agent is an intermediary between the enterprise and its customer, and a source of effective, utilitarian information encountered at different virtual destinations.

Figure 13.10 shows the new technology trends in implementing portals. The emphasis is on collaborative technologies to create communities of practice; advanced human computer interaction to enhance performance; and intelligent agents to automate the search function.

▪▪▪▪ Implications for Knowledge Management

WHO IS BUILDING ENTERPRISE PORTALS?

META Group conducted a survey of 350 organizations (respondent organizations had at least 500 employees) to find how widely enterprise portals are being deployed, how the portals are being utilized, and what services and vendors organizations use for portal deployment. More than 80 percent of the respondents knew the term *portal,* and one in three currently either have a portal installed or have one under development. Large organizations (more than 10,000 employees) have a significantly higher portal installation rate.

WHO SPONSORS ENTERPRISE PORTALS?

New portal sponsorship is shifting away from IT—which drops from 63.3 percent of sponsorship of existing portals to 46.6 percent for planned portals—and toward the marketing/sales group (20.6 percent versus 6.7 percent), which is a strong indicator of the influence of e-commerce on portal development. The line of business has increased from 2.5 percent of share to 9.2 percent, while the corporate staff sponsorship has remained the same.

IMPLEMENTATION ISSUES

Although technology issues can be categorized in many different ways, the codification versus collaboration paradigm also provides a particularly useful structure for understanding current trends in information technology. For globally distributed organizations

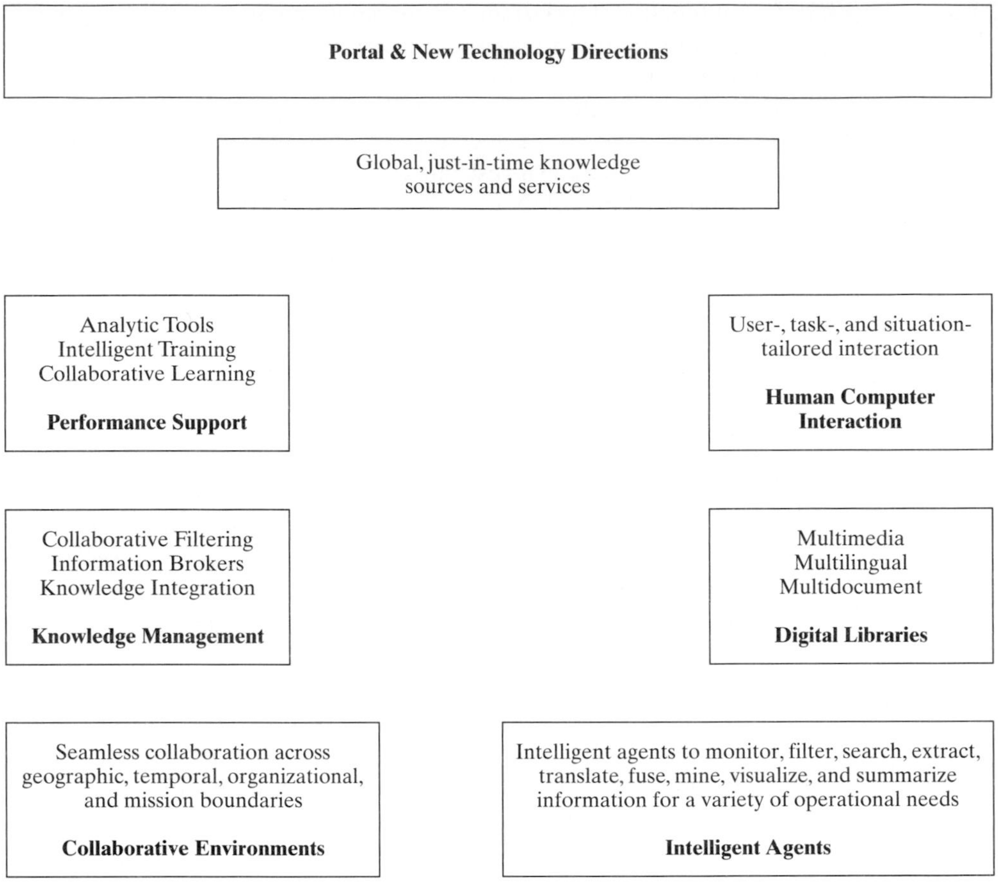

```
┌─────────────────────────────────────────────────────────────────┐
│                                                                   │
│               Portal & New Technology Directions                  │
│                                                                   │
└─────────────────────────────────────────────────────────────────┘


                    ┌──────────────────────────────┐
                    │   Global, just-in-time knowledge │
                    │      sources and services        │
                    └──────────────────────────────┘


  ┌─────────────────────────┐              ┌─────────────────────────┐
  │    Analytic Tools       │              │  User-, task-, and situation- │
  │  Intelligent Training   │              │     tailored interaction │
  │  Collaborative Learning │              │                         │
  │                         │              │   **Human Computer**    │
  │  **Performance Support**│              │    **Interaction**      │
  └─────────────────────────┘              └─────────────────────────┘


  ┌─────────────────────────┐              ┌─────────────────────────┐
  │  Collaborative Filtering│              │      Multimedia         │
  │   Information Brokers    │              │     Multilingual        │
  │  Knowledge Integration   │              │     Multidocument       │
  │                         │              │                         │
  │ **Knowledge Management**│              │  **Digital Libraries**  │
  └─────────────────────────┘              └─────────────────────────┘


  ┌─────────────────────────┐              ┌─────────────────────────────────┐
  │  Seamless collaboration across │       │ Intelligent agents to monitor, filter, search, extract, │
  │ geographic, temporal, organizational, │ │ translate, fuse, mine, visualize, and summarize │
  │    and mission boundaries       │      │ information for a variety of operational needs │
  │                                 │      │                                 │
  │ **Collaborative Environments**  │      │      **Intelligent Agents**     │
  └─────────────────────────┘              └─────────────────────────────────┘
```

▪ ▪ ▪ ▪ ▪ ▪ ▪ **FIGURE 13.10:** New Trends in Portal Technologies

SOURCE: Conover, Joan. "Using Portal Technology to Fuse Corporate Information Knowledge Management, Information Management, Data Warehousing," New Technology Digital Library. www.c3i.osd.mil/km/proceedings/53.ppt, Date accessed August 2002.

(that is, most international development organizations) that rely on the Internet as a medium for the sharing of knowledge, the issue of bandwidth is fundamental. At this point in the evolution of the Internet, bandwidth is a chief constraining factor for many applications. The determination of an organization's overall KM strategy will provide guidance for the implementation of appropriate technology. Hansen, Nohria, and Tierney (1999) present a valuable model to help guide thinking about managing organizational knowledge by distinguishing between "codification" versus "personalization" strategies. This dichotomy is useful in making the critical decisions required to ensure the right technological mix.

Codification focuses primarily on computer use, whereby knowledge is carefully coded and stored in databases for easy access (see Chapters 7 and 9). By contrast, the personalization KM strategy makes use of computers to help people communicate knowledge, not to store it. The emphasis is on knowledge sharing via direct person-to-person contacts.

BANDWIDTH

Current trends point toward a steady decrease in the cost of Internet access. The rapid and pervasive spread of Internet communication coupled with the evolution of faster and cheaper technology is resulting in improved access to the Internet at lower costs.

This trend has been slowest at manifesting itself in Africa. However, even their Internet access is spreading rapidly and is becoming much less expensive, especially in capital cities.

Given the importance of collaboration and the creation of communities of practice as a method for knowledge sharing, it is worth investigating the costs of a significant increase in bandwidth for regional offices that could support the following:

- Desktop videoconferencing
- Internet telephony
- Improved access to information systems based at headquarters
- Other collaborative tools
- Access to more sophisticated information resources

Most of the technological tools now available tend to help dissemination of know-how, but they offer less assistance for knowledge use. Tools that assist in knowledge creation are even less developed, although collaborative work spaces offer promising opportunities by enabling participation, across time and distance, in project design or knowledge-base development; those most knowledgeable about development problems—the people living them on a day-to-day basis—can actively contribute to their solutions. Some of the more user friendly technologies are the traditional ones—face-to-face discussions, the telephone, electronic mail, and paper-based tools such as flip charts. Among the issues that need to be considered in providing information technology for knowledge-sharing programs are the following:

- *Responsiveness to user need.* Continuous efforts must be made to ensure that the information technology in use meets the varied and changing needs of users.
- *Content structure.* In large systems, classification and cataloguing become important so that items can be easily found and quickly retrieved.
- *Content quality requirements.* Standards for admitting new content into the system need to be established and met to ensure operational relevance and high value.
- *Integration with existing systems.* Because most knowledge-sharing programs aim at embedding knowledge sharing in the work of staff as seamlessly as possible, it is key to integrate knowledge-related technology with preexisting technology choices.
- *Scalability.* Solutions that seem to work well in small groups (such as HTML Web sites) may not be appropriate for extrapolation organization-wide or on a global basis.
- *Hardware–software compatibility.* Hardware–software compatibility is important to ensure that choices are made that are compatible with the bandwidth and computing capacity available to users.
- *Synchronization of technology with the capabilities of users.* This is important so as to take full advantage of the potential of the tools, particularly where the technology skills of users differ widely.

PORTAL PRODUCT SELECTION

Creating an enterprise portal vendor shortlist can save time and effort typically devoted to large-scale market scans. Once a portal vendor shortlist has been created, each vendor should be evaluated through the use of scenarios that test key business functionality, based on architectural fit, vendor viability, and product features. Table 13.4 shows the features of some products and the best way to use them.

TABLE 13.4 Portal Vendors

Vendor	KM Portal Product	Feature Summary	Best Uses
Lotus/IBM	Lotus Raven 1.0 (in beta)	• Intelligent taxonomy; builder automates document clustering; learns your preferences; expertise locator links authors to content • QuickPlace collaboration tool for instant messaging, app sharing, and virtual meetings • Assigns value to data based on how often it is used • Portal replication • Facilitates content management	• Self-creating and refining taxonomies • Personnel resources linked to data sources • Advanced collaboration • Easy portal repurposing • Rapid application development with associated KM packages
Open Text	MyLivelink Portal 1.0 with Livelink 8.5.1 KM software	• Integrated work flow and project management with task lists and Java-based process maps • Quick integration of features from other apps via widgets • Quick portal deployment with more than 600 syndicated application component gadgets, which can be freely distributed	• Integrated KM • Document management and work flow • Custom collaboration spaces (personal, project, or enterprise)
Plumtree	Plumtree Corporate Portal 4.0	• Automatic population of mapped taxonomies with filtered content • E-mail, voice, and wireless notification of content updates • Integration with LDAP directories • E-room tools for collaboration and virtual communities	• Easy and extensive content and application integration • Scalability • Advanced security and access control • Trainable taxonomies • Voice and wireless data access • Customization and extensibility
Woolamai	WebMeta Engine 1.0	• Quick integration of corporate portals with data and other apps without specialized training • Intuitive, flexible portal interface • Knowledge taxonomy adapts to data views; provides relevance filtering • Data-mining functionality • Web site statistics monitor site activity	• Usability • Tracking site statistics • Content streaming to wireless devices

▪ ▪ ▪ ▪ ▪ ▪

SUMMARY ▪ ▪ ▪ ▪

- A portal is a secure, Web-based interface that provides a single point of integration for and access to information, applications, and services for all people involved in the enterprise, including employees, partners, suppliers, and customers.
- Born with search engines such as Yahoo! and Alta Vista, portals have since made their way into enterprises, bringing together not only information from the Internet, but in-house data as well. These portals, which are known as enterprise

knowledge portals (EKPs), aim to offer a single, uniform point from which all of an enterprise's data sources can be accessed.

- The term *data sources* encompasses structured data (such as databases, Lotus Notes, and so forth) and unstructured data (such as e-mails, files, and archives); it also includes the data resulting from specific processes and enterprise applications (such as ERP and CRM tools). Today, the EIP market is thriving, and many vendors are betting big on portals' well-founded ability to fulfill enterprise needs.

- Content management in the EKP context requires directory and indexing capabilities to automatically manage the ever-growing store of structured and unstructured data residing in data warehouses, Web sites, ERP systems, legacy applications, and so forth. Using metadata to define types of information, good content management can serve as the backbone for a system of corporate decision making where business intelligence tools mine data and report findings back to key players in the enterprise. Content management may also involve going outside the enterprise, employing crawlers that find pertinent data via the Internet, incorporating it into existing systems, indexing it, and delivering it to appropriate analysts, knowledge workers, or decision makers.

- The collaborative functionality of EKPs can range from tracking e-mail to developing workplace communities. Some EKPs might allow workers in different parts of the world to easily create virtual meeting rooms where they can conference by chat, voice, or video communication.

TERMS TO KNOW ▪▪▪▪

Bandwidth: The term used to describe the speed of a network connection. A fast connection allows the user to view images and videos, and interact with remote sites as if they were local.

Browser: A software application used to locate and display Web pages.

Content management system (CMS): A system used to manage the content of a Web site.

Document management system: The computerized management of electronic as well as paper-based documents.

Electronic collaboration: A process through which project partners can contribute jointly to works in progress via e-mail, groupware, and public networks.

Electronic mailing list: A list of e-mail addresses identified by a single name, such as *mail-list@sandybay.com*. When an e-mail message is sent to the mailing list name, it is automatically forwarded to all the addresses in the list.

Enterprise application integration (EAI): The process that integrates applications inside an organization or applications of many organizations in a seamless fashion.

Enterprise information portals: Portals that tie together multiple, heterogeneous internal repositories and applications as well as external content sources and services into a single browser-based view that is individualized to a particular user's task or role.

Enterprise knowledge portal: An electronic doorway into a knowledge management system.

Extensible markup language (XML): A specification developed by the W3C designed especially for Web documents.

Groupware: A generic term used to describe applications that support and facilitate the work of teams and groups of people.

Intelligent agents: Programs used extensively on the Web that perform tasks such as retrieving and delivering information and automating repetitive tasks.

Intranet: A network based on TCP/IP protocols (the Internet) belonging to an organization, usually a corporation, accessible only by the organization's members, employees, or others with authorization.

Knowledge repository: The software system that is a collection of internal and external knowledge inside the knowledge management system.

Knowledge repository model: Model that describes the 2-step knowledge transfer procedure of person-to-repository and repository-to-person.

Metadata: Data about data, such as indices or summaries.

Organizational knowledge base: The collection of knowledge related to the operation of an organization.

Personalization: Software systems that allow an Internet site to provide the user with a Web page that reflects the interests, needs, and actions of the user.

Portal: A Web page that offers links to other Web sites. Portals can be broad or narrow, specific or general.

Search engines: Software agents whose task is to find information by looking at keywords or by following certain guidelines or rules.

Teleconferencing: Conferring with a number of people via telephone or computer systems.

Vertical portal: Electronic exchanges that combine upstream and downstream e-commerce activities of specialized products or services.

Video mail: Application that enables users to transmit photos, sounds, and video.

Voice portals: Gateways that allow customers and employees to use ordinary phone lines to access and request information.

Work flow: The defined series of tasks within an organization to produce a final outcome.

Test Your Understanding ▪ ▪ ▪ ▪

1. Why is there a need for portals? How are portals similar to the concept of data warehouses and data marts?
2. What are the advantages and disadvantages of having your portal on the Internet instead of an intranet?
3. List the differences between knowledge and information portals. Discuss the benefits of each.
4. Discuss the strategic and technological fit required for an organization to implement a portal.
5. Discuss the advantages and disadvantages of purchasing a portal from a vendor. Make sure you explore vendor Web sites such as Viador (www.viador.com) and Autonomy (www.autonomy.com).
6. Discuss the differences between static and dynamic portals. When would you use each each?
7. Discuss how you can use content management to sort knowledge from external and internal sources. Illustrate with examples.
8. Discuss the issues that can arise when implementing a portal. Focus on technology, management, corporate strategy, and end users.
9. Give examples and uses of portals for B2B, B2C, B2G, C2C, and C2G.
10. List a number of possible ways a portal can be made accessible, given current technological trends. Focus on five of these technologies and discuss their strengths and weaknesses.

Knowledge Exercises ▪ ▪ ▪ ▪

1. In the past, companies used electronic data interchange (EDI) to communicate with suppliers and customers. Discuss how portals can be used to replace the functions of EDI.
2. An audit firm needs to develop a system that allows auditors and public accountants to search accounting standards, share knowledge, communicate, and share Word and Excel files between the head office and clients' sites. As a consultant, you have been asked to recommend such a system. What would you suggest?
3. A hardware retailer wishes to offer real-time support to customers via the Internet. Suggest how a knowledge portal, equipped with chat and CRM, can be used to accomplish this. What additional support can the hardware retailer offer? What information can he give to the manufacturer?
4. A multinational conglomerate has a centralized human resources department in Cleveland, Ohio. The human resources director wishes to launch a new set of multilingual policies to all employees, according to their function,

category, and grade. The director also wishes to have employees interact and give feedback on the policies. Suggest a computerized solution.

5. Discuss how synergy between different strategic business units can be harnessed and utilized by knowledge portals.

6. Discuss how portals can offer a solution to the centralized versus decentralized information dilemma. What forms of knowledge can be collected centrally, and what should be left decentralized? Why?

7. How can personalized portals use data-mining techniques? Suggest how knowledge management and data mining can be integrated on a portal, and give supporting examples.

8. Challenge: Establish e-learning portals for customers and partners to help those audiences succeed with their NCR products and to generate new revenue for NCR.

Strategy:

Use THINQ e-learning solutions to launch and track courses and provide community features—such as chat rooms and message boards—around the courses.

Results:

NCR has extended nearly 4,000 online and classroom courses to more than 2,000 registered users and is meeting its e-learning revenue goals.

NCR has come a long way in the 117 years since it introduced the first mechanical cash register, but the $6 billion company's tremendous success still hinges on the individual customer relationship. Today, NCR helps companies harness the vast amount of customer information they collect at the sales counter, over the phone, at the ATM, and on the Internet. With this information, businesses can satisfy each customer's unique needs, often automatically, and transform customer transactions into rich customer relationships.

From the dawn of the cash register through NCR's leadership in data warehousing, the company's offerings have always been sophisticated. Accordingly, it has always been important for NCR to help customers learn how to reap the full potential of their NCR hardware and software. It is also important for NCR partners to completely understand the company's products so they succeed in selling and implementing them.

NCR has traditionally offered classroom training for customers and partners to achieve these goals. Recently the company started offering courses over the Internet. These classes combine the incisive content of NCR's classroom training programs with the reach and efficiency of the worldwide network, letting students anywhere in the world take a class any time they can access a Web browser. In addition to helping customers and partners succeed, this e-learning program also generates new revenue for NCR.

NCR evaluated a number of e-learning tools for the job of powering its two customer and partner e-learning portals. One portal is the Teradata Education Network (TEN), an e-learning Web site for the company's data-warehousing customers. The other is the external NCR University (NCRU), which extends award-winning NCR employee e-learning to partners. After a rigorous review, NCR selected THINQ to build and power the portals, which offer customers and partners Web-based, self-paced training, course tracking, employee-learning reporting, live virtual classes, hosted educational chats, a reference library, message boards, and instructor-led courseware registration.

"Employee training is important, but it just scratches the surface of e-learning's potential," said Janet Perdzock, program manager, Global Learning Operations of NCR. "These initiatives improve our customers' and partners' businesses, enrich our relationships with those audiences, and generate significant new revenue for us. THINQ provides a bridge to our courses, content, and other back-end systems and is a key ingredient in our success."

NCR chose THINQ over other e-learning vendors because of THINQ's long experience in the learning industry, its integrated product, reputation, flexibility, affordability, and ability to interoperate with NCR's existing infrastructure. THINQ's satisfied customers also tipped NCR's decision.

The NCRU portal for partners went live in July 2001 and offers 3,600 courses, including 859 NCR proprietary Web-based training courses, NETg information technology courses, NETg desktop computing courses, and multilanguage courses. The portal offers CDs, books, tapes, and classroom courses—all filtered based on each company's profile. Since the launch, NCRU has signed up 766 users at 49 companies who have completed 375 courses. They can create individual learning plans, register online, and view their entire training histories. Counting users who registered for a previous "interim" site prior to July 2001, the NCRU portal for customers and partners has 1,528 authorized users.

NCR's Teradata Education Network (TEN) learning environment went live March 30, 2001, to its membership-based learning community. Teradata Education Network is exceeding all projections with more than 1,300 members, more than 1,000 user sessions every week, and more than 660 course completions in the first 6 months. One-third of all Teradata companies have an associate who is a member of TEN, and TEN is on track to meet its revenue goal for 2001. A 13-month membership to the site comes in many shapes and sizes, depending on the customer's need. An individual membership can cost as little as $895, and a corporate membership can cost as little as $6,795. Not only do members receive access to the learning community, but they also are provided with access to over 50 Teradata courses. Members get into message boards, access white papers, take virtual classroom courses, and review recorded virtual classroom presentations.

Unlike most online training programs, Teradata Education Network allows students from around the globe to communicate with other students and make direct contact with instructors. One of the most powerful aspects of the network is the access to knowledgeable Teradata professionals worldwide, giving students a chance to stay current in an ever-changing market.

In the future, NCR plans more curriculum-mapping/skill-building capabilities and additional, customized portals for specific customers or partners. It also plans thorough profiling of individual users and corporations to better meet their e-learning needs.

"Customers were asking for an alternate way to train without leaving the office that would supplement their classroom learning," said Adam Zaller, program manager of e-learning for Teradata Customer Education. "Our customers say the Teradata Education Network learning community is like having 'Partners,' our annual user conference, 365 days a year. It's a community of customers helping each other, a revenue stream for the company, and a great way to help our technology solve critical business problems in the real world. Our customers and our prospects are now a lot more aware of education and what we have to offer. We anticipate usage to continue to grow, revenue to expand, and the program to eventually cover the globe."

a. Discuss the advantages of Teradata as a learning option. What advantages does it have over conventional learning in terms of content delivery, convenience, and growth opportunities?

b. Discuss the possible disadvantage of having a purely electronic learning solution. How can the human element be incorporated?

    c. Suggest ways for NCR to incorporate curriculum-mapping/skill-building capabilities and customized portals for specific customers or partners, as mentioned in the case.

    d. Suggest ways in which Teradata can be used to train some of its divisions and departments. Can Teradata also be used to train line, middle, and upper management? If so, how can they go about this, and what content can they use?

        SOURCE: THINQ 2002

9. With the help of a corporate portal, the U.S. Postal Service (USPS) delivers quality KM.

At many organizations, corporate portals are seen as a convenient way to centralize proprietary information and make it easily accessible to employees. As such, portals can serve as an ideal knowledge management tool where employees can tap into a wealth of corporate know-how. Unfortunately, many portals fall short. Instead of serving as sleek KM vehicles, all too often portals resemble black holes where information gets dumped, never again to see the light of day.

For those striving to dust off their dormant corporate portals and transform them into a KM tools, John Gregory has a few sound words of advice. Gregory, a market research analyst for the U.S. Postal Service in Arlington, Virginia, is in charge of MarketTracks, a knowledge retrieval and competitive intelligence portal used by 1,000 sales and marketing employees.

Since 1994, the postal service has offered employees centralized sales and marketing information, first in the form of a client/server system and then, beginning in 1997, on the Web. Over the years, the organization has honed a practical strategy for creating useful, relevant online resources that actually work as advertised—they help employees do their jobs rather than hinder them.

As Gregory sees it, there are a few mysteries to solve when it comes to figuring out how to create and sustain a useful portal. When considering content, Gregory assembled focus groups of users and asked them what they wanted to get out of a portal. In most organizations where 1,000 employees are the target audience, not everyone needs or wants to see the same information. As a result, personalization of content became an important criteria.

Once he examined the content issues, Gregory turned his attention to vendors and specific technologies. Vendor selection, Gregory says, is an area having many pitfalls, but it is one that often gets short shrift. As a result of lackadaisical vetting processes, many companies are saddled with software that does not fit their needs or vendors that do not work well with them. The end result is money down the drain. "It can be enormously expensive to roll out a full-featured portal," Gregory says. "But it doesn't have to be that expensive."

For example, Gregory ruled out Plumtree's portal software because the postal service did not need its entire suite and balked at the prospect of paying for add-ons as they were introduced. Instead, the postal service served as a beta tester for Epicentric, trying out the company's enterprise portal software among a small group of employees.

"There's a lot to be said for being an early adopter," Gregory says, adding that the chance of having a good relationship with a vendor is greatly enhanced by doing so.

Even with careful vendor choices, Gregory says the odds are against most portals. "A major flaw is design," he says.

Gregory says that good design means first figuring out what people are going to do with a portal by focusing on function rather than content. Essential to function is navigation that is well planned and efficient.

"Navigation isn't just a box marked 'search,'" he says. "There's got to be the taxonomy, links, site map, and a help feature as well."

The navigation should never become static, however. As organic entities, portals need to change and adapt as the organization does, a lesson that the USPS is putting to good use.

"People think of a portal as a database and end up putting up everything that they've got instead of what users need," Gregory says. "A portal really is an organic corpus of knowledge."

SOURCE: Santosus 2002.

a. Suggest ways in which content can be managed so that it can be personally available to an employee.
b. Discuss the advantages and disadvantages of being an "early adopter" and how it may impact organizations such as USPS.
c. Discuss the advantages and disadvantages of designing a portal on the basis of functionality instead of content.
d. What does the author mean by "navigation should never become static"?

REFERENCES ■ ■ ■ ■

Bolds, Robert. "Enterprise Information Portals: Portals in Puberty," white paper, *KMWorld*, vol. 2, July/August 2001, www.kmworld.com/publications/whitepapers/portals/bolds.htm, Date accessed August 2002.

Bryan, Martin. "An Introduction to the Extensible Markup Language (XML)." SGML Centre, 1997, www.personal.u-net.com/~sgml/xmlintro.htm, Date accessed December 2002.

Conover, Joan. "Using Portal Technology to Fuse Corporate Information Knowledge Management, Information Management, Data Warehousing," New Technology Digital Library, www.c3i.osd.mil/km/proceedings/53.ppt, Date accessed August 2002.

Davydov, Mark M. "The Second Wave of EIP," *Intelligent Enterprise*, vol. 3, no. 4, March 1, 2000.

Denning, Stephen. "What Is Knowledge Management?" World Bank Knowledge Management Board, 1998, www.apqc.org/free/whitepapers/index.htm, Date accessed August 2002.

E-Gov Knowledge Management Conference. "Using Army Knowledge Online for Mission Success," April 11, 2000, www.army.mil/ako/webbriefing.ppt, Date accessed August 2002.

Enterprise Knowledge Portal, www.askmecorp.com, Date accessed August 2002.

"Enterprise Knowledge Portals to Become the Shared Desktop of the Future," www.itweb.co.za/office/bmi/9903300919.htm, Date accessed August 2002.

Finkelstein, C. "Building Enterprise Portal Using XML," The Data Warehouse Institute Conference, 2001.

Firestone, J. "Enterprise Knowledge Portals," White Paper 8, www.dkms.com, Date accessed August 2002.

Hansen, Morten, Nohria, Nitin, and Tierney, Thomas. "What's Your Strategy for Managing Knowledge?" *Harvard Business Review*, March-April 1999, p. 106.

Honeycutt, Jerry. "Knowledge Management Strategies," Redmond WA: Microsoft, 2000, p. 167, 176.

IBM. "Portals: An Overview," www-1.ibm.com/services/kcm/cm_portal.html, Date accessed August 2002.

IBM. "Portals, Knowledge, and Content Management," www-1.ibm.com/services/kcm/know_mngt_con.html, Date accessed December 2002.

IDC, "Knowledge Management Survey," 1999.

Mack, R., Ravin, Y., and Byrd, R. J., "Knowledge Portals and the Emerging Digital Knowledge Workflow," IBM Systems, vol. 40, no. 4, 2001, researchweb.watson.ibm.com/journal/sj/404/mack.pdf, Date accessed August 2002.

Meta Group, "Business Collaboration," www.metagroup.com/cgi-bin/inetcgi/commerce/productDetails.jsp?oid_29277, Date accessed August 2002.

Santosus, Megan. "In the Know," *CIO.com*, February 19, 2002. www.cio.com/knowledge/edit/K021902_portal.html. Date accessed December 2002.

Sestina, A., Graham H., Weaver Smith, B., and Sorg, S. "Technology for Knowledge Management," www.bellanet.org/km/report/KMFinal14.doc?ois=y;template=lists_word.htm, Date accessed August 2002.

Shein, E., "The Knowledge Crunch," *CIO*, May 1, 2001, www.cio.com/archive/050101/crunch.html, Date accessed August 2002.

Shilakes, C. C., and Tylman, J. "Enterprise Information Portals. In: In-depth Report," Merrill Lynch, 1998, www.sagemaker.com/company/downloads/eip_indepth.pdf, Date accessed 2002.

THINQ, "Case Study: NCR," www.thinq.com/pages/cus_case_ncr.htm, 2002, Date accessed December 2002.

www.brint.com, Date accessed August 2002.

Yahoo! Home Page, www.yahoo.com, Date accessed September 5, 2002.

PART V: ETHICAL, LEGAL,
AND MANAGERIAL ISSUES

CHAPTER

14

Who Owns
Knowledge?
Ethical and
Legal Issues

Contents

Don't ask what you can do,
ask what you should do.
—H. JEFFERSON SMITH

▪▪▪▪ # In a Nutshell

Julie, a knowledge developer of a bank, was asked by her company's marketing department for access to the customer mortgage information base. They wanted to use this information, which included household income, debt history, and other personal items, in a marketing knowledge base to help target appropriate customers for new bank services.

Although several mortgage managers complained that such information was not supposed to be used for marketing purposes, Julie delivered the information anyway. She justified her actions by saying that it was not her job to rule on the uses of information, but to expedite their exchanges.

The corporation was soon contacted by a local newspaper reporter, who had heard of the marketing campaign. He wanted some details about the marketing plan for a story on privacy and confidentiality. The result was a potentially embarrassing public relations disaster that had to be quickly and deftly handled by the CEO. After the incident, the CEO reprimanded Julie for not taking responsibility to ensure proper information flow. He made it clear that it was her duty to bring such issues to the attention of senior executives.

In this real incident, a custodian of a company's knowledge base was confronted with an ethical and potentially legal dilemma: how to manage sensitive information, how to be the corporation's knowledge conscience, and how to handle tough corporate questions regarding the consequences of knowledge-based applications.

By adopting a proactive approach grounded in sound ethical and legal reasoning, knowledge developers can extend their leadership from the technological arena into the domain of knowledge ethics. Knowledge managers who assume the moral stewardship of knowledge initiatives can provide long-term benefits to both their departments and their companies.

Unethical acts raise legal and litigation issues as well. Cases involving knowledge-based systems will depend on who owns knowledge, who is held liable, and on what basis liability is determined. The laws also vary depending on whether a knowledge system is considered a product or a service. Warranties and the laws enforcing such assurances protect employees and users in various ways.

The material covered thus far has examined the principles, procedures, tools, and methodologies of knowledge management. Each chapter discussed the managerial implications of this evolving concept and how it might serve productivity of the firm. However, other questions arise at each stage of development: Who owns knowledge? What are the ethical issues involved in building and managing knowledge-based systems? How does an organization address knowledge as a property right related to employee knowledge or expertise? What are the legal implications of knowledge management?

▪▪▪▪ Knowledge Owners

In an oral culture where literacy does not exist, knowledge is not owned by anyone: It is performed. For example, the skills involved in boat building are passed from one craftsman to another through apprenticeship and tribal arrangements. In contrast, in literate societies the invention of writing separated text from performance and knowledge from the knower. A manuscript, for example, can be stored and retrieved. By separating knowledge from the knower, knowledge can be owned by separate individuals. The printing press later severed the connection between the author and the transmission of knowledge.

Following this separation, copyright laws were created in the eighteenth century as a way of preserving intellectual property. The author began to get paid for his or her ideas and was given the right to protect the work's integrity by owning the right to modify, correct, or retract the content. Knowledge is not what you see, but what you say. Your knowledge is the result of your grasp of information from observing in the field. Your knowledge is your own, because you arrive at it by yourself and draw your own conclusions. (see Box 14.1) If you think that you can gain knowledge by simply remembering what an expert says, then ask yourself if you could learn Russian by memorizing a Russian dictionary.

In a corporate environment, the three possible owners of knowledge are the expert, the employing organization, and the user who acquires the knowledge automation system. Other situations in which knowledge ownership could be an issue in the future include the following:

1. If an expert sells personal knowledge
2. If an expert is unwilling to release knowledge gained on the job

KNOWLEDGE FOR SALE

In any environment, there is a price for knowledge (see Box 14.2). Imagine that a firm has hired a consulting group to build a knowledge automation system for a new area of the business. Because a resident expert does not exist, the consulting group is forced to locate and hire an outside expert to build the system. In this scenario, the expert would be the rightful owner of the knowledge if no prior agreements were established. Both the company and the expert are open targets for liability and ownership lawsuits. If an agreement made before developing the system allows the expert to receive royalties, then ownership and liability are obvious. To avoid this situation, the company should make arrangements to "purchase" the expert's knowledge outright. Chances are that experts may agree to it in order to escape future liability.

RELEASING KNOWLEDGE GAINED ON THE JOB

Charles Amble worked for General Motors (GM) as a maintenance engineer for more than 20 years. To avoid losing his know-how, GM developed a knowledge automation system named *Charley* in order to capture Amble's expertise in vibration analysis. Because this expert was willing to cooperate with GM during the knowledge capture phase, knowledge developers were successful in building the system. The knowledge-based system provided GM with quick, standardized diagnoses of complex vibration maintenance problems and substantial savings in all manufacturing plants, because all plant mechanics were given access to the knowledge needed to diagnose these problems. Does the company have the right to Amble's knowledge? Who owns the knowledge in this scenario?

▪▪▪▪▪▪ BOX 14.1 ▪▪▪▪▪▪

CLARIFYING KNOWLEDGE OWNERSHIP

WHO OWNS KNOWLEDGE?

"Knowledge is not what you see, but what I say."

If I said that, your answer would likely be, "Oh yeah?" You'd wonder who gave me the right to decide things for you. However, what if I said the same thing differently? "The storehouse of knowledge is too vast for any one person to comprehend, so we must accept what the experts tell us." In other words, "Knowledge is not what you see, but what the experts say."

An expert is one who has good knowledge in some area. It is not your knowledge, but his. He has observed, identified, confirmed, and combined evidence into a grasp of the subject. If he tells it all to you, then he has informed you of his knowledge. You have been given information. To make the information into knowledge, you must observe, identify, confirm, and combine it into a grasp of the subject.

"I know how to get there," says a friend. "Take the Central Freeway south, get off at Main, and turn right." "Okay!" you say. "Now I know how to get there." If you are already familiar with the area, you do know, because you can mentally verify the information by checking it against your observations. If you are unfamiliar with the area, you must take the drive to verify the information. Otherwise, what you have is not knowledge but directions.

Your knowledge is your own, because you arrive at it yourself by making your own observations and drawing your own conclusions. You need to check out the information provided by experts. Pretending that experts implant knowledge in you is tempting when it seems like a quick way to get smart. In fact, it is a quick way to get dumb. It is confusing information with knowledge. It is reciting lines and doing what you are told.

Anyone can claim to be an expert, and many do. If knowledge is owned by experts, then there must be an expert with the knowledge of who the experts really are. However, anyone could claim to be that expert, too. In the end, it will always be up to you to decide for yourself who knows what they are talking about and who does not. How do you do that? You check it out.

To check out information, you trace it to its base in sensory evidence and fit it in with everything else. You see where it came from and how it relates. If it came from the unsupported word of an expert, then it is not knowledge but opinion. Informed opinion tells you where to look for evidence. It cannot tell you what to think, no matter how much you may want it to do so.

SOURCE: Excerpted from Sedgwick, James. *The Certainty Site*, Oxford Press, 2001, p. 5, home1.gte.net/cpq1szzy/whoownsknowledge.htm, Date accessed August 2002.

▪▪▪▪▪▪

Amble developed the knowledge by using the resources made available by the firm, but he also developed personal reasoning and deductive abilities at the same time. Unless he had signed a preemployment contract or intellectual property agreement releasing his ownership of knowledge, he is the owner of knowledge. From the expert's point of view, a preemployment contract or intellectual property agreement helps to limit personal liability for the knowledge automation system. GM would also want an intellectual property agreement so that it could have title to the savings realized by the knowledge automation system.

▪ ▪ ▪ ▪ ▪ ▪   BOX 14.2   ▪ ▪ ▪ ▪ ▪ ▪

WHAT PRICE KNOWLEDGE

The sale of assets from failed Internet start-ups has captured recent headlines, focusing public attention on the difficulty of putting a price tag on intangible assets. Intellectual property represents a growing proportion of a company's value, whether that company is alive or dead.

A key in determining true corporate worth is enterprise value, which for a publicly traded corporation is simply what is left when its book value is subtracted from its market capitalization. "That number expressed as a fraction of market cap has been steadily rising for 20 years," says Alex Arrow, chief financial officer of the Patent & License Exchange, Inc., in Pasadena, California. "General Electric, for example, now has probably less than $40 billion in cash, buildings, and machinery, a small fraction of its approximately $400 million in market capitalization."

Beyond book value, a large portion of a corporation's remaining worth lies in the knowledge it possesses. Companies such as Qualcomm, Inc., and Texas Instruments, Inc., have found greater value in licensing their know-how than in making products of their own, observers say. Houston-based Bryan Benoit is responsible for the intellectual property e-business (called the *Intellectual Property Exchange*) of PricewaterhouseCoopers LLP. He commented, "Intellectual property is difficult to value because it's an asset that can be used by more than one company in more than one way simultaneously."

As for the big picture, Benoit observes that two complementary forces are driving the interest in intangibles. "Our economy is knowledge-based, and the trend is for it to become even more so over time," he says. "The other force is that because of that first force, investors are becoming more interested in the value of intangibles."

SOURCE: Rapport, Marc. "The Price of Knowledge," *Knowledge Management*, August 2001, p. 14.

▪ ▪ ▪ ▪ ▪ ▪

BECOMING AN EXPERT VIA A CORPORATE KNOWLEDGE-BASED SYSTEM

Jim DeMong has worked as a timber bucker for Roland Pacific for the past 12 years. DeMong's job requires him to make many tactical decisions when cutting trees into logs and then allocating them to appropriate manufacturing facilities. As an expert, DeMong knows just how to cut each tree into various log lengths and then distribute the logs among the different mills in the most efficient and cost-effective way. Each mill produces a different end product such as lumber, plywood, or paper. As a result, his knowledge is invaluable to Roland Pacific. Wrong cutting and allocation decisions could drastically change the profit contribution from each tree.

What is unique in this situation is how DeMong acquired his knowledge. Several years ago, Roland Pacific introduced a knowledge automation system to train and assist its timber buckers with their jobs. The new system was installed in the office where timber buckers spent a few hours a week simulating actual tree-cutting decisions and evaluating the resulting costs associated with each decision. Because the system was portable, it was also used in the field to make real-time cutting and allocation decisions.

DeMong used this knowledge-based system extensively during the first 2 years with the firm. However, for the past few years, most of the decisions he made were his own. They were virtually identical to the system's decisions. Does the company have a right to DeMong's knowledge? Can the company prevent him from using this knowledge if he leaves the company to start his own business or work for a competitor?

Again, unless DeMong signed some type of intellectual property agreement that would release ownership of his knowledge, he owns the knowledge and has a right to use it as he wishes. Intellectual property agreements are also important to the expert in order to avoid strict liability. This brings up legal issues that are covered in the next section.

■■■■ Legal Issues

Every legitimate business operates in a legal environment. Contracts, taxation, and copyrights are among the issues that fall under the legal system. Many questions that arise from knowledge ownership are not settled, but new laws can change the rules and plug loopholes in this emerging area. In an age of prolific litigation, employees and employers should be aware of the legal ramifications arising from knowledge sharing.

The excitement generated by knowledge capture and knowledge sharing has also led to substantial financial investment in knowledge ownership and the technology that makes it available. This includes e-mail infrastructure, intranets, stand-alone knowledge automation systems, and knowledge repositories. In an age of prolific litigation, users and developers should be aware of the legal ramifications arising from knowledge sharing and knowledge automation in general. Consider the following situations:

- An attorney, using a knowledge base, advises his client of the tax forms to file and what to include in his articles of incorporation to qualify as a federally tax-exempt corporation. The client is later sued by the Internal Revenue Service (IRS) for back taxes.
- A physician diagnoses a patient after consultation with her medical knowledge-based system. The patient is treated but soon dies as a result of misdiagnosis and improper treatment.
- A large computer firm sells a local area network to a client after using a knowledge-based system to identify the proper configuration. When the system is installed, the client-user discovers that the configuration is wrong and that the equipment, as it stands, is worthless.
- A knowledge-based system used by an architect incorrectly determines the stress requirements of an expensive new public building. The completed structure later collapses, killing dozens of people.
- A radiation machine guided by a knowledge-based advisory system calculates the dosage in the treatment of cancer patients. Two years after treatment, hundreds of patients die due to radiation overdose. The problem was located in a faulty programming module.

Each of these cases is real. These unfortunate situations lead to questions such as "Who owns knowledge?" "Who is liable in such situations and for what reasons?" This section examines the legal aspects of knowledge ownership.

THE LIABILITY QUESTION

Regardless of where knowledge originates, when it is misused, liability will become an issue. The blame may fall on the knowledge developer who might have tapped the wrong knowledge or on the expert who provided the wrong knowledge. It could also be the fault of the knowledge repository that produced the wrong solution. In day-to-day business, tort and contract theories present challenging questions for organizations and the legal community. If a knowledge repository produces the wrong solution, which causes losses or injury to others, the resulting damage often leads to litigation dealing with **strict liability** or **negligence**. Each individual involved in the process (company, knowledge developer, or expert) is potentially vulnerable and subject to legal scrutiny.

Liability of the Knowledge Developer

In knowledge design or software development, the developer is often responsible for knowledge accuracy and reliability. In building the knowledge-based environment, a variety of errors may become embedded in the system: Some are nontrivial and others are out-of-bounds errors. An *out-of-bounds error* is one that occurs because either the software did not have the expertise to address the particular problem or the developer improperly condensed the captured knowledge. A *nontrivial error* has a large financial impact on the business, especially if the knowledge is used by employees company-wide. The consequence is decommissioning the system or facing litigation.

Because the developer relies on his or her experience to develop the product or software and a malfunction occurs, the developer is vulnerable to charges of personal liability under the doctrine of *respondeat superior* (an employer–employee relationship). If the designer is an employee of the organization that sells the software, the employing firm is involved in the negligence action. In the end, the company is responsible for certifying the system before it is released for company use.

Liability of the Expert

Another possible target for litigation is the expert, because his or her knowledge is codified in the system. Should the system be faulty, liability will surely follow. The competency of the expert, however, is difficult to evaluate; because of their individual experiences, feelings, and instincts, even experts addressing the same problem do not always agree on all issues. Experts open up their knowledge to scrutiny, even when the resulting system is far removed from the expert's control. For example, in one incident where a walkway at a new hotel collapsed, the two structural engineers in charge were found guilty of negligence.

With each situation, expert involvement and potential liability vary. For example, could a court of law hold an expert liable if the expert were an employee of the firm that developed the knowledge-based system for resale? If the expert is an outside consultant, who would be liable? As of yet, answers to these questions are unknown, because only one case involving knowledge-based system liability has been tried in court to date.

Liability of the User

Even end users of a knowledge-based system are not immune from a lawsuit. They are directly responsible for proper use of the system. Within the duties of their jobs, refusing to comply with the system's directions will increasingly come into question. By not properly using an available resource by affirmative duty, users could be negligent by omission or "passive negligence." For example, the use of a knowledge automation system in medical diagnosis could place as affirmative duty the responsibility for using the system. It could also be used in court as support for a diagnosis, even though the diagnosis was incorrect.

THE BASIS OF LIABILITY

Although the focus in this book has been on knowledge management principles and procedures, the nature of knowledge and knowledge capture and use have not yet reached a point where new legal remedies are required. Meantime, the old familiar liability issues are still applicable. Tort law is a major area of concern, with the issue of strict liability and negligence falling under it.

Tort Law in Knowledge Management

Torts are wrongful acts subject to civil action. **Tort law** is a special area of law that remedies wrongs between parties. In knowledge management and knowledge ownership, it involves settling contract problems between the employee as an expert and the employing organization in terms of knowledge ownership. Tort cases have already been brought up in a court of law against businesses. Most of the cases have been related to negligence, misrepresentation, and trademark violations.

Negligence is failing to take certain action, causing injury or material losses to another. For example, fearing lawsuits, loss of secrets, or loss of intellectual property, many banks are now scanning employee e-mail messages at least randomly. There have been several high-profile court cases where e-mail has turned up as evidence. A business could conceivably be found negligent if it did not exercise due care in monitoring and safeguarding its intellectual property.

Misrepresentation is a tort area that tags to fraud. Similar to false advertising in intent, claiming that a certain knowledge product will perform certain functions when in fact it could not is misrepresenting the product. Likewise, if a salesperson fails to disclose the negative aspects of a product when he or she knew all along about such weaknesses, they would be subject to prosecution.

Knowledge—A Product or a Service?

In terms of legal ownership of knowledge, the question of whether knowledge is a product or a service attracts varied opinions. If one views knowledge as what you say, not what you see, then knowledge can be treated as a service. One legal opinion suggests that if knowledge is codified in a package and sold as a mass-marketed item, then it is a product. If the package is custom-designed, then it is viewed as a service.

The resolution of this issue is important for users and knowledge developers. If a knowledge repository is a product, proving negligence is unnecessary to hold the developer liable. The **Uniform Commercial Code (UCC)**, however, allows the developer to limit liability for defective knowledge bases through a disclaimer of warranties in the contract. For these liability activities, the loss falls on the defendant (developer), regardless of fault, as a cost of doing business.

Conversely, if a knowledge repository is a service, the contract law of the state in question would apply, rather than the UCC. Negligence principles should be used. A negligence cause of action is more difficult to prove, because the plaintiff must show the aspect of the process that caused the defect and prove that failure to use sufficient care caused the defect.

Many legal experts want knowledge-based systems to be considered as services in order to avoid the strict liability associated with products. For example, a medical knowledge base mass-produced to hospitals throughout the country could be classified as a product. However, such a system should not be presumed to have the physician's intuitive capabilities, knowledge of the particular patient, or perception of the subjective factors. Knowledge-based systems that require the user and the system to make a diagnosis jointly will most likely be considered a service. A summary of these relationships is presented in Table 14.1.

COPYRIGHTS, TRADEMARKS, AND TRADE NAMES

In terms of **copyright and trademark violations**, this is an area that falls under **intellectual property** law. It includes software, books, music, videos, trademarks, copyrights, and Web pages. There is a growing controversy over who owns the intellectual property of product design, creative advertisements, and the like.

TABLE 14.1 Knowledge as a Product or a Service in Litigation Issues

Product	*Service*
• Off-the-shelf software	• Custom-designed software
• Mass-marketed software	• Negligence principles used
• Custom-designed but affects a large number of customers	• Negligence cause of action more difficult for plaintiff to prove
• Proving negligence unnecessary to holding developer liable	• For liability, law of state applies, rather than UCC
• UCC liability limit allowable via disclaimer of warranties	

Copyright is ownership of an original work created by an author. It is a form of intellectual property protection that covers the "look and feel" and content of printed media like articles and textbooks as well as software programs and software packages. **Copyright law** gives the author or creator of a *tangible* product the right to exclude others from using the finished work. That is why authors and publishers place a copyright notice after the title page, although a notice does not make the work freely available.

A copyright owner has exclusive rights to his copyrighted work. They include the right to copy, duplicate, and distribute the work in any form. He or she has the right to modify the work in an effort to create a new work. In addition, a copyright owner has the right to show the work at a public place or by means of a film or television show. This includes showing the work on the Web. Such rights are protected by law; a copyright owner can recover damages in a federal district court.

Several other works are protected—literary works; musical works; dramatic works; pictorial, graphic, and sculptural works; Web sites; sound recordings; and architectural works. Knowledge-based programs and most compilations may be registered as "literary works." There are several categories of material, however, that are not eligible for copyright protection. For example, works consisting entirely of information considered common property and containing no original authorship are not copyrighted. Familiar symbols or designs or mere listings of ingredients or contents are also not copyrighted.

A copyright is good for the life of the author plus an additional 70 years after the author's death. In the case of joint authorship where the authors did not work for hire, the term lasts for 70 years after the last surviving author's death. There are also specific conditions and laws to protect people from copying someone else's work without permission. For example, an author can quote up to 250 words without permission, provided he or she gives recognition to the author of the quoted work. The same procedure applies to copying material on other people's Web pages. Beyond that, you need permission from the copyright holder to quote or to copy. A magazine that copied only 300 words of former President Gerald Ford's 200,000-word autobiography got into trouble. It was found guilty of copyright violation (Emery 1997).

In knowledge management, a knowledge repository and the way it is organized are considered a compilation and are copyrightable. A compilation's copyright protects all components within it. An original compilation of names and addresses that are now in the public domain is also copyrightable. The same applies for logos and trademarks. By international agreements, only an expression can be copyrighted, not facts. The biggest problem is not from the text content, but from images and programs. On the Web, for example, images are easy to download or cut and paste into any other page; pirating images is an everyday affair.

A word, a picture, or an image that identifies a product or service is intellectual property and is protected by a **trademark**. The term *trademark* means registration of a company's **trade name** so that others cannot use it. It is also a word or a symbol that distinguishes a good from other goods in the market. As shown in Figure 14.1, "For Dummies" is a trademarked name; "IDG Books" is a trademarked logo; and the icon on the left is a trademark symbol of the same firm.

Who owns a trademark (or a copyright) is often a contractual matter. Trademark protection is a maze of federal and state laws that have to be reviewed carefully before securing protection. Some trademarks might be registered in one state, but not in others, and some states have individual laws covering trademarks. Copyright and trademark examples are shown in Figure 14.2.

Related to the copyright issue, if a company hires an outside firm to develop its Web site, the contract should clearly give the company all intellectual property rights. The Web designer provides a "work made for hire." If the design is done in-house, the employment contract should also make it clear that any creative work performed by employees belongs to the company. For a $30 fee, anyone can copyright work with the Library of Congress. Its Web site address is www.loc.gov/copyright (see Figure 14.3).

The resolution of this issue is important for users and developers of Web sites. If a Web site representing a body of knowledge is a *product,* proving negligence is unnecessary to holding the developer liable.

WARRANTIES

The UCC is the foundation of commercial contract law in all states, except Louisiana. As such, it defines the concepts of product law and contains provisions for computer contracts in the form of warranties. A **warranty** is an assurance made by the seller about the goods sold. An additional safeguard to the UCC is the federal *Magnuson-Moss Consumer Product Warranty Act,* enacted in 1975. It clarifies the issues relating to warranty information disclosure requirements and regulates the limitation of

▪▪▪▪▪▪▪ **FIGURE 14.1:**   An Example of a Trademark and a Trade Name

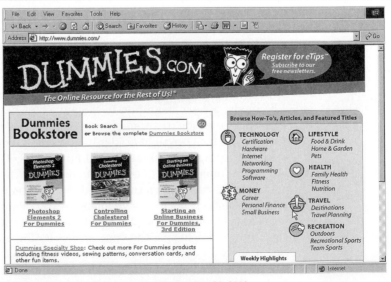

SOURCE: www.dummies.com. Date accessed November 30, 2002.

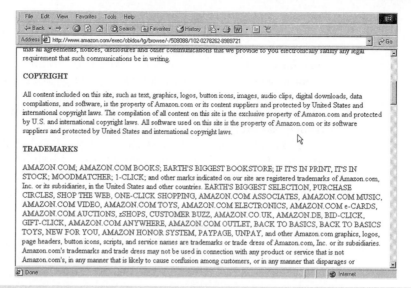

■ ■ ■ ■ ■ ■ ■ **FIGURE 14.2:**   Copyright and Trademark Statements

SOURCE: www.amazon.com. Date accessed August 2002.

implied warranties. Both the UCC and the warranty act identify the various types of warranties that can exist and serve as references for further information on the subject.

Of the two types of warranties, an **express warranty** is offered orally or in writing by the maker of the product. It is usually part of a sale. The buyer purchases the goods in part because of a statement by the seller with respect to the quality, capacity, or some other characteristic of the package. An express warranty need not be an expressed statement. It may be found in the seller's conduct.

■ ■ ■ ■ ■ ■ ■ **FIGURE 14.3:**   Library of Congress Copyright Web Site

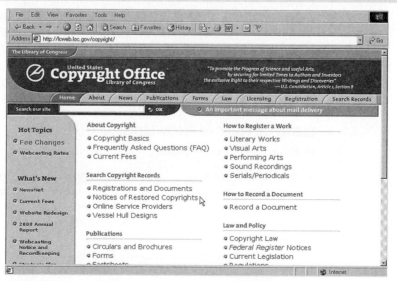

SOURCE: www.loc.gov/copyright. Date accessed December 2, 2002.

An **implied warranty** arises automatically from the fact that a sale has been made and that the good will do what it is supposed to do. For example, a knowledge base should be fit for the ordinary purposes for which it is used. This implied warranty of *merchantability* indicates that the Web site should do what it is expected to do. The other aspect of implied warranty is one of *fitness*. A knowledge base should be fit for the particular use intended by the buyer. Violation of this warranty is probably not common among knowledge developers, although it may be more common among companies that do customized programming.

Disclaimers and warranties are closely related. A **disclaimer** is the seller's intention to protect the business from unwanted liability. Many software packages are labeled "as is," meaning they are sold without warranty of any kind regarding performance or accuracy. More pronounced disclaimers go so far as to state that neither the developer, retailer, or anyone affiliated with the developer is liable for damages even if the developer has been forewarned of the possibility of such damages.

Even though disclaimers are clearly stated, their legal status is fuzzy at best. The main issue centers on whether the knowledge in question is a product or a service. In either case, the courts are adverse toward excluding warranty disclaimers or attempts by the knowledge developer to avoid their applications as unconscionable. Express warranty disclaimers are effective, provided they are conspicuously placed and in writing.

A knowledge-base client can reasonably look toward warranties as protection if damage is caused through the use of a product purchased through a company's Web site. However, showing reason why warranty exclusion should not be accepted is difficult. In fact, two states have enacted "shrinkwrap" laws, which hold that all warranties made or disclaimed on the license found inside the shrinkwrapping are legal and final. Cases involving warranties also require that the user show who is at fault and why, which is a difficult task. The knowledge automation system in question must necessarily be considered a product under UCC rules for warranty issues to be relevant.

STRICT LIABILITY

Tort theory is based on several issues, namely that the producer of a product is in the position to reduce risks and insure against injuries that could result. As with warranties, a software package must be considered a product for the tort theory of strict liability to apply. If this criterion is met, developers, manufacturers, and distributors could all be held liable for injuries even though reasonable care standards have been satisfied. For example, even though no errors are found in a Web site, the Web designer could still be held liable under the tort theory of strict liability should damages or losses result from the use of the Web site. Imposition of this theory protects the Web visitor regardless of whether anyone is at fault, in a strict sense. The major legal issues are summarized in Table 14.2.

LEGAL DISPUTES IN KNOWLEDGE MANAGEMENT

In knowledge management, several disputes may arise that have legal implications:

- An employee delivers a problem solution based on years of proven experience, but the company fails to support the work or process. As a result, the product in question fails the customer test of approval.
- A company has a quality standard for a procedure, but the employee purposely shows reluctance to cooperate to meet the standard.
- A company engineer does not like the established design, but the company is reluctant to make changes. As a result, the sale of the product falls behind due to new competition.

TABLE 14.2   Legal Issues of Knowledge-Based Systems

- An expert owns his or her knowledge of the work if no prior agreement was established.
- A preemployment contract or intellectual property agreement can limit the expert's own liability for the knowledge automation system.
- If a knowledge developer builds the system and a problem arises, he or she is subject to charges of personal liability under the doctrine of *respondeat superior.* If the developer is a company employee, the organization is also involved in the negligence action.
- If a knowledge-based system is a product, proving negligence is unnecessary to hold the developer liable. The UCC allows developers to limit liability for defective work via a disclaimer of warranties in the contract. For these liabilities, the loss falls on the developer, regardless of fault, as a cost of doing business.
- If a knowledge-based system is a service, the contract law of the state would apply, rather than the UCC.
- Cases involving warranties require that the user show who is at fault and why.
- The knowledge base in question should be considered a product under UCC rules for warranties to be relevant or for tort theory of strict liability to apply.

WEB LINKING AND DOMAIN NAME DISPUTES

In electronic commerce, unique knowledge about a product, a company, or a service resides in Web sites. The infrastructure of the Internet is designed around **hyperlinks**—text or an image whose address can be linked to another Web page for reference. When one clicks on the link, it automatically goes to the attached location and the designated Web page. This "jumping from one site to another" raises legal issues that include the following:

- Referencing a linked site without permission from the site owner
- Retrieving or downloading information from a linked site without referencing or permission
- Unauthorized use of a company's registered trademarks
- Adding a Web program to a company's Web site without permission

Inappropriately referencing a Web site is not a clear-cut issue; it depends on the intent of the referencing. For example, one bank's Web site advertised online automobile loans. When a visitor entered the amount she wanted to borrow (in this case, it was $47,000 for a Mercedes), the Web site asked the visitor to click on the "referral" button, giving the impression that her application would get special attention. Instead, she ended up on the Web site of a large bank in another state that specializes in "jumbo" auto loans. The visitor was unhappy about this runaround and promptly clicked away from both sites.

One New Jersey bank Web site posted a question on its homepage: "Want to compute your mortgage rate on a house? Click here." The software module that did the calculation was registered to a Chicago bank. The networking algorithm detected unauthorized use of the package by the New Jersey bank Web site and promptly sued for damages. The case was settled out of court; the New Jersey bank was forced to delete the referral to the mortgage calculator.

Domain names have been viewed as representing the intellectual capital of a business. Disputes over who owns a domain name have been with us since business hit the Internet. In 1992, the U.S. government contracted with Network Solutions, Inc. (NSI), which also goes by the name **InterNIC (Internet Network Information Center)**, to manage the top-level domains. Initially, domain names were assigned on a first-come, first-serve basis. However, this caused companies or individuals to register for domain names that they had no use for and hold them for future sale at exorbitant prices. Since 1995, the policy has changed. Domain names are still issued on a first-come, first-serve basis, but applicants are reminded in writing that such issuance does not duplicate or replace the legal right of another party such as a registered trademark to use the name.

The low-cost fee of $70 for 2 years of registration has caused several individuals to register and hold known names hostage for big money. One poacher, for example, registered for 200 domain names, including his former employer's. However, he kept losing cases filed against him by firms defending their right to use their trademark name. The general rule for resolving domain name disputes is to determine the date that the claimant first used his trademark or the effective date of his validated trademark registration. If the registered holder appears to have infringed on the registered trademark owner, then NSI assigns the registered holder a new domain name. The court is the only other avenue to seek relief (see Box 14.3).

Here are some ideas regarding domain names and trademarks:

- Find out whether the proposed domain name infringes upon any trademarks. The fact that one registers for a domain name does not in itself give the owner the legal right to use it.
- Secure federal trademark registration of the proposed domain name. Once it clears against possible claims of infringement, then it should be registered as a trademark with the U.S. Patent and Trademark Office.
- Register the proposed domain name with InterNIC (Internet Network Information Center)—the agency that represents the U.S. government in assigning domain names.

▪ ▪ ▪ ▪ ▪ ▪ **BOX 14.3** ▪ ▪ ▪ ▪ ▪ ▪

THE COST OF POACHING

In what is thought to be the first ruling on a potent provision of a recently signed cybersquatting legislation, a U.S. judge has empowered Bell Atlantic Corp. to take possession of nearly 2 dozen Internet addresses. Under the ruling, verbally issued by a magistrate judge, Bell Atlantic can transfer the registered domain names, said Sarah Deutsch, chief intellectual property counsel for Bell Atlantic.

In entering his order, the judge relied on the Anticybersquatting Consumer Protection Act, which gives trademark owners a powerful weapon to combat cybersquatters, those who register various permutations of company names with "bad faith intent." Key to the New York telephone company's case was a provision that explicitly allows trademark owners to take legal action directly against domain-name holders, without the necessity of hauling each alleged transgressor into court.

Although trademark owners have praised the legislation, critics worry that it goes too far and may end up snaring Internet entrepreneurs and others who innocently register names similar to a trademark. Individuals whose last name happens to resemble a corporate moniker, for example, are concerned that they will be dragged into court and forced to pay a huge fine for registering an address with their own last name.

SOURCE: Adapted from Plitch, Phyllis. "Court Order Lets Bell Atlantic Wrest Domain Names from Cybersquatter," Dow Jones & Company, February 2, 2000.

▪ ▪ ▪ ▪ ▪ ▪

- In the event of a poached domain name, bring a lawsuit to force InterNIC to reassign the name.
- Get permission before linking to other Web sites. There are issues of liability in linking to other Web sites without such permission.

THE MALPRACTICE FACTOR

Most people have heard of litigation involving doctors who have been sued for malpractice. As a result, surgeons and other professionals pay high premiums for malpractice insurance. **Malpractice** in knowledge management is negligence applied to knowledge developers for design defects in systems tailored specifically for professional use. For experts to be held liable for malpractice, they must be considered professionals, belong to a profession in which standards of care have been established, and owe a certain duty of care to those for whom they work.

At present, neither standardization nor certification that recognizes knowledge developers as professionals has been established; therefore, they are not yet liable for malpractice. Some people argue that knowledge developers should be licensed as a condition to building knowledge-based systems (see Box 14.4).

The discussion of liability and knowledge-based systems would not be complete without bringing up the potential liability for failure to use knowledge-based systems. Professionals may be held liable for not using such a system when it is available. One such case is T. J. Hooper. Hooper's tugboat lost the barges it was towing in a storm that the captain would have known about had the boat had a radio aboard. Even though a radio was not a required item, Hooper was found liable for the loss of the barges.

In another classic case, that occurred during the Persian Gulf war, the failure to comply with expert systems resulted in benefits. The U.S. intelligence community, relying on knowledge-based systems and satellites, found that only 25 percent of a key bridge in Baghdad had been destroyed. A call was made to General H. Norman Schwarzkopf, asking him to send a squadron to destroy the bridge. The general refused on the ground that the 25 percent damage had severed one span, therefore rendering the entire bridge useless. Sending solders to destroy the bridge would expose them to unnecessary risks or even casualties (Awad 1996).

■ ■ ■ ■ ■ ■   BOX 14.4   ■ ■ ■ ■ ■ ■

THE LIABILITY OF WEATHER FORECASTING

A case involving the National Weather Service (NWS) illustrates the potential danger of hyping knowledge automation system technology. According to the evidence, four fishermen consulted a weather forecast released by the NWS before embarking on an expedition. Unfortunately, even after years of study, the prediction of weather still proves to be an inexact science. The fishermen were confronted with an unpredicted storm. All four men died. Their families sued the U.S. government for $1.25 million and won. Certainly, one who develops a knowledge-based system should be aware that the system may be held to certain standards.

SOURCE: Awad, E. M. *Building Expert Systems.* Minneapolis, MN: West Publishing Co., 1996, p. 346.

■ ■ ■ ■ ■ ■

If knowledge-based system developers are professionals, they may be sued for malpractice. What about knowledge-based systems that have evolved to the level of legitimate professionals? Could they not also be held liable for malpractice? If such systems can be held liable for anything, then perhaps malpractice claims against them would be reasonable. For example, if a legal knowledge-based system has taken on all of the attributes and functions of a judge, then it should be held liable for malpractice just as a human judge would be. This scenario may be stretching the imagination a bit, but suing a knowledge-based system for malpractice may become a reality.

Malpractice is only one aspect of the liability that may exist in a world in which knowledge systems have reached their full potential. Others will undoubtedly be discovered to fill the legal gap that has been created by this new technology. Soon, new legal reasoning and new laws will be needed.

Anyone to whom liability for knowledge systems can reasonably be traced will bear responsibility. Picture a company that develops and sells a knowledge system that assists in the diagnosis of medical diseases. Over the next 10 years of its use, the program repository encounters enough new diseases or new situations that it is able not only to expand its knowledge base but also to modify itself in such a way that the code could no longer be attributable to the original developer. If an injury occurred in such a situation, logically, the correct "person" to hold liable would be the knowledge base. Again, holding such a system liable for anything may seem rather far-fetched, but it may not necessarily be out of line as laws change to reflect the influence of this technology in everyday life.

Another area that may be viewed under malpractice relates to a growing list of corporations that export their intellectual property abroad to shelter income and evade U.S. taxes. It is not clear how many patents or trademarks U.S. firms hold offshore, because the practice started in the mid-1990s. According to a source detailed in Box 14.5, a large Bermuda law firm promotes its expertise, spelling out the advantages of holding intellectual property offshore.

▪▪▪▪ The Ethics Factor

Organizations throughout the United States are troubled by ethical problems. High ethical standards in a learning organization strengthen its competitive position. The CEO plays the most significant role in setting ethical standards for employees. This section focuses on ethical issues in knowledge-based systems.

WHAT IS ETHICS?

The word *ethics* is not easy to define. It means different things to different people. To begin to discuss the concept, a common definition is needed. **Ethics** is one or all of the following: fairness, justice, equity, honesty, trustworthiness, and equality.

Stealing, cheating, lying, or backing out on one's word are all descriptive of a lack of ethics. Something is ethical when a person feels it is innately right, which is a subjective judgment. For example, "Thou shalt not steal" is a belief held by most people; however, a single parent who steals a loaf of bread to feed starving children may be forgiven for the behavior even though it is illegal.

An unethical act is not the same as an immoral or an illegal act, although one may lead to the other (see Box 14.6). For example:

1. Cheating on one's federal income tax return is more *illegal* than immoral, although it is implicitly unethical.
2. Cheating on a friend is more *immoral* than illegal, although it is tacitly unethical.

▪ ▪ ▪ ▪ ▪ ▪   **BOX 14.5**   ▪ ▪ ▪ ▪ ▪ ▪

SENDING INTELLECTUAL PROPERTY ABROAD

While Washington lawmakers are cracking down on traditional offshore corporate maneuvers to avoid taxes, another strain has sprouted that could be costing Uncle Sam billions: Companies are stashing their intellectual property abroad to shelter income from overseas sales.

Computer companies, drug firms, and others that derive most of their value from research and ideas find the tactic particularly attractive. For example, Columbia Laboratories, Inc., a small pharmaceutical firm in Livingston, New Jersey, for years has been transferring patents to Bermuda, a tiny island in the Atlantic Ocean. When two U.S.-based Columbia researchers patented a constricted-artery treatment in the mid-1990s, they turned over the rights to subsidiary Columbia Laboratories (Bermuda) Ltd.

One reason: Royalties from sales of the products made outside the United States would flow to the Bermuda subsidiary and could be parked there tax-free.

Here is how the deals typically work:

1. U.S. parent company sets up offshore holding company (IHCo) located in a low-tax jurisdiction such as Bermuda.

2. Offshore unit buys stake in parent's Buy-In Payments Intangibles Cost-Sharing existing intangibles such as trademarks, Arrangement patents, or other intellectual property. Future intangibles are developed jointly by parent and IHCo under cost-sharing arrangements.

3. Offshore unit licenses intangibles to subsidiary A, typically in a third country, which then collects royalties from foreign subsidiaries (B, C, D) that sell parent company's products to foreign customers.

4. Royalties are returned by A to IHCo, which forwards one portion back to U.S. parent and keeps its own portion offshore to avoid U.S. taxes.

(Diagram:)
- ① **U.S. Company**
- **Buy-In Payments** → **Intangibles** **Cost-Sharing Arrangement**
- ② **IHCo (low-tax jurisdiction)**
- ③ ④ **Subsidiary A Country A**
- **Foreign Subsidiaries B, C, D**
- **Foreign Customers**

SOURCE: Excerpted from Simpson, Glenn. "A New Twist in Tax Avoidance: Firms Send Best Ideas Abroad," *The Wall Street Journal*, June 13, 2002, p. A10ff.

▪ ▪ ▪ ▪ ▪ ▪   BOX 14.6   ▪ ▪ ▪ ▪ ▪ ▪

THE SAGA OF A YACHT

During the February board of directors meeting of a commercial bank, the first agenda item was a review of the statement of condition (expenses, revenues, and so forth) of the bank for the previous month. Joan, a new member of the board, noticed a line item under "entertainment" in the amount of $14,000. She thought to herself, "Here is a local bank of 240 employees. What kind of entertainment is going on at the bank to add up to this much expense?" She had seen the same figure during last month's meeting.

Out of curiosity, she asked the chairman of the board, "Mr. Chairman, I'd like to know more about the entertainment expense item. Could this be back from the Christmas party, reflected as a January expense?" The bank president, who was a member of the board snapped, "Well, as you know Joan, the bank incurs all kinds of entertainment expenses. Why don't you stop by my office after the meeting and I'd be happy to explain it further."

After the meeting, Joan and the bank president had a brief chat. The president explained, "Joan, the entertainment item is the bank's monthly contribution to the chairman's entertainment of bank customers, bank officers, and community leaders on his yacht. The chairman has certain privileges." Joan then asked, "For a bank this size, how can one justify this much expense each month? What kind of entertainment adds up to $14,000 per month? How long has this been going on?" The president, his face turning red with irritation, said, "I really don't want to elaborate further about this. Remember, you are new on the board. I wouldn't advise asking the chairman about it. I'd let it go. The bank is making enough money. The chairman has 70 percent equity in the business. What more explanation do you want?"

Sensing futility in the attempt, Joan later discovered that the monthly charge was a dockage fee for the chairman's 190-foot yacht. As a board member, she felt responsible for assuring integrity in bank management. What made this situation more difficult for Joan was that for the past 6 years, there had not been one occasion where entertainment on the yacht was related to the bank in any measurable way. She is now in a quandary wondering whether she should continue on the board or resign.

▪ ▪ ▪ ▪ ▪ ▪

3. Submitting a "padded" bill to a client is more *unethical* and possibly illegal, although it is considered immoral.
4. Stealing an item from a store is illegal, immoral, and unethical in various ways.

Incidents like these are related to one's value system, beliefs, and culture. Laws are often created to combat unethical acts that threaten societal image and survival. They are also used to reinforce existing ethics. Ethics creates a strong sense of professionalism. Ethical misbehavior among knowledge developers is no greater or less than it is among the mass public (see Box 14.7).

A model of acceptable behavior, with ethics as a factor, is shown in Figure 14.4. If a person falsely reports a donation to a charitable organization, it is considered both illegal and immoral (quadrant A). This action implies a lack of ethical standards and personal values. In quadrant D, rescuing hostages from a foreign country might be illegal (and dangerous) by that country's laws but be moral (and implicitly ethical) in terms of justice under U.S. laws. Deciding what is moral, legal, or ethical creates a constant struggle.

▪▪▪▪▪▪ **BOX 14.7** ▪▪▪▪▪▪

WHO DECIDES OPERATIONAL ETHICS?

A knowledge-based system built for a commercial bank uses 17 criteria to determine whether an applicant qualifies for a mortgage loan. For several years, the bank has been criticized by state auditors for not granting enough loans to minorities or to people living in minority districts. A review of the knowledge-based system also revealed that most mortgage loans favor applicants who are married rather than those who are single, separated, or divorced.

When the discriminating knowledge rules were pointed out, the knowledge developer said, "I developed this system based on the vice president of mortgage loan's thought process. He reviewed several prototypes and approved the sys-

tem. Why don't you talk with him?" In addressing the equity question, the vice president replied, "I make decisions on mortgage loans based on guidelines from the board of directors. Our chairperson is a major stockholder and pretty much the owner of the bank. She does not live in the area and wants to make sure we make secured loans. Why don't you talk to the president about it?"

In a meeting with the president the next day, the president said, "I'm surprised you're bringing up bank policy. We paid for a knowledge-based system to comply with our requirements. So, what is the fuss all about?"

However, the question raised here still remains: Is the system unethical, illegal, or both?

▪▪▪▪▪▪

ETHICAL DECISION CYCLE

Knowledgeable people with common sense are expected to be people of ethics. They consider a number of elements when they make ethical decisions:

1. *The nature and essence of the act.* Is the act fair, reasonable, or conscionable?
2. *The consequences of the action or inaction on the parties involved.* Who gains by the act, who loses, and by how much?
3. *The far-reaching consequence of the action or inaction on the organization, community, and society.* Will the act, if left unchecked, lead to societal ills?

Figure 14.5 summarizes the three major steps of a hypothetical ethical decision cycle. A person faces a situation and must evaluate alternative approaches that lead to a decision to commit an act. The outcome is initially reviewed by the person. If it is believed to be rewarding, fair, and just, chances are it will be repeated, and vice versa. The outcome in general becomes known to others (groups, organizations, and society) who would condone or condemn the outcome. The result of this feedback is eventual advancement and refinement of ethics within families, the workplace, and society in general.

MAJOR THREATS TO ETHICS

Ethics are more openly discussed as a serious concern today than they were in the past, because the threats have steadily increased. As shown in Figure 14.6, the main threats are as follows:

- Faster computers and PCs
- Sophisticated telecommunication and computer networks

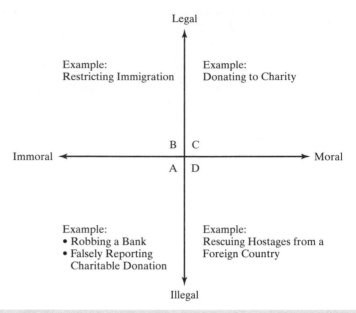

Legal

Example:
Restricting Immigration

Example:
Donating to Charity

B | C

Immoral ←——————————————→ Moral

A | D

Example:
• Robbing a Bank
• Falsely Reporting
  Charitable Donation

Example:
Rescuing Hostages from a
Foreign Country

Illegal

■ ■ ■ ■ ■ ■ ■ **FIGURE 14.4:** Model of Acceptable Behavior

- Massive integrated knowledge bases
- Ease of access to information and knowledge bases
- The view that captured knowledge is a competitive weapon

With these threats, ethical dilemmas of dimensions not imagined 10 years ago are facing today's firm, stretching standard ethical considerations to the limit. In fact, technological advancements have resulted in the need to reevaluate ethical standards and their implications for privacy, confidentiality, accuracy, and integrity.

Knowledge hoarding, unauthorized e-mail access, and sale of competitive knowledge are serious ethical issues. Also, taking out life insurance policies on employees to benefit the company when the employee dies is questionable ethics (see Box 14.8). In 2002, a senior vice president at a major credit card company was dismissed for

■ ■ ■ ■ ■ ■ ■ **FIGURE 14.5:** Ethical Decision Cycle

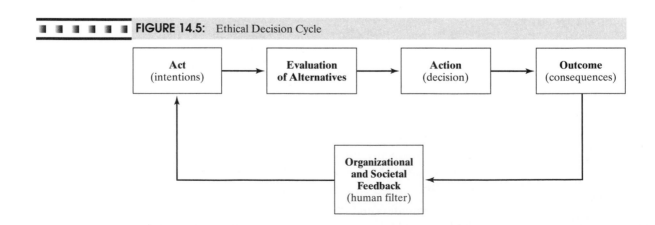

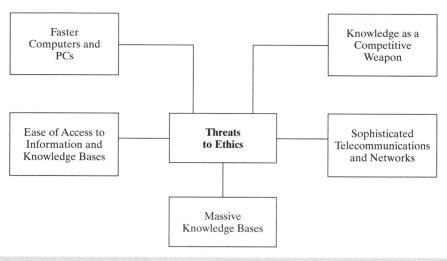

allegedly using his position and company affiliation to promote his side business and pressure company suppliers into buying products from him—all of which were carried out using e-mail and fax. Because no one knows more about information technology and has better access to the company's knowledge base than the head of the IT department, should the head of the IT department be the one to establish and enforce ethical standards for the company as a whole?

▮ ▮ ▮ ▮ ▮ ▮   **BOX 14.8**   ▮ ▮ ▮ ▮ ▮ ▮

THE ETHICS OF EMPLOYEE INSURANCE

Felipe M. Tillman loved music. One of his jobs was a brief stint in the early 1990s at a Camelot Music store in Tulsa, Oklahoma. In 1992, Felipe, then 29 years old, died of complications from AIDS. He never bought life insurance, so his family received no death benefit. However, CM Holdings, Inc., then the parent company of Camelot Music, did. It received $329,302.

CM Holdings took out life insurance policies on thousands of its employees, with itself as the beneficiary. Most workers covered this way do not know it, nor do their families. "If someone is going to use your name for something, even though you're an employee of theirs, you should know what's going on in your name," says Anthony Tillman, who was surprised to learn that his brother's death benefited Felipe's one-time employer. "It isn't fair."

Companies can use the death benefits for anything they like. CM Holdings used $168,875 of the death benefit on Mr. Felipe Tillman for executive compensation, court documents show. The documents also show that $280 went to Star County Children's Services to help cover child-support payments for a nephew of Camelot Music's founder, who was working at the company at the time.

SOURCE: Excerpted from Schultz, Ellen, and Francis, Theo. "Worker Dies, Firm Profits—Why?" *The Wall Street Journal*, April 19, 2002, p. A1.

▮ ▮ ▮ ▮ ▮ ▮

▪▪▪▪ Improving the Climate

Learning organizations can take several approaches to improve ethical behavior in the firm as a whole:

1. To ensure ethical behavior throughout the firm, top management should act as the role model.
2. A code of ethics should be established, taking into consideration the state of technology of the organization. The goals should be realistic, achievable, and agreed upon by the employees. Each organizational level should create an acting ethics program within the company's code of ethics and one that befits the nature of the operation.
3. Unethical behavior should be promptly dealt with based on criteria and procedures set in advance.
4. The firm should set up and support a strong ethics training program for all new employees and reinforce the code of ethics on a regular basis.
5. The organization must provide motivation to focus on honesty, integrity, fairness, and justice as goals that are just as important as money or the so-called "bottom line."

WHERE TO START?

Once the meaning of ethics has been agreed upon, the next step is to decide who is going to lead the "ethics movement." With knowledge workers, learning organizations have used two approaches: bottom-up and top-down. The *bottom-up* approach inculcates ethical behavior at the employee level with full support of top management. As employees follow ethical practices, the entire organization benefits. The impact creates waves of appreciation up the chain of command and benefits the entire firm over the long run.

The *top-down* approach suggests that actions of the company start with the CEO. By virtue of personal acts, decisions, and overall behavior, the top corporate officer sets the tone for the kind of image the corporation will adopt. Corporate obligations extend to a variety of **stakeholders** (such as customers, employees, and vendors), and these obligations are generally recognized as being central to the ethical standards of the firm. Carrying out these obligations requires a comprehensive ethics code that is understood and supported in every sector and at each level of the organization.

Take the case of Boeing Aircraft's chief executive William Allen. In September 1945, he resigned from his law firm to lead Boeing Aircraft to focus on postwar products after World War II. Allen had served as a company attorney for 20 years and director for 14 years. He is remembered as a man of great sincerity, honesty, and integrity. It was a great environment for knowledge sharing. When he accepted the offer of president, he offered the following resolution as a reflection of his personal values:

- Do not be afraid to admit that you don't know.
- Be definite—tell it like it is.
- Try to promote honest feelings toward the company around Seattle.
- Don't talk too much . . . let others talk.
- Be considerate of your associates' views.
- Above all, be human—keep your sense of humor and learn to relax.

Like Allen, the firm acquired a reputation as a highly ethical firm whose employees developed a strong sense of values and integrity in the way they approached their work and shared their ideas and knowledge. His term in office is remembered as a period of "uncompromising high standards and clean ethics." Employees always knew where they stood. It shows that an ethics program should be "rolled out" from the top down the line, which contributes to making each manager an effective ethics leader.

CODE OF ETHICS

Business ethics are closely tied to corporate culture and values, which means that a code of ethics should represent the entire company. The code should be all encompassing and stable over time. It does not make sense, for example, to change the code for every new situation that arises.

Once a code of ethics has been posted and approved by management and employees, it becomes a commitment to behave within its guidelines on a day-to-day basis. An honest workplace where managers and employees are held accountable for their behavior and trust one another is the best environment in which to promote ethical corporate behavior. To keep the ethical climate healthy, an organization must stress regular self-assessment and encourage open debate within the workplace. Such a step can be a sure winner in knowledge exchange and knowledge sharing.

Self-assessment is a question-and-answer procedure that allows individuals to appraise and understand their personal knowledge about a particular topic. In the case of ethics, it is not an exercise to satisfy others. The goal is to think about ethics and adjust one's behavior accordingly. It should be an educational experience for the participant.

One self-assessment procedure asks a participant to assess a scenario and judge whether an ethics issue is involved. The response is recorded on a special form and later compared to the judgment of a panel of experts. The following story is an example.

St. John's Corporation manufactures computerized voting machines and has won several contracts from southern states to install them well before the next presidential election. Alpha Corporation programs the machines for St. John's and carries out the installation on the sites. An Alpha engineer, Smith, is visiting St. John's plant one day and learns that problems in the construction of the voting machine could result in miscounts as high as one in 10 under heavy volume. Smith reports this finding to her supervisor, who informs her that it is St. John's problem, not Alpha's. Smith does nothing further.

> *Question:*   Is an ethics issue involved?
>
> *Opinion:*   Participants nearly unanimously agreed that doing nothing further
>   would be unethical. Use of inaccurate voting machines could
>   invalidate elections and potentially harm the general public trust.
>   Responsible (ethical) behavior and good business practice are not
>   inconsistent. The engineer should pursue the matter further.

THE PRIVACY FACTOR

Privacy is a basic American value. It is also one of the most pressing concerns of knowledge workers today and an issue that is inadequately addressed in knowledge management. Cyberspace, originally intended for scientists, is now dominated by virtually everyone who has access to a computer. What makes knowledge and information so valuable is that most of it is gathered discreetly. Private information is being documented and sold without the knowledge owner's permission or awareness. Obviously, a learning organization has an ethical responsibility to inform users of what information is being captured and how it is being used.

The thought of being monitored is unsettling. Hidden video cameras, phone taps, and e-mail analysis are all examples of technologies that are considered to be unethical (and sometimes illegal), because they allow information to be captured about individuals without their knowledge.

The FTC (Federal Trade Commission) has identified five principles of privacy protection, which are widely recognized in the United States, Canada, and Europe:

1. *Notice*. Employees have the right to be told in advance about any personal information being gathered.
2. *Choice*. Employees should have the final say regarding the use of personal information, other than the processing of such information.
3. *Access*. Employees should be able to access and correct any personal information captured in company files or databases.
4. *Security/integrity*. Employees' personal information should be processed, stored, and transmitted in a secure way so as to assure integrity at all times.
5. *Enforcement*. The courts should back employees if any of these principles are violated.

There are three categories of concern regarding information and knowledge privacy. The first involves the electronic knowledge that businesses store about consumers, vendors, and employees. Who owns such knowledge? The second is the security of electronic knowledge transmission. Encryption has been promoted as a secure way to transmit information or knowledge over the Internet. The third concern is the unauthorized reading of personal files. Public key infrastructure (PKI) and other technologies are used to control unauthorized access.

▪▪▪▪ Implications for Knowledge Management

One conclusion from the discussion on legal and ethical issues is that the legal rules that define who owns knowledge are yet to be clarified. The questions that come up before various technical, organizational, academic, and government groups dealing with knowledge management are "What rules should be instituted to govern knowledge ownership?" "Who will make and enforce those rules?" "What shape should copyright protection take in a world of costless, instantaneous, and undetectable copying?"

If one looks at communication networks, they are essentially defined by a set of rules—the "network protocols," which specify the characteristics of the messages to be transmitted, the media through which they can travel, and how the messages are routed through the media to their destinations. Because knowledge management is not a set of interrelationships among people or procedures, it is difficult to protect it when it is simply in the human mind. The legal implications will continue to be problematic.

Another area of concern is the long-range effect of continued knowledge hoarding as a way to safeguard knowledge embezzlement. So far, learning organizations have differentiated themselves on the basis of what is unique to the way they put knowledge to work.

Regardless of the laws that might assure integrity and protection for the employee with knowledge and the company that employs him or her, the ultimate goal in knowledge management is to nurture, promote, and protect the type and quality of knowledge that contributes to the firm's competitive advantage. The Internet makes it so much easier to trade and go global, but unfortunately it is also easier to abuse protected knowledge and, therefore, violate the laws.

In developing knowledge automation systems, knowledge developers, experts, and corporations may choose to ignore legal issues on the basis that the likelihood of litigation is remote. On the other hand, responsible system developers can become more proactive by approaching knowledge repositories and systems building with ethics and integrity. Having integrity includes never overselling the system or making outlandish claims. The zeal with which knowledge-based systems are built should be tempered with the realization that they are based on human knowledge and ideas, which are less than perfect.

Finally, management must focus on legal and employee protection issues surrounding knowledge ownership. For example, the issue of ethics may be tangential to running a business, but without it there could be serious erosion of the company's customer base. Value America had that very problem seal its fate: It went bankrupt. Also, ethics may mean one thing in one country and another in the country where business is conducted. It is important to develop a code of ethics unique to the country or region.

SUMMARY ▪ ▪ ▪ ▪

- Ethics may include any of the following: fairness, justice, equity, honesty, trustworthiness, and equality. Something is ethical when a person feels it is innately right, which is a subjective judgment. An unethical act need not be immoral or illegal, although one act may imply another.

- Several issues represent major threats to ethics. These include faster computers, sophisticated networks, ease of access to information, and transparency of software. Software copyright infringement, unauthorized e-mail access, and sale of competitive information are also serious ethical issues. To improve the corporate ethics climate, top management should act as the role model, establishing a realistic code of ethics and a strong training program.

- A code of ethics is a declaration of principles and beliefs that govern how employees of a corporation must behave. The code should be all encompassing and stable over time. Once posted, it becomes a commitment for the organization as a whole. Self-assessment allows periodic adjustments in the code.

- In an age of litigious proliferation, users and developers should be cognizant of legal issues arising from knowledge ownership and knowledge-based system use or misuse. The key issue is determining who owns the knowledge. Depending on interpretation and the laws, it could be the user, the expert, the organization, or the knowledge developer. With no prior agreements, the expert is the rightful owner of knowledge and can be the target for litigation resulting from a faulty knowledge-based system. A preemployment contract releasing ownership to the firm would help limit the liability of the expert.

- The issue of whether a knowledge-based system is a product or a service depends on interpretation. If the software is custom-designed, then it is a service and the contract laws of the state in question would apply. If it is off-the-shelf software, it is a product, which means proving negligence is unnecessary to holding the developer liable.

- The Uniform Commercial Code (UCC) offers provisions for computer contracts in the form of warranties. Warranties may be implied or expressed. Implied warranties expect the product to do what it is intended to do, which is covered under implied warranty of merchantability or fitness. Express warranties are presented orally or in writing by the seller.

- Knowledge developers are open to malpractice—negligence due to design defects and resulting damages. At present, neither standardization nor certification recognizes knowledge developers as professionals. In this respect, they are not yet liable for malpractice. Sooner or later, knowledge developers should be licensed to build knowledge-based systems.

TERMS TO KNOW ■ ■ ■ ■

Code of ethics: A declaration of principles and beliefs that governs how employees of a corporation are to behave.

Copyright: Ownership of an original work created by an author; a form of intellectual property protection that covers the "look and feel" and content of printed media like articles, textbooks, and software packages.

Copyright law: A law that gives the author or creator of a tangible product the right to exclude others from using the finished work.

Disclaimer: Renunciation of a claim or power vested in a person or product.

Ethics: Justice, equity, honesty, trustworthiness, equality, and fairness; a subjective feeling of being innately right.

Express warranty: Warranty offered orally or in writing by the maker of the system or product.

Fraud: An intent to deceive; for example, knowing in advance of a material fact about a product that is covered up in a sale.

Implied warranty: Presumed warranty; certain implied facts that represent the product.

Malpractice: Negligence or professional liability of a certified professional related to design defects in systems tailored specifically for professional use.

Misrepresentation: A tort area that tags to fraud.

Negligence: Omission to do something, which a reasonable person, guided by those considerations that ordinarily regulate human affairs, would do; lack of reasonable conduct and care.

Product liability: A tort that makes a manufacturer liable if its product has a defective condition that makes it unreasonably dangerous to the user or consumer.

Self-assessment: A question-and-answer procedure that allows individuals to appraise and understand their personal knowledge about a particular topic.

Stakeholder: Customer, employee, vendor, or distributor who has a vested interest in a company, a product, or a system.

Strict liability: A seller is liable for any defective or hazardous products that unduly threaten a user's safety.

Tort: Wrongful act, subject to civil action; a legal wrong committed upon a person or a property independent of a contract; a wrongful injury to a person, a person's reputation, or a person's property.

Trademark: Registration of a company's trade name so that others cannot use it; a word or a symbol that distinguishes a good from other goods in the market.

Uniform Commercial Code (UCC): A law drafted by the National Conference of Commissioners on Uniform State Laws that governs commercial transactions.

Warranty: A promise made by the seller that assures certain facts are truly representative of a product or service, subject to certain limitations.

TEST YOUR UNDERSTANDING ■ ■ ■ ■

1. In your own words, describe how ethics relates to knowledge.
2. Review material on the Internet, and write an essay detailing the latest views of ethics in knowledge management.
3. In what respect is an ethical act different from an immoral or legal act? Give examples of your own.
4. Distinguish between:
   a. product liability and tort laws
   b. out-of-bounds and nontrivial errors
   c. code of ethics and self-assessment
   d. implied and express warranties
5. Explain briefly the ethical decision cycle. In what respect is it viewed as a cycle?
6. In your own words, discuss the major threats to ethics. Is one threat more serious than others? Be specific.
7. How can a code of ethics be applied in an organization? What are some of the barriers?
8. Suppose you were asked to set up a code of ethics for a learning organization. How would you proceed? What steps would you take to do the job?
9. Visit a company in your community, and investigate whether it is a learning organization. What ethical issues exist in the firm? Write a brief report on your findings.
10. What is the purpose of self-assessment? How does it contribute to a corporate code of ethics?

11. Is a knowledge-based system a product or a service? Explain the pros and cons of this issue and its implications for litigation.

12. Describe the circumstances under which knowledge developers might be sued for malpractice in the future.

KNOWLEDGE EXERCISES ▪ ▪ ▪ ▪

1. The chapter suggests three possible owners of knowledge. Who are they? Do you agree?

2. In what ways will knowledge ownership be an issue in the future?

3. Who would be held liable for a defective knowledge-based system? Discuss in detail.

4. How different do you think a learning organization views or upholds standards of ethics compared to other organizations?

5. Do you think litigation is the best route to protect knowledge ownership? Form a group with your peers, and brainstorm the pros and cons.

6. The Internal Revenue Service acquires demographic data about tax-paying citizens in an effort to elicit relationships to their tax returns. In your opinion, is this effort an unethical act? Illegal act? Immoral act? Discuss.

7. Shoppers at a national retail chain are asked for their ZIP codes as part of the checkout process. This information is used to determine the pattern of business coming from various regions in the community. As a result, the store decides on its products, prices, and specials to maximize sales volume. Shoppers are not told why ZIP codes are solicited. Is the store's action ethical? How does it compare to the use of cookies in Web shopping?

8. The board of directors of a commercial bank had an attorney whose job was handling cases of bad loans and other legal matters affecting the bank. The attorney's main line of business was real estate. Cases requiring specific expertise were referred to attorneys in tow at the recommendation of the bank's attorney.

   One day, a case came up in which an employee sued the bank and one of its vice presidents for sexual harassment. The bank's attorney decided to handle the case himself. After a lengthy trial, the court ruled in favor of the employee. The jury awarded her $350,000 in damages.

   When asked why he did not have another attorney try the case, the bank's attorney replied that he thought he was saving the bank money by trying it himself, even though he had no prior experience with sexual harassment cases. At the outset, he did not think the case had much substance. The bank, on the other hand, was not happy with the results and blamed the attorney for botching the case.

   a. Could any aspect of the attorney's decision to handle the case be considered unethical, immoral, or illegal?

   b. Should the attorney be fired by the bank? Why or why not?

   c. Visit a local law library or talk to a local attorney and determine whether the bank attorney violated the American Bar Association's code of ethics.

9. A knowledge-based repository was installed in the loan department of a local commercial bank to determine the qualifications of auto loan applicants. The knowledge captured was based on the department vice president's experience. The bank paid the knowledge developer (an outside consultant) in full for the knowledge database.

   Four months later, the developer learned through one of the bank employees that the bank had modified the knowledge base to develop a real estate loan knowledge-based system on its own. The junior loan officer took the software home and spent time learning how to build a knowledge-based system. He then worked with the senior vice president of the real estate department to build the new database. Several modules of the auto loan database that check for the applicant's assets, salary, place of employment, and so on were copied into the new system. The approach to the system and the procedure were identical.

The developer filed a lawsuit against the bank, seeking damages and the right to ownership to the system. The bank, in turn, filed a countersuit, claiming it purchased the knowledge package outright and, therefore, owed the developer nothing.

a. What went wrong in this case?
b. Was an implied or express warranty part of the auto loan knowledge base?
c. Are any ethical, moral, or legal considerations at issue here?
d. Who do you think owns the knowledge in the real estate repository?
e. Based on the material presented in the chapter, how do you think the court would rule?
f. Who owns the procedure used to build the knowledge base? Is it proprietary?

REFERENCES ■■■■

Amazon.com, "Conditions of Use," www.amazon.com/exec/obidos/tg/browse/-/508088/002-2707765-6824853, Date accessed August 2002.

Awad, E. *Building Expert Systems*. Minneapolis, MN: West Publishing Co., 1996, p. 346.

Brent, Doug. "History of Ownership," www.ucalgary.ca/ejournal/archive/rachel/v1n3/v1n3.html, Date accessed August 2002.

Emery, Vince. *How to Grow Your Business on the Internet*, 3rd ed. New York: Coriolis Group Books, 1997, pp. 121–140.

Kull, Michael D. "Get a Competitive Edge with Knowledge Management," *The Law Marketing Portal*, www.lawmarketingcom/news/km.cfm, Date accessed August 2002.

Kurland, Norman. "Ownership: Knowledge as a Capital Asset," cog.kent.edu/archives/ownership/msg02255.html, Date accessed August 2002.

Louis-Jacques, Lyonnette. "Legal Research on International Law Issues Using the Internet," www.lib.uchicago.edu/~llou/forintlaw.html, Date accessed August 2002.

Mason, Richard O. "Four Ethical Issues of the Information Age," www.misq.org/ archivist/vol/no10/issue1/vol10/no1/mason.html, Date accessed August 2002.

Okerson, Ann. "Who Owns Digital Works?" www.mhhe.com/socscience/english/holeton/chap8/okerson.mhtml, Date accessed August 2002.

Platt, Nina. "Knowledge Management: Can It Exist in a Law Office?" www.llrx.com/features/km.html, Date accessed December 3, 2002.

Plitch, Phyllis. "Court Order Lets Bell Atlantic Wrest Domain Names from Cybersquatter," Dow Jones & Company, February 2, 2000.

Powell, Adam. "*MP3: Legal and Ethical Issues*," hotwired.lycos.com/webmonkey/99/06/index1a.html.

Rapport, Marc. "The Price of Knowledge," *Knowledge Management*, August 2001, p. 14.

Schultz, Ellen, and Francis, Theo. "Worker Dies, Firm Profits—Why?" *Wall Street Journal*, April 19, 2002, p. A1.

Sedgwick, James. *The Certainty Site*. Oxford Press, 2001, p. 5, home1.gte.net/cpq1szzy/whoownsknowledge.htm, Date accessed December 2002.

Simpson, Glenn. "A New Twist in Tax Avoidance: Firms Send Best Ideas Abroad," *The Wall Street Journal*, June 13, 2002, p. A10ff.

www.loc.gov/copyright, Date accessed December 2, 2002.

CHAPTER 15

Managing Knowledge Workers

Contents

He who receives an idea from me, receives
instruction himself without lessening mine; as
he who lights his taper at mine, receives light without darkening me.
—THOMAS JEFFERSON

▪▪▪▪ In a Nutshell

We are living in a continuously changing world fraught with uncertainty, market fluctuations, and aggressive competition. Today's emerging age of knowledge economy and knowledge management has created a new breed of company employees, whose intellectual capital is the accumulated experience, commitment, and potential for developing and maintaining the learning organization. Such a breed is referred to as the *knowledge worker*. A knowledge worker puts people first. He or she leverages technology to maximize efficiency and corporate success round the clock. According to one source, knowledge workers already make up one-third of the U.S. workforce. It is the fastest growing employment sector of wealthy countries.

The driver of success in the new knowledge economy is knowledge. It is impressive that people can earn a living by working with something as intangible as knowledge. In 1959, management expert Peter Drucker popularized the term *knowledge worker,* which was invented by Fritz Machlup, a Princeton economist. Although the term is widely used, there is confusion about its meaning—even among knowledge workers. In this chapter, we define knowledge workers, their attributes, job qualifications, potential, and how they should be managed. This is the crux of knowledge management as an emerging challenge for the learning organization.

▪▪▪▪ What Is a Knowledge Worker?

In reviewing the literature, several views and definitions have been proposed for the knowledge worker. Here is a representative sample:

- A knowledge worker is someone who uses IT in conducting day-to-day business and one that has direct impact on the efficiency and productivity of the job and the work process (Awad 1996).
- A knowledge worker is someone who follows a process requiring knowledge from both internal and external sources to produce a product that is distinguished by its specific information content (Kappes and Thomas 1993).
- Anyone who makes a living out of creating, manipulating, or disseminating knowledge is a knowledge worker (Bennett 2001).
- Individuals who have seriousness of purpose and are in the upper part of the talent and knowledge curves are knowledge workers. (Packaged Business Solutions, Inc. 2001).
- Individuals who add to a company's products and services by applying their knowledge are knowledge workers (Drucker 2001).
- A knowledge worker is anyone who works for a living at the tasks of developing or using knowledge (SearchCRM.com 2002).
- A knowledge worker knows what can actually be accomplished (see Box 15.1, Dove 1998).
- A knowledge worker is one who gathers data/information from any source; adds value to the information; and distributes value-added products to others (Kappes and Thomas 1993).
- Knowledge workers are people who use their heads more than their hands to produce value (Horibe 1999).

These definitions have several threads in common. Knowledge work embodies experience, innovation, creativity, and transformation of experience into knowledge for leveraging products and services. Our definition of a knowledge worker is a person

▮ ▮ ▮ ▮ ▮ ▮   BOX 15.1   ▮ ▮ ▮ ▮ ▮ ▮

THE KNOWLEDGE WORKER

Just exactly what is a knowledge worker, anyway? A little reading and you come away thinking it means people who work principally with computers—that seems to be the most vocalized worldwide–need for special skills and talent. The *Fortune* article talks about a school in Canada with a telling dropout problem. They train video-game developers and lose promising students to corporate scouts. Note two things here: These are not college-educated people, and they do not even finish their "technical" training. So, where does this knowledge come from that makes a knowledge worker so valuable?

Let's look at this knowledge worker concept more closely. This may be one of the latest buzz-words, but knowledge workers have always been here. Business essentially is the application of knowledge to produce/provide something that someone else is willing to buy. If you don't "know" how to do this, it doesn't work. If anyone else "knows" how to do it better, it won't work for long. When someone "knows" a new way to do it, everybody else is in for a shock.

That last item is what puts the spotlight on today's knowledge worker. Our collective knowledge is changing much faster today. The value of corporate experience is being recognized, and companies put their best into the corporate consulting pool. Though these people may have other knowledge of value, knowing what can actually be accomplished is the leverage they offer.

SOURCE: Dove, Rick. "The Knowledge Worker," 1998, www.parshift.com/library.htm#Other%20publications, Date accessed December 3, 2002.

▮ ▮ ▮ ▮ ▮ ▮

who transforms business and personal experience into knowledge through capturing, assessing, applying, sharing, and disseminating it within the organization to solve specific problems or to create value. He or she is the "product" of experience, values, processes, education, and the ability to be creative, innovative, and in tune with the culture of the corporation. For example, horse trailer salespeople do not sell trailers, but they do sell horse transportation solutions. They have to know their customers' business, the shows they attend, distances to haul horses, frequency of use, and the horse trailer line before they propose the right trailer to meet a customer's requirements. In this respect, the salesperson becomes a knowledge worker. Managers, lawyers, doctors, systems analysts, and accountants are all knowledge workers (see Figure 15.1).

PERSONALITY AND PROFESSIONAL ATTRIBUTES

A knowledge worker incorporates several personality and professional attributes:

- Holds unique values and understands and adopts the culture of the organization
- Aligns personal and professional growth with corporate vision and the achievement of strategic goals
- Adopts an attitude of collaboration and sharing
- Has innovative capacity and a creative mind
- Has a clear understanding of the business in which he or she is a part
- Is willing to learn, unlearn, and adopt new ways that result in better ways of doing a job
- Is in command of self-control and self-learning
- Is willing to tolerate uncertainties and grow with the company

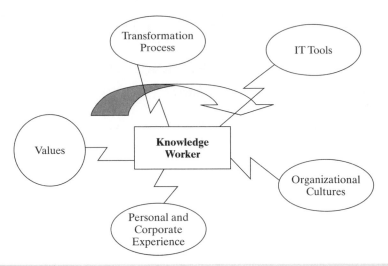

■ ■ ■ ■ ■ ■ ■ **FIGURE 15.1:** Makeup of the Knowledge Worker

Corporations preparing their human capital to be knowledge workers in a competitive environment must consider several core competencies of the self-directed knowledge worker:

- *Thinking skills.* A knowledge worker is expected to possess strategic thinking skills that shed potential on the work performed or the ideas provided on the job. Strategic thinking means having a vision of how the product can be better, how the company can improve by the value-added contributions of it employees, and how continuous learning contributes to a knowledge worker's career, loyalty to the firm, and satisfaction on the job. The organizational behavior literature cites two ways of thinking: right-brained thinkers, who tend to be intuitive and non-linear in their approach to problem solving, and left-brained thinkers, who are known for logic and decision making based on facts. For either type of thinker, the point is for the knowledge worker to stretch his or her thinking to achieve worthwhile results.
- *Continuous learning.* Knowledge work implies innovation through continuous learning on the job, professional seminars, and working in an environment conducive to creativity and advancement. This implies unlearning and relearning to be in tune with the fast-changing business. It also means the learning corporation must provide both the support and the funding for allowing its employees to continue to learn, in the hope that the outcome is better products or better quality service, or both. In one professional's words, "Learning is about working and working is about learning" (Frank 2002).
- *Innovative teams and teamwork.* As competition becomes more intense, the problems facing today's corporation become more complex, requiring innovative teamwork and joint decision making for solutions. Teamwork requires collaboration, cooperation, and coordination, based on a knowledge-sharing attitude and commitment to knowledge exchange. A prerequisite for successful teamwork is management support and attractive rewards, both intrinsic and extrinsic. For a career-oriented knowledge worker, intrinsic rewards (such as recognition) go farther than extrinsic rewards (such as salary increases or stock options) in the long run.

- *Innovation and creativity.* The spirit behind innovation and creativity is for knowledge workers to expand their vision and "dream" a new or a different product or service for the advancement of the firm. For that to happen requires open and equal opportunities to explore, to test, and to try things out. It means a solution focus mind-set, a passion to create knowledge, and a strong desire for idea generation and follow-up. From management's view, it means providing an environment in which knowledge sharing is encouraged within the framework of people's abilities and potential to succeed on behalf of the firm. The ultimate goal is to focus on creating tomorrow's product or service that the knowledge worker wants for the firm.

- *Risk taking and potential success.* Innovation and creativity mean risk taking. Maintaining the status quo requires minimum risk, but it also breeds no change for the betterment of knowledge workers or the organization. Like investing in stocks, the higher the risk, the greater the chance of higher return on investment. It could also result in a greater loss. What the knowledge worker or management must do is first share and exchange the best knowledge available, work together as a team, and make a joint decision with a calculated risk. In risk taking, you have to be willing to lose as much as you hope to gain. Vision, experience, and seasoned knowledge enter the picture in risk taking for the forward-looking firm. It is part of what a learning organization has to undergo to gain and advance its employees' knowledge base.

- *Decisive action taking.* With all these factors considered, decisive action taking means that knowledge workers should be willing to embrace professional discipline, patience, and determination. Motivation is a critical factor in keeping the focus on a product or a service for the future. Analyzing choosing among alternatives, testing, and the selling of change must come before final adoption (Garfinkle 2002).

- *A culture of responsibility toward knowledge.* This core competency means loyalty and commitment to one's manager or leader. Knowledge workers must consistently support their leaders, their peers, and the company as a whole. When a problem arises, a knowledge worker is expected to take the problem to a responsible source, discuss or brainstorm it, settle on a "best solution" outcome, and let it go at that. In traditional organizations, employees with problems or grievances often gripe about them through the rumor mill, which breeds misinterpretation or misunderstanding. This route finds no winners.

  Related to this core competency is a subculture of referrals and knowledge exchange. By that, we mean identifying knowledge workers who have specialized knowledge for certain problems and who are willing to provide such knowledge on call. A network of knowledge sources and knowledge availability is a critical component of the learning organization.

▪▪▪▪ Business Roles in the Learning Organization

By learning organization, we mean an organization of people with ingrained commitment to improve their capacity, to create, and to produce—who respond to uncertainty, to challenges in the marketplace, and to change in general. Senge defines a learning organization as "a group of people continually enhancing their capacity to create what they want to create" (Senge 2002). Malhotra defines it as an "organization with an ingrained philosophy for anticipating, reacting, and responding to change, complexity, and uncertainty" (Malhotra 2000). In brief, the rate of learning of an organization may become the most critical source of competitive advantage.

To a learning organization, data and information are givens. We have seen successes in data processing and information processing from the 1960s to the 1980s. The focus then was on efficiency, where computers replaced human redundant arithmetic (algorithmic) work. There were quantitative savings and everyone benefited. In the 1990s, information was collated, processed, and converted into relevant (nonalgorithmic) knowledge for the decision maker. At this level, the focus shifted from quantitative to qualitative performance-oriented value-added decision making. Captured and processed knowledge became the fundamental building block for today's learning organization, where everything operates creatively in real-time as problems arise. Personalization in electronic commerce and just-in-time (JIT) inventory management are examples of today's learning organization. The applications are smart enough to personalize the information based on the user's current location and needs (see Figure 15.2).

MANAGEMENT AND LEADERSHIP

In knowledge management, we distinguish between managers and leaders. Traditional managers focus on the present. They are action-oriented, spending most of the time delegating, supervising, controlling, and ensuring compliance with set procedures. They were once workers or superemployees and were promoted to managers. When they manage subordinates, they know all aspects of the business, because they were once there. The goal of management is stability on the job and meeting deadlines.

In contrast, smart managers focus on organizational learning to ensure operational excellence. Because of continuing change and improvements in the workplace, they cannot be expected to have mastered the work of subordinates. As a result, they take on the role of leaders, where change is the primary goal. Clearly, the challenge is to get the department or the organization moving in the direction of the goal(s) in line with the rate of change. Their focus is on the future, developing strategies and sharing vision through effective communication with knowledge workers. Learning becomes the key focus for the organization's survival and growth.

▪ ▪ ▪ ▪ ▪ ▪ ▪ **FIGURE 15.2:** From Data Processing to Self-Learning—A Trend

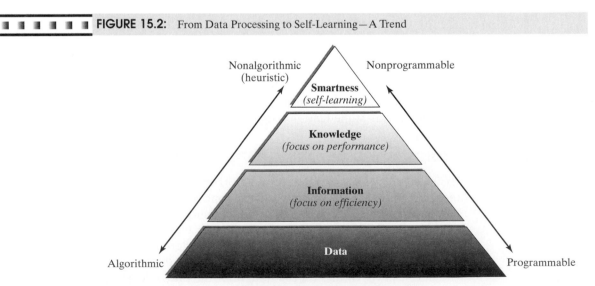

From Data Processing to Self-Learning

When it comes to leadership, the leader's role in a learning organization is more of a facilitator than a supervisor, a teacher than an order giver, a steward of the collective knowledge of his or her staff than a reporter to top management, and a designer more than the traditional role of merely seeing things done. A leader also has responsibility for knowledge workers who are continually expanding their capabilities to mold their future. This has human resources management implications, where the leader has a serious commitment to learning.

Learning and teaching are two faces of the same coin. In teaching, the focus is on knowledge transfer from the instructor to the learner. The instructor is supposed to be the expert. The role is to deliver quality content and to communicate content with potential. The interaction should instill serendipity and thinking about better ways of handling problems. Learning should promote a new way of thinking, not just facts. The key is not listening and retaining ideas or knowledge, but raising questions that might trigger new ways of decision making or problem-solving. When this is applied in a learning organization, the smart manager becomes the instructor, and the knowledge workers become the learners. A smart manager provides opportunities for knowledge workers to brainstorm ideas, exchange knowledge, and come up with new ways of doing business. All that is carried out in a culture amenable to change. As a leader, a smart manager personally leads discussions, poses questions, and provides constructive feedback. The end result is sending a signal to knowledge workers that knowledge is to be shared, not hoarded, especially among coworkers. As Ralph Waldo Emerson, the American essayist, noted over 100 years ago: "I pay the schoolmaster, but 'tis the schoolboys that educate my son" (Gavin 2002).

WORK MANAGEMENT TASKS

A key ingredient in management and leadership is the way managerial experience is processed. Smart managers learn from their experience rather than being bound by their past habits. The trick is not so much focusing on what managers learn, but how they learn what they learn—the process of learning. With this in mind, managers in a learning organization recognize and reward creative thinking, openness, and creativity. Work management tasks include the following:

- Searching out, creating, sharing, and using knowledge in everyday activities
- Managing knowledge workers and cultivating their knowledge-oriented activities to achieve effective results by using time and mental resources efficiently
- Maintaining work motivation among knowledge workers
- Ensuring readiness to work, especially during an emergency
- Allocating effort and switching control among tasks
- Managing collaboration, coordination, and concurrent activities among knowledge workers
- Sharing information and integrating work among knowledge workers (Davis 2001)
- Hiring or recruiting bright, knowledge-seeking individuals that keep the intelligence "pump" primed for future achievements of the firm

It should be noted that measuring productivity of knowledge workers is not that simple. Traditional productivity measures are inadequate and inaccurate. At best, they are subjective and indirect. For example, how would one decide between two knowledge workers who plugged the same leak in an oil well? Is it by the shortest time taken? The least costly approach? The most durable weld? Work efficiency addresses cost reduction in terms of time and effort. In contrast, work effectiveness emphasizes increased value in meeting the requirements of the task. Both are important, but the approach to productivity measures is bound to be different.

In managing knowledge workers, a manager must consider several factors that limit knowledge worker productivity and ways to get around them:

- *Time constraint.* Time is the enemy of successful knowledge workers. There is always more work to do. As a result, either quality suffers or completion time lags. Obviously, such stress can work against one's motivation to contribute.

- *Working smarter and harder and accomplishing little.* This frustrating result is often triggered by limited time, limited staff support, or financial constraints. Management can do a lot to alleviate this type of productivity problem.

- *Knowledge workers doing work that the firm did not hire them to do.* The way to get around this is for the smart manager to explore the specificity of the task or the job, match the task to the knowledge of the worker, and eliminate the nonessentials. Unlike manual or skilled labor, knowledge workers are hired because they know something the firm does not. This means that a knowledge worker is expected to open up to the organization, explain what they know and do not know, and provide the goals that their knowledge will produce for the firm.

- *Work schedule.* Heavy work demands invariably affect a knowledge worker's attention span, motivation, and patience, regardless of pay or benefits. The manager should be careful in planning work schedules and work rotation to assure cooperation and successful completion of jobs on schedule.

- *Motivation against knowledge work productivity.* Knowledge workers are not all programmed to follow the ideals proposed by management. Avoiding task uncertainty or job complexity can pose productivity problems and affect the productivity of other knowledge workers if their work depends on one another's input. Motivation is also affected in situations where urgency supercedes motivation. If productivity takes a nosedive, the knowledge worker can always blame it on the time constraint, lack of adequate input, and the like.

In summary, knowledge worker productivity is a challenge, requiring tender care, personal attention, consistent recognition, and timely rewards. Managing knowledge workers requires expertise in handling specialists with control of corporate knowledge as the core asset of business. Strategic planning means carefully selecting a knowledge worker when they join the organization, matching the knowledge worker's vocational needs with the requirements of the job, monitoring progress and improvements made over time, and ensuring stability and tenure on the job.

▪▪▪▪ Work Adjustment and the Knowledge Worker

Smart managers strive to ensure the right match between the vocational needs of their knowledge workers and the requirements of their jobs. The goal is to assure stability of the workforce and continuity on the job in the interest of the corporation. One approach to work adjustment is a model developed by a group of counseling psychologists at the University of Minnesota who were concerned with the general problem of adjustment to work (Dawis, Lofquist, and Weiss 1968). The model is based on the concept of "correspondence" or a match between the individual and his or her work environment.

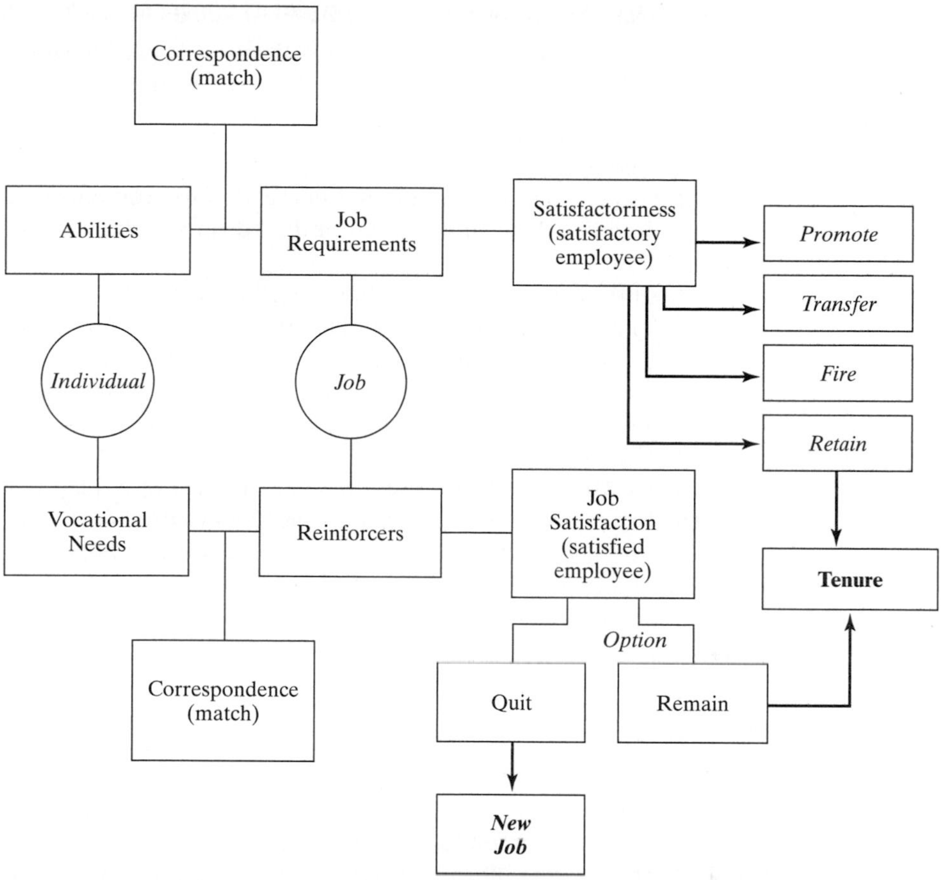

▪ ▪ ▪ ▪ ▪ ▪ ▪ **FIGURE 15.3:** A Work Adjustment Model for Knowledge Workers

Achieving and maintaining correspondence with the work environment are viewed as basic motives of human work behavior. As shown in Figure 15.3, correspondence begins when the individual brings certain skills (abilities) that enable him or her to "respond" to the requirements of the job or the work environment. On the other hand, the work environment provides certain rewards (reinforcers such as wages, prestige, personal relationships, and so forth) in response to the individual's requirements. When both the individual's and the work environment's minimal requirements are mutually fulfilled, correspondence exists.

When the individual achieves minimal correspondence, he or she is allowed to stay on the job and have an opportunity to work toward a more optimal correspondence and to stabilize the correspondence relationship. For example, an experienced teller in a commercial bank who handles customer problems effectively day after day is rewarded with a promotion in pay and rank to senior teller and on to head teller and beyond. It is presumed that the teller is satisfied on the job and is also considered a satisfactory employee (satisfactoriness) by the bank. When this relationship (correspondence) continues, it contributes to job tenure and stability of the bank as an entity.

PROFILE OF VOCATIONAL NEEDS AND REINFORCERS OF KNOWLEDGE WORKERS

In a 2002 preliminary study (Awad 2002) of select knowledge workers in the teller department of a medium-size bank, knowledge workers reported several vocational needs:

1. Achievement or a drive to accomplish worthwhile, complex tasks and a feeling of accomplishment
2. Use of their abilities on matters related to problem-solving and solutions rather than problem implementation based on a stable set of predetermined, mechanistic tasks
3. Authority exercised in terms of telling peers and others what to do
4. High pay and the prestige that goes with high compensation
5. The congenial atmosphere created by knowledge workers as coworkers
6. The freedom to try out their own ideas and create a new way of doing things
7. Recognition by both department officials and peers for work done
8. The chance to exercise responsibility in planning one's work and the work of others
9. The drive to do different things (variety) within the job scope from time to time
10. The social status that accompanies knowledge work where one can be important (somebody) in the eyes of customers and peers alike
11. Creativity or a chance to try out his or her own ideas, because no two customers or customer inquiries are ever the same

In contrast to the knowledge worker, traditional tellers' vocational needs relate to the following dimensions:

1. Handling a stable set of predetermined, relatively mechanistic tasks such as withdrawals and deposits
2. Independence on the job, in terms of doing their work alone rather than with coworkers; minimum socialization
3. The security of a steady job
4. Opportunities for advancement

With these vocational needs, the reinforcers are the efforts on the part of the employer to meet these needs and support the motivational factor that is part of the knowledge worker in general.

SMART LEADERSHIP REQUIREMENTS

Knowledge work requires smart leadership that can facilitate effective use of knowledge, where time and timing become critical in the competitive environment. Obviously, when dealing with smart people, you need a smart manager on your side. The critical point here is the *knowledge chain,* where a smart manager will focus not only on the intellectual capital of the corporation but also on the *return on time.*

The knowledge chain is a series of steps that determine the potential of a learning organization. One approach offers five key steps:

1. *Assessment of the core competency of the organization.* The key question for the smart manager is "What are we doing (not what we make) that makes us what we are?" This addresses the company's current inventory of skills, competencies, and talent. In today's global market, products must be regularly reinvented, reshaped, or refashioned to meet continuing changes in consumer tastes and preferences and to deliver the next more successful product or service in time to beat the competition. In Andrew Carnegie's words "The only irreplaceable capital an organization possesses is the knowledge and ability of its people. The productiv-

ity of that capital depends on how effectively people share their competence with those who can use it" (Koulopoulos and Frappaolo 1999).

2. *Response to the organization's internal shortcomings.* Traditional organizations are known for controlling and often suppressing new ideas. Even when they do not, in most cases, managers take credit for innovations rather than the employee(s) in the department or division. A truly learning organization encourages new ideas and knowledge sharing among employees through job coordination and effecting change in time to meet or beat market demands. Implied in this step is an assessment of how quickly core competency can be put to effective use to introduce a product to the market or respond to external company demands. A smart manager should have a grip on where the company's core competencies lie and how to take advantage of and reward its return on time.

3. *Vivid knowledge of the external market and the tricky nature of competition in the marketplace.* A classic example is Amazon.com. Soon after Amazon.com was founded, top management began to realize that in order to keep customers they needed to give advice to book buyers by posting book reviews and reviews of other purchasers on the Web site. Amazon.com also decided to post information about books with similar authors or topics. This unique approach, where human and computer intelligence are coordinated for marketing strategy, paid hefty dividends.

   A smart manager in a learning organization must assess the external environment and introduce innovative features that demonstrate his or her company's superiority over the competition.

4. *Online response to the company's external environment.* This includes the company's customers, vendors, suppliers, community, government agencies, threats, and opportunities. One of the main problems with e-merchants is their inability to deliver merchandise on time or in time to be useful or satisfactory to the customer. A smart manager knows the serious nature of this link in the knowledge chain and will make every effort to fulfill this step effectively. To do so means setting strategies and procedures, especially for emergency situations, to ensure the organization's viability.

5. *Measure the return on time.* Knowledge has already become the most important factor of production. Learning organizations have realized that having tacit knowledge and putting such knowledge to good use is what powers today's knowledge economy. A smart manager recognizes the fact that the traditional way of commanding workers to put their tacit knowledge to work for mere pay no longer works. The approach to knowledge content is to voluntarily share it for the organization to compete, innovate, and succeed. The magic ingredient is innovation. Philip Kotler, a noted marketing specialist, said, "Every firm should work hard to obsolete its own product line before the competitors do" (Koulopoulos and Frappaolo 2000). Innovation and unique ideas increase returns through product design knowledge and redesign. The return on time is like a feedback loop that judges the effectiveness of new knowledge over time.

▪ ▪ ▪ ▪ Technology and the Knowledge Worker

Knowledge work focuses on thinking, using information for processing, and recommending value-added change. The primary activities of knowledge work are assessment, decision making, monitoring, and scheduling. A knowledge worker is a manager, a supervisor, or a clerk who is actively involved in thinking, processing information, analyzing, creating, or recommending procedures based on experience and cumulative knowledge. For example, a stockroom clerk's job may be highly structured; therefore, it provides limited knowledge work. In contrast, a head teller job in a bank entails a significant amount of knowledge work, including the following:

1. *Assessing* the amount of cash available in the teller's drawer before the lunch break
2. *Deciding* on the procedure to use in handling irate customers
3. *Monitoring* cash supply for the drive-in tellers on Friday, when employees of a local plant cash their paychecks
4. *Scheduling* lunch breaks of available tellers during the flu season

Most people have an innate ability for problem-solving. However, routine activities often make it difficult to concentrate on the creative phase of problem-solving. This situation can be improved in an IT environment that provides the following:

1. A knowledge-based retrieval system that generates knowledge and ideas quickly
2. Interactive functions to derive feasible solutions
3. Functions to communicate a knowledge worker's activities to the appropriate people at the appropriate time via technology such as e-mail or an intranet

IT plays a role in the learning organization in three key processes: knowledge capture, information distribution, and information interpretation. In knowledge capture, a place for IT is in market research and competitive intelligence systems. Scenario-planning tools can be employed to generate the possible futures (Malhotra 1996). Likewise, the use of e-mail, intranets, and bulletin boards can facilitate information distribution and interpretation. The accumulated archives of such traffic can develop the basis for organizational memory.

It should be noted that the mere availability of technology does not assure a learning organization. Take the example of a multibillion-dollar bank, where the author complained about a cash deposit that would not appear on the customer's online banking screen until the following day, after the deposit had been processed. The bank's senior vice president of operations replied, "Well, everything, whether cash or checks, must be held overnight and cannot be made available for the customer before the next day." When asked, because the deposit was in cash, how the customer could withdraw some of this money during the day when the computer did not reflect a deposit. The answer was, "We try to discourage customers from doing so. We don't want any customer who makes a deposit in the morning to withdraw money later in the same day."

The contrast is a smaller bank in the same community, where a customer can view any deposit, withdrawal, or other activity within seconds from anywhere—by the teller, via ATM, or through the customer's personal computer using the bank's online banking system. Obviously, true online banking favors the latter bank, based on the policy of full customer service. In fact, the latter bank provides newer, quicker, and cheaper services for its customers on a regular basis.

The ultimate goal of technology is to serve organizational memory and to create a working environment that provides these conditions. There are various types of equipment and software unique to a knowledge worker's tasks. They include intelligent workstations, e-mail, and local area networks. E-mail and local area networks have been covered in Chapter 3. The intelligent workstation automates repetitive, tedious tasks, freeing the knowledge worker's time for more creative work. Through the keyboard or the mouse, the end user performs a host of functions, ranging from customer tracking to creating illustrated reports and from calendaring to working with knowledge-based systems. The single most used application for the executive workstation, however, is the electronic spreadsheet.

The capabilities of today's intelligent workstation fall in line with linear thinking—processes that are carried out step by step in a specific sequence. The learning organization depends on the knowledge worker to synthesize the information and develop conclusions. In addition to the mundane tasks, an intelligent workstation should perform the following functions:

1. *Administrative support functions.* These functions include such tasks as maintaining tickler files, scheduling meetings, and maintaining electronic telephone directories. With the position of private secretary on the wane, professionals are taking on a number of support tasks.
2. *Personal computing functions.* These include spreadsheets and business graphics.
3. *Intelligent databases.* These databases allow knowledge workers to create and maintain information on an ad hoc basis. Today's intelligent databases easily handle files, voice messages, and message-switching.

With knowledge worker time at a premium, learning organizations are offering flexible schedules through telecommuting. The case summarized in Box 15.2 illustrates the role of technology and networking in today's knowledge worker's performance and lifestyle.

A knowledge worker is expected to possess professional experience and technical know-how in order to access, update, and disseminate information and ideas from databases and knowledge bases. The computer should be owned by the knowledge

▪ ▪ ▪ ▪ ▪ ▪   **BOX 15.2**   ▪ ▪ ▪ ▪ ▪ ▪

FLEXIBLE SCHEDULING THROUGH TECHNOLOGY

THE BEST PLACE TO WORK

John Lewis, junior partner at a nationwide consulting firm, became the father of twins. He and his wife already had a boy and a girl from previous marriages. The new additions meant more demands on both parents. In response, John's company told him to work from home when necessary. This meant scheduling meetings with clients by phone and planning meetings with his staff around slack times. John happens to run a $35 million development project with a new client, and working from home turned out to be as effective as working from the office.

Without telecommuting, via e-mail and teleconferencing technology, John might have had to leave his job downtown (a 20-mile drive each way) and look for another job with a company closer to his home. Accommodating employees this way to avoid losing them is one reason why this consulting firm ranks among the top 25 employers for benefits and low turnover.

Among the unique benefits consulting firms offers knowledge workers like John Lewis are extended leaves of absence so they can pursue academic degrees or a lifelong dream. In fact, such a firm gives its employees a chance to set their performance goals, review them with their managers, and periodically perform self-assessment to see how well they're meeting their goals and to determine ways to correct deviations from the goal. The shared responsibilities, teamwork, and collegiality of the firm are well known among competitors, vendors, and customers. In fact, it has been known to generate more business and ensure security and stability of the workforce.

SOURCE: Excerpted from Zetlin, Minda. "Best Places to Work," *Computerworld,* May 6, 2002, p. 40ff.

▪ ▪ ▪ ▪ ▪ ▪

worker rather than by the company. Knowledge workers should keep their software and be able to take their computer from one job to another. One would expect them to customize and handle jobs within their range of experience.

Since the late 1990s, several software packages have become available; their intent is to emulate a knowledge worker's tasks. For example, KnowledgeWorker from Datum Consulting is designed to store the experience and skills of company employees. Through an Internet browser, you can create a secure picture of the unique developments on jobs, projects, work flows, team communications, and the like. The integrated components include a knowledge library that manages documents that are easily navigable via a Web browser; a business work flow to manage business processes; a digital dashboard to promote collaboration and knowledge sharing; and a search engine that allows users to surf a company's corporate information as if they were surfing the Web (Datum Consulting 2002).

KNOWLEDGE WORKER'S SKILLS

In addition to technical skills and abilities, a knowledge worker is expected to have both professional experience and soft traits such as a sense of cultural, political, and personal aspects of knowledge in the business. The personal aspects include open, candid, and effective communication skills, a warm and congenial personality that accommodates knowledge sharing in a group setting, sensitivity to the political pressures in the department or organization in general, and accommodating the job as well as peers within cultural constraints. These are people who want a challenge and to be on a winning team. They employ and create knowledge, and that is a high-demand intuitive skill. They prefer to be employed by a company that creates knowledge, not one that employs knowledge. All of these might seem ideal, but they can be a reality from the recruiting phase to the maintenance phase of human resources management.

Lawyers, consultants, and scientists are all knowledge workers. One difference between knowledge workers and white-collar workers is the level of education and specialized training. As a rule, the majority of knowledge workers have a university degree. The question of whether a knowledge worker should have a vocational degree versus a university degree continues to be a point of debate. Because knowledge work is about creating, manipulating, and sharing knowledge in the workplace, it is obvious that one needs more education than stacking products on supermarket shelves. Like it or not, employers continue to be more impressed with paper qualifications than practical experience. A paper qualification might not assure competence, but it is a door opener with long-term potential for the applicant.

A university degree is often not needed in a specialized area of work, such as dousing oil well fires or designing and running a high-level video- and audio-oriented Web site. More specifically, most employers expect the university degree to be in the area of the assigned job or department. Like medicine, a patient expects the specialist, not the paramedic, to handle serious surgery. One problem with today's higher education, however, is that most students prefer to take courses with a vocational (hands-on) drift, thinking that such experience will land a good job. To sit back and think through a concept or a strategy is a chore to many students.

▪▪▪▪ Role of Ergonomics

With regular use of the computer day after day, end-user performance and comfort are closely interrelated. No matter how sophisticated the electronic support, a knowledge worker can achieve full productivity with proper design of the work environment.

Ergonomics is a key issue here. Ergonomics involves comfort, fatigue, safety, understanding, ease of use, and any other areas that affect welfare, satisfaction, and performance of knowledge workers working with user-machine systems.

The list of factors that affect the ergonomics of knowledge workers falls into three categories:

1. *Environmental issues that include proper lighting, layout, and temperature.* Indirect lighting, covering windows near the workstation with blinds or curtains to reduce the glare, and positioning terminals at right angles to windows—all contribute to work productivity.

2. *Hardware issues that focus on furniture, comfortable seating, and well-designed workstations.* An ergonomically acceptable chair should be adjustable and supportive. Proper lumbar (lower back) support eases back strain over extended hours of work (see Figure 15.4). The workstation itself might have a built-in swivel to tilt to the angle of the user.

3. *Knowledge worker–system interface.* This addresses software, user training, and easy-to-follow documentation.

The knowledge worker–system interface emphasizes several features:

1. *Minimum worker effort and memory.* This means that information should be entered only once and nonproductive work eliminated. Documentation should also be available online in the form of a help routine. User manuals should be clear, complete, and easy to follow.

2. *Best use of human patterns.* Workstations should consistently place similar information on screens in the same position, by familiar screen formats, and so on. The knowledge worker should use a consistent approach and terminology for all functions. Performing these functions should require minimum training.

3. *Prompt problem notification.* The knowledge worker should be alerted to changes taking place that might adversely affect problem solution. For example, if a file is approaching capacity (say, 90 percent), a message should be displayed to indicate the status of the file.

4. *Maximum task support.* Task documentation should be complete and readily available so that the knowledge worker is not required to use other resources for task performance.

▪ ▪ ▪ ▪ ▪ ▪ ▪ **FIGURE 15.4:**   Ergonomic Environment and Features—The Basics

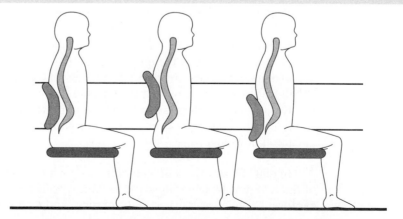

Demand for systems with good ergonomic designs continues to increase, pointing to the growing importance of the human factor. The benefits that ergonomics contribute to productivity are not readily quantifiable, partly because it is not easy to measure productivity.

▪▪▪▪ Role of the CKO

Some experts feel that KM, by definition, should be centralized; others prescribe that a specialized person be accountable for knowledge creation, transfer, organization, dissemination, and overall management. Toward that end, many large corporations such as General Electric, Dow Chemical, Texas Instruments, and Chevron Corporation have created a full-time position of chief knowledge officer (CKO) (see Box 15.3).

As the knowledge management czar, the CKO has the main mission of identifying knowledge within the company and encouraging workers to share it. Specifically, his or her main functions include the following:

- Maximize the returns on investment in knowledge—people, processes, and technology
- Share best practices and reinforce the goodness of knowledge sharing among employees on a regular basis
- Promote and improve company innovations and the commercialization of new ideas
- Minimize "brain drain" or knowledge loss at all levels of the organization

An effective CKO must be good at communications, interpersonal skills, technical skills, and people management. He or she must be a thinker, enforcing the big picture for top management. Other attributes include being an evangelist, a facilitator, and a juggler (Flash 2001). Interpersonal skills instrumental in CKO work include the following:

- *Teaching and selling.* This includes educating the user on technology; selling and promoting change through demos; seminars; and specialized behavioral training. In the end, the CKO must make the user want to "buy" change.
- *Communicating.* The CKO must speak the language of the user, mediate, work with management at all levels, and be politically sensitive.
- *Understanding.* This includes identifying problem areas and determining their impact, grasping employee expectations, and being sensitive to the impact of the KM system on people.

The key technical skills are as follows:

- Broad knowledge of business practice in general and the ability to translate technical information at the employee level
- Dynamic interface, making effective use of technical and nontechnical elements in KM design, especially if the CKO is the chairperson of the KM team
- Knowledge of information technology, information systems, software, and technology in general; knowing how information works and how it is transformed into knowledge

In real life, we expect greater emphasis on interpersonal skills during the early phase of the KM development life cycle. Technical skills become important during knowledge capture, knowledge storage, data mining, and knowledge organization. In addition

▪ ▪ ▪ ▪ ▪ ▪ **BOX 15.3** ▪ ▪ ▪ ▪ ▪ ▪

ROLE OF THE CHIEF KNOWLEDGE OFFICER

Agencies are looking beyond chief information officers to take advantage of the reams of information stored in a multitude of systems. To meet the challenge, some agencies are creating a new post: chief knowledge officer. The groundbreaking for the foundation of knowledge management within agencies occurred with the June 1999 appointment of Shereen Remez as the General Services Administration's—and the government's—first CKO.

Admiral George Naccara, the Coast Guard's CIO, said the guard is selecting a CKO who will also serve as deputy CIO. Knowledge within the Coast Guard is transitory because personnel move from station to station, taking expertise with them, he said. The CKO will help ensure that knowledge is not lost and improve critical decision support, he said.

Remez said knowledge management requires data sharing at an enterprise-wide level and bridging local islands of information. For example, she plans to implement portals through which users could make requests and a Web crawler that would gather information overnight. She also said successful implementation of KM consists of five components: business purpose and measurement of results; strategy; leadership; a culture of sharing; and technology. However, the emphasis in her office is on the human component—where the knowledge worker is most important. "Knowledge management will continue to grow as we see continued pressure on the government to perform more efficiently. It will allow us to reuse and innovate ways to use knowledge."

Susan Hanley, knowledge management director for American Management Systems, Inc., of Fairfax, Virginia, has said that to succeed, a CKO must leverage an organization's technological infrastructure to meet the data requirements of users and customers. Remez says that citizens are demanding the same type of service from the government.

SOURCE: Excerpted from Date, Shruti. "Agencies Create CKO Posts to Get in the Know," *Government Computer News,* November 8, 1999, pp. 1–2, www.gcn.com/vol18_no36/news/950-1.html, Date accessed October 20, 2002.

▪ ▪ ▪ ▪ ▪ ▪

to these skills, academic preparation and a career in knowledge management are prerequisites for filling this emerging position in industry. For example, to help prepare people for CKO work, the University of California–Berkeley's School of Information Management Systems offers graduate courses for knowledge managers. They include offerings in social science, management theory, and information technology. A list of these and other courses are available on UC Berkeley's Web site at www.sims.berkeley.edu.

In terms of roles, the CKO performs multiple roles such as:

- *Agent of change.* This requires having the style to sell the change from knowledge hoarding to knowledge sharing. The style ranges from that of persuader to imposer of change, depending on employees' level in the organization and the leverage of the CKO.
- *Investigator.* This includes identifying the real problem(s) in knowledge sharing and mapping out procedures for alternative solutions.
- *"Linking pin."* This means performing the role of liaison between employees' expectations and how a KM system must perform to meet those expectations.
- *Listener.* This includes reaching people, interpreting their thoughts, and drawing conclusions from interactions. Listening is the other side of effective communication.

- *Politician.* This means solving a problem by not creating another—an art in itself. A successful CKO knows who to contact, what to say, and how to use his or her knowledge to maximize the use of corporate knowledge for profitability and performance. Diplomacy and finesse in dealing with employees and managers can also improve the acceptance of a new KM system environment.

In 1999, many organizations had no staff devoted to knowledge management. Today, the number of people dedicated to KM is growing rapidly, although the title "CKO" remains rare (Flash 2001). Box 15.4 summarizes where CKOs come from and why organizations decide to hire one. When it comes to the serious decision to appoint a full-time CKO, the least the CIO should do is to support the cause. The CIO is not only the leader of KM efforts, but also the guarantor of its success.

▪▪▪▪▪▪ **BOX 15.4** ▪▪▪▪▪▪

DESCRIBING THE JOB OF THE CKO

WHO IS THE CKO?

Given the range of responsibilities involved, it is not surprising that the backgrounds of actual chief knowledge officers vary. David Owens, CKO of the St. Paul Cos., an insurance company in St. Paul, Minnesota, is a former teacher. SAIC's Greenes is a geophysicist who moved through management positions into human resources. Dow Chemical Co.'s Jim Allen worked as a manager in research and development before becoming director of KM under the CIO of the Midland, Michigan, company.

The career routes that knowledge leaders take to their positions show a similar diversity. Scott Shaffer, project manager for knowledge management at Northrop Grumman Corp. in Los Angeles, rose through the ranks of the company and took on a knowledge leadership role that evolved over time. After 17 years with the defense contractor, Shaffer took a position as program manager on the B-2 stealth bomber program in 1997. He became concerned about how the company would maintain its knowledge about the B-2 over the life of the aircraft, especially after the engineers who had designed it left.

"At the time, we didn't know about knowledge management, but we discovered it," Shaffer says. He helped to identify the experts who had worked on the B-2 and used video recordings to capture their knowledge. The team indexed the interviews on the company's Web sites to make them available to others.

In 1999, Hallmark Cards, Inc., realized that its customer research division had built vast repositories of data and information, but no one knew what to do with it all. The company appointed Tom Brailsford manager of knowledge leadership in charge of creating a KM infrastructure to tie the fragmented sources together and convince the corporate culture to embrace this knowledge. The result was an intranet site called *Voice of the Marketplace*, which includes customer research data that is accessible throughout the company.

No matter who the knowledge leaders report to, CKOs agree that to succeed they must have support at the top. Getting executive support can be difficult because it is not easy to demonstrate the explicit financial benefits of knowledge management. "My CEO has to make a leap of faith and say 'I believe this is right,' even though I can't prove it in dollars and cents," says Sam Saint-Onge of Clarica Life Insurance Company.

SOURCE: Excerpted from Flash, Cynthia. "Who Is the CKO?" *Knowledge Management,* May 2001, pp. 37–41.

▪▪▪▪▪▪

▪ ▪ ▪ ▪ Managerial Considerations

Regardless of the product, service, size, or culture of the organization, managing knowledge workers is unique. It requires a special breed of managers and a new set of responsibilities and challenges. Included in the managerial phase are job definitions, job performance evaluations, and an attitude to accommodate the value system and the culture of the organization. For the organization, it means facilitating collaboration among work groups and promoting the productivity potential of technology. For the knowledge workers, it means managing task schedules; automating repetitive, labor-intensive jobs; and providing an environment where knowledge workers can concentrate on challenging and creative work. In this case, the managers should support intelligent work and articulate, recognize, and reward the knowledge worker for the contributions they make at the time when they make them.

BECOMING A CHANGE LEADER

The greatest difficulty in dealing with people is not so much convincing them to accept new ideas, but in getting them to abandon old ones. Managing knowledge workers is no different. If one asks a knowledge worker "What do you expect your job to offer?" he or she is likely to cite the following:

- An opportunity to do creative work
- A chance for independence of decision making
- Good and conducive interpersonal work environment
- Management support
- Intrinsic rewards like recognition and appreciation of quality work
- Potential for advancement
- Supportive company policies
- Greater responsibility and autonomy on the job
- Variety in the job

For the change leader, the end result is likely to be improvements in efficiency and performance, improvement in focus by devoting more time to the primary functions of the job, and reduction in the amount of work that must be done. From the organization's side, what could block the change are fewer knowledge workers available to do the work, lack of up-to-date technology and support, inconsistent decision quality, and high turnover.

With that in mind, it is important that a change leader consider the following:

- *Focus less on problems and more on successes and opportunities.* A negative attitude with a focus on problems rather than successes is the wrong recipe for a knowledge worker manager. Certain problems can be tabled, while other problems must be addressed as they occur. A change leader must prioritize each problem, decide on its severity, and determine who, when, and where it must be resolved. This means that problems must be viewed in the context of the larger picture for the product, department, or organization as a whole. Likewise, successes have to be touted, and knowledge workers behind them should be recognized to promote excitement and motivation for others to follow.
- *Adopt an attitude that views challenges as opportunities.* One of the unique expectations of a change leader is strategic thinking and a knack for professional discipline. Challenges will come up at times when they are least expected. They also bring with them unexpected difficulties. A change leader must find a way of presenting or supporting challenges as ones with potential opportunities for a new product or better service, despite the risks that invariably accompany challenges.
- *Work on creating tomorrow's business instead of hammering on yesterday's problems.*

▪▪▪▪ Managing Knowledge Projects

Managing the human dimension of knowledge work is the most challenging job a knowledge manager can have. Knowledge managers coordinate special knowledge projects designed to take a product or a service a step forward under competitive pressures. The main managerial functions include drafting knowledge teams, deciding on customer requirements, identifying project problems, and ensuring successful value-added results. The role goes beyond management. A knowledge manager is expected to possess psychological, technical, and business skills. He or she needs to be on top of all these aspects, depending on the project.

Of all the challenging skills, the main challenge is assembling the knowledge team. As described in Box 15.5, the focus is first on people, processes, and cultural aspects of the job. The use of technology to facilitate knowledge sharing comes later in the team's operations. Overall, a knowledge manager must leverage the strength of each team member by the assignments made, the leadership provided, and the support given.

THE SOFT SIDE ALWAYS WINS

People will always be people. A knowledge manager must recognize certain challenges that have to be faced throughout a knowledge project. Convincing people to share individual experiences has been an elusive idea for most organizations. In a learning organization, where knowledge work reigns supreme, imagine the benefits of the following:

- The newest recruit in a customer service department addressing customer complaints as effectively as the most senior representative
- Any salesperson in the field counting on the collective knowledge of the experienced staff anytime, anywhere

Managing knowledge projects, where knowledge workers are involved, requires the knowledge manager to focus on the following:

- Encourage every team member to create new knowledge in the interest of the project. New knowledge creates wealth, which is the backbone of a learning organization.
- Help knowledge workers do their jobs. A knowledge manager must help them understand the company's business environment and its strategic orientation, and how they can apply them to the project at hand.
- Allow knowledge workers to participate in major company decisions, which can pay off in intrinsic and extrinsic benefits for the company and employees alike. This includes company image building, improved quality products, and stronger identification with a successful employer.
- Encourage knowledge workers and employees in general to learn as they earn a living on a day-to-day basis. This is made possible through on-the-job learning, job rotation, training sessions, and self-training (see Box 15.6).

An organization that manages to connect employees to employees and employees to managers to collectively solve problems makes the momentum unstoppable. However, we know from experience that once an organization grows larger, it tends to become more impersonal, which impedes knowledge sharing. This is where the challenge becomes obvious for the knowledge manager; that is, the challenge is managing the connection among people, processes, and technology on a full-time basis. It is also focusing not only on knowledge availability and dissemination like what one finds in a

▪ ▪ ▪ ▪ ▪ ▪   BOX 15.5   ▪ ▪ ▪ ▪ ▪ ▪

DRAFTING KM TEAMS

KNOWLEDGE TEAM FORMATION

By definition, it takes at least two people to share something. When that something is knowledge applied to the goals of a larger enterprise, the sharing multiplies and the number of people involved must increase. Therefore, most organizations make establishing a project team an early priority in their knowledge management initiatives.

Choosing and recruiting the right people for the team is a vital task that will have enduring consequences. Accomplishing corporate business objectives requires a mix of skills, experience, and stakeholders interests, so the team members usually will come from multiple disciplines. Team developers also must consider issues of trust across departments and business units as well as between individuals.

When helping clients to implement knowledge management projects, consultants at Chicago-based Andersen suggest staffing teams with individuals from the business process in question and from the human resources and information technology departments. A team needs members from all three sectors. "You don't find all these skills in one person, so you have to ensure that all are represented," says Christina Schultz, manager of global knowledge services at Andersen.

A team member's primary duty within the group is as important as his or her qualifications. From his KM project experience, Fred Merrill, a consultant at Ariel Performance Centered Systems,

Inc., in Fort Lauderdale, Florida, has derived six key roles, which he calls "hats," that one team member or another must play. In principle, one person might wear more than one hat if the team is small.

1. Business leads specialize in understanding the measurable results to be obtained.
2. Organizational leads specialize in communication plans, motivational incentives, and other organizational needs.
3. Superusers can influence the user community and provide practical feedback.
4. Interface design leads specialize in computer/human interaction and integrating content into work processes.
5. Training leads specialize in cognitive needs, learning strategies, and repurposing legacy content.
6. Technical architects specialize in technology installation and administration.

After you have selected the right team members, you may have to negotiate their availability for the project. Several KM experts advocate full-time devotion from members, at least in the early stages. A team member replacement plan must be worked out at an early stage so it is ready to activate, if necessary. The team also must capture the knowledge that it generates in the process of working on the project, to guide future projects, and for transfer to managers who will later take on responsibility for the company's KM efforts. This, after all, is the purpose of knowledge management.

SOURCE: Excerpted from Robb, Drew. "Draft Your Dream Team," *Knowledge Management,* August 2001, pp. 44–50.

▪ ▪ ▪ ▪ ▪ ▪

knowledge-based system, but also on creating a way to reach out to and learn from one another within the organization and with others in the know.

The bottom line is that an employee has to be convinced of the goodness of knowledge sharing before the creative process becomes a reality. Woodrow Wilson once said, "I use not only the brains I have, but all that I can borrow." For the knowledge manager, the crux of knowledge sharing is externalization or transforming captured tacit knowledge to explicit knowledge for others to learn from and use anytime, anywhere.

■ ■ ■ ■ ■ ■   BOX 15.6   ■ ■ ■ ■ ■ ■

IMPORTANCE OF SELF-TRAINING

SELF-TRAINING

What happens to all the money that companies spend on pumping their employees full of new knowledge? On average, U. S. companies put 78.6 percent of their employees through training programs. Companies spend an average of $677 per worker. All in all, training costs U. S. businesses approximately $50 billion annually.

It is questionable whether that money is well spent. For example, Motorola, Inc., found that employees tend to retain only 15 percent of what they learned within 3 weeks after taking a corporate education course. To address the retention problem, brainX.com hired experts in learning theory, curriculum design, and educational psychology and incorporated their ideas into a new software design. The company adopted a premise put forth in studies on education that the most powerful way to learn new information is to create questions based on the material and practice answering those questions.

The company released the brainX Digital Learning System, which is a personal knowledge management system. The software mimics two behaviors: browsing the Web and highlighting printed materials. When a user has collected material, brainX automatically formulates a study plan and begins quizzing. Then, the system shows the correct answer and asks the user whether he or she got it right with ease, with difficulty, by guessing, or not at all.

This type of system has applications beyond training, such as refreshing employees' memories for periodic compliance of safety testing and harvesting knowledge from seasoned employees and making it available throughout the organization. "Companies need an easy way to capture the knowledge in experts' heads in a way that makes it easy for others to learn," Dan Lewolt, founder of brainX.com says. "We are not storing documents that no one else can use but capturing the key pieces of knowledge in those documents, as identified by the experts."

SOURCE: Excerpted from Barth, Steve. "Worker, Teach Thyself," *Knowledge Management,* August 2001, pp. 65–66.

It is also the question of culture and trust that must be dominant in the decision-making environment and the factors that help build community in the organization.

In one medium-size bank, a strong community culture was discovered. Early one week, one-third of the bank tellers submitted their resignations. They were all going to a new bank across the street for higher salaries, bonuses, benefits, opportunities for advancement, and the like. To survive the "gash" in the teller line, four of the remaining tellers got together and devised an emergency schedule that handled the normal customer traffic without noticeable delay. For example, they staggered the lunch schedule so that only one teller would be absent for no more than 15 minutes. They also borrowed two former tellers from the loan department to help out. The security guards were also asked to escort customers with basic deposits or withdrawals to a special service window to expedite the traffic. As a result, the "fast checkout" window was adopted as a great idea for customer service.

The instinct for survival is a good test in any organization, where intelligent, caring, and trusting employees band together in the interest of the entity. They often come up with creative ways to repair the wounds that otherwise could leave the organization bleeding. They share what they know to survive and move on for a better tomorrow.

The bottom line is *sharing, cooperating, coordinating,* and *collaborating* for a common goal (see Box 15.7).

Of these elements, sharing what you know is the most challenging for the knowledge manager. To maintain knowledge sharing, he or she must reinforce and continue to instill the goodness of sharing and how every knowledge worker benefits with this new approach to survival and growth. The knowledge manager must deliver consistent signals that knowledge sharing is what the organization supports and rewards. There must also be a demonstration of the value of sharing through unique incentives, bonuses, and so forth. It means the human resources department must work in a

---

▪ ▪ ▪ ▪ ▪ ▪   **BOX 15.7**   ▪ ▪ ▪ ▪ ▪ ▪

IMPACT OF KNOWLEDGE SHARING

A CASE FOR KNOWLEDGE SHARING

The Executive Office of Health and Human Services (EOHHS) is the Commonwealth of Massachusetts' largest secretarial, consisting of 15 agencies and a budget of roughly $9 billion. EOHHS acts as the policy and steering arm to departments covering functions as diverse as children, benefits, disabilities, and public health.

Those agencies operate in close proximity, but in terms of technology and knowledge collaboration, they may as well be situated on opposite sides of the Atlantic. Henry Swiniarski, the state's assistant secretary for EOHHS, gives examples of some of the many agencies involved in home visiting programs. "Most of these agencies are entirely disconnected," says Swiniarski. "We didn't know who was servicing whom, and multiple interviews were going on covering the same information about the same people. As a result, the knowledge of one agency was largely unavailable to others."

Sharing information does not necessarily come easily in government. A hierarchical structure and silo-like IT organization mean that each department can operate like an information fiefdom. The leader runs his or her own staff, interagency collaboration is typically weak, and data resides in huge repositories only accessible to one or two technical staff with the know-how to run

the system. Not only does that arrangement impede the flow of data outward, it also makes it difficult to share internally.

Things came to a head in 1993, when seven youths were murdered on the streets of Boston by other juveniles. Investigation revealed that although various agencies addressed the problem, they were incapable of solving the problem individually. "These people knew each other but didn't normally work closely together," says then Commissioner of Youth Services William O'Leary, a prime mover in MassCARES—a joint technology/KM initiative designed to centrally coordinate state health and human services information, share it among multiple agencies, and use it to provide better care across the state. "There was a commitment to collaborate. We got everyone on the same page in terms of how we could get data, how we could share information, and how we could develop prevention strategies to reduce violence."

The results were surprising and immediate. They found out something that individual agencies had no way of ever discovering—a handful of individuals were responsible for most of the city's violence. By identifying those responsible and organizing better targeted and more closely coordinated actions, the problem was resolved. For the next 2 years, the city experienced no further youth shootings.

SOURCE: Excerpted from Robb, Drew. "MassCARES Seeks to Unite Disparate State and Local Agencies," *Knowledge Management,* June 2002, pp. 24–25.

▪ ▪ ▪ ▪ ▪ ▪

creative way to assure the extrinsic and intrinsic returns on knowledge sharing. The ultimate goal is to practice knowledge sharing as a two-way, reciprocal type of interface between the knower and the one who wants to know. Because knowledge has value, the company should subject it to the same economic factors and the resulting rewards that cement relationships and contribute to tenure and stability on the job.

In terms of incentives, various methods have been tried; some succeeded and others failed. Much of what ends up being the right set of incentives depends on company culture, company policies, and financial considerations. Based on our experience in the field, the following points should be considered:

- Link incentives to a team approach, where the performance of the team on the project will determine the size and nature of the incentive. It is assuming that the team is working together and sharing their knowledge in the interest of the project, where their collective strengths represent the quality of the results.
- Use awards or symbols of recognition for teams as well as individuals for unique contributions, whether it is a new method that saved time and money or a new idea that led to the creation of a new product or service. Awards tend to be motivational, because recognition is an important human need. They carry little monetary value, but when recognized through the company newsletter or Web site, an employee of the month program, or special parking space to recognize that special employee, they have far-reaching effects toward employee satisfaction and stability on the job.
- Flextime is an approach where the company allows the team to decide on when to work, when to quit, and so forth. The move away from the traditional 8 A.M. to 5 P.M. schedule implies trust in the team's judgment and also freedom for deciding the time frame for the particular problem under discussion.
- Monetary rewards, bonuses, and special prizes can be a hit with the winning team, especially when publicized throughout the company. This can be an effective management tool to jump-start a new knowledge management initiative.

From the knowledge manager's view, the ultimate goal is personal advancement of the knowledge worker's career path. The incentives provided should be heavily based on sharing and reciprocity, not individual contributions. If compensation is based solely on the individual's contributions, it could easily erode the sharing spirit and revert team spirit to knowledge hoarding and disintegration.

▪ ▪ ▪ ▪ Implications for Knowledge Management

It should be obvious by now that we are moving into an age where business is measured not in terms of historical performance, but in terms of how it makes use of the knowledge and intellectual capital of its knowledge workers. New human management challenges arise from the increasing demand for knowledge workers. This means encouraging productive knowledge to come forward and encouraging employees to learn. This is where mutual trust and employee loyalty become critical.

Knowledge management is about companies realizing anew the assets that have never appeared in the balance sheet but are vital to their future success. These hidden assets are the people with know-how. In the 1990s, the geometric growth of companies like Microsoft was based on intellectual property and the outcomes created in the way of products and services.

How a company performs depends not only on its financial capital but also on how it invests its intellectual capital. Its valuation is the sum of the talent, knowledge, patents, image, and brands that far outweigh money, brick, or mortar. Intellectual capital is measured by capturing, consolidating, sharing, and managing knowledge workers' tacit knowledge, knowledge repositories, and intelligent databases. Companies that make effective use of their knowledge workers will prosper, and those that do not will struggle. The ultimate goal is to harness employee knowledge and effectively turn it into intellectual capital that can increase and assure a company's competitive edge.

From the knowledge worker's view, as they begin to recognize the value of their knowledge, they will change their relationship with their employer from employer–employee to customer and partner. They become the source of an organization's competencies.

For a company employee to become a knowledge worker, it is important that he or she become special to the employing organization. This means that the company will have to pay a high price to replace a person's skills and knowledge. In fact, training and development can no longer be viewed as a benefit at the discretion of the employer, but as a part of employment that will increase the worth of the knowledge worker over time. By the same token, as knowledge work becomes an increasingly costly item in a company's budget, learning organizations will be under continued pressure to look for more creative ways of making every bit of knowledge count.

SUMMARY ▪ ▪ ▪ ▪

- The driver of success in the new economy is knowledge. Knowledge embodies experience, innovation, and creativity.
- A knowledge worker holds unique values, aligns personal and professional growth with corporate vision, adopts an attitude of collaboration and sharing, has innovative capacity and a creative mind, is willing to learn, is in command of self-control, and is willing to tolerate uncertainties and grow with the company.
- There are several core competencies of the self-directed knowledge worker: thinking skills, continuous learning, innovative teamwork, creativity, risk taking, decisive action taking, and a culture of responsibility toward knowledge.
- When discussing business roles in the learning organization, management and leadership become important. Smart managers focus on organizational learning to ensure operational excellence. In contrast, the leader's role is more of a facilitator, a teacher, a steward of the collective knowledge of the staff, and a designer.
- A key ingredient in management and leadership is the way managerial experience is processed. Work management tasks include searching out, creating, sharing, and using knowledge in everyday activities; maintaining work motivation; ensuring readiness to work; allocating effort and control-switching among tasks; managing collaboration; sharing information; and hiring bright, knowledge-seeking individuals.
- In managing knowledge workers, a manager must keep in mind time constraints, working smarter and harder but achieving little, knowledge workers doing the wrong job, work schedule and deadlines, and motivational forces against knowledge work productivity.
- Smart managers strive to ensure the right match between the vocational needs of their knowledge workers and the requirements of their jobs. A proper match results in worker satisfaction and hopefully a satisfactory employee as viewed by management. Vocational needs are many; they include achievement, ability utilization, recognition, and the like.

- Knowledge is a series of steps that determine the potential of a learning organization. The ultimate goal is to encourage knowledge workers to focus on thinking, using information for processing, and recommending value-added change.
- Technology plays a major role in knowledge work. It facilitates information availability and information processing for creative thinking and intuitive planning. The use of e-mail, intranets, and bulletin boards can facilitate information distribution and interpretation. With technology in mind, a knowledge worker is expected to possess professional experience and technical know-how to access, update, and disseminate information and ideas from databases and knowledge bases.
- There are several environmental, hardware, and knowledge worker–system interface factors that affect the ergonomics of knowledge workers. The goal of ergonomics is to provide minimum worker effort, make best use of human patterns, and provide maximum task support.
- To be a change leader, several factors should be considered: a focus on successes and opportunities, adopting an attitude that views challenges as opportunities, and creating tomorrow's business instead of hammering on yesterday's problems.
- When it comes to managing knowledge projects, the human factor becomes important. Convincing people to share individual experiences continues to be an elusive item in most organizations. A knowledge manager must build trust to discourage people's tendency to hoard knowledge, allow knowledge workers to participate in major company decisions, recognize and respect the experts, ensure that the technology meshes with the knowledge worker's culture and company strategy, and keep knowledge up to date.
- In terms of incentives, a knowledge manager must try various methods that work best for the knowledge worker, especially in a team environment. Incentives should be linked to a team approach, and awards should be used to recognize value-added work. Monetary rewards, bonuses, and special prizes can be a hit with the winning team, especially when publicized throughout the company.
- A major implication for knowledge management is that knowledge management is about companies realizing anew the assets that have never appeared in the balance sheet but are vital to their future success. These hidden assets are the people with know-how. How a company performs in the future depends not only on its financial capital but also on how it invests its intellectual capital.

Terms to Know ▪ ▪ ▪ ▪

Achievement: A drive to accomplish worthwhile, complex tasks and a feeling of accomplishment.

Creativity: Trying out one's own ideas in an effort to come up with new ones.

Ergonomics: The science of providing a physical environment (such as lighting or swivel chairs) for human comfort at work.

Knowledge worker: A person who transforms business and personal experience into knowledge through capturing, assessing, applying, sharing, and disseminating it within the organization to solve specific problems or to create value.

Leader: In a learning organization, a facilitator, a teacher, a steward of the collective knowledge of his or her staff, and a designer.

Smart manager: A person whose main job is to focus on organizational learning to ensure operational excellence.

Traditional manager: An action-oriented person who focuses on the present and spends most of the time delegating, supervising, controlling, and ensuring compliance with set procedures.

Work adjustment: An individualized model that prescribes achieving and monitoring correspondence between an employee's vocational needs and the reinforcers of the job.

TEST YOUR UNDERSTANDING ▪▪▪▪

1. What is a knowledge worker? Do you agree with any of the definitions in the chapter? Why or why not?
2. List and briefly explain personality and professional attributes of the knowledge worker.
3. The self-directed knowledge worker must consider several core competencies. Explain three core competencies of your choice. Why are they called core competencies?
4. Elaborate on the business roles in the learning organization.
5. In what ways are data and information considered as givens?
6. What is the difference between management and leadership? Traditional managers and smart managers?
7. How are learning and teaching related?
8. What do work management tasks focus on?
9. Explain the main factors that limit knowledge worker productivity and ways to get around them.
10. Explain the work adjustment model. How does it relate to the knowledge worker?
11. Briefly list the vocational needs and reinforcers of knowledge workers.
12. How does creativity relate to achievement?
13. Elaborate on smart leadership requirements.
14. What is meant by return on time? How does it relate to the knowledge chain?
15. Briefly explain the key steps in the knowledge chain.
16. How does technology assist the knowledge worker?
17. What should an intelligent workstation do?
18. List the knowledge worker's key skills. Do you agree with them?
19. In what way does ergonomics relate to the knowledge worker?
20. What does it take to become a change leader?
21. "Managing knowledge projects requires a set of qualifications and responsibilities." Elaborate.
22. Explain the various incentives that might be successful for the knowledge worker.
23. What implications can you draw from the chapter for knowledge management?

KNOWLEDGE EXERCISES ▪▪▪▪

1. Discuss the similarities and differences between the traditional manager and the knowledge manager.
2. Try to verify the personality and work attributes of the knowledge manager by doing research on the Internet. Report your findings to the class.
3. Is a college degree important for knowledge work? Discuss your beliefs with the class.
4. Cite three companies that qualify as learning organizations. What makes them unique?
5. Does a leader's job include management? If so, why do we need managers?

REFERENCES ▪▪▪▪

Apfel, Ira. "Hiring Changes," www.potomactechjournal.com/displayarticledetail.aspl, Date accessed October 20, 2002.

Appleton, L., and Gavin, C. *Intellectual Asset Valuation*. Boston, MA: Harvard Business School Publishing, 2000.

Awad, E. M. *Building Expert Systems*. Minneapolis, MN: West Publishing, 1996, p. 471.

Awad, E. M. "Select Attributes of the Knowledge Worker in Banking." Unpublished manuscript, 2002, pp. 1–18.

Baltazar, Henry. "Overcoming KM's Obstacles," *Knowledge Management*, February 18, 2002, pp. 43–44.

Barth, Steve. "Worker, Teach Thyself," *Knowledge Management*, August 2001, pp. 65–66.

Bennet, Bill. "Just Who Are Knowledge Workers?" November 11, 2001, Australia.internet.com/r/article/jsp/sid/11300, Date accessed August 2002.

Bhushan, Navneet. "Creating Next-Generation Enterprises," *EAI Journal*, May 2002, p. 10ff.

Chaleff, Ira. "Process Improvement for Knowledge Workers," www.ibt-pep.com/afsmart.htm, Date accessed August 2002.

Date, Shruti. "Agencies Create CKO Posts to Get in the Know." *Government Computing News*, November 8, 1999, www.gcn.com/vol18_no36/news/950-1.html, Date accessed October 20, 2002, p. 1–2.

Datum Consulting. "Knowledge Workers," www.datum consulting.com/solutions_kw_architecture.asp, Date accessed August 2002.

Davis, Gordon B. "An Emerging Issue: Knowledge Worker Productivity and Information Technology," Information Science Conference, Krakow, Poland, June 20, 2001.

Dawis, Rene V., Lofquist, Lloyd H., and Weiss, David. "The Theory of Work Adjustment." Minneapolis, MN: University of Minnesota, 1968.

Dove, Rick. "The Knowledge Worker," www.parshift.com/library.htm#Other%20publications, Date accessed December 3, 2002.

Drucker, Peter. "Who Is the Knowledge Worker?" www.pbsilink.com/knowledgeworkers.htm, Date accessed August 2002.

Dvorak, John C. "Know-Nothing Knowledge Workers Must Go!" *PC Magazine*, May 20, 2002, pp. 12–15, www.pcmag.com/article/0,2997,s%3D1500%26a%3D22201,00.asp, Date accessed August 2002.

Flash, Cynthia. "Who Is the CKO?" *Knowledge Management*, May 2001, pp. 37–41.

Flash, T. "Personal Chemistry," *Knowledge Management*, August 2001, pp. 36–43.

Frank, J. T. "Strengths of K-Professionals," www.kwx.com.my/kwx/asp/articles02/articles02/articles0207.asp, Date accessed December 3, 2002.

Garfinkle, Joel. "Steps to Becoming a Change Leader," www.kwx.com.my/kwx/asp/articles02/articles_0203.asp, Date accessed August 2002.

Gravallese, Julie. "Knowledge Management," www.mitre.org/pubs/edge/april_00/index.htm, Date accessed August 2002.

Hall, Mark. "Build a Long-Term Work Relationship," *Computerworld*, May 6, 2002, p. 46ff.

Hildebrand, Carol. "Does KM = IT?" www.cio.com/archive/enterprise/091599ic.html, Date accessed August 2002.

Horibe, F. *Managing Knowledge Workers*, New York: John Wiley & Sons, Inc., 1999.

Horvath, Dean. "Knowledge Worker," searchcrm.techtarget.com/sDefinition/0,290660,sid11_gci212450,00.html, Date accessed August 2002.

Kappes, Sandra, and Thomas, Beverly. "A Model for Knowledge Worker Information Support," *Knowledge Worker Information Management*, September 1993, pp. 1–4, www.cecer.army.mil/kws/kstoc.htm, Date accessed August 2002.

Koulopoulos, Thomas, and Frappaolo, Carl. *Smart Things to Know About Knowledge Management*. Oxford: Capstone Publishing Limited, 1999.

Maccoby, Michael. "Knowledge Workers Need New Structures," www.maccoby.com/Articles/KnowledgeWorkers.html, Date accessed August 2002.

Malhotra, Yogesh. "Knowledge Management, Knowledge Organizations, and Knowledge Workers: A View From the Front Lines," April 2001, www.brint.com/interview/maeil.htm, Date accessed August 2002.

Robb, Drew. "Draft Your Dream Team," *Knowledge Management*, August 2001, pp. 44–50.

Robb, Drew. "MassCARES Seeks to Unite Disparate State and Local Agencies," *Knowledge Management*, June 2002, pp. 24–25.

Russom, Philip. "An Eye for the Needle," *Intelligent Enterprise*, January 14, 2002, pp. 27–30.

Sebra, Bill. "Electrifying Your HR Management," www.knowledgeworkers.com/news/news_258.cfm, Date accessed August 2002.

Wesley, Doug. "Retaining Workers in the Knowledge Economy," www.findarticles.com/cf_dls/m0FWE/10_4/66276585/p1/article.jhtml, Date accessed December 3, 2002.

Zetlin, Minda. "Best Places to Work," *Computerworld*, May 6, 2002, p. 40ff.

What More Do We Need to Know?

Contents

Today's knowledge manager wants to know the reality of tomorrow, not just the reality of today. In a strategic sense, knowledge management in the next 5 to 10 years is likely to be shaped by many initiatives that we do not know for certain. Before we talk about future KM initiatives, our view of today's KM foundation is shown in Figure E.1.

■ ■ ■ ■ ■ ■ ■ **FIGURE E.1:** Today's Knowledge Foundation

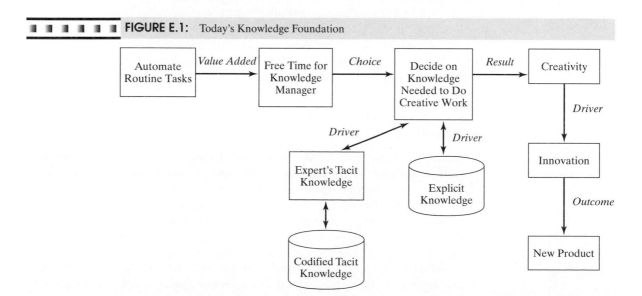

The first step is to automate and routinize basic tasks that can be handled with minimum effort by technology. This allows the knowledge manager to concentrate on higher-order decision making or decide on the knowledge needed to do creative work. Creativity is the driver of innovation, which should result in a new product or improved service over time. Knowledge for creative work comes from knowledge repositories and other sources.

What we now know is this: Knowledge management is a prerequisite for competition. It is the critical element for innovation. Consider Japan's industrial growth in the 1960s as compared to today's production of Lexus and Camry vehicles, among others. Technology alone did not do the trick. Products were initially not differentiated from competitors. When Toyota, for example, began to focus on quality, reliability, and dependability at a competitive price, it took on the U.S. market. In fact, American car manufacturers began to rethink their way of building cars to compete with a new way of doing business.

▪ ▪ ▪ ▪ The Shareability Factor

The greatest factor in knowledge management is sharing tacit knowledge. The challenge is not so much availability but willingness to share with others. We have known for years that tacit knowledge can be captured and stored before it is shared. Unfortunately, because knowledge tends to become richer, not leaner, over time, it must be kept up to date, which can be a problem. Also, the key is not availability of tacit knowledge, but how it is used. This is a major parting point from knowledge automation systems.

Another component of the shareability factor is organizational control. A traditional organization assigns certain authority, power, influence, and control to each managerial level. Sharing knowledge will require decentralized intelligence to empower knowledge workers to function more quickly and intelligently. Doing so requires transplanting vast volumes of decision making to lower levels. The problem is that the farther down the line intelligence is transported, the more "diluted" it becomes. When it reaches the intended level, only content is transported, not context. It is like going to a museum to view the paintings. They are nothing more than artifacts containing basic information about their composition or age. It is left for the visitor's imagination to draw conclusions about their prominence.

One conclusion is that shareability is more than mere availability of repositories or warehouses where the burden is on the knowledge worker to find the relevant expertise and decide how it should be applied. To achieve context, knowledge management must shift emphasis to cultivating expertise. The shift is fraught with two key misconceptions.

Misconception 1. Generalizing expertise will reach a wide audience; this is often not true. Consider this scenario:

> *One of the authors recalls a consulting assignment, involving a $200,000 hardware installation for a small bank. The vendor was known for giving no discount on the product, service, or support. Sensing that the order could go to a competing bidder, the sales representative came up with the offer of writing the installation under a 6-month testing, which meant no charge. Instead of giving the client the 20 percent discount that was refused by headquarters, the value of the 6-month period of use was worth the discount when considering the interest saved on the $200,000 at 10 percent for 6 months, plus savings on maintenance and support, to be worth $20,000. The sales rep drafted this indirect discount so*

that other sales reps could apply the same, with no reference to the customer or to the plan as a direct discount. The list was then posted on the KM portal available only to sales reps under the heading "one-time discount procedure for sales exceeding $200,000."

Misconception 2. The more knowledge is available, the more likely individuals will find what they need to solve a business problem. Humans in general do not have the patience to surf or scan hundreds of documents to locate the desired item. Also, as more documents are stored in a repository, the number of dated documents also increases. This means finding a way to filter useless documents would be required at a high cost, which is difficult to justify.

Another problem with knowledge search is that knowledge workers do not always know how to search effectively for the right document to meet specific needs. With an ever-increasing number of knowledge repositories, there is an inevitable increase in the number of "hits." This is where frustration sets in, and people want to find an easy and a quick way out.

One way to address this problem is for a select team of company experts to identify repository content that provides the most value to the company business in general. They could apply the 20/80 rule, where the top 20 percent of the content will satisfy 80 percent of the queries or problems. In addition, an online environment would continuously purge old documents through filtering. Technology may be employed to filter out the waste and organize existing resources based on value, frequency of use, and so forth. This helps ensure targeted knowledge to authorized users.

▪▪▪▪ The Human Element

People do not devote much time or show much interest in contributing to a knowledge base. This is especially true with top performers. They perceive their own knowledge as something they own. Why would they want to share it? In addition, most people do not know enough to distinguish between what should and should not be shared. Even if they did, not everything people share is necessarily valuable. However, if only a few contributors dominate a knowledge repository, it can discourage the participation of a majority of a company's experts.

To encourage experts to contribute to the knowledge management initiative, it is important for experts to be treated as experts. This means recognition and appreciation of the contributions they make, for the way they think, and how they explain things. Experts are not the most humble people or the easiest to understand. In fact, many experts with whom we have worked with over the years tend to be moody and get restless when asked to extend sessions or repeat something they have explained. However, there is a powerful emotion attached to being recognized as an expert.

This brings up important issues in knowledge management. King et al. (2002) conducted a study to identify and evaluate important knowledge management issues and how they should be managed. Table E.1 summarizes the top 20 KM issues as reported by survey respondents. The issues were factor analyzed into four grouping issues: Executive and strategic management; operational management; costs, benefits, and risks issues; and standards in KM technology and communication networks. The prediction is that these issues and their respective grouping represent the basis for effective management in the future.

Knowledge organizations face an investment choice as they consider knowledge management applications. The ingredients in knowledge management applications are

TABLE E.1. KM Issues

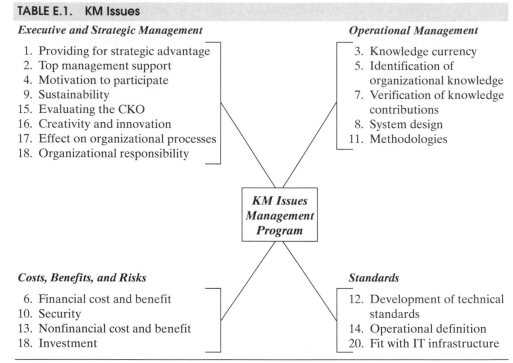

Executive and Strategic Management

1. Providing for strategic advantage
2. Top management support
4. Motivation to participate
9. Sustainability
15. Evaluating the CKO
16. Creativity and innovation
17. Effect on organizational processes
18. Organizational responsibility

Operational Management

3. Knowledge currency
5. Identification of organizational knowledge
7. Verification of knowledge contributions
8. System design
11. Methodologies

KM Issues Management Program

Costs, Benefits, and Risks

6. Financial cost and benefit
10. Security
13. Nonfinancial cost and benefit
18. Investment

Standards

12. Development of technical standards
14. Operational definition
20. Fit with IT infrastructure

Note: Numbers reflect priority ranking of each issue

SOURCE: King, W. R., Marks, P. V., and McCoy, Scott. "The Most Important Issues In Knowledge Management," *Communications of the ACM*, September 2002, p. 95.

technology and content. Our preference is to employ technology to provide knowledge managers direct access to a lower volume of high quality content that is tailored to the exact needs of the solicitor. Sophisticated indexing, for example, goes a long way toward providing the knowledge needed at the time needed, and in the proper format. Experts should also be interviewed, and their new or updated knowledge should be captured on a regular basis to ensure quality and dependability of the knowledge repository. This means that knowledge management needs to be managed and leveraged; this can only be achieved when paying attention to the best source of knowledge—people.

▪▪▪▪ There Is More to Know

Knowledge managers think ahead. They want to know how to strategize for tomorrow's business and how to continue using technology to leverage resources. Based on the authors' years of experience and existing literature, several trends are worth noting:

- Knowledge is productive only when it is captured in people's minds. Because most knowledge is acquired on the job, through training and in interaction with people, it behooves every organization to nurture and invest in the skill level of employees so that they become more productive in present and future jobs. With proper incentives and benefits, this is the kind of investment that promotes loyalty and discourages defection.

- More and more companies are discovering that leveraging knowledge is best served through decentralized intelligence. This means empowerment of knowledge workers and funneling tacit and explicit knowledge to the level where the actual work is performed. This type of decentralization is expected to make organizations more responsive to a changing environment, where the time for decision making is measured in seconds, not hours. Companies that have human knowledge updated regularly will find greater opportunities for creativity and innovation through the unique ideas that inevitably result.

- It is worth repeating that the driving force of knowledge work is creativity—an essential driver for innovation. The key is not so much the amount of knowledge available, but how knowledge is used. This is a major parting point from knowledge automation systems. Creativity is breaking loose from the traditional way of doing business. Recruitment and compensation strategies are being revised to address the creativity imperative. Aspiring candidates with potential will be highly sought. Technology will continue to take over routine and redundant work, freeing knowledge workers to concentrate on human insight and foresight.

- We believe that knowledge management will be an entry requirement for competitive advantage and that the future will belong to innovators, not copycats. This, of course, will be expensive: Recruiting intelligence is not cheap or easy. The pressure will increase on human resource managers and recruiters to scout for the right sources of talent and secure a continuing stream of candidates to support the long-term needs of the corporation.

- For years, we have been working on the assumption that corporate capital is the enabler of the enterprise. Capital continues to be important, especially when it comes to funding new projects and investing in equipment and technology. However, the trend is toward using corporate knowledge in a global competitive market. Knowledge management requires action, foresight, and focused strategic planning.

▪▪▪▪ The Social Factor

Knowledge management is seen as being passive, in that it is composed of facts and heuristics that can be stored, retrieved, and transferred with little concern for the context in which it will be used. Most of the writings and practices in knowledge management seem to focus on the content of knowledge management systems, overlooking how knowledge is presented or communicated. We believe that knowledge management is more than getting the right information to the right person at the right time. Managing knowledge occurs within a complex structured social context. That is, there must be social and human factors in the creation and exchange of knowledge (Thomas et al. 2002).

In the field of computer-supported cooperative work (CSCW), knowledge work was found to involve communication among communities of people and the social practices that occur in a particular context. For example, Orr studied the practices of photocopier technicians and found that their technical knowledge was socially distributed across the technicians of the firm and disseminated by storytelling, by memos, and by graphic sketches (Orr 1996). Another study brought up a variety of social factors that affect communication of knowledge among coworkers and illustrated how greater shared background helps in establishing common grounds for knowledge sharing. The rate of motivation also happens to be a factor in knowledge sharing. Failure of motivation was reported to be a major factor adversely affecting the adoption of groupware in most cases.

It is important to think of knowledge management as not just a bunch of isolated facts stored in documents, knowledge bases, or repositories; knowledge management is shaped by social and human factors that require the involvement of the contributor and the recipient of knowledge. Communication occurs when individuals or groups are motivated by personal and social motivators that make it convenient and appropriate to share experiences and arrive at consensus in a problem-solving context.

Given the role of technology in transferring and disseminating knowledge, the true picture of knowledge is one where people voluntarily explore, use, and adopt knowledge for the good of the project and in the best interest of the firm. Such a knowledge community includes people who know one another. They use storytelling, war stories, and other forms of narrative to enrich professional relationships, using specific techniques. This type of exchange is bound to lead to building social capital, cooperation, coordination, trust, and solidarity among professional peers. Cultural, organizational, and political factors must be considered in knowledge transfer and knowledge exchange.

Viewing knowledge management continues to be a problem. Some emphasize intellectual capital; some focus on technology; others associate different views of knowledge with personality types. Dueck did a major study in which he found that a person's temperament is a major influence on how that person views knowledge management (Dueck 2001). Briefly, he found that "corporate guardians" (caretakers, caregivers) are concerned with security of knowledge to ensure that no knowledge is lost. Everyone in the organization uses the same technology and speaks the same language for solidarity and unity in front of the customer. The other group consists of the "utilitarian rationals," who live for their work and focus on competence and the need to see daily improvements. They are not always sensitive to interpersonal exchange. They need databases and hate soft knowledge.

For knowledge management to be established in an organization, the so-called guardians will try to set standards; however, some professionals are likely to resist, because they view the "right" knowledge management approach as a function of a person's temperament.

In the final analysis, we feel the right approach to knowledge management is a unified approach, involving technological, social, human, and organizational elements that lead to economic value. Each element and temperament has to be part of the mix, the exchange, or the approach. The behaviorists have to accept the use of technology for storing and disseminating knowledge; the technologists have to understand that "tacit knowledge" and expertise are the foundations of knowledge management. The inner personalities of the experts must blend with those in technology to make things happen. It is the future of the organization, not its past or present, that is the goal of knowledge management.

▪ ▪ ▪ ▪ One Final Note

We have been undergoing dynamic and somewhat turbulent changes in the business environment. Malhotra (2002) referred to it as the world of "re-everything," tantamount to performing maintenance on a passenger train while the train is moving at top speed. What used to be predictable and programmable is becoming less relevant to survival. The question is how does a company manage a business that has the capability of questioning its executives' logic and revising their heuristics in real time as the business senses dynamic changes in the product or the environment? The concept of strategy and advance planning has shifted from predicting the future to what to do in the event of a surprise on a daily basis.

With the increasing return on intangible assets becoming more prominent, there is a pronounced shift from the "brick and mortar" to the "click and mortar," as seen in e-commerce, e-business, supply chain management, customer relation management, and the value chain for most companies worldwide. One may speculate that tomorrow's firms may far exceed the current logic of e-technologies as business becomes interlocked with learning and with digital storefronts along the Internet—the information highway.

REFERENCES ▪▪▪▪

Davenport, Tom. "From Data to Knowledge," www.cio.com/archive/040199_think_content.html, Date accessed August 2002.

Davenport, Tom. "Knowledge Roles: The CKO and Beyond," www.cio.com/archive/040196/davenport_content.html, Date accessed November 30, 2002.

Dueck, Gunter "Views of Knowledge Are Human Views," *IBM Systems Journal*, vol. 40, no. 4, 2001, pp. 885–88.

Dyson, Esther. "Intellectual Value," www.wired.com/wired/archive/3.07/dyson.html, Date accessed November 30, 2002.

King, W. R., Marks, E. V., and McCoy, Scott. "The Most Important Issues in Knowledge Management," *Communications of the ACM*, September 2002, pp. 93–97.

Malhotra, Yogesh. "Knowledge Management and E-Business in the New Millennium," January 2000, www.brint.com/ advisor/a011700.htm, Date accessed November 29, 2002.

Olsen, Bjorn. "Mismanagement of Tacit Knowledge: Knowledge Management, the Danger of Information Technology, and What to Do About It," www.program.forskningsradet.no/skikt/johannessen.php3, Date accessed August 2002.

Thomas, J. C., Kellog, W. A., and Erickson, T. "The Knowledge Management Puzzle: Human and Social Factors in Knowledge Management," *Communications of the ACM*, October 2002, pp. 863–84.

VisionCor. "The Human Element: Knowledge Management's Secret Ingredient," www.visioncor.com, Date accessed October 2002.

Index